Municipal Government
in North Carolina

Second Edition
1995

Edited by
David M. Lawrence and
Warren Jake Wicker

INSTITUTE *of* GOVERNMENT

The University of North Carolina at Chapel Hill

THE INSTITUTE OF GOVERNMENT of The University of North Carolina at Chapel Hill is devoted to teaching, research, and consultation in state and local government.

Since 1931 the Institute has conducted schools and short courses for city, county, and state officials. Through monographs, guidebooks, bulletins, and periodicals, the research findings of the Institute are made available to public officials throughout the state.

Each day that the General Assembly is in session, the Institute's *Daily Bulletin* reports on the Assembly's activities for members of the legislature and other state and local officials who need to follow the course of legislation.

Over the years the Institute has served as the research agency for numerous study commissions of the state and local governments.

Michael R. Smith, DIRECTOR
William A. Campbell, ASSOCIATE DIRECTOR

FACULTY

Stephen Allred	Joseph E. Hunt
A. Fleming Bell, II	Kurt J. Jenne
Frayda S. Bluestein	Robert P. Joyce
Mark F. Botts	Jeffrey S. Koeze
Joan G. Brannon	Patricia A. Langelier
Anita R. Brown-Graham	David M. Lawrence
Margaret S. Carlson	Charles D. Liner
K. Lee Carter, Jr.	Ben F. Loeb, Jr.
Stevens H. Clarke	Janet Mason
Anne S. Davidson	Richard R. McMahon
Anne M. Dellinger	Laurie L. Mesibov
James C. Drennan	David W. Owens
Richard D. Ducker	John Rubin
Robert L. Farb	John L. Saxon
Joseph S. Ferrell	Roger M. Schwarz
Cary M. Grant	Thomas H. Thornburg
Milton S. Heath, Jr.	A. John Vogt
Cheryl Daniels Howell	Michael L. Williamson

© 1982, 1996
INSTITUTE OF GOVERNMENT
The University of North Carolina at Chapel Hill
∞ This publication is printed on permanent, acid-free paper in compliance with the North Carolina General Statutes.
Printed in the United States of America
00 99 98 97 96   5 4 3 2 1
ISBN 1-56011-248-4 (paperback)
ISBN 1-56011-280-8 (hardback)
♲ Printed on recycled paper.

Contents

Preface

NORTH CAROLINA has some 520 cities and towns according to the census. Of these, almost 500 are active enough to qualify for state street aid. In this volume all are usually termed *cities* whatever their size or however they may identify themselves. They do vary greatly in population, from Charlotte's 445,000 to a dozen cities such as Bear Grass, Grandfather Village, and Speed that have populations of less than 100.

The state's cities are served by 520 mayors, 2,540 governing board members, more than 4,200 key administrators, and over 40,000 other employees. Together they provide municipal services to about 3.3 million people, or almost half of all the people in North Carolina. Both the problems that these cities face and the administrative structures and practices that they have developed to deal with those problems differ enormously. Nevertheless, all North Carolina cities operate within the same general legal framework. This book sets forth that framework and also suggests the range of administrative organization and practice among North Carolina cities.

The book is designed primarily to meet the needs of elected officials and key administrators—those who are chiefly in charge of the day-to-day operation of the state's municipalities. But citizens, civic leaders, high school and college students, and many city employees will also find the book helpful. It tells how cities are established and organized; what their powers, functions, and financial resources are; and how they operate in North Carolina.

The book is a general introduction to North Carolina city government. Although it may give more detail about powers, practices, and procedures than most citizens need, it does *not* contain all the detailed information in many areas that responsible city officials will want to have available. For example, all aspects of the property tax are discussed in a single chapter, which is enough information about the assessment and the collection of property taxes to meet the needs of most governing board members and city managers. A city tax collector or an attorney with a property tax problem, however, will want to have available the Institute's books entitled *Property Tax Collection in North Carolina* and *Property Tax Lien Foreclosure Forms and Procedures*. (Many chapters of this volume contain a list of publications that discuss the chapter's subject in greater detail.)

The basic principles of street construction, fire fighting, solid waste collection, and operation of a recreation program are essentially universal. They are about the same in California, Kansas, and New York as in North Carolina, and an extensive national professional and technical literature discusses them. But the states differ in what they authorize cities to do in providing these services. This book gives only limited information about the technical or engineering aspects of most functions; it focuses on the legal, financial, and administrative aspects of city government that are distinct to North Carolina, within which the more universal principles for providing each service or function must be applied. For example, the reader will find in these pages a description of a city's powers to provide streets, the revenue measures that may be used to finance them, and an outline of different financing practices. The reader will *not* find a discussion of street engineering—how wide or how thick streets should be or what materials should be used to build them. Similarly the legal requirements for budgeting and accounting are set forth in some detail, but little is said about accounting equipment or the factors to consider in selecting a computer. Again, the focus is the needs of elected officials and key administrators.

A distinctive feature of North Carolina government is that essentially all local government responsibilities are placed in cities and counties. North Carolina has fewer special districts, authorities, and other political subdivisions than most states do. As a result, local officials must understand the relationship between city and county governments and the ways in which they work together to serve their overlapping populations. The appendix to this volume briefly describes North Carolina county government. The new student of local government in North Carolina might wish to read that appendix immediately after reading the introductory chapter and before turning to the chapters that treat specific functions and services. The first chapter and the appendix are intended to provide the background against which specific functions and services and their relationships are understood.

For sixty-five years the Institute of Government has been issuing guidebooks, manuals, special studies, reports on various aspects of city government, and outlines and materials for use in training programs for city officials. This volume had its beginnings in 1969 when some items were collected into a publication entitled *Materials on Municipal Government in North Carolina.* In 1982 the materials were revised and expanded and issued in the present format as *Municipal Government in North Carolina.* This volume, the second in the current format, represents an updating and a revision (with some enlargement) of the previous edition.

In the past twenty-five years the Institute has also published three editions of a text entitled *County Government in North Carolina,* the most recent one in 1989. Thus the two chief forms of local government in the state are the subjects of comprehensive treatment in textbook form.

With five exceptions the authors of the chapters in this book are all members of the Institute of Government faculty. The author of chapter 21, "Law Enforcement," is Ronald Lynch, a former member of the Institute faculty who served as head of professional development for the sheriff's department in Orange County, Florida, until his recent retirement. Three of the authors are former staff members of the North Carolina League of Municipalities. For many years the League has joined with the Institute in providing materials used in programs for newly elected mayors and council members and other municipal officials. S. Leigh Wilson and Fred Baggett, coauthors of chapter 5, "Governance in Mayor-Council Cities," were previously the director and the general counsel, respectively, of the League. Wilson is now retired, and Baggett is city attorney for High Point. Sherman Pickard, coauthor of chapter 22, "Fire Protection," was a long-time member of the League staff. He retired recently after nine years as Raleigh's fire chief. The author of chapter 26, "Parks and Recreation," is Candace Goode, director of the Recreation Resource Service, North Carolina State University. We thank them all.

> DAVID M. LAWRENCE
> WARREN JAKE WICKER
> Professors of Public Law and Government
>   Institute of Government
>   The University of North Carolina
>   at Chapel Hill

Fall 1995

I
Introduction

1 Introduction to City Government in North Carolina

Warren Jake Wicker

Contents

A CONSIDERATION of city government's role in North Carolina requires more than simply examining the services and the functions provided by municipal governments. First, terms must be clearly defined. There is no legal distinction in North Carolina between a *city*, a *town*, and a *village*. The all-inclusive term for them is *municipality*. A municipality may call itself by whichever designation it chooses; it usually specifies that choice in its charter. *City* typically refers to a large municipality, *town* to a small one. In this volume *city* refers to municipalities of all sizes, both large and small.

The terms *urban* area, *city*, and *city government* are often used interchangeably, with occasional confusion as a result. Precisely used, *urban* refers to how land is developed, connoting a place where there are residences, commercial and institutional activity, or industry. It contrasts with *rural*, which suggests that the dominant land use is agriculture or forestry. *City* is a place designation, and often the urban area that the casual observer describes as "the city" includes areas that are outside the boundaries of the legal city within which the *city government* has jurisdiction. Urban areas in the United States may cover a number of separate local governmental jurisdictions. For convenience this volume generally uses *city* to mean *city government* when it is clear that the legally incorporated city government is the subject.

City government is but one of the governments that affect the lives of urban residents, and government itself, including city government, is but one of the institutions in society that affect the individual's life. Under the American federal system, state governments are primarily responsible for all governmental functions not delegated to the federal government in the Constitution. Each of the fifty state governments has divided responsibility for all activities under its control between itself and its local units of government—counties, townships, cities and towns, special districts, and authorities. The pattern of responsibility may differ from state to state, but the state and one or more units of local government are responsible for the major governmental activities required in every community, such as the following:

Administration of the courts   Public libraries
Airports   Public water supply
Civic facilities such as   Public welfare
    auditoriums
Conduct of elections   Recording of documents
Fire protection   Regulation of land use
                                          and development
Law enforcement   Regulation of personal
                                          conduct

Parks and recreation	Sewage collection and disposal
Public education	Solid waste collection and disposal
Public health	Streets and highways

This is not a comprehensive list, but it indicates the scope of state and local governmental responsibilities that must be met by the various units of government that have been developed since the nation was founded.

It was accepted from the earliest days of colonial government that governmental administration could not all be efficiently centralized in the colonial capital. Therefore, following the English tradition, the colony established county governments for the local administration of many of the functions of government considered essential throughout the colony: administration of the court system, law enforcement, the conduct of elections, care of the poor, and maintenance of roads. County government always preceded cities and towns.

Later, as settlements began to develop around seaports, trading centers, and county seats, the people who lived in them began to need services that the county governments could not or would not provide for everyone in the county. Again following the English tradition, independent municipal corporations (the city, the town, and the borough) were created that had the power to provide and finance the additional governmental functions needed when people live close together. This simple pattern of government, involving the state, counties, and cities and towns, was in effect at the time of the American Revolution, although counties were somewhat further decentralized into administrative areas for listing taxes, conducting elections, and organizing militias.

School districts, other special districts, and authorities were later created in North Carolina but have never been as widely used here as elsewhere in the nation. Substantially independent school districts in North Carolina were abolished in 1931, and other kinds of special districts have not often been formed. The two most common special districts today are the sanitary district and the rural fire protection district. Around the nation a great many authorities have been created in this century, principally to operate revenue-producing enterprise activities. North Carolina also has a few authorities—for

Table 1-1
Local Governmental Units in the United States and North Carolina, 1992

Type of Unit	United States	North Carolina
Counties	3,043	100
Municipalities	19,279	516[a]
Townships	16,656	—
School districts	14,422	—
Special districts[b]	31,555	321
Total	84,955	937

Source: Bureau of the Census, *1992 Census of Governments,* GC92-1 (1) (Washington, D.C.: Government Printing Office, 1994), table 3.

a. The Bureau of the Census's count of municipalities includes thirty-five that were inactive by North Carolina standards—that is, not active enough to receive state street aid.

b. The Bureau of the Census includes authorities in the tabulation of special districts.

example, those involved with housing, airports, and water and sewer services.

The 1868 constitution tried to introduce township government into North Carolina, the township being a subdivision of the county with independent governmental powers and responsibilities. Although townships are still a feature of the governmental structure in New England and in some middle Atlantic and midwestern states, they were effectively abolished in North Carolina after the 1875 amendments to the state's constitution authorized the General Assembly to eliminate them. Townships remain, but only as administrative areas within the counties, chiefly for tax-listing and election purposes.

The types and the number of local governments in the United States and North Carolina found in the 1992 census of governments are given in table 1-1. North Carolina averages about nine local governmental units per county, whereas the nation averages some twenty-eight units per county. Today, as in Revolutionary times, North Carolina state and local governmental responsibilities are largely carried out by the state and by county and city governments. The extent of those responsibilities, of course, has greatly increased since the Revolution.

Development of North Carolina City Government

Because the units of government have changed little in 200 years, one might conclude that no major changes have occurred in governmental structure or functions during that period. In fact, though, the functions for which these governmental units are responsible have been considerably reshuffled, as a brief account of the development of city government in North Carolina indicates.

Growth in the Scope and the Standard of Municipal Activity

The Early Town

The colonial town, serving several hundred people, had few functions. It organized a town watch, established a volunteer fire department, built public wells, kept the streets in repair, occasionally (as in Fayetteville and Wilmington) built a town market, and passed ordinances to protect the public health and safety. North Carolina towns, largely trading centers and county seats, did not grow with pre–Civil War industrialization, as many northern cities did. By 1850 only one North Carolina city, Wilmington, had a population of 5,000. As a result, North Carolina cities and towns were a full half-century delayed in encountering a demand for such major municipal functions as water systems and paid police departments.

1865–1900

Between 1865 and 1900, water and sewer systems were first introduced, largely through franchised private companies. Public transportation, such as streetcar systems, was introduced under similar franchises, as were electric and telephone systems. Street lighting first became common. The large cities began to spend a lot of money on paving streets, just as the large counties began to pave the roads that led out from the cities. Public health regulations received an increased emphasis. Schools were operated by school districts, with better and more expensive schools in the cities and the towns. Wilmington reached a population of 10,000 in 1870, followed by Asheville, Charlotte, and Raleigh in 1880.

1900–1920

During the first two decades of the twentieth century, there were several new developments. Streets and roads were paved as the automobile became commonplace. More and more water and sewer systems came under public ownership as private companies found it difficult to maintain high-quality systems and still produce a profit. A number of cities acquired their own electric systems. Full-time police departments were established, and full-time paid fire brigades began to supplement the efforts of volunteer companies. The first building codes were adopted. Public support for local libraries began, largely in response to Carnegie Foundation grants-in-aid for library construction. Public health departments were first established. In 1910, Charlotte and Wilmington became the state's first cities with a population of 25,000.

1920–1930

The national prosperity of the twenties was reflected in great physical expansion in water and sewer systems, street construction, and city halls and auditoriums. The statewide system of primary highways connecting principal cities and towns was established. Schools were built. Municipal bonded indebtedness shot up. Zoning was introduced. A wave of new subdivisions featured paved streets and water and sewer lines, all paid for from special assessments. The state's municipal population increased by some 45 percent, and Asheville, Charlotte, Durham, Greensboro, and Winston-Salem all reached a population of 50,000 or more.

1930–1945

The Great Depression broke the expansion bubble. All services were cut back, but debt service obligations became a heavy burden. Defaults on bond obligations led to the creation of the Local Government Commission. Poor property tax collections threatened continued operation of county road systems and public schools; as a result, the state assumed responsibility for nonmunicipal roads in 1931 and for a minimum level of public education in 1933. Independent school districts were abolished. Federal public works programs built many municipal improvements, including the first water and sewer systems in many small towns. Federal aid led to uniform county responsibility for public welfare and encouraged development of health departments. State aid for city streets and for public libraries appeared in the late thirties. Recreation programs and airports became municipal functions. During the 1930s the municipal population increased at about one-third the rate in the booming twenties; even so, by 1940, Charlotte had over 100,000 people.

1945–1960

The postwar period was a time of rapid urban growth and a very rapid expansion of municipal facilities, first to make up deficiencies left from the Depression and later to meet new demands. Capital expenditures to increase water supplies and extend water systems, extend sewer systems and build sewage disposal facilities, pave and rebuild streets, and expand fire protection facilities were very heavy. Service standards for law enforcement and fire protection, garbage collection, and other primary services were raised. The trend toward exclusive county responsibility for public health just about ran its course. Charlotte passed the 200,000 population mark in the 1960 census.

The 1960s

During the sixties, cities—especially medium-size and large ones—continued to grow, but their rate of population increase was lower than in any previous decade in the twentieth century. Between 1960 and 1970 the state's municipal population increased by 14.0 percent, compared with a 27.1-percent increase for the previous decade. By 1970 almost 43 percent of the state's population lived inside municipal boundaries. As a result of growth, inflation, higher service levels, and public salaries being raised to a level more in line with private-sector salaries, municipal expenditures continued to increase during the decade. As the expenditures rose, so did tax receipts, and the expansion of the property tax base came very close to keeping pace with the expenditure trend. Consequently the effective property tax rates in most cities were no higher at the end of the decade than they were at the beginning.

In terms of powers and functions, the major changes of the 1960s resulted from legislation adopted by the 1959 General Assembly. An annexation procedure incorporating the principle that what is urban should become municipal was approved; it is viewed by students of local government as a model for the nation. Under this procedure a municipal governing board, by ordinance and without referendum, may annex contiguous territory that meets the statutory standards of "urbanly developed" if the municipality can demonstrate its capacity to provide its standard services to the territory. Model legislation on major thoroughfare planning was also enacted in 1959. It fixed responsibility for thoroughfare planning and for adoption of a major thoroughfare plan by the municipal governing board and the state's Department of Transportation. The 1959 legislation also significantly expanded the powers of both cities and counties to plan, to zone, and to regulate land development, and it provided for increased joint and cooperative activities by city and county governments.

In 1967 the Local Government Study Commission was established. From it came a host of recommendations for both constitutional amendments and statutory changes. All were generally designed to provide increased flexibility and freedom of action for county and municipal governments.

1970–1995

In the quarter-century since 1970, major events and changes on the national and global scenes have greatly influenced city government in North Carolina. Environmental concerns flowered in the 1970s. In January 1970, President Richard M. Nixon signed the National Environmental Policy Act, and on April 22 of the same year, the nation marked the first Earth Day. Other legislation soon followed: the Clean Air Act, the Clean Water Act, a Marine Mammal Protection Act, the Endangered Species Act, a Safe Drinking Water Act, a Toxic Substances Control Act, and more, plus a stream of acts by the several states, including North Carolina.

Energy became a major concern worldwide with the oil crisis of the mid-1970s. Federal general revenue sharing started in 1972 and ended in 1986. In 1973 the Vietnam War ended. The use of computers became commonplace in both business and government. The CD-ROM (compact disc, read-only memory), now a part of daily lives, first came to market in the early 1980s. Voice mail, e-mail, and the Internet changed how Americans worked in offices, in factories, and on farms as well as how they relaxed and what they did for entertainment.

Major world events had their influence also. The Berlin Wall came down and the Cold War ended. The Soviet Union dissolved into a score of independent nations. The global economy, long heralded by futurists, became a reality for ordinary citizens, who watched their television made in Japan while tying their shoes made in China and slipping on their clothing assembled in Honduras from American-made materials.

Intergovernmental relations in the United States changed. Federal financial support for cities peaked, relative to other municipal revenues, in 1978. Federal budget deficits grew during most of the period, and the national debt reached alarming levels in the view of many observers. A relative decline in defense expenditures was not enough to match the growing outlays for entitlements, especially for Social Security, Medicare, Medicaid, and welfare.

Federal mandates, especially those relating to environmental protection and social justice, increased greatly throughout the quarter-century. By the middle of the 1980s, there was growing concern about unfunded mandates, that is, federal requirements that imposed costs on state and local governments without federal appropriations to meet the costs. By the early 1990s the national organizations representing the states, counties, and cities had mounted major campaigns to reduce or eliminate unfunded mandates. In 1993 they staged the first Unfunded Mandates Day to focus attention on the practice. The efforts bore fruit in early 1995 when Congress enacted legislation to eliminate or reduce future unfunded mandates.

Against this national and world background, North Carolina cities were undergoing major changes as well. In the early 1970s North Carolina also adopted numerous environmental measures, almost all of which required increased outlays by local governments. The state statutes governing cities and counties were revised and updated in the early 1970s. The state's constitution was amended in 1973 to provide more flexibility in local government financing. By the 1980s environmental concerns and prodding by federal legislation had led to more stringent standards for solid waste disposal and extensive efforts at reduction and recycling of solid wastes. All these efforts brought greatly increased costs.

By 1995 about half of all North Carolinians lived in the state's cities and towns. Cities handled the growth with attention to their traditional services. Water and sewer services were expanded, including more services outside city boundaries. Streets and highways were improved, often with developers putting the initial improvements in place. Emphasis on planning and land use control increased. Outlays for the arts, culture, and recreation were upped. Most of the large cities started bus systems.

The period between 1970 and 1995 saw the continued spread of the council-manager form of city government and the county manager form for counties in North Carolina. The number of council-manager cities more than doubled, from 90 in 1970 to 182 in 1994. In 1970 some 20 counties had the county manager form; by 1994 all but 3 of the 100 counties used the county manager form, and those 3 had a full-time administrator.

Changes were also occurring in municipal governing bodies and the municipal workforce. Among the large cities there was a modest move to some form of district election of city council members from the still more common (then and now) at-large manner. The number of cities using partisan elections also increased slightly. There were more marked increases in the number of women and African-Americans elected to city offices. Similar changes took place in the municipal workforce; proportional increases in the number of women and minorities were widespread, especially in the technical and middle-management areas.

The growth of cities and the changes in the economy in the past twenty-five years created the need for city and county governments increasingly to undertake cooperative arrangements. Hundreds of arrangements developed in this period, varying from one unit contracting with another to the merger of functions. (See chapter 10 for a more detailed discussion.)

Councils of governments were authorized in 1976; and under the impetus of federal grant requirements, councils or other regional agencies were created, collectively known as *lead regional organizations* (LROs) and together covering all areas of the state. There were originally seventeen regions; one was divided in 1979 to make eighteen. North Carolina LROs tend to have more extensive functions and larger budgets and staff than LROs in other states do. Although legally creatures of local governments, LROs are financed from federal and state funds as well as from local moneys.

North Carolina's population, along with the populations of most other Sunbelt states, increased more rapidly than the national popula-

Table 1-2
Municipal, Nonmunicipal, and Total Populations, and Number of Cities and Towns in North Carolina, 1900–1990

Year	Municipal Population (in millions)	Nonmunicipal Population (in millions)	Total Population (in millions)	Muni. Pop. as % of Total Pop.	No. of Cities & Towns
1900	0.21	1.68	1.89	11.1	341
1920	0.73	1.83	2.56	28.5	468
1940	1.23	2.34	3.57	34.4	365
1960	1.91	2.65	4.56	41.9	411
1980	2.50	3.37	5.87	42.6	458
1990	3.20	3.43	6.63	48.3	481

Sources: Total populations for all years, municipal populations and number of cities for 1900, 1920, and 1940, from Bureau of the Census, *Historical Statistics of the United States, Colonial Times to 1970*, pt. 1 (Washington, D.C.: Government Printing Office, 1975), 33; Bureau of the Census, *1990 Census of Population and Housing, North Carolina* (Washington, D.C.: Government Printing Office, 1991), table 1; Bureau of the Census, *Summary Characteristics for Governmental Units and Standard Metropolitan Statistical Areas, North Carolina* (Washington, D.C.: Government Printing Office, 1982), table 1. Municipal populations and number of cities for 1960, 1980, and 1990, including only cities active enough to qualify for state street aid, from North Carolina Department of Transportation, Division of Highways, Planning and Environmental Branch, *Incorporated Municipalities, Municipal Officials and State Street Aid Allocations*, pt. 2 (Raleigh, N.C.: NCDOT, 1994), 3.

tion during this period. The state's municipal population increased at a slightly higher rate than the total population. Nevertheless, the state's population continues to be dispersed. The population of North Carolina and its distribution between city and noncity areas during this century appear in table 1-2.

Growth in Municipal Revenues

Concurrent with this gradual development in the scope and the standard of municipal activity has been the gradual growth in the municipal financial base. The colonial town supported its activities from fees, charges, fines and penalties, and revenue from the sale of lots. Around 1800, property, poll, and license taxes were introduced, but tax levies for cities and towns were very small until after the Civil War. Following 1865, with the demand for paved streets and utilities came special assessments and water charges. Sewer charges date from about 1920, and license taxation expanded at about the same time. State financial aid was virtually unknown until the Great Depression, but it has become a significant source of municipal revenue, especially since the cities' share of the state's gasoline tax and franchise tax was increased in the early 1970s. Federal revenue sharing was introduced in 1972, then eliminated fourteen years later. The most significant change in municipal revenues came in 1967, when Mecklenburg County was authorized to piggyback a 1-percent local sales tax on the state's general sales tax. Since then the rate has doubled, and the tax is levied in all 100 counties under arrangements by which the proceeds in each county are shared between the county government and the cities within it.

The Current Role of the City: Summary

Against this background the role of municipal government may be defined more precisely:

1. The city has a major function to protect the individual and the public as a whole. It carries out this responsibility through police and fire services, through ordinances that protect the safety of individuals and the public at large from the acts of other persons, and through ordinances that protect the use and the value of property.
2. The city is a provider of services. It provides a local street system; operates the water and sewer systems; collects solid wastes; sometimes builds and operates essential facilities like electric and gas distribution systems, airports, and auditoriums; and contributes to its citizens' cultural and leisure-time activities by supporting libraries, parks, and recreation programs.
3. The city is a major factor in the continued economic development of the community. It shares responsibility with the state for the street and highway system that is the key to effective transportation. It builds and operates the water and sewer systems without which urban development is impossible. It often directly supports economic and industrial development bodies, sometimes alone and at other times in

cooperation with other cities or with counties. It provides the civic facilities like parking, auditoriums, and airports that make the city attractive as an economic center. It helps rebuild its own obsolete sections and improve its housing stock. Through all its activities it helps to build an attractive, convenient, and appealing community.

Comparative Roles of City and County Governments

As the foregoing discussion indicates, the distribution of governmental responsibilities in North Carolina continues to reflect the pattern developed in colonial days, assigning to city and county governments almost all local government responsibilities. The result is that both city and county governments are now units of local self-government, with broad powers and considerable discretion in how they carry out those powers.

Three factors that bear on the present roles of city and county governments help explain how they have evolved. First is the role of North Carolina state government, which has been strong since colonial days but even stronger since 1930. Table 1-3 shows the comparative roles of the state and local governments and the changes since 1900 as illustrated by their taxing levels. In the past twenty-five years the national trend has been for the states to raise increasing shares of the state and local revenues. By the early 1990s about a dozen other states had taken the dominant role in raising revenues for state and local purposes.[1]

The second key influence on the present roles of city and county governments also stems from the historical assignments previously described. The early pattern called for local functions and services needed by all people to be assigned to county governments and those needed in urban areas to be assigned to city governments. To a very large extent, all functions *have* been assigned to city or county governments; other forms of local government were not used or have been discarded, as road districts and independent school districts were.

The third influence has been the changing social and economic conditions and the needs of a population that either (1) is dispersed among a great many small (by national standards) cities, or (2) lives outside a municipality. Some 48 percent of North Carolina's popu-

Table 1-3
Nonfederal Taxes Levied by State and Local Governments in North Carolina,
Selected Years, 1900–1992

Government	Percentage				
	1900	1929	1978	1982	1992
State	23.2	32.1	74.8	74.1	72.1
Counties	53.0	39.6	18.1	18.5	21.1
Cities	23.8	16.0	5.8	6.3	6.0
Districts	NA[a]	12.3	1.2	1.1	0.8
Total	100.0	100.0	99.9	100.0	100.0
Total tax revenue (in millions)	$4.6	$97.1	$3,708.7	$5,367.7	$12,967.6

Sources: Calculations for 1900 and 1929, from North Carolina State Tax Commission, *Report of the State Tax Commission* (Raleigh, N.C.: the Commission, 1900, 1929). Calculations for 1978 and 1982, from North Carolina Department of Revenue, *Statistics of Taxation 1978* and *Statistics of Taxation 1982* (Raleigh, N.C.: NCDOR, 1978, 1982), tables 2, 3, 69, 70, 87; tables 2, 3, 74, 86. Calculations for 1992, from North Carolina Department of Revenue, unpublished information.

Note: State calculations include all taxes collected and either retained for state use or shared with local governments. All local sales taxes are counted as county taxes because they are levied by the counties. District taxes are, in most cases, levied for districts by city and county governments. Chief among those included in this class are taxes for school district supplements, sanitary districts, and fire districts.

a. District percentages included with county percentages for 1900.

lation lives in a city. In the nation about 62 percent of the country's population resides inside municipal boundaries.[2] Increasingly, however, North Carolina citizens who live beyond a municipal boundary need essentially the same types of local governmental services as those who live inside cities. The state's response, within the tradition that calls for all functions to be assigned to either cities or counties, has been to authorize counties to perform the same services and functions as were first authorized for cities.

State actions in authorizing cities and counties to provide services and functions needed in an increasingly urban society, and local government's responses, follow a pattern. Four stages may be observed:

1. Urban citizens recognize a need, and the state empowers city governments to provide the service or the function. Often in this stage the initial authorization is for one city or

only a few cities under special legislation. Later the authorization is extended to all cities.

2. In accord with changes in the economy, citizens who live outside cities find that they also need the service or the function, and the state authorizes counties to undertake the activity. As with cities in stage 1, a few counties may lead the way by securing special legislation several years before all counties are included in the authorization. For example, county authority to provide water and sewer services and solid waste collection and disposal followed this pattern.

3. Some counties undertake the activity independently, while others join with cities in either administration, financing, or both.

4. The county government assumes full responsibility for the function on a countywide basis.

This four-stage pattern has not been followed exactly for every service or function, but its general outline is evident in the development of many city and county activities. For example, libraries were originally authorized only for cities. Counties were then empowered to support and operate libraries, and joint libraries were frequently created. Today almost all public libraries are county responsibilities at the local level. Hospitals were originally functions of city government; today they are county functions. Solid waste collection and disposal started with cities; now disposal is largely a county function, and county collection activity is increasing. Water and sewer services were originally city functions; every county in the state has now participated to some extent in providing them. Parks and recreation services started as city programs, but today are often provided by counties; a few city and county programs have been consolidated into county programs. Fire protection was originally a city service, and that is still true for high-level fire protection, but county government support for rural fire protection is widespread.

Both city and county governments now have very broad powers and under the state's Interlocal Cooperation Act may exercise them separately or jointly. The extent of their dual authority appears in table 1-4. Two-thirds of the services and the functions listed are authorized for both governments. In practice there is less overlap. As noted earlier, libraries and hospitals are now almost exclusively county government activities. City governments, on the other hand,

Table 1-4
**Chief Services and Functions Authorized for City and County Governments
in North Carolina**

Services and Functions Authorized for Counties Only

1. Agricultural extension
2. Community colleges
3. County home
4. County surveyor
5. Drainage of land
6. Forest protection
7. Juvenile detention homes
8. Medical examiner/coroner
9. Mental health
10. Public health
11. Public schools
12. Railroad revitalization
13. Register of deeds
14. Social services
15. Soil & water conservation

Services and Functions Authorized for Both Cities and Counties

1. Aging programs
2. Air pollution control
3. Airports
4. Alcoholic rehabilitation
5. Ambulance services
6. Animal shelters
7. Armories
8. Art galleries & museums
9. Auditoriums & coliseums
10. Beach erosion control & hurricane protection
11. Bus lines & public transportation systems
12. Civil defense
13. Community action
14. Community appearance
15. Community development
16. Drug abuse programs
17. Economic development
18. Fire protection
19. Historic preservation
20. Hospitals
21. Human relations
22. Industrial promotion
23. Inspections
24. Jails
25. Law enforcement
26. Libraries
27. Manpower
28. National guard
29. Off-street parking
30. Open space
31. Parks
32. Planning
33. Ports & harbors
34. Public housing
35. Recreation
36. Rescue squads
37. Senior citizens programs
38. Sewage collection & disposal
39. Solid waste collection & disposal
40. Storm drainage
41. Urban redevelopment
42. Veterans services
43. Water
44. Watershed improvement

Services and Functions Authorized for Cities Only

1. Cable television
2. Cemeteries
3. Electric systems
4. Gas systems
5. Sidewalks
6. Street lighting
7. Streets
8. Traffic engineering

Note: Both units have authority to undertake the necessary supporting functions and activities—finance, tax collection, personnel, purchasing, and so forth—and to construct buildings and other facilities necessary to provide the listed services. The authority cited in the table is qualified in some cases, and in some cases one unit's action may limit the other's. The table does not include regulatory or franchising authority.

are the only ones significantly involved in urban redevelopment and public transportation.

The Pattern of Government in North Carolina

The pattern of government in each state—the division of responsibilities, powers, and functions between the state government and the various units of local government—has developed differently, in accordance with each state's traditions, circumstances, and political judgments. The states' patterns of government are often similar, but they also differ in characteristic ways. Ten North Carolina characteristics may be cited; taken together, they distinguish this state's pattern of government from the patterns found elsewhere.

1. *Primary state responsibility for financing education and highways.* Two functions for which state and local financial outlays are large—education and highways—are both financed primarily at the state level in North Carolina, and from taxes imposed by the state. All states support these two functions from the state treasury to some extent, but few to the degree that North Carolina does. In most states the local share of financial responsibility is much greater. Moreover, the major local tax is generally the property tax. In North Carolina the property tax is much less important in financing these two functions than in the nation at large.

2. *Primary county responsibility for areawide, or "people," services at the local level.* A number of major services and functions, especially health, education, and welfare, are needed by people in both rural areas and urban areas. In North Carolina the local responsibility for these services and functions is vested in the county, the one type of unit that covers the entire state. In contrast, in other states these services and functions may be vested locally in counties, cities, special districts, or a combination thereof.

3. *Primary city responsibility for the high levels of some services that are needed in urban areas*—fire protection, law enforcement, refuse collection, water and sewer services, and street maintenance and improvement. In this characteristic, North Carolina is much like other states, although some states use

local authorities or special districts to provide water and
sewer services, fire protection, and the like.

4. *County authority to provide urban types of services.* North Carolina counties have extensive authority to provide water and
   sewer services, solid waste collection and disposal, recreation, and other services needed by urban areas. This permits the county government, if it chooses, to provide these
   services in the urbanized fringe areas of cities, pending annexation, or throughout the county in unincorporated communities as may be necessary. Increasingly, county governments in North Carolina are doing just that. In many other
   states these functions could be undertaken in such areas
   only by forming special districts or authorities.

5. *Extensive city and county authority to regulate and direct urban development.* Both cities and counties in North Carolina are
   broadly authorized to undertake planning programs and to
   regulate land use through zoning and subdivision control.
   Most cities have extraterritorial jurisdiction with respect to
   these controls. Local units in other states also have such
   powers, but not all states grant such wide authority.

6. *Flexibility in city-county and multi-unit arrangements.* Cities and
   counties in North Carolina also have broad authority to take
   joint or parallel action or to contract with one another for
   performance of functions that both are authorized to undertake. Such agreements may range from the joint financing
   of a water line to the merging of tax collection offices.

7. *A model system for major thoroughfare planning.* Under a procedure established in 1959, each municipality and the state's
   Department of Transportation jointly develop and adopt a
   major thoroughfare plan for the municipality and its surrounding area. North Carolina's system is a nationally recognized approach that has served as a model for procedures
   adopted elsewhere.

8. *A less-regressive, more-responsive state-local revenue system than most
   states have.* The major taxes in North Carolina are the property tax, the general sales tax, the individual and corporate
   income taxes, and the gasoline tax. The property tax is levied by local governments only, the general sales tax by local
   and state governments, and the income and gasoline taxes
   by the state only. Rates for the sales and income taxes are
   average to high compared with rates for the same types of

taxes in other states, whereas rates for the property tax are low compared with those found elsewhere. The property tax is also relatively less important in North Carolina than it is elsewhere. Because the property tax is substantially regressive and income taxes are progressive, the resulting system in North Carolina is less regressive than most state-local structures in the nation. In terms of responsiveness to economic growth, the property tax everywhere tends to lag growth more than taxes directly tied to economic activity, such as income and sales taxes. Thus North Carolina's total revenue structure tends to be more responsive than most states' tax programs.

9. *Reliance on general-purpose local governments.* At the local level in North Carolina, almost all governmental responsibilities have been vested in county and municipal governments, two general-purpose units. Over 95 percent of expenditures of local governmental units in North Carolina are made through these two units. In most other states, special districts, school districts, and authorities are relatively much more important. The result is that North Carolina's urban areas do not have the multitude of overlapping units frequently found elsewhere.

10. *Comprehensive and flexible procedures for municipal annexation.* As noted earlier, in 1959, North Carolina adopted annexation procedures that are based on the general principle that whatever becomes urban in character should become municipal as well. This axiom accords with the view that essentially all local governmental functions should be provided by either a county government or a city government, according to the allocation of responsibilities between these two types of units just described. To make this approach effective, procedures permitting cities to annex areas that need municipal services are necessary. Without such annexation powers, urban types of services must be provided in some other way—through counties, special districts, new incorporations, or the like—or not provided at all. To solve the problem of competing city annexations when two cities are growing together, cities may execute annexation agreements that delineate the limits of their future annexation. Orderly growth of municipal boundaries may thus replace hurried annexations and fights over areas of growth. The

North Carolina procedures are regularly cited as a model throughout the nation, and despite occasional complaints from persons being annexed, they are usually considered to be successful by students of urban development.

To summarize, the North Carolina pattern of local government reflects an arrangement that is flexible and provides for much local control. It is state oriented in financing and has produced essential taxing equity between taxpayers inside and outside municipal boundaries. The pattern has tended to reduce rural-urban conflict and has resulted in a relatively simple governmental structure, with few units of government and limited overlapping jurisdictions.

Forms of City Government

The *form* of city government refers to how the government is organized to make policy and to administer its affairs. Historically, both legislative and administrative responsibilities have been vested in the city governing board.

Textbooks on municipal government typically cite four or five forms of city government: a *mayor-council* form, which is often listed as two forms, a *strong mayor–council* form and a *weak mayor–council* form; a *council-manager* form; a *commission* form; and a *town meeting* form. Students of municipal government do not agree on what a pure example of each form would be, and variations in all the forms are widespread. Moreover, the terms used to designate the different forms are not standard. For example, some writers describe the strong mayor–council form as the *strong-mayor* form, and the *weak mayor–council* form as the *mayor-council* form. That approach is used in this book.

The strong-mayor form makes the mayor a true executive and gives the legislative powers to the city council. The National Civic League lists the strong-mayor and council-manager forms as the two most likely to promote effective administration.[3] The league recommends that the mayor in the strong-mayor form have the following powers:

1. To hire and fire department heads
2. To prepare the budget for the council's consideration
3. To administer the adopted budget
4. To veto acts of the council, subject to an override by an extraordinary majority.

The strong-mayor form is frequently found in the nation's large cities and less frequently in small and medium-size cities.[4] There are no strong-mayor city governments in North Carolina in a strict and formal sense. A number of small cities without a manager have a mayor who, in fact, carries out functions and responsibilities very similar to those legally vested in the mayor under the strong-mayor form.

The mayor-council (or weak mayor–council) form has an elected city council and typically a separately elected mayor. The council establishes policy, and the mayor may have some overall administrative responsibility but little authority. The mayor, in a formal sense, has few special powers for either preparing the budget or administering it. Department heads are typically appointed by the council. In a few mayor-council cities, the council appoints an administrator who may function very much as a city manager but without the legal status that goes with that title in a council-manager city. The mayor-council form is the one most widely used in small cities in North Carolina. The same pattern is found in the nation.[5] (See chapter 5 for a longer discussion of mayor-council government.)

In the council-manager form the council is the policy-making body and appoints the manager, who is the chief administrator. The mayor, usually elected separately, presides over the council but has few independent powers. Limited powers of appointment are the most common. The manager is responsible for preparing the budget and for administering it in accord with the council's directions. The manager hires and fires employees and supervises all departments. Minor variations are common. For example, the council may appoint the clerk, the attorney, or some other officer. All but one (Mint Hill) of North Carolina's cities with a population over 10,000 have the council-manager form, and so do a majority of those with a population between 2,500 and 10,000. The council-manager form predominates nationally in cities with a population between 10,000 and 250,000.[6] (See chapter 4 for a full discussion of council-manager government.)

The commission form typically calls for the voters to elect from three to seven persons. Each one serves full-time as the head of a city department, and as a group, they serve as the city's governing board. Although no North Carolina city has the commission form by charter, several small municipalities have informally modified their mayor-council form to carry out their operations in a manner much like the commission form. In these cases, for example, one board member

Table 1-5
Forms of Government of North Carolina Cities, by Population, 1994

Population Class (1990)	Cities	Mayor-Council Cities	Council-Manager Cities
25,000 & over	22	0	22
10,000–24,999	28	1	27
5,000–9,999	33	3	30
2,500–4,999	75	26	49
1,000–2,499	116	81	35
500–999	99	88	11
Under 500	147	139	8
Total	520	338	182

Source: David M. Lawrence, comp., *Forms of Government of North Carolina Cities,* 1994 ed. (Chapel Hill, N.C.: Institute of Government, The University of North Carolina at Chapel Hill, 1994), 40.

may be designated the street commissioner, another the finance commissioner, and so on. These board members serve as the contact point for the municipal staff in their areas of designated responsibilities and may give directions according to prescribed policies. The commission form was first used early in this century and became fairly widely used, but it has declined in popularity in recent years. Nationwide, fewer than 3 percent of the cities with populations over 2,500 now use it.[7] A few North Carolina cities at one time used commission government, but none has done so since World War II. (The *style* of the governing board—*board of commissioners, board of aldermen,* or *council*—is unrelated to the form of government. Any of the three styles may be used in either the mayor-council or the council-manager form.)

The town meeting, in which citizens meet to enact ordinances, levy taxes, and elect certain officials, developed in New England and is still used there. As cities and towns have grown, the form has been modified. The representative town meeting, involving elected representatives, is sometimes used, and many towns appoint a town manager to administer the town's affairs. North Carolina has no town meeting cities.

Table 1-5 shows the forms of government used in North Carolina cities by population class, and table 1-6 gives data on the composition and the election of city governing boards. North Carolina's pattern is much like the nation's. Mayors are generally elected directly by the people, and they tend to serve short terms. Governing boards

Table 1-6
Composition of City Councils and Manner of Election in North Carolina Cities,
by Population, 1994

	Population Class							
	25,000 & Over	10,000–24,999	5,000–9,999	2,500–4,999	1,000–2,499	500–999	Under 500	Total
Number of Cities	22	28	33	75	116	99	147	520
Style of Corporation								
City	20	18	15	9	4	2	1	69
Town	2	10	16	66	110	96	135	435
Village	0	0	2	0	2	1	11	16
Style of Governing Board								
Board of commissioners	0	3	8	37	73	72	101	294
Board of aldermen	3	6	4	13	19	13	18	76
Council	19	19	21	25	24	14	28	150
Type of Election								
Nonpartisan								
Election by plurality	7	17	22	63	109	96	144	458
Election & runoff	3	8	5	3	3	3	1	26
Primary & election	7	2	3	5	3	0	2	22
Partisan primary & election	5	1	3	4	1	0	0	14
Election of Mayor								
By the people	22	26	32	75	107	91	135	488
By & from city council	0	2	1	0	8	5	9	25
Other	0	0	0	0	1	3	3	7
Mayor's Term								
Two years	14	17	24	52	71	69	120	367
Four years	8	11	8	23	40	27	22	139
Other	0	0	1	0	5	3	5	14
Number of Council Members								
Five	2	7	17	45	67	76	76	290
Four	1	3	6	15	26	12	33	96
Six	9	6	7	13	11	3	3	52
Three	0	0	0	1	8	7	34	50
Seven	3	6	3	1	3	1	0	17

continued on next page

Table 1-6, *continued*
Composition of City Councils and Manner of Election in North Carolina Cities,
by Population, 1994

	Population Class							
	25,000 & Over	10,000– 24,999	5,000– 9,999	2,500– 4,999	1,000– 2,499	500– 999	Under 500	Total
Number of Council Members, *continued*								
Eight	4	6	0	0	0	0	0	10
Twelve	1	0	0	0	1	0	0	2
Eleven	1	0	0	0	0	0	0	1
Nine	1	0	0	0	0	0	0	1
Two	0	0	0	0	0	0	1	1
Council Members' Terms								
Staggered four-year	10	16	19	50	76	50	45	266
Two-year	9	5	10	22	32	43	92	213
Four-year	3	3	3	1	7	4	8	29
Other	0	4	1	2	1	2	2	12
Election of Council Members								
At large	6	14	23	62	108	97	146	456
Combination of at large & from districts	8	6	5	4	1	0	0	24
At large but with district residence requirement	2	4	2	7	5	0	1	21
From districts	4	4	2	2	2	1	0	15
Combination of at large & at large but representing districts	2	0	1	0	0	1	0	4

Source: David M. Lawrence, comp., *Forms of Government of North Carolina Cities,* 1994 ed. (Chapel Hill, N.C.: Institute of Government, The University of North Carolina at Chapel Hill, 1994), 40–42.

are usually small. Elections are largely nonpartisan and at large, as might be expected given that so many cities are comparatively small. The trend recently has been toward four-year staggered terms and away from two-year terms.

Summary

City governments in North Carolina play a major role in providing the services and the functions that are needed in an increasingly urban society. They are created by the state, and their powers and functions are authorized by the state. Although many cities provide about the same package of services, each city has considerable flexibility in determining what functions it will undertake and at what level. Within the general limitations prescribed by the state, city councils have wide discretion in providing the services and the functions that will best serve the needs of their communities.

Additional Resources

Adrian, Charles R. "Forms of City Government in American History." In *The Municipal Yearbook 1988*, 3–12. Washington, D.C.: International City Management Association, 1988.

Adrian, Charles R., and Ernest S. Griffith. *A History of American City Government: The Formation of Tradition, 1775–1870*. New York: Praeger Publishers, for the National Municipal League, 1976.

Bureau of the Census. *1992 Census of Governments*, GC92(1)-1, *Governmental Organization*. Washington, D.C.: Government Printing Office, 1994.

Griffith, Ernest S. *A History of American City Government: The Progressive Years and Their Aftermath, 1900–1920*. New York: Praeger Publishers, for the National Municipal League, 1974.

The Municipal Year Book. Washington, D.C.: International City/County Management Association, published annually.

Shafroth, Frank. "The Reagan Years and the Nation's Cities." In *The Municipal Yearbook 1989*, 115–28. Washington, D.C.: International City Management Association, 1989.

Notes

1. Bureau of the Census, *Governmental Finances: 1990–91*, Series GF/91-5 (Washington, D.C.: Government Printing Office, 1993), table 28.

2. Bureau of the Census, *1992 Census of Governments; Government Organization*, GC92(1)-1 (Washington, D.C.: Government Printing Office, 1994), table 8.

3. National Civic League, *Forms of Local Government* (Denver, Colo.: National Civic League Press, 1989).

4. *The Municipal Year Book 1994* (Washington D.C.: International City/County Management Association, 1994), xii.

5. *The Municipal Year Book 1994,* xii.

6. *The Municipal Year Book 1994,* xii. ·

7. *The Municipal Year Book 1994,* xii.

II
Organization and Administration

2 The Legal Nature of the City and Its Governing Board

David M. Lawrence

Contents

THIS CHAPTER describes the legal character of the city government and the city's relationship to the General Assembly. It also discusses the governing board—its structure, its meetings, its forms of action, and its procedures.

The word *city* describes at least two entities: one physical or geographical, the other legal. The physical city is a place, an urban community, whose constantly changing boundaries are defined by patterns of land use, of commuting, of economic dependence. The legal city is a governmental entity whose boundaries are defined by law. Although these two sorts of cities overlap, they are almost never identical. In some cases, more frequently in small communities, the physical city exists alone. More often the physical city outgrows its legal counterpart, and sometimes several legal cities share governmental responsibility in a single urban community. The focus in this chapter is the legal city.

The City as Municipal Corporation

In law a city is a *municipal corporation.* Under the law a corporation is a *person* (an artificial one, to be sure)—an entity separate from its owners. In this respect a municipal corporation is no different from a business corporation, and the benefits that cause businesses to organize into corporations explain why city governments also organize in this way. First, a corporation continues in existence without regard to changes in its ownership. Owners may die or leave the corporation, and new owners may join, but the corporation's existence continues unaffected. This attribute facilitates long-term projects and commitments by the enterprise, whether it is a manufacturing company or a city. Second, the corporate form permits a limited commitment of assets by the owners; the corporation must meet its obligations from its own resources, not those of its owners. Their liability is limited—to the amount of their investment in business corporations, by tax-rate limits in municipal corporations. Third, the corporate form facilitates the delegation of management responsibility from the corporation's owners to its board of directors or governing board and administration.

Most business corporations are organized for economic purposes with the intention of returning a profit to their owners—their shareholders. Municipal corporations, on the other hand, are part of the governmental structure of the state, organized to provide public services and regulate activities in a specific community. Perhaps the most notable difference between municipal corporations and business corporations lies in the involuntary character of "ownership" of the former. A person becomes an owner—a stockholder—of a business corporation by the voluntary act of purchasing that corporation's stock. Ownership is given up by simply selling the stock. But a person joins a municipal corporation involuntarily. This corporation's owners include everyone who lives within its borders, and the only way one can escape ownership is to move away.

Cities and the General Assembly

Cities exist, of course, in an intergovernmental context that includes the national government, the state government, and other local governments, such as counties. Of these other sorts of government, the state is by far the most important to cities, and within North Carolina state government the most important actor is the General Assembly. Cities owe their very existence to the General Assembly, and the General Assembly can almost at will abolish them, change their borders, modify their structures, or grant or take away their powers. In this state there is no inherent right of local self-government, nor is there the sort of home rule that permits cities elsewhere to write their own charters. The basic framework of government in North Carolina—what is done by government, who does it, and how it is financed—is set by legislative action.

Because cities gain their authority to act—to provide services, to regulate activities, to raise revenues—from the General Assembly, a city that wants to begin a new activity must be able to point to legislative authorization to do so. It is not enough (as it is with private corporations) to say that there is no prohibition on what the city wants to do; instead, the law must expressly or implicitly permit the city to act.

The General Assembly authorizes cities to act through two general types of legislation: general laws and local acts. A *general law* is one that applies statewide to all cities or to all cities in a particular class, such as all cities with a population of 5,000 or more. Most of the basic general laws that govern cities were either first written or exten-sively revised in the last two decades; therefore they provide sufficient authority for the large majority of cities to do nearly all that they might wish to do.

But if a city wants to do something new or to undertake a familiar task in a way not permitted by general law, it may seek a local act au-thorizing the new power or procedure. A *local act* is an act of the leg-islature that applies to one city or county or occasionally to a few cit-ies or counties. Under the General Assembly's courtesy system, if the delegation that represents the city or the county involved supports the local bill, the rest of the legislature normally defers to the delegation's wishes and passes it. As a result, local acts are easier to enact than general laws are, and they sometimes serve the important function of permitting local experimentation with a program that could not be enacted statewide. For example, in 1967, Raleigh re-ceived authorization by local act to annex areas that were not adja-cent to the city limits. Other cities received similar authority in 1969 and 1971, and in 1974 an act was passed to permit such annexations statewide.

The City Governing Board

A city's governing board—variously called the *council*, the *board of commissioners*, or the *board of aldermen*—holds ultimate authority to act for the city. It decides what services the city provides and at what level. It establishes the city's fiscal policy by adopting the annual budget ordinance, and it levies the city's taxes. It adopts the city's ordinances. In addition to exercising these sorts of broad policy-making responsibilities, a city governing board typically decides nu-merous separate administrative matters. Thus it may authorize the city to enter into a contract, buy or sell a parcel of property, award the successful bid on a purchase or a construction project, or accept the dedication of a street.

As it takes all these actions—and many others—the governing board must act as a collective body. Just as the city itself has a legal existence separate from its residents, so too a city council is a body separate from its members. The members may act as the governing board only when properly convened, in a legal meeting. An indi-vidual member may not act on the board's behalf, at least not without specific authorization from the board itself. Moreover, a majority of the entire membership may act on the board's behalf only at a meeting of the board called and held pursuant to law.

Governing Board Structure

There is no typical structure for a city governing board in North Carolina. Each board's structure is set out in the city's charter, and charters exhibit great variety in what size the boards are; in whether the members are elected by district or at large; in whether elections are partisan or nonpartisan, by majority or plurality; and in whether terms are for two years or four. Despite the absence of a model, it may be useful to describe the patterns found in board structures and the trend of change in recent years. (Table 1-6, pages 25–26, contains summary figures on the structures of the governing boards of North Carolina cities.)

Size

Boards range in size from three members to twelve, although only four have more than eight members. By far the most popular size is five.

Length of Members' Terms

All terms are for either two years or four, the larger number of boards having four-year terms. Most boards with four-year terms stagger elections so that about half the members are elected every two years; and most changes in recent years have been to the staggered four-year term.

Election at Large or by District

Nearly all boards—almost 90 percent statewide—are elected from the city at large. Only among the larger cities does some form of district election of board members occur widely.

Election on a Partisan or Nonpartisan Basis

More than 90 percent of the governing boards are elected on a nonpartisan basis. Most of these, particularly those in the smaller cities, are elected on a plurality basis, without a primary.

Changing of the Board's Structure

A city governing board's structure may be changed through any of four methods. First, the General Assembly may change the structure by amending the city's charter. Although the legislature retains full legal control of the process, as a practical matter any such amendment would normally be enacted only at the request of the affected board. Second, the governing board itself may change its structure simply by adopting an ordinance. Such an ordinance is adopted following a public hearing on the proposed change. Third, the governing board may adopt such an ordinance, whose effectiveness is conditioned on approval by the city's voters. The governing board itself might decide to require voter approval for the change to be effective; or voters might force a referendum by submitting a sufficient number of signatures: 10 percent of the city's registered voters or 5,000, whichever is less. Fourth, the voters may initiate such a change by submitting petitions that both propose the change and call for a referendum on the proposal. This method also requires the signatures of 10 percent of the city's registered voters or 5,000, whichever is less. Each of the methods that may be carried out locally is limited to the specific options set out in the applicable statute, G.S. 160A-101 through -111.

The Mayor

North Carolina's mayors enjoy very few formal powers. With but few exceptions these powers consist of presiding at governing board meetings, voting to break ties at those meetings (and at no other time), and signing documents on behalf of the city. (A slowly increasing number of mayors vote on all matters, not just to break ties.) The strong-mayor system used in many of the nation's large cities, under which the mayor is charged with actually running city government, is simply not found in this state.

Despite having so few formal powers, many mayors do exercise great influence in the operation of their cities. The office of mayor is viewed by both the electorate and those who serve in city office as the chief political office in city government, and by the force of that perception and their personality, many mayors effectively lead their governing boards. Moreover, in small cities without a manager, the mayor often serves as de facto chief administrator simply because he or she is willing to work long hours in the town hall.

All but a few North Carolina mayors are elected by the city's voters. Those few are elected by the governing board itself from its own membership.

Governing Board Meetings

Regular Meetings

G.S. 160A-71 directs each city's governing board to fix the time and the place of its regular meetings. (If the board fails to act, the statute provides that meetings shall be held on the first Monday of each month at 10:00 A.M.) The open meetings law (see the discussion under the heading Special Meetings, later in this chapter) requires that the governing board's schedule of regular meetings be filed with the city clerk and that any changes in it be filed at least seven days before the day of the first meeting under the changed schedule. This filing constitutes the only required notice of regular meetings.

Organizational Meeting

After each city election the governing board must organize itself. In the absence of any board action, the organizational meeting is held at the board's first regular meeting in December following the election. However, G.S. 160A-68 permits a board to establish an earlier date if it wishes. It may schedule the meeting for any time during the period beginning on the day that the election results are officially determined and published, and ending on the day that the board holds its first regular meeting in December. At the organizational meeting, the newly elected and reelected members and the mayor, if appropriate, must take the oath of office. In addition, the board must elect a mayor *pro tempore* (and in cities in which the board elects the mayor, the mayor). G.S. 160A-70 specifies that the mayor *pro tempore* is to serve at the pleasure of the governing board.

Special Meetings

Special meetings of a governing board may be called in either of two ways. First, if a board is convened in a regular meeting or a duly called special meeting, it may schedule a special meeting. Second, the mayor, the mayor *pro tempore*, or any two members of the board may call such a meeting. They may do so by preparing and signing a written notice of the meeting—setting out its time, its place, and the subjects to be considered—and causing this notice to be delivered to each board member (or to his or her home). Under G.S. 160A-71 this notice must be delivered at least six hours before the meeting, but as discussed later, the open meetings law requires forty-eight hours' *public* notice of a special meeting.

In general, a governing board may take any action at a special meeting that it may take at a regular meeting. A few exceptions do exist, however. For example, it must adopt ordinances awarding or amending franchises at regular meetings, and it must take action on several procedures for selling property at regular meetings. (Even so, a board may *discuss* these matters at a special meeting; it simply may not act.) Because of these exceptions, before taking any action at a special meeting, a board should consult its attorney to ascertain whether it may properly take the action.

As mentioned earlier, the open meetings law establishes additional procedures that must be followed for each special meeting of the governing board, no matter how it is called. Except in an emergency G.S. 143-318.12 requires forty-eight hours' public notice of any special meeting, to be given in two forms. First, the notice, which must include the time, the place, and the purpose of the meeting, must be posted on the board's principal bulletin board. Second, the notice must be mailed or delivered (not telephoned) to anyone who has made a written request for notice. In an emergency, only the local news media need be informed of the meeting, and that may be done by telephone or in the same way board members are informed.

Rules of Procedure

Each governing board has the power to adopt its own rules of procedure. Exercise of this power can help prevent arguments over procedure that cannot otherwise be satisfactorily resolved. Boards often base their rules on *Robert's Rules of Order* or similar sources; however, they should be careful to adapt these models, which are primarily intended for large groups, to the special needs of a small board. For this purpose they will find an Institute of Government publication entitled *Suggested Rules of Procedure for a City Council* very helpful.[1]

One procedural rule that is useful, even if the board does not adopt a full set of rules, is a standard agenda that establishes the order of business at board meetings. Such an agenda organizes the matters to come before the board, setting forth every item that must be discussed and grouping similar subjects. A model for a standard agenda is set out in *Suggested Rules of Procedure for a City Council.*[2]

> Adoption of the agenda
> Approval of minutes of prior meeting
> Public hearing(s)
> Administrative reports
> Committee reports
> Unfinished business
> New business
> Informal discussion and public comment

Governing Board Action

Forms of Action

City governing boards take action in a variety of forms: ordinances, resolutions, motions, and orders. Textbooks usually define *ordinance* as a permanent rule of conduct imposed by a city on its citizens. Thus ordinances may limit the amount of noise that citizens may make, regulate how they may use their land, or require their businesses to treat sewage before discharging it into the city's system. In North Carolina, cities also appropriate money and levy taxes by ordinance.

The other sorts of actions are less precise in their meaning. Textbooks often define *resolutions* as expressions of board opinion on administrative matters and *motions* and *orders* as actions resulting in or expressing a decision. Thus a board might set out the city's policy on extension of utilities by resolution while approving specific extensions by motion or order. In practice the distinction is not always so carefully drawn; often one board takes actions by order or motion that another takes by resolution.

Quorum

As noted earlier, a governing board may take action only during a legally constituted meeting. A meeting is legally constituted only when a quorum is present. G.S. 160A-71 defines *quorum* as a majority of the actual membership of the council, including the mayor but excluding vacant seats. For example, if a city is governed by a five-member board plus the mayor, the actual membership of the group is six and thus a quorum is four. If one seat is vacant, however, the membership becomes five and a quorum three.

Once a quorum has been attained and the meeting convened, a member may not destroy the quorum by simply leaving. G.S. 160A-74 provides that if a member withdraws from the meeting without being excused by a majority vote of the remaining members present, he or she is still counted as present for purposes of a quorum. In addition, the member is counted as voting aye on all matters that come before the board after he or she leaves.

Voting Rules

The number of board members who must vote for a measure in order for that measure to pass differs according to a number of factors: whether the measure is an ordinance or some other form of action; when the measure first comes before the council; and whether any members have been excused from voting on the measure. G.S. 160A-75 establishes the applicable rules.

Ordinances: The Day of Introduction

To be adopted on the day that it is introduced, an ordinance, or an action no matter how labeled that has the effect of an ordinance, must be approved by a vote of at least two-thirds of the actual membership of the governing board, excluding vacant seats. In determining the membership, the mayor is not counted unless he or she has the right to vote on all questions before the board. Thus if a board has seven members and is presided over by a mayor who votes only to break ties, five members must vote in favor of an ordinance for it to be adopted on the day that it is first introduced. If there is a vacant seat, however, the actual membership is then six, and only four votes are required to adopt the ordinance on that first day.

Given this special rule pertaining to the day of introduction, what constitutes introduction? The statute states that the day of introduction is the day on which the board first votes on the subject matter of the ordinance. Examples of such a vote might include a vote to hold a hearing on the ordinance, to refer it to committee, or to try to pass it.

Ordinances: The General Rule

After the day on which it is introduced, an ordinance may be adopted by an affirmative vote equal to at least a majority of the board membership; vacancies do not affect the number necessary for approval. However, if a member has been properly excused from voting on a particular issue (see the discussion under the heading Excusing of Members from Voting, later in this chapter), on that issue the number required for approval is a majority of the number of members not excused. For example, a six-member board normally requires an affirmative vote of four members to adopt an ordinance. But if one member is excused on a particular issue, the board is treated as having only five members on that issue, and only three need vote affirmatively for the measure to pass.

Although the mayor is not counted in determining how many members constitute the board (unless he or she is elected by and from the board), if there is a tie, the mayor's vote is counted in determining whether the requisite majority vote has been attained. Thus if a six-member board divides three to three on an issue and the mayor votes affirmatively to break the tie, the measure has received the four votes necessary for its adoption.

G.S. 160A-75 requires this sort of majority on a few other measures besides ordinances: (1) any action having the effect of an ordinance, no matter how it is labeled; (2) any measure that authorizes an expenditure of funds or commits a board to one, other than the budget ordinance or a project ordinance; and (3) any measure that authorizes, makes, or ratifies a contract.

Resolutions and Motions

With the exceptions just noted, the general law makes no special provision for the sort of vote necessary to adopt measures other than ordinances. (Some charters do require that resolutions or other actions receive the same vote as ordinances.) In that circumstance the rule is that action may be taken by a majority of those present and voting, as long as a quorum is present. Thus if a board has eight members, its quorum is five; and if only five members are present, a resolution or a motion might normally be adopted by a vote of only three of the five.

Excusing of Members from Voting

G.S. 160A-75 permits a board member to be excused from voting in two circumstances in which there is a potential conflict of interest: (1) when the question involves his or her own financial interest and (2) when it involves his or her official conduct. Unless the board has adopted a procedural rule authorizing a member to be excused by the mayor or to excuse himself or herself, such an abstention should be allowed only by vote of the remaining board members. If a member is excused, that member should neither vote nor participate in any way in the deliberations leading up to the vote.

Unless a board member is excused, he or she must vote unexcused abstentions are not permitted. If a board member persists in abstaining without being excused, G.S. 160A-75 directs that the member be counted as voting aye.

The rules for mayors are slightly different. If a mayor is elected by and from the board, he or she is a board member and must vote. But a mayor who may vote only to break a tie has the option of not voting at all. The rule against unexcused abstentions does not apply to such a mayor. If he or she refuses to break a tie, the measure is defeated.

Minutes

G.S. 160A-72 requires that the governing board, through the city clerk, keep "full and accurate" minutes of its proceedings. Although the statute does not detail what full and accurate minutes should include, the proper content of board minutes is suggested by their purpose, which is to provide an official record, or proof, of governing board actions. Therefore at a minimum the minutes should include two sorts of material: (1) the actions taken by a board, stated specifically enough to be identified and proved; and (2) proof of any conditions necessary to action, such as the presence of a quorum.

As noted, the purpose of minutes is to provide an official record, or proof, of council action. In a judicial proceeding, the minutes are the only competent evidence of council action, and as such, they may not be attacked on the ground that they are incorrect. Once approved, minutes may be modified in only two ways: (1) a person may bring a legal action alleging that the minutes are incorrect and seeking a court order to correct them; and (2) much more common, a council may itself modify its minutes if they are found to be incorrect.

Appointments: Officers, Boards, and Commissions

Generally in a city with a city manager, the governing board appoints the manager, the city attorney, and the city clerk, and the manager appoints all other city officers and employees. In a number of cities with managers, the board also appoints the tax collector and the finance officer. In a city without a manager, the board appoints all department heads and normally delegates to them the appointment and the supervision of other employees.

The board and the mayor are also responsible for appointments to the various boards and commissions of city government, such as the planning commission, the parks and recreation commission, and the civil service board. (In most cases the board makes the appointments; the mayor, however, is by statute the appointing official for the housing authority.) For some boards and commissions the number of members and the length of their terms are set out by statute; for others, these matters are established by city ordinance.

Ordinance Books and Codes

G.S. 160A-78 requires that all cities maintain an *ordinance book*, separate from the minute books, in which all ordinances are placed when adopted. If a city has codified its ordinances, ordinances are placed in the ordinance book when they are adopted and remain there until they are placed in the codification. If a city has not codified its ordinances, they are placed in the ordinance book permanently.

G.S. 160A-77 requires cities with populations over 5,000 (and permits smaller cities) to codify their ordinances. A *city code* is a compilation of a city's ordinances systematically arranged by subject into chapters or articles; it is the municipal parallel to the North Carolina General Statutes. In requiring larger cities to codify their ordinances, the law assumes that these cities will have so many ordinances that particular ones would be difficult to locate in a simple ordinance book. If a city of less than 5,000 people finds itself in that situation, then it too should codify its ordinances.

It is crucial that a city place its ordinances in either an ordinance book or a code. Unless an ordinance is found in one or the other, G.S. 160A-79 will not permit the courts to enforce it.

Open Meetings

The North Carolina open meetings law (G.S. 143-318.9 through -318.18) extends to all "public bodies." In city government the term *public bodies* includes the governing board itself; each committee of the board, whether it is a standing committee or an ad hoc committee; and each group established by action of the governing board, such as a planning board, a zoning board of adjustment, a parks and recreation commission, and a human relations commission.

All *official meetings* of public bodies must be open to the public (unless closed sessions are permitted). Such meetings occur whenever a majority of the members of a public body gather to take action, hold a hearing, deliberate, or otherwise transact the business of the body.

The law permits a public body to meet in closed session for a variety of reasons:

1. *When the public body is involved in an adversarial relationship,* so that the other party may not gain an unfair advantage from discussion or action in open session. Thus closed sessions are permitted—
   a. To discuss the terms of acquisition of real property;
   b. To discuss litigation to which the city or a city employee is a party or in which the city or a city employee has a substantial interest; and
   c. To plan, conduct, or hear reports about investigations of illegal criminal conduct.
2. *When an open session might lead to substantial invasions of personal privacy.* Thus closed sessions are permitted to discuss the qualifications, the performance, the fitness, and so forth of public officers and employees and to consider information contained in records made confidential by law.
3. When the public body needs to meet in closed session for certain specified reasons—for example, to discuss matters

relating to the location or the expansion of industries or other businesses, or to consult with its attorney about matters within the attorney-client privilege.

If a public body wishes to hold a closed session, the body must first meet in open session and then vote to hold the closed session. It is not sufficient for the presiding officer simply to announce that a closed session will be held. The motion to hold the session must state the session's general purpose.

There are two remedies for correcting violations of the open meetings law. The first is an injunction. Any person may seek aninjunction to stop the recurrence of past violations of the law, the continuation of present violations, or the occurrence of threatened future violations. The second is the invalidation of any action taken or considered in violation of the law. Although such invalidation is not automatic, a trial judge does have the option of entering such an order.

Additional Resources

Lawrence, David M. *North Carolina City Council Procedures.* Chapel Hill, N.C.: Institute of Government, The University of North Carolina at Chapel Hill, 1981.

———. *Open Meetings and Local Governments in North Carolina.* 4th ed. Chapel Hill, N.C.: Institute of Government, The University of North Carolina at Chapel Hill, 1994.

———, comp. *Forms of Government of North Carolina Cities.* 1994 ed. Chapel Hill, N.C.: Institute of Government, The University of North Carolina at Chapel Hill, 1994.

Notes

1. A. Fleming Bell, II, *Suggested Rules of Procedure for a City Council* (Chapel Hill, N.C.: Institute of Government, The University of North Carolina at Chapel Hill, 1986).

2. Bell, *Suggested Rules,* 6.

3 Incorporation, Abolition, and Annexation

David M. Lawrence

Contents

IN NORTH CAROLINA, incorporation and abolition of cities are actions that only the General Assembly may take. The legislature has, however, delegated to cities broad authority to expand their boundaries through annexation.

Incorporation

In North Carolina a city may be established—that is, incorporated—in only one way: by an act of the General Assembly. Such an act establishes the initial borders of the city and enacts its charter. No standards restrict the legislature's discretion in incorporation. It may incorporate an area with very few people or with a largely rural character; it may even incorporate an area in anticipation of development, before any city in fact exists. The single constitutional restriction on the General Assembly's power of incorporation is found in Article VII, Section 1, of the state constitution. That provision stipulates that if a community lies within 1 mile of the limits of an existing city of 5,000 people or more, within 3 miles of a city of 10,000 or more, within 4 miles of a city of 25,000 or more, or within 5 miles of a city of 50,000 or more, then the General Assembly may incorporate that community only on approval of three-fifths of the members of each house. This provision reflects a state policy that favors annexation by existing cities of urban areas near their borders, over incorporation of new cities.

When a legislator agrees to assist a community in securing incorporation legislation, the legislator may proceed in either of two ways. The simpler way, and still the more common, is to introduce a bill incorporating the community, then to shepherd that bill through the General Assembly. Alternatively the legislator may first refer the proposal to the Joint Legislative Commission on Municipal Incorporations, a legislative agency established under G.S. 120-158 through -174. The commission reviews the proposal and makes a recommendation to the General Assembly on whether or not the community should be incorporated. The statute contains a number of standards—pertaining, for example, to proximity to existing cities, size, urban character, and economic resources—and if a community fails to meet all the standards, the commission is required to make a negative recommendation. Even if a negative recommendation is made, however, the General Assembly may still incorporate the community; the commission's recommendation in no way binds the legislature.

When the General Assembly incorporates an area, it may immediately do so or it may first require the approval of the area's residents. The decision of whether or not to require residents' approval rests with the General Assembly; local voters have no inherent constitutional right to approve an incorporation.

North Carolina has been an actively growing state in recent years, and the growth is reflected in the number of requests to the General Assembly to incorporate communities as cities. From the 1981 session through the 1994 session, the General Assembly enacted incorporation legislation for forty-nine communities. Of these, thirty-nine have become active cities. Voters in ten communities voted incorporation down.

Abolition

Just as only the General Assembly may incorporate a community, so too only the General Assembly may abolish, or disincorporate, a legally established city. It does so by repealing the city's charter. In practice the General Assembly takes such an action only on the request of the affected community, normally because the city government has ceased to operate. A 1971 omnibus act repealed the charters of ninety-five inactive towns,[1] but numerous others are technically still in existence.

Annexation

North Carolina's annexation laws are a central part of the state's policies for providing government services in urban areas, policies that favor the expansion of existing cities over other ways of providing those services. Only cities are authorized by law to provide the full range of basic urban services: water supply and distribution, sewage collection and treatment, law enforcement, fire protection, solid waste collection and disposal, and street maintenance and improvement. Counties are not authorized to provide street maintenance and improvement, and no types of special districts are authorized to provide either law enforcement or street maintenance and improvement. Furthermore, as is noted in the discussion on incorporation, the law favors expansion of existing cities over incorporation of new ones. Not only does the state constitution restrict the General Assembly's ability to incorporate new cities in the proximity of existing ones, but the state's annexation statutes facilitate the orderly expansion of the state's cities.

Methods of Annexation

There are four methods by which a city may annex nearby territory: annexation by legislative act, voluntary annexation of areas contiguous to the city, voluntary annexation of areas not contiguous to the city but nearby, and annexation at the city's initiative of contiguous areas that are developed for urban purposes. With only very minor exceptions,[2] these methods are available to all the state's 500-plus cities. In general, a city may annex any territory qualifying under the various procedures as long as that territory is not part of another, active city. [Under G.S. 160A-1(2), which defines *city* and *incorporated municipality* for purposes of G.S. Chapter 160A, to be considered active in this context, the other city must have held its most recent election for council.] A city may annex territory that is within a sanitary district or another special district,[3] or territory that is within another city's extraterritorial jurisdiction for land use planning. County boundaries are not a bar to annexation; some thirty cities lie within two or more counties.

Most annexations in North Carolina are voluntary, under one of the two voluntary procedures. Nearly all these annexations are relatively small, however, often comprising the property of only one person or very few persons. The greatest number of persons and the greatest amount of property are annexed under the involuntary, city-initiated procedure.

Annexation by Legislative Act

The General Assembly may at any time enlarge the boundaries of a city by local act. This approach, which is available to all cities, was the original method used to effect annexations and before 1947 was the only method available. Although the legislature has essentially complete discretion in annexing territory to existing cities, in practice it almost never does so except at the request of the city involved. At present, legislative annexation is especially useful for areas that need annexation but for some reason cannot be annexed under any of the other procedures. Annexation of public facilities surrounded by areas of limited development, annexation of areas involving lakes or rivers, annexation of unincorporated "doughnut holes" in the middle of a city, and realignment of existing boundaries to match service areas all fall into this class.

Voluntary Annexation of Contiguous Areas

G.S. 160A-31 authorizes a city to annex any area contiguous to its borders on receipt of a petition signed by all the owners of real property within the area proposed for annexation. The procedure is simple. Once a petition is presented and certified by the city clerk as sufficient, the council holds a public hearing on whether or not the statutory requirements—contiguity and signatures by all the owners of the subject property—have been met. If the council determines that the requirements have been met, it may adopt an ordinance annexing the property. This method is especially suited to annexations of small areas, new subdivisions (before lots have been sold), and tracts with a limited number of property owners.

Two points should be made about the procedure. First, the petition must contain the signature of *all* the owners of each lot or tract included in the petition. If a married couple own a property, for example, both must sign. Second, the supreme court has held that a property owner may withdraw his or her signature at any time before the council has adopted the annexation ordinance.[4] If that happens, the council may not simply annex the remaining property listed in the petition. Rather, because the council no longer has before it a petition signed by all the owners of the property listed in the petition, such a withdrawal invalidates that petition, and a new petition must be submitted including only property whose owners still desire annexation. The same is true if ownership of some of the property changes between the time the petition is signed and the time the city seeks to act. Again the council no longer has before it a petition signed by all the owners of the property listed in the petition, and submission of a new petition is necessary.

Voluntary Annexation of Noncontiguous Areas

Areas near an existing city often develop in an urban manner, but are separated from the city by undeveloped territory, so they are not subject to annexation by methods that limit annexation to contiguous areas. Frequently these areas are in the normal path for city growth, and property owners in the area desire the advantages of city services—water and sewer system, police and fire protection, solid waste collection, and street maintenance. Also, early annexation of the areas is an advantage to the city because it enables the city to plan for the orderly expansion of basic facilities to serve both these areas and the intervening areas that will develop in time.

North Carolina has responded to this situation by permitting voluntary annexation of such noncontiguous, or *satellite*, areas. The procedure was first developed and authorized for Raleigh by local act in 1967. Over the next several years eleven other cities secured similar local act authority from the legislature. In 1974, in response to the likelihood of further requests for local acts, the General Assembly enacted general enabling authority for satellite annexation (G.S. 160A-58 through -58.8), repealing the various local acts.

The procedure for satellite annexation is comparable to that for voluntary annexation of contiguous areas. Once a petition signed by all the owners of the listed property has been received and certified by the city clerk, the council holds a public hearing on the petition's sufficiency and the annexation's desirability. [G.S. 160A-58.1(a) provides that the petition need not be signed by owners of property exempt from property taxation, by railroad companies, by public utilities, or by electric or telephone membership corporations.] If the council determines that the petition is adequate and the property involved qualifies under the statutory standards, it may adopt an ordinance annexing the property. The statute sets out the following four standards that the property must meet:

1. The nearest point on the proposed satellite area must be no more than 3 miles from the city's primary limits.
2. No point within the proposed satellite area may be closer to another city than to the annexing city.
3. The total satellite area or areas of the city may not exceed 10 percent of the area of the city within its primary limits.
4. The city must be able to provide the full range of city services to the satellite area.

The fourth standard deserves elaboration. One situation in which satellite annexation is sometimes sought is when the annexing city allows the sale of beer and wine or mixed drinks and the surrounding county does not. Owners of restaurants or grocery or convenience stores then seek annexation of their single lot or tract in order to sell beer or wine or mixed drinks. Sometimes these owners will assure the annexing city that they do not care about receiving city services and indeed will sign a waiver of such services. City officials need to understand that such a waiver probably does not obviate the statutory responsibility of the city to be able to provide services and actually to provide them, and such a waiver most certainly does not bind subsequent owners of the property.

Annexation Subject to Development Standards and Service Requirements

North Carolina's principal annexation statute, enacted in 1959 and codified as G.S. 160A-33 through -56, seeks to balance the state's interest in the orderly expansion of city boundaries to include developed and developing urban territory, against residents' and property owners' interest in receiving services equitably. The balance effected permits a city to annex an area if the area is developed in an urban manner and if the city can and has plans to provide services to the area on the same basis as it provides services within the existing city. The North Carolina procedure has been recommended by the United States Advisory Commission on Intergovernmental Relations since 1967 as a model for the nation.

To be subject to annexation, an area must meet three general conditions:

1. It must be contiguous to the existing city. Satellite annexations are not permitted under this procedure.
2. One-eighth of the external boundary of the area must coincide with the existing city boundary. This requirement is intended to avoid "shoestring" or "balloon" annexations, in which a large developed area is connected to the city by only a thin string of land, such as a road right-of-way.[5]
3. The area may not be part of an existing, active city.

In addition to these general standards, the area must be developed for "urban purposes" as defined in the statute. The statute sets out three standards under which an area meets the requirement that it be developed for urban purposes:

1. The first applies to all cities, regardless of size, and measures urban character by the uses to which land is put and the degree to which land has been subdivided. The *use test* requires that at least 60 percent of all *lots and tracts* be in

urban uses: residential, commercial, industrial, institutional, or governmental. The *subdivision test* requires that at least 60 percent of the total *acreage* of land that is vacant or in agricultural, forest, or residential use be subdivided into lots or tracts of 5 acres or less in size.

2. The second standard applies only to cities with populations in excess of 5,000. It looks solely to population and defines as urban any area with a population density of at least two persons per acre.

3. The third standard, also applicable only to cities with populations greater than 5,000, measures urban character by a combination of population and degree of land subdivision. It first requires a population of at least one person per acre. It then requires that at least 60 percent of the *acreage* be subdivided into lots and tracts of 5 acres or less in size, and that at least 65 percent of the *lots and tracts* be no more than 1 acre in size.

Finally, the city must be able to provide "major" services to the annexation area on the same basis as it provides these services to the existing city. The statute defines major services as police protection, fire protection, street maintenance, solid waste collection, water distribution, and sewerage collection and treatment. A city need not do more for the annexation area than it already does for the existing city, however. If it does not provide one or more of the major services, instead relying on other governments or private parties to do so, it may continue that reliance in the annexation area.

When a city proposes to annex an area under these procedures, it begins by preparing a report that shows the character of the area and its plans for extending and financing major services to the area. After notice to the residents and the property owners of the area, the city council holds a public hearing on the proposal, explains the report, and listens to public comment. If the statutory standards are met, if the city can extend and finance the necessary services, and if the procedures have been followed, the city may annex the area by ordinance.

The Effect of Annexation on Existing Public Services

When a city annexes an area, in the absence of a statute protecting private service providers, the city becomes entitled to be the primary provider of municipal services in the annexation area. A case several years ago involving a Winston-Salem annexation illustrates this point. Forsyth County had franchised a number of private solid waste collectors to collect residential and commercial solid wastes in the area annexed. On annexation, and in conformity to its duties under the annexation statutes, Winston-Salem itself began to collect solid wastes in the area. Because the city service was financed from taxes, which the residents had to pay in any event, the effect was to put the private haulers out of business in the annexation area. When they sued the city, the North Carolina Supreme Court held that the county franchises expired on annexation and that the city had no duty to cooperate with the private collectors or to compensate them for lost business.[6] In the absence of a statute, the same rules would apply for other privately provided services.

A number of statutes have been adopted that modify this basic principle. These statutes protect volunteer fire departments and private solid waste collectors. They do not apply evenly to all annexation procedures, however.

Contracts with Fire Departments

If an area being annexed under the standards-and-services procedure is being served by a volunteer fire department, the annexing city must make a good faith effort to negotiate a contract with the fire department for the latter to continue to provide fire protection in the annexation area for five years. The statute defines what constitutes a good faith effort and permits the fire department, if its officials think it has not received a good faith offer, to appeal the matter to the state's Local Government Commission. If the commission agrees with the fire department, it must delay the annexation until the city makes the necessary offer.

If a city annexes property on petition, however, or if the annexation is effected by legislative act, there is no statutory requirement to contract with a volunteer fire department.

Fire Department Debt

If a city has annexed territory under any of the *statutory* procedures, voluntary or involuntary, and has not contracted with a volunteer fire department or has done so and the contract has expired, then the city may be responsible for a portion of the outstanding indebtedness of the volunteer department. The city's responsibility extends to any fire department debt that existed when the city began the annexation proceeding. The city's share of the debt repayment obligation is determined by the assessed valuation of the area annexed and served by the fire department in relation to the assessed valuation of the total area served by the fire department. Thus if the city's annexation area represents 5 percent of the valuation of the fire district served by the fire department, then the city must pay 5 percent of the department's debt obligation. This requirement does not apply to legislative annexations.

Contracts with Solid Waste Collectors

The result of the Winston-Salem case, described earlier, has been reversed by statute, but only in legislative annexations and in annexations done pursuant to the standards-and-services procedure. If a private solid waste collector has been doing a substantial amount of business—at least fifty residential customers or at least $500 per month of nonresidential business—in an area annexed by a city, then the collector is entitled either to have the city contract with it to continue collecting solid wastes on the city's behalf for two years, or to have the city make good the losses occasioned by the annexation (defined as 12 times the firm's average monthly revenues in the annexation area). As with fire departments, the private firm enjoys a right to appeal to the state's Local Government Commission if the city does not offer a contract or compensation. This requirement does not apply to any voluntary annexations.

Taxation of Newly Annexed Property

G.S. 160A-58.10 sets out the rules to be followed in extending property taxes to areas annexed under any of the statutory methods. (Annexations effected by legislative act are frequently made subject to G.S. 160A-58.10 as well.) These rules apply to taxes for the fiscal year during which the annexation becomes effective.

Basically, owners of annexed property are liable for city taxes for that fiscal year on a prorated basis. The city determines what each property owner's tax liability would have been had the property been in the city for the entire fiscal year, then prorates that amount based on the number of full months remaining in the fiscal year on the effective date of annexation. For example, an annexation becomes effective on March 17. At that time there are three full months remaining in the fiscal year: April, May, and June. Therefore an owner who would have been liable for $600 of city taxes had his or her property been in the city the entire year, will be liable for three-twelfths of an entire year's taxes, or $150. After that first year, property in the annexation area is taxed in the same manner as all other property in the city.

The preceding paragraph sets out the rules for determining the *amount* of tax owed by property owners in the annexation area. There are additional rules about the *date* on which those taxes are due. If the annexation occurs on or after July 1 and before September 1, the taxes are due on September 1, in the same manner as all other property taxes in the city. But if the annexation occurs on September 1 or later in the fiscal year, then the prorated taxes are not due until the next September 1.

Annexation Disputes Between Cities

Sometimes more than one city is interested in annexing the same parcel or parcels of property, and sometimes the owners of property in the area much prefer annexation by one city over annexation by another. The courts have established a doctrine of *prior jurisdiction* to determine which of two such cities is entitled to carry out the annexation. Under this doctrine, the city that takes the first formal statutory step toward annexation is entitled to complete its procedure without interference by the other. If this results in a valid annexation, then the other city no longer has any rights of annexation over the disputed area.

The first formal step differs depending on the nature of the annexation. If it is a nonvoluntary annexation under the standards-and-services procedure, the first formal step is the city's adoption of the *resolution of intent.* If it is a voluntary annexation, the first formal step is not as clear, but it appears to be the moment when the annexation petitions are presented to the city's governing board.[7]

The statutes also permit cities that would rather avoid annexation fights of this sort to enter into agreements under which each city is granted a zone of territory that it has exclusive authority to annex (G.S. 160A-58.21 through -58.28). These agreements may extend for up to twenty years, and a city must give five years' notice to withdraw from one. If a city attempts to annex territory in violation of such an agreement, any other city party to the agreement may bring an action to enforce it and thereby invalidate the annexation.

Deannexation

There are no statutory procedures under which a city may deannex territory. Rather, if a city wants to subtract some part of its existing territory, the only way it may do so is to seek a local act of the General Assembly effecting the deannexation. Such acts are quite rare and as a practical matter are only enacted at the request of the affected city.

Notes

1. 1971 N.C. Sess. Laws ch. 740.

2. Three small towns are subject to exceptions to the general annexation laws. The charter of Walnut Creek, in Wayne County, prohibits the town from annexing by any method; thus only the General Assembly can currently add territory to Walnut Creek. 1975 N.C. Sess. Laws ch. 687. The town of Bridgeton, in Craven County, may not annex territory unless it receives a petition from the owners of the property to be annexed or a majority of the voters in the area proposed for annexation approve the annexation. 1985 N.C. Sess. Laws ch. 92. The town of Holden Beach, in Brunswick County, is permitted, but not required, to condition a nonvoluntary annexation on approval by a majority of the town's voters. 1991 N.C. Sess. Laws ch. 638.

3. *See* State *ex rel.* East Lenoir San. Dist. v. City of Lenoir, 249 N.C. 96, 105 S.E.2d 411 (1958).

4. Conover v. Newton, 297 N.C. 506, 256 S.E.2d 216 (1979).

5. Even meeting the one-eighth requirement may not be enough if a court considers the resulting annexation to be shoestring in nature. In Amick v. Town of Stallings, 95 N.C. App. 64, 381 S.E.2d 221 (1989), the court invalidated an annexation that did meet the one-eighth requirement by proposing to annex a thin strip (50 to 150 feet wide) along more than 7,400 feet of existing city boundary, then extending a shoestring to annex two outlying subdivisions. The court held that the resulting annexation would have contravened the contiguity requirements of the annexation law.

6. Stillings v. City of Winston-Salem, 311 N.C. 689, 319 S.E.2d 233 (1984).

7. *See, e.g.,* City of Burlington v. Town of Elon College, 310 N.C. 723, 314 S.E.2d 534 (1984).

4 Governance in Council-Manager Cities

Kurt Jenne

Contents

NORTH CAROLINA has a long tradition of using a professional manager to assist the elected mayor and city council in governing their city. Hickory and Morganton first adopted the council-
manager plan as part of their charters in 1913, just one year after the
first charter adoption of the plan in the country by Sumter, South
Carolina. Another twenty-three North Carolina cities had adopted
the plan by 1940, and two or three more adopted it each year from
the 1940s through the 1960s. By 1994, all but 30 of the 158 cities with
a population over 2,500 had appointed a manager under their charters. Table 4-1 shows that the council-manager plan is more prevalent
in the state's large cities. The small communities tend to favor the
mayor-council form (see chapter 5). As of 1994, 99 of the state's 100
counties had adopted the similar county manager form of government for their jurisdictions.

Origins of the Council-Manager Form of Government

The council-manager form of government was created as part of
an effort to reform the corruption in American local government at
the turn of the century. Nineteenth-century Jacksonian democracy
with its aversion to concentrated power in government had created
a system (the so-called long ballot) by which popularly elected officials filled most critical administrative positions. Few of these officials
had the requisite skills or any incentive to cooperate with other

Table 4-1
Prevalence of the Council-Manager Form of Government in North Carolina Cities, by Population, 1994

	Population Class							
	25,000 & Over	10,000– 24,999	5,000– 9,999	2,500– 4,999	1,000– 2,499	500– 999	Under 500	Total
Cities	22	28	33	75	116	99	147	520
Council-manager cities	22	27	30	49	35	11	8	182

Source: David M. Lawrence, comp., *Forms of Government of North Carolina Cities*, 1994 ed. (Chapel Hill, N.C.: Institute of Government, The University of North Carolina at Chapel Hill, 1994), 40.

officials to run an efficient or effective government. This created a leadership void that was quickly filled by party machines, with political bosses controlling and manipulating voting. In return for delivering the vote, the bosses told elected officials how to run operations, invariably in a way that benefited them and their friends. Public affairs were organized and conducted on the basis of personal favors, political deals, and private profit. Machine politics laid such waste to municipal treasuries and resulted in such inefficiency that it became a blatant affront to middle- and upper-class notions of a broader public good as the guiding principle of government. To change this, progressive reformers promoted widespread citizen access to accountable elected officials through such devices as the short ballot, the strong mayor, nonpartisan at-large elections, the initiative, the referendum, and the recall.

At the same time, reformers sought to introduce into local government the application of business and scientific management principles that were hugely popular at the time. One vehicle for doing this was the council-manager plan, originated by reformer Richard Childs in 1910[1] and officially incorporated into the Model City Charter of the National Civic League in 1915. The plan sought to bring to governance a balance of democratic political accountability and honest, competent administration. In a move away from the reformers' previous support of the strong-mayor concept, it called for a small accountable elected body, without a strong elected chief executive, to employ a politically neutral, expert manager to serve at its pleasure. The manager would give objective, rational advice to the council and then faithfully execute whatever decisions the council made for the welfare of the citizens, using sound business practices to administer efficiently the day-to-day affairs of government.

The main elements of the plan have changed very little in almost eighty years. Today the criteria of the International City/County Management Association (ICMA) for officially recognizing a jurisdiction as a council-manager city include that the manager serve at the pleasure of the entire city council (not the mayor alone); have direct responsibility for the operation of governmental services and functions; have joint responsibility, in partnership with the council, for policy formulation; have direct responsibility for budget preparation and implementation; and have appointment, removal, and administrative authority over principal department heads.[2]

Adoption of the Council-Manager Form of Government in North Carolina

The council-manager form of government is one of two forms that cities in North Carolina may adopt under the General Statutes [G.S. 160A-101(9)]. The other form, mayor-council, in which there is no requirement for the governing board to employ a professional manager, is discussed in chapter 5. It is fairly typical for very small communities to operate under the mayor-council form, usually because their small size and administrative simplicity make the constant attention of a professional manager neither necessary to make things run well nor worth the cost. Once a community reaches a population of a few thousand, however, it usually begins to see benefits that it can realize by employing a full-time professional. Among communities that decide a change is warranted, some cities change their form of government and hire a city manager; others hire a chief administrator without changing the form of government right away and then after some successful experience with that arrangement, make the full transition to the council-manager form. No charter amendment is required for a city council to hire an administrator, but if a city wants to adopt the council-manager form, it may do so by amending its charter in any one of four ways: by ordinance; by ordinance subject to a referendum; by initiative petition and a referendum; and by special act. These options are discussed in the following sections.

Options for Amendment of the Charter

Amendment by Ordinance

A city council may simply pass an ordinance adopting the council-manager form of government (G.S. 160A-102). This is the option most commonly used by cities today. To exercise it, a council must first adopt a resolution of intent that describes the proposed charter amendment and, at the same time, call a public hearing to be held within 45 days. The council must publish a notice of the hearing and a summary of the proposal at least 10 days before the hearing is to take place. After the hearing, the council may not take action before its next regular meeting, but it may act on the ordinance at that meeting or at any time after that. If the council adopts the ordinance, the council must publish a notice summarizing its substance and the effects of the action within 10 days of adoption.

Thus under this option a council may simply adopt an ordinance after following the specified procedure, without any actual vote of the people. However, adoption by this method may have to be confirmed by a referendum if enough of the voters want it so (G.S. 160A-103). If a valid petition is filed with the city clerk within 30 days after the council publishes the notice of its adoption of the ordinance, an election must be held on the question between 60 and 120 days following the receipt of the petition. To be valid, the petition must include the signatures of 10 percent or 5,000 of the city's registered voters, whichever is less. If the election supports the ordinance, the ordinance takes effect; if not, it becomes void.

Amendment by Ordinance Subject to a Referendum

A city council may on its own initiative make its ordinance subject to a referendum (G.S. 160A-102). Council members might think that the council-manager form would be in the best interest of the community, but want to give the citizens an opportunity to confirm or deny that judgment. In this case the council follows the same procedures described earlier for the simple passage of an ordinance without a referendum; however, on passage of the ordinance the council simultaneously adopts a resolution calling a referendum election on the issue. The election must be held within 90 days of adopting the ordinance. If the council takes the initiative to call an election in this manner, then it must publish a notice of the election at least 30 days before voter registration closes, and does not have to publish a separate notice of the ordinance's passage. If a majority of those voting in the election support the ordinance, it is put into effect; if not, it becomes void.

Amendment Following Initiative Petition and a Referendum

The voters themselves may initiate a referendum to change the form of government (G.S. 160A-104). If a petition that is valid by the same standards described earlier, is initiated by citizens and submitted to the city council, the council must call a referendum election on the issue between 60 and 120 days after receiving the petition. The council need not pass any ordinance before the election, but must publish a notice of the election, including a description of the issue to be voted on, 30 days before registration closes. If the election decides in favor of the proposed changes, then the council must pass an ordinance putting them into effect. In this case the ordinance is immune to a petition to put it to a vote after the fact as provided in G.S. 160A-102.

Amendment by Special Act

A city council may ask the General Assembly to enact a bill amending the city's charter. The special act may require a referendum or not. This method is seldom used anymore because of the ease with which a city can decide the matter under the general law described earlier. Among the sixty-five local acts passed in this manner by 1975, sixty of them required referenda.

Requirement to Keep the Change for Two Years

G.S. 160A-107 requires that a city that changes its charter by any of the first three general law provisions, keep the change in effect for at least two years after adoption. The purpose of this provision is to give the new arrangement an opportunity to get through the inevitable tremors of change and to prove itself. In the case of moving to the council-manager form, this provides an opportunity for the council, the mayor, and the manager to work through new ways of doing things and to figure out how to make the arrangement work well for everyone involved. The transition is seldom easy. Old habits are hard to change quickly, and the powers and duties assigned to the city manager by statute are ones that others on the council or staff may have been exercising for a long time, making them difficult to relinquish under the new arrangement. Adjustment of the roles that various elected and appointed officials play under the new form of government is usually a more complex and difficult undertaking than the change in the charter that preceded it.

Roles of the City Council, the Mayor, and the City Manager

A few assumptions implicit in the council-manager plan have influenced North Carolina's and other states' general laws regarding this form of government and affected the way in which elected officials and managers perceive their roles in relation to each other. The plan, for the most part, assumes that the city council fairly represents the electorate, that a clear public interest can be found to guide most decisions, and that therefore the council can, with some degree of consensus, give the manager clear direction for carrying out its policies. The plan has always promoted separation of the council's responsibility for political judgments and policy direction from the manager's responsibility for administration in accordance with the council's overall policy guidance and his or her own politically neutral expertise. By these assumptions the plan seeks to create that effective balance between objective, honest, expert governmental operation and democratic access and control through the authority and the accountability of the elected body.

Many of these underlying assumptions have always been difficult to realize in reality and are becoming even more problematic in the political and social landscape of the 1990s. A task force of city and county managers from all over the country convened by ICMA in 1993 to examine council-manager relations began its work by talking about the forces of change that were affecting the council-manager form of government. Managers suggested that citizens seemed to be losing respect for both politics and government itself and that the public whom managers served was increasingly fragmented into interest groups with competing narrow agendas, an unwillingness to cooperate, and a tendency to vie for absolute control. As a result, managers saw themselves faced with mixed signals and sometimes unresolvable conflicts of expectations from elected officials and citizens. They felt that directly elected mayors often viewed managers as competition in the arena of local leadership and that the old business traditions of the profession had themselves evolved into such a state of "thriving on chaos" that managers who played by the old rules might find themselves characterized as impediments to progress.[3]

These changes and managers' attempts to adjust to them have led to confusion over what the absolutes of the council-manager plan are—which of the elements in the idealized version are essential to its integrity and which can be changed or adapted to the needs of politics in local government henceforth. Today many managers and elected officials seem to be seeking ways to forge a true partnership in governance, one that recognizes that council members, mayors, and managers are mutually dependent on one another, share responsibility for most of the aspects of governance, yet divide some responsibility for fulfilling certain expectations in order to make the whole system work for the benefit of the community. But such partnerships must often be formed and sustained in an arena in which personal interests, district interests, and confrontational politics make it difficult or impossible to obtain the kind of political consensus that used to exist on many councils. The responsibilities of the council, the mayor, and the manager that come from the law, from the managers' professional code, from realistic notions of roles in policy and administration, and from commonly understood expectations of behavior can be helpful in understanding how this partnership might work and how it is often challenged in the context of the council-manager form of government.

Statutory Responsibilities

The City Council

Regardless of the form of government, G.S. 160A-67 provides that "except as otherwise provided by law, the government and general management of the city shall be vested in the council." The city council has the authority to confer powers and duties on both the mayor and the manager in addition to those conferred on them by law. Further, under G.S. 160A-146 the council has the authority to organize and reorganize city government. Except when expressly prevented by other laws, the council can ". . . create, change, abolish, and consolidate offices, positions, departments, boards, commissions, and agencies . . . to promote orderly and efficient administration of city affairs . . ." Finally, G.S. 160A-147 provides that in a council-manager city, the council as a body appoints the city manager to serve at its pleasure. Thus by statute the city council has the primary responsibility to establish the general framework under which the government can meet the needs of the community, and as the employer of the manager, it is the body to whom the manager is directly responsible and accountable.

The Mayor

G.S. 160A-101(8) gives a city the option of electing the mayor separate from election of the members of council, in a vote of the people, to serve from two to four years; or having the council select the mayor from among its members to serve at its pleasure. In either case the statutory powers and duties conferred on the mayor are few. Most of the significant powers held by a mayor in North Carolina are created by individual city charters, by action of the city council, or by the mayor's own political stature. G.S. 160A-67 confers on the mayor all powers and duties enumerated in the General Statutes as well as any others conferred on him or her by the council. This statute recognizes the mayor as the official head of the city for purposes of serving civil process, and most federal agencies extend this same recognition for purposes of official correspondence or actions such as grant awards or enforcement of federal laws and regulations. G.S. 160A-69 requires the mayor to preside at council meetings, and G.S. 160A-71 gives the mayor the power to call special meetings of the council. If the mayor is elected by the people, he or she may be given the right to vote on all matters before the council or only the right to vote to break a tie. If the mayor is selected from the council, he or she does not give up his or her vote as a member of the council and may vote on all matters.

Sometimes when the manager has resigned or been fired by the council, the mayor seems like a natural choice as a stand-in until another manager can be found; however, G.S. 160A-151 expressly makes the mayor (and any member of the council) ineligible to serve as manager, interim manager (temporarily filling a vacancy), or acting manager (serving in the manager's absence). Under this provision the mayor could always resign his or her office and be appointed as manager, but could not hold the elected and appointed offices at the same time.

The City Manager

North Carolina's laws authorizing the council-manager form of government, like those of most of the states, drew on the provisions contained in the National Municipal League's Model City Charter. Consequently the specifications of the powers and duties of the city manager found in North Carolina's General Statutes (G.S. 160A-148) are fairly typical of those found nationwide, and are consistent with the general elements of the council-manager plan:

Section 148. Powers and duties of manager. The manager shall be the chief administrator of the city. He shall be responsible to the council for administering all municipal affairs placed in his charge by them, and shall have the following powers and duties:

(1) He shall appoint and suspend or remove all city officers and employees not elected by the people, and whose appointment or removal is not otherwise provided for by law, except the city attorney, in accordance with general personnel rules, regulations, policies, or ordinances as the council may adopt.

Most city charters in North Carolina provide for the council to appoint the city clerk and the city attorney, although the Greensboro charter makes the manager responsible for both of these appointments. A few council-manager cities, like New Bern, have charters that require the council to appoint the chief of police, a very high-profile and sensitive position. Otherwise, except for the clerk and the attorney, the manager is responsible for the appointment, the disciplining, and the removal of all administrative personnel. Managers consider this to be one of their most important authorities because if the council is to hold them responsible and accountable for the performance of administrative units, they feel that they must, in turn, have hiring and firing authority over the personnel directly responsible for the units' work. An important qualification to this authority is that it must be exercised in accordance with whatever personnel rules the council adopts.

(2) He shall direct and supervise the administration of all departments, offices, and agencies of the city, subject to the general direction and control of the council, except as otherwise provided by law.

This provision makes the manager clearly responsible for the direct supervision of city operations, in accordance with whatever laws, regulations, policies, direction, and guidance the council might give. The council's control is intended to be general in nature, with the manager exercising professional judgment on how to carry out the council's intent. Obviously this can be a difficult line to draw clearly, and its actual practice varies from city to city depending on a variety of factors like tradition, confidence in the person who serves as manager, individual personalities and styles, and the issues involved. Charlotte and Rocky Mount have charter provisions prohibiting council members from giving orders to or trying to influence the actions of the manager's subordinates, but this is a normal expectation under the council-manager form. Otherwise, employees might be confused or paralyzed by conflicting directions, and the manager might legitimately object to being held accountable for the results. To make sure the tenet is honored, some managers have insisted that there be no contact between employees and council members without their permission. This usually proves frustrating for everyone, however: employees feel that they are being deprived of their citizenship, the manager finds that he or she has to devote too much time to managing traffic, and council members regard it as unduly restrictive of their ability to keep track of the pulse of government or to get simple information. Most managers find it effective to have an understanding that the council will not give directions to employees, but that members are free to seek information and keep up with employees' activities and outlook.

(3) He shall attend all meetings of the council and recommend any measures that he deems expedient.

The manager does not actually have to attend all meetings of the council in person; however, this provision acknowledges that one of the manager's fundamental responsibilities is to give professional advice and counsel to the council in its deliberations or, at the very least, to ensure that the council has access to and understands the information it needs to make informed choices in the matters coming before it. Thus the expectation is that the council will have access to the advice of the manager or the manager's designee any time it gathers. Most managers will not miss a meeting if they can help it and will be careful to secure the concurrence of the mayor or the entire council if they must be absent. They will also make sure that an assistant or whoever is chosen to act in their place is fully able and prepared to give the council the support it needs.

(4) He shall see that all laws of the State, the city charter, and the ordinances, resolutions, and regulations of the council are faithfully executed within the city.

This general supervisory role of the manager is self-explanatory.

(5) He shall prepare and submit the annual budget and capital program to the council.

In a council-manager city the manager is also the budget officer (G.S. 159-9) and is required by G.S. 159-11 to prepare a budget for consideration by the council in whatever form and detail the council might specify. This is, of course, a *recommended* budget and capital program, which the council may modify as it wishes before adopting the budget ordinance (see chapter 13).

(6) He shall annually submit to the council and make available to the public a complete report on the finances and administrative activities of the city as of the end of the fiscal year.

In practice this is usually done more often than once a year. The manager commonly makes quarterly administrative reports to the council, and some councils receive monthly financial statements.

(7) He shall make any other reports that the council may require concerning the operations of city departments, offices, and agencies subject to his direction and control.

(8) He shall perform any other duties that may be required or authorized by the council.

These responsibilities too are self-explanatory.

The ICMA Code of Ethics

The professional city manager has another set of expectations governing his or her behavior: a code of ethics originally developed in 1924 by the International City Managers' Association (the original name of ICMA)[4] and modified periodically since then. The ICMA Code of Ethics is a point of pride among professional managers. Any manager admitted to the association is bound by its ethical tenets and is subject to censure by or even expulsion from the association for violations of this professional code. Overall, the code seeks to enforce and balance what ICMA believes to be the prerogatives that the professional manager must have to do his or her job properly and the obligations that the manager must meet in order to honor the authority of the council and promote the overall welfare of the citizens.

The twelve tenets of the Code of Ethics are as follows:[5]

1. Be dedicated to effective, responsive local government by responsible elected officials and professional general management.
2. Be a constructive, creative, and trusted public servant.
3. Be dedicated to the highest ideals of honor and integrity.
4. Recognize the chief function of local government as serving the best interests of all citizens.
5. Propose policies, give the council all the information it needs to make decisions, and carry out the council's decisions and policies.
6. Give credit to the council for establishing policies; accept responsibility for carrying them out.
7. Refrain from involvement in local electoral politics.
8. Continually improve his or her own and others' professional competence.
9. Keep citizens informed and promote effective communications and public service.
10. Resist any encroachment on his or her professional responsibilities.
11. Handle all personnel matters on the basis of merit.
12. Seek no personal favor.

Recent censures of managers for violations of the tenets illustrate how they are applied by the profession. A city manager in Texas was publicly censured for falsifying an expense report (violating tenets 2, 3, and 9). He was held accountable, even though he had been directed by an elected official to submit the misinformation. Private censures have involved job-hopping (violating tenet 4), publicly engaging in the election process (violating tenet 7), failing to disclose complete and accurate information about background and qualifications on the résumé (violating tenet 3), and joining in real estate investments in the jurisdiction in a manner that could appear to be a conflict of interest (even though there was no indication of actual conflict of interest in this case) (violating tenet 12).

Roles and Relationships in Policy and Administration

Although both the law and the ICMA Code of Ethics prescribe responsibilities for the manager and the council, they are very general and do not go far in describing exactly how these officials should actually interact with one another in order to be effective in the division of labor set out in these tenets. Popular wisdom used to promote the notion of a strict dichotomy between policy making and administration: the elected body should make policy, and the administration should carry it out, each without interference from the other as it performed its functions. The dichotomy probably arose originally from a misinterpretation of a highly respected paper by Woodrow Wilson in which he advocated the use of appointed officials to relieve legislators of the burden of administrative functions.[6] The fact that the popular interpretation of this dichotomy theory reduced council-manager relations to a simple, easy-to-follow formula, probably accounts for its perpetuation. However, as anyone who works in local government for very long soon realizes, matters are just not that simple. The city manager often has training, analytical skills, experience in other jurisdictions, and an in-depth knowledge of the city and its governmental operations that would be extremely helpful to the council in establishing policy. On the other hand, when constituents complain about the quality of a service or the treatment they receive from city employees, a member of the council is unlikely to feel that it is an administrative matter that does not concern him or her. John Nalbandian, a respected scholar of local government who has served as mayor of Lawrence, Kansas, has observed,

> The practical world of city management often suggests a more complicated view [than the dichotomy theory]. The manager is deeply involved in policy-making as well as implementation, responds to a multitude of community forces as well as to the governing body, and incorporates a variety of competing values into the decision-making process.[7]

Figure 4-1.
Dichotomy-Duality Model
Mission-Management Separation with Shared Responsibility
for Policy and Administration

Dimensions of Governmental Process

**Illustrative tasks
for Council**

Determine "purpose,"
scope of services, tax
level, constitutional
issues.

Pass ordinances,
approve new projects
and programs, ratify
budget.

Make implementing
decisions (e.g., site
selection), handle
complaints, oversee
administration.

Suggest management
changes to Manager;
review organizational
performance in
Manager's appraisal.

**Illustrative tasks for
administrators**

Advise (what city "can"
do may influence what it
"should" do), analyze
conditions and trends.

Make recommendations
on all decisions, formu-
late budget, determine
service distribution
formulae.

Establish practices and
procedures and make
decisions for implement-
ing policy.

Control the human,
material, and informa-
tional resources of
organization to support
policy and administrative
functions.

The curved line suggests the
division between the Council's
and the Manager's spheres of
activity, with the Council to the
left and the Manager to the
right of the line.

The division presented is
intended to approximate a
proper degree of separation
and sharing. Shifts to either
the left or right would indicate
improper incursions.

Source: "Dichotomy and Duality: Reconceptualizing the Relationship Between Policy and
Administration in Council-Manager Cities," *Public Administration Review* 45 (January/
February 1985), 228.

A more realistic relationship between elected officials and
managers in policy and administration has been depicted by James H.
Svara, as shown in figure 4-1.[8] This depiction recognizes that there
is no strict dichotomy; rather, there is involvement of both elected
and administrative officials at all levels of policy and administration.
The involvement and the responsibility of each are proportionately
different depending on the level at which they occur. At the highest

level the city council is responsible for setting the overall direction, or *mission*, of city government, including its purpose, scope, and philosophy. Figure 4-1 suggests that although the council has a clearly dominant role in this function, the manager can bring knowledge and experience to the table that enhances the council's ability to make informed choices and decisions. The council must enact *policy* to achieve the mission that it sets for city government. It does this through functions like budgeting, capital improvement programming, comprehensive planning, and the making of laws and policies regarding city life and governmental operations. Although the council has the final responsibility for adopting budgets, plans, and ordinances, the manager and his or her staff play a major role in developing technical studies and estimates, and analyzing the impact of alternative choices. Thus these kinds of policy making are a shared responsibility in reality. In government, how something is done is often as important to citizens' satisfaction with the outcome as what is done. Consequently, although the manager and the staff are responsible for implementing the policies adopted by the council, elected officials still have a stake in how those policies are carried out—that is, in *administration* and *management*. After making a decision to build a new community center and budgeting funds for it, the council will almost always have a continued interest in how the facilities actually look and work. It will be concerned about how well the scheduling of work on a downtown streetscape project minimizes disruption of business for merchants. It will always have an interest in how overall employee morale is affected by internal operating policies developed by the administration.

Thus figure 4-1 describes a partnership at every level of endeavor, with the elected body shouldering most of the responsibility, authority, and initiative at the mission level, the administration shouldering most of it in internal management, and the two sharing it significantly in policy and administration. In practice the line that is depicted in figure 4-1 is symbolic; it would be expected to vary among jurisdictions and within a particular jurisdiction over time for the reasons described earlier. Some councils want the manager to push aggressively for policies that he or she thinks necessary; other councils want the manager to stay in the background and respond to council initiatives. Some councils feel the need to be intimately familiar with day-to-day occurrences in city business; others want to concern themselves with administrative matters only when those matters might create public controversy. Agreement between elected and appointed officials on where the line is drawn is an essential element of a good relationship and has to be checked out frequently to make sure everyone understands.

The elected officials have to consider more than their own personal preferences and operating styles in this matter, taking into account how citizens perceive the relationship between elected and appointed officials. Citizens' most important expectation is that the council will either represent or at least be attentive to their interests. If administrators do not satisfy this expectation on behalf of the council by their service and behavior, citizens will usually expect the council to take a more dominant role, whereas if citizens' needs are being met routinely, they may be satisfied with elected officials taking a more passive role on a day-to-day basis.

Today it may be harder for either the council or the administration to please everyone, harder for the council to achieve consensus on many issues that might have been routine in the past, and therefore harder for the council to give the manager clear direction at all times. This, in turn, makes it harder for the manager to administer the city in a way that satisfies the entire council. Some observers of local government bemoan the increase in confrontational politics on the part of constituents and the trend back to district representation on councils, as undermining the principles of broad representation of the public good and efficient administration. Others, however, point out that these developments are just a surfacing of the reality of constituent politics and make for more open, fairer representation of all the diverse interests in the community, instead of just those of a powerful privileged few or an exclusive majority. Nevertheless, many managers feel it is now more difficult than it used to be to obtain and maintain the kind of clear consensus and direction from the council that is one of the fundamental assumptions of the council-manager form of government.

Common Expectations among the City Council, the City Manager, and the Mayor

Specific expectations and practices among the council, the manager, and the mayor vary greatly from community to community, depending on the social and political norms, the traditions, and the local codes. They can also vary over time in a particular community with changes in the personalities involved as elected officials turn over and managers come and go. However, experience and research have shown that in some critical aspects of the partnership, there are fairly consistent expectations across jurisdictions and over time. For the most part these expectations may be regarded as basic and necessary to defining roles and maintaining a healthy relationship between the elected council and the manager.

Expectation 1: The Manager Is a Valued Advisor to the Council

Both the General Statutes and the ICMA Code of Ethics require the manager to give policy advice to the council and to carry out its policy decisions; however, neither tenet deals specifically with some subtle but important aspects of this process. The General Statutes require the manager to "recommend any measures that he deems expedient," and the Code of Ethics requires him or her to "submit policy proposals" and give "facts and advice" to help the council make decisions and set goals. Councils expect the manager to offer balanced and impersonal advice: to provide all relevant information that is reasonably available on the different options, to present the pros and the cons of each option, to explain the professional reasoning that leads him or her to a recommendation, and to base that reasoning on established professional, technical, or legal principles, not on personal beliefs, no matter how strongly held, unless the council specifically solicits them. Even the appearance or the suspicion that the manager is being selective in the information he or she gives, personally biased in the judgment he or she renders, or manipulative of the council's decision in the way he or she presents material, can severely damage the manager's credibility and thereby his or her effectiveness.

Most managers feel responsible for arguing for a professionally compelling course of action no matter how unpopular it might be with the public or with the council itself. This often requires the manager to have the courage to make an unpopular recommendation that might not have very good prospects of being accepted. Many managers must have in mind at those times the human propensity for striking out at the messenger who bears bad news. Often council members or citizens who are upset over the facts that are presented or who disagree with the recommendations might, at best, attack the validity of the advice, at worst, attack the competence, the motives, or the character of the manager who gives the advice. One of the most difficult tests of a professional manager as policy advisor is to remain cool and undefensive during heated debate over the information and the recommendations that he or she has brought to the council.

Once the council has made a decision, the manager must get behind it fully and make sure that the administration does the same. The General Statutes require the manager to see that all actions of the council are "faithfully executed," and the Code of Ethics requires him or her to "uphold and implement" all the council's policies. This sometimes requires the manager aggressively to implement something that he or she thinks is a bad idea. If the manager believes that the direction the council has given is illegal or if it is professionally or personally repugnant, and if the manager cannot dissuade the council from its action, he or she can, of course, resign. If the manager chooses to stay, however, he or she is obliged to assist the council in carrying out its will. Sometimes the manager will be put in the awkward position of arguing strenuously for a course of action that the council subsequently rejects, and then having the press ask what he or she thinks of the council's decision. Unless reasoned debate has changed the manager's mind, to agree completely with the council will make the manager look like a toady. On the other hand, to criticize or denigrate the council for its decision will violate the Code of Ethics and court legitimate censure. Most professional managers who find themselves in this situation acknowledge the differences in judgment that were exhibited in the deliberations and try to explain the reasoning that brought the council to the decision it made. In other words, they will help the council explain its decision to the public and help the public understand the council's point of view. Obviously, carrying out this important responsibility often takes great emotional maturity.

Expectation 2: The Council and the Manager Jointly Strive for Good Service to Citizens

Service to citizens is the litmus test of municipal operations, and it is where the dichotomy theory miserably fails the test of reality. Regardless of what the council accomplishes, if the government does not satisfactorily deliver basic services to citizens, citizens will be dissatisfied with the council, and the council in turn will be dissatisfied with the manager and the administration. Everyone's fate rises or falls with citizens' satisfaction over services. Therefore one of the most important responsibilities of the manager is to be aggressive in ensuring that his or her administration provides the very best service possible to the community. Careful planning, budgeting, and management help, but the manager cannot be everywhere at all times to supervise day-to-day execution, so he or she has to create in the organization a culture of responsiveness, both in providing routine service to citizens and in handling special requests and complaints. This usually involves pushing down to the lowest levels of the organization the responsibility and the authority to make decisions and to act, being supportive of people who take initiative, and helping people learn from mistakes made in good faith. The manager must take personal risks on behalf of employees and fully accept responsibility with the council when things go wrong.

On the other hand, if the manager is going to accept such responsibility, he or she should be able to expect that council members will give the system a chance to work and will channel complaints through the manager. The gratitude that an elected official might enjoy as a result of personally wading into a problem and doing something is ordinarily short-lived and transitory. More lasting credit usually comes from citizens' recognition that the council has created and maintains a responsive workforce as an essential ingredient of efficient and effective governance. Even when an administration is very good at responding to citizens' needs, people will ask their elected officials for help, usually in good faith, but sometimes with manipulation in mind. Managers expect council members to determine whether the citizen has tried administrative remedies and to steer the citizen into the system if he or she has not. If the administration has in fact been unresponsive, then the manager expects to be informed and to have the opportunity to get the problem fixed, and the manager will give the council member the necessary information to follow up with the citizen if he or she wishes.

Expectation 3: Elected Officials' Relationships with Employees Are Carefully Managed

Observing a chain of command in answering service needs is desirable from the standpoint of managing resources effectively. The problems that can arise when elected officials intervene directly in service operations include confusing employees with conflicting directives or priorities from supervisors and elected officials, weakening or destroying clear accountability for work results, and short-circuiting coordinated plans developed by the supervisor responsible for day-to-day operations. This does *not* mean that elected officials should not have periodic or even regular contact with city employees. To prohibit such contact would be to ask employees and elected officials to give up some of their basic rights as members of the community, and would make it harder to build harmony among the critical people in city government. It would also be inefficient. To funnel all communication through the manager would waste his or her time with unnecessary traffic and would be terribly awkward and inconvenient for elected officials.

A common arrangement to protect planned workflow and still reap the benefits of regular interaction is to encourage direct contact between elected officials and employees for routine inquiries or requests that do not affect administrative workloads, and to route more significant requests through the manager. This permits elected officials to obtain routine information that they need quickly and accurately from the persons who are closest to the action and most informed about details—just as citizens can (or should be able to do!). It also provides the opportunity for regular informal communication between elected officials and employees, helping each become more familiar, more comfortable, and more trusting of the other over time. Anything an elected official wants from employees that will involve significant and unplanned expenditures of time or money, or disrupt agreed-on work schedules, is taken up with the manager so as not to put employees on the spot. Then the manager and the member can make informed choices about whether the request should take outright precedence over existing commitments, whether something could be done that would meet the official's needs but not be disruptive, or whether it should not be done at all, given other commitments. The manager and the elected official who made the request might also agree to submit the question to the whole council to decide as a body whether a change in resource allocation would make sense or not.

Sometimes managers have attempted to cut off direct contact between elected officials and employees to counteract members of the council who meddle with or harass employees, or employees who are manipulative and disloyal. Like most treatments of a symptom alone, such an approach usually does little or nothing to solve the problems that underlie these dysfunctional behaviors. Often it makes matters worse by creating a siege mentality among administrators, anxiety among employees, and distrust and frustration among elected officials.

Expectation 4: The Council Acts as a Body and Is Dealt with as a Body

One of the tricky aspects of dealing with a council is that by law, it takes official action as a body, yet it is made up of three to thirteen individual politicians (counting the mayor) with various constituencies, personal interests, and personalities. Without benefit of consensus or at least formal support of a majority of the council, individual elected officials often find it hard to refrain from imposing their own personal agendas on the administration. Most managers will welcome, discuss, and frequently respond directly to suggestions at any time from individual council members, as long as they do not conflict with the pleasure of the council as a whole. However, if a request sets new directions or requires allocation of funds or staff time not anticipated by the council, the manager will usually ask the member making the proposal to put it to the entire council for consideration. It is important for the manager to treat all members alike in this respect. There will always be some council members whom the manager likes better, gets along with better, or agrees with more than others. Unless he or she is scrupulous in avoiding even the appearance of favoritism, however, the manager can seriously undermine his or her effectiveness by permanently alienating the members who feel slighted or barred from some inner circle, real or imagined. Even in the case of routine requests for information, most managers will keep all members informed of transactions with individuals by sending copies of written responses or summaries of opinions rendered or actions agreed to in conversation, to all members for their information.

One area in which the manager must take initiative in this matter is in keeping members up-to-date on day-to-day events. Elected officials do not like surprises. It is embarrassing for an elected official to be asked about some newsworthy item of city business and have to admit that he or she does not know much about it. It is unforgivable for someone to be the *only* member of the council who is ignorant about it! Councils expect their managers to be sensitive, alert, and responsive to their needs for current information, including making occasional extraordinary efforts that might be necessary to make sure that every member of the council has the same level of information and understanding.

Expectation 5: The Manager and the Council Give Each Other a Chance to Prove Themselves

One of the implicit foundations of council-manager government is that a professional manager, who is dedicated to serving whatever elected body is seated by the people, will provide smooth transitions, some institutional stability and memory, and some changes, as different individuals or groups join and leave the council. Nevertheless, it is sometimes hard for council members who have sought election because they too want to bring about changes, to trust the loyalty of the manager to the new members or to have confidence in the ability of the manager to help bring about the changes they want. In short, the manager is sometimes viewed as inextricably tied to the old way of doing things and assumed to be an impediment to progress. Most managers strive to change the direction of administration in whatever way the council decides (they can resign if they feel they cannot serve the new council's agenda in good conscience). Therefore managers expect newly elected officials to give them a chance to prove that they can serve the new council as well as the old one.

On the other hand, sometimes after an election the manager finds himself or herself working for one or more council members who as candidates roundly criticized the way in which the community was governed and managed. During their campaigns, some of those council members may have called for the manager's dismissal. Few elected officials would dispute that even if they had prior municipal involvement on volunteer boards or commissions, the view of government from the inside is very different than the view from the outside. Candidates, on taking office, usually learn that the simplicity and the surety of campaign rhetoric seldom stand up to the complexity of governance or management. Realizing this, experienced and mature managers will withhold judgment on members whose campaigning seems threatening and will set about to prove that they can serve the new council as well as they served the old. They will hope that given a chance, they will eventually earn the trust and the confidence of the new members as those members learn the realities of governing, gain skill as legislators, and observe the manager's performance at close hand.

Expectation 6: The Manager and the Council Freely Give and Seek Feedback

One of the key ingredients for building and maintaining a relationship of trust and confidence is open communication. City managers and elected officials invariably find themselves caught up in a whirlwind of daily activity. There never seems to be quite enough time to do everything and especially to do it all just right. So both elected officials and managers make mistakes; they overlook side effects of actions taken in the heat of urgency, and they say or do things that convey messages they never intended. All these occurrences can generate dissatisfaction, disappointment, offense, anger, and distrust if they are not recognized and resolved appropriately. The key to dealing effectively with such matters is to work hard to maintain open communication among elected officials and the manager. The jobs of both elected official and manager can make the persons holding them feel very isolated. The manager, accountable to a council of citizens and responsible for a city workforce, might feel apart from both, a part of neither. The elected official, held accountable by fellow citizens for the city's administration, might feel that he or she has very little direct role to play in making sure things go well. Open communication is one effective cure for these feelings of isolation. Managers must provide all council members with accurate, relevant, and timely information, and council members must take initiative to ask questions and make their interests, positions, and feelings known to the manager.

Most managers appreciate clear signals about how well they are satisfying the elected officials whom they serve, even when those signals are negative. Being criticized is not pleasant, but it is in fact more comforting than inferring all kinds of unexpressed dissatisfaction from elected officials' behavior. Many people find it easier to give faint compliments or remain silent than to confront others—even subordinates—with criticism; however, dissatisfaction withheld is usually hard to conceal for very long without being revealed indirectly by behavior or rumor. This kind of indirect revelation almost always produces at least some inaccuracy and misinterpretation regarding facts, feelings, and underlying motivations; distracts the manager, who becomes unduly preoccupied with figuring out where he or she stands; and often has the effect of shutting down communication and producing an increasing spiral of tension between the manager and the elected official involved. On the other hand, when a council member openly directs constructive criticism at the manager—gets the issue out on the table—the manager can ask questions, provide information that the member might not have, and respond to his or her concerns. Such dialogue gives council members the opportunity to clarify their expectations of the manager by means of concrete examples as they come up, and it gives the manager more certainty about what he or she has to do to satisfy the council and how well he or she is succeeding. Each council and its manager have to work out for themselves how publicly they are willing to give and receive this individual feedback. They should come to an agreement early in the manager's tenure and confirm or modify it when there is turnover on the council.

Many elected officials appreciate the same candor from the manager when they are behaving in a way that frustrates effective management. This attitude is by no means universal, however, and most managers are very careful to determine the comfort zone of a particular body and its individual members in offering them constructive criticism. Nevertheless, the benefits of freely giving and accepting feedback are potentially as great for elected officials as for the manager.

The Special Role of the Mayor

As noted earlier, the role of the mayor in a council-manager city in North Carolina is largely limited to serving as ceremonial head of the government and presiding over its affairs.[9] Not only does the mayor have no veto over council actions and no executive authority; in some jurisdictions he or she may not even vote on matters coming before the council. Yet many mayors in council-manager cities continue to be very influential in exerting political leadership and in facilitating the work of both the council and the administration by assuming roles for themselves that are not specifically prescribed by statute.

Political Leadership

In the vast majority of council-manager cities in North Carolina (175 of 182, as of 1994), candidates run specifically for the office of mayor. Only a handful (7) still select the mayor from among the members of the elected council. Just by being elected to office apart from the council, the mayor assumes a certain amount of political clout and an image of leadership in the eyes of the public. Therefore, regardless of the paucity of powers granted to the office by statute, most mayors in council-manager cities enjoy at least some of the popular image of the executive mayor and are in a position to exert political leadership in the affairs of the council if they have the skill and the disposition to do so. This might include proposing policy, organizing public support of or opposition to issues, mediating solutions to political struggles, and encouraging the manager to accomplish certain tasks. The actual performance of mayors in this situation seems to be highly personalized, depending on both the style of the mayor and the degree to which the council is willing to cooperate with the mayor's exercising such informal authority.

Facilitative Leadership

If the mayor wins the trust and the confidence of council members and the manager, then he or she is in a good position to enhance the performance of both elected and appointed officials by helping them channel their individual and collective energies into productive actions. By staying abreast of council members' interests, positions, and feelings, the mayor can help stimulate thought and discussion among them, and facilitate understanding and possibly consensus on issues. In turn, the mayor is in a position to communicate developing council consensus on issues to the manager and to provide an effective sounding board by which the manager can sense the climate on the council for ideas, options, or issues that he or she and the staff are considering. The bigger the council, the more time and energy this can save for the manager, but the harder it can be to develop consensus or even to discern or predict any meaningful or dependable pattern among members' opinions. By the same token, if the manager can demonstrate the merit of an idea to the mayor, then the mayor can be effective in promoting understanding of the issue, possibly helping move the council toward its acceptance. This facilitative role becomes harder if the council suffers from fractiousness born of political conviction, representation of a divided constituency, or personal animosity. In addition, managers who are lucky enough to have a mayor who takes on this kind of facilitative role, are usually very careful not to let it replace regular and direct contact with individual council members, recognizing how important that contact is to their relationship with the whole council.

Executive Leadership

Both of the foregoing roles cast the mayor as a central figure in the affairs of the city—the "first among equals" on the governing board. Councils typically accept the notion that the mayor will spend more time with the manager than any one council member and will play a preeminent role among them in representing the city to the public and other governments. However, there is an important boundary that most mayors observe in order to maintain their relationship of trust with the council and the manager. Although the mayor may encourage administrative actions or suggest policy interpretations on the basis of his or her position as first among equals, he or she must be careful not to violate the council's prerogatives. Indeed, the manager is accountable to the entire council and is ethically bound to ensure that at least a majority of the council concurs, before taking actions that would deviate significantly from the council's established policies, expectations, or norms. The original council-manager plan purposely precluded a separately elected mayor because of the possibilities for conflict between a strong chief administrator and a strong political executive—like two stars struggling for the center of the stage. However, in the judicious combination of political leadership and facilitation of the process of governance, an effective mayor can complement a competent manager and an active council in a working relationship of harmony and trust.

The Search for an Effective City Manager

Hiring a city manager is one of the most important actions that a council may be called on to take. From the preceding description of how the manager and the council work together, it should be evident that their working relationship can have a significant influence on the effectiveness of the local government that they serve. Whether a council is hiring its first manager or replacing one who has resigned or been fired, it can take several basic steps to ensure that it makes a good choice:

1. *Determine the future needs of the community and city government.* It is well worth the council's time to spend a few hours discussing what it thinks will be the future demands on the manager's position. What will be happening in the community? What will the prominent or controversial issues be? What will the workforce be like, and how will it change? The answers to these questions are likely to be different for every community. By thinking about them, the council increases the probability that it will find somebody who has the right talents to deal with the issues facing its particular city.

2. *List the critical skills that are required to deal with those needs.* Almost 4,000 men and women have met ICMA's stringent criteria for professional membership, and many more capable public administrators working in the public and private sectors are not members. Many of the applicants for a city manager position will have educational credentials and experience that are at least adequate and often impressive, but no two of them will be exactly the same. Each applicant will have slightly different strengths and weaknesses. The challenge facing the council is to choose from many capable applicants the person who comes closest to having the unique set of skills and abilities that is needed to deal with its city's issues and personality.

3. *Recruit and screen applicants.* This step typically includes setting a salary range within which the council is willing to negotiate, advertising to attract persons with the attributes it seeks, screening applications, and deciding on and arranging to interview a set of top candidates. Normally the council needs a staff person to assist it in this process, and it is important that this be somebody who has the confidence of the entire council. Care must be taken to preserve the confidentiality of the applications[10] unless and until the applicants release the city from that obligation. The council typically seeks a release in the interview stage when it becomes

very difficult to ensure confidentiality to any applicant. Some councils have arranged for five to ten semifinalists to have screening interviews with a committee of the council or to have videotape interviews conducted by a contractor, after which they invite three to five finalists for an interview with the whole council. Most others have found it effective to narrow the field down to three to five finalists simply by reviewing and discussing the applications.

4. *Interview applicants.* The structure of the interview process varies quite a bit in practice, from simply interviewing each candidate to bringing all the candidates and their spouses in together to see various aspects of the community, meet key people in and outside city government, and participate in an assessment center, or highly structured interview. At the very least the interviews should be structured to allow council members to make reliable judgments about the important attributes that they have agreed they need in a manager, and to make valid and consistent comparisons among the candidates. G.S. 143-318-11(6) in the open meetings law allows these interviews to be conducted in a closed session.[11]

5. *Hire the manager.* After the interviews the council will usually try to reach consensus on one candidate, with perhaps a backup if the chosen candidate does not accept an offer. Many managers insist on consensus before they will accept a council's offer, feeling that anything less would make their position too tenuous to survive the stress and the strain that the demands of governance and management put on the relationship between the council and the manager. Some managers, however, are willing to start with no more than the tentative security of support from a simple majority. Sometimes the council chooses to send one or more members to the leading candidate's community for confirmation of its impressions, but usually it simply arranges for a final background investigation while it negotiates the terms and the conditions of employment with the prospective manager. When these negotiations are complete, the other candidates are notified, and the council takes formal action in open session to hire the successful candidate. The entire recruitment, screening, selection, and hiring process can normally be completed in about six months.

6. *Conclude an employment agreement.* An increasing number of cities in North Carolina have formal employment agreements with managers. Sometimes called *contracts,* they may set out a variety of conditions specific to the manager's employment, such as leave, use of a car for official business, expense accounts, participation in professional activities, and virtually anything else that establishes a clear understanding between the council and the manager about the responsibilities, the benefits, and the privileges of the office. Many councils now include severance provisions in these agreements, which specify the manager's responsibilities for notifying the council in advance of his or her intention to resign, and provide a lump-sum severance payment in the event that the manager's employment is involuntarily terminated for reasons other than illegal behavior. These agreements do not and cannot guarantee any tenure to the manager, inasmuch as G.S. 160A-147(a) provides that the council shall appoint the manager to serve at its pleasure.

Establishment and Maintenance of a Good Relationship

The relationship between a council and a manager can enhance or impede the process of governance significantly, so it is important that they devote some time to establishing and maintaining a good one. As soon as possible, they should establish what they expect of each other beyond the very general tenets of statutory and professional responsibilities. No two councils are exactly alike, nor are any two managers. No matter how much previous experience a new manager has had or how many managers a particular community has had, the relationship between a particular council and a particular manager is certain to be different in some ways than any either of them has previously experienced.

Soon after a new manager is hired, if a significant turnover in council occurs, or a new mayor is elected, the council, the mayor, and the manager will find it useful to discuss their specific expectations of one another. Such a discussion allows them to understand what each thinks he or she needs from the others to be effective in carrying out major responsibilities. The mayor's and the council's expectations of the manager provide a sound basis for them to be effective in both formally evaluating the manager and giving the manager informal feedback about his or her specific behavior and general performance. Most councils find it effective and convenient to conduct a formal evaluation of the manager once a year, usually associated with their consideration of adjustments in the manager's compensation. Typically the evaluation is held in closed session, with the manager present when his or her performance is discussed and rated with respect to general behavior and the achievement of specific tasks or objectives previously set out by the council.[12]

More and more councils are using retreats to set out these initial expectations among themselves and the manager and to achieve other purposes that contribute to effective governance. The idea behind a retreat is for the council and whomever else it wants to join it, to convene at a time and a place other than those of its regular meetings[13] to deliberate about matters that are difficult to fit into the crush of routine formal business that fills its regular agendas. Councils commonly use retreats to identify agreements and differences among members in their beliefs and goals for the community, to plan how they will achieve common goals and accommodate differences, and to understand one another's expectations about working together.[14] Most councils and managers that have tried retreats have found them to be an effective way to build a unity of effort that is difficult to develop in the course of regular meetings.

ઢ   ઢ   ઢ

The council-manager form of government has a long and successful history in the United States and especially in North Carolina. Like any governmental arrangement, it has potential advantages that are not automatically realized in practice; however, it provides many advantages to the process of governance if the elected officials and the manager work together in a good faith effort to observe the tenets on which the system is based. The General Statutes constitute a clear foundation for the council-manager form of government, but they are only a starting point in a very complex working relationship. Using the council-manager form successfully depends on the council and the manager establishing clear expectations, maintaining good communication, and developing a sense of shared vision and teamwork on behalf of the community.

Additional Resources

Publications

International City/County Management Association. *Employment Agreements for Managers: Guidelines for Elected Officials.* Washington, D.C.: ICMA, 1984.

————. *Employment Agreements for Managers: Guidelines for Managers.* Washington, D.C.: ICMA, 1992.

————. *Partnerships in Local Governance: Effective Council-Manager Relations.* Washington, D.C.: ICMA, 1989.

————. *Recruitment Guidelines for Selecting a Local Government Administrator.* Washington, D.C.: ICMA, 1987.

Nalbandian, John. *Professionalism in Local Government.* San Francisco: Jossey-Bass, 1991.

Svara, James H. "Contributions of the City Council to Effective Governance." *Popular Government* 51 (Spring 1986): 1–8.

————. "The Responsible Administrator: Contributions of the City Manager to Effective Governance." *Popular Government* 52 (Fall 1986): 18–27.

Organizations

International City/County Management Association, 777 North Capitol Street, NE, Washington, DC 20002

National League of Cities, 1301 Pennsylvania Avenue, NW, Washington, DC 20004

North Carolina League of Municipalities, Albert Coates Local Government Center, 215 North Dawson Street, Raleigh, NC 27602

North Carolina City and County Management Association, P.O. Box 3069, Raleigh, NC 27602

Notes

1. Richard Childs first articulated the plan in a proposal to combine the commission form of government with a professional city manager. (The commission form of government became popular after its successful use in resurrecting Galveston, Texas, from almost complete destruction from a hurricane in 1900.) Childs drafted a bill incorporating the plan and persuaded the Lockport (N.Y.) Board of Trade to sponsor its introduction in the New York State Legislature with the public support of reform organizations. Thus the earliest version is known as the Lockport Plan.

2. See "ICMA Local Government Recognition," in *Who's Who in Local Government Management, 1994–1995* (Washington, D.C.: ICMA, 1994), 434.

3. These were the main conclusions drawn by participants in the initial meeting of the ICMA Task Force on Council-Manager Relations, in San Francisco in February 1993. They formed the basis of the task force's inquiry into how ICMA could help foster citizen support for the council-manager form of government and strengthen the partnership between elected officials and appointed administrators.

The task force's conclusions were summarized in three parts in the *ICMA Newsletter* 74, no. 10 (17 May 1993), no. 11 (31 May 1993), and no. 13 (28 June 1993).

4. Originally called the International City Managers' Association, ICMA has modified its name twice since 1924. In 1969 it changed *Managers'* to *Management* to recognize the inclusion of members who are deputies, assistants, directors of councils of governments, and local government chief administrative officers who do not have the title or the traditional authority of a manager. In 1991 it included a reference to county managers, who had become a significant proportion of the membership—thus the International City/County Management Association. Because of tradition and widespread recognition of the original acronym, ICMA, the association decided to continue it in that form.

5. Adapted from "ICMA Code of Ethics with Guidelines," in *Who's Who in Local Government Management, 1994–1995* (Washington, D.C.: ICMA, 1994), 4–5.

6. Woodrow Wilson, "The Study of Administration," *Political Science Quarterly* 2 (June 1887): 197–222. When Wilson wrote that "administration lies outside the proper sphere of politics. Administrative questions are not political questions. Although politics sets the tasks for administration, it should not be suffered to manipulate its offices" (p. 210), he was arguing for the provision of administrative support to legislative bodies, not prescribing a strict separation of duties between the two.

7. John Nalbandian, *Professionalism in Local Government* (San Francisco: Jossey-Bass, 1991), xiii.

8. A more thorough discussion of the relationships among the council, the manager, and the mayor over a continuum from mission to management as depicted in figure 4-1, can be found in a series of articles written for *Popular Government* by James H. Svara: "Understanding the Mayor's Office in Council-Manager Cities," 51 (Fall 1985): 6–11; "Contributions of the City Council to Effective Governance," 51 (Spring 1986): 1–8; and "The Responsible Administrator: Contributions of the City Manager to Effective Governance," 52 (Fall 1986): 18–27.

9. Svara's study of the five largest cities in the state showed these two roles of the mayor to be overwhelmingly the ones identified with the office: 82.8 percent of respondents saw the mayor as "performer of ceremonial tasks," and 51.7 percent saw the mayor as "presiding officer." No other role exceeded 36 percent [James H. Svara, *Official Leadership in the City: Patterns of Conflict and Cooperation* (New York: Oxford University Press, 1990), 108].

10. *See* Elkin Tribune v. Yadkin County Bd. of Comm'rs, No. 431PA91 (N.C. June 25, 1992). The court held that applications for employment were personnel records under G.S. 153A-98 and therefore their disclosure was prohibited.

11. The council must nevertheless follow all the other procedural requirements contained in Article 33-C. These interviews are typically conducted in closed session. However, it is not required that they be so conducted, and there has been one recent exception to this practice: in 1993 the Wilmington City Council chose to conduct its final interviews in open session.

12. For a detailed treatment of the evaluation process, see Margaret S. Carlson. "'How Are We Doing?' Evaluating the Performance of the Chief Administrator," *Popular Government* 59 (Winter 1994): 24–29.

13. A retreat must still meet all the requirements set out in the open meetings law.

14. For a more thorough discussion of retreats, see Kurt Jenne, "Governing Board Retreats," *Popular Government* 53 (Winter 1988): 20–26.

5   Governance in Mayor-Council Cities

S. Leigh Wilson, Fred P. Baggett, and Warren Jake Wicker

Contents

THE MAYOR-COUNCIL FORM of government is the original form of general-purpose local government in this country, descended from the English borough mayor-and-council system and instituted in the first American colonies. Throughout its long history and in its many variations—such as a bicameral council, a weak versus a strong mayor's office, and an at-large or a ward system—it has been successfully employed from the smallest colonial town dependent on ferry tolls for operating expense, to the modern megalopolis with a multi-billion-dollar budget.

Pre-Revolutionary towns were typically chartered by the colonial governors, who also usually named the mayor, and councils were elected by the town's voters. With independence the state legislatures chartered towns, and the mayor was usually selected by the elected council from among its members. The council as a group made all the decisions concerning town issues, and the mayor, in great contrast to the English counterpart, was not a preeminent figure and held no independent authority. This same principle prevails today in North Carolina cities under the mayor-council form of government.

Following the new federal government model of separate election of the president, the practice of directly electing the mayor began in some small towns, spread to the large cities in the country during the rise of Jacksonian Democracy in the first half of the nineteenth century, and was firmly entrenched by mid-century. In many large cities throughout the country, there was a concomitant shift of power from the council to the independently elected mayor. The council remained the primary deliberative and legislative body, but in these strong-mayor cities, the mayors gradually assumed important individual powers like limited or absolute veto power, direct control of some or all of the city departments, and budgetary responsibility. This trend was far from universal, and many cities and towns, especially the small ones, continued under the traditional weak mayor–council system in which the council (including the mayor) exercised all the power as a body and the mayor's individual duties were largely ceremonial.

As cities grew in wealth, responsibilities, and bureaucracy, the spoils system emerged, and popular dissatisfaction grew in those cities that experienced corruption, inefficiency, and political favoritism. In light of the mayor-council form's historical as well as continued popularity, these difficulties may be blamed as much on the people in government—or more probably the size of the government—as on the form of government. The problems were real, however, and in the first decade of the twentieth century, there emerged the commission form of municipal government and then the council-manager form of government as alternatives. Until then, the mayor-council plan had been the exclusive form of municipal government in the United States. The council-manager form has steadily increased in popularity since its inception, and it now is the principal form of municipal government in American cities with populations of 10,000–500,000. The mayor-council form, as either the strong-mayor or weak-mayor type, predominates in cities in the smaller (less than 10,000) and larger (over 500,000) population classes.

Advantages and Disadvantages of the Mayor-Council Form of Government

The primary advantage of the mayor-council form of government is that it brings government closer to the voters. The people who have the responsibility of not only formulating city policy but also actually operating the gears of government are directly elected by the citizens. The elected leaders are solely accountable for the direct administration as well as the oversight of municipal functions.

On the other hand, there are two major weaknesses inherent in the plan as it is used in North Carolina (the weak-mayor form). The first is the absence of any real concentration of executive authority and responsibility because decision making ultimately rests with the city council as a group. Responsibility for operating the city is divided among and shared by all members of the council, making it administration by committee. Strong, consistent direction depends on maintaining general agreement, which may be difficult at times. This diffusion of authority and responsibility has even been perceived as an advantage of the plan: the difficulty of concerted and decisive action makes it unlikely that the government can do much harm!

The second weakness in the mayor-council form of government is that good politicians are not necessarily good administrators. Those who are elected may be popular with the voters, but amateur at running a municipality, and even if inept administration later brings rejection at the polls, the result is usually a new set of popular but inexperienced administrators.

However, the continued use of the mayor-council form of government belies these weaknesses and indicates that it can and does work where conscientious elected officials work together for the welfare of the city. As a practical matter, many small towns cannot afford to employ an experienced professional administrator. This form of government is best suited for and most often used by small towns, where municipal functions are few and not sophisticated and can be well provided by an elected council and relatively few employees.

Extent of Use in North Carolina

Numerically the mayor-council form is the principal form of local government in North Carolina today. In 1994 it was used by 338 cities. It predominates among cities with populations of less than 2,500. The council-manager plan has been the exclusive form in large cities in North Carolina (those with populations over 25,000) since the late 1940s, and it is used by most cities with populations of 2,500–25,000. Cities in this range have also tended over the last forty years to shift from the mayor-council plan to the council-manager plan.

In 1994, only one city with a population between 10,000 and 25,000, Mint Hill, had the mayor-council form of government, and Mint Hill appointed a town administrator to supervise all departments. In the next lower population class, 5,000–10,000, only three of thirty-three cities—Hamlet, Spring Lake, and Williamston—used the mayor-council form, and all three also had appointed town administrators to supervise departmental operations. The distribution of mayor-council cities in cities with populations under 5,000 in 1994 is shown below in table 5-1.

Operation of the Plan

Organization of the City Council

Designation and Composition

The city council is designated as the *board of aldermen*, the *board of commissioners*, or the *town* or *city council*. The designation used makes no difference; the choice is merely a matter of custom and local preference.

The number of council members varies from two to twelve; small cities sometimes have three council members and a mayor; large cities usually have four or five council members and a mayor. Most councils are elected on a nonpartisan basis and at large by all the

Table 5-1
Prevalence of the Mayor-Council Form of Government in Small North Carolina Cities, by Population, 1994

	Population Class				
	2,500–4,999	1,000–2,499	500–999	Under 500	Total
Cities	75	116	99	147	437
Mayor-council cities	26	81	88	139	334

Source: David M. Lawrence, comp., *Forms of Government of North Carolina Cities*, 1994 ed. (Chapel Hill, N.C.: Institute of Government, The University of North Carolina at Chapel Hill, 1994), 40.

city's qualified voters. However, two or more electoral districts may be established from which some or all of the council members are elected. The district candidates may be elected exclusively by residents of the district in which they live or by the electorate at large.

The members of most city councils have four-year staggered terms to ensure a degree of continuity in municipal affairs and prior experience among at least some members of the council. Two-year terms for council members is a close second in popularity of terms of office.

Organizational Meeting

A new council takes office at its first regular meeting in December after the November election, at which time the members take the oath of office and organize the government for the conduct of business. The council must appoint a mayor *pro tempore* to preside over it and to fulfill the other duties of the mayor when he or she is absent or incapacitated.

Officers and Employees

A city's charter ordinarily states that certain officers and employees will be appointed by the city council, and specifies their duties. The General Statutes require that the following officers be appointed and have the described general duties in addition to any other duties specified by the council.

Clerk (G.S. 160A-171). The clerk is responsible for giving the proper notices of regular and special meetings of the council, keeping an accurate journal of the council's proceedings, and being the custodian of all city records. A deputy clerk may (but need not) be appointed to perform whatever duties the council specifies (G.S. 160A-172).

Budget officer (G.S. 159-9). The budget officer receives budget requests from the various city departments, prepares a proposed budget for submission to the council, and complies with other requirements concerning budget preparation and administration prescribed by the General Statutes. Unlike cities with a council-manager form of government, under which the city manager is the budget officer, cities with the mayor-council plan may designate any city officer or employee (including the mayor, if he or she agrees) as budget officer.

Finance officer (G.S. 159-24). The finance officer may also be called *accountant, treasurer,* or *finance director.* He or she has the general responsibility to keep the accounts and disburse the city's funds in a manner consistent with the General Statutes' provisions pertaining to the finance officer's duties. These duties may be conferred on the budget officer.

Attorney (G.S. 160A-173). The council must appoint a city attorney to be its legal advisor. He or she serves at the council's pleasure.

Tax collector (G.S. 105-349). The tax collector has the general responsibility to collect property, privilege license, and all other taxes due the city and to fulfill the other duties imposed by the General Statutes concerning tax collection. Any officer or employee may be appointed tax collector except a member of the council; the finance officer may be appointed to that office only with the Local Government Commission's consent. Many cities, both large and small, contract with the county to collect their taxes.

Appointments to Boards and Commissions

Either the city council or the mayor makes initial appointments and fills vacancies on all separate boards and commissions that are authorized by special or general laws of the state. Planning boards, boards of adjustment, and parks and recreation commissions are examples of the separate boards and commissions to which the council is authorized to make appointments. Members of housing authority boards are appointed by the mayor. The number of board or commission members and their terms of office are established by general law authorizing such boards or by ordinance implementing the authority granted by statute. In addition, the council is authorized to create special citizen advisory committees, such as a human relations committee, and to appoint their members.

Appointment of Department Heads and Employees

The council is responsible for establishing the city operating departments deemed necessary or desirable and for appointing, suspending, and removing department heads and all other city employees. It may delegate to an administrative officer or a department head the authority to appoint, suspend, or remove employees assigned to that department (G.S. 160A-155). In cities with populations of less than 5,000, the mayor and the members of the council may serve as department heads or other city employees and may receive reasonable compensation. In cities with populations of 5,000 or more, they may not (G.S. 160A-158).

Typical city departments are police, fire, water, streets, sanitation, recreation, and inspections. The council may combine the responsibilities of departments, or appoint one person to supervise several departments or to fill duties in more than one department (G.S. 160A-146). For example, a public works director may be appointed to supervise both the street and the sanitation department, or the fire chief may also be assigned the duties of building inspector.

Supervision of Officers and Employees

In organizing, directing, and supervising the various functions or departments of municipal government, the city council may use one of several administrative or organizational plans unless the charter provides otherwise. Whatever type of administrative plan is used, it is important for the council to define clearly the responsibility of each officer or department; to coordinate, as far as possible, the activities of each; to establish clear lines of authority between the council, the department heads, and employees; and in general, to establish a sound administrative plan that will enable the council to supervise all municipal activities adequately.

Three basic administrative plans are used in cities under the mayor-council form of government: (1) the entire council directly supervising all departments; (2) one council member assigned to supervise each department; and (3) committees of the council supervising one or more functions or departments.

Direct Supervision of All Departments

When direct supervision is used, the council appoints and removes all department heads and directs and supervises them in carrying out their duties. Each department head or officer reports directly to the council and is responsible to it for the operation of his or her department. This plan is widely used but can be cumbersome if the city has many departments. It is probably best suited to small cities with not more than three or four departments or functions that require the council's direct supervision.

Assignment of Council Members to Departments

Under this administrative arrangement a designated city council member has charge of a department and may exercise such administrative control over the operation of the department and its head as the council may direct. The department head or officer is directly responsible to that council member rather than to the entire council. The member reports to and recommends measures to the entire council regarding the department's affairs. This system expedites the administration of departmental affairs, but council members may become more concerned with their department than with the total operation and administration of all departments, which is the council's principal responsibility.

Committee System

Under this organizational plan the city council creates committees of the council to study and make recommendations concerning the operation of the respective departments; in some places these committees are given the authority to supervise departmental operations. When this system is used, the committees are normally assigned general areas of responsibility that may include several departments. For example, supervision of police, fire, and inspection services might be assigned to a public safety committee that is composed of several council members.

The number of committees and their membership will vary depending on the council's size, the number of departments, and other factors. If the charter is silent regarding requirements for committees, the council may establish committees and assign them such duties, consistent with the charter and general laws of the state, as it deems best. Suggested committee structures for a council consisting of a mayor and five council members appear in table 5-2.

The Role of the Mayor

The mayor is directly elected by the city's qualified voters except in a few places where election is by the city council from its members. The mayor is recognized as the head of the municipal government and usually is its spokesperson, but he or she has only the limited authority granted by the city's charter and the general laws of the state. He or she presides at meetings of the council, is the city's representative for ceremonial purposes, and has whatever other powers and duties the city council assigns, if any. Any power and influence that the mayor enjoys usually result from force and vigor of personality rather than from legal authority. Unless the city charter provides otherwise, a mayor elected directly has the right to vote on council matters when there is a tie vote of the council, but a mayor elected by the council from its members votes on all council matters (G.S. 160A-69).

Adoption of the Mayor-Council Form of Government

The mayor-council and council-manager plans are the two alternative forms of municipal government available by general law and in use in North Carolina. The form of government is set forth in a city's charter. An initial charter is an act of the General Assembly.

The General Statutes provide a method for a city to change its own form of government by a local ordinance that amends the charter (G.S. 160A-101 through -110). Thus a city that has either the council-manager or the mayor-council form of government may adopt the other form by following the statutory procedure for amending its charter. The procedure calls first for a resolution of intent to amend the charter and then a public hearing on the issue before the amending ordinance may be adopted. The ordinance

Table 5-2
**Alternative Plans for Organizing a City Council Composed of a Mayor and
Five Council Members**

Three-Committee System

The council is organized into three committees: Finance, Public Works, and
Public Safety. The committees' responsibilities are as follows:
Finance: budgets, taxation, recreation, and library
Public Works: streets, transportation, water and sewer, electric light and power,
stormwater drainage, and solid wastes
Public Safety: police, fire, health and sanitation

Alternative Organization Plans

	Finance	Public Works	Public Safety
Plan 1	Mayor	Commissioner 1 (mayor *pro tempore*)	Commissioner 2
	Commissioner 2	Commissioner 4	Commissioner 3
	Commissioner 3	Commissioner 5	Commissioner 4
Plan 2	Commissioner 1 (mayor *pro tempore*)	Commissioner 4	Commissioner 3
	Commissioner 2	Commissioner 5	Commissioner 4
	Commissioner 3	Commissioner 2	Commissioner 5
Plan 3	Mayor	Commissioner 1 (mayor *pro tempore*)	Commissioner 4
	Commissioner 2	Commissioner 3	Commissioner 5

Number of Committee Assignments per Member, by Plan

	Plan 1	Plan 2	Plan 3
Mayor	1	0	1
Commissioner 1 (mayor *pro tempore*)	1	1	1
Commissioner 2	2	2	1
Commissioner 3	2	2	1
Commissioner 4	2	2	1
Commissioner 5	1	2	1

Comments

Plan 1 requires the mayor to serve on the Finance Committee; this is often advantageous. Also, plan 1 requires only three members to serve on two committees. Plan
2 requires four members to serve on two committees. Plan 3 requires that each
member serve on only one committee; this is desirable, but a committee composed
of only two members is often unworkable.

Table 5-2, *continued*
**Alternative Plans for Organizing a City Council Composed of a Mayor and
Five Council Members**

Two-Committee System

The council is organized into two committees: Finance and Public Safety, and
Public Works. The committees' responsibilities are as follows:
Finance and Public Safety: budgets, taxation, recreation, library, police, fire, and
health and sanitation
Public Works: streets, transportation, water and sewer, stormwater drainage,
electric light and power, and solid wastes

Alternative Organization Plans

	Finance and Public Safety	Public Works
Plan 1	Mayor	Commissioner 1
		(mayor *pro tempore*)
	Commissioner 2	Commissioner 4
	Commissioner 3	Commissioner 5
Plan 2	Commissioner 1	Commissioner 4
	(mayor *pro tempore*)	
	Commissioner 2	Commissioner 5
	Commissioner 3	Commissioner 2

Number of Committee Assignments per Member, by Plan

	Plan 1	Plan 2
Mayor	1	0
Commissioner 1 (mayor *pro tempore*)	1	1
Commissioner 2	1	2
Commissioner 3	1	1
Commissioner 4	1	1
Commissioner 5	1	1

may be made effective either with or without voter approval, at the
council's option. If the council does not provide for a vote on the
ordinance, a referendum on the issue must be called if enough voters sign a petition requesting it. The General Statutes also provide
a procedure for an initiative petition, under which an election on the
form of government may be called on petition of sufficient qualified
voters; the new form of government is established if the voters approve it. Chapter 4 discusses these options in more detail.

Carefulness in Speaking for the Council

Members of city councils should be careful when talking with the news media, citizens' groups, and even individuals to make certain that their comments reflect the council's view rather than their personal opinion. Opinions and statements of position expressed by council members are usually taken to be those of the entire body. If a council member misstates the city's position, assumes a council position that has not actually been taken, or incorrectly predicts a council position or action, the result can be embarrassment, mistrust, and resentment on the part of the listener and other council members, as well as the public. Citizens often do not distinguish between the thoughts of an individual council member and those of the council as a whole, nor do they remember that one council member's feelings may not be shared by the others. The listener may infer that what is actually only a personal expression of opinion is an authoritative pronouncement of official city policy. On important or sensitive city matters requiring clarity and careful explanation, it may be desirable for the council to designate one of its members as spokesperson; a written statement agreed on by the whole council that is available for distribution may be advisable for some situations.

Additional Resources

Adrian, Charles B., and Ernest S. Griffith. *The Formation of Traditions, 1775–1870.* New York: Praeger Publishers, for the National Municipal League, 1976.

Griffith, Ernest S. *A History of American City Government: The Progressive Years and Their Aftermath, 1900–1920.* New York: Praeger Publishers, for the National Municipal League, 1974.

International City/County Management Association. *The Municipal Year Book.* Washington, D.C.: ICMA, published annually.

6   The City Clerk and City Records

A. Fleming Bell, II

Contents

THE POSITION of city clerk is one of the oldest in municipal government, dating at least to biblical times. For example, the book of Acts in the Christian New Testament records that when a conflict arose between the people of Ephesus and the missionary Paul and his companions, the town clerk quieted the crowd and prevented a riot.[1]

The term *clerk* has long been associated with the written word. Indeed, an archaic definition of a clerk is a person who can read, or read and write, or a learned person, scholar, or person of letters. *Clerk* can also mean cleric or clergyman; during the Middle Ages the clergy were among the few literate people in many European communities.

Those who can read and write can keep records for their fellow citizens; so it is that modern-day municipal clerks are the primary official record keepers for their cities and towns. All municipalities in North Carolina must have a clerk (G.S. 160A-171), and the most important municipal records maintained by the clerk, such as minutes of board meetings, must be kept permanently for the use of future generations.[2] The city council may also provide for a deputy clerk, who may perform any of the powers and duties of the clerk that the council specifies (G.S. 160A-172).

In addition to creating and maintaining records, city clerks and their deputies have a variety of other duties. The diverse responsibilities of clerks are the focus of the first part of this chapter; the second part addresses specific legal requirements for municipal records.

The City Clerk

Appointment

The municipal clerk generally works directly for the city council, keeping the city's records, giving notices of meetings, and performing various other functions as the council requires. In mayor-council cities the clerk is almost always appointed by the council. In council-manager cities, situations vary. Some city charters in such cities provide for appointment of the clerk by the council, although in recent years some charters have been revised to specify that the clerk is to be appointed by the manager.

In the absence of a charter provision in a council-manager city, the manager will probably appoint the clerk, although the clerk will still perform duties for the council. G.S. 160A-148(1) specifies that the manager is to appoint and suspend or remove, in accordance with any council-adopted general personnel rules, regulations, policies, or ordinances, all nonelected city officers and employees "whose appointment or removal is not otherwise provided for by law, except the city attorney." G.S. 160A-171 states, "There shall be a city clerk," but it does not specify how the clerk is to be appointed, so the provision for appointment by the manager probably applies. However, both G.S. 160A-171 and G.S. 160A-172, which deals with deputy clerks, state that these officials are to perform duties required (G.S. 160A-171) or specified (G.S. 160A-172) by the *council.*

Record Keeping and Notice Giving

Minutes

One of the clerk's most important statutory duties is "to keep a journal of the proceedings of the council" (G.S. 160A-171)—that is, to prepare and maintain the minutes of council meetings in a set of minute books. The powers of a municipality are exercised by the city council, and the minutes of the council's meetings are the official record of what it does.

The minutes must be "full and accurate" [G.S. 160A-72; G.S. 143-318.10(e)], for they are the legal evidence of what the council has said and done. The council "speaks" only through its minutes, and their contents may not be altered nor their meaning explained by other evidence.[3]

"Full and accurate" does not generally mean, however, that a verbatim transcript of a meeting's proceedings must be made. Rather, the minutes must record the results of each vote taken by the council (G.S. 160A-72), and they should also show the existence of any condition that is required before a particular action may validly be taken. The full text of each motion should be recorded, including the full text of all ordinances and resolutions passed by the council. This permanent, unchanging record of council actions can be extremely important in later years to supplement and back up other information sources, such as ordinance books and codes of ordinances, which are frequently revised.

Other details are also important. The minutes should state that the meeting was legally convened and should show that a quorum was present at all times during the meeting. The late arrival and the early departure of members (including whether someone leaving was excused by the remaining members) should be noted. A list of the members who voted each way on a particular question (the "ayes and noes") must be included if any member so requests (G.S. 160A-72).

The minutes should also show that any other legally required conditions for taking action were met—for example, that a properly advertised public hearing was held on a proposed rezoning or that an ordinance received a sufficient number of votes to be adopted finally on first reading. As another example, if a formally bid contract is awarded, a list of the bid proposals must be included in the minutes [G.S. 143-129(b)].

As noted earlier, minutes generally do not need to include a verbatim transcript or even a summary of the discussion that took place at the council meeting. Indeed, including a detailed record of comments may well be counterproductive; the council may find itself spending an excessive amount of time at its next meeting discussing the details of this record, which could have been omitted altogether.

A verbatim transcript of council proceedings may be required in one limited instance. When the council is sitting as a quasi-judicial body—for example, when it is considering issuance of a special use permit under a zoning ordinance—it must act somewhat like a court, and a full transcript of the proceedings must be provided if requested by one of the parties appearing before the council.

Council meetings need not be audio- or video-recorded by the city. (Persons attending the meeting may make their own recordings if they desire.) If the clerk or another city official does make a tape, it may be disposed of after the minutes of that meeting are approved. Should the city attorney or the council wish that meeting tapes be retained for a longer period, the council should establish a clear, uniform policy for the clerk's guidance. The city's tape of a meeting is a public record available for public inspection and copying, just like the minutes.

Minutes made of a closed session may be sealed by the city council for as long as necessary to avoid frustrating the purpose of the session [G.S. 143-318.10(e)]. A recorded vote to seal the minutes is advisable. Many clerks maintain sealed closed-session minutes in a separate minutes book. The council's public minutes should record the motion to go into closed session, including the information required by the open meetings law [G.S. 143-318.11(c)], and the fact that the council came out of the session.

Draft copies of council minutes are generally sent by the clerk to the council members several days before the meeting at which they are to be considered for approval. The circulated draft minutes are a public record that must also be made available for public inspection.

Council members should carefully review the minutes and bring their suggested changes and corrections to the meeting for consideration by the full council. Although the clerk records the draft minutes for the council, the council itself, acting as a body, must finally determine what the minutes will include. The minutes do not become the official record of the council's actions until it approves them.

The council may correct minutes that it has already approved if it later finds that they are incorrect.[4] In such a case the correction should be noted in the minutes of the meeting at which the correction is made, with an appropriate notation and cross-reference at the place in the minutes book where the provision being corrected appears.

Under the open meetings law, "full and accurate" minutes must also be kept of the meetings of other "public bodies" that are part of municipal government. Included are all city council committees, all other boards and committees of the city that perform either legislative, policy-making, quasi-judicial, administrative, or advisory functions, and all subcommittees of these other boards and committees. The council should establish procedures to ensure that the minutes of these various boards are properly recorded and maintained. The minutes of these various public bodies may be kept either in written form or, at the option of the public body, in the form of sound or video-and-sound recordings [G.S. 143-318.10(e)].

Other Records

Among the other records of council actions maintained by the city clerk are the ordinance book and the code of ordinances (governed by G.S. 160A-78 and -77 respectively). A true copy of each city ordinance must be filed in an appropriately indexed ordinance book. This book is separate from the minutes book and is maintained for public inspection in the clerk's office. If the municipality has adopted and issued a code of ordinances, its ordinances need be filed and indexed in the ordinance book only until they are codified.

Every municipality with a population of 5,000 or more must adopt and issue a bound or looseleaf code of ordinances. The code must be updated at least annually unless there have been no changes. Separate sections may be included for general ordinances and for technical ordinances, or the latter may be issued as separate books or pamphlets. Examples of technical ordinances are those pertaining to building construction; installation of plumbing, electric wiring, or cooling and heating equipment; zoning; subdivision control; privilege license taxes; the use of public utilities, buildings, or facilities operated by the city; and similar ordinances designated as technical by the council.

The council may omit from the code classes of ordinances that it designates as having limited interest or transitory value (e.g., the annual budget ordinance), but the code should clearly describe what has been left out. The council may also provide that certain ordinances pertaining to zoning district boundaries and traffic regulations be maintained on official map books in the clerk's office or in some other city office generally accessible to the public.

Ordinance books and codes are intended to make the city's laws readily accessible to its citizens. Accordingly ordinances may not be enforced or admitted into evidence in court unless they are properly filed and indexed or codified. It is presumed, however, that the proper procedure has been followed unless someone proves to the contrary [G.S. 160A-79(d)].

The clerk is the custodian of all other city records in addition to minutes and ordinances (G.S. 160A-171). Council resolutions, city contracts, council and mayoral correspondence, signed oaths of office, copies of legal and other notices, financial and personnel records, and a variety of other miscellaneous documents (e.g., records of going-out-of-business sales for which the clerk has issued licenses) are all to be maintained in the clerk's office or under the clerk's guidance. As the custodian of the records, the clerk has primary responsibility for ensuring that municipal records are kept safely, are accessible for use by the public and city officials (except as restricted by law), and are disposed of in accordance with the *Municipal Records Retention and Disposition Schedule.* The general rules governing city records are considered in some detail in the final section of this chapter.

Notices

The clerk is required by statute to give notice of council meetings, and he or she is usually responsible for a variety of other public notices as well. Notice of the regular meetings of all public bodies that are part of city government (including the council) is given through regular meeting schedules, which are kept on file in the clerk's office. The clerk handles the posting and the distribution of special meeting notices for the council and frequently for other city boards, and often oversees the legal advertisements required for public hearings, bid solicitations, bond orders, and other matters.

Other Statutory Duties

Clerks have specific statutory responsibilities besides those related to record keeping and notice giving. For example, the clerk and the mayor are the only two municipal officials who may administer oaths of office [G.S. 11-7.1(a)(5), (7)]. (The clerk should also take such an oath.)

In addition, the clerk is responsible for enforcing within the municipal limits the state's law regulating all going-out-of-business and distress sales [G.S. 66-77(a)]. This task can be very difficult. The clerk must deal with the false advertising claims of merchants who are not really going out of business, and he or she must ensure that unhappy failing merchants comply with what they may well regard as intrusive state requirements.

General Assistance to the Council

Research and General Assistance

As well as the responsibilities previously outlined, clerks are to "perform any other duties that may be required by law or the council" (G.S. 160A-171). The clerk is frequently called on to find answers to questions for individual council members or for the council as a whole. He or she may be asked to learn how others have solved a particular problem, to find sample ordinances for the municipal attorney, or to search the minutes for information about the actions of a previous council. Individual council members also look to the clerk for help in arranging official appointments and making official travel plans.

Acting as researcher and information provider is both a rewarding and a difficult part of the clerk's responsibilities. Council members can help the clerk serve them more effectively by remembering the limits of the clerk's role. For example, a professional clerk generally does research and provides information for the benefit of the entire council. Seeking assistance from the clerk to win a squabble with another council member is inappropriate. Also, although clerks expect to make travel arrangements and perform other official tasks for individual council members, each member should be careful not to demand more than his or her fair share of the clerk's time and energy.

Preparation for Meetings

One of the most important services that the clerk provides to the council is assistance with preparations for meetings. The clerk is usually involved in preparing the tentative agenda for council meetings and compiling background information for the council's agenda packet. He or she may also arrange for taping of meetings and may set up other audiovisual equipment and the meeting room.

Clear procedures for handling these matters can serve both the council and the clerk. The council should establish and enforce a realistic schedule for placing items on the agenda that allows the clerk time to compile and duplicate background materials, and it should clearly state any preferences concerning the order of items on the agenda. It should support the clerk in complying with public and press requests for information about upcoming meetings and for access to tapes and other records of prior meetings (see the discussion under the heading Access for Inspection and Copying, later in this chapter).

Information Source

The clerk is sometimes described as "the hub of the wheel" in local government because of the central role that he or she plays in the governmental communication network.[5] Clerks provide information daily to council members, city employees, citizens, and the press. A clerk in a medium-size North Carolina city has the following thoughts about her position:

> Basically my office is an information office. I am in the center of things because as clerk I am usually more accessible than the mayor, council members, and other city officials. I have immediate access to information because I am on the front line in the city council meetings. I communicate daily with the mayor, the city manager, and

various department heads, depending on what is going on. My office has quite a bit of contact with the newspapers, and we get anywhere from fifteen to twenty calls a day from the general public.[6]

Dealing with such a wide variety of information requests requires tact, judgment, empathy, organizational skills, energy, and a good sense of humor. Although the clerk works *for the council,* he or she is truly providing *public* service, from helping the press understand the meaning of a complicated motion, to assisting a citizen in finding the correct individual to help with a complaint, to keeping department heads advised of council actions and keeping council members informed of administration proposals. As local government becomes larger and more complicated, the clerk's role as a professional, dispassionate provider of information to citizens, government officials, and the media becomes more and more important.

Combination of the Clerk's Position with Other Jobs

Many municipal clerks perform tasks besides those that have been described. Clerks are often tax collectors or finance officers for their cities, and some also serve as purchasing agents, personnel directors, or managers.[7] In North Carolina's smallest towns the clerk may be the only administrative official and have to function in every role, from substitute operator of the waste treatment plant to zoning administrator.

Wearing many hats can be both stressful and invigorating for a clerk. If clerks are to perform well the varied duties of their office or to combine their position effectively with other roles, they must be given appropriate authority and adequate financial rewards along with the broad responsibilities.

Professionalism and Continuing Education

Municipal clerks have one of the most active professional associations of public officials in North Carolina. The North Carolina Association of Municipal Clerks is dedicated to improving the professional competency of municipal clerks through regular regional and statewide educational opportunities and through a nationally recognized certification program. The association operates a mentor program to provide guidance for new clerks, and it gives clerks a chance to work with other municipal officials through permanent representation on the Board of Directors of the North Carolina League of Municipalities.

City Records

Definition

As noted in the earlier discussion of the clerk's record-keeping responsibilities, municipal governments create and maintain a wide variety of records. Some of the preservation and access requirements for municipal and other government records are set out in the main body of the public records law, G.S. Chapter 132.

G.S. 132-1 defines *public record* very broadly as all "documents, papers, letters, maps, books, photographs, films, sound recordings, magnetic or other tapes, electronic data processing records, artifacts, or other documentary material, regardless of physical form or characteristics made or received pursuant to law or ordinance in connection with the transaction of public business by any agency of North Carolina government or its subdivisions." The last phrase includes "every public office, public officer or official (State or local, elected or appointed), institution, board, commission, bureau, council, department, authority or other unit of government of the State or of any county, unit, special district or other political subdivision of government."

The phrase "made or received pursuant to law or ordinance in connection with the transaction of public business" should also be given a broad interpretation. It appears to mean that public records include not only records that are required by law to be made or received, but also records that are simply kept in a public office by public officials in carrying out lawful duties. Thus practically all documentary material in municipal offices is covered by the public records law and its requirements for preservation of and access to records. These two topics are considered in turn.

Safekeeping, Retention, and Disposition

The city clerk is the custodian of all city records. He or she is responsible for following the general safekeeping requirements of G.S. 132-7: "Insofar as possible, custodians of public records shall keep them in fireproof safes, vaults, or rooms fitted with noncombustible materials and in such arrangement as to be easily accessible for convenient use. All public records should be kept in the buildings in which they are ordinarily used." The clerk is responsible for supervising the use of records and ensuring that they are not lost or damaged.

These custodial responsibilities should be carried out under the direction and with the approval of the city council, which is ultimately responsible for the records. It is often helpful for the council to adopt standard procedures concerning matters such as the time and the manner of access to records, the procedures for copying them, and the care of records that are located in other city offices and hence not in the clerk's direct custody. As discussed under the heading Access for Inspection and Copying, such rules should be designed only to safeguard the records and to minimize the disruption of public offices. They should not unduly restrict public use and copying of records, except in specific instances when restrictions on access are allowed.

Municipal records may be disposed of only in accordance with the *Municipal Records Retention and Disposition Schedule*, published by the Division of Archives and History of the North Carolina Department of Cultural Resources, the state agency with overall responsibility for public records. The *Schedule* sets out the minimum amounts of time that various records must be kept. Records that must be retained permanently are kept in the city or sent to the state archives in Raleigh. Other records may be destroyed with the city council's permission according to the *Schedule*'s timetables, once the council has agreed with the Department of Cultural Resources that it will follow the *Schedule*.

By agreeing to the *Schedule*, a municipality receives blanket permission to dispose of its records at the specified times, rather than having to seek the department's permission whenever it wants to throw anything away. Variations from the *Schedule* are sometimes approved by the department at the request of a particular city.

A council's vote to permit the destruction of specific records in accordance with the *Schedule* should be recorded in the minutes, and a permanent list of the records destroyed should be kept in the minutes or elsewhere. Preservation and destruction are the only legal options available for public records. They may not be given to private individuals, local historical societies, or other groups that request them.

The city records that must be kept permanently—most notably, the minutes of council meetings—will be microfilmed on request at no charge by the Division of Archives and History. A security copy of the microfilm is stored by the division so that the local records can be replaced if they are ever damaged or destroyed. Many municipalities regularly send copies of their minutes to Raleigh for this security microfilming.

Access for Inspection and Copying

Most of the records of municipalities must be made available for public inspection. However, some records are exempt from inspection because of a specific statute. Examples of statutory exemptions are those for most municipal personnel records (G.S. 160A-168), those for certain attorney-client records (G.S. 132-1.1), those for certain law enforcement records (G.S. 132-1.4), and those for specified records concerning industrial development (G.S. 132-6, -9).

Unless a record is exempted from disclosure, it must be made available for inspection and examination "at reasonable times and under reasonable supervision by any person" [G.S. 132-6(a)], not just by residents of the city or those with a special interest in the record. The use that a person plans to make of city records is irrelevant to his or her right of inspection [G.S. 132-6(b)], with one exception. A person obtaining geographic information systems records may be required to agree in writing not to use them for trade or commercial purposes (G.S. 132-10).

Making public records available for inspection is an important legal duty of city clerks and other custodians of records. Generally no fee should be charged for the right of inspection.

Adequate space for inspection should be provided, and inspection should generally be allowed during most hours for which the office is open. The originals of the public records must usually be made available.[8]

The right of access is a right to make reasonable requests to inspect the particular records maintained by the custodian. The person requesting the records may not require creation or compilation of a record that does not exist [G.S. 132-6.2(e)]. Thus the clerk is not required to sort or tabulate individual paper or computer files to place them in an order more usable by the person requesting them. Nor is he or she required to make a transcript of a tape recording just because the person requesting the tape would like to have its information in written form. If the custodian voluntarily elects to create or compile a record as a service to a person requesting it, he or she may negotiate a reasonable charge for doing so [G.S. 132-6.2(e)].

Records custodians are required to make copies of records when requested, as well as to make the records available for inspection. Copies must generally be furnished "as promptly as possible" [G.S. 132-6(a)].[9] If the records requested contain confidential as well as public information, the custodian must separate the two [G.S. 132-6(c)]. The person requesting copies may elect to obtain them in any medium (e.g., computer disc or paper copy) in which the city is capable of providing them [G.S. 132-6.2(a)].

Fees for copies of public records usually may not exceed the actual cost to the city of making the copy. In general, personnel and other costs that the city would have incurred had the copying request not been made may not be recovered [G.S. 132-6.2(b)], although there are exceptions for certain requests that involve extra work.[10] Fee schedules should be uniform and established in advance.

As noted earlier, reasonable regulations to protect the records and to minimize disruption of public offices are permissible as long as the rights of access, inspection, and copying are not unduly limited. For example, cities need not respond to requests for copies of records outside their usual business hours [G.S. 132-6.2(d)]. Like fee schedules, such regulations should be established in advance by the council, or by the clerk pursuant to policies established by the council. Persons desiring access to the city's records should be informed of the rules. Ad hoc rule making should be avoided to prevent arbitrary and unreasonable limitations on the rights of access, inspection, and copying.

The law establishes special rules for electronic data-processing records. These include requirements for indexing computer databases [G.S. 132-6.1(b)] and for purchasing data-processing systems that do not impair or impede the accessibility of public records [G.S. 132-6.1(a)], and provisions governing the way in which copies of computer databases are to be supplied [G.S. 132-6.2(c)].

Any person who is denied access to public records for purposes of inspection and examination, or who is denied copies of public records, may seek a court order compelling disclosure or copying [G.S.132-9(a)]. If the records have been withheld without substantial justification, the city may in some cases be required to pay the person's attorney's fees [G.S. 132-9(c)]. On the other hand, attorney's fees may be assessed against the person bringing the action if the court determines that the legal action was frivolous or was brought in bad faith [G.S. 132-9(d)].

Additional Resources

Lawrence, David M. *Interpreting North Carolina's Public Records Law.* Chapel Hill, N.C.: Institute of Government, The University of North Carolina at Chapel Hill, 1987 (2d ed. forthcoming).

Notes

1. Acts 19: 23–41.

2. North Carolina Department of Cultural Resources, Division of Archives and History, *Municipal Records Retention and Disposition Schedule* (Raleigh: the Division, 1983).

3. *See* Norfolk S. R.R. v. Reid, 187 N.C. 320, 326, 121 S.E. 534, 537 (1924) (minutes of county commissioners).

4. *Id.* at 326–27, 121 S.E. at 537–38 (1924).

5. Carolyn Lloyd, "The Hub of the Wheel," *Popular Government* 55 (Spring 1990): 36–43.

6. Lloyd, "The Hub," 38.

7. A. Fleming Bell, II, "Facts about North Carolina's Clerks," *Popular Government* 55 (Spring 1990): 43. This article includes information about the percentages of clerks performing various other duties.

8. Inspection or copying of records that, because of age or condition, could be damaged during inspection or copying may be subjected to reasonable restrictions intended to preserve the records. G.S. 132-6(f).

9. In the case of computer databases, the law provides that (1) persons may be required to submit requests for copies in writing, and (2) the records custodian is to respond to all such requests "as promptly as possible." If the request is granted, the copies are to be provided "as soon as reasonably possible." G.S. 132-6.2(c). It is unclear whether the latter phrase means something different from "as promptly as possible."

10. *See* G.S. 132-6.2(b), -6(c). The latter statute establishes a timetable for cities to bear the cost of separating confidential from nonconfidential information.

7 Personnel Administration

Stephen Allred

This chapter is a revision and update of the chapter, "Personnel Administration," by Donald B. Hayman, professor emeritus of the Institute of Government, in the first edition of *Municipal Government in North Carolina*. The author gratefully acknowledges his indebtedness to the previous author and appreciates the opportunity to build on that earlier work.

Contents

MUNICIPAL PERSONNEL ADMINISTRATION in North Carolina is a function of the North Carolina General Statutes, federal statutes, the United States Constitution, the North Carolina Constitution, decisions of state and federal courts, and the personnel ordinances and policies adopted by the cities themselves. Personnel functions carried out by cities include classification of positions, recruitment and selection of employees, performance evaluation, pay-and-benefits administration, and discipline. Public personnel administration includes everything concerned with the human resources of city government. The General Assembly has delegated broad authority for personnel administration to cities, essentially reflecting the view that providing a framework within which cities may determine their individual personnel policies is better than prescribing numerous specific requirements. This chapter provides an overview of the law governing personnel administration by North Carolina cities.

Responsibility under the General Law

Mayor-Council Form of Government

G.S. 160A-155 states that the council in mayor-council cities shall appoint, suspend, and remove the heads of all city departments and all other city employees. However, the council may delegate to any administrative official or department head the power to appoint, suspend, and remove city employees assigned to his or her department. For cities with a population of 5,000 or more, neither the mayor nor any member of the council may serve as the head of any city department, even on an acting or interim basis (G.S. 160A-158).

Council-Manager Form of Government

Many North Carolina city charters establish the council-manager form of government, which is discussed in detail in chapter 4. In 1994 there were 182 city managers in the state, virtually all cities with a population over 10,000 having managers. The trend in North Carolina has increasingly been to adopt the manager plan.[1]

Other Statutory Provisions Regarding the Power to Appoint

G.S. 160A-147 authorizes a city council to appoint a city manager to serve at its pleasure. Irrespective of the size of the city, neither the mayor nor any member of the council may serve as the manager, on a permanent or temporary basis (G.S. 160A-151).[2] For cities with a city manager, the General Statutes delegate the appointment authority to the manager. G.S. 160A-148(1) provides that the city manager shall appoint, suspend, and remove all city officers and employees who are not elected by the people and whose appointment or removal is not otherwise provided for by law, except the city attorney, in accordance with such personnel rules as the council may adopt.

Organization of the Personnel Function

Cities take the authority to determine their organization and establish personnel policies from G.S. Chapter 160A, Article 7. G.S. 160A-162 authorizes a city council to create, change, abolish, and consolidate city offices and departments and to determine the most efficient organization for the city, with only three limitations. First, the council may not abolish any office or agency established and required by law. For example, a council may not abolish the office of city attorney; G.S. 160A-173 requires a city to have one. Second, the council may not combine offices when forbidden by law. For example, G.S. 160A-151 provides that neither the mayor nor any member of the council may serve as the city manager, even on a temporary basis. Third, the council may not discontinue or assign elsewhere any functions assigned by law to a particular office. For example, G.S. 160A-171 establishes the office of the city clerk and prescribes certain duties that may be performed only by the clerk or a deputy clerk.

In mayor-council cities the council must appoint or designate a personnel officer or confer the personnel duties on some city administrative officer. The personnel officer is responsible for administering the position classification and pay plan in accordance with general policies and directives adopted by the council [G.S. 160A-162(a)]. When there is a city manager, he or she is responsible for the personnel function unless a personnel director has been appointed.

G.S. 160A-165 authorizes the creation of a personnel board and restricts it to two functions: (1) to administer tests designed to determine the merit and the fitness of candidates for appointment and (2) to conduct grievance and disciplinary appeal hearings. Because many tests have been challenged as discriminatory, few if any personnel boards administer employment tests. On the other hand, a number of North Carolina cities have established personnel boards to hear employee grievances and appeals. Typically the board is composed of citizens who are not city employees. The board conducts hearings and recommends actions on grievances or appeals for the consideration of the city manager or the council.

Quite apart from personnel boards, civil service commissions have been established by some cities through local acts of the General Assembly. These commissions, composed of appointees who serve fixed terms, review all recommended personnel actions, including hirings, promotions, and dismissals. Civil service commissions were once common in North Carolina. Today only Asheville and Raleigh have civil service commissions with authority over all nonadministrative employees. In Charlotte, Statesville, and Wilmington the commissions have authority over police and fire employees only.

Position Evaluation

In cities with a manager, G.S. 160A-162(a) provides that the city manager is responsible for preparing position classification and pay plans for submission to the council, and for administering the classification and pay plans. In mayor-council cities the classification and pay functions are the responsibility of the personnel officer or some other administrative officer. However, in neither case do the General Statutes prescribe the type of classification system to be used (point system, position classification, factor evaluation system, etc.) or the format of the pay plan (number of pay grades, amount of increases, positions covered, etc.).

Public and private employers in the United States use a variety of job evaluation methods: position classification, whole-job ranking, point rating, factor comparison, and factor ranking. Any of these methods may be adopted by a North Carolina city. Irrespective of the method used, job evaluation is inherently a subjective process. It is not surprising that classification determinations frequently lead to disagreements among employees, supervisors, and personnel departments about the proper characterization of a job.

1. *Position classification,* the most commonly used evaluation method among North Carolina cities, is a means of creating a hierarchy of jobs. Within the organization a job analysis is conducted to determine the major characteristics and dimensions of each job. By observing the major tasks involved in a job and interviewing incumbents in the position and similar positions, the classification specialist determines the responsibilities, the skills, the knowledge, and the abilities required for the position, and then designates the job as being at a certain level in the overall hierarchy of positions.
2. *Whole-job ranking* involves a ranking by managers of all positions in an organization, from the lowest to the highest. One whole-job ranking method is to compare each position with every other position, one by one, and assign a numerical value to the higher position; another is to analyze each position according to certain factors and rank it.
3. *Point rating* is a process of identifying the factors to be used in determining compensation levels, defining the factors,

and then indicating the degree to which the factors are present in the positions to be classified. Point rating is becoming increasingly popular among North Carolina cities.

4. *Factor comparison* contrasts jobs using the same selected dimensions. The factors used are typically mental requirements, physical requirements, skill requirements, responsibility, and working conditions.

5. *Factor ranking* is a method developed by the federal government to classify civil service jobs. It consists of a comparison of all positions on designated variables, such as knowledge required, amount of supervision required, complexity, scope and effect of personal contact, and physical requirements. Guide charts are developed to help the classifier determine the appropriate ranking for each position, with point values assigned for each factor.

Compensation

Action by the Council

G.S. 160A-162 establishes the general authority of a city council to "fix or approve the schedule of pay, expense allowances, and other compensation of all city employees." The same provision authorizes the adoption of position classification plans by the council. The council controls compensation by adopting the position classification plan, adopting the pay plan, adopting personnel rules governing the administration of the pay plan, adopting the budget that appropriates funds to the several departments and establishes expense allowances, and reviewing reports of the manager and the city's independent auditor.

Recommendations and Administration by the Manager

G.S. 160A-162 states that in cities with the council-manager form of government, the manager is responsible for preparing classification and pay plans and administering them after adoption by the council. A pay plan is simply a list of job titles and a schedule of the amount of money to be paid to whoever performs the prescribed duties of each position during a fixed period. The plan establishes pay rates for positions, not persons.

In *Newber v. City of Wilmington*,[3] the North Carolina Court of Appeals interpreted the pay provisions of the statutes to bar the payment of stand-by and on-call time to a police officer when the Wilmington City Council had not previously authorized the payment. Stated the court, "G.S. 160A-148(1) prohibits the city manager from unilateral adoption of a policy establishing the funding for stand-by and on-call duty for any city department. The manager's role is limited to recommending position classification and pay plans to the city council for their ultimate approval."[4]

Minimum Wage and Overtime Requirements

In designing their compensation plans, cities must be aware of the minimum wage and overtime requirements of the federal Fair Labor Standards Act (FLSA).[5] The FLSA is administered and enforced by the United States Department of Labor.

The FLSA originally applied only to private employers engaged in commerce. In 1974 it was amended to cover state and local governments. In 1976 in *National League of Cities v. Usery*,[6] the United States Supreme Court held that the federal government had no power under the Tenth Amendment to interfere with "traditional" functions of state and local governments, including the power to determine wage rates to be paid to their employees. In 1985, however, the Supreme Court reversed its earlier decision and held in *Garcia v. San Antonio Metropolitan Transit Authority*[7] that the FLSA did govern wage and overtime practices of state and local governments.

This is not to say that all other employees are subject to all FLSA requirements. The critical inquiry under the FLSA is whether a given individual is *exempt* or *nonexempt*. Exempt employees are subject to the FLSA's equal pay provisions and record-keeping requirements; they are not, however, subject to the act's minimum wage and overtime provisions.

The act provides that salaried[8] executive, administrative, and professional employees are exempt from its minimum wage and overtime provisions.[9] Two tests, the *long test* and the *short test*, have been adopted by the Department of Labor to determine whether an employee meets one or more of these exemptions.[10] An employee is exempt if he or she meets either one of the tests.

The typical nonexempt employee is entitled to overtime compensation at the rate of one and one-half hours for every hour worked over forty in a seven-day workweek. A partial exemption from the FLSA requirements is found at Section 207(k), which permits a city to pay overtime for law enforcement personnel[11] only for hours in excess of 171 in a twenty-eight-day cycle and for firefighters[12] only for hours in excess of 212 in a twenty-eight-day cycle. The act also provides a complete overtime exemption for any employee of a local government engaged in law enforcement or fire protection if that local government entity has fewer than five employees during the workweek in either capacity.[13]

For all employees, compensation may be in the form of money or compensatory time. Section 207(o) of the FLSA permits cities to give compensatory time off rather than monetary overtime pay at a rate of not less than one and one-half hours for each hour of employment for which overtime would be required. However, such an arrangement is permitted only when the employees agree to accept compensatory time in lieu of money.

In the case of police officers or firefighters, sleep time may be excluded from compensable hours of work for Section 207(k) employees who are on a tour of duty for more than twenty-four hours.[14] For example, a tour of duty of twenty-four hours and fifteen minutes is sufficient to constitute "more than 24 hours on duty" for purposes of determining whether or not sleep time may be excluded.[15] There must be an express or implied agreement between the employer and the employees to exclude such time; in the absence of an agreement, all sleep time is compensable.[16]

Comparative Salary Studies

Personnel ordinances frequently direct managers to make annual comparative studies of the pay plan and recommend changes to the council. The factors that a manager considers may be divided into two groups. First, if the manager is checking the appropriateness of a salary range for a single class of positions, he or she should consider changes in the following: (1) duties and responsibilities, (2) minimum qualifications, (3) working conditions, (4) hours of work, (5) turnover, (6) difficulty in recruiting qualified applicants, and (7) salaries paid for comparable work by other employers in the competitive labor market areas. Second, if a manager is studying the need for a general revision of the pay plan, he or she should consider changes in the following: (1) cost of living, (2) benefits paid by competitors, (3) economic conditions in the area, (4) cost of implementing a revised pay plan, and (5) availability of funds.

Salary Increases

City councils may provide for salary increases for all employees or for a class of employees as part of the annual budget. Many cities in North Carolina have implemented pay systems that have a merit pay component. For example, since 1975, Greensboro has had a system that bases salary increases solely on the performance record of each employee. Other cities use across-the-board systems that reward all employees equally, regardless of individual performance. Another widespread practice in North Carolina cities is the use of longevity pay, under which employees receive additional pay increases on the basis of number of years of service.

Equal Pay and Comparable Worth

All municipal employees, whether exempt or nonexempt, are covered by a 1963 amendment to the FLSA known as the Equal Pay Act.[17] The act states that an employer may not pay an employee of one sex less than it pays an employee of the opposite sex for work that is performed under similar working conditions and that requires equal skill, effort, and responsibility. To be considered equal work under the act, jobs need not be identical, only substantially equal.[18] The Equal Employment Opportunity Commission, which has enforcement responsibility for the act, states in its regulations that the question of "what constitutes equal skill, equal effort, or equal responsibility cannot be precisely defined."[19] Each element constitutes a separate requirement, all of which must be met for the equal pay standard to apply. An employer must show substantial differences, not minor ones, to justify pay differences.

The *equal skill requirement* is measured in terms of job performance, taking into consideration experience, training, education, and ability. The critical focus is on the position, not the incumbent.

Thus even if an incumbent has particular skills exceeding those needed for adequate job performance, those skills may not be taken into consideration in determining equal skill requirements between two jobs.[20]

The *equal effort requirement* examines the amount of physical or mental exertion needed to perform a job. The degree of effort, not the type of effort (i.e., physical versus mental), is measured to determine equality.[21]

The *equal responsibility standard* focuses on the degree of accountability required for adequate job performance. Emphasis is placed on the importance of the job obligation.[22]

The Equal Pay Act requires only equal pay for equal work; it does not require equal pay for work of comparable worth. The notion of *comparable worth* originates in the political movement to raise the ratio of wages in traditionally women's jobs to wages in traditionally men's jobs. Proponents argue that society is dominated by men, has steered women into certain jobs, and has kept the wages in those jobs below what the jobs are actually worth to the employer because most of the incumbents are women. The solution, they contend, is to apply job analysis techniques to determine the relative worth of jobs.

In its purest form, comparable worth involves a comparison between workers of one sex in one job category with workers of the other sex in a totally different job category. Proponents argue that although the work is not the same, it is of comparable worth to the employer.[23]

A less-rarefied concept of comparable worth involves a comparison between workers of one sex in one job category with workers of the other sex in a similar job category. Proponents argue that although the two groups are not performing work that meets the legal standard of the Equal Pay Act (that the jobs require equal skill, effort, and responsibility and be performed under similar working conditions), the work is nonetheless of comparable worth to the employer.

Legal claims of comparable worth have met with virtually no success in recent years.[24] As a result, proponents of comparable worth have turned to legislatures rather than courts for relief, again with little success. The North Carolina General Assembly has not indicated a willingness to adopt comparable worth as the basis of pay systems for public employees.

Fringe Benefits

Fringe benefits are defined as benefits granted to an employee by an employer that involve a money cost without affecting the wage rate. Fringe benefits represent from 25 to 40 percent of the total compensation package of the average city. In light of this significant cost, *fringe benefits* is a misnomer.

Discretion in Choice of Benefits

North Carolina cities have some discretion in choosing what type of benefits to offer to employees. Under G.S. 160A-162(b) they may provide benefits for all employees or for any class of officers or employees and their dependents. Premiums for hospital, medical, or dental insurance may be paid by the employer, the employee, or both. If a government employer pays the entire premium, G.S. 58-58-135 requires all eligible employees (except those who are deemed unsatisfactory to the insurer) to be insured. Similarly, group accident insurance may be provided by the city, and premiums may be paid by the employer, the employees, or both. If any part of the premium is paid by the employees, the covered group must be structured on an actuarially sound basis (G.S. 58-51-80). Under G.S. Chapter 143, Article 12A, municipal employees who work in law enforcement and related fields are entitled to a death benefit of up to $25,000, payable to a beneficiary.

Local Government Employees' Retirement System

A major benefit available to municipal employees is the Local Government Employees' Retirement System (LGERS), established at G.S. Chapter 128, Article 3.[25] G.S. 128-23 permits a city to elect to have its employees become eligible to participate in the retirement system if a majority of employees vote to do so. The term *employee* is defined at G.S. 128-21(10), and in the implementing regulations, to include all officers and employees in a regular position that requires not less than 1,000 hours of service per year.[26] The employer must file an application for participation in the retirement system with the LGERS Board of Trustees and agree to meet the terms of membership. A resolution approved by the board of trustees is then passed by the local city council.

An employee may retire at age sixty with five years of creditable service or at any age with thirty years of creditable service [G.S. 128-27(a)(1)]. A firefighter may retire at age fifty-five with five years of creditable service. Law enforcement officers may retire at age fifty with fifteen years of creditable service or at age fifty-five with five years of creditable service [G.S. 128-27(a)(5)].

Law enforcement officers who retire after July 1, 1992, also receive a service retirement allowance computed as follows: if retirement is at age fifty-five with five years of service, or at any age after thirty years of service, the allowance is 1.70 percent of average final compensation (highest four-year average) multiplied by years of service [G.S. 128-27(b10)(1)]. Other employees who retire after July 1, 1992, receive a service retirement allowance computed as follows: if retirement is at age sixty-five with five years of service, or at any age after thirty years of service, or after age sixty with twenty-five years of service, the allowance is 1.70 percent of average final compensation (highest four-year average) multiplied by years of service [G.S. 128-27(b10)(2)]. A reduced benefit is paid for earlier retirement [as set forth in G.S. 128-27(b8)(2) for law enforcement officers, in G.S. 128-27(b7)(2a), (2b), and (3) for other employees].

In addition to the regular retirement benefits paid to employees under LGERS, law enforcement officers are entitled to two other retirement benefits. First, the city makes a 5-percent contribution to a Section 401(k) retirement plan for each officer.[27] The state contributes approximately $12 a month to the plan, collected from a portion of court costs (G.S. Ch. 143, Art. 12D, covers law enforcement officers of state agencies and local governments; G.S. Ch. 143, Art. 12E, provides retirement benefits for local government law enforcement officers). Second, the city must pay a special separation allowance to law enforcement officers who retire after January 1, 1987. The allowance is computed as follows: the last salary multiplied by .85 percent, multiplied by the number of years of creditable service. This allowance is payable to all officers who (1) have completed thirty or more years of creditable service or have attained age fifty-five with five or more years of creditable service, (2) have not attained age sixty-two, and (3) have completed at least five years of continuous service as a law enforcement officer immediately before service retirement (G.S. Ch. 143, Article 12D).

Social Security

Another benefit provided to virtually all municipal employees is coverage under the Social Security Act.[28] The General Statutes authorize establishment of plans for extending Social Security benefits to state and local government employees (G.S. 135-21 covers state employees, G.S. 135-23 local government employees). The Social Security Act, in turn, provides that states may obtain coverage for political subdivisions by executing agreements with the secretary of the United States Department of Health and Human Services. The initial decision to participate in Social Security, then, is a voluntary one by the government employer.

Recent congressional actions have ensured the continued participation of cities in the Social Security system. In 1983, Congress amended the Social Security Act to prevent termination of coverage agreements on or after April 20 of that year. The Supreme Court upheld Congress's action as constitutional in *Bowen v. Public Agencies Opposed to Social Security Entrapment.*[29] The result is that all government employers providing Social Security coverage are required to continue to do so. Having elected to participate in the system, government employers may not revoke that election. In 1990, Congress enacted the Omnibus Budget Reconciliation Act,[30] which provides that all employees of state and local governments who are not members of a retirement system are covered by the Social Security Act after July 1, 1991.[31]

Personnel Rules and Conditions of Employment

Policies

G.S. 160A-164 sets out a nonexclusive list of personnel policies that a council may adopt by rules, regulations, or ordinances. The statute requires that policies "promote the hiring and retention of capable, diligent, and honest career employees," but imposes no other restrictions. Thus a city council may choose to adopt personnel policies governing leave, overtime, training, HIV (human immunodeficiency virus) in the workplace, residency, or any other issue. The important point is that the General Assembly has not mandated that North Carolina cities establish any personnel policy other than classification and pay plans.

Hours Worked

Most municipal employees are on a standard forty-hour work-week. Some cities have a schedule of thirty-seven and one-half hours, and others require as few as thirty-five hours a week. Some cities have adopted flextime programs, which allow employees to begin work any time between 7 and 9 A.M., work eight hours, and then leave for the day.

Vacation and Other Leave

Most cities provide paid leave to employees. Typically nine to twelve days a year are designated as paid holidays. In addition, employees usually earn sick leave and vacation leave. Some cities also grant petty leave (periods of less than a day), court leave, and funeral leave. Under G.S. 160A-164 the decision to establish personnel policies allowing various types of leave rests solely with the city. If a city provides vacation leave for employees, however, G.S. 95-25.12 requires that it grant the leave or payment in lieu of leave.[32] However, under G.S. 95-25.12 and -25.13 the city may establish a written policy requiring the forfeiture of vacation leave in specified circumstances.

Military leave is time off from regular duties to participate in the activities of a reserve component of the United States armed forces. Municipal employees are entitled to unpaid leave for this activity under Title 38, Section 2024, of the United States Code. The leave of absence is to be granted "for the period required to perform active duty for training or inactive duty training," and the employee must then be permitted to return to his or her position "with such seniority, status, pay, and vacation as such employee would have had if such employee had not been absent for such purposes."[33]

Maternity leave policies adopted by cities must meet the requirements of the Pregnancy Discrimination Act of 1978.[34] That act prohibits disparate treatment in employment of pregnant women. Specifically the act (1) requires employers to treat pregnancy and childbirth the same as they treat other causes of disability under fringe benefit plans, (2) prohibits terminating or refusing to hire or promote a woman solely because she is pregnant, (3) bars mandatory leaves for pregnant women arbitrarily set at a certain time in their pregnancy and not based on their individual inability to work, and (4) protects the reinstatement rights of women on leave for pregnancy-related reasons. The act also makes it unlawful for an employer to differentiate between pregnancy-related and other disabilities for purposes of fringe benefits, including leave policies. The general rule that emerges from the Pregnancy Discrimination Act is that a city must treat a pregnant employee the same as it treats other employees with a temporary disability.

Recruitment and Selection

The responsibility for adopting specific requirements for recruitment and selection is placed on the individual city, not mandated by the General Statutes. The decision to advertise positions, to post vacancy announcements, to interview candidates using panels, and to make outreach efforts to improve minority recruitment is one freely made by the city, not required by federal or state law. Obviously, however, the city's recruitment and selection decisions are less likely to be challenged successfully under federal statutes prohibiting discrimination if they are based on a system that reaches a large applicant pool and gives full and fair consideration to all candidates.

Title VII of the Civil Rights Act of 1964

The federal legislation that has had the greatest effect on municipal recruitment and selection is Title VII of the Civil Rights Act of 1964.[35] Originally applicable only to private employers of fifteen or more employees, the act was amended in 1972 to apply to public employers irrespective of the number of employees hired. Title VII bars employers from hiring or dismissing or making other decisions with respect to terms and conditions of employment on the basis of race, color, religion, sex, or national origin.[36] Only when religion, sex, or national origin is a *bona fide occupational qualification* (BFOQ), reasonably necessary to the operation of the business,[37] is an exception made. Title VII is enforced by the United States Equal Employment Opportunity Commission.

Uniform Guidelines on Employee Selection Procedures

The federal government published the *Uniform Guidelines on Employee Selection Procedures* in 1978 to provide employers with one set of standards to help them determine whether they were meeting the requirements of Title VII as it related to recruitment and selection.[38] These guidelines provide that a recruitment policy or practice that has an "adverse impact" on the employment opportunities of any race, sex, or ethnic group is illegal under Title VII unless the adverse impact is justified by a business necessity.

The guidelines establish a rule of thumb for determining whether an employer's recruitment policies have an adverse impact, by comparing the selection rates for different groups. This rule, known as the four-fifths rule or the 80-percent rule, states that if the selection rate for one group is not at least 80 percent of the selection rate for another group, then the policies have an adverse impact on the lower-rated group. For example, a city might hire three of every five white applicants referred for a position, but only one of every five black applicants—selection rates of 60 percent for whites and 20 percent for blacks. A comparison would show the city's recruitment policies to have an adverse impact because a 20-percent rate is less than four-fifths of a 60-percent rate.

A showing of an adverse impact does not in and of itself prove discrimination. Still, when such differences in selection rates exist, a city should consider increasing its efforts to equalize the rates. Conversely, even if a government employer can show that black applicants are selected at a rate equal to at least 80 percent of the rate for white applicants, it may still be liable for individual cases of discrimination in hiring. A bottom-line defense that the employer has met its overall objective of having relatively equal rates of hiring will not withstand an otherwise valid showing of individual discrimination.[39]

Affirmative Action

Affirmative action is the deliberate use of race and sex preferences in selection or promotion.[40] Affirmative action may result from an employer's voluntary decision to adopt an affirmative action plan or from a consent decree or a court order requiring its use. Affirmative action is not the use of informal or ad hoc preferences, even for good motives; that is discrimination prohibited under Title VII of the Civil Rights Act of 1964.[41]

Affirmative action plans have been challenged under both Title VII of the Civil Rights Act of 1964 and the United States Constitution. By and large, however, affirmative action as a legal remedy to past discrimination has survived both types of challenges.

The first Supreme Court case to examine the affirmative action issue was not decided until 1978 and did not involve affirmative action in employment. Nonetheless, that case, *Regents of University of California v. Bakke,*[42] upheld the principle of affirmative action and stands for the proposition that government may take race into account to remedy past racial injustice, at least when appropriate findings of past discrimination have been made by a court, an administrative agency, or a legislative body. In *Bakke* the affirmative action taken was to set aside 16 of 100 seats in the entering class at the University of California medical school for minority applicants. The Court upheld the consideration of race in admissions as not violative of the Constitution's equal protection clause; however, the Court struck down the use of strict quotas.

In 1979 the Court decided its first case on affirmative action in employment, *United Steelworkers of America v. Weber.*[43] In that case a white employee sued his employer and his union, challenging a voluntarily adopted job training program that mandated a one-for-one quota for minority employees. The Court upheld the program, ruling that Title VII's ban on racial discrimination did not prohibit voluntary affirmative action plans. The Court set forth four criteria to guide employers in adopting affirmative action plans: (1) that a showing of prior discrimination had been made, (2) that the plan was reasonably related to remedying the prior discrimination, (3) that the plan did not trammel the rights of the majority-race workers or serve as a complete bar to their advancement, and (4) that the plan was a temporary measure to eliminate an existing racial imbalance.

In 1986 the Supreme Court issued its decision in *Wygant v. Jackson Board of Education.*[44] The Court held that for a public employer, a voluntary affirmative action plan must comply with the equal protection clause of the Constitution and that an affirmative action plan's requirement that white employees with greater seniority be laid off while black employees with less seniority be retained was unconstitutional. The justification offered for the plan, that black students needed black teachers as role models, was found insufficient to justify layoffs of white teachers with more seniority.

One year later in *Johnson v. Transportation Agency, Santa Clara County*,[45] the Court held that a public employer's voluntary affirmative action plan that did not establish quotas but did allow consideration of sex as one factor when evaluating qualified job applicants for positions in which women were underrepresented, was lawful under Title VII. The sex-conscious relief was found justified by the existence of a manifest imbalance[46] reflected in sex-segregated job categories and by the fact that the rights of innocent third parties were not unnecessarily trammeled, nor were those parties barred from further advancement. Significantly the Court in *Johnson* added that a public employer using an affirmative action plan in which race or sex was one factor in the decision to promote or hire, was not required to prove or admit that it had illegally discriminated in past employment decisions.

At least five rules for voluntary affirmative action plans emerge from the Supreme Court's affirmative action cases:

1. Plans with race or sex preference are lawful under Title VII if they are designed to correct manifest imbalances reflecting underrepresentation of minority groups in traditionally segregated job categories.
2. A public employer is not required to admit past discrimination in order to adopt an affirmative action plan. However, "societal discrimination" or the "role model" theory will not support race-conscious plans.
3. Race or sex may be considered as one factor in a decision to promote or hire; however, no unqualified individuals may be considered.
4. The plan may not unnecessarily trammel the rights of white or male employees or applicants, or create an absolute bar to their advancement.
5. Plans must be temporary and be aimed only at attaining a balanced workforce, not at maintaining a permanent race or sex balance.

Preparation of an Affirmative Action Plan

Cities have substantial latitude in preparing voluntary affirmative action plans. Among the items that might be included in a plan are the following:

1. A statement of affirmative action policy
2. A determination and a statement of responsibility for preparing, adopting, administering, and distributing a plan
3. An analysis of current personnel practices and a determination of whether they unnecessarily screen out qualified members of protected groups
4. An analysis of the municipal work force and the applicant pool by race and sex
5. An identification of job classes and departments in which protected groups are underrepresented
6. A plan to increase representation of protected groups by specific actions, such as increasing publicity about job openings, developing upward-mobility programs, targeting recruitment efforts, implementing training opportunities, and eliminating invalid screening procedures.

Other Federal Antidiscrimination Acts

In addition to the Civil Rights Act of 1964, federal legislation exists to outlaw racial discrimination in the making of employment contracts, to ensure protection of federal civil rights, to bar age discrimination, and to require accommodation of disabled individuals.

The Civil Rights Acts of 1866 and 1871

After the Civil War, Congress passed two civil rights enforcement statutes to give effect to the Thirteenth, Fourteenth, and Fifteenth amendments to the United States Constitution. These acts, codified at Section 1981 and Section 1983 of Title 42 of the United States Code, have been used by plaintiffs to bring claims of discrimination in employment separate from Title VII.

The Civil Rights Act of 1866 is found at Section 1981. It provides that "all persons . . . shall have the same right . . . to make and enforce contracts . . . as is enjoyed by white citizens." This language allows a plaintiff to sue a government or private employer for discrimination in employment on the basis of race or national origin.[47] A city is not liable for a discriminatory hiring decision of one of its employees unless that decision is traceable to an official policy or practice of the local government employer.[48]

The Civil Rights Act of 1871 is found at Section 1983. It provides that "[e]very person who, under color of any statute, ordinance, regulation, custom or usage, of any State or Territory, subjects, or causes to be subjected, any citizen of the United States or other person within the jurisdiction thereof to the deprivation of any rights, privileges or immunities secured by the Constitution and laws, shall be liable to the party injured in an action at law, suit in equity, or other proper proceeding for redress." The Supreme Court has described the purpose of Section 1983 as "to interpose the federal courts between the States and the people, as guardians of the people's federal rights."[49] Section 1983 does not provide an independent source of rights, however; it is a vehicle by which one can challenge a city's action as violating a right protected under some other statute or under the United States Constitution. Cities may be sued under Section 1983 for deprivation of constitutional or federal rights only if the plaintiff can show that the deprivation was caused by an established government custom or by a policy statement, ordinance, regulation, or decision officially adopted and promulgated by the body's officers,[50] either by formal governing board action or by the policy decisions of upper-level administrators.

The Age Discrimination in Employment Act

The Age Discrimination in Employment Act of 1967 (ADEA)[51] prohibits discrimination on the basis of age for all persons age forty and above. Specifically the ADEA makes it unlawful for an employer to do the following:[52]

1. To fail or refuse to hire, or to discharge any individual or otherwise to discriminate against any individual with respect to compensation, terms, conditions, or privileges of employment because of such individual's age
2. To limit, segregate, or classify employees in any way that would deprive or tend to deprive any individual of employ-

ment opportunities or otherwise adversely affect his or her status as an employee because of such individual's age
3. To reduce the wage rate of any employee in order to comply with the ADEA.

The ADEA is enforced by the Equal Employment Opportunity Commission.

Statutes Prohibiting Discrimination on the Basis of Disability

The Rehabilitation Act of 1973[53] prohibits discrimination in employment against handicapped persons. The act defines the term *handicapped person* as any person who "(i) has a physical or mental impairment which substantially limits one or more of such person's major life activities, (ii) has a record of such an impairment, or (iii) is regarded as having such an impairment."[54] *Major life activities* is defined by the United States Department of Labor, Office of Federal Contract Compliance, as "communication, ambulation, selfcare, socialization, education, vocational training, employment, transportation, adapting to housing, etc."[55] The act, which covers only recipients of federal contract funds,[56] bars discrimination against otherwise qualified handicapped persons in any program or activity receiving federal financial assistance.[57] The term *program or activity* includes a department, an agency, a special-purpose district, or another instrumentality of a state or local government.[58]

Closely related to the Rehabilitation Act of 1973 is the Americans with Disabilities Act (ADA) of 1990.[59] The ADA prohibits discrimination against individuals with disabilities. Title I of the act prohibits discrimination in employment; the other titles prohibit discrimination in public services and transportation, public accommodations, and telecommunications.

The Rehabilitation Act of 1973 covers only recipients of federal funds. The ADA has no such limitation. Employers with at least fifteen employees are covered as of July 26, 1994.

Title I of the ADA prohibits covered employers from discriminating against a qualified individual with disabilities in any aspect of employment, including hiring, promotion, dismissal, compensation, and training. Specific prohibitions include (1) limiting, segregating, or classifying a job applicant or an employee in a way that adversely affects the opportunities or the status of such an individual because of a disability; (2) using standards or criteria that have the effect of discriminating against persons with disabilities; (3) denying job benefits or opportunities to someone because of his or her association or relationship with a person who is disabled; (4) not making reasonable accommodations; (5) using employment tests or selection criteria that screen out persons with disabilities and are not job related; and (6) failing to use tests that accurately measure job abilities.

Training

Many North Carolina cities have personnel policies that provide training and educational leave for employees. Several large cities now have full-time training officers and training divisions. Training may be offered either on site (by the city or by a contractor) or off site (by an educational institution or other provider). Educational leave may be granted for up to a year, with or without pay, to equip employees to perform current duties better or to perform duties to which they expect to be assigned.

The North Carolina Supreme Court held nearly fifty years ago[60] that a city might spend public funds to train its employees. Cities, like private-sector employers, recognize the need to provide high-quality and timely training to all levels of employees if they are effectively to meet the demands of the public.

Defense of Employees

G.S. 160A-167 allows cities to provide for the legal defense of employees or officers and to pay judgments entered against them, but does not require cities to do so. However, a city may not simply decide informally whether or not to provide for the legal defense of its employees. G.S. 160A-167(c) requires the city council to adopt uniform standards under which claims may be paid, in advance of any agreement to provide a defense or make a payment. These standards must be made available for public inspection.

Workers' Compensation

G.S. Chapter 97, the North Carolina Workers' Compensation Act, is an employer-financed program of benefits to provide for medical coverage, rehabilitation expenses, and loss of income for employees who have job-related injuries or illnesses (covered occupational diseases are found at G.S. 97-53). At G.S. 97-2(2) it encompasses cities, providing coverage for injury "arising out of and in the course of the employment" [G.S. 97-2(6)].[61]

Employees receive full coverage for medical and rehabilitation treatment, and two-thirds of their salary for lost time at work. Income benefits begin on the seventh calendar day after the lost time begins; however, if the lost time exceeds twenty-one days, income benefits are then also paid for the first seven days (G.S. 97-28). Income replacement continues until the employee returns to work or reaches the maximum medical improvement. In the case of permanent and total disability, income replacement is a lifetime benefit, continuing until the employee's condition changes or the employee dies (G.S. 97-29).

When an injury or an illness results in permanent partial disability, a lump-sum settlement based on a schedule set out in G.S. 97-31 is paid to the employee. Death benefits are paid to survivors of job-related injuries or illnesses. Survivors of employees who served as law enforcement officers or firefighters receive a higher-level benefit for job-related death (G.S. 97-38).

Cities may choose to be fully insured or to self-insure for these benefits. Employees whose workers' compensation claims are denied have the right to appeal to the North Carolina Industrial Commission and to state court. An award of the Industrial Commission is binding on all questions of fact, but may be appealed to the court of appeals on errors of law (G.S. 97-86). The review of the court of appeals is limited to two questions: (1) whether there was any competent evidence before the agency to support its findings of fact; and (2) whether the findings of fact supported the commission's conclusions of law.[62]

Traditionally North Carolina courts have held the Workers' Compensation Act to provide the exclusive remedy available to an injured employee, even when the injury has been caused by gross negligence or the willful, wanton, or reckless behavior of the employer (G.S. 97-10.1).[63] In 1991, however, the North Carolina Supreme Court held in *Woodson v. Rowland*[64] that the Workers' Compensation Act was not the exclusive remedy for an employee who was killed or injured when the employer engaged in conduct knowing that it was substantially certain to cause serious injury or death. Such misconduct, held the court, was tantamount to an intentional tort, and in such a circumstance a plaintiff might maintain a civil action against the decedent's employer.

Unemployment Compensation

G.S. Chapter 96, Article 2, sets forth an employer-financed program to provide partial income-replacement benefits to employees who lose their jobs or have their work hours reduced to less than 60 percent of their last schedule. The program is authorized by the Federal Unemployment Tax Act, which levies a tax of 6.2 percent of payroll, with tax credits of up to 5.4 percent for state unemployment taxes paid. The program is administered by the North Carolina Employment Security Commission. State and local government employers are covered under the program [G.S. 96-8(5)p]. Contributions by employers are made as provided by a schedule set out at G.S. 96-9.

Individuals are eligible for benefits if they register for work and continue to report at the Employment Security Commission employment office, make a claim for benefits, and are able and available to work [G.S. 96-13(a)]. An individual may be disqualified for benefits if he or she has left work voluntarily and without good cause attributable to the employer [G.S. 96-14(1)]. Further, if the Employment Security Commission determines that an individual was discharged for misconduct connected with the work, then benefits will be denied [G.S. 96-14(2)]. The term *misconduct connected with the work* is defined at G.S. 96-14(2) as

> conduct evincing such willful or wanton disregard of an employer's interest as is found in deliberate violations or disregard of standards of behavior which the employer has the right to expect of his employee, or in carelessness or negligence of such degree or recurrence as to manifest equal culpability, wrongful intent or evil design, or to show an intentional and substantial disregard of the employer's interests or of the employee's duties and obligations to his employer. . . . [The term also includes] reporting to work significantly impaired by

alcohol or illegal drugs; consuming alcohol or illegal drugs on employer's premises; conviction by a court of competent jurisdiction for manufacturing, selling, or distribution of a controlled substance punishable under G.S. 90-95(a)(1) or G.S. 90-95(a)(2) while in the employ of said employer.

Unionization and Employee Relations

G.S. Chapter 95, Article 12, is a comprehensive ban on collective bargaining by public employees. One provision, G.S. 95-97, which purports to prohibit public employees from becoming members of trade unions or labor unions, was held unconstitutional in *Atkins v. City of Charlotte*[65] and is of no effect. Thus despite the statute, municipal employees may exercise their First Amendment right of association and speech by belonging to labor unions. In contrast, G.S. 95-98, which makes contracts between any city and any labor organization "illegal, unlawful, void, and of no effect," was upheld in *Atkins v. City of Charlotte* as a valid and constitutional exercise of the legislature's authority. Nothing in the statute affects the right of employees and labor organizations to present their views to city councils and officials, however, to the same extent that other citizens may.[66] Finally, G.S. 95-98.1 and G.S. 95-98.2 prohibit strikes by public employees, and G.S. 95-99 makes the violation of Article 12 a misdemeanor. The constitutionality of these latter provisions has never been tested.

Restrictions on Political Activity

G.S. 160A-169 prohibits certain partisan political activities by municipal employers and employees. The act bars employees, while on duty or in the workplace, from using official authority or influence to interfere with or affect the result of an election or a nomination for political office, or to coerce, solicit, or compel contributions for political or partisan purposes by another employee. The statute also provides that no employee may be required to contribute funds to political campaigns, and that no employee may use local government funds or facilities for partisan political purposes.

In addition to rights under the General Statutes, municipal employees enjoy First Amendment free speech protection, including the right to engage in political activity. The courts have limited the circumstances in which political party affiliation may be used as a basis for personnel actions, such as hiring and dismissal of employees, to instances in which it can be shown that "affiliation with the employer's party is essential to the employee's effectiveness in carrying out the responsibilities of the position held."[67] When partisan political activities are undertaken by employees, the employer (and ultimately the courts) is required to strike the balance between the First Amendment right of the employee to speak on matters of public concern and the city's right to a workplace free from undue disruption.[68]

Discipline, Dismissal, and Grievances

The Fourteenth Amendment to the United States Constitution guarantees that no state shall "deprive any person of life, liberty, or property, without due process of law."[69] The United States Supreme Court has held that this guarantee of due process extends in two distinct circumstances to a public employee's job security. First, when a public employee has a vested property interest in the job (for example, the requirement under G.S. 126-35 that employees subject to the State Personnel Act may be discharged only for "just cause"), the employee may be removed only after notice, an opportunity to respond, and a demonstration that cause exists.[70] Second, when a public employer dismisses an employee for reasons "that might seriously damage his standing and associations in his community" or that might stigmatize the employee and foreclose "his freedom to take advantage of other employment opportunities,"[71] the public employee has been deprived of his or her liberty interest under the Fourteenth Amendment. If the employer makes public such stigmatizing charges, the employee is entitled to notice and an opportunity for a hearing to clear his or her name.[72]

Cities may create a property interest in employment by enacting personnel ordinances that confer on employees the understanding that they may be disciplined or dismissed only for poor performance or misconduct. For example, in *Howell v. Town of Carolina Beach*,[73] the North Carolina Court of Appeals held that the personnel manual enacted by the town through its ordinance procedure gave rights comparable to those of state employees under the State Personnel

Act, and that the summary dismissal of an employee had violated his due process rights.

If a city creates a property interest in employment, what process is due the public employee under the Fourteenth Amendment? In brief, due process requires that (1) the employee be given notice of the charges against him or her, (2) the employee be given an opportunity to respond to those charges before being dismissed, and (3) the decision of whether or not to uphold the charges be made by an impartial decision maker.[74] This means that the municipal employer must specify the reasons for the proposed dismissal in such a way that the employee clearly understands the basis for the action. It further requires that the employer give the employee a reasonable amount of time to prepare a response to the proposed action, with the assistance of counsel if necessary. Finally, it requires that the employer conduct a predismissal hearing with an impartial decision maker, at which the employee may present evidence and arguments against the proposed dismissal. The decision maker then decides whether or not to uphold the charges.

Personnel Records

G.S. 160A-168 governs a city's release of information from the personnel files of three groups: current employees, former employees, and applicants for employment. The term *personnel file* is defined very broadly at G.S. 160A-168(a) to include "any information *in any form* gathered by the [employer] . . . relating to [the employee's] application, selection or nonselection, promotions, demotions, transfers, suspension, and other disciplinary actions, evaluation forms, leave, salary, and termination of employment" (emphasis added). No matter where or in what form the information maintained on an employee is kept—in the personnel office or elsewhere, in a file folder or on computer tape—the release of it is governed by G.S. 160A-168.

Information Permitted to Be Released

Whether a given type of information in an employee's personnel file is open or confidential is determined by the status of the person or the agency requesting the information. The information that may be released to each type of person or agency requesting it is as follows:

The general public. Eight items in an employee's personnel file must be disclosed to the public when requested [G.S. 160A-168(b)]:

1. The employee's name
2. The employee's age
3. The date of the employee's original employment or appointment
4. The employee's current position title
5. The employee's current salary
6. The date and the amount of the most recent increase or decrease in the employee's salary (but not the date and the amount of any previous salary change)
7. The date of the employee's most recent promotion, demotion, transfer, suspension, separation, or other change in position classification (again, however, not the date of any previous change in position or disciplinary action)
8. The office or the station to which the employee is currently assigned.

Employees. An employee has the right to have access to any information contained in his or her personnel file "in its entirety," except letters of reference solicited before the employee was hired. Also exempt from disclosure to the employee is information concerning medical disabilities that a prudent physician would not disclose to a patient [G.S. 160A-168(c)(1)].

Applicants, former employees, or their agents. An applicant for employment, a former employee, or an agent of either may examine the applicant's or the former employee's personnel file to the same extent that an employee may examine his or her own file. No information about applicants may be disclosed to the public, however.[75]

Government officials. The broadest right of access is afforded to a person having supervisory authority over the employee, who may examine all material in the employee's personnel file. This provision allows not only an employee's immediate supervisor, but also others in the chain of command, to have access to the personnel file. Similarly members of the city council and the council's attorney, as well as officials of federal or state agencies, have the right to examine a personnel file when the custodian of the personnel records deems it "necessary and essential to the pursuance of a proper function" [G.S.

160A-168(c)(3)]. Thus no city council member or other official has a right to look at a personnel file merely to satisfy his or her curiosity; rather, some legitimate need must exist to warrant the examination.

Party with a court order. Finally, a party to a judicial or administrative proceeding involving an employee may, on obtaining a proper court order (not a subpoena), inspect and examine a particular portion of an employee's personnel file that otherwise would be confidential.

Exceptions to the Rule of Confidentiality

The General Statutes contain two exceptions to the rule that all matters not specifically listed as open to inspection are confidential. The first exception is found in G.S. 160A-168(c)(7), which provides that personnel information otherwise confidential may be disclosed by the city manager if "the release is essential to maintaining public confidence in the administration of city services or to maintaining the level and quality of city services." In such a case the manager, with the concurrence of the city council, may "inform any person or corporation of the employment or nonemployment, promotion, demotion, suspension or other disciplinary action, reinstatement, transfer, or termination of a[n] . . . employee and the reasons for that personnel action." To illustrate, if a former employee falsely tells a newspaper reporter that he was dismissed for exposing corruption by the local city council, the act permits the council to correct the record by informing the newspaper of the actual basis for the employee's dismissal. However, if the manager decides to disclose the circumstances of the employee's dismissal, he or she must first propose disclosure to the council, which must determine whether release of the information in this case is "essential." If the council agrees that disclosure is warranted, the manager must prepare a memorandum stating the circumstances that require disclosure and specifying the information to be disclosed. The memorandum itself then becomes a public record and is maintained in the employee's personnel file. Only after this process is completed may the manager discuss the reasons for the employee's dismissal with the newspaper reporter.

The second exception is found in the open meetings law (G.S. Ch. 143, Art. 33C), which provides that the terms of any settlement of a "pending or potential judicial action or administrative proceeding" in which a public body is a party or has a substantial interest shall be disclosed [G.S. 143-318.11(a)(4)]. Disclosure is required even when the parties to the judicial action agree to keep the terms of the settlement confidential.[76]

In addition to the provision of the open meetings law, the 1989 General Assembly amended G.S. Chapter 132, the Public Records Act, to provide that the term *public records* includes "all settlement documents in any suit, administrative proceeding, or arbitration instituted against any agency of North Carolina government or its subdivisions" [G.S. 132-12.2(a)].[77] The act further prohibits settlement agreements between government employers and plaintiffs that contain confidentiality clauses.

An exception to the requirement that settlement records be made public is found at G.S. 132-12.2(b). A judge, an administrative judge, an administrative hearing officer, a board, a commission, or an arbitrator may order or permit the sealing of a settlement document if he or she concludes that (1) the presumption of openness is overcome by an overriding interest and (2) such overriding interest cannot be protected by any measure short of sealing the settlement.

The personnel records acts governing North Carolina public employees also provide that employees may sign a written release permitting the city or the county to give information about the employee to prospective employers or others [G.S. 160A-168(c)(6)]. In the preceding example, if such a release was in place, the manager could disclose the circumstances of the dismissal to any party authorized by the release without making a written determination that disclosure of the information was essential.

æ   æ   æ

North Carolina cities exercise the personnel function under the limits of the General Statutes, federal statutes, and the requirements of the common law. The challenge is to administer personnel policies in a way that is both legally defensible and efficient for all parties concerned.

Notes

1. See North Carolina League of Municipalities, *State of Our Cities and Towns* (Raleigh, N.C.: the League, January 1994), vi.

2. When a vacancy is created in the office of the city manager, the council is

authorized to "designate a qualified person to exercise the powers and perform the duties of manager until the vacancy is filled" (G.S. 160A-150).

3. 83 N.C. App. 327, 350 S.E.2d 125 (1986), *cert. denied,* 319 N.C. '225, 353 S.E.2d 402 (1987).

4. *Id.* at 330, 350 S.E.2d at 127.

5. 29 U.S.C. §§ 201–219, 52 Stat. 1060 (1938), as amended.

6. 426 U.S. 833 (1976).

7. 469 U.S. 528 (1985) (holding that federal minimum wage and overtime laws might constitutionally be applied to state and local governments and that attempt to define certain governmental activities as "traditional" had proven unworkable in period since *Usery* was decided).

8. 29 C.F.R. § 541.118(a) (1994) provides that employees are considered paid on a salary basis if they regularly receive each pay period a predetermined amount not subject to reduction because of variations in the quality or the quantity of work performed. A series of federal court decisions in 1990 and 1991 held that if an employer made deductions from an employee's paycheck for absences of less than a full day, the employee was not truly salaried and was thus nonexempt. *See, e.g.,* Abshire v. Kern County, 908 F.2d 483 (9th Cir. 1990), *cert. denied,* 111 S. Ct. 785, *reh'g denied,* 111 S. Ct. 1341 (1991); Hartman v. Arlington County, 903 F.2d 290 (4th Cir. 1990). In 1991 the Department of Labor was besieged with requests to amend the regulations to permit deductions for absences of less than a day for employees designated as exempt, and agreed to do so by amending the regulations. 29 C.F.R. § 541.5d (1994) now expressly permits state and local government employers to make deductions for absences of less than a day without endangering the exempt status of the employees for whom the deductions are made.

9. 29 U.S.C. § 213 (1994).

10. The tests may be found at 29 C.F.R. § 541 (1994).

11. Defined at 29 C.F.R. § 553.11 (1994) as an employee who (1) is a uniformed or plainclothes member of a body of officers or subordinates; (2) has been empowered by statute or local ordinance to enforce laws designed to maintain public peace and order, protect life and property from accident or willful injury, and to prevent and detect crimes; (3) has been given the power of arrest; and (4) has graduated from a special course of instruction or will undergo on-the-job training. Civilian dispatchers who work for a public safety department have been held not to be covered by the Section 207(k) provision and therefore to be entitled to overtime compensation for all hours worked over forty in a week [W.H. Op. Ltr. (Oct. 10, 1990)].

12. Defined at 29 C.F.R. § 553.210 (1994) as an employee who (1) is employed by a fire department or district; (2) has been trained as required by statute or ordinance; (3) has authority to engage in fire prevention, control, or extinguishment; and (4) performs fire prevention, control, or extinguishment. In Schmidt v. County of Prince William, 929 F.2d 986 (4th Cir. 1991), the court held that firefighters assigned to a one-year training period as dispatchers were engaging in fire-fighting support activities and therefore were subject to Section 207(k) of the FLSA.

13. 29 U.S.C. § 213(b)(20) (1994). This provision is explained in the Department of Labor regulations at 29 C.F.R. § 553.200 (1994).

14. 29 U.S.C. § 207(o) (1994); *see also* 29 C.F.R. § 553.15 (1994).

15. W.H. Op. Ltr. (Sept. 11, 1987).

16. 29 C.F.R. § 553.222(c) (1994).

17. 29 U.S.C. § 206(d) (1963).

18. Corning Glass Works v. Brennan, 417 U.S. 188 (1974); 29 C.F.R. § 1620.13(a) (1994).

19. 29 C.F.R. § 1620.14(a) (1994).

20. 29 C.F.R. § 1620.15(a) (1994).

21. 29 C.F.R. § 1620.16(a) (1994).

22. 29 C.F.R. § 1620.17(a) (1994).

23. *See, e.g.,* Lemons v. City and County of Denver, 620 F.2d 228 (10th Cir.), *cert. denied,* 449 U.S. 888 (1980) (comparing worth of nurses to that of tree trimmers).

24. *See, e.g.,* American Nurses Ass'n v. Illinois, 783 F.2d 716 (7th Cir. 1986); AFSCME v. Washington, 770 F.2d 1401 (9th Cir. 1985).

25. The pension rights of LGERS members may be modified by the legislature without violating the constitutional prohibition on impairment of contracts when the impairment is reasonable and necessary to serve an important public purpose [Simpson v. North Carolina Local Gov't Employees' Retirement Sys., 88 N.C. App. 218, 363 S.E.2d 90 (1987), *aff'd mem.*, 323 N.C. 362, 372 S.E.2d 559 (1988)].

26. N.C. ADMIN. CODE tit. 20, ch. 02C § .0802 (1990).

27. In Abeyounis v. Town of Wrightsville Beach, 102 N.C. App. 341, 401 S.E.2d 847 (1991), the court held that the employer, not the employee, had to fund the Section 401(k) plan, and that a budget ordinance that gave a 1.5-percent raise to town police and a 3.5-percent raise to all other municipal employees, with the 2.0-percent difference being used to fund the Section 401(k) plan, violated G.S. 143-166.50(e).

28. 42 U.S.C. § 301–2007 (1994).

29. 477 U.S. 41 (1986).

30. Pub. L. No. 101-508, 104 Stat. 1388 (1990).

31. The regulations implementing this change are found at 29 C.F.R. pt. 31 (1994).

32. Narron v. Hardee's Food Sys., 75 N.C. App. 579, 331 S.E.2d 205, *cert. denied,* 314 N.C. 542, 335 S.E.2d 316 (1985).

33. 38 U.S.C. § 2024(d) (1994).

34. 42 U.S.C. § 2000e(k) (1994).

35. 42 U.S.C. §§ 2000e–2000c4 (1994).

36. 42 U.S.C. § 2000e-2(a)(1) (1994).

37. 42 U.S.C. § 2000e-2(e)(1) (1994). Although the act provides for the BFOQ exception, in practice, employers have found this exception extremely difficult to meet.

38. 29 C.F.R. § 1607 (1994).

39. Connecticut v. Teal, 457 U.S. 440 (1982).

40. The Equal Employment Opportunity Commission defines *affirmative action* as "actions appropriate to overcome the effects of past or present practices, policies, or other barriers to equal employment opportunity" [29 C.F.R. § 1608.1(c) (1994)].

41. Lilly v. City of Beckley, 797 F.2d 191 (4th Cir. 1986) (invalidating informal affirmative action plan under which municipality gave preference to minority applicants, without proof that plan had remedial purpose of hiring qualified minorities).

42. 438 U.S. 265 (1978).

43. 443 U.S. 193 (1979).

44. 476 U.S. 267 (1986).

45. 480 U.S. 616 (1987).

46. 480 U.S. at 640.

47. In St. Francis College v. Al-Khazraji, 481 U.S. 604 (1987), and Shaare Tefila Congregation v. Cobb, 481 U.S. 615 (1987), the United States Supreme Court held that Section 1981 claims were not limited to race discrimination, but included claims by persons "who [were] subjected to intentional discrimination solely because of their ancestry or ethnic characteristics," such as Arabs (*St. Francis College*, 481 U.S. at 613).

48. Jett v. Dallas Indep. School Dist., 491 U.S. 701 (1989).

49. Mitchum v. Foster, 407 U.S. 225, 242 (1972).

50. Monell v. New York Dep't of Social Serv., 436 U.S. 658, 694 (1978).

51. 29 U.S.C. §§ 621–631 (1994).

52. 29 U.S.C. § 623(f)(1) (1994).

53. 29 U.S.C. §§ 701–796i (1994).

54. 29 U.S.C. § 706 (1994).

55. 41 C.F.R. § 60-741 app. A (1994).

56. Consolidated Rail Corp. v. Darrone, 465 U.S. 624, 636 (1984).

57. 29 U.S.C. § 794(a) (1994).

58. 29 U.S.C. § 794(b)(1)(A) (1994).

59. 42 U.S.C. § 1201 (1994).

60. Green v. Kitchen, 229 N.C. 449 (1948).

61. The employee must prove that he or she suffered an injury by accident, that the injury arose from employment, and that the injury was sustained in the course of employment [Gallimore v. Marilyn's Shoes, 292 N.C. 399, 233 S.E.2d 529 (1977)].

62. McClean v. Roadway Express, 307 N.C. 99, 296 S.E.2d 456 (1982).

63. Barrino v. Radiator Specialty Co., 315 N.C. 500, 340 S.E.2d 295 (1986); Harless v. Flynn, 1 N.C. App. 448, 162 S.E.2d 47 (1968).

64. 329 N.C. 330, 407 S.E.2d 222 (1991).

65. 296 F. Supp. 1068 (W.D.N.C. 1969).

66. Hickory Fire Fighters Ass'n, Local 2653 v. City of Hickory, 656 F.2d 917 (4th Cir. 1981).

67. Jones v. Dodson, 727 F.2d 1329, 1334 (4th Cir. 1984) [citing Branti v. Finkel, 445 U.S. 507 (1980), and Elrod v. Burns, 427 U.S. 347 (1976)]. *See also* Rutan v. Republican Party of Illinois, 110 S. Ct. 2729, 111 L. Ed. 2d 52 (1990).

68. *See, e.g.,* Joyner v. Lancaster, 815 F.2d 20, 23 (4th Cir.), *cert. denied,* 484 U.S. 830 (1987) (upholding discharge of captain in Forsyth County sheriff's department based on his disruption of working relationship).

69. U.S. CONST. amend. XIV, 1.

70. Cleveland Bd. of Educ. v. Loudermill, 470 U.S. 532, 541–42 (1985).

71. Board of Regents v. Roth, 408 U.S. 564, 573 (1972).

72. *Id.*; Bishop v. Wood, 426 U.S. 341, 348–49 (1976); Boston v. Webb, 783 F.2d 1163, 1166 (4th Cir. 1986); McGhee v. Draper, 564 F.2d 902, 909 (10th Cir. 1977).

73. 106 N.C. App. 410, 417 S.E.2d 277 (1992).

74. Cleveland Bd. of Educ. v. Loudermill, 470 U.S. 532 (1985).

75. Elkin Tribune v. Yadkin County Bd. of County Comm'rs, 331 N.C. 735, 417 S.E.2d 465 (1992).

76. News & Observer Publishing Co. v. Wake County Hosp. Sys., 55 N.C. App. 1, 12–13, 284 S.E.2d 542, 549 (1981), *petition for discretionary review denied,* 305 N.C. 302, 291 S.E.2d 151 (1982), *cert. denied,* 459 U.S. 803 (1982).

77. The term *settlement documents* is broadly defined at G.S. 132-12.2(c) to include "correspondence, settlement agreements, consent orders, checks, and bank drafts."

8   Elections

Robert P. Joyce

This chapter is a revision and update of the chapter, "Elections," by H. Rutherford Turnbull III, a former Institute of Government faculty member who is now codirector of the Beach Center on Families and Disability at the Univeristy of Kansas at Lawrence, in the first edition of *Municipal Government in North Carolina.* The author gratefully acknowledges his indebtedness to the previous author and appreciates the opportunity to build on that earlier work.

Contents

CITY ELECTIONS are conducted under state law, usually by county officials, at city expense. The state law, enacted by the North Carolina General Assembly, is found primarily in Subchapter IX (Municipal Elections) of Chapter 163 of the General Statutes. It is enforced and interpreted by the State Board of Elections, which has the authority to overturn the results of city elections when necessary, and to order new elections. The state law and the interpretations of that law by the State Board of Elections determine what kinds of elections may be held, who may register, who may vote, how votes are counted, how outcomes are determined, and how protests may be lodged.

The county officials who conduct city elections are the county board of elections, employees in the county board office, and precinct officials appointed by the county board. In a small number of cities, city elections are conducted by a city board of elections.

The city expense, in most cases, is a reimbursement that it pays to the county board of elections to cover the direct costs the county board incurred in conducting a city election. In cities that conduct their own elections, the expenditure is made directly by the city.

Kinds of Elections Authorized

In North Carolina, only the elections specifically authorized by statute may be held. Even if it appears to a city council that a vote of the people on some matter would be useful—say, where to locate a new city park—unless that vote is one of the types of referenda generally authorized for cities, it cannot be held without special legislation specifically authorizing that particular vote. Because locating a city park is not an issue that falls within the general referendum authorization, a city council could conduct such a vote only if the General Assembly passed a local act specifically authorizing it to do so.

The General Statutes authorize two basic types of city elections: (1) the election of city council members and usually the mayor[1] and (2) special elections, such as votes on permitting beer and wine sales, commonly called referenda, that apply only to the particular city.

City Council Elections

Under the uniform municipal elections law (G.S. Chapter 163, Subchapter IX), a city may elect its governing board by one of four methods: partisan elections, nonpartisan plurality elections, nonpartisan primary and general elections, and nonpartisan elections and runoffs. Under all four methods, candidates file for election between noon on the first Friday in July and noon on the first Friday in August. General election day is Tuesday after the first Monday in November in odd-numbered years. Under the first three methods there is always an election on that day; under the fourth method there may not be.

Types of City Council Elections

Partisan Elections

Of the 520 cities in North Carolina, only 14 use partisan elections.[2] Those 14 include Asheville, Charlotte, Concord, Kinston, and Winston-Salem, however, which among them encompass more than 650,000 citizens.

In cities with partisan elections, candidates file to run for party nomination in primary elections held on the sixth Tuesday before the November general election. A second primary, if necessary, is held on the third Tuesday before the general election. On general election day, the nominees of the parties appear on the ballot. In addition, candidates may appear on the ballot as unaffiliated through a petition signed by 4 percent of the voters in the city. The results of partisan municipal elections are determined just as the results of partisan state and county elections are (see table 8-1).

Nonpartisan Plurality Elections

Currently, 458 of North Carolina's 520 cities use nonpartisan plurality elections, the simplest of the four methods.[3] There is only one vote, on general election day. Whoever receives the most votes wins, even if no one gets a majority. If several candidates are seeking one seat, the highest vote getter wins (see table 8-1). If two or more seats are being contested as a group (as in an at-large council election) and there are more candidates than open seats, then the number of candidates equal to the number of open seats, who receive the highest number of votes are elected.

Nonpartisan Primary and General Elections

Only 22 cities use nonpartisan primary and general elections, but that number includes Burlington, Durham, Fayetteville, Goldsboro, Greensboro, Hickory, and High Point, which together

Table 8-1
Dates for City Elections, When Voting for a Single Seat

Type of Election	Sixth Tuesday before General Election Day	Fourth Tuesday before General Election Day	Third Tuesday before General Election Day	General Election Day
Partisan elections (14 cities)	First primary, by party, to select party nominees	No vote this day	Second primary, by party if necessary	Election between party nominees
Nonpartisan plurality elections (458 cities)	No vote this day	No vote this day	No vote this day	Election among all candidates; highest vote getter wins
Nonpartisan primary and general election (22 cities)	No vote this day	Primary to narrow field to two candidates, if necessary	No vote this day	Election between final two candidates
Nonpartisan election and runoff (26 cities)	No vote this day	Election; candidate with majority declared winner; if no candidate has majority, second-place finisher may demand runoff	No vote this day	Runoff between final two candidates, if necessary

encompass 575,000 people.[4] On the fourth Tuesday before general election day, a vote is taken to narrow the field to two candidates for each position to be filled (or if several seats are being filled as a group, to narrow the field to twice as many candidates as there are seats open). If only one or two candidates file for a single seat (or if fewer than twice as many candidates file for two or more seats open as a group), then the candidates who have filed are declared nominated, and no primary is held. If a primary is held, however, then the two candidates receiving the highest number of votes for a single office are declared nominated (even if one of them receives a majority and the second-place finisher receives a minority), and twice the number of candidates as there are seats in a group election are declared nominated. The election is then held on general election day, with the highest vote getters winning (see table 8-1).

Nonpartisan Elections and Runoffs

The 26 cities using this method include Raleigh, Rocky Mount, and Wilmington. There is an election on general election day only if a runoff is necessary. On the fourth Tuesday before general election day, an election is held among all candidates. A candidate receiving a majority (which in elections for more than one seat voted on as a group, is calculated by dividing the total vote cast for all candidates by the number of seats and then by two), wins. If no candidate receives a majority, the highest vote getter is declared elected unless the second-highest vote getter requests a runoff by noon on Monday following the election. The runoff is then between those two (see table 8-1). In multiple-seat group elections, candidates with a majority win.[5] If too few gain majorities to fill all seats, then the highest vote getters without majorities, equal to the number of remaining seats to be filled, are declared elected unless the next-highest vote getters equal in number to those remaining seats (or some of them) demand a runoff. The runoff is then between the highest non-majority-vote getters and the candidates demanding a runoff.

Filing Fees

A candidate filing for city election must pay a filing fee (or submit a petition as described in the next paragraph) at the time the notices of candidacy are filed. The fee is set by the city council not later than the day before filing begins. The minimum amount that the council may set is $5; the maximum is 1 percent of the annual salary of the office sought.

Instead of paying a filing fee, a candidate may present a petition to the appropriate board of elections. If the election is partisan, the petition must be signed by 10 percent of the registered voters of the city (or of the district if the election is from wards) who are of the same political party as the candidate, or by 200 registered voters of the city (or of the district if the election is from wards), whichever number is greater. It must be submitted by noon on Monday before the filing deadline for the primary. If the election is nonpartisan, the petition must be signed by 10 percent of the registered voters of the city (or of the district if the election is from wards) regardless of party. It must be submitted at least sixty days before the filing deadline for the primary or the election.

Special Elections

In addition to conducting city council elections, cities may conduct special elections, commonly known as *referenda*, as permitted by the North Carolina General Statutes. The authorized special elections are (1) alcoholic beverage elections for sale of beer, sale of unfortified wine, establishment of Alcoholic Beverage Control (ABC) stores, and sale of mixed beverages (G.S. 18B-600 through -605), (2) issuance of bonds (G.S. 159-48, -49) and levy of tax to supplement the revenue of a revenue bond project (G.S. 159-97), (3) levy of city property tax (G.S. 160A-206 through -209), and (4) city charter amendments (G.S. 160A-101 through -110). Before calling a special election, the city council must adopt a resolution specifying the details of the election and deliver the resolution to the board of elections—city or county—that conducts elections for the city. A special election may be held at the same time as any other election, but not within thirty days before or thirty days after another election. The statutes authorizing each kind of special election contain details regarding procedures for calling and conducting that election.

Without special legislation, only the kinds of special elections specified in the statutes may be held. There is some special legislation authorizing other kinds of special elections either on an ad hoc basis (such as a local act of the General Assembly authorizing a particular city to conduct a one-time referendum on some particular topic) or as part of the city charter (some North Carolina cities have provisions in their charters for recall elections for city officeholders, for example).

Eligible Voters

Qualifications

Every person who is eighteen years old as of the date of the general election, who was born in the United States or has been naturalized as a citizen, who has been a resident of the city for thirty days before the election, and who is not a disqualified felon, is eligible to vote if registered. Cities may not add a qualification, such as a requirement that to vote, a resident of the city must own property in the city.[6] Also, they may not expand the right to vote in a way that includes nonresidents, such as allowing nonresident freeholders to vote.[7]

Registration

Citizens need register only once to vote in all elections. Voters remain registered and eligible to vote unless they are convicted of a felony or move from the city. A registered voter who fails to vote in two consecutive presidential elections and all elections in between, is subject to initiation of a process that may result in cancellation of his or her registration. Whether a city's elections are conducted by the county board of elections or by a city board, the county board's registration records are used for city elections.

Absentee Voting

Absentee voting is permitted in municipal elections only if the election is conducted by the county board of elections and the city council chooses to permit it. To permit absentee voting, the council must adopt a resolution calling for it at least sixty days before an election. That choice remains in effect for future elections until the council rescinds it by resolution adopted sixty days before an election. Absentee voting is not permitted in municipal elections conducted by a city board of elections.

The Board Responsible for Conducting City Elections

If a city elects its council on a partisan basis, its elections must be conducted by the county board of elections. If a city uses nonpartisan elections, however, it may choose to have its elections conducted by its own city board of elections. Whichever system is used, the board conducting the elections is subject to the oversight of the State Board of Elections.

State Board of Elections

By statute the State Board of Elections has general supervision over primaries and elections in North Carolina. It has the authority to make rules that all elections officials must follow in conducting elections. It appoints all members of county boards of elections and advises county and city boards on how to conduct elections. On its own motion or in response to complaints that have first been heard by the local elections board, it investigates violations of election laws or other improprieties. It may order corrections, including, when necessary, holding the election again. When it believes that criminal conduct has occurred, it refers the matter to appropriate prosecutorial officials for possible prosecution. It determines the form and the content of ballots, instruction sheets, pollbooks, tally sheets, abstract and return forms, certificates of election, and other forms to be used in elections. It furnishes county and city boards of elections with many of the kinds of forms used in elections and makes others available for counties and cities to purchase. It prepares ballots for state and national offices and for referenda on constitutional amendments and other statewide propositions, and instructs local boards on printing local ballots. It canvasses primary and general election returns for national, state, and district offices and for constitutional amendments, and declares the results.

The five members of the State Board of Elections are appointed for four-year terms by the governor in May just after the governor has taken office. No more than three may be of the same political party. The practical result is that when the governor is a Republican, the state board has three Republicans and two Democrats, and vice-versa when the governor is a Democrat.

County Boards of Elections

The county board of elections supervises and conducts all elections within a county (unless one or more cities in the county use their own city board). The county board supervises voter registration, establishes precincts and sets polling places, appoints precinct officials to conduct the election on election day, employs regular employees to run the board office, hears the appeals from those denied registration and the protests of those who believe irregularities have occurred in the election (though only the state board may order a new election), examines the sufficiency of petitions for unaffiliated candidates or formation of political parties or other purposes, contracts for printing ballots, provides the required notices concerning an upcoming election, purchases voting equipment, maintains custody of equipment and records, canvasses election returns, and issues certificates of election.

The three members of the county board of elections are appointed by the State Board of Elections for two-year terms beginning in June of odd-numbered years, from lists provided by the state chair of each political party. No more than two members may be of the same party. The practical result is that when the governor is a Democrat, and therefore the state board has a majority of Democrats, all 100 county boards have two Democrats and one Republican, and vice-versa when the governor and the majority of the state board are Republicans.

The expenses of the county board in conducting elections—that is, in purchasing and maintaining equipment, printing ballots, publishing notices, paying office employees and precinct officials, and so on—are covered by a budgetary appropriation of the county commissioners. When the county board conducts city elections, the city is obligated to reimburse the county for the costs of the election. If the city and the county cannot agree on a formula for determining the amount of the reimbursement, the state board may prescribe it.

City Boards of Elections

Of North Carolina's 520 cities, fewer than 150, most of them small, have their own city boards of elections. Those city boards conduct council elections and special elections that affect the city only.

City boards of elections have, with respect to city elections, all the powers and the duties conferred on county boards of elections in their conduct of national, state, district, and county elections. Only cities with nonpartisan elections may use city boards of elections.

City boards of elections are composed of three registered voters of the city appointed by the city council for two-year terms beginning in June of even-numbered years. If the city has registered voters of more than one political party, then no more than two members of the city board may be of the same party.

The Federal Voting Rights Act

Congress passed the federal Voting Rights Act of 1965[8] to combat practices that prevented or inhibited black citizens and members of other minority groups from voting and from electing candidates of their choice. Section 2 of the act is applicable everywhere in the United States. Section 5 is applicable only in selected parts of the country, including forty North Carolina counties.

Provisions Applicable Everywhere

Under Section 2, no state, county, city, or other jurisdiction may set voting qualifications or use election procedures that adversely affect the voting rights of minorities. Since amendments to the Voting Rights Act in 1982, it has been clear that someone claiming a violation of Section 2 does not have to show that the qualifications or the procedures are used with the *intent* of discriminating. He or she need only show that there is an *effect* of discrimination, regardless of the reason that the qualification or the procedure was adopted in the first place.

The most common claim of discrimination under Section 2 in the last few years has involved the use of at-large voting to elect boards of county commissioners and city councils. A city that has a significant black population, for example, and that uses at-large voting for city council is vulnerable to a claim that the at-large system has the effect of discriminating against black voters if two factors are present: (1) blacks have been elected to the city council in numbers below their proportion of the population and (2) there is a history of racially polarized voting. In such a case a court may conclude that the effect of the at-large system is discriminatory, regardless of the intent behind its adoption or retention. The remedy may be to require the city to switch to a system of electing council members from districts (commonly called *wards*). Courts have been creative in requiring other changes, such as eliminating staggered terms to permit more effective "single-shot" voting. If several seats are open at once in an at-large election, and if black voters vote for only one candidate while white voters vote for several, blacks increase the likelihood of electing the candidate whom they favor.

Provisions Applicable in Forty North Carolina Counties

Section 5 of the Voting Rights Act imposes an additional requirement on selected counties in the United States—forty of which are in North Carolina—and on the cities and other jurisdictions within those counties. Before any change in any election procedure may be enforced there, the change must be approved by the United States Department of Justice. (The alternative exists of seeking approval from the federal court for the District of Columbia, but is not favored because it is slower and more expensive.) The approval is commonly referred to as *preclearance*. Examples of changes requiring preclearance include a switch to or from an at-large election system, any change in the term of office of the mayor or council members, annexations, the moving of polling places or precinct lines, new office hours of the board of elections, and the changing of voting equipment.

The Justice Department will review the proposed change to determine whether it would be retrogressive—that is, whether after the change, minority voters would be in a less favorable position to elect candidates of their choice. The department seldom objects, but it is most likely to object to annexations, alterations in district lines, changes from district to at-large elections, and changes to staggered terms.

Cities in the following North Carolina counties must obtain preclearance of voting changes: Anson, Beaufort, Bertie, Bladen, Camden, Caswell, Chowan, Cleveland, Craven, Cumberland, Edgecombe, Franklin, Gaston, Gates, Granville, Greene, Guilford, Halifax, Harnett, Hertford, Hoke, Jackson, Lee, Lenoir, Martin,

Nash, Northampton, Onslow, Pasquotank, Perquimans, Person, Pitt, Robeson, Rockingham, Scotland, Union, Vance, Washington, Wayne, and Wilson.

State law specifies that the city attorney is responsible for submitting changes in that city for preclearance. Once the Justice Department makes its final decision on a city's preclearance request, the city attorney must file the notification letter with the North Carolina Office of Administrative Hearings for publication in the *North Carolina Register*. Before the law was made clear regarding who must submit changes for preclearance, it commonly happened that changes were simply not submitted. All changes since November 1, 1964, require preclearance. On discovering some old change that was never submitted, a city should immediately submit it. Without preclearance, even long-used changes are by law without effect. Until they are approved by the Justice Department, their current status will remain in doubt.

Additional Resources

Constitution of North Carolina, Articles I, VI.

Crowell, Michael. *Guide to Elections Outside Chapter 163*. Chapel Hill, N.C.: Institute of Government, The University of North Carolina at Chapel Hill, 1984.

Joyce, Robert P. *Precinct Manual*. Chapel Hill, N.C.: Institute of Government, The University of North Carolina at Chapel Hill, published biennially.

North Carolina General Statutes Chapter 163, Articles 23, 24.

Notes

1. Mayors are elected by the people in 488 of North Carolina's 520 cities. In 25 cities the mayor is selected by and from the city council. Seven cities use some other method [David M. Lawrence, comp., *Forms of Government of North Carolina Cities*, 1994 ed. (Chapel Hill, N.C.: Institute of Government, The University of North Carolina at Chapel Hill, 1994), 40].

2. *See generally* Lawrence, *Forms of Government*.

3. *See generally* Lawrence, *Forms of Government*.

4. *See generally* Lawrence, *Forms of Government*.

5. It is possible in a group election for more candidates to receive a majority than there are open seats. In that case the candidates receiving the greatest number of votes, equal to the number of open seats, are elected.

6. Smith v. Town of Carolina Beach, 206 N.C. 834, 175 S.E. 313 (1934).

7. Wrenn v. Town of Kure Beach, 235 N.C. 292, 69 S.E.2d 492 (1952).

8. The two main provisions of the Voting Rights Act, Section 2 and Section 5, are codified at 42 U.S.C. §§ 1973 and 1973c (1994), respectively.

9 Civil Liability of the City and Public Servants

Jeffrey S. Koeze

This chapter is a revision and update of the chapter, "Civil Liability of the City and City Officials," by Michael R. Smith, now director of the Institute of Government, in the first edition of *Municipal Government in North Carolina*. The author gratefully acknowledges his indebtedness to the previous author and appreciates the opportunity to build on that earlier work.

Contents

THE EXPENSE and the trouble of lawsuits are unavoidable costs of doing municipal business. Anyone with a pencil, a piece of paper, and the filing fee can bring a lawsuit. Also, if a city runs a police department, a fire department, a park, or any other municipal service long enough, someone will make a mistake and damage something or somebody. The job for municipal public servants is therefore not the impossible task of eliminating lawsuits, but the merely difficult task of providing municipal services while minimizing the cost and the disruption that lawsuits bring. The first step in accomplishing that task is learning the basic legal principles that control the liability of cities and their public servants. This chapter sets forth those principles. The chapter generally uses the term *public servants* to refer to all the people who do the city's work, from elected members of the city council to the lowest ranks of line staff. At times, however, it distinguishes *employees* from *officials*, and *elected officials* from *other municipal workers*. In these cases the meanings of the terms used should be clear from the context.

The chapter deals with two basic areas of liability: tort liability under North Carolina law and liability under federal law for violations of the Civil Rights Act of 1871[1] (often called Section 1983, which refers to its location in the United States Code).[2] Except perhaps for employment-related claims, these two kinds of claims are the most common ones brought against municipal public servants and governments. However, there is a universe of both state and federal claims that this chapter cannot begin to address: environmental claims, tax claims, a variety of other civil rights claims, and contract claims, to mention a few.

The discussion that follows is an introduction to a complex subject. The many twists and turns in this area of the law cannot be and are not fully described. Furthermore, at this writing, cases pending before the North Carolina courts, and the recent and anticipated replacement of several justices of the United States Supreme Court, may mean important changes in the law described herein.

This chapter uses the following framework to discuss state law tort and Section 1983 liability:

- Tort liability under North Carolina law
  Liability of the city
  Liability of public servants
- Section 1983 liability
  Liability of the city
  Liability of public servants

A public servant and the city may under certain circumstances be sued under North Carolina law and found liable for intentional wrongful acts or for *negligence* (failure to exercise reasonable care under the circumstances) if those acts or that negligence causes personal injury or property damage. Similarly a city or its public servants may be sued under Section 1983 for official conduct that causes a person to be deprived of a federal statutory or constitutional right. If a court finds that a public servant wrongfully caused harm to another individual, it may require a payment of *compensatory damages,* a sum of money to make up for the injured person's loss. If the official action was malicious or especially reckless, the court may punish the responsible public servant by requiring payment of *punitive damages,* a sum of money that is greater than the amount needed to compensate the injured person for the loss.[3]

Separate sets of rules—state and federal—determine whether a city and its public servants may be required to pay damages to someone harmed by official action. Some overlap between the two sets of rules means that certain official actions may violate both of them and make the city and its public servants potentially liable under state and federal law. (However, the person who brings the lawsuit may be compensated only once for the injuries.) The rest of this chapter examines what a plaintiff must establish under state and federal law to recover damages from a city or any of its public servants.

Tort Liability under North Carolina Law

General Background

Liability in state court, as noted earlier, may arise for either intentional acts or negligence that causes personal injury or property damage. The North Carolina courts have classified these harmful acts as civil wrongs, as opposed to criminal offenses, and a person may recover damages for injuries or other harm caused by them. Such civil wrongs are called *torts*.

Tort law makes persons who injure others pay for the harm that they inflict. Individuals who are harmed through no fault of their own are not required to bear the loss; instead, the person whose wrongful act caused the harm must pay compensatory damages to the injured party. Another purpose of tort law is to deter people from engaging in conduct likely to cause personal injury or property damage. Tort law assumes that people will be more careful in conducting their day-to-day activities if they have to pay for any harm that results.

In considering how the law of torts affects the liability of municipal public servants and cities, it is important to understand the two types of civil wrongs that may be remedied by an award of damages in a civil tort lawsuit: intentional torts and negligence.[4]

Intentional Torts

Intentional torts are intentional wrongful acts that cause personal injury or property damage and give rise to civil liability for damages. Some common torts of this type are battery, false imprisonment, and defamation.

Battery

The intentional touching or striking of another person without either that person's consent or a legally recognized authorization is the intentional tort of *battery*. In an illustrative case an elderly man named Munick tried to pay his water bill with cash that included a wrapped roll of fifty pennies.[5] The water department manager became outraged, threw the pennies to the floor, and ordered Munick to pick them up. When he did not respond, the manager locked the office door, slapped him in the face, pulled him into a back room, and then beat and choked him. The state supreme court found that Munick could recover damages for a battery because the attack was unprovoked and without legal excuse.

Striking another person without consent is not always a battery. For example, a law enforcement officer may use reasonable force to effect a legal arrest [G.S. 15A-401(d)(1)]. Therefore an officer who uses such force and strikes a suspect to prevent an escape does not commit a civil battery. However, if more force is employed than is reasonably necessary to make the arrest, the officer may be sued in state court for the intentional tort of battery and be required to pay damages.[6]

False Imprisonment

False imprisonment is restraining the movement of another without that person's permission or without a legally recognized authorization. In one case of false imprisonment, an inmate was kept in the county jail beyond the court-ordered release date.[7] In another case a mayor was found liable for false imprisonment for ordering a police officer to arrest and detain a man for thirty to forty minutes without legal justification.[8]

Defamation

Defamation is written or oral communication that injures a third party's reputation. Defamation in writing is called *libel*; oral defamation is called *slander*. Defamation includes accusations that a person is a criminal, statements that injure someone in his or her occupation, and claims that an individual has an offensive disease. For example, it would be defamation for a city emergency medical services worker to spread a false rumor that a particular person has a sexually transmitted disease. Defamation could also be established if the city manager falsely told a local newspaper that an employee had been dismissed for stealing.[9]

A public servant who is sued for making a public statement that harms someone's reputation has two defenses. First, the truth of a statement is an absolute defense to liability for damages in a defamation lawsuit. Second, a person may avoid liability for a false statement by showing that it was made under circumstances that gave rise to a *qualified privilege*.[10] A qualified privilege exists when (1) the person who makes a statement has a valid interest in making it or a legal duty to make it, and (2) the person makes it to someone with a corresponding interest or duty. Public servants with a qualified privilege to make a particular statement will not be held liable for defamation unless they act with malice in making it.

Negligence

The law imposes a duty on all people, including public servants, to use reasonable care in conducting their daily affairs. They are negligent if they fail to do so and their conduct causes personal injury or property damage. If this failure to use reasonable care under the circumstances directly causes harm and the harm was a predictable result of that misconduct, the person harmed is entitled to compensation. The main exception to this rule permits a person who is sued for negligence to invoke the defense of *contributory negligence*— a legal rule that bars recovery by any individual whose own negligence, however slight, contributes to his or her injury.

Negligence is the careless performance of any act. It may occur in an infinite variety of situations. Whether particular conduct is negligent cannot be determined in the abstract; the jury must decide in each specific case whether the defendant acted as a reasonably prudent person would have under the same circumstances.

Some examples may help illustrate the operation of these rules. In one case, two local government employees drove a truck that spewed a thick insecticide fog along a road.[11] The fog totally blocked the view of approaching traffic. No warning signs were displayed to give oncoming vehicles notice of the hazard. A man rounded a curve into the fog and slowed his truck, but he was blinded by the fog and sideswiped a car that had pulled off the road to wait for the fog to clear. The North Carolina Supreme Court held that a jury could find that the two employees were negligent—had not exercised reasonable care under the circumstances—in creating a hazardous condition likely to cause injury to highway travelers.

In another case a county jailer took custody of a sick and helpless man who had been arrested and placed him in a cell with another man who was violently insane.[12] During the night the latter used a leg torn from a table in the cell to beat the helpless inmate, and he died the next morning. The state supreme court ruled that a jury could find that the jailer had failed to act reasonably—in other words, that he was negligent—in placing a helpless individual in the same cell with a violent one.

In still another case an employee was cutting grass in a rocky area of a government-owned park, using a ten-year-old mower without a front guard.[13] The mower threw out a rock that hit a man and fractured his skull. The park superintendent testified that he had seen rocks thrown from beneath the mower thousands of times. The North Carolina Supreme Court found that it was not reasonable under the circumstances—in other words, that it was negligent—for the local government to allow operation of the mower without a guard because it should have anticipated that eventually someone would be injured.

Liability of the City

Private employers must pay damages for any harm caused by the negligence of their employees who are acting within the scope of their employment (see the discussion under the heading Scope of Employment, later in this chapter). However, a North Carolina city's liability for the torts of its public servants depends on whether they were engaged in a governmental function or a proprietary activity. A city is not liable for the torts of an employee who harms someone while carrying out a governmental function; it is liable if the employee commits a tort while engaged in a proprietary activity.

The state supreme court has distinguished between governmental and proprietary activities as follows:

> Any activity . . . which is discretionary, political, legislative or public in nature and performed for the public good in behalf of the State, rather than to itself, comes within the class of governmental functions. When, however, the activity is commercial or chiefly for the private advantage of the compact community, it is private or proprietary.[14]

Unfortunately this distinction is difficult to apply and often results in arbitrary characterizations of city activities. For example, if a city employee negligently causes an accident while en route to fix a pothole, the city is liable, but if the employee negligently causes an accident while en route to fix a traffic signal, the city is not liable. The absence of a precise standard makes it difficult to predict whether a city will be liable for the torts of an employee who is engaged in a particular activity. Because the North Carolina courts rely heavily on mechanical adherence to legal precedent and unarticulated public policies when making the distinction between governmental and proprietary, one must examine how the courts have historically viewed particular activities to determine whether the city will be held liable in a specific case.

Governmental Activities

A city may not be held liable and required to pay damages under state law for the tortious actions of its employees if a governmental activity is involved.

Law enforcement. It is well established that law enforcement is a governmental function because it is performed for the general welfare of the state. In one case, for example, the plaintiff sued the city after one of its law enforcement officers illegally arrested him in a brutal manner.[15] The state supreme court ruled that the government could not be held liable because the officer who injured the plaintiff was performing a governmental function.

Jails. In an early case the city successfully asserted its governmental immunity in a lawsuit by a man who became sick when he spent a cold winter night in an unheated jail cell.[16]

Public libraries. In a 1965 case the state supreme court found that a woman who was injured on a cracked library step could not recover damages under state law because operating a public library was a governmental function.[17]

Traffic signals. In an illustrative case a woman who was injured when her car collided with a city-owned truck negligently driven by a city employee on his way to install a bulb in a traffic light, could not recover damages from the city because the state supreme court ruled that the employee was engaged in a governmental function at the time of the accident.[18]

Fire protection. The establishment and the operation of a fire department are governmental functions. As a result, persons who are injured by negligently maintained fire equipment may not recover damages against the city.[19]

Electric power for street lights. A city engages in a governmental function when it furnishes electricity for street lights.[20] Thus a person who touches a live electrical wire that has fallen from a street light is not entitled to recover damages, even if the city negligently fails to keep the wire in a safe condition.

Proprietary Activities

A city may be held liable and required to pay damages under state law for the tortious actions of its employees in carrying out proprietary functions.

Airports. A city-county airport employee negligently shot and killed a man. The state supreme court ruled that his survivors could sue the city and recover damages for the wrongful act of its employee because constructing, operating, and maintaining a public airport were proprietary functions.[21] The court suggested, however, that the employee's function would have been characterized as governmental (law enforcement) and the city would have been immune from liability if the employee had been appointed as an airport guard with full police powers.

Golf courses. Maintaining and operating a public golf course have also been characterized as proprietary functions.[22] In the case cited, a caddie was allowed to sue and recover damages from a local government when he was injured on a defective bridge. Two factors contributing to the holding that running a golf course was proprietary were that doing so was not a traditional function performed by cities and it generated more than incidental income.

Hospitals. A young woman died when the doctors in a public hospital negligently gave her a transfusion with the wrong type of blood. The North Carolina Supreme Court held that operating a public hospital was a proprietary function because fees were charged and its operation was not a service traditionally performed only by local governments. As a result, the woman's survivors could recover damages from the hospital for the negligent acts of its employees.[23]

Sale of electric power and natural gas for profit. A boy died after touching an uninsulated electric wire that was too close to the ground. The town had installed the wire and had contracted to supply electricity to an amusement company. The state supreme court held that supplying electric power for profit was a proprietary function that exposed the town to liability for negligence.[24] The courts have held the same to be true of activities related to the distribution and sale of natural gas.[25]

Streets and sidewalks. The town negligently graded a street next to a man's property and destroyed several brick walls on his land. The court allowed the man to collect damages from the town because maintaining city streets was a proprietary function, even though it was for the public good.[26]

The Effect of Fee Collection on the Characterization of an Activity

Collecting user fees is a popular method of paying for a number of municipal functions, but it can have the unfortunate side effect of increasing a city's potential liability. Although the law remains unsettled, collecting user fees or other income may cause a court to characterize an activity as proprietary rather than governmental. The following cases involving parks and solid waste disposal illustrate this point.

Public parks. A child playing in a public park was injured when she fell from a seesaw that had negligently been permitted to become unsafe. The local government involved received income from park charges that amounted to less than 1 percent of the park's total operating costs. The court considered this income incidental, and found that the park's operation was a governmental function for which the unit could not be held liable in tort.[27] In contrast, in another case a local government received income from park charges that amounted to 11 percent of the park's entire operating cost. The court held that this income was substantial. It characterized the park's operation as a proprietary function for which the local government could be held liable in a tort lawsuit.[28]

Water and sewer service. In 1909 the North Carolina Supreme Court ruled that maintaining a free public sewer was a governmental function and that therefore the City of Asheville was not liable for causing cases of typhoid fever by negligently discharging sewage into a creek.[29] In 1980 the North Carolina Court of Appeals followed that rule when it decided that the City of Lenoir was not liable for sewage backing up into a resident's home.[30] However, charging a fee for residential and commercial sewer service, as is common practice, almost certainly makes this activity proprietary. Similarly, charging a fee for water makes providing it a proprietary function.

Solid waste disposal. In one case a woman was seriously injured when she was struck by a garbage truck negligently operated by an employee of the sanitation department of a city.[31] The court held that garbage collection was a governmental function and that the plaintiff therefore could not recover damages from the city. The fee charged for waste disposal did not make garbage collection a proprietary function because it covered only actual expenses.

In another case the fees charged by a local government for disposing of solid waste at its landfill paid a little over 9 percent of the landfill's operating cost. Methane gas created by decomposing garbage exploded and killed several people in a nearby building, and the government was sued. Even though garbage collection and disposal are usually characterized as governmental functions, the state supreme court held in this instance that because the fee charged generated more than incidental income, the operation of the landfill had become a proprietary function. The local government therefore could be required to pay for injuries caused by the negligent operation and maintenance of its landfill site.[32]

These cases illustrate the confusion over the effect of fees on the classification of a function as governmental or proprietary. In the first case the city removed garbage only for its own residents and collected a fee permitted by statute. In the second case the city received some of its income by contracting with a county for the disposal of the county's garbage. This was considered a significant distinction.

These distinctions are not necessarily compelling reasons for granting immunity in one case and not the other. The second case arose later, and reveals increased hostility by the courts to the doctrine of governmental immunity. The holding probably means that the receipt of fees is now more likely to result in a denial of immunity than it was in the past. A city improves its chances for immunity slightly if a fee is authorized by statute and if the activity serves only its residents.

Waiver of Governmental Immunity

The General Assembly has authorized cities to waive the defense of governmental immunity by purchasing liability insurance (G.S. 160A-485). Cities do this for two primary reasons. First, as just illustrated, for many activities it is difficult to be certain in advance that governmental immunity will protect the city from liability. Second, by purchasing liability insurance, a city provides a remedy for citizens who otherwise could not be compensated for injuries caused by the negligence of the city's employees in performing governmental activities. An award of damages against a city on a tort claim that arises from governmental activities may not exceed the liability insurance coverage. (See the discussion under the heading Insurance against Civil Liability, later in this chapter.)

Scope of Employment

A city is not liable for the torts of its employees if the harm occurs while they are acting outside the scope of their employment. Determining what is inside and what is outside the scope of employment is sometimes difficult. In one case, for example, Black Mountain was sued when a boy died after falling from a town truck negligently driven by a town golf course employee.[33] The accident occurred while the employee drove the truck on a pleasure trip down a public road against the explicit orders of his supervisor. The North Carolina Supreme Court held that the town was not responsible for his negligence because at the time of the accident, he was acting outside the scope of his employment.[34]

Another case took a broader view of the scope of employment. A city sanitation worker beat a woman who argued with him about his work. The court stated that an act could be within the scope of employment "even if it is contrary to the employer's express instructions, when the act is done in the furtherance of the employer's business and in the discharge of the duties of employment."[35] Even though the sanitation worker's conduct was an intentional tort and a crime, the court left it up to the jury to decide whether or not he was acting within the scope of his employment.

Special Immunity Rules

The Public Duty Doctrine

The *public duty doctrine* holds that certain municipal activities do not create liability to individual members of the public. The most common application of the public duty doctrine is to law enforcement. Courts routinely hold that individual victims of crime are not entitled to recover damages for the failure of law enforcement officers to prevent the crime from happening. The duty to prevent crime extends to the public generally and cannot be enforced by individuals against a city.

A good example of the application of the doctrine is a case in which a person injured in a car accident sued the Town of Mount Airy for having failed to serve arrest warrants for driving violations on the driver of the car that caused the accident. The court held that the town had no duty to the injured person to serve the warrants, and hence was not liable for damages for failing to prevent the accident.[36]

The exceptions to the public duty doctrine allow liability for negligence when a special relationship between the city and a person gives rise to a duty—for example, between the police and a confidential informant—or when the city creates a duty for itself by making a promise—such as promising one person protection from another.[37]

The public duty doctrine has the potential to be an important source of liability protection for cities and for public servants, but it will be some time before the courts decide enough cases to lay out the doctrine's scope and application fully.

The Doctrine of Discretionary Immunity

The *doctrine of discretionary immunity* provides that North Carolina courts will not review decisions that have been left by law to the discretion of a local legislative body. Although this type of immunity is sometimes characterized as one of the governmental functions within the broader doctrine of governmental immunity,[38] it is more appropriately discussed separately as a special category of immunity.

The power of cities to enact ordinances offers a good example of how courts apply the discretionary immunity doctrine. A court will not substitute its judgment for that of a local governing body by imposing liability on the unit for the exercise or the nonexercise of the unit's ordinance-making power. For example, Charlotte's board of aldermen once temporarily suspended an ordinance against the use of fireworks inside the city limits. A man's building was destroyed when fireworks landed on the roof and caught fire. He sued the city to recover damages, alleging that the board's negligence in suspending the ordinance caused his loss. The state supreme court denied recovery against the city on the grounds that a local government was not liable for the exercise or the nonexercise of a discretionary power, such as the power to enact ordinances.[39]

Nuisance and Inverse Condemnation

A city that engages in an activity that substantially and unreasonably interferes with the use and the enjoyment of someone's land commits a tort called *nuisance*. A city may be required to pay for damage to another's land caused by a nuisance even if the damage comes about through the performance of a governmental function. For example, in one case a town's sewage treatment plant smelled so bad that the value of the plaintiff's nearby home was permanently reduced.[40] The state supreme court held that the plaintiff was entitled to recover damages from the city to compensate him for the reduction in value.

A city may also be liable for lowering someone's land values under federal and state constitutional provisions that prevent government from taking a person's private property without just compensation. If city activities permanently and substantially reduce the value of land, a court may say that the city has in effect taken the property and must pay compensation to the property owner.[41]

This kind of taking is sometimes called *inverse condemnation* to distinguish it from condemnation or outright appropriation of land for public use. As an example of this approach, the state supreme court has ruled that inverse condemnation, not nuisance, provides the sole remedy available to a landowner for interference with his property by aircraft overflights involving a city-owned airport.[42]

Violation of Rights Enjoyed under the North Carolina Constitution

A city may not claim the protection of governmental immunity when it is sued for violating the rights of an individual under the North Carolina Constitution. For example, if a city fired an employee for exercising free speech rights protected under the state constitution, the city could not defend its action by claiming governmental immunity.[43]

Liability of Public Servants

A city does its work through the actions of its elected officials, appointed officials, and employees, and just as the city may be held responsible for those actions, so may the public servants themselves. A public servant may be sued for negligence in an official capacity, that is, as the representative of the city, and also in a personal or individual capacity. Damages awarded in personal capacity suits would, in the absence of insurance coverage or a city policy to the contrary, be paid from the public servant's personal assets rather than from the city's funds.

All public servants are liable for damages caused by their intentional torts.[44] For example, both the highest-ranking city official and the lowest-ranking employee are personally liable for damages if they assault someone.[45] No public policy interests are served by granting public servants immunity from liability for damages for intentional wrongful acts.

On the other hand, there are legitimate policy reasons for granting certain public officials immunity from liability for harm caused by their negligence. The main public policy concern is that those whose duties involve the exercise of discretion might be hesitant to take necessary official actions if they could be held personally liable for harm caused by their simple negligence. The result of this reluctance to act would be a less efficient government. The law of personal liability reflects this concern about exercise of discretion: whether public servants may be held liable for the consequences of their negligent acts depends entirely on the nature of their responsibilities.

Liability of Policy-Making Officials

North Carolina public officials whose governmental duties require the exercise of judgment and discretion are not liable for harm caused by their negligence in carrying out those duties. Unfortunately the legal definition of who is a public official is somewhat uncertain. In *Pigott v. City of Wilmington*[46] the North Carolina Court of Appeals held that a public official was someone whose position was created by legislation, who normally took an oath of office, who performed legally imposed duties, and who exercised a certain amount of discretion. The court directed that all these factors be taken into account in deciding whether someone was a public official. Since *Pigott*, however, the court of appeals has emphasized one factor—whether the position was created by statute—almost to the exclusion of all others.[47] In fact, the court of appeals has never found a person whose duties were not specifically spelled out in the General Statutes to be a public official.

Public officials may be required to pay damages only if they cause injury by an action taken for corrupt or malicious reasons.[48] For example, a building inspector is immune from liability for negligently ordering the destruction of a building out of conformance with the city building code,[49] but not for maliciously doing so.[50]

Stated another way, a municipal official may not be held personally liable for an honest judgment made in the exercise or the nonexercise of a discretionary governmental power. For example, a local social services director was found immune from a claim that he negligently failed to train and supervise his employees properly.[51] This good faith or discretionary immunity can be overcome only if the injured person demonstrates malice—that is, demonstrates that the public official acted recklessly or with an improper motive, for example, by hiring a plainly unqualified person on the basis of nepotism rather than merit.[52]

It is an open question whether policy-making public officials may be held personally liable for the negligent performance of or the failure to perform ordinary day-to-day tasks that are part of their responsibilities. In many states the law distinguishes between an official's policy-making or discretionary functions, which are protected by qualified immunity, and ministerial tasks, for which qualified immunity is unavailable.[53] In a 1979 case the North Carolina Court of Appeals appeared to reject that distinction, finding that the Nash County Register of Deeds was immune from liability arising from a claim brought by a person who had fallen down some steps in the office of the Register of Deeds while looking at records alleged to have been placed in a dangerous spot at the top of a stairwell.[54]

City officials also enjoy governmental immunity for the negligent failure to perform a ministerial duty imposed by a statute, such as the duty to receive an adequate bond from an employee, unless a statute specifically provides otherwise.[55]

Liability of Regular Employees

Unlike policy-making officials, city employees who work under the general direction of a superior and exercise little discretion in performing their duties may be held personally liable for any injury caused by their negligence. This rule is based on the assumption that such employees have clearer, simpler responsibilities than policy-making officials have and therefore are less likely to be made hesitant to act by fear that they might be held liable for possible negligence.

In a case that provides an example of the operation of this rule,[56] government employees negligently drove a street sweeper past the open doors of a store and blew dirt into it. Much of the merchandise was ruined. The state supreme court held that the operators of the sweeper could be required to pay for damage caused by their negligence, giving the following explanation:

> [A] mere employee doing a mechanical job . . . must exercise some sort of judgment in plying his shovel or driving his truck—but he is in no sense invested with a discretion which attends a public officer in the discharge of public or governmental duties, not ministerial in their character . . . . The mere fact that a person charged with negligence is an employee of others to whom immunity from liability is extended on grounds of public policy does not thereby excuse him from liability for negligence in the manner in which his duties are performed, or for performing a lawful act in an unlawful manner.[57]

Similarly in another case the state supreme court held that a county jailer could be required to pay damages to an inmate whose thumb he negligently caught in a cell door.[58] City employees are most often held responsible for negligence in the operation of city vehicles and other equipment.

In a recent series of cases, the North Carolina Court of Appeals has tried to change the rules governing the liability of public servants.[59] Although the reasoning of these cases is obscure, their result seems to be that public servants are immune from liability for damages arising from actions taken within the scope of employment. In effect, the court of appeals has extended the immunity of public officials to public employees. These cases are inconsistent with decisions of the North Carolina Supreme Court (*Miller*, for example) and may not survive supreme court review.

Liability under Federal Law

General Background

Section 1983 authorizes a person to sue and recover damages against a city or its governing board members, officials, and employees for violating one of the person's federal constitutional or statutory rights, when the violation is caused by official conduct. By providing a remedy under federal law for the violation of rights that are protected by a federal statute or the United States Constitution, Section 1983 creates a framework of liability that is separate from that of state tort law. Thus Section 1983 may allow for a finding of liability in some cases in which there is none under state law. In other cases, however, an official action may violate both sets of liability rules and expose the public servant and the city to liability under state and federal law.

Federal liability rules serve many of the same functions as state liability rules. Compensation of victims is an example: a person who violates someone's federal rights may be required to compensate the injured party, just as an individual who commits a civil wrong under state law may be required to do. In addition, the federal rules, like the state rules, are designed to deter city public servants from violating someone's legal rights. In analyzing how the federal liability rules affect the civil liability of cities and their public servants, one must first examine the type of official conduct that can give rise to liability under Section 1983.

Violation of Constitutional Rights

Section 1983 permits a person to sue and recover damages if the city or any of its public servants violate his or her federal constitutional rights. Several common constitutional violations are violation of the First Amendment rights of free speech and free political affiliation, violation of the Fourth Amendment right of freedom from unreasonable searches and seizures, and violation of the Fourteenth Amendment right of due process.

First Amendment Rights of Free Speech and Political Affiliation

The Constitution's First Amendment protects everyone's freedom of speech. A public servant violates this protection if, for example, he or she prevents a person from holding a nonobscene protest sign at a political rally.[60] The free speech right also protects public employees who speak out on matters of public concern.[61] A city employee may sue under Section 1983 if, for example, he or she is fired or disciplined for writing a letter to the newspaper about the misuse of city funds.[62]

The same principle also prohibits firing or otherwise punishing most city employees because of their political party affiliation.[63] Grounds for a Section 1983 lawsuit would exist if, for example, the party controlling the city council decided to dismiss the public works director because the director was a member of the other party.[64]

Fourth Amendment Rights of Freedom from Unreasonable Searches and Seizures

The Fourth Amendment to the United States Constitution guarantees everyone's right to be free from unreasonable searches and seizures. This right is violated if a law enforcement officer arrests (an arrest being one kind of seizure) someone without a solid basis, called *probable cause*, for believing that the person committed a crime. An officer may also violate Fourth Amendment rights by searching a person or a person's property without a search warrant. In one case, for example, the plaintiff alleged that a law enforcement officer had violated his constitutional rights when the officer broke into his home unannounced, searched the entire house without a warrant, shot and killed the family dog, arrested the owner, and pushed him out into public with a gun pointed at his head. The federal district court held that the plaintiff could recover damages under Section 1983 for this violation of the Fourth Amendment.[65]

Fourteenth Amendment Right of Due Process

The Fourteenth Amendment to the Constitution provides that no person may be deprived of life, liberty, or property without *due process of law*. For the most part, due process concerns itself with the procedures that the government must follow before depriving someone of life, liberty, or property. The complicated rules for criminal trials are one example of due process.

In other contexts the due process clause requires that those who are to be deprived of liberty or property receive prior notice of the reasons for the deprivation and an opportunity for a hearing to consider those reasons. *Property* and *liberty* are defined broadly for purposes of this guarantee. For example, under the personnel ordinances of some cities, city employees may not be fired without good cause.[66] Such an ordinance gives them a "property" interest in their jobs,[67] and the city must give them a hearing on the grounds for discharge before they may be fired.[68]

Due process also protects persons from arbitrary actions by the government. For example, a developer was permitted to sue under Section 1983 for violations of due process when a local government governing board intervened to prevent the routine issuance of a building permit to which he was entitled under state law.[69] For a claim to be actionable under Section 1983, the plaintiff must prove that the city took away a liberty or property interest created by state or local law, through arbitrary or capricious conduct or an abuse of discretion.[70]

Violation of Statutory Rights

Section 1983 also authorizes a person whose rights under a federal statute have been violated to sue for and recover damages.[71] In one case, for example, the Supreme Court held that an error in billing low-income housing tenants for their utilities might violate the Housing Act of 1937 and result in a recovery of damages under Section 1983.[72] In another case a man alleged that social service workers improperly reduced his Aid to Families with Dependent Children benefits because they misinterpreted the Social Security Act. The United States Supreme Court held that he could sue for damages in federal court under Section 1983.[73]

Liability of the City

The rules that govern a city's liability under federal law for violating federal constitutional or statutory rights differ from those that govern a city's tort liability under state law. State tort law holds a city liable for any actions of its employees within the scope of their employment whenever they are carrying out functions for which the city does not have governmental immunity. In contrast, a city may be required to pay money damages in a lawsuit brought under Section 1983 if the violation of federal rights is caused by the city's official policy,[74] regardless of whether the city would enjoy governmental immunity under state law.

What does it mean to say that a violation of federal rights is caused by a city's official policy? A city may, for example, be held liable if someone's federal rights are violated by the implementation of an ordinance, a regulation, or a decision officially adopted by the city's governing board.[75] Thus a city might be held liable if the council were to enact an arbitrary zoning ordinance in violation of federally protected constitutional property rights.

Acts less formal than passing an ordinance can also establish official policy, such as adopting personnel policies, passing formal resolutions of the governing board giving support to particular persons or conduct, or issuing instructions to the city manager.[76] In addition, a governing board's failure to act can establish official policy.[77] The most common lawsuit of this kind involves governing boards that are alleged to have failed to control persistent, widespread customs of police misconduct.

A city may also be required to pay damages under Section 1983 if someone's federal rights are violated by a city board or a public servant given decision-making authority under state or local law in the area involved,[78] or if the governing body delegates its authority to another board or public servant.

An isolated act of a public servant who has no authority to make policy for the city does not establish official policy, and the city is not liable for that act.[79] For example, a city is not liable under Section 1983 every time a law enforcement officer makes an illegal arrest or conducts a warrantless search in violation of someone's Fourth Amendment rights. To recover damages from the city, the person arrested or searched would have to prove that the arrest or the search represented the official policy of the city.

Liability of Public Servants

Public servants may also be sued individually in a Section 1983 lawsuit if they violate someone's federal rights. In some cases, however, they may be entitled to the protection of either absolute or qualified immunity from personal liability for damages. (In contrast, the city is never entitled to immunity from liability for damages in a Section 1983 lawsuit if its official policy caused the violation of someone's federal rights.)[80]

Liability of Governing Board Members

Members of local legislative bodies are absolutely immune from personal liability for damages if the body's legislative acts violate someone's federal rights.[81] This absolute immunity means that city governing board members may never be required to pay damages for acts taken within the scope of their legislative duties. In contrast, they may be held personally liable for acts taken within the scope of their administrative duties, although qualified immunity may sometimes protect them (see the discussion under the next heading, Liability of Other Public Servants).

The legal distinction between an administrative and a legislative act is difficult to draw, but an example may help illustrate it.[82] Because passing an ordinance is a legislative action, city council members are absolutely immune from personal liability if the council enacts a personnel ordinance that lists Republican political-party affiliation by a city employee as cause for dismissal, even though it interferes with an employee's First Amendment right to affiliate freely with any political party. However, enforcing a personnel ordinance is an administrative action, and council members who vote to dismiss an employee under an unconstitutional ordinance are individually liable for that action.[83]

Liability of Other Public Servants

A public servant who is not a member of a governing board and who violates someone's federal rights while performing his or her official duties (and city governing board members who are performing administrative tasks) are entitled to qualified immunity from personal liability.[84] Such immunity is necessary to ensure that public servants will make decisions without fear of personal liability for honest mistakes in judgment. The qualified immunity defense provides that a public servant may not be held personally liable in a Section 1983 lawsuit unless his or her conduct violates clearly established statutory or constitutional rights about which a reasonable person in similar circumstances would have known.[85] In other words, public servants are shielded from Section 1983 liability if they could reasonably have thought that their conduct was lawful. The qualified immunity defense protects public servants if the law governing their conduct is unclear at the time they act, even if a court later declares their conduct unconstitutional.

For example, a city manager has dismissed an employee. The personnel ordinance provides that employees may be dismissed only for cause (that is, for a good reason). The manager gave the dismissed employee neither a reason for the action nor a hearing to challenge it. A year before the dismissal the United States Supreme Court held that public employees who might be dismissed only for cause had a property interest in their job and had to be granted a due process hearing before they might be dismissed. When the employee brings a Section 1983 lawsuit against the manager on the basis of not receiving due process, the manager claims entitlement to qualified immunity from liability for damages on the basis of never hearing about the Supreme Court decision. The manager loses the argument because a reasonable person under the circumstances would have known about the constitutional requirement of a hearing. Although qualified immunity offers complete protection to public servants who violate someone's constitutional rights, it protects them only if they could not reasonably have predicted that their conduct was unlawful.

Insurance against Civil Liability

One prudent way to protect the city treasury and municipal public servants from potentially crippling state or federal damage awards, and from the huge expenses that can result from defending a lawsuit, is to purchase liability insurance. The General Assembly has authorized cities to purchase insurance to protect themselves and any of their officers, agents, or employees from civil liability for damages (G.S. 160A-485). The city council has absolute discretion in deciding which liabilities and which public servants, if any, will be covered by this insurance.

A fundamental reason for purchasing liability insurance is the need to protect the city against liability in state court for damage resulting from negligence in proprietary activities. Insurance can also protect a city from liability for damages under Section 1983 for violations of federal rights.

Another reason to obtain liability insurance is to give members of the public, who currently cannot recover damages from the city for injuries caused by governmental activities, an opportunity to be compensated for the harm done to them. The defense of governmental immunity that is available to cities under state law is waived to the extent that they are protected by liability insurance.

A judgment for damages entered against a city under state law on a tort claim that arises out of a governmental activity may not under G.S. 160A-485 exceed the coverage of the city's liability insurance. However, a judgment against a city on a tort claim that arises out of a proprietary activity, or under Section 1983, may exceed the coverage of the liability insurance because a city has no immunity from those claims. The city attorney therefore should examine any existing liability insurance policy to determine whether it sufficiently protects against liability for damages from all sources. For example, a liability insurance contract should cover the city's liability for damages caused by violations of federal constitutional and statutory rights, as well as its liability for damages under state tort law.

As important as its paying damages and providing a source of compensation for the public, liability insurance typically requires the insurance company to pay the costs of defense of any lawsuit, whether or not the city actually ends up losing the lawsuit. If a suit is brought, the insurance company must pay for an attorney to investigate the merits of the suit, negotiate an out-of-court settlement, and prepare and defend the suit at trial. In addition, many policies require the insurance company to pay all court costs associated with a lawsuit, including the plaintiff's attorney's fees if the plaintiff prevails.

Defense of Employees and Payment of Judgments

Provision of Defense

Each city is authorized, but not required, to provide for the defense of any civil or criminal action brought against current or former public servants in state or federal court on account of alleged acts or omissions committed in the scope and the course of their employment (G.S. 160A-167). A city may provide a defense through the city attorney or a private attorney. Also, as discussed earlier, the city may purchase liability insurance that requires the insurer to defend lawsuits brought against certain public servants. Whether to provide a defense at all is of course the city council's decision.

Payment of Judgments

Each city is also authorized, but not required, to pay all or part of any settlements or judgments in lawsuits against public servants for acts committed in the scope and the course of their employment (G.S. 160A-167). No statutory limit is placed on the amount of money that a city may appropriate to pay a settlement or a judgment. However, funds may not be appropriated to pay a public servant's settlement or judgment if the governing board finds that the individual acted or failed to act because of fraud, corruption, or malice.

The city must meet certain procedural requirements before it may pay a public servant's settlement or judgment. (No such requirements need be met before providing for the defense.) First, notice of a claim or litigation must be given to the city before a settlement is reached or a judgment is entered, if it is to pay the settlement or the judgment. Also, before the settlement or the entry of a judgment, the city council must adopt a set of uniform standards under which claims against public servants will be paid. These standards must be available for public inspection.

Notes

1. 42 U.S.C. § 1983 (1988).

2. The question of what law applies to a particular claim is largely independent of the court in which the lawsuit is brought. State courts handle some claims brought under federal law, including Section 1983 claims, and federal courts handle some claims brought under state law. *See* Howlett v. Rose, 496 U.S. 356 (1990); 28 U.S.C. § 1332(a)(1) (1988).

3. North Carolina law provides that a local government may not be required to pay punitive damages unless payment is expressly authorized by statute. Long v. City of Charlotte, 306 N.C. 187, 293 S.E.2d 101 (1982). Punitive damages may be recovered from a city in a wrongful death lawsuit because it fits within that narrow exception. Jackson v. Housing Auth., 316 N.C. 259, 341 S.E.2d 523 (1985). The U.S. Supreme Court has decided that punitive damages may *not* be awarded against a local government in a Section 1983 lawsuit. City of Newport v. Fact Concerts, Inc., 453 U.S. 247 (1981).

4. A number of the court decisions used to illustrate principles in this chapter involve lawsuits against counties rather than cities. These illustrations are relevant because the same rules of civil liability generally control the outcome of lawsuits against the two types of government units.

5. Munick v. City of Durham, 181 N.C. 188, 106 S.E. 665 (1921).

6. State v. Mobley, 240 N.C. 476, 83 S.E.2d 100 (1954). In Houston v. DeHerrodora, 192 N.C. 749, 136 S.E. 6 (1926), for example, police officers who chased the plaintiff in their car and fired twenty shots at him before identifying themselves as police officers were held liable for battery and required to pay $2,000 in damages.

7. *See* Williams v. State, 168 N.Y.S.2d 163 (Ct. Cl. 1957) (awarding damages for false imprisonment to prison inmate who had been detained for one and one-half years after his maximum sentence expired).

8. Blackwood v. Cates, 297 N.C. 163, 254 S.E.2d 7 (1979); *see also* Hoffman v. Clinic Hosp., 213 N.C. 669, 197 S.E. 161 (1938) (per curiam).

9. *See* Jones v. Brinkley, 174 N.C. 23, 93 S.E. 372 (1917).

10. *See* Presnell v. Pell, 298 N.C. 715, 260 S.E.2d 611 (1979); Towne v. Cope, 32 N.C. App. 660, 233 S.E.2d 624 (1977). In some instances, state statutes expressly extend this qualified privilege to designated public servants. For example, the 1987 General Assembly created a privilege for written communications made by members of nursing home advisory committees. *See* G.S. 131E-128(i).

11. Moore v. Town of Plymouth, 249 N.C. 423, 106 S.E.2d 695 (1959).

12. Dunn v. Swanson, 217 N.C. 279, 7 S.E.2d 563 (1940).

13. Glenn v. City of Raleigh, 246 N.C. 469, 98 S.E.2d 913 (1957).

14. Millar v. Town of Wilson, 222 N.C. 340, 23 S.E.2d 42 (1942).

15. McIlhenney v. City of Wilmington, 127 N.C. 146, 37 S.E. 187 (1900).

16. Moffitt v. City of Asheville, 103 N.C. 237, 9 S.E. 695 (1889); *see also* State *ex rel.* Hayes v. Billings, 240 N.C. 78, 81 S.E.2d 150 (1954).

17. Siebold v. Kinston-Lenoir Public Library, 264 N.C. 360, 141 S.E.2d 519 (1965).

18. Hodges v. City of Charlotte, 214 N.C. 737, 200 S.E. 889 (1939).

19. Peterson v. City of Wilmington, 130 N.C. 76, 40 S.E. 853 (1902).

20. Baker v. City of Lumberton, 239 N.C. 401, 79 S.E.2d 886 (1954).

21. Rhodes v. City of Asheville, 230 N.C. 134, 52 S.E.2d 371 (1949).

22. Lowe v. City of Gastonia, 211 N.C. 564, 191 S.E. 7 (1937).

23. Sides v. Cabarrus Memorial Hosp., 287 N.C. 14, 213 S.E.2d 297 (1975); *see also* Casey v. Wake County, 45 N.C. App. 522, 263 S.E.2d 360, *disc. review denied*, 300 N.C. 371, 267 S.E.2d 673 (1980) (holding that provision of birth control in county family planning clinic is governmental function).

24. Harrington v. Commissioners of Wadesboro, 153 N.C. 437, 69 S.E. 399 (1910).

25. Gregory v. City of Kings Mountain, 117 N.C. App. 99, 450 S.E.2d 349 (1994).

26. Millar v. Town of Wilson, 222 N.C. 340, 23 S.E.2d 42 (1942).

27. Rich v. City of Goldsboro, 282 N.C. 383, 192 S.E.2d 834 (1972).

28. Glenn v. City of Raleigh, 246 N.C. 469, 98 S.E.2d 913 (1957).

29. Metz v. City of Asheville, 150 N.C. 748, 64 S.E. 881 (1909).

30. Roach v. City of Lenoir, 44 N.C. App. 608, 261 S.E.2d 299 (1980). *But cf.* Williams v. Town of Greenville, 130 N.C. 93, 40 S.E. 977 (1902) (holding city liable for tort of trespass when water backing up at clogged culvert causes property damage).

31. James v. City of Charlotte, 183 N.C. 630, 112 S. E. 423 (1922). *See* Broome v. City of Charlotte, 208 N.C. 729, 182 S. E. 325 (1935).

32. Koontz v. City of Winston-Salem, 280 N.C. 513, 186 S.E.2d 897 (1972).

33. Rogers v. Town of Black Mountain, 224 N.C. 119, 29 S.E.2d 203 (1944).

34. *See also* Lertz v. Hughes Bros., 208 N.C. 490, 181 S.E. 345 (1935), in which the employer was held liable for an automobile accident that occurred when an employee took a joy ride in the course of running an errand for an employer; Munick v. City of Durham, 181 N.C. 188, 106 S.E. 665 (1921).

35. Edwards v. Akion, 52 N.C. App. 688, 693, 279 S.E.2d 894, 897, *aff'd*, 304 N.C. 585, 284 S.E.2d 518 (1981) (per curiam).

36. Martin v. Mondie, 94 N.C. App. 750, 381 S.E.2d 481 (1989); *see also* Braswell v. Braswell, 330 N.C. 363, 410 S.E.2d 897 (1991), *cert. denied sub nom.* Hunt v. North Carolina, 112 S. Ct. 3045 (1992); Hull v. Oldham, 104 N.C. App. 29, 412 S.E.2d 72 (1991). For a case applying the public duty doctrine to the work of building inspectors, see Lynn v. Overlook Developers, 98 N.C. App. 75, 389 S.E.2d 609, *aff'd on other grounds*, 328 N.C. 689, 403 S.E.2d 469 (1991).

37. *Braswell*, 330 N.C. at 371, 410 S.E.2d at 902.

38. *See, e.g.*, Blackwelder v. Concord, 205 N.C. 792, 795, 172 S.E. 392, 393

(1934) ("[t]he exercise of discretionary or legislative power is a governmental function, and for injury resulting from the negligent exercise of such power a municipality is exempt from liability").

39. Hill v. Board of Aldermen, 72 N.C. 55 (1875); *see* Moye v. McLawhorn, 208 N.C. 812, 182 S.E. 493 (1935).

40. Glace v. Town of Pilot Mountain, 265 N.C. 181, 143 S.E.2d 78 (1965).

41. *See* Gray v. City of High Point, 203 N.C. 756, 166 S.E. 911 (1932); *cf.* Williams v. Town of Greenville, 130 N.C. 93, 40 S.E. 977 (1902).

42. Long v. City of Charlotte, 306 N.C. 187, 293 S.E.2d 101 (1982). A related rule provides that a city does not enjoy governmental immunity if it undertakes to abate a nuisance on private property and the property owner can later prove that a nuisance did not in fact exist. *See* Rhyne v. Town of Mount Holly, 251 N.C. 521, 112 S.E.2d 40 (1960) (holding that city may be required to pay for trees wrongfully cut down by city workers enforcing local ordinance requiring landowners to cut weeds and brush twice a year).

43. *See* Corum v. Appalachian State Univ., 330 N.C. 761, 413 S.E.2d 276, *cert. denied sub nom.* Durham v. Corum, 113 S. Ct. 493 (1992).

44. One exception to this rule concerns the intentional tort of defamation. As discussed earlier, public servants with a qualified privilege to make a particular statement will not be held liable for defamation unless they act with malice.

45. *See* Blackwood v. Cates, 297 N.C. 163, 254 S.E.2d 7 (1979) (holding mayor personally liable for intentional tort of false imprisonment).

46. 50 N.C. App. 401, 273 S.E.2d 752, *disc. review denied,* 303 N.C. 181, 280 S.E.2d 453 (1981); *see also* State v. Hord, 264 N.C. 149, 141 S.E.2d 241 (1965); Wiggins v. City of Monroe, 73 N.C. App. 44, 326 S.E.2d 39 (1985).

47. *See* Hare v. Butler, 99 N.C. App. 693, 700, 394 S.E.2d 231, 236, *disc. review denied,* 327 N.C. 634, 399 S.E.2d 121 (1990); Harwood v. Johnson, 92 N.C. App. 306, 31011, 374 S.E.2d 401, 404 (1988), *aff'd in part, rev'd in part,* 326 N.C. 231, 388 S.E.2d 439 (1990); *see also* EEE-ZZZ Lay Drain Co. v. North Carolina Dep't of Human Resources, 108 N.C. App. 24, 422 S.E.2d 338 (1992).

48. Hipp v. Ferrall, 173 N.C. 167, 91 S.E. 831 (1917).

49. *See* Pigott v. City of Wilmington, 50 N.C. App. 401, 273 S.E.2d 752, *disc. rev. denied,* 303 N.C. 181, 280 S.E.2d 453.

50. *Wiggins,* 73 N.C. App. at 44, 326 S.E.2d at 39.

51. *Hare,* 99 N.C. App. at 700–01, 394 S.E.2d at 237.

52. Betts v. Jones, 208 N.C. 410, 181 S.E. 334 (1935).

53. E. McQuillin, *The Law of Municipal Corporations,* 3d. ed. (Deerfield, Ill.: Clark Boardman Callaghan, 1993), sec. 53.22.10, p. 273.

54. Robinson v. Nash County, 43 N.C. App. 33, 257 S.E.2d 679 (1979). *But see* Smith v. State, 289 N.C. 303, 331, 222 S.E.2d 412, 430 (1976); Moffitt v. Davis, 205 N.C. 565, 568, 172 S.E. 317, 318 (1915); Hipp v. Farrell, 169 N.C. 551, 554–55; 91 S.E. 831, 832–33 (1915); Wiggins v. City of Monroe, 73 N.C. App. 44, 326 S.E.2d 39 (1985). Interestingly, the *Robinson* court quotes *Hipp* in its discussion of discretionary immunity. *Robinson,* 43 N.C. App. at 38, 257 S.E.2d at 682.

55. Etheridge v. Graham, 14 N.C. App. 551, 188 S.E.2d 551 (1972).

56. Miller v. Jones, 224 N.C. 783, 32 S.E.2d 594 (1945).

57. *Id.* at 787, 32 S.E.2d at 597.

58. Davis v. Moore, 215 N.C. 449, 2 S.E.2d 366 (1939).

59. *See, e.g.*, Gregory v. City of Kings Mountain, 117 N.C. App. 99, 450 S.E.2d 349 (1994); Robinette v. Barriger, 116 N.C. App. 197, 447 S.E.2d 498, *appeal filed* (1994); Taylor v. Ashburn, 112 N.C. App. 604, 436 S.E.2d 276 (1993); Dickens v. Thorne, 110 N.C. App. 39, 429 S.E.2d 176 (1993); Whitaker v. Clark, 109 N.C. App. 379, 427 S.E.2d 142, *disc. rev. denied*, 333 N.C. 795, 431 S.E.2d 142 (1993).

60. Glasson v. City of Louisville, 518 F.2d 899 (6th Cir.), *cert. denied*, 423 U.S. 930 (1975).

61. See Stephen Allred, *Employment Law: A Guide for North Carolina Public Employers* (Raleigh, N.C.: Institute of Government, The University of North Carolina at Chapel Hill, 1992), 190–203.

62. *See, e.g.*, Pickering v. Board of Educ., 391 U.S. 563 (1968).

63. Rutan v. Republican Party, 497 U.S. 62 (1990).

64. See Allred, *Employment Law*, 204–08.

65. Ellis v. City of Chicago, 478 F. Supp. 333 (N.D. Ill. 1979).

66. See Allred, *Employment Law*, 31.

67. Board of Regents v. Roth, 408 U.S. 564 (1972).

68. Cleveland Bd. of Educ. v. Loudermill, 470 U.S. 532 (1985); Bishop v. Wood, 426 U.S. 341 (1976). See Allred, *Employment Law*, 225–30.

69. Scott v. Greenville County, 716 F.2d 1409 (4th Cir. 1983).

70. *Id.* at 1419.

71. There are two exceptions to the use of a Section 1983 lawsuit to remedy alleged violations of federal statutes by municipal public servants. First, a lawsuit under Section 1983 is not possible if the federal statute allegedly violated provides an exclusive remedy for its own enforcement. Middlesex County Sewerage Auth. v. National Sea Clammers Ass'n, 453 U.S. 1 (1981). Second, no Section 1983 lawsuit is permitted if the federal statute allegedly violated does not create an enforceable right. Pennhurst State School and Hosp. v. Halderman, 451 U.S. 1 (1981).

72. Wright v. City of Roanoke Redevelopment and Housing Auth., 479 U.S. 418 (1987).

73. Maine v. Thiboutot, 448 U.S. 1 (1980).

74. Monell v. Department of Social Serv., 436 U.S. 658 (1978). An extensive discussion of the principles of municipal liability under *Monell* and subsequent Supreme Court decisions appears in Spell v. McDaniel, 824 F.2d 1380 (4th Cir. 1987), *cert. denied sub nom.* City of Fayetteville v. Spell, 484 U.S. 1027 (1988).

75. *See, e.g.*, Matthias v. Bingley, 906 F.2d 1047, *modified*, 915 F.2d 946 (5th Cir. 1990) (per curiam).

76. See S. Nahmod, *Civil Rights and Civil Liberties Litigation*, 3d ed., vol. 1 (Colorado Springs: Shepard's/McGraw-Hill, 1991), 429–30.

77. *See* Avery v. County of Burke, 660 F.2d 111 (4th Cir. 1981).

78. Dotson v. Chester, 937 F.2d 920 (4th Cir. 1991).

79. As noted earlier, a city may be held liable under state law for torts committed by its employees solely because it is the employer, without regard to whether or not the employees were carrying out official city policy. In fact, under state law the city may be liable even if the employee is acting contrary to official policy. Edwards v. Akion, 52 N.C. App. 688, 693, 279 S.E.2d 894, 897, *aff'd*, 304 N.C. 585, 284 S.E.2d 518 (1981) (per curiam).

80. Owen v. City of Independence, 445 U.S. 622 (1980).

81. Bruce v. Riddle, 631 F.2d 272 (4th Cir. 1980).

82. On the legislative-administrative distinction, see Scott v. Greenville County, 716 F.2d 1409, 1422–23 (4th Cir. 1983).

83. *See, e.g.*, Gross v. Winter, 876 F.2d 165 (D.C. Cir. 1989).

84. *See* Wood v. Strickland, 420 U.S. 308 (1975). Absolute immunity is available to local government employees under narrow circumstances. An example is law enforcement officers who testify in criminal trials. *See* Briscoe v. LaHue, 460 U.S. 325 (1983).

85. Anderson v. Creighton, 483 U.S. 635 (1987). In *Anderson* the Supreme Court stated that qualified immunity protected public servants from Section 1983 liability "so long as their actions could reasonably have been thought consistent with the rights they are alleged to have violated." *Id.* at 638.

10 Interlocal Cooperation, Regional Organizations, and City-County Consolidation

David M. Lawrence and Warren Jake Wicker

Contents

GOVERNMENT OFFICIALS frequently discover that some facilities and services can more efficiently be operated or provided through collaboration among two or more local governments. North Carolina cities have entered into a wide variety of agreements establishing such collaboration. The number and the success of joint efforts have led to continuing interest in consolidation of governments themselves, especially cities with counties, but no city-county consolidations have yet occurred in North Carolina.

Interlocal Cooperation

Cooperation among local governments has become common in recent years. As urbanization has spilled beyond city limits, cities and counties have found it useful to cooperate in providing urban services to unincorporated neighborhoods. The cooperation might take the form of county contributions to city services, city provision of services to unincorporated areas through contracts with the county, or jointly financed and operated services. In addition, cities have continued to cooperate among themselves in providing services.

Cooperation offers several advantages:

1. It may be the most efficient and least expensive way to provide a new service. As a small town begins inspection services, a contract with an ongoing city or county inspection department can provide experienced services immediately, with no administrative overhead. To take another example, a city by itself may not need or be able to afford specialized services like the more sophisticated types of police activities on a full-time basis; if it joined with the county and one or more other cities in the county, however, such a service might be financially feasible and fully used.

2. Through cooperation, governments may achieve economies of scale, lowering the per-unit cost of a service and perhaps providing it at a higher level. A good example is a city-county utility operation.

3. Cooperation permits a more effective response to problems that refuse to respect jurisdictional lines—for example, air pollution that drifts across governmental boundaries.

4. By cooperating, two units may coordinate functions that each has been carrying on independently. Water and sewer services just beyond city limits are an example of this coordination; counties must often work with cities to establish policies on extensions, supplies, costs, and the like.

5. Cooperation permits local governments to adjust inequitable situations. For example, cities often provide recreation programs used by people from throughout the county, so many counties contribute to these programs.
6. Cooperation is flexible. It can usually begin by simple action of governing boards. A unit may engage in several cooperative ventures, each differing from the others in scope, administrative structure, and financial support. A cooperative relationship established for one service may provide a model for another, but it in no way establishes a mold.

Types of Cooperation

Cooperation between local governments may assume a variety of forms. The most frequent categories are contributions, mutual aid contracts, transfer of functions, service contracts, joint agreements, and new units of government.

Contributions

Occasionally one government will provide a program that benefits the property or the citizens of another government, but without financial support from those beneficiaries. In that case the government that benefits might contribute funds to the government that provides. County support of a city recreation program is such a contribution.

Mutual Aid Contracts

Mutual aid contracts involve two or more governments agreeing to come to one another's aid (if possible) in police or fire emergencies or natural disasters.

Transfer of Functions

Sometimes a county and a city, each authorized to perform a particular function, will agree that the county should assume total responsibility. This process has frequently occurred with libraries, hospitals, and most recently solid waste disposal.

Service Contracts

The category of service contracts includes all agreements in which one government contracts with another to provide a service, either an administrative service to the receiving government itself or a direct service to the citizens of that government. A county might contract to collect the taxes of a city, or a city might contract to inspect buildings throughout the county or treat the sewage of a second city.

Joint Agreements

The line between joint agreements and service contracts is often thin, but in theory the former involves two or more units exercising jointly a power that each could exercise individually. A city and a county might employ a joint manager, or two cities a joint recreation director. City-county planning boards fit in this category, as do councils of governments and other regional councils.

New Units of Government

On occasion, two or more local governments may cooperatively create a new political subdivision, intended to provide a service to citizens of each of the creating governments. This form of cooperation is not often found in North Carolina, but examples include some airport authorities, water and sewer authorities, metropolitan water or sewerage districts, and regional housing authorities.

Authority for Cooperation

The General Assembly, through a series of statutes, has provided ample authority for cooperation by cities. Table 10-1 sets out the principal statutes authorizing cities to cooperate with other local governments.

Provisions of Interlocal Agreements

Some types of cooperative arrangements are quite simple. When one government contributes to a continuing program of another, the contributing government typically does not concern itself with the administration of the program; it simply includes an appropriation in its budget ordinance. The amount of the appropriation may have been negotiated, but the negotiations probably did not extend to how the program is run. The same disinterest in administration would probably attach to a transfer of function; once the transfer had been made, the function would become the sole responsibility of the recipient government.

Other arrangements, however, become more complex, and negotiations may be difficult. Questions arise concerning financing, operations, administration, property, and many other matters. This chapter cannot suggest correct solutions because the needs, the administrative structures, the traditions, and the services involved all differ. Nor can it suggest all the questions. But it can point out the most common decisions that two negotiating governments might face (see table 10-2 pages 202–3). Perhaps the list could then suggest other questions more particular to the situation.

Regional Organizations

The conditions that have given rise to cooperative relationships between local governments have also prompted the development of substate regional organizations. The development of highway systems, the operation of water and sewer facilities, the protection of air quality, and the regulation of land use are examples of activities that when undertaken by one unit, will affect people and property in neighboring units. Sometimes, as noted in the preceding section, these common interests may be recognized and managed by cooperative relationships. At other times, however, the administration of some joint interests may be accomplished most effectively by creating a joint, regional agency.

Impetus for Regional Organization

By 1960 an increasing number of federal agencies required some form of regional planning and the creation of multicounty organizations to administer categorical programs under their jurisdictions. State agencies, of course, had a long history of dividing the state into administrative regions. In 1961 the General Assembly authorized the creation of regional planning commissions (G.S. 153A-391, -400) and economic development commissions (G.S. 158-8, -15) by general law. These actions built on the successful experience with regional plan-

Table 10-1
Statutes Authorizing Cities to Cooperate with Other Local Governments

Function	G.S. Citation
General Powers of Cooperation	
Administrative and governmental powers	160A-460 through -464
Property transactions	160A-274
Buildings	153A-164
Councils of governments	160A-470 through -478
Consolidation study commissions	153A-401 through -405
Elections	
Registration	163-288
Conduct	163-285
Officials	163-281(a)
Voting machines	163-151
Planning and Regulation of Development	
Transfer of territorial jurisdiction	160A-360
Planning contracts	160A-363
Historic preservation commissions	160A-400.7
Appearance commissions	160A-451
Open space	160A-404
Inspection services	160A-413
Housing	157-39.5
Community development	160A-456
Regional planning commissions	153A-391 through -398
Regional economic development commissions	158-8 through -15
City-county redevelopment commissions	160A-507.1
Environmental Matters	
Air pollution control	143-215.112
Sedimentation control	113A-60
Public Safety	
Law enforcement	
Training	160A-289

continued on next page

ning and economic development organizations that had been established in previous years by local legislation. Today's most frequently used form of regional organization, the regional council of governments, was authorized by legislation in 1971 (G.S. 160A-470, -484).

The big push for multicounty regional organizations, however, came from the federal government after Congress enacted the Intergovernmental Cooperation Act of 1968. This act encouraged the states to establish a uniform system of areawide planning and development districts. Regional review of local grant and program propos-

Table 10-1, *continued*
Statutes Authorizing Cities to Cooperate with Other Local Governments

Function	G.S. Citation
Public Safety, *continued*	
Law enforcement, *continued*	
Auxiliary police	160A-283
Personnel and equipment	160A-288
Local confinement facilities	153A-219
Fire protection	160A-293
Civil disorders	14-288.12, -288.14
Civil preparedness	166A-7, -10
Ambulance services	153A-250
Animal shelter	160A-493
Hospitals	131E-7
Social Services	
Human relations programs	160A-492
Manpower programs	160A-492
Community action programs	160A-492
Senior citizens	160A-497
Library Services	153A-270
Recreation, Generally	160A-355
Regional sports authorities	160A-479 through -479.17
Public Enterprises	
Airports	63-56; 153A-278
Water services	153A-278
Sewer services	153A-278
Solid waste services	153A-278; 160A-192(b)
Utility emergencies	160A-318
Public transportation systems	153A-278
Electric power generation	159B-4 through -59
Regional public transportation authorities	160A-600 through -625
Regional solid waste management authorities	153A-421 through -432

als, as required by Circular A-95 of the Office of Management and Budget, became a standard procedure. In the following year, 1969, the General Assembly directed the Department of Administration to cooperate with " . . . the counties, the cities and towns, the federal government, multi-state commissions and private agencies and organizations to develop a system of multi-county, regional planning districts to cover the entire State . . ." [G.S. 143-341(6)(i)]. This charge was part of the department's broader role in undertaking and supporting state and regional planning and development.

Table 10-2
Common Decisions Facing Negotiating Governments

Administrative Structure	Should the units jointly supervise the function, or should one simply contract with the other to supervise it for both?
Finances	Are user charges to be levied?
	Should the agreement establish the schedule of charges?
	Should the agreement establish the basis of charges?
	How should charges be modified?
	Should charges be the province of the operating government alone?
	On what basis are costs to be divided?
	What should be included as costs attributable to the activity?
	What will be the timing and the manner of payment between governments?
	What budgeting procedures should be established?
	Are special assessments to be used? On what basis?
	In capital projects, who will make expenditure decisions?
Operations	What will be the territorial scope of activity?
	What performance levels will be expected? Can they be modified? How?
	In capital projects, will the parties mandate specific features?
	On facilities, what limitations or priorities on use will be necessary?
Personnel	How are personnel to be selected?
	Whose employees will they be?
	Should there be special provisions in regard to position classification, pay plan, fringe benefits, etc.?

continued on next page

Lead Regional Organizations

In May 1970, Governor Robert Scott, by executive order, designated seventeen multicounty regions. One of these, Region G, was divided in 1979 to add Region I. There have been eighteen regions since that time. Following the designation of the multicounty regions, many state agencies took action to align their regional administrative organization with the new regional designations. Cities and counties in the regions also moved to create a new regional organization or to reshape an existing one to fit the new pattern. In 1971 the state announced a policy of designating a single

Table 10-2, *continued*
Common Decisions Facing Negotiating Governments

Property	How will decisions to buy real or major personal property be made?
	How are sites to be selected?
	How are specifications to be established?
	How will acquisition be made?
	Who will own the property?
	How will property be disposed of?
Miscellaneous	What reports will be required?
	What records must be retained?
	What rights of inspection should be allowed?
	How will potential tort liabilities be paid?
Joint agencies	How will joint agencies be structured?
	What will the size of the coordinating body be?
	What will the terms of members be?
	Who will appoint them?
	How often will the body meet?
	What powers and duties will be conferred on/delegated to the body?
	What provisions should be made for budgeting?
	What reports and records will be required?
Duration	How long will the cooperative activity continue?
Termination and renewal	What should be the provisions for renewal and termination?

organization in each region as the *lead regional organization* (LRO). This organization is open to all cities and counties in the region and is the organization through which many state and federal programs are channeled. In 1992 five of these LROs were planning and economic development commissions, and thirteen were councils of governments.

The governing bodies of the LROs comprise representatives from the member governments. In 1991 their staffs varied in size from eleven to sixty persons, with an executive director as the administrative head. Because the LROs may not levy taxes, they must depend on membership dues, earnings from technical assistance, and grants from other governments for their financial support. Although the LROs are created by local governments, their financial support is primarily from the state and federal governments. Annual membership contributions from local governments in 1991 met about 8 percent of their support. State and federal grants in that year accounted for some 82 percent of their support. The remainder came from charges for technical assistance and miscellaneous receipts. Cities that are members of their LRO typically contribute $.30–$.35 per capita in annual membership dues.

Individual budgets of the LROs in 1991 ranged from a low of $410,000 to a high of $2,013,000. The combined budgets of all eighteen LROs totaled just under $20,000,000, or about $3 per capita on a statewide basis.

Programs and activities of the LROs vary. All engage in economic planning and development, provide intergovernmental review, serve as a data center for the region, administer programs for the aging in cooperation with state and federal agencies, and advise and assist counties in providing emergency medical services. Most participate in administering community development block grants and the Job Training Partnership Act, and provide technical assistance in local solid waste and land use planning, housing, and programs to enhance water quality. For a number of LROs, transportation services, regional transportation planning, management consulting, and land and water conservation are significant activities. In short, although the LROs focus principally on planning and coordinating activities and technical assistance in the areas within which they work, they are also available to carry out almost any function or activity that their members may wish.

City-County Consolidation

City-county consolidation is the merger of a county government with one or more city governments. As a general rule, the city government is abolished and the county government is legally transformed into one that has all the powers and the functions previously held by both governments. Authority for counties and cities to create special commissions to study consolidation and other forms of cooperative action, including the drafting of a charter for a consolidated government, is found in Article 20 of G.S. Chapter 153A.

Table 10-3

Results of City-County Consolidation Referenda in North Carolina

Governmental Units Involved	Date of Referendum	Number For	Number Against	Percentage For	Percentage Against
Wilmington and New Hanover County	March 28, 1933	1,189	4,128	22	78
	February 27, 1973	4,040	11,722	26	74
	October 6, 1987	7,051	10,337	41	59
	October 10, 1995	11,377	15,923	42	58
Durham and Durham County	January 28, 1961	4,115	14,355	22	78
	September 10, 1974	6,198	13,124	32	68
Charlotte and Mecklenburg County	March 22, 1971	17,313	39,464	31	69
Asheville and Buncombe County	November 2, 1982	12,642	20,883	38	62

Source: Official election returns

The History of City-County Consolidation

City-county consolidation has a long history in the United States. New Orleans City and Parish were consolidated in 1813; Boston and Suffolk County in 1821; and Philadelphia City and County in 1854.

In North Carolina, *interest* in city-county consolidation has a long history, beginning with a 1927 plan, never submitted to the voters, to consolidate Charlotte and Mecklenburg County. Since that time, consolidation plans have been placed before the electorate four times in Wilmington and New Hanover County, twice in Durham and Durham County, and once each in Charlotte and Mecklenburg County and Asheville and Buncombe County. All the plans were rejected, but the margins of defeat have decreased in the places that have had more than one consolidation attempt. The results of the eight referenda on consolidation are shown in table 10-3.

In every case, voters inside the city proposed for consolidation were more favorable toward the merger than those outside. However, only in the three most recent votes—Wilmington and New Hanover County in 1987 and 1995, and Asheville and Buncombe County in 1982—have a majority of the voters inside the city involved favored merger.

Other moves toward city-county consolidation in the four counties mentioned earlier have been made in the past sixty years, but they all stopped short of producing a charter that was the subject of a referendum. Interest in consolidation, as evidenced by the creation of study groups, has also been present in recent years in a number of other cities and counties, including Brevard and Transylvania County, Elizabeth City and Pasquotank County, Fayetteville and Cumberland County, Roxboro and Person County, and Sanford and Lee County.

Advantages and Disadvantages of City-County Consolidation

The persons who have supported consolidation have done so on the grounds of efficiency. They note that the county is a single local social and economic community, and they argue that it could be better served by one local government than by two. They see better coordination of all governmental services and improved management of growth flowing from consolidation. Merger would also result in greater equity in taxation, in their view, because it typically involves the use of service districts with taxation tied to service levels. Proponents argue as well that a single governing board, serving all citizens for all local governmental purposes, would be more responsive and responsible. Furthermore, they assert, consolidation would eliminate city-county conflicts and the objections to municipal annexation decisions being made by a governing board not responsive to those being annexed.

The opponents of consolidation, for their part, have put forth a host of objections. Citizens outside the central city have feared that merger would result in their being "swallowed up" by the "big city." They note that a merged government would be a larger one, and argue that this would mean a less-responsive and less-efficient government. The fear of higher taxes, especially among residents outside the city, has usually been a major objection to consolidation.

Most of the plans for consolidation proposed in North Carolina have called for changes in the manner in which the governing board was elected and for the merger of administrative departments and offices. These proposed changes have caused some citizens to fear a loss of political influence or jobs or both. Members of rural fire departments and employees of sheriffs' offices, for example, have usually opposed consolidation.

Residents of small towns in counties proposed for merger with the central city have usually opposed consolidation, even though their towns were to continue to exist after the merger. They have seen the initial consolidation as a first step that might eventually lead to the merger of their towns and a loss of their identity.

ea   ea   ea

The efforts at city-county consolidation have not yet culminated in a merger of any governments. Almost all of them, however, have been a factor in promoting city-county cooperation by the merger of functions or by an increase in the joint use of facilities.

III
City Finance

11 Revenues

David M. Lawrence

Contents

CITIES must raise *revenues* to support the services they provide. Revenues increase a city's net worth or financial resources. Revenues are usually cash receipts, but not all cash receipts are revenues. For example, when a city redeems an investment, one asset, the investment, is changed for another, cash. Except for interest earnings from the investment, the city's net worth does not increase, and no revenues accrue. Likewise, when a city issues bonds, its cash receipts increase by the amount of the bond proceeds, but the city also incurs a debt or a liability equal to the proceeds. The addition to cash receipts in this case is balanced by the liability, and neither the city's net worth nor its revenues are increased.

The major types of revenues available to North Carolina cities are local taxes, state-shared taxes, user charges, other local fees and charges, and federal and state grants and aid. *Taxes* are compulsory charges that governments levy on persons or property. They need not bear any relation to the benefit from public services received by the taxpaying persons or property. The most important taxes for North Carolina cities are the property tax, the local-option sales tax, and state-shared taxes. Property taxes normally constitute from one-third to one-half (occasionally, even more) of general fund revenues for most North Carolina cities. Cities with a system for electric power distribution often subsidize general government activities with net earnings from the system, and in these cities the property tax on average contributes a smaller portion to annual revenues than it does elsewhere. The local-option sales tax typically contributes between 10 and 15 percent of annual general fund revenues. The three state-shared taxes—the franchise tax, the gasoline tax, and the beer and wine tax—contribute from 10 to 20 percent of general fund revenues for the state's medium-size and large cities and up to 25 percent of such revenues for small cities.

User charges are levied on those who avail themselves of certain city services, in proportion to the benefit received from the services. Water supply and distribution and sewage collection and treatment are the most important city activities supported by user charges. Other user charges levied by this state's cities are for electric power and gas distribution, solid waste collection and disposal, off-street parking, mass transit, ambulance services, cemeteries, recreation and cultural activities, airports, and several other functions.

Besides taxes and user charges, cities have other local revenue sources available to them. The more important of these are fees levied to cover the cost of regulation, special assessments, profits from alcoholic beverage control (ABC) stores, and investment earnings.

Finally, North Carolina cities receive intergovernmental grants and aid. One major change in public finance since the early 1980s has been the reduction in federal aid to local governments. Nationwide, direct federal aid to local governments as a percentage of general revenues from local sources fell from more than 17 percent in 1979 to less than 6 percent twelve years later.[1]

Local Taxes

As creations of the legislature, cities may impose only the local taxes specifically authorized by the General Assembly. The following local taxes are available to them under the general law: the property tax, the local-option sales and use tax, the privilege license tax, the cable television franchise tax, the animal tax, the motor vehicle license tax, and the charge for 911 services. In addition, a number

of cities either levy taxes or receive shares of other local taxes authorized by local act of the legislature.

The Property Tax

The property tax is levied against real and personal property and
generally is an obligation of the property, not its owner. That is, if the
tax is not paid, the usual enforcement procedure is to sell the property and pay the tax from the proceeds of the sale. Table 11-1 shows
total city property tax levies in North Carolina in recent years. Part
of the annual increase in property tax levies evident in that table is
due to increases in the tax rate, and the other part to growth in the
tax base, that is, the value of property.

Tax Base

The property tax base consists of real property (land, buildings,
and other improvements to land); personal property (business
equipment, automobiles, etc.); and the property of public service
companies (electric power companies, telephone companies, railroads, airlines, and certain other companies). Not all property is
subject to taxation. Government-owned property is exempt under
the state constitution.[2] In addition, the General Assembly may exempt property from taxation or classify property to exclude it from
the tax base, give it a reduced valuation, or subject it to a reduced
tax rate. It must do so, however, only on a statewide basis.[3] A local
government may not itself exempt or classify or otherwise give a tax
preference to property within its jurisdiction.

Table 11-1 shows the assessed value of property subject to taxation in North Carolina's cities. The data in the table indicate that the
municipal property tax base has grown at a slightly faster rate than
the total property tax base. This may reflect the general aggressive-
ness of North Carolina municipal annexation policies.

Once every eight years the county tax assessor must revalue the
real property in the county. Twelve or thirteen counties undergo this
process each year. Between revaluations, growth in the real property
tax base results only from new construction. Personal property and
public service company property are revalued annually. The revaluation of real property only once every eight years presents a difficult

Table 11-1
Property Taxation in North Carolina, 1984–85 through 1993–94

| | Municipal Property Tax Levies | | Assessed Value of Taxable Property | | | |
| | | | Countywide Total | | City Share | |
Year	Amount (in millions)	Percent Increase from Prior Year	Amount (in billions)	Percent Increase from Prior Year	Amount (in billions)	Percent Increase from Prior Year
1984–85	$423	—	$158.9	—	$ 74.7	—
1985–86	465	10	175.9	11	84.0	12
1986–87	518	11	191.9	9	92.1	10
1987–88	561	8	208.9	9	102.0	11
1988–89	574	2	214.9	3	105.4	3
1989–90	621	8	231.6	8	114.2	8
1990–91	688	11	248.2	7	122.9	8
1991–92	742	8	269.7	9	137.3	12
1992–93	750	1	288.7	7	147.1	7
1993–94	780	4	302.8	3	155.1	5

Source: Patricia C. Seawell, North Carolina Department of Revenue, Tax Research Division, telephone conversation with author, 30 June 1995.

problem in budgeting and finance for North Carolina local governments. The revaluation is occasionally completed late, creating uncertainty about what the tax base will be for the budget year following revaluation. Politically it often makes taxpayers antagonistic toward government because first, the assessed valuation of much property increases so much at one time, and second, the revaluation also shifts the incidence of the property tax from personal property and property of public service companies to real property. Chapter 12 offers a full discussion of the process and the issues related to the octennial revaluation.

Tax Rate Limitations and Voter Approval

Property taxes levied for certain purposes are subject to rate limitations and in certain cases must be approved by the voters. These restrictions are pursuant to Article V, Section 2(5), of the state constitution, which says:

> The General Assembly shall not authorize any county, city or town, special district, or other unit of local government to levy taxes on property except for purposes authorized by general law uniformly applicable throughout the State, unless the tax is approved by a majority of the qualified voters of the unit who vote thereon.

This provision means that unless the General Assembly specifically authorizes the levy of property taxes for a particular purpose, and does so on a statewide basis, property taxes may be levied for that purpose only with voter approval.

To implement Article V, Section 2(5), the General Assembly has enacted G.S. 160A-209. This statute places functions that cities are authorized to undertake in three groups. Cities may levy property taxes for Group I functions without restriction on tax rate or amount. The only important function in Group I is debt service. Cities may levy property taxes for Group II functions without a vote, to a maximum rate of $1.50 per $100.00 valuation of taxable property. Group II functions appear in table 11-2. A city may hold a referendum on the levy of property taxes for any Group II function. If such a referendum passes, the tax levied under it does not count against the $1.50 limitation. A city may also hold a referendum to raise the $1.50 limitation. Group III functions include all authorized activities that the General Assembly has not specified as either Group I or Group II functions. The statute does not list Group III functions, but the most important ones for cities appear in table 11-3. If the voters approve the levy of property taxes for a Group III function, any tax levied for that function does not count against the $1.50 rate limitation.

Tax-Levy Formula

The formula for setting the property tax rate and enacting property taxes is relatively simple. One determines the amount of property tax revenue that must be *collected* to balance the budget, considering estimated expenditures and the amount of money that other revenue sources are likely to yield. (The full property tax levy—the total dollar value of the tax enacted—is seldom collected. Most North Carolina cities and towns collect 95 to 99 percent of the levy.) In calculating the amount of tax expected to be collected, the city may not use an estimated collection percentage that exceeds the current year's collection percentage [G.S. 159-13(b)(6)].

Table 11-2
Group II Functions, for Which Property Taxes May Be Levied by a City
without a Vote, within a $1.50 Rate

Administration	Jails
Air pollution	Joint undertakings with other local
Airports	governments for any Group II function
Ambulance service	Libraries
Animal protection and control	Mosquito control
Arts programs and museums	Off-street parking
Auditoriums, coliseums, and	Open space
convention centers	Parks and recreation
Beach erosion and natural disasters	Planning
Bus lines and mass transit systems	Police
Cemeteries	Ports and harbors and cooperative programs
Civil defense	with North Carolina Ports Authority
Community development	Public housing
Debts and judgments	Senior citizens programs
Defense of employees and officers	Sewage collection and disposal
Drainage	Solid waste collection and treatment
Economic development	Streets
Elections	Traffic control and on-street parking
Electric power	Urban redevelopment
Fire protection	Water resources development in federal
Gas transmission and distribution	water resources development projects
Historic preservation	Water supply and distribution services
Hospitals	Watershed improvement projects
Human relations	

Table 11-3
Group III Functions, for Which a City May Levy Property Taxes Only After an
Approving Vote of the People

Armories	Manpower programs
Cable television	Mental health and alcoholism programs
Community action programs	Sedimentation control
Employment service offices	Joint undertakings of any of preceding
	functions

To illustrate the procedure for determining the tax levy and rate, a city must collect $700,000 in property tax revenue to balance its budget, and its finance officer expects 96 percent of the property tax levy to be collected. Being a little conservative, the finance officer assumes that the collection percentage for the coming budget year will be 95 percent. She divides the $700,000 of required property tax revenue by .95, which yields a property tax levy of $736,800. She then divides the $736,800 levy by taxable valuation—say, $80,000,000—which yields $.009210. This figure is multiplied by 100 to produce a tax rate of $.921 cents per $100.00. Fractional cents may be but are usually not levied in the tax rate. To check her arithmetic, the finance officer multiplies the $80,000,000 by .00921, which yields $736,800, the levy; and 95 percent of the levy is $700,000 in collected property taxes.

Collection of Property Taxes and Cash Flow

Property taxes are due on September 1, but taxpayers may delay payment until January 5 without incurring a penalty. In one county in a recent year, 5 percent of the tax levy was paid in August; 4 percent in September and in October; 15 percent in November; 36 percent in December; 28 percent in January; and 6 percent in all other months of the year.[4] Such a concentration of property tax collections in the middle of the fiscal year is typical of most North Carolina cities and counties. It means that they must rely on fund balances and other revenue sources to finance expenditures during the first part of the fiscal year.

Uniformity of Taxation and Service Districts

With one exception the state constitution requires that the city property tax rate be uniform throughout the city. The uniformity rule applies only to the levy of the tax, not to the use of its proceeds, which may be spent wherever needed. The exception arises from Article V, Section 2(4), of the state constitution, which authorizes the General Assembly to permit counties and cities to define special service districts within their borders and to levy additional taxes in those areas to provide services or facilities that are not offered throughout the unit, or that are offered at a lower level in the rest of the unit.

Pursuant to this constitutional provision, the General Assembly has enacted the Municipal Service District Act of 1973, G.S. Chapter 160A, Article 23. It authorizes cities to define a part of the city as a service district, to levy a property tax in the district additional to the citywide property tax, and to use the proceeds to provide services to the district. A service district is in no way a separate unit of government. It is simply a geographic designation, a defined part of the city in which the city levies extra taxes and provides extra services. Cities may define a service district for any of the following functions:

1. Beach erosion control and flood and hurricane protection works
2. Downtown revitalization projects
3. Drainage projects
4. Off-street parking facilities
5. Sewage collection and disposal systems
6. Watershed improvement projects

A city may define any number of service districts in order to provide one or more of the preceding functions. In fact, however, of the approximately thirty-five cities that have established districts since the Municipal Service District Act was enacted, almost all have done so for downtown revitalization. Such downtown districts may be used for projects to finance services, such as additional police patrols or more frequent solid waste collection, and capital improvements. A downtown revitalization project may also include promotional and development activities to further the economic well-being of the downtown.

A service district does not have its own governing body separate from the city council. It is governed by the council of the city that establishes it.

G.S. 160A-537 establishes the standards for creating a service district. A district is defined by simple action of the council. No petition from district residents is required, although a council could establish a policy of defining districts only when it receives such a petition. Nor need a vote be held within the district in order to create it. A council has only to find that the district needs the proposed service or services "to a demonstrably greater extent" than the rest of the city. Usually a city sets the effective date for a new service district at the beginning of the first new fiscal year after its council adopts the resolution approving the district, though the council may postpone that date. Once the district becomes effective, the unit must "provide, maintain, or let contracts for" the service or services involved within a reasonable time, not to exceed one year.

Reimbursements

As noted earlier, the General Assembly establishes the kinds of property that will be included in the property tax base, through its power to exempt, and to classify and exclude, property from taxes. Traditionally when the General Assembly has sought to subsidize an activity or a group by excluding property from the tax base, it has placed the fiscal burden of the subsidy on local governments, through reduction in their tax bases. In recent years, however, the legislature has sometimes coupled tax-base exclusions with state reimbursement to local governments of some or all of the lost tax revenues.

The earliest of these reimbursements partially compensates local governments for taxes lost to the so-called homestead exemption, under which the principal residence of certain older or disabled taxpayers is partially excluded from the tax base. There has since been a series of reimbursements triggered by the exclusion from the tax base of retailers', wholesalers', and manufacturers' inventories. By 1992–93 the annual statewide total of such reimbursements to cities was about $75 million.[5]

During the state's budgetary difficulties in 1990 and 1991, local governments became very concerned that one way in which the state might attempt to balance its own budget would be to reduce or eliminate reimbursement payments. Although that has not yet happened, it remains a threat. Local officials would prefer a stable, locally controlled revenue source to continued reliance on reimbursement payments. Therefore the future of reimbursements is uncertain.

Payments in Lieu of Taxes

The state constitution exempts from taxation property owned by the federal government or by the state or a local government. Occasionally, however, the government that owns the property makes payments in lieu of taxes to the government that could have taxed the property had it been privately owned. Most of these payments are directed by statute. For example, the federal housing law requires each local housing authority to make payments in lieu of taxes to the city or cities in which its projects are located. A city may use such payments for any public purpose.

Table 11-4
North Carolina Local-Option Sales and Use Tax Revenue,
1984–85 through 1993–94

Fiscal Year	County Government Share		City Government Share	
	Amount (in millions)	Percent Increase	Amount (in millions)	Percent Increase
1984–85	$308.6	—	$127.0	—
1985–86	340.9	10	144.7	14
1986–87	409.8	20	173.7	20
1987–88	515.4	26	219.5	26
1988–89	580.7	13	250.9	14
1989–90	611.3	5	264.7	6
1990–91	624.8	2	271.7	3
1991–92	640.8	3	269.2	0
1992–93	677.6	6	282.3	5
1993–94	740.7	9	300.3	6

Source: Patricia C. Seawell, North Carolina Department of Revenue, Tax Research Division, telephone conversation with author, 3 July 1995.

The Local-Option Sales and Use Tax

The local-option sales and use tax is in fact two taxes. The *sales tax* is basically a tax on the retail sale or lease of tangible personal property and on the rental of motel and hotel rooms. The *use tax* is an excise tax on the right to use or consume property in North Carolina or elsewhere. The use tax produces about 10 percent of the total sales and use tax yield. Table 11-4 shows the total amounts of sales and use tax proceeds received by counties and cities in recent years. The large increases in the mid-1980s was due in part to a half-percent increase in the rate of tax.

Although cities share in the proceeds of the local sales and use taxes, they do not levy the taxes; rather, counties do, and all 100 counties now levy the full amount authorized. North Carolina has three separate local sales and use taxes; together they total 2 percent. (The state levies a 4-percent sales and use tax for its own purposes; thus the total sales tax in North Carolina is 6 percent.) The three separate local sales and use taxes are distributed differently and carry different expenditure requirements, and for that reason they must be discussed separately. The three taxes, characterized by the articles in G.S. Chapter 105 under which they are levied, are the *Article 39 one-cent tax*, the *Article 40 half-cent tax*, and the *Article 42 half-cent tax*.

Each of the local sales and use taxes is collected by the state, along with the state's comparable tax. After collection costs (slightly less than 1 percent of collections) are subtracted, the net proceeds are allocated among the 100 counties. Net proceeds of the Article 39 tax are returned to the county of collection. Net proceeds of the Article 40 and Article 42 taxes, however, are placed in a statewide pool and allocated among the counties on a per capita basis.

The allocation of the proceeds among governmental units in the county is based on either of two distribution formulas: per capita or ad valorem (property) tax. The county commissioners select the distribution formula and may change it in April of each year, to take effect in the ensuing fiscal year. The per capita formula uses the annual population estimates of the State Department of Administration. The county's total population is added to the population of all cities in the county. This adjusted population figure is divided into the sales and use tax revenue available to the county to determine the county's per capita sales and use tax amount. The resultant figure is then multiplied by the population of the county and each city within it to determine each unit's share of the county's allocation. Under the ad valorem tax formula, the dollar amounts of ad valorem taxes levied by the county and each city in the county are added. The proportion that the levy of each of these units bears to the total levy of all the units in the county is the proportion of the county sales and use tax revenue that each unit receives. Ad valorem tax figures used in the formula are those of the fiscal year immediately preceding the year in which the distribution is made. For the 1994–95 fiscal year distributions, 62 counties used the per capita formula, and 38 used the ad valorem tax formula for the allocation of local sales and use tax proceeds.[6]

Cities may spend the proceeds of the Article 39 one-cent tax for any public purpose that they are authorized to undertake. The proceeds of the second half-cent tax, however, are partially earmarked— 40 percent for the first five years the tax is in effect and 30 percent for the next five years.[7] The earmarked money must be used for water and sewer capital outlay. (If a city has no need of the money for this purpose, it may seek the approval of the Local Government Commission for a waiver of the earmarking.) The counties did not initially levy this half-cent tax at the same time, so the two five-year periods begin at slightly different times in different counties. A general notion of the status of each earmarking period may be gained, though, by noting that the General Assembly authorized the tax in 1986, and almost all counties acted to levy the tax within a few months.

Other Local Taxes

Other local taxes permitted by general law are the privilege license tax, the local franchise tax, the animal tax, the motor vehicle license tax, and the charge for 911 services. In addition, some cities may by local act of the legislature levy occupancy taxes, and one city may levy an admissions tax. Although none of these local taxes are significant in the overall revenue picture for North Carolina's cities, they produce hundreds of thousands of dollars and up to several million dollars each for some of the state's largest cities. Revenue from the taxes authorized by general law may be spent for any public purpose. Revenue from the taxes permitted by local act is usually earmarked for specific purposes.

The Privilege License Tax

The privilege license tax is imposed on the privilege of carrying on a business or engaging in certain occupations, trades, employments, or activities. Under G.S. 160A-211 a city may levy privilege license taxes except as specifically restricted or prohibited by law. The restrictions and the prohibitions appear primarily in Article 2, Schedule B, of G.S. Chapter 105 and arise when the state levies a tax on a business or an occupation.

In devising local privilege license taxes for businesses and occupations, cities have much flexibility. The basic rate of taxation must be uniform for each class of taxpayer (that is, for each occupation and business), but may differ among classes. Some authorities recommend that privilege license taxes be based on gross receipts and be uniform on all businesses and occupations, and increasingly cities are adopting that measure for the tax. The privilege license tax is paid once a year, and the license period usually runs for the fiscal year. An Institute of Government publication entitled *North Carolina City and County Privilege License Taxes* is a useful guide to this subject.[8]

The Cable Television Franchise Tax

Under federal and state law, a city may levy a tax on franchised cable television companies up to 5 percent of gross receipts.

The Animal Tax

Cities may levy taxes on the privilege of keeping domestic animals (G.S. 160A-212). These taxes evolved from local dog taxes, and most cities still tax only dogs. A city is free to decide which domestic animals to tax and to set the rate of the tax. Rates usually do not exceed $5 per animal.

The Motor Vehicle License Tax

G.S. 20-97 authorizes cities to levy a motor vehicle license tax on the privilege of keeping a motor vehicle within the city. For almost all cities this tax may not exceed $5 per vehicle per year.

The Charge for 911 Services

Cities may impose a charge on telephone subscribers for certain costs associated with 911 services. (These charges are typically levied throughout a telephone exchange, and because an exchange rarely follows city boundaries, they are more likely to be levied by counties than cities.) The telephone company collects the charges.

Taxes Permitted by Local Act

Local governments in about seventy counties are permitted by local act to levy occupancy taxes, which are taxes on the occupancy of hotel and motel rooms. Although most of these taxes are levied by county governments, a few are levied by cities, and cities frequently receive a share of the tax, even if the county levies it. In most cases the local act authorizing the tax limits the use that the levying government may make of the proceeds, often to travel- or tourism-related programs, but in some instances it may use the money for any public purpose.

A local act of the General Assembly permits Greensboro to levy a tax on admissions to the Greensboro Coliseum. No other local government may currently levy such a tax.

State-Shared Taxes

State taxes that are shared with cities are the state franchise tax, the gasoline tax, and the beer and wine taxes. Together these taxes contribute from 10 to 25 percent of a city's general fund revenue. Of these state-shared taxes the franchise tax is the most important. It yielded $121.6 million for North Carolina's cities in 1993–94, compared with $92.2 million from the gasoline tax, and $12.4 million from the beer and wine taxes.[9]

The Franchise Tax

Under Schedule C of the Revenue Act (G.S. 105-114 through -129), the state levies franchise taxes on electric, gas, telephone, and telegraph utilities, on railroads and street transportation companies, and on certain business corporations. The franchise taxes on electric, gas, and telephone utilities are shared with cities. The state taxes these companies at a rate of 3.22 percent of gross receipts, over and above the regular state sales tax, and shares with each city an amount equal to 3 percent of such receipts on the sales of service within the city's boundaries. The money is distributed quarterly.

State franchise tax collections and the cities' share of these collections have grown considerably over the last decade. Table 11-5 shows the cities' share. Cities may spend state franchise tax revenue for any public purpose.

The Gasoline Tax

North Carolina's state gasoline tax is now $.17 per gallon, plus the greater of 7 percent of the average wholesale price or $.035 per gallon. From this revenue an amount equal to the proceeds of $.0175 per gallon, plus an additional 6.5 percent of the net proceeds of the North Carolina Highway Trust Fund, is distributed among the state's cities.[10] The legislation that first established this distribution is known as the Powell Bill (after its principal sponsor in the North Carolina Senate), and the moneys distributed to the cities are often called Powell Bill funds.

The available funds are distributed according to a two-part formula. Three-quarters of the local proceeds are distributed among cities on a per capita basis and one-quarter according to the number of miles of nonstate streets in each city. Street mileage information

Table 11-5
City Revenues from State-Shared Taxes, 1983–84 through 1993–94

Fiscal Year	Franchise Tax Amount (in millions)	Franchise Tax Percent Increase	Gasoline Tax Amount (in millions)	Gasoline Tax Percent Increase	Beer and Wine Taxes Amount (in millions)	Beer and Wine Taxes Percent Increase
1983–84	$ 84.7	—	$43.2	—	$ 9.2	—
1984–85	90.3	7	45.4	5	9.6	4
1985–86	96.5	7	47.2	4	10.4	8
1986–87	105.2	9	54.8	16	11.2	8
1987–88	109.4	4	63.8	16	11.4	2
1988–89	110.6	1	66.7	5	11.8	4
1989–90	120.2	9	67.6	1	12.0	2
1990–91	121.6	1	81.2	20	12.6	5
1991–92	116.6	4	81.9	14	11.3	– 10
1992–93	118.3	1	88.1	8	11.7	4
1993–94	121.6	3	92.2	5	12.4	6

Source: Data for 1983–84 through 1990–91 and 1993–94, from Patricia C. Seawell, North Carolina Department of Revenue, Tax Research Division, telephone conversation with author, 3 July 1995, and from unpublished reports, NCDOR; for 1991–92 and 1992–93, from North Carolina League of Municipalities.

comes from annual reports by each city to the State Department of Transportation; annual population estimates come from the State Department of Administration. In 1993 the distributions were $21.10 per capita and $1,459 per mile. Only active cities are eligible to receive state gasoline tax money.[11] The money is distributed annually, around October 1.

Table 11-5 shows city revenues from the state gasoline tax in recent years. Most of the growth has come from increases in the tax or in the cities' share of the tax.

Cities may use gasoline tax revenue only for maintaining, repairing, and constructing streets or thoroughfares, including bridges, drainage, curbs and gutters, sidewalks, and other necessary appurtenances to streets. Street maintenance includes street cleaning and snow removal. Permitted construction expenditures include all phases of construction: right-of-way acquisitions; legal and engineering expenses; salaries, wages, and fringe benefits; materials for construction; payments to contractors, and so forth. Cities may also use gasoline tax money for traffic control devices and signs, debt service on street bonds, and the city's share of special assessments for street improvements. They may not use it for street lighting, on- or off-street parking, traffic police, or thoroughfare planning.

Beer and Wine Taxes

The state levies a number of taxes on alcoholic beverages. These include license taxes, excise taxes on liquor, and excise taxes on beer and wine.[12] The state shares 23.75 percent of its basic excise tax on beer, 62 percent of its net excise tax on unfortified wine, and 22 percent of its excise tax on fortified wine with cities and counties. A city or a county is eligible to share in beer or wine excise tax revenues if beer or wine may legally be sold within its boundaries. If only one beverage may be sold, the unit shares in the tax for only that beverage. General law permits beer and wine to be sold statewide, but allows any county to hold a referendum on prohibiting the sale of either beverage (or both) within the county. The statutes also allow a city in a dry county to vote to permit the sale of beer or wine within its boundaries.

Distribution of state beer and wine tax revenue that is shared with local governments is based on the population of eligible cities and counties. Counties are given credit only for their *nonmunicipal* population. Table 11-5 shows city beer and wine tax revenue for recent years. Since 1983–84 such revenue has grown slowly but steadily. By 1994, 61 counties and 411 cities were receiving some share of the tax. The money is distributed annually, around Thanksgiving. Cities may spend state-shared beer and wine tax revenue for any authorized public purpose.

User Charges

Revenues from user charges finance, in whole or in part, numerous local government functions. *User charges* means charges to those who voluntarily receive or use certain governmental services or facilities. In this context the phrase does not include fees that are incidental to a regulatory program.

Many revenues from user charges are placed in the general fund and are available to support any general fund activity or program. Charges for recreation and cultural activities, ambulance services, cemeteries, and even solid waste collection are budgeted in the general fund in most cities. User charges for these and most general fund services typically cover only a small portion—that is, from 5 to 25 percent—of the cost of providing the service.

Some activities supported by user charges are set up and operated as public enterprises. A *public enterprise* is an activity of a commercial nature that could be provided by the private sector. Most public enterprises are self-supporting or predominantly so. North Carolina cities may operate public enterprises for water supply and distribution, sewage collection and treatment, electric power generation and distribution, gas production and distribution, solid waste collection and disposal, public transportation, off-street parking, airports, cable television, and stormwater (G.S. 160A-311 through -322). A city must set up a separate accounting fund for each enterprise that it owns or operates,[13] and user-charge revenue generated by the enterprise must be deposited in that fund and applied first to pay operating expenses, debt service, and capital outlay for the enterprise [G.S. 159-136(b)(4)]. If any user-charge revenue from the enterprise remains, it may be transferred from that enterprise fund and made available to support general government activities or another enterprise. In establishing user-charge rates for public enterprises or any function supported by user charges, a council may consider the rates of private companies that provide comparable services; for example, the rates for city electric and gas systems are typically set at or near private-market levels.

Reasons for Charging Fees to Users

User charges are feasible for any service that directly benefits individual users, is divisible into service units, and can be collected at a reasonable cost. For example, garbage collection provides a direct benefit to each user (his or her garbage is removed), the service is divisible into units (so many containers emptied at each residence), and the individual users can be charged for each container serviced. To take another example, golfers on a city golf course receive a benefit or a service that is primarily individual; therefore cities typically charge them a fee equal to or almost equal to the cost of their use of the course.

User charges also allocate limited services and resources efficiently. For example, free water, financed by general taxes, tends to be wasted. But when people are charged for water, they use it more economically.

Cities often impose user charges for services that are heavily used by nonresidents—for example, airports, parking facilities, cultural facilities, coliseums, and convention centers. The city cannot tax these people, but it can levy charges on them to recoup its cost for providing a service that directly and individually benefits them.

Types of User Charges

Water and Sewer Services

In North Carolina the most important municipal services that are supported by user charges are water supply and distribution and sewage collection and treatment. The gross receipts generated by the charges for these services contribute 15 to 25 percent of most cities' annual revenue. Almost all cities meter water consumption and charge for water use on this basis. Sewer charges are usually set at some percentage—often at or close to 100 percent—of the water cost. Sewer services to large industries are increasingly metered, and the charge for service to them is based on how much sewage is treated and how difficult it is to treat. A city may charge higher rates for water and sewer services provided outside its boundaries, and such higher outside rates are common; they range from 50 to 100 percent higher than in-town rates. City water and sewer system rates are not subject to regulation by the State Utilities Commission.

Nearly all city water and sewer systems in North Carolina are operated as public enterprises. A water and sewer system is self-supporting when its charges for service plus other recurring revenues—for example, interest earned on water and sewer investments—equal or exceed operating expenses, interest on outstanding water and sewer debt, and depreciation. An increasing proportion of North Carolina's water and sewer systems are self-supporting. In recent years many cities have received grants from the state Clean Water Bond program and from the United States Environmental Protection Agency to construct water and sewer systems; to receive the grants, the cities had to agree to keep their water and sewer systems self-supporting.

Electric Power and Gas Services

Seventy cities in North Carolina operate electric power distribution systems, and eight have natural gas distribution systems. These cities buy power or gas wholesale from private utility companies, joint power agencies, or other *electric cities* (the term for cities that distribute electric power). They then distribute and sell it retail to households and businesses within their boundaries and sometimes in unincorporated areas outside their city limits.

Most of the state's electric cities participate in generating their own power through joint power agencies. North Carolina has two active joint power agencies. One is made up of nineteen electric cities in the central and western parts of the state. This agency owns a 75-percent interest in Unit Two of Duke Power's Catawba nuclear power station. The second active joint power agency is in eastern North Carolina; it is composed of twenty-one electric cities once served by Carolina Power and Light Company and eleven cities once served by Virginia Electric Power Company. It owns between 12.44 and 18.33 percent of five generating facilities (plus a number of canceled plants).

Cities that have electric power and gas systems charge for these services on the basis of metered usage by customers. The cities set their utility rates at about those of private power and gas companies in their areas. Because they do and because the cities do not pay property taxes or federal and state income taxes, their utility systems are normally profitable, although the size of electric system profits has decreased in recent years. Part of these surpluses is spent for capital improvements for the electric and gas systems, and the rest is typically transferred to the general fund to finance general government activities. As with water and sewer services, electric power and gas system rates are not subject to State Utilities Commission regulations.

Solid Waste Collection and Disposal

Cities are authorized to collect and dispose of solid wastes. In practice, cities commonly carry on collection programs, whereas counties provide disposal facilities. Revenues from collection services include the basic service fee, charges for additional or special services, and proceeds from the sale of bags or the rental or the sale of commercial or industrial solid waste containers. A city may charge higher fees for collection outside its borders; but if the county wishes, it may regulate the city's extraterritorial fee schedule through its authority to franchise and regulate collection in unincorporated areas. Revenue generated by disposal facilities comes from fees per weight of load. Recent changes in state law that mandate a reduction in solid wastes entering the waste stream have caused increasing numbers of cities to institute fee-supported collection services. The hope is that if a person's solid waste collection costs are sensitive to the amount of waste generated, people will recycle more, use products with less elaborate packaging, and otherwise reduce the amount of waste generated.

Public Transportation

Cities may also own and operate public transportation systems, although only a few cities now do so. The principal local revenue source for transportation is fares. City fare schedules are not subject to State Utilities Commission regulation. Because public transportation is a Group III function, the voters must approve any subsidy from property tax proceeds for a public transportation system.

Off-Street Parking

Cities may provide off-street parking and charge for the privilege of parking in such a facility on either a short- or a long-term basis. The revenue from these charges usually supports all operating costs and sometimes all debt service costs for off-street parking.

Airports

Cities have authority to own and operate airports. A variety of fees, charges, and rentals raise revenue for an airport operation: landing fees; rentals of hangar space, terminal space, and land; franchise fees for ground transportation services; sale of gasoline, aircraft materials, and the like; and parking receipts.

Cable Television

Cities are authorized to establish and operate cable television systems, and one—Morganton—started doing so in 1992. The fees charged to subscribers are the basic revenue source.

Stormwater

Recent federal law has required large cities in North Carolina and elsewhere to increase their stormwater management programs significantly. A number of cities are in the final stages of establishing programs that will be operated as enterprises, with the principal revenue being a monthly charge to property owners, added to the water and sewer bill.

Ambulance Services

Although cities may provide ambulance services, the statutes give priority to their provision by counties. The principal ambulance charge is a per-trip fee.

Cemeteries

Cities may operate cemeteries. The revenue sources for cemetery operations are the sale of plots and perpetual care, and fees for opening and closing graves and for setting monuments and markers.

Recreation and Cultural Activities

Cities may operate recreation programs, art galleries, museums, auditoriums, coliseums, convention centers, libraries, and the like. Many cities have recreation programs, but only a few have established the other facilities listed. A variety of support sources are available in this category of service: admission charges, concessions, facility rentals, and parking receipts. For most recreation and cultural programs, user charges are not the principal means of support; rather, the programs are largely financed by tax proceeds. Auditoriums and coliseums can be more readily supported by user charges. G.S. 153A-264 entitles any resident of a county or a city that operates or contributes to a public library to free use of the library; user charges are therefore generally inappropriate for libraries.

Other Local Revenues

Other local revenues for cities consist of fees that are incidental to regulation, special assessments, profits from ABC stores, investment earnings, and revenues from other miscellaneous sources—for example, penalties from enforcement of municipal ordinances.

Fees Incidental to Regulation

Local governmental regulatory programs frequently have associated fees and charges. The person being regulated is required to meet some or all of the costs occasioned by the regulated action. Programs that often have such fees and charges are building inspection, land use regulation, health and sanitation regulation, and the like.

The authority to impose reasonable charges for regulatory activities is subsumed in the power to regulate.[14] There is no general statutory limit to such charges, although occasionally the amount of a regulatory fee is set by statute. A rough limit to reasonableness for these fees is the amount necessary to meet the full cost of a regulatory program. Fees and charges for regulatory programs may be used for any public purpose that cities are authorized to undertake. Street parking-meter receipts are the exception; G.S. 160A-301(a) limits the use of these receipts to expenditures for enforcing traffic and parking ordinances and regulations.

Special Assessments

Special assessments are levied against property to pay for public improvements that benefit that property. Like user charges and unlike property taxes, special assessments are levied in some proportion to the benefit received by the assessed property. Unlike user charges, special assessments are levied against property rather than persons— and typically for public improvements rather than for services. Although special assessments are a relatively minor revenue source in the overall revenue picture of North Carolina's cities, contributing only about 1 percent or so to annual revenues, they are significant in reimbursing the cities that use them for such projects as extensions to water system lines and street improvements.

Under G.S. 160A-216, cities may levy special assessments to finance the following public improvements: streets, sidewalks, water systems, sewer systems, storm sewer and drainage systems, and beach-erosion control and hurricane flood-protection works. A few cities may, by local act, levy special assessments to finance street lights and to keep lots free of weeds.

The amount of each assessment must bear some relationship to the amount of benefit that accrues to the assessed property. The most common basis of assessment is front footage: each property is assessed on a uniform rate per foot of property that abuts on the project. Other bases include the size of the area benefited or the value added to the property because of the improvement. Many cities levy special assessments under local acts that authorize other bases of assessment.

The council may levy special assessments without a petition except for street and sidewalk improvements. For such improvements the council must first receive a petition requesting the assessments from a majority of the property owners to be assessed who represent over half of the front footage of the property to be improved. (By charter provision a number of cities may assess for street and sidewalk improvements without a petition.)

Special assessments may be and often are paid in annual installments along with interest on the amount outstanding in any year. Special assessment revenue, including the interest portion, generally is not earmarked and may be used for any public purpose. Local improvements are often financed from special assessment revolving funds; assessment revenues generated from finished projects are used to finance new improvements.

Special assessments may not be levied until the improvement being financed has been completed. Therefore the city must advance its own funds to construct the improvement.

Profits from ABC Stores

Both cities and counties may establish and operate ABC stores. By mid-1994, 107 cities had their own ABC systems, which produced net profits of $10.8 million that year. (In mid-1994 there were 47 county ABC systems, which produced $15.7 million in net profits.)[15] Net profits equal gross sales less state taxes, the per-bottle add-on tax, the cost of goods, the contributions for ABC law enforcement and education and rehabilitation programs for alcoholics, and operating expenses. About 80 percent of the net profits is distributed to the units that are authorized to share in the profits. The rest of the profits is kept by the ABC systems as working capital.

ABC profits are constitutionally subject to no limitations except public purpose. Local acts of the General Assembly frequently earmark all or some portion of a system's profits, however.

Investment Earnings

G.S. 159-30 authorizes cities to invest their idle cash. Funds for investment come from bond proceeds, capital and operating revenues, and fund balances. Local governments' most common investments are certificates of deposit in banks and savings and loan associations, obligations of the United States Government (called *Treasuries*), and obligations that mature no later than eighteen months from the date of purchase of certain agencies set up under federal law (called *Agencies*). The interest earned on investments must be credited proportionately to the funds from which the moneys that were invested came. Investment income has become a much more important revenue source in recent years because of high interest rates and more sophisticated case management practices by North Carolina local governments. North Carolina's cities often earn investment income, exclusive of income on invested bond proceeds, that is the equivalent of 5 or more cents on the property tax rate.

Minor Sources

Cities have many minor sources of local revenue. For example, many units receive payments from other local governments for joint or contractual programs. Some units receive funds from the management of their property, such as from leasing of city-owned building space or land, or sale of surplus equipment. Cities receive refunds on the state gasoline and sales taxes that they pay. Occasionally a city receives a bond forfeiture from a prospective vendor or a contractor.

Federal and State Aid

The previous edition of this book, published in 1982, included a discussion of federal aid. Since that time, however, the federal aid system of the 1970s has virtually disappeared. General revenue sharing has been repealed. The number of categorical grants and block grants available to local governments has been significantly reduced, as have the amounts of money appropriated by Congress for remaining grant programs. The great part of federal financial assistance reaching local governments now comes through the state, appropriated by the General Assembly and sometimes accompanied by matching state moneys. For the most part, then, the federal aid system has become indistinguishable from the state aid system. Furthermore the preponderance of such aid goes to counties rather than cities. Therefore a discussion of federal aid is no longer justified.

Nor is there an extensive program of purely state aid to cities. There are no programs that have wide distribution patterns; rather, programs of state aid to cities are categorical in nature and, except for the Clean Water program, relatively small.

Clean Water

The state has provided funds to local governments since 1977 to assist in wastewater treatment or collection projects and in water supply and distribution systems. The state money was initially provided from a state bond issue, then from current appropriations, and most recently from a second bond issue. By and large the state assistance has been used to reduce the local share in projects that are primarily funded with federal moneys.

Other Programs

Other programs of state aid include airport construction grants and public transportation grants, administered by the Department of Transportation; water resources development grants, administered by the Department of Environment, Health, and Natural Resources; and as a kind of indirect support to cities, grants to volunteer fire departments and rescue squads, administered by the Department of Insurance.

Additional Resources

Lawrence, David M. *Local Government Finance in North Carolina*, 2d ed. Chapel Hill, N.C.: Institute of Government, The University of North Carolina at Chapel Hill, 1990.

Notes

1. Bureau of the Census, *Government Finances, 1978–79* (Washington, D.C.: Government Printing Office, 1979), 64; and *Government Finances, 1991–92* (Washington, D.C.: Government Printing Office, 1992), 1.

2. N.C. CONST. art. V, §§ 2(2), (3).

3. *Id.*; G.S. 105-275 through -278.9.

4. These data were supplied by the county finance director.

5. North Carolina League of Municipalities, *North Carolina Municipal Reimbursements and State-Collected Local Revenues for Fiscal Year 1992–93* (Raleigh, N.C.: the League, 1994), 20.

6. Patricia C. Seawell, North Carolina Department of Revenue, Tax Research Division, telephone conversation with author, 3 July 1995.

7. A similar portion of the proceeds of the first half-cent tax was also earmarked, but that earmarking expired after ten years.

8. William A. Campbell and David M. Lawrence, *North Carolina City and County Privilege License Taxes*, 3d ed. (Chapel Hill, N.C.: Institute of Government, The University of North Carolina at Chapel Hill, 1990; 4th ed. forthcoming).

9. Patricia C. Seawell, North Carolina Department of Revenue, Tax Research Division, telephone conversation with author, 3 July 1995.

10. G.S. 136-41 through -41.3; 1981 N.C. Sess. Laws ch. 690.

11. North Carolina Department of Transportation, *1993 North Carolina State Street Aid Allocations to Municipalities* (Raleigh, N.C.: NCDOT, October 1993), 3–4.

12. North Carolina Department of Revenue, Tax Research Division, *Statistics of Taxation 1980* (Raleigh, N.C.: NCDOR, 1981), 172.

13. Water and sewer systems operated as a consolidated enterprise may be accounted for in the same fund. G.S. 159-26(b)(4).

14. Homebuilders Ass'n of Charlotte v. City of Charlotte, 336 N.C. 37, 442 S.E.2d 45 (1994).

15. Mike Herring, North Carolina Alcoholic Beverage Control Commission, telephone conversation with author, 14 June 1995.

12 Administration of the Property Tax

William A. Campbell and Joseph S. Ferrell

Contents

FROM COLONIAL TIMES to the present, North Carolina has used taxes on land and other forms of property to finance the operations of government. At one time, property taxes were the major revenue source for both the state and its local governments. Today the property tax is levied only by local governments, but it remains an important element of North Carolina's overall system of taxation. When all state and local taxes are combined, the property tax ranks third in importance. In the 1992–93 fiscal year, North Carolina taxpayers paid $2.6 billion in property taxes, $4.4 billion in state income taxes, and $3.3 billion in state and local sales taxes. Cities rely on the property tax as the major source of local tax revenue.

Most of the day-to-day administration of the property tax is handled by county officials. Some cities collect their property tax levies, but many cities contract with the county for this purpose. The major involvement that most cities have with the property tax occurs at budget time when the tax is levied and its yield in the upcoming fiscal year is estimated.

Section 1, Characteristics of the Property Tax

Two characteristics of the property tax distinguish it from other forms of taxation and underlie the methods of determining tax liability and enforcing collection. The first characteristic is that the property tax is levied on property itself, not on the owner. The second is that the tax is measured by the value of the property as a marketable item, not by the owner's ability to pay. Thus it is often called an *ad valorem* tax, from the Latin phrase meaning "according to value."

The concept of the property tax as being levied on property itself underlies the legal principle that the property tax lien—that is, the obligation to pay the tax—attaches directly to land and other forms of real property. The nature of the lien and other methods of enforcing collection are discussed in section 2 of this chapter. Calculating tax liability according to the value of the item taxed lies behind the complex administrative structure needed to inventory taxable property, estimate its value, and assess it for taxation. These aspects are discussed in section 1 of this chapter.

The Tax Base

North Carolina local governments have no power to devise and impose taxes on their own authority; they acquire all of their taxing power by delegation from the General Assembly. The federal and state constitutions restrict the General Assembly's power to devise tax schemes and to delegate the taxing power to local government units. The federal Constitution forbids the states to tax property outside their borders, property moving in interstate commerce, and property being imported from or exported to a foreign country as long as the importation or exportation process continues. For the purposes of this chapter, the North Carolina Constitution's restrictions on the structure of the property tax base are more important. The General Assembly may select the kinds or the classes of property to be taxed, but it must do so by laws that are uniform throughout the state. It may not delegate the power to classify property for taxation to local governments, and it may not exercise that power with an act that applies in less than all local taxing units. Furthermore, once the General Assembly chooses a class of property for taxation, the class must be taxed *by uniform rule*, which means that property in any given class may have only one value for tax purposes and must be taxed according to the same rules by each local taxing unit in which it may be situated. The state constitution itself exempts all publicly owned property from taxation, and it authorizes the General Assembly to exempt or grant preferential tax treatment to other types of property as long as it does so by uniform, statewide legislation.

Against the background of these constitutional limitations, the North Carolina General Assembly has exercised its full power to subject property to ad valorem taxation. The law provides that all property within the jurisdiction of the state is subject to taxation unless it is specifically exempted by the constitution itself or a statute enacted in accordance with the constitutional limitations described earlier. All the many categories of property thus subjected to taxation are known collectively as the *tax base*.

Very little privately owned property is automatically excluded from taxation in North Carolina. Even though the General Assembly may have enacted legislation excluding a certain class of property from the tax base, in most cases the owner must claim the benefit by applying for it to the county assessor, who, on the basis of the written application, determines whether the property qualifies for the benefit claimed. Most of the excluded classes of business personal property require an annual application. Most of the other types of exempt and excluded property require an application that need not be renewed unless circumstances change in ways that would affect the property's continued eligibility. Government-owned property and a few other types, such as cemeteries and business inventories, require no application for exemption.

Appraisal, Assessment, and Tax Rate Defined

G.S. 105-273 defines *appraisal* and *assessment*. As used in North Carolina property tax law, the words *to appraise* mean to determine market value, and the words *to assess* mean to fix tax value. The two terms represent two processes or steps in the taxing procedure: first, all property must be appraised; then it must be assessed for taxation.

G.S. 105-284 requires that unless property falls within a special class entitled to preferential treatment, it be assessed at 100 percent of its appraised value. Ultimately this means that market value (as determined by the county assessor's appraisal) and tax value are the same, except in the few cases in which property is classified for taxation on a different basis. For example, real property designated as a historic structure or site by a local historic properties ordinance is eligible to be assessed for taxes at 50 percent of its appraised value.

The third concept necessary to an understanding of how property is taxed is the tax rate—the factor that determines the amount of taxes due on taxable property. In North Carolina, tax rates are customarily expressed in dollars per $100. A typical municipal tax rate might be $.70 per $100, which means that for every $100 in value of taxable property, $.70 is due in taxes.

Local taxing units determine their annual tax rates by dividing the total amount of tax revenue needed to balance the budget by the total assessed value of taxable property in the unit. This decimal fraction is then applied to the assessed value of taxable property belonging to each taxpayer. The result is the tax due from the taxpayer's property for the current fiscal year. For example, a taxpayer owning property with a total assessed value of $40,000 in a city whose tax rate is $.70 per $100 will owe $280 in city property taxes (the decimal-fraction equivalent of a rate of $.70 per $100 is .007; $40,000 × .007 = $280).

Assessment Systems

Broadly conceived, ad valorem taxes are levied for the benefit of North Carolina local governments on virtually all kinds of property, real, tangible, and intangible, but there are distinct assessment systems for the property (both real and personal) of public service companies, motor vehicles, and the general mass of real and personal property. Although the primary focus of this chapter is the legal status and the administrative structure of the tax levied on the general mass of real and personal property, a full understanding of the importance of ad valorem taxation in North Carolina must include awareness of how and by whom the other major categories of property are taxed.

Intangible Personal Property

From 1937 to 1955 the major types of intangible personal property were taxed by the state for the benefit of local governments and were exempt from local property taxes. These types included stocks and bonds, accounts receivable, and notes and other evidences of debt. The 1995 General Assembly repealed the intangibles tax and exempted from local property taxes the forms of intangible personal property that had been subject to the intangibles tax. Forms of intangible personal property that have not been specifically exempted from local property taxes remain in the general mass of property subject to local taxation. These include leasehold interests in exempt real property, franchises, trademarks, and patents.

Public Service Company Property

G.S. 105-333 through -344 governs listing, appraisal, and assessment of public service company property. Most of the real and personal property belonging to regulated public utilities is listed, appraised, and assessed for taxes by the state Department of Revenue. Taxable values as determined by the state are then certified to local taxing units, which levy taxes on these companies at the same rate as they levy taxes on the general mass of taxable property. Public service companies subject to this assessment system include railroads, electric power companies, telephone and telegraph companies, natural gas distribution companies, petroleum and natural gas pipelines, airlines (with respect to flight equipment only), bus companies (with respect to rolling stock only), and motor freight carriers (with respect to rolling stock only). Public service company property comprises about 7 percent of the statewide property tax base.

Motor Vehicles

G.S. 105-330 through -330.8 governs listing, appraisal, and assessment of motor vehicles. Taxation of the great majority of motor vehicles in the state is administered entirely by the county. The county assessor lists and appraises all registered vehicles located in a city, and the county tax collector bills and collects the taxes on behalf of the city each month. The tax due date is linked to the registration or the renewal of registration of each vehicle, so each month the taxes on approximately one-twelfth of all vehicles located in a city become due. Each month the county finance officer remits a check to the city for the motor vehicle taxes collected during the previous month. The county may retain up to 3 percent of the municipal taxes collected as an administrative charge.

Real and Personal Property in General

All property not included in one of the special assessment systems described earlier and not exempted from taxation by the state constitution or an act of the state legislature is subject to ad valorem taxation through a listing, appraisal, and assessment system that is centered on the county assessor. The remainder of this chapter discusses that system in detail.

Property Tax Listing and Assessing

The county is the basic government unit for appraising and assessing property for taxation, not only by the county itself, but also by cities and special taxing districts within its borders. In North Carolina, property has only one tax assessment, which is used by all taxing units that are entitled to tax it. For this reason, municipal governing boards and officials have virtually no role to play in appraisal and assessment.

Administrative Structure

The General Assembly has prescribed a statewide standard official framework for assessment in each county. The statutes that provide the tax assessment and collection framework, or *machinery*, are commonly and collectively known (in this chapter and elsewhere) as the Machinery Act.

At the heart of this administrative structure stand the 100 county assessors. Above them are the county commissioners, who name them, pay them, and provide them with assistance. Beneath the assessors stand their assistants (appraisers, clerks, and listers, for example), whom they select and supervise. The work of the county assessor is subject to review in the first instance by the county board of equalization and review, which in most counties is composed of the board of county commissioners sitting in another capacity. The primary task of the board of equalization and review is to hear and decide taxpayers' appeals. At the state level, over and above the county officials, is the Department of Revenue and the Property Tax Commission. As an administrative agency, the department is charged with supervising the valuation and the taxation of property by local units of government and, in limited cases, with appraising property for local taxation. The Property Tax Commission, on appeal, has power to review and change listing and valuation decisions made by local officials or the Department of Revenue.

The Listing Process

Under G.S. 105-301 through -312, all taxable property, both real and personal, must be listed for taxation each year, and it is the owner's legal responsibility to list what he or she owns with the appropriate taxing units. Failure to comply with the listing requirement results in an automatic penalty: 10 percent of the amount of tax that will become due for the following fiscal year. If the owner fails to list his or her property, the assessor is required to do so in the owner's name.

Roles of the County and the City in the Listing Process

G.S. 105-326 through -328 governs the role of cities in the listing process. Real and personal property must always be listed with county officials. The *abstract*—that is, the listing form—must indicate the city and the special districts, if any, in which the property is also situated. The county commissioners are almost always the tax-levying authority for special districts; they therefore perform the listing function for those districts as well as for the county.

Cities have a choice in listing property. They may copy their listings from the county records, or if they prefer, they may set up their own machinery for securing lists of property subject to municipal taxation. Cities that copy their listings from county records remain responsible for deciding for themselves whether specific property should be listed for taxation or be granted immunity. This responsibility is independent of county decisions about the same property. If a county and a city differ on whether certain property is entitled to exemption or other preferential treatment, the owner may appeal to the Property Tax Commission for resolution of the dispute.

Although a city may elect to do its own listing, it must accept the property valuations fixed by the county authorities unless it lies in more than one county. (In that case the statute grants special appraisal authority to the city.) The requirement that cities accept county valuations of property has led most of them to copy county listings rather than make their own.

The Location of Property for Listing Purposes: A Matter of Jurisdiction

G.S. 105-301, -304, and -305 determine where property is taxable. By its nature, real property is fixed in one location; thus the law logically provides that taxable real property must be listed in the county in which it is situated. If real property is located within the boundaries of a city or a special tax district, that fact must be indicated on the abstract when the property is listed.

On the other hand, the very essence of personal property is its movability. Determining the place where it is taxable demands more complicated rules. In general, if personal property is within the jurisdiction of the state, the Machinery Act makes the owner's North Carolina residence (or lack of residence) the key fact in determining where his or her personal property is to be listed. Thus the local unit in which the owner resides ordinarily has the right to tax his or her personal property. If the property is held or used at the owner's business premises, however, it must be taxed there. This requirement makes it essential to determine the "residence" of business firms as well as of individuals.

Duty to List

In general, all taxable property must be listed in the name of the person who owned it on January 1 of the particular year, and it is the owner's duty to list the property by completing a listing form and signing an affirmation stating that the form is accurate and complete (G.S. 105-308). The regular listing period runs through the month of January. Extensions of time in which to list may be obtained on written application filed during the regular listing period. Extensions may not run later than April 15.

Property Not Subject to Taxation: Requests for Tax Relief

Under G.S. 105-282.1, exempt and excluded property is not required to be listed, but owners of such property have the burden of demonstrating to tax authorities that it qualifies for this preferential treatment by filing a request for tax relief. This is normally done during the regular listing period. (No request need be made for government-owned and certain other types of property.)

For most of the property currently granted tax immunity or other preferential treatment by the Machinery Act, requests for relief must be made only once, then revised thereafter when improvements or additions are made or a change in use occurs. However, for some types of business-related exempt and classified property, annual requests for relief must be made.

As the requests are made or revised, tax officials are expected to review them to ensure that the property in question qualifies for the relief requested. If a request for relief is required but has not been made, the property involved is treated the same as property for which a required listing was not made.

The Valuation Process

Statutory Elements of Value

The North Carolina Constitution contains no instructions on how property is to be valued for tax purposes. It simply states that if property is taxed, the General Assembly may divide it into classes, and as long as the taxes are uniform in their application within a class, they will be upheld.

Market-Value Standard

Although the state constitution is silent on the valuation process, the Machinery Act specifies in detail the valuation standard, the factors to be considered in arriving at an estimate of value, and the procedures that assessors must follow in appraising property for taxes. All property not singled out for preferential treatment is subject to a single valuation standard. G.S. 105-283 defines the *market-value standard* as follows:

> All property, real and personal, shall as far as practicable be appraised or valued at its true value in money. . . . that is, the price estimated in terms of money at which the property would change hands between a willing and financially able buyer and a willing seller, neither being under any compulsion to buy or to sell and both having reasonable knowledge of all the uses to which the property is adapted and for which it is capable of being used.

The standard draws no distinction between real and personal property and allows no room for arbitrary methods of appraisal that are not directly based on the operation of the free market.

Use-Value Appraisal of Farmlands

In 1973 the General Assembly enacted the only instance in the Machinery Act of a departure from the market-value standard of tax appraisal (G.S. 105-277.2 through -277.6). Land used for agricultural, horticultural, or forestry purposes, if it meets certain other qualifications, may be taxed on the basis of its value in its present use, even though it may have a greater market value for other uses. G.S. 105-277.2 defines *present-use value* as "the value of land in its current use as agricultural land, horticultural land, or forestland, based solely on its ability to produce income, using a rate of nine percent (9%) to capitalize the expected net income of the property and assuming an average level of management."

Market value still plays an important part in the taxation of farmlands, however. If they cease to be used for agricultural, horticultural, or forestry purposes, or if title to them passes to someone outside the immediate family of the owner, a *deferred tax* must be paid. The amount of this tax is the difference between the taxes paid based on the use value and the taxes that would have been paid based on the market value for the preceding three years. The county has responsibility for performing use-value appraisals when requested, just as it must make market-value appraisals.

Time for Appraisal

G.S. 105-285 through -287 establishes the time for appraisal.

Personal Property

Personal property must be appraised each year when it is listed for taxation. The law assumes that the true value of personal property fluctuates rapidly; therefore the law insists that the value of personal property be examined annually. This annual appraisal may be a simple process, as in determining the value of an automobile, or it may be highly complex, as in selecting an appropriate depreciation rate for unusual industrial machinery. The day as of which the value of property is to be determined is January 1.

Real Property

The North Carolina law adopts a different attitude toward real property. It assumes that real property values do not fluctuate rap-

idly and, accepting some of the practical arguments against too-fre-
quent appraisal, requires that all real property be reappraised only
every eight years.

G.S. 105-286 divides the counties of the state into eight groups
and establishes an *octennial revaluation schedule*, that is, a base revaluation year for each group. Each county must conduct a general revaluation of real property in the base year for its group and every
eighth year thereafter. This establishes the minimum level of effort
required of the county.

A county may find it desirable to revalue real property before the
end of its current eight-year cycle. The law places no obstacles in the
path of a county wanting to do so. Several counties are moving toward
cycles of four or five years rather than eight. The legal effect of conducting a revaluation earlier than the law specifies is simply to require
that the next revaluation take place within eight years thereafter; the
county is not thereafter bound to adhere to the shorter cycle.

Appraisal Techniques

Having established market value as the appraisal goal, the North
Carolina tax statutes go on to indicate what factors should be considered in determining the value of property (G.S. 105-317, -317.1).
With regard to personal property, the appraiser must consider the
following for each item (or each lot of similar items): replacement
cost; sale price of similar property; age; physical condition; productivity; remaining life; obsolescence; economic utility (that is, usabil-
ity and adaptability for industrial, commercial, or other purposes);
and any other factor that may affect its value. Although this statement is not entirely satisfactory, it is valuable as a guide for the appraiser. In effect, it requires him or her to employ every reasonable
standard available in deciding on the true value of personal property.

County appraisers have developed many techniques for estimating the market value of various types of personal property. Industry
pricing guides are available for such major categories as motor vehicles, mobile homes, boats, and aircraft. For machinery and equipment the current value may be estimated by depreciating the original cost to acquire the item according to a standard depreciation
schedule. This technique is further refined in many counties by fac-
toring or "trending" the original cost to current market levels before
applying the standard depreciation factor.

Mass Appraisal of Real Property

A general revaluation of real property is a big undertaking. The typical county has more than 40,000 parcels of land that must be individually appraised. The process must begin early enough to have the results ready in time for tax billing in the revaluation year, but not so early that the value estimates will be out of date by the time they take effect. Also, the cost of the revaluation must be reasonable. A person who is borrowing money from a lending institution to buy a new house can expect to pay about $275 for an appraisal of the house and the lot. A tax appraisal must cost much less than that. Most counties want it done for $16 to $18 per parcel (these figures assume that the revaluation does not entail extra features such as installing a new computer-based office system). Obviously, to accomplish a job of such magnitude at reasonable cost requires specialized appraisal techniques that rapidly, efficiently, and economically yield a high degree of accuracy.

Development of an Appraisal Manual for Establishing Market Value

G.S. 105-317 lays out the essential elements of a modern mass appraisal system that accomplishes the objective just summarized. The foundation of the system is the assessor's *appraisal manual*—or as the statute describes it, a "uniform schedule of values, standards, and rules to be used in appraising real property in the county." The manual is formulated from two basic sources: the local real estate market and nationally developed data on the cost of building construction, adjusted to reflect local building costs. The manual identifies a large number of characteristics exhibited by real property in the county and indicates the dollar amount that each characteristic can normally be expected to contribute to the value of a given parcel of land or a given building according to a unit of measure appropriate to the characteristic. For example, the appraisal manual contains a land schedule. For agricultural land or forestland the appropriate unit of measure is usually the acre, whereas urban land is typically measured by square footage, front footage (the number of feet of a lot that front on a street), or standard-size lot (such as the 100-foot by 200-foot lot often found in newer subdivisions). Buildings are usually measured by square footage.

The value increments attributed to the various units of measurement vary considerably. Some land may be worth $5,000 per acre, other land only $400 per acre. Buildings of top-quality construction may be priced at $70 or more per square foot, lower-quality buildings at $40. Other characteristics may increase or reduce the value indicated by the basic unit of measurement. Agricultural land may be decreased in value by poor soil or topography. The value of an urban residential lot may be adversely affected by other development in the neighborhood. The value of buildings is always adjusted to reflect accrued depreciation.

The characteristics just mentioned are but the tip of the iceberg; a well-conceived appraisal manual will identify many more. The manual is a comprehensive, complex document designed to enable the assessor to estimate the value of thousands of parcels and buildings accurately, efficiently, and rapidly by means of a manageable number of characteristics that influence value.

Developing the appraisal manual is the single most important step in a revaluation. The manual's designation of the property characteristics to be examined and the value increment to be attributed to each determines the accuracy with which the assessor can estimate the fair market value of real property in the county. If the manual sets values too high, most properties will be appraised higher than market value. If the values are too low, most properties will be underappraised. If too few characteristics are used, the accuracy of appraisals will vary widely from parcel to parcel. If too many are used, the assessor may not be able to complete the job on time. Because the appraisal manual is so important, the Machinery Act requires that it be formally approved by the board of county commissioners. The act also permits any property owner of the county to test the validity of the appraisal manual before the Property Tax Commission.

Development of a Special Schedule for Establishing Present-Use Value

Similarly the assessor establishes a special schedule for appraising eligible agricultural land, horticultural land, and forestland at its present-use value. For this purpose he or she has available a statewide valuation manual prepared by the Department of Revenue with the assistance of the Use-Value Advisory Board, which is composed of representatives of the Agricultural Extension Service, the state Department of Agriculture, and the state Division of Forest Resources. This manual is based on the net income per acre that can be anticipated from growing corn and soybeans in each soil type found in the state. Use of the Department of Revenue's manual is not mandatory, but it carries great authority.

Approval of the Manuals

After the manuals on market value and present-use value have been prepared and a public hearing has been held, the board of county commissioners adopts them and places a newspaper notice stating that it has done so. Property owners then have thirty days to challenge the manuals by appeal to the state Property Tax Commission on grounds that the manuals do not adhere to the appropriate statutory valuation standard (that is, that they will produce values that are too high, too low, or inconsistent). The commission has the power to order the board of county commissioners to revise the manuals if they do not adhere to the statutory valuation standard—and it has done so on occasion. The commission's decision may be appealed to the North Carolina Court of Appeals.

Preparation of Record Cards

After the manuals are adopted, the assessor prepares a record card for each parcel of land in the county. On this card he or she notes all the characteristics of the parcel that will be considered in making the appraisal. Although land and the buildings on it are appraised separately, data for both appear on the same property record card. The Machinery Act specifically directs the assessor to show on the card all characteristics considered in appraising the parcel, points out that they must be consistent with the appraisal manual, and requires that the data be accurate.

Collecting data about property characteristics is called *listing* the property. For buildings this process consists of measuring their outside perimeter, showing special features such as air conditioning and the number of bathrooms, and recording such crucial factors as depreciation and quality or grade of construction. For agricultural land and forestland, the process is similar but simpler. Characteristics of such land usually include the number of acres in the tract, its road frontage if the manual identifies this as a relevant characteristic, its fertility or productivity grade, and any crop allotments. Much of this information can be gathered by persons who are not trained appraisers; for example, no advanced training is needed to measure a house or compute the number of acres in a tract of land from the tax map. Other computations, such as estimating depreciation, require trained and experienced personnel.

Appraisal of Property

After the basic data have been gathered and recorded on the property record card, the parcel is appraised. G.S. 105-317 requires that a competent appraiser do this for each parcel individually. The first step is usually carried out mechanically. The property characteristics gathered by the listers are used to compute a preliminary value estimate according to the value increments set out in the manual for those characteristics. This value is tentatively recorded on the property record card. The appraiser then takes the cards into the field and revisits each property. This procedure, known as the *review*, is the critical fine-tuning step in which the training, the experience, and the judgment of the appraiser play a large part. Recognizing the crucial importance of appraising property on the basis of accurate data, G.S. 105-317 gives each property owner the right to have the assessor (or one of the assessor's agents or employees) actually visit and observe the property to verify the accuracy of characteristics on record for it.

Notice to Property Owners

The Machinery Act requires that when the final review has been completed, the assessor send each property owner a written notice of the appraised value on each parcel owned by that person. At this point, nearly all assessors allow for a period of informal appeals that is not required by law. Typically the value notice sent to taxpayers states that they may contact the assessor for an appointment to review the appraisal if they believe it to be in error. Most counties engage the services of a professional appraisal company to assist in the revaluation, although the legal responsibility remains entirely in the hands of the assessor appointed by the county commissioners. If professional appraisers have helped in the revaluation, taxpayers may obtain an appointment with the company appraiser, at which they may be able to persuade him or her that a mistake was made in measurement, calculation, or judgment. The time allowed for these informal appeals is within the discretion of the assessor.

Formal Appraisal and Assessment

When the informal appeal process is over, the assessor formally appraises and assesses each parcel. Ideally the appraisals are adopted before January 1 of the revaluation year. This may not always be possible because the appraisal may take more time than was planned or there may be more informal appeals than were expected. In any event, after the assessor has adopted the appraisals, the taxpayer may appeal directly to the assessor at any time before the county board of equalization and review convenes.

Valuation Appeals

G.S. 105-322 governs listing and valuation appeals. The county board of equalization and review is the local body charged with hearing property tax valuation appeals. It also has the power to correct the tax lists or to increase or reduce values on its own motion if it finds such action to be warranted. As explained earlier, in most counties the board of equalization and review is the board of county commissioners sitting in another capacity. In some counties, however, the board of commissioners has created a special board to hear appeals. In some others a special board has been created by local act of the General Assembly. In all counties the primary work of the board of equalization and review is essentially the same: to hear and decide valuation appeals. The board convenes no earlier than the first Monday in April and no later than the first Monday in May. It sits for at least four weeks and may meet longer if needed. It may not sit later than July 1 except to decide appeals filed before that date. Before the board convenes, it must publish its hours of operation in a newspaper. It must also publish any change in that schedule.

A taxpayer appealing a listing or an appraisal may simply appear at a scheduled meeting of the board of equalization and review, but writing or calling for an appointment is always preferable. Proceedings before a county board of equalization and review are informal. However, the appealing taxpayer should expect that the board will want specific testimony on why the taxpayer is entitled to the relief he or she is seeking. The most persuasive evidence in a valuation appeal is the testimony (oral or written) of a qualified appraiser who disagrees with the assessor's appraisal.

The Property Tax Commission hears appeals from the county boards of equalization and review across the state. The commission's hearings are more formal than those of the county boards, but are still relatively informal compared with court proceedings. Testimony is recorded and may be transcribed, documentary evidence is formally introduced, and both sides (the county and the taxpayer) are usually represented by attorneys. An appellant taxpayer who believes that the Property Tax Commission made an error of law in reaching its decision on his or her property may appeal further to the North Carolina Court of Appeals. Normally this is the court of last resort; however, the North Carolina Supreme Court will hear a property tax appeal if it believes that a major issue of law in the case warrants its attention.

Adjustment of Real Property Values in Nonrevaluation Years

The North Carolina plan for taxing property envisions annual appraisal of personal property and octennial appraisal of real property. Yet for the sake of equity and uniformity, some parcels of real property may need reappraisal in a year in which general revaluation of real property is not undertaken. G.S. 105-287 directs the assessor in a nonrevaluation year to reappraise specific parcels in order to correct clerical or mathematical errors in the former appraisal; correct appraisal errors resulting from misapplication of the county's appraisal manual; or recognize an increase or a decrease in value resulting from some factor other than normal depreciation, economic changes affecting property in general, or certain improvements such as repainting and landscaping. Reappraisals made under the authority of G.S. 105-287 must conform to the appraisal manual adopted in the last revaluation year so that they will represent market or present-use value as of January 1 of the revaluation year, rather than current value. Also, these appraisals take effect as of January 1 of the year in which they are made and do not affect previous tax years.

Discovered Property

To *discover* property, as the expression is used in the tax statutes, means to find that an item of taxable property has not been listed for taxation during the annual listing period established by law, or has been listed at a substantial understatement of value, quantity, or other measurement. Under G.S. 105-312 it is the duty of the assessor to see that all property not properly listed during the regular listing period is accurately listed, assessed, and taxed. The assessor is also required to file reports of such discoveries with the governing boards of all taxing units affected by the discovery at such times and in such form as those boards may require.

The fact that cities have statutory authority to conduct their own tax listing, rather than obtain their tax lists from the county, means that they also have authority to discover unlisted property independently of county officials. For example, a city may disagree with the county assessor's ruling that certain business personal property does not have a tax situs within the city, or a city may disagree with the county assessor's action approving an exemption for certain property. In such cases the city may proceed to discover the property for municipal taxation. When a city council decides to undertake a discovery, it must designate some official, usually the city tax collector or the city clerk, to perform the duties assigned by law to the county assessor, and the council itself must undertake the duties assigned by law to the county board of equalization and review or the board of county commissioners.

When a city identifies unlisted real or personal property to be discovered, the city assessor must first sign an abstract listing it and, in accordance with the best information available, make a tentative appraisal of it. If the property has been listed for county taxes, the city assessor must adopt the county's appraisal of the property. The assessor must then mail a notice to the person in whose name it has been listed. This notice must give the name and the address of that person, a brief description and a tentative appraisal of the property, and a statement to the effect that the taxpayer has thirty days in which to object to the listing and the appraisal.

If the taxpayer objects in writing within the thirty-day period, the assessor must arrange a conference to give the taxpayer an opportunity to present any evidence or argument regarding the discovery. The assessor must make a final decision within fifteen days, and the taxpayer has fifteen days (measured from the time at which he or she is officially notified of the decision) to appeal that decision. Both the listing and the appraisal are subject to the right of appeal to the city council and from there to the Property Tax Commission.

When property is found not to be listed for a given year, it has often not been listed for a number of years, or perhaps it has never been listed. Accordingly there is a statutory presumption that it should have been listed by the same taxpayer for the preceding five years. The taxpayer can overcome this presumption by showing that the property was not in existence, that it was actually listed for taxation, or that it was not his or her duty to list the property during all or some of the years in question.

The penalty for failing to list property for taxes is an amount equal to 10 percent of the tax for each listing period that has elapsed since the failure to list occurred. For example, if a taxpayer failed to list his or her property for 1990 taxes and was subjected to discovery procedures in September 1995, the penalty for the 1990 failure to list would be 60 percent of the tax. If the taxpayer had failed to list the same item of property for each of the intervening years, the penalty rates would be 50 percent for 1991, 40 percent for 1992, and so on down to 10 percent for 1995.

Special cases may arise in which the city council feels that the statutory provisions place an undue burden on the property owner. In such situations the council is empowered to reduce the penalty (or even the principal amount of the tax) to what it finds to be equitable. This is true whether the discovery has been made by county officials on behalf of the city or by the city through its own officials. This authority does not arise until the discovery procedures have been completed, and it may be exercised only on written petition of the taxpayer. The assessor has no authority to waive any part of the penalty or the tax, and the board may not delegate such authority to him or her. Because each request for relief is unique, the board should act on it separately. Cities that obtain their tax lists from the county typically delegate to the board of county commissioners the authority to rule on discovery appeals.

Section 2, Collection of the Property Tax

The Office of Tax Collector

Cities with special legislation or a charter provision that provides a method for selecting tax collectors must adhere to the provisions of that legislation or provision relating to the tax collector's selection and term of office [G.S. 105-395(c)]. In the absence of special legislation, the city council of each city must appoint a tax collector, for a term to be determined by the appointing body, to collect the taxes levied by the city [G.S. 105-349(a)]. Ordinarily, collectors are named early enough in the fiscal year to prepare themselves to take over the new taxes when the time comes for collection.

Often persons charged with tax collection also have other duties or are elected to other offices. The Machinery Act, the legislation that provides for city and county property taxation (G.S. Ch. 105, Subch. II), declares the office of tax collector to be "an office that may be held concurrently with any appointive or elective office other than those hereinafter designated, and the governing body may appoint as tax collector any appointive or elective officer who meets the personal and bonding requirements [discussed under the next heading, Qualification as Tax Collector]" [G.S. 105-349(e)]. Only two restrictions are placed on double-office-holding by collectors, but they are important:

> A member of the governing body of a taxing unit may not be appointed tax collector, nor may the duties of the office be conferred upon him. A person appointed or elected as treasurer or chief accounting officer of a taxing unit may not be appointed tax collector, nor may the duties of the office of tax collector be conferred upon him except with the written permission of the secretary of the Local Government Commission who, before giving his permission, shall satisfy himself that the unit's internal control procedures are sufficient to prevent improper handling of public funds. [G.S. 105-349(e)]

Historically the clerk in many small towns has served as treasurer and tax collector and has performed the duties commonly assigned to a financial officer or an accountant. The Machinery Act disallows these combinations unless a city can satisfy the secretary of the Local Government Commission that its internal control procedures are sufficient to prevent mishandling of funds. In addition, G.S. 128-1.1 limits to two the number of offices that one person may hold concurrently.

Pay for tax collectors varies greatly in both amount and basis. Most cities pay their collectors salaries, often with a modest travel allowance in addition. A few collectors are paid wholly from commissions on collections. The Machinery Act provides simply that "[t]he compensation and expense allowances of the tax collector shall be fixed by the governing body" of the taxing unit [G.S. 105-349(d)].

Qualification as Tax Collector

Governing bodies of cities are not free to assign collection responsibility for any tax year to an individual unless the person selected can meet the prescribed legal standards [G.S. 105-352(b)]:

Before the tax receipts for the current year are delivered to the tax collector, he shall have:

(1) Delivered to the chief accounting officer of the taxing unit the duplicate receipts issued for prepayments received by the tax collector.

(2) Demonstrated to the satisfaction of the chief accounting officer that all moneys received by the tax collector as prepayments have been deposited to the credit of the taxing unit.

(3) Made his annual settlement . . . for all taxes in his hands for collection.

(4) Provided bond or bonds as required by [law] for taxes for the current year and all prior years in his hands for collection . . . .

This could hardly be plainer. Proper settlement for prepayments, proper settlement for prior years' taxes, and a proper bond to cover the new and old taxes that the tax collector is to collect are prerequisites to delivery of the tax books to the collector. The word *settlement* as used in this connection has a technical meaning (see the discussion under the heading Settlements, later in this chapter).

The courts have not defined *satisfactory bond* for a local tax collector. A useful test might be a reasonable approximation of the maximum amount of money that the collector will have in his or her hands at any one time, plus a reasonable allowance for cumulative losses.

By law, any member of a governing body who votes to deliver the tax receipts to the tax collector before the collector has met the requirements just listed is individually liable for the amount of taxes charged against the tax collector for which he or she has not made satisfactory settlement. Any member who so votes is also guilty of a misdemeanor punishable by fine or imprisonment, or both, in the discretion of the court [G.S. 105-352(d)(1)].

Removal of the Tax Collector

Collectors who cannot meet the bonding and settlement requirements outlined in the preceding section are not entitled to serve and may be removed or simply not permitted to enter on collection work. However, cases may arise in which it is questionable whether a collector should be permitted to remain in office, even though he or she has met the statutory prerequisites and conditions. The manner in which a tax collector may be removed depends on the source of law under which he or she holds office. Because the Machinery Act preserves local legislation relating to the selection of tax collectors [G.S. 105-395(c)], pertinent provisions of the special act or charter creating the tax collector's office in a given city may control the circumstances and the procedures under which he or she may be dismissed. Governing bodies of units subject to such local legislation should seek the advice of their attorneys before attempting to remove a tax collector from office, especially if the collector is an elected official. The Machinery Act gives the city council express authority to remove the tax collector from office during the tax collector's term for good cause after giving notice in writing and an opportunity to appear and be heard at a public session of the council [G.S. 105-349(a)]. *Cause* in this sense refers to reasons recognized by the law and sound public policy as sufficient warrant for removal—that is, legal cause, not merely cause that the appointing power in exercising its discretion may deem sufficient. Moreover, the cause must relate to and affect the administration of the office and must be restricted to something of a substantial nature directly affecting the rights and the interests of the public.[1] For example, misappropriation of funds would be cause for discharge.

Deputy Tax Collectors

City councils are free to decide whether to name deputy tax collectors. They also have the authority to set the term and the pay of each deputy collector as well as the amount of his or her bond. Most important, unless the council specifically limits the scope of the deputy's authority, he or she has the authority to perform, under the direction of the tax collector, any act that the tax collector may perform [G.S. 105-349(f)].

Necessary Collection Records

The words *tax records* as used in the Machinery Act have a precise and technical meaning. Two records are included: the *scroll*, which the law defines as the record of property valuations; and the *tax book*, which the law defines as the record of taxes due. The two may be combined [G.S. 105-319(a)], and they customarily are. This combined record is usually called the scroll, but not always. City records must be kept "in some public office of the municipality designated by the governing body of the city or town" [G.S. 105-319(a)]. The law permits the governing body to give the collector a copy of the scroll when he or she is charged with collection [G.S. 105-319(a)].

Apart from the tax records, the most important document in the collection process is the *tax receipt.* The primary purpose of the tax receipt is twofold: to furnish the taxpayer with evidence of payment and to furnish the tax collector with the payment information necessary to support a credit in the settlement. Depending largely on the complexity of the accounting procedures of a particular city, receipts may be prepared in sufficient copies to provide a tax notice, possibly a second notice, an official receipt for delivery to the taxpayer on payment, an auditor's copy, and an office or permanent copy. The law specifies the minimum information to be shown on the receipt given the taxpayer [G.S. 105-320(a)]. One of the required entries is "[t]he rate of tax levied for each unit-wide purpose, the total rate levied for all unit-wide purposes, and the rate levied by or for any special district or subdivision of the unit . . . ."[G.S. 105-320(a)]. This breakdown may not be finally determined until shortly before the deadline for setting the tax rate (July 1 for all units; see chapter 13); thus to avoid delay in having receipt forms printed, the statute allows this information to be furnished on a separate sheet of paper, properly identified, when the official receipt is delivered on payment [G.S. 105-320(A)(6)].

North Carolina law does not require that property owners be sent or receive bills or notices of taxes due. On the contrary, "[a]ll persons who have or may acquire any interest in any real or personal property" are charged with notice that their property is or should be listed for taxation, that taxes are or may become a lien thereon, and that if taxes are not paid, the proceedings allowed by law may be taken against the property. This notice is conclusively presumed, whether or not such persons have actual notice (G.S. 105-348). In only one place does the Machinery Act mention tax notices: G.S. 105-350(8) empowers the governing body in its discretion at any time to require the collector to send out tax bills or notices. This practice is a means for improving collections and one that should always be used; nevertheless, no property owner has an enforceable right to a bill or a notice, and his or her failure to receive one cannot be considered a valid reason for not enforcing the full tax claim (principal and interest).

Reports of Progress in Collection

The tax collector must keep adequate records of all collections [G.S. 105-350(4)], and at least as often as each regular meeting of the governing body, must submit a report showing the amount collected on each year's taxes with which the tax collector is charged, the amount remaining uncollected, and the steps being taken to encourage or enforce payment [G.S. 105-350(7)]. Collectors usually comply with this reporting requirement, but governing board members often disregard the reports. Having to make a periodic statement with respect to their efforts may spur collectors to action, and a periodic record placed before it of what is being done and what has and has not been collected is information that no responsible board would ignore. The board can draw comparisons between the current year's position and positions on the same date in prior years, with useful results.

Due Dates for Taxes: Periods Covered

As pointed out earlier, city property taxes are due and payable on the first day of September of the fiscal year for which they are levied [G.S. 105-360(a)]. They are legally collectible until their collection is barred by the statute of limitations. The statute of limitations requires all taxing units to initiate an action to enforce any legal remedy provided for the collection of tax claims within ten years of the date on which taxes are due (G.S. 105-378).[2]

The period of time for which taxes are levied, or the period that taxes for a particular year are said to "cover," has occasionally caused confusion. Units of local government operate on a fiscal year beginning July 1 and ending June 30; property is listed for taxation each year in January. Property is listed at the beginning of the calendar year to be taxed by the unit to support its operations in the fiscal year opening next after January 1; and for enforcement purposes the lien of taxes levied for that fiscal year attaches to real property on January 1 [G.S. 105-355(a)].

Order of Collection

The tax books and receipts are to be turned over to the collector between July 1 and September 1 if he or she has been able to meet the requirements pertaining to settlement and bond already discussed [G.S. 105-352(a)]. An important feature of this *turning over* or *charge* is the order of collection. The city's governing body is to issue the order, deliver a copy to the collector, and insert a copy in its minutes [G.S. 105-321(b)]. The wording of the order is prescribed by statute [G.S. 105-321(b)]:

STATE OF NORTH CAROLINA

COUNTY (or City or Town) OF _____

To the Tax Collector of the City of _____ :

    You are hereby authorized, empowered, and commanded to collect the taxes set forth in the tax records filed in the office of _____ _____ and in the tax receipts herewith delivered to you, in the amounts and from the taxpayers likewise therein set forth. Such taxes are hereby declared to be a first lien upon all real property of the respective taxpayers in the City of _____, and this order shall be a full and sufficient authority to direct, require, and enable you to levy on and sell any real or personal property of such taxpayers, for and on account thereof, in accordance with law.
    Witness my hand and official seal, this _____ day of _____ 19_____ .

_____   (SEAL)
Mayor, City (or Town) of _____
Attest:

_____
Clerk to the City (or Town) of _____

Examination of the order indicates that it commands the collector to collect, declares the already-existing fact that taxes are a first lien on real property, and requires the collector to "levy on and sell" any real and personal property owned by the taxpayers if necessary to enforce collection. The order enumerates the lawful means for collecting taxes that the collector is, by virtue of his or her position, required to employ. Even if the governing body fails to issue the order of collection, the collector has full power and responsibility to levy, garnish, and prepare the necessary information on which the governing body may order sale of liens against real property and, eventually, initiate foreclosure [G.S. 105-350, -366, -369, -373 through -375].

Property Tax Lien

The North Carolina Supreme Court has defined a *lien* as "the right to have a demand satisfied out of the property of another."[3] This right runs against the property rather than against the owner. As used in the property tax laws of this state, the lien for taxes runs in favor of the local governmental unit and may be enforced against the property of the taxpayer.

Each year the city acquires a lien against all *real* property that each taxpayer owns within the city on January 1; this lien attaches automatically, by operation of law, without any effort on the collector's part [G.S. 105-355(a)]. On the other hand, the taxing unit does not obtain a lien against *personal* property until the collector takes action to levy or garnish [G.S. 105-355(b)].

Because the lien attaches to real property as of January 1, obviously it attaches not only before the tax becomes due but also before the exact amount of the tax can be known. Thus until the amount of the tax is computed, the lien is indeterminate, but this in no way impairs either its validity or its priority. The lien against real property, it will be seen, includes not only the taxes levied on the real property itself but also the taxes levied on all the taxpayer's personal property by the taxing unit. Of the taxpayer's total tax bill, as it will be determined between July and September of the ensuing fiscal year, the only amount that does not attach to a given parcel of realty on January 1 is the amount levied on other parcels of real property. In addition, "[a]ll penalties, interest, and costs allowed by law shall be added to the amount of the lien for the principal amount of the taxes" [G.S. 105-355(b)].

The lien for taxes attaches to *personal property* of the taxpayer only when the property is *seized* by the tax collector, either under levy or under attachment and garnishment. Once attached, however, the lien against personal property includes all taxes due the city, not merely those levied on the particular item seized, nor merely those levied on the personal property of the taxpayer [G.S. 105-355(b)].

Once the lien attaches to either real or personal property, affirmative action is required to obtain its release. Ordinarily the tax lien on real property continues "until the principal amount of the taxes plus penalties, interest, and costs allowed by law [has] been fully paid" [G.S. 105-362(a)]. This is true with regard to personal property seized under levy or attachment as well as real property subjected to the automatic lien. Nevertheless, it is possible for a careless or untrained collector to release the taxing unit's lien by failing to require taxpayers and other interested persons in each instance to pay the full amount secured by the lien before he or she issues a full-payment receipt. Because the lien is the city's security, great care should be exercised to ensure that collectors adhere to the law, and a diligent collector should be given full support by the city council.

The lien of the property tax against real property is superior to all other liens and rights (except certain liens for other taxes), regardless of the claimant and regardless of whether the other liens or rights were acquired before or after the lien for taxes [G.S. 105-356(a)(1), (2)]. Furthermore, once the lien has attached to real property, its priority is not affected by transfer of title, by death, or by receivership of the property owner [G.S. 105-356(a)(3)].

As already pointed out, taxes, interest, penalties, and costs become a lien on personal property from and after levy or attachment and garnishment. What is the priority of such a lien when it attaches? The Machinery Act makes a distinction between (1) the status of a lien for taxes on the specific property seized and (2) the status of a lien for taxes on other property: the portion of the lien that is for taxes levied on the specific personal property is superior to all other liens and rights, both prior and subsequent [G.S. 105-356(b)(1)]; the portion that is for taxes levied on property other than the specific personal property is inferior to prior valid liens and perfected security interests, but superior to all subsequent liens and security interests [G.S. 105-356(b)(2)].

Payment of Taxes

As a general rule, tax collectors are authorized to accept nothing in payment of taxes except existing national currency [G.S. 105-357(a)]. They may take a check (and all collectors do), but they do so at their own risk. Thus a collector who accepts a check in payment of taxes is permitted to issue the receipt immediately or withhold it until the check is collected [G.S. 105-357(b)]. Sometimes collectors require a certified or cashier's check as an alternative to withholding the receipt until an ordinary check has cleared.

When a collector has taken a check in payment of taxes, has issued a receipt, and has had the check returned unpaid, the taxes are treated as being unpaid. In such a case the collector has the same remedies for collection that he or she would have had if the receipt had not been issued (plus the right to bring a civil suit on the check), provided that the collector has not been negligent in presenting the check for payment [G.S. 105-357(b)].

In the course of their work, tax collectors are often asked for information on whether some individual owes taxes or whether any taxes are outstanding against a given parcel of real property. There is only one statutory provision on this subject in North Carolina, and it applies only to taxes that constitute a lien on real property. The statute requires the tax collector to give written statements of the taxes that constitute a lien on specified real property when requested to do so by (1) an owner of the property, (2) an occupant of the property, (3) a person having a lien on the property, (4) a person having a legal interest or estate in the property, (5) a person or a firm having a contract to purchase or lease the property, (6) a person or a firm having a contract to make a loan secured by the property, or (7) the authorized agent or attorney of anyone in one of the first six categories. Before furnishing the statement, the collector should require the requester to identify the person in whose name the property was listed for each year for which tax information is desired. Of course, the collector need not furnish such a statement unless the taxes have become due and are "in his hands for collection" [G.S. 105-361(a)].[4]

When a qualified person requests and obtains a written statement and actually relies on it by (1) paying the amount of taxes certified as a lien on the property, (2) purchasing or leasing the property, or (3) lending money secured by the property, then in relation to that person a lien will exist against the property only to the extent that taxes and special assessments are stated to be due in the certificate. An understatement of the tax liability in the certificate causes the lien to be released to the extent of the amount of the understatement. Thus although the city's claim for the full amount of taxes due is in no way released or compromised by the taxpayer's reliance on an erroneous certificate, the tax collector should exercise care in preparing a certificate to avoid surrendering the city's security for payment.

Once a lien is lost, collectors are liable on their bond for any loss that the city suffers [G.S. 105-361(b)]. It must be emphasized that the statutory provisions are exclusive with respect to both the kind of information that may be compelled and the persons who are entitled to it: no one other than members of the enumerated categories is entitled to a binding certificate, and no one at all can force the collector to state the amount of personal property taxes (other than those constituting a lien on the specified real property in which a qualified person is legally interested) owed by any taxpayer. Finally, an oral statement made by the tax collector about the amount of taxes, penalties, interest, and costs due binds neither the tax collector nor the city [G.S. 105-361(d)].

Partial Payments

Unless the city council directs otherwise, the tax collector is required to accept partial payments on taxes and to issue partial-payment receipts for the amounts accepted (G.S. 105-358). The council may by resolution prohibit acceptance of partial payments altogether, and in no event is the city required to accept partial payment on taxes for any year before the annual budget estimate for that year has been filed [G.S. 105-358, -359(b)]. In addition to its power to refuse acceptance of partial payments, the city council has explicit authority to prescribe by regulation an amount or a percentage of the entire tax as the required minimum for a partial payment, as long as the amount or the figure adopted applies uniformly to all tax bills (G.S. 105-358). If partial payments are accepted, the statute requires that they be applied first against accrued interest, penalties, and costs, if any, and then against the principal amount of the tax (G.S. 105-358).

Prepayments

Taxpayers are permitted to pay taxes before they are legally due. That is, taxpayers may prepay. Unlike the situation with regard to partial payments, the city has no discretion to refuse a tender of full payment of a tax after the annual budget estimate has been filed [G.S. 105-359(a), (b)]. However, the obligation to accept

Table 12-1
Interest Schedule for Late Payment of Taxes

If taxes are paid . . .	Then the interest rate is . . .
From September 1 through January 5	0
During the remainder of January	2%
During February	2¾%
During March	3½%
Thereafter	3½% plus ¾% per month, the additional ¾% being added on the first day of each month

prepayments carries with it no requirement that the taxpayer be given a discount for early payment. If the council chooses to provide discounts for prepayment—that is, for payment before September 1—it may do so by adopting a resolution or an ordinance, not later than the first day of May preceding the due date of the taxes to which the resolution or the ordinance first applies, specifying the amounts of the discounts and the periods during which they are to be applicable [G.S. 105-360(c)(1)]. The resolution or the ordinance must be approved by the Department of Revenue, and the discount schedule must be published at least once in some newspaper that has a general circulation in the taxing unit [G.S. 105-360(c)(3)]. The Department of Revenue will not approve a discount schedule if in its opinion the rates are excessive or the discount period is unreasonable [G.S. 105-360(c)].

Interest for Late Payment of Taxes

The substance of the statewide statute establishing interest for late payment of taxes [G.S. 105-360(a)] can be reduced to the schedule in table 12-1.

Enforcement of Collection of Property Taxes

Cities have a general power to bring suits to collect debts in their own names as governmental units. However, the tax statute itself supplies the collector, in administering the duties of tax collection, with specific legal means for enforcing collection against the taxpayer's property: in the case of real property, advertisement of the lien, followed by foreclosure; and in the case of personal property, levy or attachment and garnishment. Having these remedies, neither the collector nor the city itself, except in certain limited instances, may bring a civil action to enforce collection of property taxes.[5]

Enforcement against Real Property: Lien Advertisement and Foreclosure

The lien of taxes attaches to all the taxpayer's real property in the taxing unit as of January 1 of the year in which the property is listed and assessed; the lien encompasses the owner's personal property taxes as well as the taxes on the real property itself [G.S. 105-355(a)]. Thus when any or all of the taxes are not paid, the lien against the real property may be enforced.

Report of Delinquent Taxes Constituting Liens on Realty

In February of each year the tax collector is required to report to the governing body of the taxing unit "the total amount of unpaid taxes for the current fiscal year that are liens on real property . . . ." [G.S. 105-369(a)]. When it receives this report, the governing body must order that the liens be advertised and set a date on which advertisement is to occur [G.S. 105-369(a)].

Time and Place of Lien Advertisement

The city council may choose any date from March 1 through June 30 on which to advertise the liens. It must advertise them at least once and may advertise them additional times [G.S. 105-369(c)]. It must advertise them by posting a notice at the city hall and by publishing a notice in a newspaper of general circulation [G.S. 105-369(c)].

Foreclosure

Foreclosure of the lien on real property should be viewed as the collection remedy of last resort. It is a complex and expensive remedy and should be used only after the collector has attempted to collect the delinquent taxes through attachment or levy. Governing board members and tax collectors must realize that there is nothing automatic about foreclosure. It requires affirmative action.

The first action is for the council to decide which of the available foreclosure methods it will employ. For this it will need the city attorney's advice. Two methods of foreclosure are available under North Carolina law: one is characterized as being "in the nature of an action to foreclose a mortgage" [G.S. 105-374(a)], and the other is described as an action "*in rem*" [G.S. 105-375(a)].

Under the first method, an action "in the nature of an action to foreclose a mortgage" is brought in the appropriate division of the General Court of Justice to foreclose the lien and to obtain an order from the court for sale of the foreclosed real estate [G.S. 105-374(a), (k)]. The courts have been zealous to protect all interested parties against loss of real property in this way; thus great care must be exercised to ensure that all interested parties receive adequate notice of the action. Such a suit requires the services of an attorney. Because it is practically impossible to discover and provide for all indicated contingencies, the most that the tax attorney can do, and the least, is to make a careful check of the records and bring in all parties who may thereby be revealed as having an interest in the property, plus all other parties who by such reasonable inquiry as the records may suggest might be discovered.

Determining how to proceed and whom to involve as necessary parties is only part of the difficulty of bringing a tax foreclosure "in the nature of an action to foreclose a mortgage." Costly title examinations must be made to determine who these proper parties are; diligent search must be made to determine where they are; and care must be taken to ensure that all necessary procedures are followed.

Under the alternative, or *in rem,* procedure, not earlier than six months after the lien sale, the council may order the collector to file with the clerk of superior court in each case a certificate showing the name of the taxpayer, the amount of the unpaid lien, the years for which the taxes are due, and a description of the property [G.S. 105-375(b)]. When docketed and indexed by the clerk in the name of the listing taxpayer, this certificate constitutes a judgment having "the same force and effect as a duly rendered judgment of the superior court directing sale of the property . . . ." [G.S. 105-375(d)]. At least thirty days before filing the certificate as a judgment, however, the tax collector is required to give notice by registered or certified mail to the listing taxpayer and the current owner at their last-known addresses, informing them that such a judgment will be docketed and that execution will be issued on it. Lienholders of record must also be given notice of the docketing [G.S. 105-375(c)]. Ten days after the notices have been mailed, if the tax collector has no indication that his or her letter was received by either the taxpayer, the current owner, or one of the lienholders, he or she must publish a notice naming the unnotified lienholders, the current owner, and the taxpayer in a newspaper of general circulation for two consecutive weeks [G.S. 105-375(c)]. Before the execution sale any interested party may appear before the clerk of superior court and move to set the judgment aside on the ground that the tax has been paid or that the tax lien on which the judgment is based is invalid [G.S. 105-375(f)].

The execution sale is to be conducted in the same manner as executions on other judgments, except that in lieu of personal service of notice on the property owner, registered or certified mail notice must be given to the last-listing taxpayer at his or her last-known address at least one week before the sale [G.S. 105-375(i)]. The purchaser at the execution sale acquires a fee-simple title, free and clear of all other interests and claims except liens for other taxes or assessments that are not discharged by being included in the purchase price and the judgment [G.S. 105-375(i)]. The procedure that is outlined here is described in the statute, G.S. 105-375, as a *proceeding in rem.*

Unfortunately no one can be certain that this alternative method of foreclosure will stand all constitutional tests. Despite the uncertainty, taxing units may use the procedure with some safety. As with all untested statutes, it is entitled to a presumption of validity. Furthermore, the statute itself contains a saving clause that would seem to insure the taxing unit against any permanent losses even if the courts should hold the procedure unconstitutional [G.S. 105-375(m)]. A good many units regularly use the procedure with marked success.

Enforcement against Personal Property: Levy and Garnishment

The remedies for use in subjecting personal property to the satisfaction of tax claims are based on actual seizure of the property. What happens after the seizure differs according to the remedy being used, but the fundamental element in the remedies remains seizure. If the personal property to be seized is tangible, the appropriate remedy is levy, followed by public sale of the property seized. If the personal property to be seized is intangible—that is, incapable of manual seizure or delivery—the remedy is attachment and garnishment.

Kinds of Taxes Appropriate for Use of Levy and Garnishment

Levy may be used against tangible personal property as a means of enforcing collection of taxes imposed on both real and personal property (that on which the taxes have been levied and any other owned by the taxpayer). Similarly, attachment and garnishment of intangible personal property is available for enforcing collection of taxes imposed on both real and personal property of the taxpayer [G.S. 105-366(a)]. Tax collectors need no special authority from the city council to use levy and garnishment; they have that authority by virtue of their office [G.S. 105-366(a)]. There are two cases, however, in which collectors have a legal duty to use one or both of these remedies before proceeding against the taxpayer's realty:

1. They must do so when "directed to do so" by the governing body [G.S. 105-366(a)(1)].
2. They must do so "[w]hen requested to do so by the taxpayer or by a mortgagee or other person holding a lien upon the real property subject to the lien for taxes if the person making the request furnishes the tax collector with a written statement describing the personal property to be proceeded against and giving its location" [G.S. 105-366(a)(2)].

Time Limitations on the Use of Levy and Garnishment

As a general rule, levy and garnishment may not be used until the tax has become delinquent [G.S. 105-366(b)]—that is, not until after the January 5 following the September 1 due date. The right to use these remedies continues, in the case of taxes that are a lien against real property, until foreclosure is initiated [G.S. 105-366(b)], and in the case of taxes that are not a lien against real property, until foreclosure is barred by the ten-year statute of limitations (G.S. 105-378).

There are four situations in which levy and attachment and garnishment may be used before the date on which the tax becomes legally due:

1. If before January 6 "the tax collector has reasonable grounds for believing that the taxpayer is about to remove his property from the taxing unit . . . ." [G.S. 105-366(c)]

2. If before January 6 "the tax collector has reasonable grounds for believing that the taxpayer is about to . . . transfer [his or her property] to another person . . . ." [G.S. 105-366(c)]

3. If before January 6 "the tax collector has reasonable grounds for believing that the taxpayer . . . is in imminent danger of becoming insolvent . . . ." [G.S. 105-366(c)]

4. "Whenever any wholesale or retail merchant . . . sells or transfers the major part of his stock of goods, materials, supplies, or fixtures, other than in the ordinary course of business, or goes out of business" and the taxes on the transferred property that will fall due on the following September 1 are not paid within thirty days after the described action [G.S. 105-366(d)(3)].

Procedure in Making of Levy

As already indicated, levy is a procedure under which tangible personal property of the taxpayer is seized, advertised, and sold to the highest bidder for cash to pay a tax claim held by the taxing unit. The present law anticipates that the levy will be made by the tax collector or by a properly authorized deputy tax collector [G.S. 105-367(b)]. Ordinarily it is not the responsibility of a law enforcement officer to make levies for taxes. Nevertheless, city councils have power to authorize tax collectors to call on the county sheriff and on municipal police officers to assist in this work [G.S. 105-367(b)]. When the council has passed a resolution to that effect, the collector "may direct an execution against personal property for taxes to the sheriff in the case of county or municipal taxes or to a municipal policeman in the case of municipal taxes" and "the officer to whom the execution is directed shall proceed to levy on and sell the personal property subject to levy . . ." [G.S. 105-367(b)]. As a matter of practice, it is much simpler not to adopt this procedure. If the collector needs protection in making the levy, a law enforcement officer can be called on to accompany him or her. Tax levies, however, should be made by tax collectors.

Procedure in Attachment and Garnishment

The key characteristic of attachment and garnishment is that it invariably draws into the collection process a third person—that is, a person other than the taxpayer and the tax collector. The third person is brought in because the item of intangible personal property to be attached is something that the third person owes the taxpayer or holds for the taxpayer. For example, an employer owes wages to the taxpayer; a bank holds money for its depositor-taxpayer. Debts owed to a taxpayer, though intangible, are nonetheless the property of the taxpayer, and it is this kind of property that the attachment and garnishment procedure enables the tax collector to reach to satisfy the unit's claim for taxes. Like levy, attachment and garnishment is designed to operate outside the courts, and the statute provides that any payment made to the tax collector by the garnishee "shall completely satisfy any liability therefor on his part to the taxpayer" [G.S. 105-368(c)].

The collector initiates the procedure by preparing a notice to be served on both the taxpayer and the person or the institution that holds the intangible item to be seized, informing them of (1) the taxpayer's name and address; (2) the amount of the tax (stating the years for which the taxes were levied); (3) the name of the taxing unit; (4) the property to be attached; and (5) by giving them a copy of G.S. 105-366 and G.S. 105-368, the law under which the collector is proceeding [G.S. 105-368(b)]. Usually the collector need take no further action; the garnishee will remit to the collector the amount demanded. If the garnishee has a "defense or set-off" to assert against the taxpayer—which he or she must state in writing under oath, sending two copies of the statement to the collector by registered mail within ten days—or if the taxpayer asserts a defense in the same manner, then the collector must decide whether to admit the defense or the set-off or to deny it, in whole or in part [G.S. 105-368(d), (f)]. If the collector denies the defense, the collector must notify the garnishee or the taxpayer, as the case may be, in writing within ten days "or within such further time as may be agreed on by the garnishee [or taxpayer] and at the same time the tax collector shall file a copy of the notice of garnishment, a copy of the garnishee's [or taxpayer's] statement, and a copy of the tax collector's objections thereto in the appropriate division of the General Court of Justice . . . where the issues made shall be tried as in civil actions" [G.S. 105-

368(d), (f)]. In most cases the person or the institution garnished pays—when it receives the collector's first notice—the taxing unit's claim against the taxpayer to the extent of the asset held. [If wages are attached, no more than 10 percent per pay period may be reached by this procedure—G.S. 105-368(a).] Only if the collector has not received the garnishee's response within fifteen days after the notice was served, or if the garnishee [G.S. 105-368(e)] or the taxpayer asserts a defense to the garnishment that the collector refuses to allow [G.S. 105-368(d), (f)], is court action necessary.

Reduction, Release, and Refund of the Property Tax

Reductions, refunds, and releases of tax claims are matters to be decided by the city's governing body; they should not be left to the discretion of the tax collector or the county tax supervisor. Furthermore, each claim should be dealt with on its own facts. Once a tax bill has been computed and turned over to the collector, it can be reduced, released, or refunded only on the specific authorization of the governing body [G.S. 105-380, -381(b), -373(a)(3)]. *Tax bill*, as used in this sentence, covers not only the principal amount of the tax but also all interest, penalties, and costs that may have accrued on the unpaid tax [G.S. 105-273(15)].

A strong public policy supports the stability of sources of governmental revenue, and property taxes constitute the major source of county and city tax revenue in this state. For this reason the statutes dealing with forgiveness of property tax claims are strict. G.S. 105-380 opens with the following statement of general policy:

> The governing body of a taxing unit is prohibited from releasing, refunding, or compromising all or any portion of the taxes levied against any property within its jurisdiction except as expressly provided in [the Machinery Act].

This is a rigid prohibition, and failure to abide by it carries personal liability for each member of the governing body:

> Any tax that has been released, refunded, or compromised in violation of this section may be recovered from any member or members of the governing body who voted for the release, refund, or compromise by civil action instituted by any resident of the taxing unit, and when collected, the recovered tax shall be paid to the treasurer of the

taxing unit. The costs of bringing the action, including reasonable attorneys' fees, shall be allowed the plaintiff in the event the tax is recovered. (G.S. 105-380)

The express provisions referred to in G.S. 105-380's statement of general policy are that releases, refunds, or reductions of tax claims must be allowed if the tax was illegal, levied for an illegal purpose, or imposed through a clerical error [G.S. 105-381(a), (b)]. Specific instances in which refunds or releases should be granted include the following (G.S. 105-381):

1. If the assessed valuation of the property taxed has been reduced under proper exercise of legal authority, a reduction in the tax bill follows as a matter of course.
2. If the property concerned is not taxable by the unit—that is, if the property is legally entitled to exemption or if it does not fall within the unit's jurisdiction—a release of the claim is justified.
3. If the property has been listed and taxed twice—that is, *double listed*—one of the duplicate claims should be released.
4. If the rate of tax or any part of it has been illegally levied (as in the following examples), a release is warranted. That is, a release is warranted if the tax—
    a. Is levied for something other than a "public purpose."
    b. Is levied without a vote of the people in a situation in which such a vote is required by law.
    c. Is levied for an amount greater than that authorized by the state constitution, statutes, or a vote of the people.
5. If the amount of the tax has been erroneously computed, through clerical or mathematical error, at a figure higher than is proper, a release or a reduction is appropriate.

City council members should familiarize themselves with these grounds.

Basically there are two situations in which governing bodies must examine the legality of taxes as applied to individual taxpayers:

1. When the taxpayer applies for a release—before he or she has paid the tax to which he or she objects
2. When the taxpayer applies for a refund—after he or she has paid the tax to which he or she objects

The procedures that must be followed before a release may be granted are relatively simple. The taxpayer must submit a written statement of his or her demand to the governing body of the taxing unit. The only time limit governing acceptance of the taxpayer's statement is that implicit in the relief requested: releases are granted only before the tax has been paid. As long as the tax has not been paid, a release may be requested regardless of when the tax first came due. Once the taxpayer's demand has been made, the governing board must decide whether legal grounds for the release exist. If it finds that grounds do exist, then it instructs the official who prepared the tax receipt to make the proper reductions and adjustments in the taxpayer's bill. When the taxpayer pays, he or she pays at the reduced amount (G.S. 105-381).

When a refund is requested—after the taxpayer has already paid some or all of the bill, but before the right to reduction or release has been determined—the problem is not so simple. In fact, under some circumstances, despite the existence of a right to reduction or release, a refund is not to be allowed. The reason is that the statutes impose a limit on the time in which a dissatisfied taxpayer must act to establish an enforceable right to a refund. To obtain a valid refund, the taxpayer must comply with the following requirements:

1. He or she must have paid the tax or a part of it equal to the amount of the refund.
2. He or she must make the demand in writing.
3. His or her demand must be delivered to the governing body "within three years after said tax first became due or within six months from the date of payment of such tax, whichever is the later date" [G.S. 105-381(a)(3)].

If the taxpayer has satisfied these procedural requirements and if the governing body finds legal grounds for a refund, then the refund must be granted—the governing body has no discretion to refuse the refund on a valid claim. On the other hand, if the procedures are not followed, then the refund should not be allowed. In fact, as already mentioned, members of the governing body who vote to make refunds when the procedures have not been strictly followed lay themselves open to possible suit and personal liability for the money refunded (G.S. 105-380).

Settlements

Webster's defines *settlement* as "an agreement composing differences."[6] This definition supplies a useful introduction to what the North Carolina law means when it speaks of the tax collector's settlement with the governing body of the taxing unit. Settlement refers to the tax collector's paying and composing the governing body's doubts and differences of opinion about the work the collector has done, as well as accounting for the funds he or she has collected.

An audit disclosing that funds collected have been properly allocated and deposited is not equivalent to a settlement. In a settlement the governing body, in addition to determining whether the collector has been honest and careful, reviews his or her efforts to collect.

The governing body may call on the collector to make a full settlement at any time [G.S. 105-350(6)]. More commonly it relies on an annual settlement or a settlement when a vacancy occurs in the office. No matter when the settlement occurs, the legal effect for the collector remains the same:

> Approval of any settlement by the governing body does not relieve the tax collector or his bondsmen of liability for any shortage actually existing at the time of the settlement and thereafter discovered; nor does it relieve the collector of any criminal liability [G.S. 105-373(e)].

Time for Annual Settlement

The tax collector is supposed to settle for the previous fiscal year's taxes after July 1 and before he or she is charged with taxes for the current fiscal year [G.S. 105-373(a)(3)]. This requirement fixes the time for annual settlement to a date shortly after the close of the fiscal year for which the taxes were levied. Although the governing body, as noted earlier, may require the collector to make settlement "at any other time," such other settlements as the governing body may require must be in addition to the mandatory settlement to be made annually in July; they may not take its place. Council members who permit settlements to be delayed until after taxes for the current year are charged to the collector should consult the following provision in G.S. 105-373(f):

> In addition to any other civil or criminal penalties provided by law, any member of a governing body . . . who fails to perform any duty

imposed upon him by [the settlement statute, G.S. 105-373] shall be guilty of a misdemeanor punishable by fine or imprisonment, or both, in the discretion of the court.

An administrative matter must also be kept in mind. Settlement must be made before the new tax books are turned over to the collector [G.S. 105-373(a)(3)]. Any member of the governing body who votes to deliver the tax receipts to the tax collector before the collector has met the requirements prescribed (including making settlement) is individually liable for the amount of taxes charged against the tax collector for which he or she has not made satisfactory settlement. Any member who so votes or willfully fails to perform any duty imposed by the settlement law is guilty of a misdemeanor punishable by fine or imprisonment, or both, in the discretion of the court [G.S. 105-352(d)(1)]. This could become serious if the collector has not been diligent in cases in which diligence might have produced results.

Settlement Procedure

Tax collectors are supposed to carry out the law as it is written; they are not policy makers. They are personally responsible for collecting the taxes in their hands, and the law gives them ample authority to seize any property that the taxpayer may own in order to collect the unit's claim. The law presumes that with this responsibility and with these remedies, collectors will do their utmost to collect—that they will, if necessary, seize whatever property of the delinquent taxpayer may be available to them. Thus the governing body rather than the collector has the responsibility for determining whether the collection work has been performed satisfactorily. Ultimately the governing body must decide in each case whether the collector has done everything that he or she could have done to reach whatever property may have been available. If the unit has no lien for taxes against real property, the collector's effort to enforce collection must be the subject of the special scrutiny described in the next section.

Insolvents

After July 1 and before he or she makes the annual settlement, the collector is supposed to present the governing board with "[a] list of the persons not owning real property whose personal property taxes for the preceding fiscal year remain unpaid," along with a statement under oath [G.S. 105-373(a)(1)b]—

1. That he or she has made a diligent effort to collect these taxes out of the personal property of the taxpayers concerned.
2. That he or she has made use of the "other means available to him for collection."
3. That where applicable, he or she has tried to make collection outside the taxing unit.
4. That he or she has included any information concerning these taxpayers that may be of interest to or required by the governing body.

This is not to be a perfunctory report. Collectors are supposed to demonstrate that they have actually done everything possible under the law to collect the taxes for which the unit has no lien against real estate. The first affirmation that collectors must make means that they have been diligent in using levy and garnishment. The second means that they have done what they could to collect by working out partial-payment schedules for taxpayers and that they have used all the procedures available to them in collecting from estates, receivers, and bankrupts. The third affirmation means that in appropriate instances they have exercised their authority to call on collectors of other units to help them make collections.

The fourth item listed is not itself an affirmation, but a reminder of two things: (1) that collectors should include facts in their report to justify their failure to collect the accounts reported; and (2) that when the governing body desires to do so, it may require collectors to furnish whatever factual information is considered useful in connection with their report.

The mere fact that a collector, in making this report, swears that he or she has used diligence in attempting to collect from the persons listed as still owing personal property taxes is not determinative of the matter. The governing body has power to reject the name of any taxpayer if, in its opinion or knowledge, the taxpayer is not insolvent. In the event of a rejection, the governing body is entitled to hold the collector liable on his or her bond for the uncollected tax [G.S. 105-373(a)(2), (3)]. Having reviewed the list submitted by the collector and having come to a conclusion about the collector's justification in asking that he or she be allowed credit in the settlement for the un-

Table 12-2
Items Required to Be Charged against and Credited to the Tax Collector

Charges	Credits
1. The total amount of all taxes placed in the collector's hands for collection, including taxes on discoveries, late listings, increased assessments, and values certified by the Property Tax Commission in the Department of Revenue	1. All sums deposited by the collector to the credit of the taxing unit or receipted by the proper official
2. All late-listing and other penalties collected by the tax collector	2. Releases allowed by the governing body (rebates, reductions, refunds, etc.)
3. All interest on taxes collected by the tax collector	3. Discounts allowed for prepayments if the principal amounts of such accounts were collected after the books were placed in the collector's hands
4. Any other sums collected or received by the tax collector, including, for example, fees allowed in levy and garnishment	4. The principal amount of taxes constituting liens against real property
5. Any fees that the tax collector may have taken for making "outside collections"	5. The principal amount of taxes found by the governing body to be uncollectible in the current year because the taxpayers who owed them were insolvent
	6. Any commissions to which the collector is entitled

collected items on the ground of the taxpayers' "insolvency," the governing body must enter in its minutes the names of the taxpayers found to be insolvent and designate them as the insolvent list "to be credited to the tax collector in his settlement" [G.S. 105-373(a)(2)].

Form of Settlement

A review of the North Carolina statutes will disclose that city governing bodies are given every opportunity throughout the year to keep abreast of the tax collector's work. The cornerstone of this scheme, mentioned earlier, is the requirement that the collector submit to the governing body at each of its regular meetings a report of the amount that he or she has collected on each year's taxes with which he or she is charged, the amount remaining uncollected, and the steps that he or she is taking to encourage or enforce payment of uncollected taxes [G.S. 105-350(7)]. If the collector is careful to comply with this requirement and if the governing body pays attention to his or her periodic reports, calling for additional information as desired, the annual settlement will follow in orderly culmination.

The law specifies the items that must be charged against the collector and the items that must be allowed as credits for him or her [G.S. 105-373(a)(3), (b)]. They are summarized in table 12-2.

The charges and the credits should balance. The collector is liable on his or her bond for any deficiency disclosed. In addition to this civil liability, he or she is subject to the criminal penalties imposed by G.S. 105-373(f): "[A]ny . . . tax collector . . . who fails to perform any duty imposed upon him by [the settlement statute] shall be guilty of a misdemeanor punishable by fine or imprisonment, or both, in the discretion of the court."

Additional Resources

Campbell, William A. *Guidebook for North Carolina Property Mappers*, 2d ed. Chapel Hill, N.C.: Institute of Government, The University of North Carolina at Chapel Hill, 1995.

——————. *Property Tax Collection in North Carolina*, 3d ed., with 1992 supplement. Chapel Hill, N.C.: Institute of Government, The University of North Carolina at Chapel Hill, 1988, 1992.

——————. *Property Tax Lien Foreclosure Forms*, 4th ed. Chapel Hill, N.C.: Institute of Government, The University of North Carolina at Chapel Hill, 1992.

Ferrell, Joseph S. "Recent Legal Developments of Interest to Property Tax Administrators." *Property Tax Bulletin* no. 43 (1975).

Ferrell, Joseph S., and Michael R. Smith. "State Jurisdiction to Tax Tangible Personal Property." *North Carolina Law Review* 56 (1978): 807–24.

Lawrence, David M. *Local Government Finance in North Carolina*, 2d ed. Chapel Hill, N.C.: Institute of Government, The University of North Carolina at Chapel Hill, 1990.

Lewis, Henry W. *The List Taker's Guide*. Chapel Hill, N.C.: Institute of Government, The University of North Carolina at Chapel Hill, 1969.

Liner, Charles D. "The Origins and Development of the North Carolina System of Taxation." *Popular Government* 45 (Summer 1979): 41–49.

Notes

1. *American Jurisprudence*, 3d ed., vol. 63, *Public Officers and Employees*, sec. 202. (Rochester, N.Y.: Lawyers Cooperative, 1972).

2. As of July 1, 1972, all taxing units became subject to the ten-year statute of limitations.

3. Thigpen v. Leigh, 93 N.C. 47, 49 (1885).

4. Taxes that are due but whose payment has been deferred under G.S. 105-277.4(c) must be included in the statement.

5. See William A. Campbell, *Property Tax Collection in North Carolina*, 3d ed. (Chapel Hill, N.C.: Institute of Government, The University of North Carolina at Chapel Hill, 1988), 103–4.

6. *Webster's Ninth New Collegiate Dictionary* (Springfield, Mass.: Merriam-Webster, 1984), 1078.

13 Budget Preparation and Enactment

A. John Vogt

Contents

NORTH CAROLINA cities budget and spend moneys under the Local Government Budget and Fiscal Control Act (LGBFCA) (G.S. Ch. 159, Art. 3). This law requires that the budget be balanced and that city moneys be budgeted before being spent. Ongoing operating expenditures and the recurring revenues that support them must be included in the annual budget. Expenditures and revenues for capital assets and for projects financed wholly or partly with federal or state grants must be budgeted either in the annual budget or in project ordinances. Revenues and expenditures of a separate fund for a city's internal services may be included in a separate financial plan for that fund or in the annual budget.

The fiscal control portions of the LGBFCA require cities to maintain accounting systems in accordance with generally accepted accounting principles as well as the rules and regulations of the Local Government Commission. The commission is an agency in the Department of State Treasurer that approves and sells local government bonds and other debt and helps local governments with financial management. The LGBFCA also requires that expenditures be made in accordance with the approved budget, that cash and other assets be safeguarded, and that a city's financial accounts be audited annually by an independent public auditor.

The LGBFCA is neither too broad to leave doubt about what are proper financial procedures nor too narrow to impede improvements in financial practices or local government services. This chapter examines the budgeting portions of the LGBFCA, including budget practices. Chapter 14 deals with capital improvement programs, capital budgets, and debt, and chapter 15 analyzes the fiscal control and cash management portions of the LGBFCA.

Definitions, and Purposes of the Budget

The LGBFCA defines the *annual budget* as "a proposed *plan* for raising and spending money for specified programs, functions, activities, or objectives during a fiscal year" (emphasis added) [G.S. 159-7(b)(1)]. The city council reviews the budget and enacts it into law by adopting the *annual budget ordinance*, which the LGBFCA characterizes as "the ordinance that levies taxes and appropriates revenues for specified purposes, functions, activities, or objectives during a fiscal year" [G.S. 159-7(b)(2)]. The *fiscal year* runs from July 1 through June 30.

The LGBFCA's definition of the annual budget as a plan suggests that one purpose of the budget is to *allocate resources rationally*. In this process the objectives for a city's services are established and ranked in priority, and then the expenditures to be incurred to reach those objectives are estimated and balanced with available resources. Officials strive to make budgetary decisions that are *cost-effective*, that is, that yield the greatest benefit with the available resources.

The budget process in actual settings often does not measure up to this ideal. Where there are major disagreements among budget makers, the budget process is likely to be more a political than a planning type of exercise. In this case, budgeting *involves much bargaining among participants who represent different points of view*, and the result may be not the most effective or rational allocation of resources, but a compromise that decision makers and different community groups resign themselves to live with for another year.

Thus the annual budget process can be an opportunity to plan programs and activities for the coming year or a vehicle to deal with differences and reach a political compromise among groups in a city about what its government should do in the next year. Usually the budget is both. In some cities and at particular times, however, one of these concepts or purposes of budgeting predominates.

Whether the annual budget serves primarily as a planning vehicle or as a means of reaching political agreement about budgetary policies, it can and should serve several specific purposes. Most basically it *sets three legal limits* on what a city government may do:

1. The most important legal limit concerns the *property tax levy*, the amount of property tax due, calculated by applying the rate—expressed as so many cents per $100 of taxable value—to the value of taxable property. Under the LGBFCA, once the city council sets the tax levy in the budget ordinance, neither the levy (by explicit reference) nor the rate (by implication) may be amended or changed during the fiscal year (G.S. 159-15). This is the only part of the annual budget ordinance that may not be amended.
2. The LGBFCA requires the annual budget ordinance to be balanced. This limit is discussed in depth later in the chapter.
3. Appropriations made in the budget ordinance set legal limits on what a city may spend. The sum of expenditures and encumbrances chargeable to an appropriation may not exceed the appropriation. The city council may also incorporate provisions in the budget ordinance that specify the manner in which appropriations must be spent.

The annual budget also provides the opportunity for officials to *review and evaluate city programs and activities*. During most of the year, officials are often hard-pressed to keep up with day-to-day duties and may not have the time to examine the full range of city programs to determine whether they are heading in the proper directions or need adjustments. Even if local officials make no changes after they review programs and activities, and the budget remains the same from year to year, such a review is valuable. It gives officials an overview of programs and a broader perspective for the decisions that they must make, issue by issue, during the following year.

The annual budget hardly ever remains the same from one year to the next. Besides having to accommodate changes in costs for continuing programs, the budget is also usually used to expand, improve, reduce, revise, or eliminate existing programs or to authorize or undertake altogether new programs.

The disadvantage of using the budget for this purpose is that preparing and approving cost estimates for just the existing programs is difficult and time-consuming enough; incorporating and executing many program or policy changes in the annual budget makes budget preparation and enactment even busier and more challenging. As a result, some proposed changes may slide through and be approved in the budget process without adequate review. This problem can be avoided if major program changes to be effected in the annual budget are considered during the year before the budget process begins. Then the budget is used mainly to implement the changes, rather than to review and study as well as implement them.

Finally, the budget can *serve management purposes*. By making appropriations to departments or divisions within departments, the budget assigns or renews the assignment of responsibility for providing services or programs for which the appropriations are made. A city council may also review and approve goals and objectives to be achieved by departments as well as dollar authorizations for them in the budget. Such board-approved goals and objectives can be translated into very specific targets for managers and supervisors to achieve during the year. All these goals, objectives, and targets taken together can constitute a plan of work that guides management efforts and for which managers can be held accountable.

The Public-Purpose Limitation

A fundamental restriction that underlies the LGBFCA is that public moneys, regardless of their source, may be budgeted and spent only for public purposes. This limitation springs from Article V, Section 2(1), of the North Carolina Constitution, enacted in 1936, which reads, "the power of taxation shall be exercised . . . for public purposes only." Rulings of the state's supreme court in the half century leading up to this constitutional provision and since have applied the provision to all public moneys, not just taxes, and have forbidden both raising and spending public moneys for private purposes.[1]

The twentieth century has been an era of expanding government responsibilities, spurred by citizens' needs and desires, and questions have been raised about whether some newly proposed programs or expenditures serve public purposes. The courts, and ultimately the state supreme court, determine what is a public purpose. Until a court does decide, a city may rely on a legislative declaration that a particular activity serves a public purpose.

In deciding whether an expenditure serves a public purpose, the courts have not tried to define what public purpose means in the abstract. They have decided public-purpose cases considering what have generally been accepted as legitimate and proper local government functions, yet recognizing that conditions change and functions that are not now considered public purposes may one day become such.

A basic principle at work in the public-purpose limitation is that some activities are reserved for the private sector of the economy, and therefore it is inappropriate for government to engage in them. In other words, the courts have accepted as public purposes, traditional government functions, or activities that are perceived as extensions of traditional functions, and have maintained a cautious attitude toward governmental expansion into traditionally private-sector functions.

Some expenditures fail the public-purpose test because the benefits that they bring to particular persons or businesses significantly outweigh any benefit to the public at large. For example, in cases in which government sought to issue bonds to build facilities for private entities, the North Carolina Supreme Court found the benefit to the private organizations to be paramount, significantly outweighing any public benefit and causing the proposed bonding programs to fail the public-purpose test.[2] These specific cases have since been reversed by narrowly drawn constitutional amendments,[3] but they still reflect the basic point that the public benefits of a particular expenditure or activity may be so slight that the courts will hold that the expenditure or the activity serves no essentially public purpose.

The public-purpose limitation does not prevent a city from appropriating money to a private agency for the performance of a public activity. Article V, Section 2(7), of the state constitution permits the General Assembly to authorize local governments to "contract with and appropriate money to any person, association, or corporation for accomplishment of public purposes only." Pursuant to this constitutional provision, G.S. 160A-20.1 expressly authorizes cities to appropriate money to any person, association, or corporation to carry out any public purpose that the city is authorized by law to undertake. (G.S. 153A-449 provides comparable statutory authority for counties.)

Although cities may contract with private agencies to provide public services, there are certain limitations or procedural requirements that they should respect or follow in doing so: First, as already noted, the activity must be one that the city itself is legally authorized to undertake. Second, in giving financial support to privately controlled agencies, a city should specify the purposes or the uses of the money and take steps to ensure that the money is spent only for these purposes or uses. Third, the city should require the private agency to account for its expenditures of the money at the end of the fiscal period or year for which the money is given.[4]

A city may contract or cooperate with other local governments for the provision of authorized public services without raising a public-purpose issue as long as the city's citizens benefit from the arrangement (G.S. Ch. 160A, Art. 20, "Interlocal Cooperation").

Budgeting and Accounting

Budgeting estimates future revenues and makes appropriations for expenditures to support an organization, a program, or a project, whereas *accounting* records revenues raised and expenditures actually made and reports on the resulting financial condition of the organization, the program, or the project. Budget estimation and decision making depend on accounting records that are accurate and consistent from one period to the next. The importance of accounting records for budgeting may become apparent only when such records are absent or deficient. Three facets of governmental accounting have important implications for budgeting by cities and other governmental entities: fund accounting, budgetary accounting, and basis of accounting and budgeting.

Fund Accounting

An accounting *fund* is a separate fiscal and accounting entity, with its own set of accounts and its own cash and other assets, liabilities, equities or fund balance, revenues, and expenditures or expenses.[5]

Governmental financial transactions are grouped into funds essentially to isolate information for legal and management purposes.

G.S. 159-8(a) requires the annual budget ordinance to be balanced by fund, as well as for the city as a whole. Individual funds may be balanced in part through interfund transfers.

G.S. 159-26(b) lists the types of funds that governments generally maintain: general, debt service, special revenue, enterprise, internal service, capital project, and trust and agency funds. Which ones and how many a particular city maintains will depend on what functions it performs and how it finances those functions, although to simplify accounting and reporting, a city should maintain as few funds as possible.

General Fund

The *general fund* is a catchall fund for all transactions not properly accounted for in another fund. The general fund typically budgets and accounts for all or most property tax revenue, most sales and use tax revenue, state-shared tax revenue, and other revenues that are not statutorily earmarked for particular purposes. Usually it also includes all or most city expenditures for law enforcement, fire protection, other public safety programs, parks and recreation programs, general engineering and maintenance, and city administration and finance. The general fund may include expenditures for solid waste collection if it is not operated as a public enterprise, and street maintenance. For purposes of budgeting, accounting, and financial reporting, there can be only one general fund.

Debt Service Funds

Debt service funds may be established for the payment of principal and interest on general obligation bonds and notes and other debt-financing instruments. Alternatively, generally accepted accounting principles permit debt service payments on such bonds, notes, or debt to be made directly from the general fund or from the applicable operating fund. Although the use of debt service funds was common in the past, a debt service fund should be used only if a city is legally or otherwise required to set aside money for debt service payments. For general obligation bonds and notes, debt service payments should generally be made from the general fund, or if such bonds or notes were issued for enterprise purposes, from the appropriate enterprise fund.

Special Revenue Funds

Special revenue funds account for the proceeds of revenue sources that are legally restricted to expenditures for specific purposes. The LGBFCA requires that a special revenue fund be established for activities supported in part or in whole with voted property taxes (property taxes levied pursuant to a voter referendum), for service districts, and for activities for which money is appropriated under grant project ordinances (see the discussion under the heading Project Ordinances, later in this chapter). Some cities use special revenue funds to budget and account for street maintenance and construction programs financed in whole or in part by Powell Bill revenue, which must be used for street-related expenditures. However, generally accepted accounting principles and Local Government Commission policies encourage the inclusion of restricted revenues like Powell Bill money in the general fund as long as a city's accounting system can track the receipt and the expenditure of the revenues in that fund.

Enterprise Funds

A separate *enterprise fund* must be established for each public enterprise operated by a city. An *enterprise* is understood to mean a public service that is financed partly or wholly through charges to users or customers and that is operated in a proprietary or business-like manner. Even when user charges cover only a portion of the cost of such a service, using an enterprise fund to account for it enables city officials to determine the extent to which the service is self-supporting. A city may establish enterprise funds for the following services: water supply and distribution, sewage collection and disposal, solid waste collection and disposal, airports, off-street parking, public transportation systems, electric generation and distribution, gas production and distribution, cable television, and stormwater and drainage systems (G.S. 160A-311).

Internal Service Funds

Internal service funds account for activities that serve other departments or parts of the same government or other governments, rather than the public. City-owned and -operated central stores or warehouses, print shops, data-processing units, and motor pools are examples of internal services. Cities may account for internal services either in the general fund or in one or more separate internal service funds. If a city wants to operate an internal service like a business and charge city departments that use the service, it will set up an internal service fund for it.

Capital Project Funds

Bond and debt proceeds may be used only for the purposes for which the bonds were issued or the debt incurred. To ensure this, *capital project funds* must be established for bond- or debt-financed projects. Such funds should also be used to budget and account for the construction of most major capital improvements, whether or not bond or debt financing is involved. A single capital project fund may be used to account for multiple capital projects as long as a city's accounting system can segregate the revenues and the expenditures for each of the projects.

Trust and Agency Funds

Trust and agency funds are used to account for assets that are held by a city as a trustee or as an agent for another governmental unit, a private organization, or one or more individuals. Others besides the city have ownership rights in the assets of these funds, although the city holds and manages the assets. Cities establish trust or agency funds for pension system assets that they manage, deferred compensation programs for city employees, and other purposes. Most trust and agency funds do *not* have to be budgeted (see the discussion under the heading Moneys Not Having to Be Budgeted, later in this chapter).

Budgetary Accounting

Commercial accounting principles do not require a firm's budget to be recorded in its accounting system. The accounts record only actual revenues and expenses. In government, however, generally accepted accounting principles call for the approved budget to be entered into a governmental entity's accounting records.[6] The LGBFCA reflects this principle of governmental accounting by directing that a local government's accounting system show "appropriations and estimated revenues as established in the budget ordinance and in each project ordinance . . . ." [G.S. 159-25(a)]. With appropriations and estimated revenues recorded in the accounting system at the beginning of the fiscal year, actual expenditures and revenues are then charged against the appropriations or the estimated revenues during the year. This whole process is called *budgetary accounting*.

Why do governments use budgetary accounting, and private firms not? In the private sector the principal yardstick of success is earnings or profit. The budget is useful as a guide to achieving that end, but meeting or staying within the budget is secondary to a private firm as long as revenues exceed expenses and a profit is earned. Thus in the private sector, revenues and profit rather than the budget generally serve to control or limit spending, and the budget is a plan but not, strictly speaking, a ceiling or a limit on spending. Therefore the budget is not recorded in a firm's accounting system. In the public sector, on the other hand, the budget is both a plan and a ceiling or a legal limit on spending, and the budget is entered into a governmental entity's accounting system.

In government, many services are financed with taxes and either do not generate revenues at all or generate revenues only in amounts that cover a portion of the service's expenditures. For most public services, therefore, revenues cannot serve as a check or a limit on expenditures. Instead, governments rely on an approved budget to legally limit spending for such services. Because the budget in government serves this important legal role, generally accepted accounting principles and the LGBFCA require that appropriations and estimated revenues from the approved budget be recorded in a local government's accounting system, and that actual expenditures and revenues be charged against the budgeted amounts. Of course, some city services, like many water and sewer systems and all or virtually all municipal electric and gas systems, generate sufficient revenues to cover their expenditures. Even so, the LGBFCA requires budgetary accounting for such self-supporting enterprise services as well as for non-self-supporting enterprises and general government functions.

Under the LGBFCA, budgetary accounting is not required for financial plans for internal service funds [G.S. 159-13.1, -28(a)]. If a city accounts for an internal service in an internal service fund, it may "budget" revenues and expenditures for the fund either in the annual budget ordinance or in a separate *financial plan.* Although the city council must approve any such financial plan, the approved amounts for revenues and expenditures in the plan are estimates and not legal limits. Consequently the LGBFCA does not require that these revenue and expenditure estimates be recorded in the unit's accounting system, although a city may choose to do so.

Basis of Accounting and Budgeting

Basis of accounting has to do with when revenues and expenditures or expenses are recorded in the accounting records and reported in the financial statements. It is of particular significance for revenue and expenditure or expense transactions that occur near the end of one fiscal year or at the beginning of the next one.[7] Basis of accounting provides criteria for determining the fiscal year in which such transactions should be recorded. There are three general bases of accounting:

1. *Cash basis,* by which revenues and expenditures are recorded when cash is received or disbursed
2. *Accrual basis,* by which revenues are recorded when they are earned, regardless of when they are received in cash, and expenses are recorded when goods or services are received and liabilities are created for them, regardless of when cash disbursements are made to pay for the goods and services
3. *Modified accrual basis,* by which revenues are recorded when they are measurable and available, and, as with the accrual basis, expenditures, with a few exceptions, are recorded when goods and services are received and the liabilities for them are created

Practically speaking, the modified accrual basis, as applied to North Carolina local governments, records many revenues when they are received in cash. However, some revenues to be received within a month or two after the start of a new fiscal year may be assigned to the prior fiscal year if their amounts can be determined (measured) at the end of the prior year and if they will be available soon enough after the close of that year to pay liabilities (bills) for expenditures incurred that year. Liabilities for many items and services received near the end of one fiscal year are often not paid until after the beginning of the next fiscal year. The quarterly payment of sales tax revenues that the state makes to cities and counties in August each year may be budgeted and accounted for in the year ending on June 30, even though it is not received in cash until August of the next fiscal year. A city can estimate the amount of the August sales tax distribution with reasonable accuracy at the end of June, and that distribution is available early enough in the next fiscal year to cover expenditures incurred before June 30 of the prior year. Therefore the August sales tax payment may be recorded as a revenue for the year ending June 30.

The LGBFCA directs that cities and other local governments use the modified accrual basis of accounting except as otherwise provided by regulation of the Local Government Commission. Generally the commission requires local governments to record revenues and expenditures using the modified accrual basis of accounting unless they have formally received permission from the commission to use the accrual basis of accounting.

Basis of accounting, as applied to budgeting, has to do with the year to which revenues and expenditures are assigned or for which they are estimated. Generally, estimates of revenues and expenditures in the budget should use the same "basis" as the recording of revenues and expenditures in the accounting system. Thus most or nearly all cities should use the modified accrual basis for budgeting revenues and expenditures. This means that cities should assign most revenues, including the property tax, to the year when they are received in cash, or if they are received shortly after the start of one fiscal year but are measurable and available at the end of the prior fiscal year, to the prior year's budget; and they should assign expenditures to the year in which the liabilities arising from those expenditures are expected to occur.

The Inclusiveness Requirement

The *inclusiveness requirement* means that a city or another local government may spend or disburse only moneys that have been budgeted [G.S. 159-8(a)]. Although the LGBFCA authorizes an exception for certain trust and agency fund moneys (see the discussion under the heading Moneys Not Having to be Budgeted, later in this chapter), the inclusiveness requirement applies to all moneys, regardless of source, including property taxes, other local taxes, state-shared taxes and revenues, user charges for specific services, federal and state grants, bond proceeds, fund balances, and any other money available to a city to fund its programs, activities, or projects. A city has several options for budgeting moneys: the annual budget ordinance, project ordinances, and financial plans. City council adoption is necessary for all these budgeting options.

The Annual Budget Ordinance

Any moneys that a city spends may be budgeted in the annual budget ordinance. If a city does not use project ordinances or financial plans for internal service funds, all city moneys that a city spends must be included in the annual budget ordinance. All revenues that support recurring operating expenditures are generally included in the annual budget ordinance, which is enacted for a July 1–June 30 fiscal year. More is written about the annual budget ordinance in subsequent sections of this chapter.

Project Ordinances

Expenditures and revenues for the construction or the acquisition of capital assets or for projects that are financed in whole or in part with federal or state grants or assistance, may be budgeted either in the annual budget ordinance or in one or more project ordinances. A *project ordinance* appropriates revenues and expenditures for however long it takes to complete the project rather than for a particular fiscal year or period (G.S. 159-13.2).

G.S. 159-13.2(a) specifies that a *capital project ordinance* may be used to appropriate revenues and expenditures for a project "financed in whole or in part by the proceeds of bonds or notes or debt instruments or a project involving the construction or acquisition of a capital asset." Practically speaking, cities are authorized to use bond or debt financing only for capital projects or acquisitions. Therefore the focus of attention here is the second part of this statutory language. What is a capital asset? According to generally accepted accounting principles, a *capital asset* is tangible property of significant value that has a useful life of more than one year. Such assets include land, buildings, improvements other than buildings, and equipment. The amount that establishes *significant value* for the purpose of identifying capital assets is determined locally and varies by size of jurisdiction. It usually falls somewhere between $100 and $1,000. Although capital project ordinances may be used to appropriate revenues and expenditures for any capital asset, such ordinances are especially suitable and primarily used for capital improvements or acquisitions that are large relative to the annual resources of a city, that take more than one year to build or acquire, or that recur irregularly, that is, once every few years or less often. Authorizing such large projects in the annual budget presents challenges that are more effectively addressed by the use of project ordinances. Expenditures for capital assets that are not expensive relative to a city's annual budget or that recur annually or with frequent regularity can usually be handled effectively in the annual budget.

A *grant project ordinance* may be used to appropriate revenues and authorize expenditures for operating or capital purposes in a project financed wholly or partly by a grant or other financial assistance from the federal or state government. According to generally accepted accounting principles, a *grant* is a gift of cash or other assets from one government or entity to another that must be used or spent for a specific purpose. A *project* is a temporary activity. Thus a grant project ordinance should be used only to appropriate moneys for federally aided or state-aided activities that serve specific purposes and are temporary in nature. Grant project ordinances are often used for multiyear grants that cities receive, such as Community Development Block Grant moneys. Grant project ordinances may not be used to appropriate state-shared taxes or other federal or state revenue or aid that is provided on a continuing basis to a city. Such revenue or aid, even if it is earmarked for a specific purpose, should be budgeted in the annual budget ordinance.

A project ordinance must identify and authorize the project, identify the revenue sources for financing it, and make all appropriations necessary to complete the project. Like the annual budget ordinance, a project ordinance must be adopted by the city council. A project ordinance may be adopted at any time during the year. A public hearing is not required in relation to the adoption of a project ordinance. Once a project ordinance has been adopted, it need not be readopted in subsequent fiscal years; it has a project life rather than an annual life. Correspondingly a project ordinance need not be balanced by year; it is balanced for the life of the project. A project ordinance may be amended at any time as long as it stays balanced. More is written about amending project ordinances later in this chapter.

A project ordinance must encompass all forecasted expenditures and revenues for the project. Revenues may include grant moneys, bond proceeds, transfers from capital reserve funds, annual revenues, fund balances, and other sources of revenue. Of course, bond proceeds and moneys from a capital reserve fund may generally be spent only for capital purposes. Annual revenues may be appropriated directly into a project ordinance, or they may be appropriated initially in the annual budget ordinance and transferred from there into the project ordinance. If property taxes are used to finance a project authorized in a project ordinance, such taxes must be levied in the annual budget ordinance and then transferred into the project ordinance. A project may not be financed partly from appropriations in a project ordinance and partly from appropriations in the annual budget ordinance. If money is appropriated initially in the annual budget to finance a project for which a project ordinance exists, it must be transferred from the annual budget into the project ordinance and reappropriated there before it can be spent for the project. Appropriations for expenditures in a project ordinance may be a lump sum, that is, a single sum for the entire project, or they may be and usually are broken down into line-item or functional categories—for example, for a capital project ordinance, land, construction, and equipment.

The annual budget must include information about capital or grant project ordinances to be approved during the year and about previously adopted capital and grant project ordinances for which appropriations are available for expenditure in the budget year. Moneys appropriated and spent under grant project ordinances must be accounted for in a special revenue fund [G.S. 159-26(b)(2)]. Moneys appropriated and spent under a capital project ordinance in which bond or other debt financing is involved must be accounted for in a capital project fund [G.S. 159-26(b)(6)]. Generally accepted accounting principles encourage the use of a capital project fund for any major capital project authorized under a project ordinance, even if bond or debt financing is not involved.

Financial Plans for Internal Service Funds

As already mentioned, an internal service fund may be established to account for a service provided by one department or part of a local government to other departments or divisions in the same local unit, and in some cases to other local governments. In small cities, internal services, if they exist within the structure of city government, are typically budgeted and accounted for in the general fund and financed with general fund revenues. However, in most large cities and in a growing number of medium-size ones, many internal services are financed by charges to other departments for the use of the services, and they are budgeted and accounted for in internal service funds rather than in the general fund.

If a city uses an internal service fund, the fund's revenues and expenditures may be included either in the annual budget ordinance or in a separate financial plan adopted specifically for the fund [G.S. 159-8(a), -13.1]. The city council must approve any financial plan adopted for an internal service fund, with such approval occurring at the same time that the council enacts the annual budget and running for the same July 1–June 30 fiscal year as the budget ordinance. In practice, a city council's approval of a financial plan often occurs simultaneously with its adoption of the annual budget ordinance; the ordinance may include a special provision indicating the council's approval of each financial plan. An approved financial plan must be balanced, and it may be amended only with the approval of the city council.

As stated earlier, estimated revenues and expenditures in an approved financial plan may be, but are not required to be, recorded in a city's accounting system. They are planned, but strictly speaking, not legal limits on revenues and expenditures and therefore do not have to be included in the accounting system. Actual spending from an internal service fund is limited by revenues to the fund that arise from charges to the departments that use the fund's services. Such charges are expenditures of the using departments for which the council approves appropriations that are recorded in a city's accounting system. Thus a city council maintains control over internal service fund expenditures for which a financial plan authorizes spending both directly through its approval of the financial plan and indirectly through budgeted appropriations to the departments that use the internal service and pay the internal service fund for that use.

Moneys Not Having to Be Budgeted

The LGBFCA permits the revenues of certain local government trust and agency funds to be spent or disbursed without being budgeted [G.S. 159-13(a)(3)]. As already mentioned, a trust or agency fund accounts for moneys or other assets that are held and managed by a city but for which the city serves only as an agent or a trustee. For example, some cities collect certain revenues as an agent for other governmental units. Although these collections are held temporarily by the city, they belong to the other units. They are therefore not revenues of the city collecting them, and it should not include them in its budget, even though it must account for them in a nonbudgeted agency fund. Many cities now set aside and manage moneys that finance special separation allowances and certain other retirement benefits for law enforcement officers. Some cities still manage full-fledged pension systems for certain employees and retirees. Moneys set aside for such allowances, benefits, or pension systems do not belong to the city or to the city alone. The employees and the retirees for whom the city is managing these moneys have ownership rights in them. Although a city must budget its initial contributions on behalf of employees or retirees into the trust fund for such a benefit or pension system, usually calculated as some percentage of payroll, once the moneys are in the fund, earnings on the assets, payments to retirees or employees, and other receipts and disbursements of the fund should not be included in the city's budget.

Some cities have trust funds that generate income or provide other revenue that finances city services or projects. For example, the income of a cemetery perpetual care trust fund, which is used to maintain a city's cemetery, should generally be included in a city's budget. Even though the law permits its exclusion, including it is recommended because the income goes to finance a city function. As another example, a city may receive a donation that the donor requires be placed in a trust fund and be spent only for a specific function, for example, the city's parks and recreation programs. Because the money is to be spent for a city function, that is, parks and recreation, income or principal withdrawn from the fund to be spent for this function should be budgeted before being spent. Such trust funds are similar to special revenue funds; therefore income or withdrawals from them for financing city services should be budgeted.

The Balanced-Budget Requirement

A fundamental requirement of the LGBFCA is that the annual budget ordinance and any project ordinance or any financial plan for an internal service fund be balanced. The next section discusses the balancing requirement for the annual budget ordinance in some depth. The balancing requirements for project ordinances and financial plans differ somewhat from the requirement for the annual budget ordinance. Later sections discuss them.

The Annual Budget Ordinance

G.S. 159-8(a) states that the annual budget ordinance is balanced when "the sum of estimated net revenues and appropriated fund balances is equal to appropriations" (for expenditures). This law requires an exact balance; it permits neither a deficit nor a surplus. Further, each of the accounting funds that together make up the annual budget—the general fund, a water and sewer fund, and so forth—must also be balanced [G.S. 159-13(b)(16)].

During budget preparation, which can begin from two to eight months or so before the budget year begins, each of the variables in the balanced budget equation (estimated net revenues, appropriated fund balances, and appropriations for expenditures) is an estimate. The law makes this explicit with regard to revenues by referring to them as "estimated" net revenues. Both revenues and appropriations for expenditures remain estimates during budget preparation and through much of the budget year. Officials will not know whether their estimates for these variables are accurate until near the end of the budget year. Indeed, except for changing the property tax levy, the city council can amend the budget ordinance to increase (assuming money is available) or decrease appropriations during the year in order to accommodate changing conditions that cause estimates in the original annual budget to become outdated. Appropriated fund balance is taken from unrestricted money that is left over at the end of the current year that is legally available to budget in the coming year. During budget preparation for the coming year, which takes place before the current year ends, legally available fund balance at the end of the current year is also an estimate. It does not become an actual figure until the end of the current year, after all revenues for the year have been collected and all expenditures have been made.

Each variable in the budget equation for the annual budget ordinance is now examined.

Estimated Net Revenues

Revenues

Generally a *revenue* is an increase in cash or other financial resources, or in a few cases a decrease in liabilities, that increases an entity's net worth or fund balance and that can be made available in the budget to support spending.[8] An increase in cash or another financial resource that is balanced by an increase in one or more liabilities or by a decrease in other resources or assets does not increase an entity's net worth or fund balance and is therefore not a revenue.

For purposes of the LGBFCA, revenues or increases in financial resources (the equivalent of revenues under the LGBFCA) for a specific fund—for example, a capital project fund—may include proceeds from bonds or other debt that may be budgeted and spent from the fund, and transfers into the fund from other funds. However, what may be a revenue or an increase in financial resources for one fund of a city may not be a revenue or an increase in financial resources for the city as a whole. For instance, if a city issues bonds and deposits the bond proceeds into a governmental capital project fund, this increases that fund's cash and fund balance or equity, and when budgeted, would be considered a fund revenue or the equivalent under the LGBFCA. However, there is no increase in equity, net worth, or fund balance (assets minus liabilities) for the city as a whole because the city's general long-term debt, recorded in the general long-term debt group of accounts, increases by the amount of the bond proceeds. Under generally accepted accounting principles, the term *revenue* does not include debt proceeds or transfers into a fund from another fund of a city. Generally accepted accounting principles refer to debt proceeds and such transfers as *other financing sources* rather than revenues per se.

Some increases in cash or financial resources may appear to be revenues, but are actually collections of receivables under generally accepted accounting principles and also the LGBFCA. For instance, when a city buys materials or equipment, it pays state sales taxes on such purchases and then files for reimbursement from the state for the state sales taxes. Such sales taxes should be recorded as receivables rather than expenditures when the purchases for which they are paid are made. When the city receives reimbursement from the state for such sales taxes, the city should classify the reimbursement as the collection of a receivable rather than as a revenue under both generally accepted accounting principles and the LGBFCA. Such reimbursements should be budgeted neither as revenues nor as expenditures.

Net Revenues

The LGBFCA refers to "estimated net revenues" in the balanced-budget equation. The word *net* refers to revenues levied or billed, less discounts or amounts that a city does not expect to collect of the totals levied or billed. For example, some cities give property tax payers discounts for paying taxes before September 1 [G.S. 105-360(c)], which are typically 1 or 2 percent of the tax levy. Moreover, cities and other units of local government seldom collect the full amounts of the property taxes that they levy or the water and sewer or other charges that they bill. The LGBFCA's explicit reference to net revenues in the balanced-budget equation directs local governments to budget only revenues that a city actually expects to collect or have available to fund expenditures during the budget year. Although not required by the LGBFCA, the annual budget ordinance may show or refer to gross, levied, or billed revenues as well as net revenues. However, the estimates of revenues used for the balanced-budget equation should be net revenues only.

Budgeting of Revenues by Major Source

G.S. 159-13(a) requires that the annual budget ordinance "show revenues by major source." Generally accepted accounting principles as interpreted by the Local Government Commission define *major source* in this statute to include at least the following revenue categories: taxes, licenses and permits, intergovernmental revenues, charges for services, interest earnings, and miscellaneous revenues. The annual budget ordinances of most cities actually show or appropriate revenues in more specific categories—current year's property taxes, prior years' property taxes, sales taxes, and so forth, for general fund revenues.

Conservatism in Estimating Revenues

For any revenue source that is listed separately in the budget ordinance, one estimate must be selected from a range of possible figures. For reasons discussed later in this section, city officials should be conservative in estimating revenues. This means selecting an estimate for a revenue source that is somewhat below the midpoint of the range for that source. Some budget officials estimate revenues conservatively for all or most revenue sources. Others choose revenue estimates at the midpoint of the range for most sources, but are conservative on one or a few of the major sources, such as the property tax or the sales tax.

Property tax revenue is often estimated conservatively by underestimating the percentage of the levy that will be collected. Thus, if a 98-percent collection percentage is anticipated for the coming year, the property tax revenue estimate in the budget might be calculated in terms of only a 97-percent collection rate. As a result, property tax revenue estimated in the budget is somewhat less than what will probably be collected.

City officials estimate revenues conservatively because the penalties for underestimating are usually less severe than those for overestimating. Probably the most significant penalty that sometimes results from underestimating is the accumulation of a fund balance that is excessive, angering taxpayers. In contrast, a range of unfortunate possibilities awaits the city that overestimates revenues. One possible consequence is having to cut appropriations and planned services that citizens were led to believe they would receive. If expenditures could not be cut and additional non-property-tax revenues could not be raised (the property tax levy may not be legally changed after the budget ordinance is adopted) to cover a shortfall caused by an overestimate of revenues, the year would end with a deficit to be funded from the next year's budget or from borrowing (strongly discouraged by the Local Government Commission). Either eventuality would likely hurt a city's standing with creditors or potential creditors. Awareness of these dangers tends to cause cities and other local governments to be conservative in estimating revenues for the budget.

Of course, a city or any local government can be too conservative in estimating revenues. There is a reasonable range of high to low forecasts for any revenue source, and budget makers cannot place their estimates below (or above) this range without being dishonest. However, because selecting this range depends as much on judgment as on calculation, there is no simple or definitive norm for determining what is an appropriately conservative estimate for major revenue sources. The extent of conservatism in estimating revenues should depend on one or more of various factors, including the following:

1. *The economic outlook.* If economists paint a bright picture for the coming year and the city is likely to benefit, the revenue estimates can be more optimistic. If the economy looks weak, however, and the weakness is likely to affect city revenues, revenue estimates should generally be more conservative.

2. *The tightness of the city's budgeting for expenditures.* If departments are expected to underspend their appropriations in the budget year, the need to be conservative in revenue estimates is reduced. On the other hand, if expenditures are tightly budgeted and departments are likely to spend all or nearly all their appropriations, revenue estimates should be more conservative.

3. *The size of fund balance and/or contingency appropriations.* If a city will close the current year with a significant general fund balance and/or significant working capital in enterprise funds that the city will carry as unappropriated operating reserves into the next budget year, revenue estimates can be less conservative than they would otherwise be. However, if a city will have little or no unappropriated general fund balance or enterprise fund working-capital reserves to back up its budget for the next year, city officials should be more conservative in estimating revenue. A contingency appropriation can serve in place of an unappropriated fund bal-

ance as an operating reserve to support the budget, and although G.S. 159-13(b)(3) limits contingency appropriations to 5 percent of all other appropriations in a fund, a city that includes contingency appropriations in its budget can be somewhat less conservative in estimating revenues.

4. *The city's size.* A large city with considerable diversity in its revenue sources and specialized financial staff can operate closer to the margin in estimating revenue than a small city with fewer revenue sources and a small financial staff can. On this basis alone, a large unit could therefore estimate its revenues somewhat less conservatively than a small one, other things being equal.

Appropriated Fund Balance

The second variable in the balanced-budget equation for the annual budget is appropriated fund balance.

Available Fund Balance

Legally available fund balance is money that is left at the end of one fiscal year that may be appropriated to finance expenditures in the next year's budget. G.S. 159-8(a) defines such fund balance as ". . . the sum of cash and investments minus the sum of liabilities, encumbrances, and deferred revenues arising from cash receipts, as those figures stand at the close of the fiscal year next preceding the budget year."

Legally available fund balance is calculated using this statutory formula. The calculation starts with an estimate of cash and investments at the end of the current year, and subtracts from them estimated liabilities, encumbrances, and deferred revenues from cash receipts at the end of the current year. All these figures are estimates because the calculation is being made for budget purposes before the end of the current year. If the estimate of available fund balance is for the general fund, typical liabilities are payroll owed for a payroll period that carries forward from the current year into the budget year, and accounts payable representing unpaid trade accounts for goods and services provided to the city toward the end of the current year. Such liabilities should be paid from the current year's moneys rather than the next year's; they will thus reduce cash and investments that would otherwise be part of available fund balance. Encumbrances arise from purchase orders and other unfulfilled contractual obligations for goods and services that are outstanding at the end of a fiscal year. They reduce legally available fund balance because cash and investments will be needed to pay for the goods and the services on order. A *deferred revenue* from a cash receipt is revenue that is received in cash in the current year, even though it is not owed to the city until the coming budget year. Such prepaid revenues are primarily property taxes. They should be included among revenues for the coming year's budget rather than carried forward as available fund balance from the current to the coming year.

Legally available fund balance is different from fund balance, equity, or net worth for financial reporting purposes as presented in the balance sheet of a city's annual financial report. Legally available fund balance includes only cash and investments. It may not include any receivables or other current assets. By contrast, fund balance, equity, or net worth for financial reporting purposes is calculated considering all assets of the fund, and includes receivables as well as cash and investments. In calculating or estimating fund balance available for appropriation into next year's budget, city officials should use the legal formula provided in G.S. 159-8(a) rather than the accounting or balance sheet amount for fund balance.

Some legally available fund balance, as defined by G.S. 159-8(a), may be restricted or reserved for particular purposes by other statutes. For example, a portion could represent Powell Bill or state gasoline tax moneys that may be spent only for street construction and maintenance. Available fund balance attributable to Powell Bill moneys will generally be reserved to show that it is not available for general purposes. It is a part of legally available fund balance under G.S. 159-8(a), but it is available only for street-related spending and not for general spending in the next year's budget. Other portions of legally available fund balance may be designated by local officials for particular purposes—for example, future capital improvements—and therefore may also not be available for general purposes in the next year's budget unless local officials remove the designations.

Sources of Fund Balance

Legally available fund balance at the end of the current fiscal year can originate from unbudgeted fund balance carried forward from the prior year or from conservative revenue estimates or underspent appropriations in the current year's budget.

Appropriated and Unappropriated Fund Balance

Fund balance that is legally available at the end of the current year that is otherwise unreserved or undesignated does not have to be appropriated into the next year's budget except under one condition. If part or all of it is needed to balance the next year's budget, considering estimated revenues and appropriated expenditures for the year, at least that much of the available fund balance must be appropriated. Otherwise, none of the legally available fund balance need be budgeted, legally speaking. A city may choose to appropriate some or all of available and unrestricted fund balance for any purpose for which the city is authorized to spend money. The city might also budget available fund balance in a contingency appropriation; as already noted, the amount of this appropriation may not exceed 5 percent of all other appropriations in a fund. If a larger operating reserve is needed, as is often the case, it must remain outside the budget as unappropriated fund balance. Alternatively, if a city does not need any fund balance to balance its budget, it may choose not to appropriate any available fund balance. Any portion of legally available fund balance that a city budgets is generally called *appropriated fund balance.* Any portion that remains outside the budget is called *unappropriated fund balance.*

Reasons for Cities to Carry Fund Balances

Cities and other local governments carry significant fund balances to provide working capital to pay vendors and others in a timely way, to meet emergency or unforeseen needs, and to be able to take advantage of unexpected opportunities requiring the expenditure of money. If a city with low fund balance attempts to issue bonds, its bond rating may be hurt because of inadequate fund balance, causing the city to have to pay more in interest than it otherwise would. Without fund balances, some cities would face a cash-flow deficit during the first half of the fiscal year because most property tax revenue, the most important general revenue source, is not received until December, whereas expenditures are evenly distributed throughout the year. With Local Government Commission approval, such a deficit may be funded by borrowing against anticipated tax or other revenues, but the interest cost of such borrowing adds to expenditures, and such borrowing is discouraged by the Local Government Commission. Cities in North Carolina have traditionally used end-of-year fund balances rather than borrowing against anticipated tax or other revenues to meet cash-flow shortfalls in the first part of the budget year. Finally, even in periods of low interest rates, a city with significant fund balance can earn investment income that helps to hold down its property tax.

Recommended Amount of Available Fund Balance

Staff of the Local Government Commission recommend that cities end a fiscal year with legally available general fund balance equal to at least 8 percent of general fund expenditures for that year. Commission staff consider the 8-percent level to be a floor, representing only about one month's expenditures and needed just to meet operating or working-capital requirements. Therefore they encourage most cities to maintain fund balances larger than this. If a city's end-of-year general fund balance falls below 8 percent of general fund expenditures, commission staff will send city officials a letter noting this fact and advising them to rebuild available general fund balance at least to the 8-percent level. If city officials fail to do so, the city may be unable to secure the commission's assistance and approval in selling bonds or other debt instruments.

In deciding how much available general fund balance a city should carry, officials should consider the experiences of other cities of similar size. Generally, small cities have larger available fund balance relative to expenditures than medium-size and large cities do. It is not uncommon for cities with several thousand or fewer people to have available general fund balance equal to 50 to 100 percent of general fund expenditures. At first glance, such fund balance seems excessive. However, it usually is not, considering the actual dollar amounts that these percentages represent in relation to the large unforeseen expenditures that small cities must occasionally make to meet emergency needs. Also, many small cities rely heavily on pay-as-you-go financing of capital improvements and build general fund balance for such financing of future capital needs. Statistics on available fund balance for municipalities of different sizes are compiled and published each year by the Local Government Commission.

The amount of available general fund balance that a particular city carries should depend on a variety of factors, including how conservatively it estimates revenues, how tightly it budgets expenditures, whether it faces a cash-flow deficit during the first half of the fiscal year, and what economic prospects are. Generally officials should increase general fund balance to the extent that revenues are estimated less conservatively, actual spending takes more of appropriations, a cash-flow deficit exists, available reserves do not exist in other funds, or economic conditions affecting local revenues and expenditures worsen. Available fund balance carried by a particular city should also depend in part on how well the city manages its fiscal affairs. The better a city manages these affairs, the more likely it can get by with a somewhat lower available fund balance.

Presentation of Fund Balance Information in the Budget

The LGBFCA explicitly requires that any appropriation of fund balance be shown in the annual budget ordinance [G.S. 159-8(a), -13(a)]. By implication the recommended budget, which must be balanced unless the city council authorizes the budget officer to submit an unbalanced budget, must also show any appropriation of fund balance that the budget officer proposes to use to balance the budget. There are, however, no additional requirements for the budget or the budget ordinance to present fund balance information. As a matter of local policy, the recommended budget for a city should include the budget officer's estimate of legally available fund balance at the close of the current year as well as any amount of this fund balance that the budget officer is proposing for appropriation into the coming year's budget. The recommended budget should also include a brief discussion of the fund balance policies that the proposed budget is following. Because available fund balance on June 30 can only be estimated at the time of budget preparation, the presentation of much of this fund balance information in the budget must be tentative. Nonetheless, such information represents a very important dimension of the budget and should be dealt with explicitly at the time of budget presentation and enactment. A city's annual financial report will eventually reveal actual fund balances on June 30 for the fiscal year preceding the budget year, changes in the city's fund balance during that year, and the amount of available fund balance appropriated into the budget, but that report will not be available for at least three months after the budget year begins.

Appropriations for Expenditures

The third variable in the balanced-budget equation is appropriations for expenditures. An *appropriation* is an estimate of future expenditures, a legal authorization to spend, and a ceiling on expenditures. Only the city council may establish appropriations; neither the budget officer nor any other administrative official may do so. The expenditure figures that appear in the budget officer's recommended budget are only proposed appropriations and breakdowns of those appropriations.

An appropriation is a specified dollar amount set forth in the annual budget ordinance or in a capital or grant project ordinance. Financial plans for internal service funds estimate and authorize expenditures. However, the estimates and the authorizations are not ceilings for expenditures and therefore are not appropriations under the LGBFCA (G.S. 159-13.1).

Lump-Sum or Detailed Appropriations

G.S. 159-13(a) provides that appropriations in the annual budget ordinance shall be by department, function, or project. This raises the question of how general or specific appropriations should be. A very detailed budget ordinance makes appropriations by line item or by individual object of expenditure. The line items or the objects of expenditure are taken from the expenditure accounts in a city's accounting system. Many small cities have annual budget ordinances with detailed line-item appropriations. Although such appropriations facilitate close control by the city council over departmental expenditures, they can cause the council to become enmeshed in the details of budget administration and correspondingly neglect the broader issues of budget development and execution.

Most medium-size and large cities make appropriations by department or by function or division within departments. This level of appropriation seems to be favored by G.S. 159-13(a), specifying that the annual budget ordinance "shall make appropriations by department, function, or project and show revenues by major source." With departmental, functional, or project appropriations, the city council delegates control over expenditures by line item to the budget officer (the manager or the administrator in cities with the council-manager form of government), who is responsible for reviewing and approving expenditures from line-item accounts and transfers of money from one such account to another within the same departmental or functional appropriation. Usually this system works well because control over expenditures by line item is usually a management responsibility.

In some cities the council permits the budget officer or the manager to delegate to department heads the authority to approve most transfers among line-item accounts within each departmental or functional appropriation, reporting such transfers to the budget or finance officer as or after they are made. In return for this flexibility, department heads are held accountable for achieving specific performance targets or objectives within appropriated funds. In units where such budget flexibility is practiced, certain transfers on or off salaries and wages lines or accounts may still have to be approved by the budget officer or staff before being made.

A lump-sum appropriation for the general fund or any fund from which more than one department or function is financed is too broad and is not in keeping with the intent of G.S. 159-13(a). Appropriation by fund is legally permissible only for a fund that finances the activities of just one department or function.

Nondepartmental Appropriations

Some appropriations authorize expenditures for nondepartmental purposes or items—for example, premium payments for property and general liability insurance, and contributions to private nonprofit organizations that carry out functions that the city itself is authorized to undertake. The LGBFCA's provision for "appropriations by department, function, or project" favors the allocation of expenditures among departmental, functional, program, or project appropriations in the annual budget ordinance. Moreover, generally accepted accounting principles require that nondepartmental appropriations be held to a minimum.[9]

Allocation of Appropriations for Shared Services

General fund departments often provide certain services to other funds. For example, the finance department, which is typically budgeted and accounted for in the general fund, often prepares and mails utility bills and processes utility payments for the water and sewer fund. Both the general fund and the water and sewer fund share the services of the finance department. Water and sewer and other utility funds should reimburse the general fund for utility billing, mailing, and collection services provided by the finance department to the utility funds. Such reimbursements should be budgeted and accounted for as expenditures (expenses) for the utility funds. On the general fund side of the transaction, some cities mistakenly budget and account for such reimbursements as revenues or "other financing sources." Generally accepted accounting principles call for these reimbursements to be accounted for as reimbursements of general fund expenditures. To avoid having to make the reimbursements, a city may allocate or split the appropriation for the finance department between the general and utility funds based on the estimated use of finance department services by each fund. Such split or allocated appropriations are in accord with generally accepted accounting principles and may be the simplest way for cities to budget and account for expenditures for shared services.

Required Appropriations

Although cities enjoy broad legal discretion over what programs and expenditures they choose to provide, and at what levels, there are limits on this discretion. First, the full amount estimated by the city's finance officer to be required for debt service during the budget year must be appropriated [G.S. 159-13(b)(1)]. During the spring the Local Government Commission notifies each finance officer of that city's debt service obligations on existing debt for the coming year. If the city does not appropriate enough money for the payment of principal and interest on its debt, the commission may order the city to make the necessary appropriation; if the city ignores this order, the commission may itself levy the local tax for debt service purposes (G.S. 159-36).

Second, sufficient appropriations must be made for continuing contracts [G.S. 159-13(b)(15)]. *Continuing contracts* are those that extend over more than one fiscal year. G.S. 160A-17 requires that in each year of such a contract, the city council appropriate sufficient funds to meet payments that come due that year under the contract. G.S. 159-13(b)(15) of the LGBFCA simply repeats that requirement.

Third, the full amount of any deficit in each fund must be appropriated [G.S. 159-13(b)(2)]. Three types of deficits may occur to which this requirement applies:

1. Despite the LGBFCA's provisions to the contrary, expenditures occasionally occur without an appropriation or exceed

appropriations, creating a deficit for that appropriation and perhaps for the entire fund. If the fiscal year ends with such a circumstance and the expenditures are otherwise authorized by law, the resulting deficit must be funded by an appropriation in the budget ordinance for the coming fiscal year.

2. Revenue estimates may turn out to be higher than actual revenue collections for a year. Although expenditures may not exceed the revenue estimates, they may exceed revenue collections. If this occurs and if the legally available fund balance in the affected fund falls below zero, a deficit exists in that fund, and sufficient moneys must be appropriated in the next fiscal year's budget to make up the deficit.

3. A deficit is created when a city appropriates more fund balance in the budget than the amount that is legally available on June 30 of the year preceding the budget year (see the discussion under the heading Available Fund Balance, earlier in this chapter). If such an overappropriation of fund balance occurs, the budget ordinance must be amended to correct this situation.

Limits on Appropriations

Several LGBFCA provisions place upper or lower limits on certain appropriations. First, as already mentioned, contingency appropriations for each fund are limited to 5 percent of the total of all other appropriations in that fund. Thus a general fund's contingency appropriation is limited to 5 percent of other appropriations in the general fund.

Second, G.S. 159-13(b)(4) requires that tax limits and earmarked revenues be respected. For example, cities must use state street aid or Powell Bill revenues for street-related expenditures only.

Third, G.S. 159-13(b)(5) states that the total of all appropriations for purposes that require voter approval for expenditure of property tax moneys under Article V, Section 2(5), of the North Carolina Constitution must not exceed the total of all estimated non-property-tax revenues (not including nontax revenues required by law to be spent for specific purposes) and property taxes levied for such purposes pursuant to a vote of the people.

Restrictions on Appropriations for Interfund Transfers

The annual budget ordinance often makes appropriations to transfer money from one fund to another. A contribution, or *transfer-out,* from one fund becomes a financial resource, or *transfer-in,* to the receiving fund. A common interfund transfer moves enterprise-fund surplus to the general fund. The LGBFCA generally permits appropriations for interfund transfers, but it sets some restrictions on them, each designed to maintain the basic integrity of a fund in light of the purposes for which the fund was established. In addition, the LGBFCA prohibits certain interfund transfers of moneys that are earmarked for a specific service. The LGBFCA's restrictions on interfund transfers for cities affect voted property tax funds, agency funds for special districts, capital project funds involving bond or debt proceeds, enterprise funds, service district funds, and overhead and revenue-generation and -collection costs.

1. *Voted property tax funds.* Proceeds from a voted property tax may be used only for the purpose approved by the voters. Such proceeds must be budgeted and accounted for in a special revenue fund and may not be transferred from such a fund [G.S. 159-13(b)(10)].

2. *Agency funds for special districts.* Moneys collected by a city for a special district belong to that district, not to the city, and such moneys may not be appropriated from the agency fund for the district to any other fund of the city [G.S. 159-14(b)].

3. *Capital projects funds involving bond or debt proceeds.* Bond or debt proceeds may be spent only for the purposes for which the bonds or the debt was issued. Therefore the statutes permit the appropriation or the transfer of bond proceeds only (1) for the purposes stated in the bond order, (2) to a debt service fund to pay debt service on the bonds, or (3) to a capital reserve fund for eventual expenditure for the purpose stated in the bond order [G.S. 159-13(b)(13)]. Expenditure of the proceeds of debt instruments other than bonds is more circumscribed; such proceeds may be spent only for the project or the purpose for which the debt was approved and issued [G.S. 159-13(b)(19)].

4. *Enterprise funds.* Appropriations to transfer moneys from an

enterprise fund to another fund may be made only if other appropriations in the enterprise fund are sufficient to meet operating expenses, capital outlays, and debt service for the enterprise [G.S. 159-13(b)(14)]. This limitation reflects the policy that enterprise revenues must first meet the expenditures and the obligations related to the enterprise. Enterprise revenues are not absolutely earmarked, however; once all enterprise expenditures have been funded by appropriations, the law permits any remaining moneys to be transferred to another fund. In recent years the bond rating agencies have expressed concern about the extent to which general funds in cities with electric utilities rely on transfers from the electric funds. A city's general fund should rely on transfers from an enterprise fund only pursuant to a council-approved policy that takes into account long-term as well as immediate prospects for both enterprise and general funds.

5. *Service district funds.* Although a service district is not a separate government, specific taxes and other revenues raised within it for the district belong to the district. Therefore no appropriation may be made to transfer moneys from a service district fund except for the purposes for which the district was established [G.S. 159-13(b)(18)].

6. *Overhead and revenue-generation and -collection costs.* Each prohibition or limitation on interfund transfers discussed in this section except the one relating to capital project funds, is subject to the modification that any fund may be charged for general administrative and overhead costs properly allocable to its activities, and for the costs of levying and collecting its revenues [G.S. 159-13(b)]. As already mentioned, a transfer of money to reimburse one fund for administrative or overhead services that it provides to other funds should be budgeted and accounted for as a reimbursement of expenditures rather than as a revenue or as "other financing sources" in the fund receiving the reimbursement. Alternatively the appropriations for departments that serve other funds as well as their own fund may be budgeted or allocated initially between the respective funds.

Project Ordinances

The LGBFCA requires a capital or grant project ordinance to be balanced for the life of the project, specifies that such an ordinance is balanced when "revenues estimated to be available for the project equal appropriations for the project," and requires the ordinance to identify the revenues for financing the project and to make the appropriations necessary to complete the project. A project ordinance may be amended at any time as long as the ordinance remains balanced (G.S. 159-13.2).

The key characteristic of a project ordinance is that it has a project life, which means that the balancing requirement for such an ordinance is not bound by or related to any fiscal year or period. Estimated revenues and appropriations in a project ordinance must be balanced for the life of the project, but do not have to be balanced for any fiscal year or period that the ordinance should happen to span.

A project ordinance does not have to be readopted after it is initially enacted, and spending authority created by a project ordinance continues in force for however long it takes to complete the project authorized by the ordinance. This could be several months to a year or longer for major equipment acquisitions or modest capital improvement projects, or a year to multiple years for major capital improvement projects. Of course, a project ordinance may be amended to change the scope of the project, to keep revenues and expenditures for the project in balance, or to accomplish other purposes.

Estimated revenues for a project ordinance may include bond or debt proceeds, federal or state grants, revenues from special assessments or impact fees, other special revenues, and annually recurring revenues. As already mentioned, annually recurring revenues may be budgeted initially in the annual budget ordinances and then transferred to a project ordinance, or appropriated directly into the project ordinance. If property tax revenue is used to help finance a project ordinance, it must be levied initially in the annual budget ordinance before being transferred to the project ordinance.

Appropriations for expenditures in a project ordinance may be general or detailed. A single lump-sum appropriation for a project fulfills the requirements of the LGBFCA. However, project ordinances for major capital improvements or large grant-financed projects generally break down appropriations into expenditure categories. For improvement projects the common categories are planning and design, land, construction, equipment and furnishings, and administrative and legal expenses. Appropriations for grant programs for operating purposes are often made by function or purpose authorized under the grant, by general line-item category, or some combination.

Fund balance is not part of the balanced-budget equation for project ordinances. Because project ordinances do not have fiscal year or period lives, they do not generate fund balances. Of course, projects are frequently completed with appropriated revenues remaining unspent. Practically speaking, such excess revenues are equivalent to a project fund balance. However, because a project ordinance's authority ends with the completion of the project, the LGBFCA's silence about such remaining project revenues suggests that a project's completion should occasion the transfer of any remaining project revenues to another appropriate project, fund, or purpose. Annual revenues budgeted in a project ordinance that remain after a project is finished may be transferred back to the annual budget ordinance. Bond proceeds remaining after a project is finished should be transferred to the appropriate fund for other projects authorized by the bond order or to pay debt service on the bonds.

Financial Plans for Internal Service Funds

The LGBFCA requires any approved financial plan for an internal service fund to be balanced. It specifies that such a plan is balanced when "estimated expenditures do not exceed estimated revenues."

Internal service fund revenues are principally charges to city departments that use the services of an internal service fund. These charges are financed by appropriated expenditures of the using departments in the annual budget ordinance. Internal service fund revenues or resources may also include an appropriated subsidy or transfer unrelated to specific internal service fund services, from the general fund to the internal service fund. Such a subsidy is often made during the start-up years of an internal service fund. It should be shown as a transfer-in rather than a revenue per se for the internal service fund. Internal service fund revenues may also include investment income and income from certain other sources.

Expenditures for an internal service fund are typically for items necessary to provide fund services, including salaries and wages; other operating outlays; lease, rental, or debt service payments and/ or depreciation charges on equipment or facilities used by the fund; and other internal service expenditures. Estimates of fund expenditures might be by purpose or function within the fund rather than by line item.

The LGBFCA makes no mention of internal service fund balance and reserves or the equivalent (fund equity), even though the approved financial plan for any such fund is for the same July 1– June 30 fiscal year as the annual budget, and even though an internal service fund's revenues may exceed its expenditures in a year, creating fund balance or reserves for that year and possibly over time. In adopting the annual financial plan for an internal service fund, a city council must decide what to do with any available balance or reserves remaining from any previous year's financial plan. The law permits such balance or reserves to be used to help finance fund operations in the next year, or if the balance is substantial, to fund long-term capital needs of the fund. Alternatively such balance may be allowed to continue accumulating for the purpose of financing major capital needs of the fund in the future, or it may be transferred to the general or another fund and be used there. Generally accepted accounting principles discourage the buildup of internal service fund balance unrelated to specific present or future needs of the fund.[10] Accumulation of large balance or reserves may also create problems if internal service fund expenditures are charged to federal grant programs. Federal regulations prohibit excessive charges to federal programs, and unexplained internal service fund balance or reserves may be interpreted by auditors as resulting from excessive charges.

The Budget Officer

Authorities on budgeting distinguish between a budget prepared by a legislative body or a governing board and one prepared by or under the direction of the jurisdiction's chief executive officer. When a local governing board formulates the budget, departmental budget requests flow directly to the board; it estimates revenues, balances the requests against available revenues, and then enacts the budget.

This can be called a *legislatively prepared budget.* On the other hand, an *executive budget* is one prepared by a jurisdiction's chief executive officer, who receives departmental budget requests, reviews and balances the requests against available revenues, and submits a recommended and balanced budget to the governing board or the legislative body for its review and approval.

The LGBFCA provides for an executive budget. It calls for each city to appoint a budget officer to be responsible for budget preparation (G.S. 159-9). By law a city's manager or administrator, if it has one, is its budget officer. The law gives the manager this responsibility because the budget is the basis for managing and providing public services. In cities without a manager or an administrator, the council must appoint a budget officer to serve at its pleasure. Any officer or employee, including the mayor, any other member of the council, the finance director, or the clerk to the council, may serve as the budget officer.

Having one official who is responsible for budget preparation focuses responsibility for timely preparation of the budget, permits a technical review of departmental estimates to ensure completeness and accuracy, and allows for administrative analysis of departmental priorities in the context of a city's overall priorities. This centered responsibility for budget preparation means that the council receives a budget already reviewed by someone who shares its overall perspective and who has the first-hand knowledge to evaluate and recommend services and priorities.

In the state's large cities the city manager often delegates many of the duties associated with budget preparation to another official or employee, for example, the finance director or a separate budget director or administrator. This is strictly an administrative arrangement, usually with the official or the employee performing these duties serving only as staff to the manager. Under the law and often in actual practice in cities with managers, the manager retains full responsibility for budget preparation and decision making, subject to council review and approval. A 1990 survey of budget practices in seventy-four North Carolina cities found that regardless of who served legally as the budget officer, the work associated with preparation of the 1990–91 budget was the responsibility of the manager or the administrator in twenty-one of these cities, the finance director in another eighteen units, the clerk to the council in fourteen units (all but one with 5,000 or fewer people), a separate budget director or administrator in eleven units (nearly all large cities), an assistant manager or administrator in six units, and other officials or employees in four units.[11]

The Annual Budget Preparation Process

The LGBFCA provides for three general stages of annual budget preparation and enactment: formulation of expenditure requests and revenue estimates by city departments, preparation of a recommended budget by the budget officer, and governing board review and enactment of the annual budget ordinance. Preceding these stages is a preliminary organizational stage.

Initiation of the Budget Process

Before the budget process begins, the budget officer, alone or often with the city council's direction and advice, generally establishes an administrative calendar for budget preparation and prescribes forms and procedures for departments to use in formulating requests. Budget officers in many cities also issue fiscal or program policies to guide department officials in formulating their budget requests.

Calendar for Budget Preparation

The LGBFCA specifies the dates by which each stage in the annual budget process is to be completed (G.S. 159-10 through -13). Departmental requests must be submitted to the budget officer before April 30. The recommended budget must be given to the city council no later than June 1, and the council must enact the budget ordinance by July 1, when the fiscal year begins. The most important of these dates is the last one.

Even if the budget ordinance is not enacted by July 1, its legal validity is not impaired once it is enacted. Similarly, even if the departments and the budget officer miss their target dates, neither the budget process nor the budget is invalid in any way. The failure of a city to enact its annual budget by July 1, however, may suggest that it is experiencing problems in managing its fiscal affairs. The Local Government Commission and the national bond rating agencies are likely to look unfavorably on such a failure if it happens year after year.

If a city fails to enact its annual budget ordinance by July 1, it must enact an interim budget to provide legal authority for expenditures made between July 1 and whenever the budget ordinance is finally approved. In one recent year a significant number of cities delayed enactment of their budget ordinances several weeks to a month or more after July 1 because they were waiting for the General Assembly to pass the state budget. Officials in these units felt that they could not enact their budgets without knowing with certainty how much revenue the state budget was going to provide to them.

The statutory dates of April 30, June 1, and July 1 for budget preparation serve as targets for establishing an administrative calendar for annual budgeting. This calendar can be established by working back from the statutory dates. It should specify who is responsible for doing what in annual budget preparation and enactment.

Several key issues arise in setting the administrative calendar. The most obvious one is how much time the calendar should provide overall for budget preparation. The larger and more complex the budget, the more controversial the issues addressed in it, and the more departmental and citizen participation in the process, the longer the calendar needs to be. Most medium- and large-size cities allow four to six months or so for budget preparation and enactment.

A second issue concerning the administrative calendar for budget preparation is whether the city council and the budget officer should, at the very start of the process, set guidelines for departments to follow in making budget requests. Although the LGBFCA does not expressly address this early role for the council and the budget officer, it does not prohibit such a practice, and more and more city councils and budget officers are using it. Such a procedure enables elected and top administrative officials to take more initiative in setting policy in the budget. It also saves department heads' time: guidelines tell them early what the council's priorities and intentions are; therefore they need not waste time generating requests that have no chance of being funded. The previously mentioned study of budget practices for 1990–91 found that city councils in fifty of the seventy-four cities surveyed, including small units as well as large ones, held meetings at or near the start of budget preparation to discuss the upcoming budget. For thirty of these fifty cities, such meetings took the form of retreats at which the council could discuss budget issues in depth. In thirty-three of the fifty cities, the council approved policies or goals to guide budget preparation at these meetings or retreats.[12]

Budget Forms and Procedures

Forms are unavoidable in budgeting: they are necessary to calculate expenditures and revenues and summarize the budget; they are important because by structuring information, they can influence the outcome of budget decisions. The budget officer has the authority to prescribe the forms and the procedures for departments to use in preparing their requests. In the words of G.S. 159-10, requests "shall be made in such form and detail, with such supporting information and justifications, as the budget officer may prescribe." In large cities the budget officer usually prepares a budget manual— including forms, instructions, and sample requests—and provides other information such as historical data for department officials to use in making their requests.

Several types of forms are basic and are found in almost any budget preparation system, regardless of a jurisdiction's size and approach to budgeting. One type lists positions and corresponding salaries and wages. A second type lists expenditures by account, object, or line item. One of the line items is a total for salaries and wages that is taken from the salaries-and-wages form; other lines list expenditures for different expenditure accounts. G.S. 159-10 requires that a budget request show actual expenditures for the prior year, estimated expenditures for the current year, and requested expenditures for the coming year. This second budget form should show expenditures by line item for each of these three years. Many cities use additional request forms that are tailored to their needs in budget preparation. The information from the various forms used for preparing budget requests is usually consolidated as the process progresses from the request stage through the recommended budget to enactment of the budget ordinance.

Departmental Requests

A departmental budget request often includes estimated receipts from fees imposed for departmental services; expenditures for salaries, fringe benefits, supplies, other operating items, and capital or permanent property items; requests for new positions or improved or new services; and in a growing number of cities, a service plan focusing on program goals and objectives and including service effort and accomplishment measures. In some cities, departmental budget requests distinguish between expenditures to continue services at current levels and those to expand or improve services. If budget reductions are to be made, departmental budget requests often identify where departmental services and the departmental budget might be cut.

Departmental Receipts

G.S. 159-10 requires that the budget request for a department include revenues or fees that it will collect in the budget year. The request must show such receipts whether they are earmarked by law or local policy exclusively to finance departmental expenditures or are available for financing any city programs or services. In many cities the finance officer actually makes the estimates of revenues to be collected by a department. If department officials make these estimates, they should be approved by the city finance officer before they become part of the budget.

Line-Item Expenditures

Salaries and wages make up the largest share of expenditures in most departmental budget requests. To estimate these requirements, department officials typically start with a list of existing authorized positions. A budget request should include an estimate of how much of the amount to be authorized for salaries and wages will not be spent because of vacancies, and it should not overlook special salary payments such as overtime, premium pay for work on holidays or on second or third shifts, and longevity pay. Decisions on salary and wage increases or adjustments are usually made on a citywide basis; therefore the money to fund them is usually not included in departmental budget requests. That money is budgeted initially in a nondepartmental account or maintained in unappropriated fund balance. After the city council approves the increases or the adjustments, or at the start of the new budget year, the money is transferred to departmental salaries-and-wages accounts.

Fringe benefits are an increasingly expensive component of most departmental budgets. Such benefits include time away from work (for example, vacations and sick leave). Although time away from work may not require specific cash outlays by a city and therefore does not of itself have to be budgeted, it may create the need for expenditures for temporary employees or even other permanent positions, which, of course, do have to be budgeted. Fringe benefits also include city contributions for Social Security, health and other insurance, retirement benefits, and other employee benefits, which all must be budgeted. Because of increasing fringe benefit costs for permanent employees, some cities are relying more on temporary or part-time employees (for whom they must usually pay only Social Security contributions) or on private contractors to perform certain city functions or work.

Supplies and operating expenditures are another component of departmental budget requests. In this category, inflation must be taken into account. On the items that a city buys, like gasoline or uniforms, inflation may run higher or lower than increases in the general consumer or wholesale price indexes. In budgeting for inflation, cities should refer to one or more of the special price indexes available to measure cost increases for supplies or services that local governments use. For instance, *American City and County* magazine publishes such indexes for different types of government functions and services.[13] Some cities require departments to use a single percentage-increase allowance to budget for inflation for all items; others permit departments to use percentage-increase allowances that vary from item to item. The percentage-increase allowance(s) can be based on knowledge of what inflation has been over the most recent fiscal year or twelve-month period, or on a forecast of what it is projected to be in the budget year.

Acquisitions of capital assets such as equipment, vehicles, and furnishings are also a significant part of most departmental budget requests. A capital or permanent property item is one that is held or used for more than one year and is of significant value, for example, worth $500 or more. In budgeting for capital or permanent property, cities find it useful to distinguish between items that replace existing equipment, vehicles, or furnishings, and items that are in addition to existing items. Replacement capital items are usually more likely to be approved and funded in the budget than additional ones. The difficulties of budgeting for expensive capital or permanent property in the annual budget have been eased somewhat with the wide availability of lease and installment purchase arrangements for financing capital items. In the past a city had to pay cash in one lump sum up front to acquire most capital or permanent property items. Now a city has the choice of paying for capital items in cash up front or in installments over several years under leases or installment purchase contracts.

Service Plans

Most medium-size and large cities and some small ones require departments to include annual service plans with their budget requests. These plans identify objectives for departmental services and activities and include performance, workload, or service effort and accomplishment measures related to the objectives. The objectives are often derived from council-approved goals for departmental services. A service plan can be the starting point—or one of them—in preparing a budget request. Too often the only formal starting point for a departmental budget request is its current year's budget. City councils are increasingly asking about the levels and the quality of services that their cities are receiving for money budgeted, and departmental service plans help answer these questions.

The survey of city budget practices for 1990–91 addressed the use of service plans, including objectives and performance or workload measures, in departmental budget requests. Of the thirty-two cities in the survey with populations above 10,000, twenty-six required the inclusion of objectives and twenty-two required the inclusion of performance or workload measures in departmental budget requests. For the forty-two cities with populations below 10,000, the numbers were nine and ten respectively.[14]

Continuation and Expansion Expenditures

Departmental budget requests may distinguish between continuation and expansion expenditures. *Continuation expenditures* are generally those that are made just to provide the same level and quality of service in the coming budget year that the department is providing in the current year. Such expenditures typically include outlays in the current year that will repeat in the budget year with adjustments for salary and wage increments, inflation or deflation on items to be purchased, rate changes on contractual obligations, necessary replacement of capital equipment, and certain nonrecurring items. *Expansion expenditures* typically include requests for new positions, for additional capital equipment or assets, and for program growth or new programs or services. Expansion expenditures are highlighted in almost any budget request and must usually be well justified to be approved and funded. The justification should refer to any law or contract that will be violated if the request is not funded; use statistics, if available, to show the need for what is being requested; indicate whether other similarly situated cities are funding the service or the item being requested; and include a forecast of probable expenditures for the request for several years beyond the coming budget year.

Identification of Budget Reductions

Resistance to tax increases and the need to provide city services more efficiently are causing more cities to require department officials to identify possible savings in operations, low-priority programs, and possible reductions in departmental budgets. This chapter addresses that important topic later under the heading Incremental and Zero-Base Budgeting and Budget Reductions.

The Recommended Budget

The LGBFCA requires that the budget officer's recommended budget be balanced unless the city council insists that an unbalanced budget be submitted [G.S. 159-11(c)]. In the latter instance the budget officer simply gives to the council the departmental requests and revenue estimates at current rates, noting the property tax rate that would have to be levied to balance the budget. Even in this circumstance, however, the budget officer should conduct at least a technical review, checking the accuracy and the completeness of departmental requests.

This minimal role for the budget officer in compiling departmental budget requests and estimating revenues does not fulfill the intent of the LGBFCA. The budget officer should be much more than a clerk who compiles budget figures and passes them on to the council. The LGBFCA calls on the budget officer to prepare a balanced budget for the city. Until this happens, the various components of the budget may exist, but the budget for the city as a whole has yet to be created. Developing that budget requires the budget officer to exercise both judgment and skill with regard to fiscal requirements, program needs, and the political environment of the city. In short, the budget officer's role in preparing a city's budget is a crucial one. A city council should expect the budget officer to review departmental requests substantively, examine revenue estimates, recommend changes in services and revenue rates or sources, and present a budget that balances the needs and the resources of the city.

The Budget Officer's Review of Requests

In setting the administrative calendar for budget preparation, the budget officer can require that requests be submitted all at once or on staggered dates. Having the requests come in on a staggered basis over several weeks spreads the work of budget review.

What, specifically, should be the focus of the budget officer's review of departmental requests? First, the budget officer or staff should make sure that all expenditure items included in the base on which departments have built their budget requests are indeed needed. The base for building a budget request is most often an updated estimate of expenditures for the current year. This base is generally calculated by starting with the current year's budget as enacted on last July 1, adjusted for amendments and actual expenditure experience from July 1 to date, and further adjusted by a revised forecast of expenditures for the remainder of the current year. In cities facing fiscal retrenchments, the budget base may be reduced to an amount equal to 95 percent or less of the revised estimate of the current year's expenditures. In a few cities the base may include all expenditures necessary to continue services at current levels into the coming budget year. In most situations this would provide a base somewhat above the revised estimate of the current year's expenditures.

Second, the budget officer should make sure that every additional dollar included in a budget request over the base is accounted for. Thus if the base—that is, the revised current year's estimated expenditures—for a particular department or program amounts to $4,200,000, and the budget request for next year for the department or the program is $4,500,000, the request should make clear how the additional $300,000 will be spent, and the budget officer should make sure that the additional money is needed.

Third, any new permanent position or capital improvement or equipment requests should be scrutinized. Although the cost of a new permanent position may be modest relative to the entire budget, approving a new permanent position represents a long-term commitment that will be expensive over time. The substantial acquisition or financing costs for most capital improvements and major equipment items require them to be examined, especially if they are associated with program expansion or the start-up of a new program, or if they will result in significant increases in operating expenditures in annual budgets in subsequent years.

Fourth, the budget officer must look carefully at the revenue side of the budget. This subject is discussed at some length under the heading The Balanced-Budget Requirement, earlier in the chapter. Two points bear repetition: (1) The budget officer should make certain that revenues estimated for each source are realistic. G.S. 159-13(b)(7) states that the annual budget ordinance "shall include only those revenues reasonably expected to be realized in the budget year . . . ." (2) The budget officer should make sure that revenues that will not recur in future years are used only for nonrecurring types of expenditures and also that any alternative revenue sources that are locally available are not overlooked.

Fifth, the budget officer should formulate or review recommendations and options for salary and wage increases or adjustments. Such increases or adjustments can take various forms. The traditional alternatives are cost-of-living and performance or merit pay adjustments. In recent years more cities are giving employees only performance pay increases. Some local governments have begun giving employees bonuses. Both cost-of-living and performance pay increases are typically added to the salary-and-wage base and continue in that base each year thereafter. Bonuses, on the other hand, are usually not built into the salary-and-wage base and therefore are not continuing commitments in subsequent years. Cost-of-living or performance pay increases can be made effective on July 1 or later during the fiscal year. The later in the year that such increases become effective, the less money they cost that year.

Finally, and most important, the budget officer must decide what property tax rate to recommend to the city council. The tax rate is almost always the focal point of any budget. In selecting a tax rate to recommend, the budget officer must resolve the following questions:

1. Should the property tax rate remain the same? If so, what effect will the unchanged rate have on fund balance and city services?
2. Should the tax rate be lowered? If so, by how much, and what effect will the lower rate have on fund balance and city services?
3. Should the tax rate be raised? If so, by how much, and how will the additional tax revenue be spent? Will it finance new or expanded services or be used just to keep existing services going? Can the property tax rate be raised, given the views of the council and the citizens?

Submission of the Recommended Budget

The budget officer must submit a recommended budget to the city council "not later than June 1." Because this should be an occasion for summarizing and explaining the budget to both the council and the public, the law urges that the budget be submitted at a formal meeting of the council, when the explanation is most likely to reach the public. Many city councils hold a regular meeting during the first full week of each month, and this meeting in June is often the occasion for budget submission, even though the meeting date will only rarely fall on June 1. This is acceptable because like April 30, June 1 is primarily a guideline, a checkpoint on the way to adopting the budget by July 1. Of course, in some cities the budget is submitted well before June 1.

When submitting the budget, the budget officer must include a budget message. This message should both introduce and summarize the budget: introduce it to the council and members of the public who wish to study it; and summarize it for those who have no time to study it themselves or are perhaps intimidated by its detail. Thus the message should emphasize the major features of the proposed budget, especially significant changes or additions from the current year's budget. G.S. 159-11(b) states that the message should include:

a concise explanation of the governmental goals fixed by the budget
    for the budget year,
important features of the activities anticipated in the budget,
reasons for stated changes from the previous year in program goals,
    programs, and appropriation levels, and
any major changes in fiscal policy.

Although a written format for the budget message is not explicitly required, it is preferable to a simple oral statement. An oral statement will summarize the budget only for those who are present when
it is made. The larger public will not benefit from the statement
except to the extent that they learn of it in the press. Normally the
budget message takes the form of a letter from the budget officer to
the council and is bound with or attached to the document presenting the full budget.

In many small cities the recommended budget takes the form of
a proposed annual budget ordinance. In most cities, however, the
budget is presented in a budget book that includes tables showing
revenues by fund and source and expenditures by fund, department,
function or program, and line item or line-item class. Some budget
books also contain organization charts; statements of policies that
have guided preparation of the budget; goals, objectives, and performance indicators and data for departments and programs; and lists
of positions authorized in the budget. The book should present full
explanations of changes or increases in the recommended budget
from expenditures for the current year. It may also contain special
sections that highlight specific challenges facing the city, such as a
slow-growing property tax base and the need to rely more on user
fees.

The budget book may present only the budget officer's recommended budget or both the requested amount and the recommended budget for each department and program. The survey of
city budget practices for 1990–91 revealed that the recommended
budget included departmental budget requests along with the budget officer's recommended budget for departments and programs in
forty-four of the seventy-four cities and towns surveyed.[15]

The budget book provides the detailed backup to the annual
budget ordinance. Once the city council approves the ordinance, the
book should be revised to reflect the changes made by the council.
The book, along with the ordinance, then serves as the budget
officer's guide in executing the budget.

When the budget is submitted, some city councils adopt it as the tentative budget. Although such a step does no harm, the LGBFCA neither requires nor provides for it. Such an adopted tentative budget is not the equivalent of the annual budget ordinance and provides no appropriation authority for spending.

On the day that the budget officer submits the budget to the city council, he or she must file a copy with the clerk to the council. The clerk must then make the copy available to all news media in the county (G.S. 159-12).

The council must schedule a public hearing on the budget after it is submitted but before the budget ordinance is adopted [G.S. 159-12(b)]. After the budget is filed and the date for the hearing is set, the clerk to the council must publish, in a newspaper with general circulation, a legal notice stating that the budget has been submitted to the council and that a copy is available for public inspection in the clerk's office. The notice should also give the time, the date, and the place of the budget hearing. The notice need not but may include a summary of the proposed budget. The statute requires no specific minimum number of days between the date on which the notice appears and the date on which the hearing is held; however, the notice should be timely enough to allow for full public participation at the hearing.

Council Review and Enactment of the Annual Budget

Council Review

Once the proposed budget is before the city council, several general legal provisions apply to council review and adoption of the budget ordinance. First, at least ten days must elapse between submission of the budget and adoption of the budget ordinance [G.S. 159-13(a)]. Second, during the interval between submission and adoption, the council may conduct its review at both regular and special meetings, and the particular notice requirements of G.S. Chapter 160A and of any local acts applying to the city may be ignored. However, the notice requirements of the open meetings law (see G.S. 143-318.12) must be met, each council member must be notified of any budget review meeting to be held, and only budget matters may be discussed at such meetings (G.S. 159-17). Third, as just noted, the open meetings law (G.S. 143-318.9 through -318.18) applies to the budget preparation and adoption process. Any public body (including a city council and its committees) with power to conduct hearings, deliberate, or take official action must do so in public unless the law specifically allows it to hold an executive session. There is no provision allowing executive sessions for the local budget process.

Council practices in reviewing the budget vary from city to city and over time in the same city. In some cities or in some years, the council may hold the one statutorily required public hearing and stop there, accepting with little question the budget officer's recommendations. The review may last only a day or a few days. Most councils, however, take a month or so to review the budget. The 1990–91 survey of city budget practices found that council review of the proposed budget generally took thirty-five to forty days in cities with populations above 25,000 and twenty to thirty days in smaller cities.[16] Council review of the proposed budget usually takes place in a series of briefings or meetings on the budget. Ordinarily, each meeting dwells on one part of the budget, and the budget officer, often with help from budget staff, the finance director, and other department heads, briefs the council on that part. Citizens and representatives of organizations or groups in the community also often comment on particular parts of the budget at these meetings. The council may make decisions on particular requests as the meetings progress, or it may hold its decisions until the review is finished.

Whether the council's review is short or long depends very much on what the recommended budget includes—that is, whether it requests new positions and programs, makes cuts in existing programs or activities, calls for a tax rate increase, and so on. The length of the review process may also depend on personal or political considerations. For example, if members of the council essentially agree on major issues and have confidence in the budget officer, their review may well be short. If the opposite is true, however, review by the council may be long and difficult.

Public Hearing(s) on the Budget

Although the city council may hold a series of budget review meetings or briefings that are called hearings, they do not satisfy the requirement for a budget hearing under G.S. 159-12(b). This law expects at least one hearing on the entire budget, primarily to allow citizens to speak to the council. As with most of the budget process, the law permits variety and flexibility in conducting the required budget hearing. The hearing may be the culminating step in the council's review of the budget. Even when this is not the case, the hearing is usually held nearer to adoption than to submission of the recommended budget. The survey of city budget practices for 1990–91 revealed that sixty-three of seventy-four cities held just the one legally required public hearing on the budget; the other eleven cities held two or more budget hearings. Of the units holding just one hearing, forty held it just before adoption of the annual budget ordinance, sixteen held it sometime during the period when the council was holding briefings on the budget, and seven held it immediately after the budget officer presented the proposed budget.[17]

Enactment of the Annual Budget Ordinance

As noted earlier, G.S. 159-13(a) directs that the budget be adopted by July 1. If this does not occur and expenditures must be made before the annual budget ordinance is adopted, G.S. 159-16 requires that the city council adopt an interim budget, making "interim appropriations for the purpose of paying salaries, debt service payments, and the usual ordinary expenses" of the city until the budget ordinance is adopted. An interim budget should not include appropriations for salary and wage increases, capital items, and program or service expansion. An interim budget may not levy property taxes, nor should it change or increase other tax, user fee, or other revenue rates. The purpose of an interim budget is to keep operations going at current levels without funding new or expanded programs or changing fiscal policy. Although there must be cash available to fund interim appropriations, the interim budget need not include revenues to balance the appropriations. Any expenditures made under an interim budget must be charged against the comparable appropriations in the annual budget ordinance once it is adopted. In other words, the interim expenditures will be funded eventually with revenues included in the annual budget ordinance. If the annual budget ordinance will be adopted a few days late but before any payroll is due or other expenditures must be made, an interim budget may be unnecessary.

The LGBFCA specifically provides that the budget ordinance may be adopted at any regular or special meeting at which a quorum is present, by a majority of those present and voting (G.S. 159-17). Any local act with other requirements may be ignored. Adoption of the budget ordinance is also not subject to the normal ordinance-adoption requirements of G.S. 160A-75.

The budget ordinance must contain appropriations for expenditures, estimates or appropriations of revenues, and the property tax levy. The ordinance must show revenues and expenditures by fund and demonstrate a balance in each fund. The property tax levy is stated in terms of a rate of so many cents per $100 of taxable value. The stated rate may also be accompanied by the dollar amount of the levy, the taxable value to which the rate will be applied to produce the dollar amount of the levy, and the percentage of the levy that is estimated to be collected. The estimated collection percentage used for the property tax in the budget may not exceed the percentage of the property tax levy collected in the year preceding the budget year. Typically the annual budget ordinance devotes a section to appropriations and revenues for each fund and one to the levy of property taxes.

Although these sections are sufficient, the annual budget ordinance may contain other sections or provisions as well. For example, it might include instructions on its administration. If the ordinance makes appropriations very broadly, it might direct that expenditures comply not only with the ordinance but also with the more detailed budget book on which the ordinance is based. If a fund mixes earmarked revenues with general revenues, or supports a function for which property taxes may not be used, the ordinance might specify the use of the earmarked funds or direct which non-property-tax revenues are to support the function in question. The ordinance may also authorize and limit certain transfers among departmental or functional appropriations within the same fund pursuant to G.S. 159-15, put certain restrictions on interfund loans within the year (the city council should approve interfund loans that remain outstanding from one fiscal year to the next), set rates or fees for public enterprises or other municipal services, and so forth.

Finally, G.S. 159-13(d) directs that the budget ordinance be entered in the council's minutes and that within five days after it is adopted, copies be filed with the budget officer, the finance officer, and the clerk to the council. Because the LGBFCA itself requires that this filing take place, the ordinance need not restate the filing requirements.

Budget Modification and Amendment

Once adopted, the annual budget ordinance is not merely a financial plan for the year but also the legal gauge against which expenditures must be measured. An expenditure must be authorized by an appropriation in the ordinance, and sufficient moneys must remain in the appropriation to cover the expenditure. Obviously, events during a fiscal year may occasion greater or less spending than anticipated for some activities, or needs may arise for which there is no appropriation or for which the existing one is exhausted.

To meet these situations, three types of changes to the annual budget may be made: first, certain budget modifications may be made without changing the ordinance; second, expenditures may be made from contingency appropriations; third, the annual budget ordinance itself may be amended. The next three sections discuss these types of changes.

An adopted project ordinance is also a legal gauge against which expenditures are measured, as well as a plan for the project. Although an approved financial plan for an internal service fund provides only estimates of fund revenues and expenditures, the LGBFCA addresses modifications to such plans. Later sections discuss amendments and modifications to project ordinances and financial plans for internal service funds.

Cities use certain control procedures to make sure that expenditures do not exceed appropriations, that actual revenues and financial resources for the budget are sufficient to cover expenditures, and that a budget deficit does not occur in executing the budget. Chapter 15 discusses the LGBFCA's provisions regarding budget control and financial management in general.

Modifications in the Annual Budget

As pointed out earlier, the budget normally exhibits greater detail than the budget ordinance. Thus an ordinance may make appropriations by department within the general fund, while the budget on which the ordinance is based may break down departmental totals into line-item categories or accounts. For example, the budget might show the following breakdown for a city's recreation department for the fiscal year:

Recreation Department		$401,400
Personnel services	$249,000	
Contractual services	41,000	
Operating expenses	74,250	
Capital outlay	37,150	

If only the total departmental figure ($401,400) appears in the annual budget ordinance, it is only that figure against which expenditures are compared by law. In other words, as long as the recreation department's expenditures do not exceed $401,400, there is no violation of the annual budget ordinance nor of the LGBFCA.

To continue the example, events during the year result in these actual recreation department expenditures:

Recreation Department		$396,200
Personnel services	$262,400	
Contractual services	41,000	
Operating expenses	47,600	
Capital outlay	45,200	

Even though two of the accounts (personnel services and capital outlay) have been overspent, neither the annual budget ordinance nor the LGBFCA has been violated because the budget ordinance's appropriation for the department ($401,400) has not been exceeded.

Contingency Appropriations in the Annual Budget

Contingency appropriations are intended for funding unanticipated expenditures. Moneys may be transferred from contingency appropriations and spent by direct authorization of the city council, by order of the budget officer, or on the basis of express delegation from the council [G.S. 159-13(b)(3)]. If the budget officer is given the authority to approve transfers from and expenditures of contingency appropriations, he or she must report any such expenditure to the council at its next regular meeting, and the report must be recorded in the council's minutes. Money transferred from a contingency appropriation and spent should be charged to the departmental, functional, or project appropriation for which it is spent and not to the contingency appropriation.

Amendments to the Annual Budget Ordinance

A city council has broad flexibility to amend the budget ordinance except that no amendment may increase a property tax levy (or the rate per $100 of taxable value) or alter a property tax payer's liability. The legal bar to amending the property tax levy and rate does not apply to other tax or revenue sources controlled by the council, although practical difficulties may be involved. Thus the privilege license tax schedule may be revised during a year, but a change would not be effective until the next license year begins in July. On the other hand, user fees and charges—such as water rates, admission fees to public recreation facilities, or landfill tipping fees—may be changed via an amendment to the budget ordinance and become effective at any time. Another change possible on the revenue side of the ordinance is the appropriation of additional fund balance if it is legally available.

If revenue estimates are increased or decreased, appropriations for expenditures or appropriated fund balance must be correspondingly adjusted so that all funds and the total annual budget ordinance remain in balance. When changes in appropriations are made, the directions and the limitations discussed earlier in this chapter must still be observed.

In amending the budget ordinance, the city council enjoys the same freedom from the procedural requirements set forth in G.S. 160A-75 or in the local charter as it does in adopting the ordinance itself. Any amendment to the annual budget ordinance must be by ordinance. There are neither notice nor public hearing requirements for amendments, and they may be adopted by a simple majority of board members as long as a quorum is present.

As with contingency expenditures, the council may delegate to the budget officer the authority to make certain amendments to the budget ordinance. Subject to restrictions set by the council, the budget officer may be permitted to transfer moneys from one appropriation to another within the same fund (G.S. 159-15). Two elements of this statutory authorization should be emphasized. First, the transfers must be within the same fund; transfers between funds by the budget officer are not permitted. Second, the transfers must be between appropriations; the budget officer may not make changes on the revenue side of the budget, such as increasing the amount of appropriated fund balance. By extension, this means that total fund appropriations may not be increased or changed by the budget officer or any other administrative official. If the power to amend pursuant to G.S. 159-15 is delegated to the budget officer, each amendment must be reported to the council at its next regular meeting, and it must record the report in its minutes.

Amendments to Project Ordinances

As mentioned earlier in the chapter, a project ordinance may make a single, lump-sum appropriation for the project authorized by the ordinance, or it may make appropriations in detail by line-item, functional, or other appropriate categories within the project. If the ordinance makes a single project appropriation, actual expenditures may exceed estimated expenditures in any budget or account category by which expenditures for the project may be classified without violating the project ordinance, as long as total expenditures do not exceed the total project appropriation. On the other hand, if the project ordinance makes appropriations by expenditure category, actual expenditures for a category may not exceed the appropriation for it without violating the project ordinance. If expenditures for a project will exceed the ordinance's appropriation, in total or for any expenditure category for which an appropriation was made, an amendment to the ordinance will be necessary to increase the appropriation and identify additional revenues to keep the project ordinance balanced. Only the city council may amend a project ordinance.

Modifications to Financial Plans for Internal Service Funds

As explained earlier, a financial plan for an internal service fund only estimates annual revenues and expenditures for the fund. The estimates are not legal limits on spending and therefore are not required to be recorded in a city's accounting system. Thus no violation of the LGBFCA occurs when actual expenditures exceed a financial plan's estimated expenditures, by category or in total. Such spending flexibility is one of the reasons for including revenues and expenditures for an internal service fund in a financial plan rather than in the annual budget ordinance.

Nevertheless, G.S. 159-13.1(d) directs that any change in a financial plan be approved by the city council. Because a financial plan does not control expenditures, one interpretation of this provision is that it requires the budget officer or staff to report to the council differences between actual revenues and expenditures and the council-approved financial plan for the internal service fund. A narrower interpretation is that it requires council approval of major changes in internal service fund financing, especially those affecting departmental usage of and expenditures for fund services, and, correspondingly, internal service fund revenues.

Line-Item and Performance Budgeting

Line-item budgeting and *performance budgeting* refer to general systems or approaches for budget preparation, presentation, and review. Although not mutually exclusive, they are often viewed as alternative budget systems. A *line-item budget* organizes information principally by expenditure account or object of expenditure, that is, by the items or the resources that a government must acquire to provide public services. A *performance budget* organizes information principally in terms of the services to be provided or the objectives to be achieved. Depending on the stage of development and the particular emphasis given to it when used, performance budgeting has been called by various names: *program budgeting, objectives budgeting, planning-programming-budgeting system, results-oriented budgeting, service budgeting,* and, most recently, *outcome-oriented budgeting.*

The LGBFCA permits cities to select the particular system or approach for budgeting that they wish to use. Most of the state's small cities rely essentially on line-item budgeting systems, although a growing number are incorporating aspects of performance budgeting into these systems. Most medium-size cities use what can be characterized as mixed line-item and performance budgeting systems. The state's large cities, that is, those with populations above 50,000, have performance or objectives-oriented budgeting systems, although there are significant line-item components even in these systems.

A line-item or object-of-expenditure budget emphasizes the relationship between money budgeted and the item or the object that the city will acquire or purchase with that money. The items or the objects are expenditure accounts that are taken from an entity's accounting system, and they are typically organized into the conventional categories of salaries and wages, benefits on salaries and wages, operating supplies, contractual services, and capital or permanent property. Office supplies, for example, would be a line item or object within the operating supplies category. A line-item budget can present information by object or line-item *category*, providing a consolidated line-item budget, or by individual line-item or object *accounts*, creating a very detailed line-item budget. Some line-item budgets are so detailed as to show expenditures for individual positions in the proposed and even in the enacted budgets.

A line-item budget is principally a control tool. It provides information that elected and top administrative officials can use to make sure that revenues are spent only for personnel or items that they approve in the budget. By reviewing requested and recommended expenditures by line, they seek to prevent the misapplication of public moneys and generally to encourage frugality in the use of public funds. As suggested earlier, the line-item budget's main tool is the departmental accounting system, with its detailed listing of expenditure accounts within each department. These line-item accounts become the categories for budgeting as well as accounting, and in a pure line-item budget format, they are *not* complemented by information about departmental goals, objectives, or activities.

Performance budgeting emphasizes the relationship between money budgeted and the objectives that a city will achieve or the services that a city will provide by spending that money. This type of budgeting attempts to be specific about the demand for public services, the level (quantity) and the quality at which services are provided, and the results obtained from providing the services. In performance budgeting, mission statements and general goals are established by the council to guide budget preparation. Objectives and performance targets based on the mission statements and general goals are formulated by program managers in making their budget requests and are approved by top administrators and the council when reviewing and approving the budget. Performance measures or indicators relating to the objectives and the performance targets are also identified in the budget. Then, while the budget is being executed, data on these measures are collected to determine the extent to which the program objectives and the performance targets have been achieved. In a full-fledged performance budgeting system, expenditure or cost data are related to performance measures to produce cost-performance ratios that officials can use for budget and management control.

Whereas line-item budgeting is oriented more toward administration and management, performance budgeting is oriented more toward policy or decision making. Because line-item budgeting shows expenditures by line or object, it emphasizes the trade-offs between spending money for one item (such as salaries and wages for permanent positions) and spending that money for another item (such as contractual services). Such trade-offs have more to do with administration and budget execution than with policy making. A performance budget, on the other hand, emphasizes the trade-offs between spending money for one function or program (like law enforcement) and spending it for another program (like street maintenance). The fundamental directions that a city takes in providing public services are often at stake in these program trade-offs. Thus the performance budget tends to be more of a policy-making tool than the line-item budget is.

Renewed interest in performance budgeting has developed in recent years. This is arising from at least three sources. First, the book *Reinventing Government* recommends that governments become mission driven and that governmental budgeting systems identify measurable objectives to be achieved with the funds that are budgeted.[18] As stated in the book, the premise that underlies these recommendations is, "What gets measured is what gets done." Second, the Governmental Accounting Standards Board (GASB), which establishes principles for governmental accounting and financial reporting, has issued a concepts statement calling on government entities to develop and include service effort and accomplishment measures in their external financial reports.[19] Such measures are generally comparable to what public officials have more commonly known as performance measures or indicators. If this GASB statement is approved in its present or a comparable form and comes to represent generally accepted accounting principles for government, it is likely to cause many local governments across the nation, including those in North Carolina, to adopt one form or another of performance budgeting. Third, the Government Finance Officers Association of the United States and Canada sponsors a Distinguished Budget Presentation Awards Program for state and local government budgets. In this program, budget documents are evaluated as policy documents, financial plans, operational guides, and communication devices. Some of the specific criteria in several of these general areas are related to performance budgeting and have the effect of encouraging governments seeking the award to incorporate aspects of performance budgeting into their budgeting systems.

In performance budgeting, the city's budget officer and staff and department officials are primarily responsible for controlling expenditures by line item. They use line-item data on amounts budgeted and spent to enforce account ceilings and to prevent the misapplication or the extravagant expenditure of public funds. The council may call for and use the line-item data at any time, but they usually do so to spot-check line-item control by administrative officials or to resolve thorny budget problems involving particular line-item expenditures. Besides the line-item budget data, the budget officer and other administrative officials use the accounting system, purchasing procedures, and other fiscal tools for enforcing line-item budget control.

All this does not mean that in performance budgeting, the city council must delegate all authority for executing and controlling the budget to the budget officer and other administrative officials. The council can and should hold that officer and the department heads accountable for achieving the objectives and the performance targets specified in the budget—and within the funds appropriated. These objectives and performance targets can be detailed and extend down to the operating levels in each department. Moreover, the council can and usually should continue to maintain general types of line-item control, such as ceilings on the number of positions in each department, function, or division, and should review specific expenditure items that are sensitive or potentially controversial. Also, as noted, the council can call for and review line-item data at any time.

A performance budgeting system is more complicated than a typical line-item one. This is why performance budgeting is more commonly used by large cities than by small ones. A performance budget requires not only line-item data for costing out objectives and programs and for maintaining administrative control of expenditures by line, but also program objectives and performance measures and data. Moreover, often several types of performance measures and data are collected and used in performance budgeting—for example, measures pertaining to the need or the demand for services; measures relating to the outcomes sought through the provision of public services; and measures dealing with the quantity and the quality of the services being provided.

In undertaking performance budgeting, some governmental units create programs and formulate performance objectives for them apart from the regular organizational structure. Creating such a separate program structure for budgeting requires "cross-walking" department and line-item expenditures into the programs in the separate program structure. Such cross-walking complicates the budget process and means that budgets are prepared and approved one way, on the basis of programs, and then executed another way, on the basis of the departmental and line-item accounting system. For most cities, objectives and performance data should generally be formulated for departments, divisions, and units in the existing organizational structure, rather than for a program structure that exists apart from the organizational structure. If the existing organizational structure meets management needs, it probably can serve budget purposes as well. If a city does use a separate program structure, the LGBFCA requires that the programs, as approved in the budget ordinance, be organized within accounting funds.

Cities that adopt performance budgeting and begin to use program objectives and measures in the budget will not see results overnight. Almost any city or other local government will need several years to refine objectives and performance measures to the point that they are reliable enough for budget- and management-control purposes. Once good performance objectives and data are available, a city should begin to build a program- or activity-based cost-accounting system that relates expenditures or costs to individual objectives or performance targets approved in the budget. This process will give the city the cost- or expenditure-performance ratios mentioned earlier. These ratios are a major payoff of performance budgeting. They may be used not only for planning and decision making, but also for control and evaluation.

Incremental and Zero-Base Budgeting and Budget Reductions

Budgeting in government over the past half-century has focused on the changes in the budget from year to year, especially on the ways in which additional funds are to be spent. Additional revenue resulting from growth in the tax base, occasional increases in the tax rate, and generally modest but continuous increases in other revenues have provided the increments to allow growth in expenditures from year to year. Some of the additional revenue available in any year is typically applied to finance expenditure increases for existing programs. The rest may be used to finance improvement or expansion in existing services or start-up of new services, or it may be returned to the taxpayers by lowering taxes. *Incremental budgeting* focuses on these issues. Expenditures for existing services in the current year that repeat in the budget year, and the revenues that finance them, are the base in incremental budgeting, and they are usually approved and funded after limited review. Precedent enters into play in this situation: if expenditures were made in the past and are being incurred in the current year, budget makers are generally willing to approve them again for the next budget year.

A growing number of citizens and taxpayers question whether the base—roughly the current year's budget—should be accepted so readily in preparing the next year's budget. They point out that the need for an existing program may have diminished, and if so, budget makers should challenge its continuation and perhaps cut it back or eliminate it altogether. Such a course would permit revenues that would have been spent for the program to be reallocated to higher-priority existing programs or to new programs, or to be returned to the taxpayers in tax reductions.

Zero-base budgeting has been advocated for reducing expenditures in existing programs and applying the money so freed to other, more pressing needs, or lowering taxes. In this kind of budgeting, the base is zero rather than the current year's expenditure and revenue level, and the current year's expenditures are not accepted as a given in preparing the next year's budget. In zero-base budgeting theory, all continuing or current-year expenditures must be justified anew each time the budget is prepared and approved.

Zero-base budgeting can be understood more fully by making two comparisons of what it calls for in theory and what it has actually achieved in practice. First, in zero-base budgeting, according to the theory, the starting point is zero, and review efforts are spread over the entire budget rather than concentrated on any one part of it. In practice, where zero-base budgeting has been tried, the starting point has not been zero but some level below the current year's budget or expenditure level—from 5 to perhaps 30 percent below the current expenditure level. This base may represent what officials consider to be a minimum level of effort for a service or a program if it is to be provided at all.

Second, in zero-base budgeting, in theory, no priorities exist when the budget process begins, and all requests, whether for ongoing programs or continuing expenditures or for new ones, are ranked during the budget process. In practice, the minimum level of service in zero-base budgeting—70 to 95 percent of the current year's expenditure level—has top priority, even at the beginning of the budget process. The process is then used to establish priorities among the requests for program expansion or new programs and also among the programs or the items in the 5 to 30 percent of the current year's budget that are not a part of the minimum level of service and expenditure. Even in zero-base budgeting, however, the ongoing expenditures that are not a part of the minimum level are usually more likely to be funded than are requests for service expansion or new programs or services.

Putting zero-base budgeting into practice entails some practical problems. First, it requires more time and work than conventional or incremental budgeting. The justification and the review of requests in zero-base budgeting focus not only on the changes from the current year's budget, but also on at least some current year's expenditures. Second, zero-base budgeting involves some political risks that are not as present in conventional or incremental budgeting. Because existing services stand to be reduced or eliminated in zero-base budgeting, the clients who benefit from these services and the employees who provide them are likely to object to proposed reductions identified in the budgeting process. If such reductions must or should be made, this ought not to dissuade the budget officer and the council from using zero-base budgeting to select and make them. However, these officials should be prepared to cope with the political repercussions.

A city can use parts of zero-base budgeting rather than the full package. Zero-base budgeting includes many elements, and some are more useful than others. One of the most useful elements is the division of a budget request into alternative levels (increments and decrements) of service and expenditure. For example, at the top of table 13-1, the current year's service level is 10,000 units, and the budget to provide it is $100,000. The request for the coming budget year presumes a minimum level of service of 7,500 units, requiring total expenditures of $79,000. The $79,000 includes $75,000 of recurring expenditures plus a $4,000 increase to cover salary and wage increases and other increased costs. Additions or increments above the minimum level are also identified. Increment 1, at 9,000 units and a cost of $96,000, is below the current year's service level. Increment 2, at 10,000 units and a cost of $107,000, is at the current year's service level. Increments 3 and 4, both at 11,000 units but one at a cost of $118,000, and the other, of improved quality, at a cost of $127,000, are above the current year's service level. They are called *betterment* increments. By presenting budget requests for public services in this way, department officials show the effects on services of reductions in or additions to their current year's budget. The type of general budget format shown in table 13-1 has been used by several North Carolina local governments at one time or another.

A few governments have applied the thorough budgetary review characteristic of zero-base budgeting to one or two programs or departments each year. After five or six years, all departments have been examined in such a thorough review. This practice is a rotating approach to zero-base budgeting. The reasons for undertaking it may have as much to do with the need periodically to assess and update departmental policies, organization, and methods as with any need to reduce or change budgets.

A city can of course cut existing services or shift funding among them without resorting to zero-base budgeting or a modified version of it. For example, officials can simply ask departments to rank existing services, activities, or items according to priority, thereby identifying expenditures that they would probably cut first if they had to make budget reductions. Alternatively officials can review programs and budgets and identify areas where they can make improvements in productivity, thereby saving money without intending to cut services. However, a caution is in order: significant and true improvements in productivity often cannot be achieved without at least some initial investments of money.

Table 13-1
Alternative Service and Expenditure Levels

	Service Level (in units)		Expenditure	
	Increment	Total	Increment	Total
Current Year	NA	10,000	NA	$100,000
Budget Year				
Base Level	NA	7,500	NA	79,000
Increment 1	1,500	9,000	$17,000	96,000
Increment 2	1,000	10,000	11,000	107,000
Increment 3	1,000	11,000	11,000	118,000
Increment 4	Quality improvement	11,000+	9,000	127,000

Budgeting for Contributions to Community Agencies

Cities and other local governments seldom provide all the local public services that citizens in their communities want or need. A great variety of private community agencies serve people in ways that city government might serve them, but often chooses not to do. Some of these agencies, like councils of churches, provide services such as a homeless shelter or a soup kitchen to disadvantaged persons or groups. Others, such as local arts councils or historical societies, sponsor cultural programs, events, or exhibits that are open to the public. Still others, like chambers of commerce or downtown business associations, promote economic development in the community or administer certain civic programs. Many of these typically nonprofit community agencies seek funding from the cities that they serve, as well as from private and other public sources.

As already discussed under the heading The Public-Purpose Limitation, cities are authorized to contribute money to private community agencies to carry out any public purpose that cities themselves are authorized by law to undertake.[20] Despite statutory authorization, city council members may disagree philosophically on whether the city should provide funds for social or other programs administered by private community agencies. Some council members may argue that funding such agencies is the responsibility, not of city government, but of the private sector or of county government. Other council members may believe that city government support of community agency programs is necessary to address specific problems or to take advantage of opportunities, and that community agency provision of these programs is likely to be more cost-effective than direct city involvement. Still other council members may not object on philosophical grounds to funding community agencies, but be unwilling to do so because city funds are already stretched too far to fund city services.

Many North Carolina cities receive significant funding requests from private community agencies. The survey of city budget practices for 1990–91 revealed that fifty-six of seventy-four cities received budget requests from community agencies for that year. Fourteen of the eighteen units *not* receiving any such requests were cities with fewer than 5,000 people. As one would expect, the number of community agencies making requests and the amount of the requests varied by size of unit.[21] There seems to be growing interest in relying more on community agencies and the private sector to meet certain public needs, and cities are likely to receive more funding requests for increasing amounts from private community agencies in the future.

How cities handle requests for funding from community agencies in the budget process is important. Are requests from community agencies treated differently than those from city departments, or do all budget requests, regardless of source, go through the same budget review process? The 1990–91 survey of city budget practices examined certain procedures for budgeting contributions to community agencies. Two of these concerned whether cities required community agencies to submit requests on city-prescribed forms and whether the city budget officer or staff reviewed community agency requests before they went to the city council. Of the fifty-six cities receiving budget requests from community agencies, only seventeen required the agencies to submit their requests on city forms. In the other units the requests were presumably submitted by letter or on an agency's own forms. In thirty-five of the cities the budget officer or staff reviewed community agency requests before the requests went to the city council.[22] Submitting budget requests from community agencies to the same procedural and review requirements as requests from city departments fosters a perception that all requests are treated on the same basis. It also enables city budget officials to review community agency requests for legality and consistency.

Even if a city does not submit budget requests from community agencies to the same procedural and review requirements as it does other requests, city contributions to any such agency should occur only under a written contract between the city and the agency. The contract should specify the purposes for which the city's contributions are to be spent and should require an end-of-year, or in some cases a more frequent, accounting of how the community agency spends city contributions.[23] If the city's contribution to an agency is more than $1,000 in a year, the city may require an independent audit of the agency's finances, although certain community agencies, like volunteer fire departments and rescue squads, are exempt from this requirement (G.S. 159-40). Of course, a city is not legally required to make contributions to community agencies, and a city could require an annual audit of any agency to which it gives funds as a contractual condition of the contribution.

In sum, officials in a city must decide (1) whether and to what extent they will contribute to the support of private community agencies; (2) what budget procedures they will require community agencies to follow in making requests for city funding; and (3) what contractual and expenditure-control requirements they will impose on community agencies to which they make contributions.

Budgeting for Annexations

Article 4A of G.S. 160A establishes statewide requirements for cities to meet when annexing territory. One requirement is that a city provide municipal services to any area that it annexes generally on the effective date of annexation and substantially on the same basis and in the same manner as it provides such services in the rest of the city. New infrastructure for water and sewer services does not have to be in place for a year or two after annexation takes effect.

Except for annexations pursuant to petition of those being annexed, the statutes require a city annexing territory to prepare a plan showing how the city will serve the area to be annexed (G.S. 160A-35, -47). Such a plan should be prepared for any annexation that will require a city to make significant capital or operating expenditures to extend services to the area to be annexed. Any such plan needs to include a cost-revenue analysis, showing the impact that the annexation will have on the city's expenditures and on estimated taxes and other revenues to be collected from property and residents in the area. The plan should also identify the types and the amounts of investments in new infrastructure and equipment that the city will have to make to serve the area, and suggest sources of financing for such investments.

Annexations of areas with substantial industrial or commercial property are generally economically beneficial for a city. The annual taxes and revenues that a city derives from such an area are usually likely to more than cover the city's recurring expenditures to extend services to the area. Annexations of areas that are predominantly residential often present break-even situations, at best, with annual taxes and revenues from such areas just covering or not covering recurring expenditures to serve them. If a city annexes an area for which it must build or acquire major new infrastructure, the costs of such investments plus the city's recurring expenditures to serve the area are likely to exceed city taxes and revenues generated from the area during the first several years after annexation. Only after several years will such an annexation begin to pay for itself. If a city is without substantial capital reserves or fund balances to finance major capital needs associated with an annexation, the city may have to issue bonds or incur other debt to finance them. If such bonds are needed for major water or sewer trunk lines and the voters must approve the bonds, a successful bond referendum must precede the effective date of the annexation [G.S. 160A-37(e)(3), -49(e)(3)].

Regulation of development in its extraterritorial planning areas can help a city avoid or reduce major expenditures for public infrastructure when annexation occurs. Through such regulation a city can require developers of subdivisions there to provide and finance streets, water and sewer lines, and certain other public infrastructure to city standards. Then when the city annexes such subdivisions, it will not be faced with the need to spend large sums to bring inadequate public infrastructure in the subdivisions up to city standards.

Many cities often extend water and sewer services to persons who live in the developing areas just outside their borders. City policies that allow for or encourage extensions ease the challenges of providing utility infrastructure to these areas when the city annexes them. Such policies can spread out the city's expenditures for infrastructure over many years as development occurs and help the city avoid having to spend major amounts for the infrastructure at or shortly after the time of annexation.

Many annexations will require the annexing city to make additional expenditures to extend law enforcement, fire protection, solid waste collection and disposal, street maintenance and improvement, and other municipal services to the newly annexed area. A city may begin to spend money to prepare to serve an area proposed for annexation once the city council passes the final annexation ordinance (G.S. 160A-40, -52).

A city annexing an area that is served by one or more rural fire departments or private waste haulers may have extra payments in relation to the city's provision of fire and solid waste collection services to the area. If an area is to be annexed without a petition—that is, if the annexation is involuntary—and if the area is part of a rural fire protection, fire service, or fire insurance district that is served by a rural fire department, the city can expect either to contract with that department to provide fire protection in the annexed area for at least five years after annexation, or to compensate the rural fire department for annual revenue loss directly attributable to the annexation over the same five years. The statutes provide alternative ways for calculating such revenue loss. If the city does not contract with the rural fire department to provide service to the annexed area, or if such a contract ends or the city ceases making payments in lieu of a contract, then the city has to pay annually a share of any debt service payments for facilities or equipment of the rural fire department if the debt existed on the effective date of the annexation. An annexing city is responsible for a pro-rata share of such debt service even if the annexation is voluntary (that is, occurring pursuant to a petition of the property owners being annexed). The city's share of such debt service would be in the same proportion that the taxable value of property in the annexed area bears to the taxable value of property in the entire fire district on the date of annexation (G.S. 160A-37.1, -37.2, -49.1, -49.2).

Similarly, if an area to be annexed is served by a private solid waste collection firm when annexation occurs, the annexing city must either contract with the firm to serve the area or the portion of it that the firm had previously served for a period of at least two years after annexation, or pay the firm, in lieu of a contract, a sum equal to one year's loss that the firm experiences as a result of not having a contract to serve the annexed area (G.S. 160A-37.3, -49.3).

Effects of the Annexation Date on Revenues

A city will realize additional tax and other revenues from most annexations that it makes. The effective date of an annexation can be very important in determining when an annexing city begins to receive such revenues. Generally an effective date of June 30 is most

Table 13-2

Effect of Annexation Date on Receipt of Tax Revenues from the Annexation

Type of Revenue	Effective Date of Annexation			
	On June 1–30 before budget year	On July 1 of budget year	After July 1 but before August 31 of budget year	After August 31 of budget year
Property Tax Revenue	A full year's levy received in budget year.	A prorated levy received in budget year.	A prorated levy received in budget year.	A prorated levy received in year after budget year.
Sales Tax Revenue: Per Capita Distribution	Begins to accrue on July 1 of budget year. First payment received in August of budget year.	Begins to accrue on July 1 of budget year. First payment received in August of budget year.	Begins to accrue on July 1 after budget year. First payment received in August after budget year.	Begins to accrue on July 1 after budget year. First payment received in August after budget year.
Sales Tax Revenue: Ad Valorem Distribution	Begins to accrue on July 1 after budget year. First payment received in August after budget year.	Prorated portion begins to accrue on July 1 after budget year. First payment received in August after budget year.	Prorated portion begins to accrue on July 1 after budget year. First payment received in August after budget year.	Prorated portion begins to accrue on July 1 after budget year. First payment received in August after budget year.

Table 13-2, *continued*

Effect of Annexation Date on Receipt of Tax Revenues from the Annexation

Type of Revenue	On June 1–30 before budget year	On July 1 of budget year	After July 1 but before August 31 of budget year	After August 31 of budget year
		Effective Date of Annexation		
Powell Bill Revenue	Begins to accrue on July 1 of budget year. First payment received around October 1 of budget year.	Begins to accrue on July 1 of budget year. First payment received around October 1 of budget year.	Begins to accrue on July 1 after budget year. First payment received around October 1 after budget year.	Begins to accrue on July 1 after budget year. First payment received around October 1 after budget year.
Franchise Tax Revenue	Begins to accrue on July 1 of budget year. First payment can be received in December of budget year.	Begins to accrue on July 1 of budget year. First payment can be received in December of budget year.	Begins to accrue on October 1 of budget year. First payment can be received in March of budget year.	Depends on effective date.
Beer and Wine Tax Revenue	Begins to accrue on July 1 of budget year. First payment received in June of budget year.	Begins to accrue on July 1 of budget year. First payment received in June of budget year.	Begins to accrue on July 1 after budget year. First payment received in June after budget year.	Begins to accrue on July 1 after budget year. First payment received in June after budget year.

advantageous for expediting revenue flow to a city from an annexation. Table 13-2 shows how the effective date of an annexation determines when a city annexing territory begins to accrue and receive additional property, sales, and state-shared tax revenues from the annexation.

Property Tax Revenue

Property tax revenue will usually constitute a major portion of additional revenues from an annexation, and an annexation's effective date can affect the amount and the time of receipt of property tax revenue in the first year or two after annexation.[24] If an annexation becomes effective on June 30 (or on any date during June), the city may levy and collect a full year's property taxes from the annexed area for the fiscal year beginning on July 1. If an annexation becomes effective sometime between July 1 and August 31, property taxes due from the annexed area for that fiscal year are prorated for the portion of the year that the annexation is effective, and they must be paid that year. The proration is based on the number of full months after the effective date of the annexation relative to the number of months in the fiscal year. If an annexation becomes effective on September 1 or later in the fiscal year, property taxes from the annexed area are again prorated for the year, following the proration method just described. However, property owners in the annexed area do not have to pay the property taxes that they owe for that year until the following fiscal year (G.S. 160A-58.10).

Sales Tax Revenue

A city annexing territory is likely to receive additional sales tax revenue as a result of the annexation. The additional sales tax revenue will depend in part on the method that the county uses to allocate sales tax revenue among specific local governments in the county. This intracounty allocation can be based on the populations served by the specific governmental entities or on their property tax levies.[25] If a county uses the per capita basis of allocation, and a city in the county annexes an area that significantly increases the city's population, the annexation is likely to increase the city's sales tax revenue significantly. This increase will come at the expense of county government and other city governments in the county. Similarly, if a county uses the ad valorem tax basis for distributing sales tax revenue, and a city in the county annexes an area that significantly increases its taxable valuation, the city is likely to receive significant new sales tax revenue as a result of the annexation. This increase too will come at the expense of county and other local governments in the county. Of course, in either case the county commissioners, following the required procedures, could change the intracounty basis for distributing sales tax revenue in order to avoid the loss of some or all of its sales tax revenue resulting from the annexation.

If a county uses the per capita basis for distributing sales tax revenue among city and county governments in the county and if an annexation is effective on or before July 1, the annexing city will begin accruing sales tax revenue from the annexed area on that July 1. The state updates its population estimates for local governments once a year effective on July 1, and population from an area that is annexed on or before July 1 will be included in the state's revised population estimate for the city for the fiscal year beginning on July 1. The state distributes local sales tax revenue collected in one quarter about six weeks into the next quarter. Thus a city annexing territory effective on or before July 1 will receive its first installment of sales tax revenue from the annexed area sometime in mid-November. If an annexation is effective after July 1—for example, on August 30—the annexing city will not begin to accrue sales tax revenue from the annexed area until the following July 1, and it will not receive any sales tax revenue from the annexed area until the following November.

If a county uses the ad valorem tax basis for intracounty allocation of sales tax revenue, such revenue resulting from an annexation will not start accruing to the annexing city until the fiscal year after the one in which the city begins taxing property in the annexed area. This is because the ad valorem tax basis of distribution uses property taxes from the prior year for the purpose of calculating the distribution of sales tax revenue for any year. Thus if a city annexes territory effective on June 30 and levies taxes on property, including that in the annexed area, for the fiscal year beginning July 1, the city will not begin to accrue sales tax from the annexed area until July 1 of the following fiscal year and will not receive any sales tax revenue from the area until November of that year.

State Gasoline Tax Revenue

Many annexations also yield additional Powell Bill, or state gasoline tax, revenue for the annexing city. The state distributes three-quarters of such revenue among cities based on city population and one-quarter based on city-maintained street mileage. Any annexation increasing a city's population or non-state-system street mileage will increase its Powell Bill revenue. This increase will come at the expense of other cities across the state. The state distributes Powell Bill revenue to cities once a year around October 1. If an annexation is effective on July 1 or before, the annexing city will receive increased Powell Bill revenue from the annexation with the next October 1 distribution. An annexation that is effective after July 1 will not yield additional Powell Bill revenue for the annexing city until October 1 of the following fiscal year.

Other Tax Revenues

Many annexations will also increase the annexing city's share of the state-levied utility franchise tax and beer and wine tax revenue.[26] Annexation will increase a city's revenues from the state franchise tax to the extent that companies subject to the tax serve customers in the annexed area. The increase occurs at the expense of the state. The state allocates franchise tax revenue to cities quarterly, with the cities' share of collections in one quarter allocated toward the end of the next quarter. An annexation that is effective on the first day of a quarter can begin to accrue additional franchise tax revenue for the annexing city on the effective date of annexation. An annexation that is effective during a quarter will not begin earning additional franchise revenue for the annexing city until the beginning of the next quarter. A city annexing territory must notify the state and companies subject to the tax in the annexed area that the city is due a share of franchise tax revenue from company sales in the area. Thus if an annexation is effective on July 1, and the annexing city notifies the state and companies subject to the franchise tax in the area by or before that date, additional franchise tax revenue from the annexed area may begin accruing to the city on July 1, and the city may receive its first increment of additional franchise tax revenue from the annexation the following December. Because of delays in notification, a city may not begin to accrue or earn additional franchise tax revenue from an annexation for a quarter or two after an annexation becomes effective.

An annexation increases a city's beer and wine tax revenue insofar as it increases the city's population. This increase occurs at the expense of the county where the annexing city is located if the county permits the sale of beer and wine in its unincorporated areas, or at the expense of cities and counties across the state if the county does not permit the sale of beer and wine. The state allocates beer and wine tax revenue once a year. In the past this allocation was made in November. Beginning in 1995–96, it will be made sometime early in the summer, probably in June. The annual allocation is based on population estimates as of July 1. Thus a city annexing territory effective on or before July 1 will receive additional beer and wine tax revenue from the annexed area probably in June. If the annexation is effective after July 1, the annexing city will neither accrue nor receive any beer and wine tax revenue from the annexed area until the following June.

Water and Sewer Service Revenue

Water and sewer service revenue can increase or decrease as a result of annexation by a city. To the extent that annexation adds customers to a water and sewer system, such revenues will increase. However, this increase may occur only gradually over several years following annexation as the city extends water and sewer lines to residents in the annexed area. If a significant number of residents in the annexed area are already customers of the city's water and sewer system and are paying rates that are, for example, double those paid by the water and sewer customers in the city, the annexation may actually cause a decline in city water and sewer service revenues, at least for a few years after annexation. Moreover, any increase in water and sewer service revenues may be partly or wholly absorbed by increased expenditures that the city incurs to serve customers who hook up to its water and sewer system as a result of annexation.

Reimbursement for Intangibles Tax

In 1995 the General Assembly repealed the intangibles tax. Before repeal, the state collected the tax and shared it with cities, counties, and certain special-purpose local governments. The state replaced the intangibles tax with an annual reimbursement to local governments of $95.3 million (the amount of the intangibles tax that the state was distributing to local governments at the time of repeal). There is no provision for growth in this reimbursement in future years. Under the reimbursement formula the $95.3 million is first allocated among the 100 counties in proportion to what each county received in intangibles tax proceeds in August 1994. It is then divided among the county and city governments in the county in proportion to each government's property tax levy in the preceding fiscal year.

If a city annexes an area and thereby increases its property tax levy relative to the county's and other cities' property tax levies in the county, the annexing city will receive additional reimbursement revenue for the intangibles tax as a result of the annexation. The annexing city will not begin to receive this additional reimbursement revenue until the year after it levies property taxes in the annexed area. The effective date of the annexation affects the annexing city's reimbursement revenue in the same way that this date affects the allocation of sales tax revenue among local governments in a county when such sales tax revenue is distributed among them in proportion to their ad valorem tax levies. (See table 13-2.)

Budgeting for Federal and State Grants

Although the amount of federal and state grants has dropped dramatically over the last fifteen years both in absolute terms and as a proportion of city revenues, such grants can be important sources for financing specific projects or programs. Cities have several devices to help them budget federal and state grants. The most important is probably the grant project ordinance, which is examined in earlier sections of this chapter.

Cities also follow certain administrative procedures to address the challenges involved in budgeting federal and state grants. One is to require department officials to secure the manager's or the city council's approval before applying for any such grant. The budget officer should also carefully analyze any federal or state grant that department or other officials apply for or say will be received in the budget year to ascertain in fact whether the grant will be forthcoming. Once the city receives notice of a grant award, the city can budget it by amending the annual budget ordinance or by adopting a grant project ordinance at that time. Another precaution in budgeting federal and state grants is for a city to maintain a locally funded contingency or reserve for programs or projects funded with federal or state grants, which can be a part of unappropriated fund balance. Such a contingency or reserve can provide a ready source of matching funds if the city is unexpectedly awarded a federal or state grant. Alternatively, if federal or state moneys are unexpectedly cut for an existing grant-funded program, but the city wishes to continue the program, the contingency or reserve gives the city the wherewithal to do so for a time while it searches for or arranges permanent funding for the program.

Finally, although most federal grants and aid are now provided on a letter-of-credit basis, by which federal funds are wired to a city to pay expenditures as they are incurred, a few federal and some state grants continue to be provided to cities on a reimbursement basis, under which a city must incur and pay expenditures for a program or a project with its own money and then apply for reimbursement of its payments from the federal or state government. In these latter instances a city must have its own front-end money to undertake the program or the project.

Multiyear Financial Forecasting

A multiyear financial forecast projects revenues and expenditures over a future planning period, usually for a term of somewhere from three to six years. If a city has a multiyear capital improvement program (see chapter 14), the forecast usually covers the same future period as that program. Most local governments' multiyear financial forecasts embrace all funds included in the budget and one-time or nonrecurring as well as annually recurring revenues and expenditures.

Multiyear financial forecasting helps city officials plan more effectively for the future. With such a forecast, officials are better able to see that decisions made in the annual budget process have implications for the long term. A forecast can be useful to officials in anticipating long-term program needs and thinking through the most cost-effective ways to meet those needs, and it can provide a context for long-range management planning. A multiyear forecast is especially important for city-operated utilities and enterprises, which are capital intensive and for which long lead times are needed to plan and put infrastructure and facilities into place. Multiyear forecasting is useful for any city that is undertaking major capital improvements. Regardless of how capital projects are financed initially, through debt or on a pay-as-you-go basis, they must ultimately be paid for from operating revenues. Future operating revenues must cover not only future operating expenditures, but also annual principal and interest payments on bonds and other debt issued to finance capital projects, as well as capital projects and outlays financed on a pay-as-you-go basis directly from future operating revenues. A multiyear forecast can reveal a city's ability or inability in the future to cover these future debt service, capital, and operating requirements.

The LGBFCA does not require a city or any other local government to prepare a multiyear financial forecast. Preparing one is a matter of local policy. In the 1990–91 survey of city budget practices, eighteen of the forty-eight cities in the sample that were asked about multiyear financial forecasting (all above 5,000 in population) responded that they had such forecasts. Multiyear forecasting was most common among the large cities; four of the state's five cities above 100,000 in population had such forecasts.[27]

In cities where multiyear revenue and expenditure forecasts are prepared, the forecasts are typically presented to the city council for review and approval. The forecast may be presented to the council in a special section of the annual budget document or in an altogether separate document. Council approval of the forecast has no legally binding effect. It does not commit the council to raise revenues or make expenditures at the levels shown in the forecast or at any other levels. Council approval is tantamount to acceptance of the forecast and indicates council recognition of the financial situation forecasted for the city.

The methodology for a multiyear financial forecast typically carries forward revenue and expenditure trends from prior years and adjusts them for events that officials know or expect will affect the trends during the forecast period. The forecast of revenues is typically by fund and by major source within each fund. For the general fund, separate forecasts would ordinarily be made of revenues from the property tax, the sales and use taxes, major state-shared taxes, and other sources. For utility or enterprise funds, separate forecasts would be made of revenues from each major operating or user charge and from other sources. The forecast of some revenues should involve a projection of the tax base—for example, taxable value for the property tax—with the forecast resulting from application of the current or an adjusted tax rate to the projected base. Most forecasts assume the continuation of current tax or revenue rates through the forecast period. The advantage of this is that it avoids assumptions about council actions during the forecast period to increase rates or charges. The disadvantage is that the forecast is likely to show imbalances between revenues and expenditures for particular years that could be difficult to explain to interested members of the public. Because of this and for certain other reasons, some multiyear forecasts assume and provide for changes in the property tax rate or other charges that the forecast shows will be necessary to balance revenues and expenditures in years during the forecast period.

The forecast of expenditures is typically by fund and by line-item category or by department and function within each fund. A forecast of expenditures by line item across departments within a fund rather than by department within a fund is less likely to influence department officials' judgments about what growth or changes in expenditures will be expected or accepted for their respective departments during the forecast period. However, such a forecast may be less accurate than one by department and line item within each department. Forecasts of expenditures can be based on carrying current per capita expenditures into the forecast period, on analyzing probable changes in expenditures in each expenditure category, or some combination of these approaches. An expenditure forecast based partly or wholly on an analysis of probable changes or increases in expenditures would have to make some assumptions about salary and wage adjustments, inflation or deflation, replacement of capital equipment and property, creation of new positions, expansion of existing programs and creation of new ones, and acquisition or construction of new capital infrastructure during the forecast period.

Additional Resources

Government Finance Officers Association. *Research Report: The Use of Performance Measures in City and County Budgets.* Chicago: GFOA, Government Finance Research Center, 1994.

Lawrence, David M. *Local Government Finance in North Carolina,* 2d ed., especially chaps. 5–8. Chapel Hill, N.C.: Institute of Government, The University of North Carolina at Chapel Hill, 1990.

Strachota, Dennis. *The Best of Governmental Budgeting: A Guide to Preparing Budget Documents.* Chicago: Government Finance Officers Association, 1994.

Notes

1. See, for example, Greensboro v. Smith, 241 N.C. 363, 85 S.E.2d 292 (1955), and the discussion of this case in David M. Lawrence, *Local Government Finance in North Carolina*, 2d ed. (Chapel Hill, N.C.: Institute of Government, The University of North Carolina at Chapel Hill, 1990), 3.

2. Mitchell v. Financing Auth., 273 N.C. 137, 159 S.E.2d 745 (1968); Foster v. Medical Care Comm'n, 283 N.C. 110, 195 S.E.2d 517 (1973); and Stanley v. Department of Conservation and Dev., 284 N.C. 15, 199 S.E.2d 641 (1973).

3. N.C. Const. art. V, §§ 8, 9.

4. Dennis v. Raleigh, 253 N.C. 400, 116 S.E.2d 923 (1960).

5. Government Finance Officers Association, *Governmental Accounting, Auditing and Financial Reporting* (Chicago: GFOA, 1994), 332.

6. GFOA, *Governmental Accounting*, 15–17, 317.

7. For a discussion of basis of accounting, see GFOA, *Governmental Accounting*, 23–24.

8. GFOA, *Governmental Accounting*, 351.

9. The Local Government Commission and independent public accountants auditing local government finances discourage the use of nondepartmental appropriations.

10. GFOA, *Governmental Accounting*, ch. 11. The Local Government Commission discourages the accumulation of fund balances in internal service funds.

11. Selected results of this survey of budget practices are summarized in A. John Vogt and Charles K. Coe, "A Close Look at North Carolina City and County Budget Practices," *Popular Government* 59 (Summer 1993): 16–28; and Charles K. Coe and A. John Vogt, "How North Carolina Cities and Counties Budget for Community Agencies," *Popular Government* 58 (Winter 1993): 26. Unpublished results of this survey are available from the Institute of Government.

12. Vogt and Coe, "A Close Look," 17.

13. See, for example, *American City and County* 110, no. 4 (April 1995): 84.

14. Vogt and Coe, "A Close Look," 21.

15. Vogt and Coe, Unpublished survey results, available from the Institute of Government.

16. Vogt and Coe, Unpublished survey results, available from the Institute of Government.

17. Vogt and Coe, Unpublished survey results, available from the Institute of Government.

18. David Osborne and Ted Gaebler, *Reinventing Government: How the Entrepreneurial Spirit Is Transforming the Public Sector* (Reading, Mass.: Addison-Wesley Publishing Company, 1992).

19. Governmental Accounting Standards Board, *Proposed Statement on Concepts Related to Service Efforts and Accomplishments Reporting* (Norwalk, Conn.: GASB, September 1993).

20. N.C. Const. art. V, § 2(7); G.S. 160-20.1.

21. Charles K. Coe and A. John Vogt, "How North Carolina Cities and Counties Budget for Community Agencies," *Popular Government* 58 (Winter 1993): 26.

22. Coe and Vogt, "How North Carolina Cities and Counties Budget," 26.

23. These requirements are mentioned in the earlier section The Public-Purpose Limitation. They are based on Dennis v. Raleigh, 253 N.C. 400, 116 S.E.2d 923 (1960).

24. Chapter 12 describes the formula and the procedures for levying the property tax. This section simply explains how the effective date of an annexation determines or influences when an annexing city begins to earn and receive additional property tax and other major revenues from an annexation.

25. Chapter 11 describes in full the per capita and ad valorem methods of distributing sales tax revenue among government entities in a county.

26. Chapter 11 describes in full these state-shared taxes and the methods that the state uses for allocating them among local governments.

27. Vogt and Coe, "A Close Look," 26.

14 Capital Improvements, Capital Budgets, and Debt

A. John Vogt and David M. Lawrence

Contents

PLANNING, financing, and providing the capital infrastructure, facilities, and equipment needed for public services are among the most important responsibilities of city officials. The North Carolina General Statutes give local governments, including cities, specific powers that are important in capital budgeting. G.S. Chapter 159, Article 4, the Local Government Bond Act, prescribes procedures for the authorization and the issuance of general obligation bonds secured by taxing power for a broad range of capital purposes.

G.S. Chapter 159, Article 5, authorizes revenue bonds secured by the net earnings of a self-supporting enterprise to finance capital projects for such enterprises. Under the security interests statute (G.S. 160A-20), installment purchase or certificate of participation debt, which is secured by the asset being financed with the debt, may be used to acquire or build capital assets. The Solid Waste Management Loan Program (G.S. Ch. 159I) authorizes special obligation debt, secured by revenues from any available source as long as city taxing power is not pledged, for certain solid waste projects. G.S. 159-18 through -22 permits the accumulation of moneys in capital reserve funds for future capital expenditures or improvements, and G.S. 159-13.2 permits the appropriation of moneys for capital projects or expenditures in capital project ordinances. Finally, one statutory duty of managers in cities with the council-manager form of government is to prepare and submit a capital program [G.S. 153A-82(5)].

Although these statutes grant major powers, they do not define or suggest what a capital budget is. Nor do they specify a process for local governments to use in capital budgeting; this absence contrasts with the provisions relating to annual budgeting, for which the Local Government Budget and Fiscal Control Act (G.S. Ch. 159, Art. 3) sets forth a process for local units to follow (see chapter 13 of this volume).

What, then, is *capital budgeting and finance*? It may be defined as a process that has the following steps. The steps are the subjects of the next six sections.

1. *Identification and classification of capital requests and expenditures.* This step consists of deciding whether particular requests are in fact capital (see next section) and whether they belong in the capital budget, as well as making sure that specific expenditure items properly chargeable to a capital project or outlay are so charged and others are not.

2. *Capital improvement programming.* This step involves planning for and scheduling major capital needs for approval, funding, and implementation over a five- to ten-year forecast period.

3. *Assessment and maintenance of a city's ability to finance capital needs.* This step involves taking the steps necessary to maintain and/or improve a city's bond or credit ratings, determining present financial condition, and forecasting the

resources that will be available to finance capital needs over the same five- to ten-year forecast period covered by the capital improvement program.

4. *Selection of the financing source(s) for individual capital projects and expenditures.* Major capital projects are typically financed by issuing bonds or other forms of debt. Other sources of capital financing include current revenues, capital reserves, and gifts or grants.

5. *Authorization of capital projects or expenditures and appropriation of funds for them.* Authorization and appropriation may occur together or in separate steps. Appropriation may be made in the annual budget ordinance or in one or more capital project ordinances.

6. *Implementation of the capital budget.* This step consists of managing the funds that have been accumulated for capital projects and expenditures; acquiring equipment; and designing, contracting for, supervising, and accounting for construction projects.

Identification and Classification of Capital Requests and Expenditures

Broadly conceived, a *capital expenditure* is an outlay of significant value that results in acquisition of or addition to a fixed asset.[1] The term *fixed asset* refers to property that is held or used for more than one year, usually for many years. *Fixed* does not mean "immobile"; an automobile is usually a fixed asset.

According to the Department of State Treasurer's *Policies Manual,*[2] which recommends fiscal policies and practices for local governments, fixed assets that are owned and used in city operations can be classified into the following categories:

1. All land or rights to land.
2. All buildings.
3. Additions to or renovations of buildings that cost $500 or more and that add value to the building or improve its utility.
4. Improvements to land other than buildings that cost $500 or more and that add value to land or improve its utility. These

improvements can include drainage systems, parking lots, and similar construction on land.

5. Equipment and furnishings that cost $500 or more. Additions to or refurbishing of equipment that costs $250 or more is also a fixed asset according to the *Policies Manual.*

Expenditures for fixed assets owned by a city and used in its operations that are for general governmental purposes should be budgeted for in the general fund, a capital projects fund, or another governmental fund, and then recorded or carried as *general* fixed assets in a city's accounting system. Expenditures for fixed assets owned by a city that are used in enterprise or proprietary fund activities should be budgeted for and recorded or carried as fixed assets in the appropriate enterprise or proprietary funds. If a city acquires or builds a fixed asset for the purpose of selling or donating the asset to another organization—for example, to the local housing authority—the city must of course budget for the expenditure but does not have to record or carry it as a fixed asset.

Cities also make major capital expenditures for infrastructure that is used by the public—streets, roads, bridges, sidewalks, drainage systems, and similar improvements. Such assets are typically immovable and have value only to the governmental entity that builds them and the public that uses or benefits from them. Expenditures for infrastructure must be budgeted for—usually in a capital projects fund—but the recording or the capitalizing of such public domain infrastructure in a city's accounting system is optional and is usually not done, except that all enterprise or other proprietary fund infrastructure is capitalized.

The general definition of capital expenditure just given says that such an expenditure must be of *significant value*—$500 as a minimum for improvements to land and for equipment and $250 for additions to or refurbishing of equipment, according to the *Policies Manual.* A city must select a specific dollar amount as a minimum expenditure for equipment and improvements other than buildings to budget and account for (capitalize) them as fixed or capital assets. The selection of this minimum is a local decision and should depend on the size of the city. For example, many small cities use a minimum as low as $100, and some large cities use one as high as $1,000 or several thousand dollars.

Generally, in governmental budgeting and accounting, only expenditures to acquire *tangible* assets or property are recorded as fixed assets.[3] Tangible assets are touchable or physical items—for example, land, buildings, and equipment. Expenditures to acquire *intangible* assets, such as a patent or a license for a specific technology, are seldom recorded as fixed assets for governmental funds in the general fixed asset account group[4] (intangible fixed assets should be capitalized in an enterprise fund).[5] Despite general practices, a growing number of North Carolina cities are recording expenditures for computer software programs as fixed or capital assets. If the software is an operating system, comes with the hardware, and without it the hardware cannot run, the software should probably be capitalized as part of the computer's costs. If the software is an application program, it may have market value of its own. In this instance the software could be capitalized separately from the hardware.

Not all capital expenditures have to be included in the capital budget. *Inexpensive capital expenditures and those that recur every year* may be reviewed in the annual budget process, approved in the annual budget ordinance, and accounted for in the general fund or in another operating fund. The meaning of *inexpensive* will vary with the size of the city. A small city might establish a dollar cutoff for this determination of anywhere from several thousand dollars to $10,000 or so, and include all capital assets with an acquisition or construction cost below this amount in its annual budget and all more costly capital assets in a separate capital budget. A medium-size or large city would use a higher cutoff—for example, anywhere from $20,000 to $50,000 or even $100,000—and put only capital assets that cost more than this amount in its capital budget. The rest of the city's capital expenditures or assets would be included in the annual budget.

Many *annually recurring capital expenditures* are made to replace vehicles or equipment. For example, some large cities replace one or more sanitation packers annually. Because each packer has a useful life of more than one year and is of significant value—that is, it costs more than the minimum dollar amount used for capitalization—each is a fixed asset, and the expenditures to acquire one or more of them are capital. But annually recurring expenditures to replace sanitation packers or other equipment or for other capital purposes, like relatively inexpensive capital expenditures, present no special problem that would prevent their inclusion in the annual budget. They can be reviewed and approved in the annual budget, which can accommodate them just as readily as expenditures for salaries, supplies, and operating items, which are also cumulatively expensive and recur yearly.

It is the very expensive, long-lived, and irregularly recurring capital projects and acquisitions that deserve the special treatment and planning called capital budgeting. Such projects and acquisitions must often be identified and planned ahead of actual need through a multiyear capital improvement program, for which careful financial planning has to occur. They require large amounts of financing, for which debt is often issued, and they are frequently budgeted in capital project ordinances and accounted for in special capital project funds.

Problems occasionally arise in deciding whether to charge specific items of cost to a capital project or expenditure. A capital project or acquisition should include all expenditures or items that are incurred to put the capital asset being built or acquired into operating condition. For construction projects these items would include all costs for labor and construction materials; planning as well as architectural and engineering design; legal services; the acquisition of land or other property for the project, including brokerage fees, and the preparation of land for construction; easements; equipment and furnishings that are affixed to the project; interest and other financing charges during construction; and project administration charges. For equipment acquisitions the capital cost or expenditure includes not only the purchase price of the equipment per se, but also any transportation charges to move the equipment to its place of intended use and costs for installation and testing, if any.

Expenditures for certain items associated with a capital asset or facility may not be charged as a capital cost of the asset. Instead, they are operating expenditures. For example, although expenditures to buy land for a landfill and ready it for use are properly charged as capital costs for the landfill, expenditures for certain closure and postclosure purposes at a landfill are considered to be operating expenditures, according to interpretations of the bond statutes and generally accepted accounting principles, and may not be included among capital costs.[6] Furthermore, although some expenditures for maintenance and repair—for example, a major repainting project on a large building—may preserve the useful lives of capital assets and seem like capital expenditures, they should be budgeted and accounted for as operating expenditures.

Capital Improvement Programming

One useful approach for planning capital acquisitions and improvements is a *capital improvement program* (CIP). A CIP forecasts future capital project and expenditure needs of a city, identifies sources of financing for those projects and expenditures, and points to the effect that the projects and the expenditures, if approved and implemented, will have on future annual budgets. A survey of North Carolina city budget practices for 1990–91 revealed that 69 percent of the cities above 5,000 in population that were surveyed, or thirty-three of forty-eight, had CIPs in that year.[7] More and more cities have instituted CIP processes in recent years to plan major infrastructure programs and in response to recommendations of the Local Government Commission and the debt rating agencies.

CIP Forecast Period and Allocation of Costs by Year

Most CIPs forecast five or six years into the future. A shorter period generally does not allow enough time to plan and obtain clearances and funding for major projects, although some, mostly small cities have successfully used three- or four-year CIPs. A few of the state's largest cities have used ten-year forecast periods, but such long forecasts involve considerable guesswork with the projection of needs for the latter part of the forecast period necessarily remaining general.

The essential feature of a CIP is the apportionment of capital expenditures among the years of the forecast period. On the CIP summary form (figure 14-1), the columns designated Prior Years and Current Year are used for capital projects that are in process. Expenditures have been incurred for them, are being incurred for them, or both; but the projects are not finished, and expenditures will be incurred for them in the coming Budget Year and possibly in one or more of the Planning Years. The column designated Budget Year lists capital expenditures that will be incurred in the next year. These expenditures may be for projects in process or for projects or expenditures that are in the final stage of review in this year's CIP, for which money will be spent in the Budget Year if they are approved. The columns on the CIP form designated Planning Years can show expenditures to be incurred in the future for multiyear projects that are in process, for projects that are getting under way in the Budget

Figure 14-1
CIP Summary Form, All Funds
Project Expenditures, Funding Sources, and Operating Budget Impact by Year

	Prior Years	Current Year	Budget Year	Planning Years					Subsequent Years	Total Project
				Year 1	Year 2	Year 3	Year 4	Year 5		
Project Expenditures by Function										
General government										
Public safety										
Streets & transportation										
Culture & recreation										
Community, physical, & economic development										
Environmental protection										
Water & sewer										
Other enterprises										
Total Expenditures for All Projects										
Funding Sources										
General fund revenues										
Enterprise fund revenues										
General capital reserves										
Enterprise capital reserves										
General obligation bonds authorized										
General obligation bonds two-thirds										
General obligation bonds to be authorized										
Revenue bonds										
Certificates of participation or leases										
Special obligation bonds										
Impact fees or assessments										
Grants, contributions, gifts, & other										
Total for All Funding Sources										
Effect of Projects on Annual Budget										
Salaries, wages, & benefits										
Other operating & maintenance expenditures										
Capital expenditures										
Debt service and lease payments										
Revenues										
Net Impact on Annual Operating Budget										

Year but will not be completed until a later year, and for projects that are scheduled to start in one of the Planning Years. The column designated Subsequent Years is for expenditures on projects that get under way in the CIP forecast period, usually in one of the Planning Years, but will not be finished until sometime after the CIP forecast period.

The CIP's phasing of projects and expenditures by year is important not only in scheduling, but also in setting priorities. A capital project or expenditure that is scheduled in the Budget Year or an early CIP Planning Year is often placed there because it has a higher priority than other projects and outlays scheduled for one or more of the later Planning Years.

As figure 14-1 suggests, CIPs often distribute costs over the years covered by the CIP based on when expenditures will be made. Alternatively, costs can be allocated among a CIP's years based on when a city council is expected to make appropriations for projects or outlays or when contractual obligations will be incurred for projects or outlays. Of course, appropriation, contracting, and expenditures for a project or an acquisition can all occur in the same year, especially if the project or the item is relatively small or modest in size. However, they often occur in different years for relatively large projects or acquisitions. A hypothetical example illustrates the difference among these alternatives. A multiyear construction project for a city will cost $3 million. All $3 million will be appropriated for the project in the coming Budget Year; $2 million in contracts will be let for it in that year and $1 million in Planning Year 1; and $1 million will be spent for the project in the Budget Year, $1 million in Planning Year 1, and $1 million in Planning Year 2. If the city's CIP allocates costs by year based on when appropriations for projects are made, the CIP will show the full $3 million in the Budget Year. However, if the CIP allocates project costs by year based on when contracts are let, it will show $2 million in the Budget Year and $1 million in Planning Year 1. If costs in the CIP are allocated by year based on spending, then the CIP will show $1 million in the Budget Year, $1 million in Planning Year 1, and $1 million in Planning Year 2. The 1990–91 survey of city budget practices found that among the thirty-three cities above 5,000 in population with CIPs, distribution of costs by year in the CIP was based on spending in thirteen cities, on appropriations in twelve, on contractual obligations in five, and on other bases in three.[8]

A CIP that distributes costs by year based on when appropriations are made focuses attention principally on the decisions that officials must make to approve projects. The approval of projects or expenditures often occurs via appropriations. Even if effective approval of a project occurs before appropriations are made for it, the appropriation of funds is usually a key step in getting the project going. A CIP that distributes costs by year based on when contracts are let or on when expenditures occur addresses both decision-making and implementation concerns: decision-making concerns because appropriations are generally associated with contracts let or expenditures made for a project in its first year, and implementation concerns because contracting and spending are integral parts of project execution. A city should use one basis for distributing costs by year in its CIP and not switch among bases for different projects.

The CIP is conceived as an annual process, and most cities that use one revise it each year. Annual review provides for a recurring assessment of capital needs and updates the CIP to accommodate new projects and expenditures. New capital requests should be anticipated before the time of need and first placed in the CIP in one of the later Planning Years (Planning Years 3, 4, or 5). Then, as the CIP process is repeated annually, the standing requests are reviewed, those that pass muster move up a year toward approval and funding, and marginal requests are weeded out. When the requests that survive reach the Budget Year, they are approved and funding arrangements are made. Of course, not all capital needs can be foreseen years in advance. Some capital requests must be approved and funded almost immediately after the need for them becomes apparent. If this happens with many projects, however, the CIP loses much of its value as a planning tool.

The CIP Preparation Process

The total time needed for CIP preparation, review, and approval may span up to six months or so in the state's largest cities. It may span only a month to several months in small and medium-size cities.

An important issue is whether the CIP process should occur before, along with, or after the annual budget process. Both processes involve much time and work, and running them simultaneously can be difficult. Some cities prepare CIPs before the annual budget process begins. In this way, decisions about major improvements that are made in the CIP process establish a framework for follow-up decisions on operating issues that are made in the annual budget. As a result, the annual budget process can be less complex and difficult. Other cities run the CIP process concurrently with the annual budget process. Indeed, CIP preparation is viewed and treated as just one part, albeit an important one, of the annual budget process in some of these cities. Linking the CIP to annual budget preparation in this way helps ensure that program operation and capital project decisions, which arise from the same general needs, are adequately coordinated. Few jurisdictions prepare their CIPs after the annual budget has been prepared and presented. The 1990–91 survey of city budget practices revealed that among the thirty-three cities above 5,000 in population with CIPs, the CIP was presented to the city council before presentation of the annual budget in fourteen cities, concurrent with presentation of the annual budget in sixteen cities, and after presentation of the annual budget in three cities.[9]

Coordination

One official in a city is typically assigned the responsibility of coordinating the preparation of the CIP. In small jurisdictions this official is typically the city manager or administrator. In medium-size and large cities, the manager is likely to delegate the responsibility to another official. The 1990–91 survey of budget practices found that the city manager or administrator coordinated the CIP process in seven of the thirty-three cities above 5,000 in population with CIPs, the budget director or a budget analyst in seven cities, the finance director in seven cities, an assistant manager or assistant to the manager in six cities, the planning director in three cities, and other officials in three cities.[10] In some cities an administrative committee composed of the manager and top staff officials oversees CIP preparation. However, even with this arrangement, one of the officials on the committee typically has day-to-day responsibility for coordinating the CIP.

A city's CIP should be coordinated with other multiyear plans that relate to the city's growth in future years. For instance, a city may have a strategic plan that addresses community growth over the next decade, a stormwater construction plan, a utility system expansion plan, neighborhood revitalization plans, annexation plans, a comprehensive-land-use development plan, or a capital or needs assessment that forecasts city capital projects five to ten years beyond the CIP planning period. A CIP often is a vehicle for implementing these and any other plans that directly address or have implications for a city's capital infrastructure needs.

A city's CIP should also be coordinated with projects in the state's Transportation Improvement Program (TIP). The TIP forecasts state highway and road construction projects seven years into the future and includes many projects that affect thoroughfare and street construction plans for cities of all sizes across the state. City officials should make sure that local transportation projects that are in their CIPs are coordinated with state projects that the TIP shows will get under way in or near their jurisdictions in the future.

Requests

The CIP preparation process typically begins with the issuance of request forms and instructions to departments and other agencies that participate in the CIP process. In most cities, only city departments may submit CIP project requests. In a few cities, special-purpose governmental entities, like a public housing authority, or community service agencies that provide services to city residents, like a homeless shelter, may be allowed or encouraged to submit project requests in the city's CIP process.

Instructions for CIP requests usually specify what types of capital projects and expenditures may be included in the CIP. Cities vary, principally according to size, in the types of capital items that their CIPs include. For example, in one city with a population of 10,000, projects or items that have a useful life of more than one year and cost $20,000 or more are included in the CIP. One of the state's largest cities limits CIP requests to projects that are for construction, renovation, or purchase of buildings, for infrastructure, for purchases of land, or for major landscaping; and that have a useful life of ten years or more and cost more than $25,000 per project. Neither purchases of vehicles nor acquisitions of freestanding equipment, no matter how large, are included in the city's CIP. Items or projects not meeting these criteria are planned, budgeted, and financed entirely in the city's annual budget process. Most other large cities in the state include nonrecurring and expensive equipment and vehicles in their CIPs and have a minimum-useful-life requirement that is shorter than ten years for CIP projects.

The description of and the justification for any CIP project or acquisition should do the following:

- Summarize the project or the acquisition and explain how it fits with the objectives and the future plans of the requesting department or agency.
- Indicate the clients whom the project or the acquisition will serve and explain the effect of the project or the acquisition on them.
- Identify any alternatives to the requested project or acquisition.
- Provide expenditure estimates for completing the project or the acquisition, and address the probability that the expenditure estimates will escalate over time.
- Identify funding sources that may be available to fund the project or the acquisition. Program officials in most city departments are not likely to be knowledgeable about suitability and availability of general financing sources for most CIP requests. Nevertheless, program officials are often in a position to identify grants or other special funding sources for CIP projects that they propose. The city's finance director and other administrative officials are generally in the best position to identify and make recommendations about the applicability and the selection of funding sources for specific CIP requests. Figure 14-1 shows the typical funding sources that are available for financing capital projects in North Carolina. The most important ones are discussed in detail under the heading Capital Financing Methods, later in this chapter. However, a comment is appropriate here about whether a CIP should include projects that are to be financed with general obligation bonds yet to be authorized by the voters, shown as General Obligation Bonds to Be Authorized in figure 14-1. The inclusion of projects to be funded with general obligation bonds that are not yet authorized presumes that the voters will approve a referendum. Nevertheless, the CIPs of some of the state's cities include this source of financing and identify projects to be funded from it. In these jurisdictions the CIP serves as a springboard for seeking voter approval of general obligation bonds for the projects or purposes to be funded from them.

- Provide a schedule for completing the project or making the acquisition, and indicate the relationship of this project to other projects in general, to other projects or acquisitions that must be completed before this one is undertaken, and to other projects that should await completion of this one.
- Comment on the status of any feasibility studies, architectural or engineering plans, land or right-of-way acquisitions, or construction already done for the project or the acquisition.
- Show the effect of the project or the acquisition on the annual operating budget, considering additional operating and maintenance expenditures and debt service or lease payments that are likely to result, and any one-time or recurring savings or revenues that the project is likely to generate.
- Indicate the project's or acquisition's priority among other CIP requests that the department is making.

Review and Approval

After CIP project and acquisition requests have been submitted, city administrative staff need to review the requests from several standpoints. Requests should be checked for appropriateness for inclusion in the CIP and for technical feasibility. Project justifications, expenditure estimates, and the impact of projects on the operating budget must be verified. The availability of proposed financing sources for particular projects needs to be confirmed, and the ability of the city to incur new debt to finance CIP projects or acquisitions should be determined. Finally, relationships among CIP requests, of CIP requests to other multiyear development plans that the city may have, and of CIP requests to capital improvement plans of other governments that serve city residents—for example, the county—need to be taken into account.

Once the review of CIP requests is finished, a recommended CIP for the city is usually prepared. This is likely to involve hard choices because the total of CIP requests is likely to exceed by far the availability of capital financing over the CIP forecast period. Even if the city were to issue debt to finance all or most CIP requests, the amount of debt that it could issue would be limited by its ability to service the debt during the forecast period and beyond. Many cities incorporate ranking criteria or systems into their CIP process to help put CIP project and acquisition requests in priority order. For example, officials in one North Carolina city use the following ranking criteria, the first criterion having the highest priority:

1. Is mandated: Is clearly and specifically required by federal or state laws or court rulings.
2. Removes hazard: Removes an existing or potential hazard that threatens public health or safety.
3. Maintains service: Permits an existing standard of service to be maintained. If the request is not funded, a decrease in service will occur.
4. Improves efficiency: Reduces operating expenditures in the annual budget.
5. Increases revenues: Yields a net gain in revenues, considering increases in gross revenues and expenditures over the useful life of the project.
6. Expands or improves existing service: Increases the population served, the quantity of the service or the product provided, or the quality of the service or the product.
7. Creates new service: Makes possible the provision of an altogether new service or program.
8. Increases convenience, and Other: Increases the ease with which a service is provided, or does not fit into another category.

Many capital project and acquisition requests are likely to be excluded from the CIP that is recommended for a city. Some requests are likely to be excluded because they are not justified or because they are not technically feasible. Others that are justified and technically feasible are likely to be excluded because they are of lower priority given the financing capabilities of the city. In some future year the latter requests may take on a higher priority and be included in the CIP. Because of this, some CIPs contain a special section or appendix that lists currently low-priority but otherwise justified CIP requests that are not included in the current CIP but may be included in it in later years.

The city manager or administrator, or if a city has no manager or administrator, another official—for example, the finance director—usually presents the recommended CIP to the city council. If this presentation occurs as part of the annual budget process, the recommended CIP is typically included in the document presenting the annual budget. In many cities the recommended CIP is presented to the council in a separate CIP document.

Whether the CIP is presented to the council in the annual budget document or as a separate document, the city council usually holds one or more review sessions focused exclusively on the CIP and capital projects or acquisitions included in it. Although there is no statutory requirement for a city council to hold a public hearing on the recommended CIP, city councils often do so to give citizens the opportunity to comment on the entire program or specific projects. The 1990–91 survey of city budget practices found that among the thirty-three cities above 5,000 in population with CIPs, councils in twelve cities held one or more public hearings on the recommended CIP. Councils in the other cities did not.[11]

After considering and making changes in the recommended CIP, councils in most cities pass a resolution approving it. The 1990–91 survey found that councils in twenty-two of the thirty-three cities above 5,000 in population with CIPs enacted such resolutions.[12] The resolution approves the CIP as a plan for the forecast period. Generally it does not represent council approval of or commitment to any one project or expenditure, nor does it of itself appropriate money for any project or expenditure. However, as already mentioned, projects and expenditures in the first year of the CIP typically become the proposed capital budget for that year, and unless such projects and expenditures are in process with appropriations made for them in prior years, they are up for council approval and appropriation.

Council appropriation of moneys for projects and expenditures in the Budget Year of the CIP can be accomplished either in the annual budget ordinance, in amendments to that ordinance, or in one or more capital project ordinances (see the discussion under the heading Use of Capital Project Ordinances, later in the chapter).

In some cities, council approval of the CIP as a plan may occur almost simultaneously with council appropriation of funds for projects and expenditures in the Budget Year of the CIP. Because of this, approval of the CIP itself and appropriation of money for projects or expenditures may be difficult to distinguish. Moreover, in cities where the council does not pass a resolution approving a CIP, appropriation of funds for projects and expenditures in the first year of the CIP can be seen as approval of the CIP itself. Nevertheless, approval of the CIP, on the one hand, and approval of CIP projects and appropriation of money for them, on the other hand, are typically and should be separate steps.

Reasons for Preparing a CIP

Why should a city undertake a CIP? There are numerous reasons:

1. Having such a program helps a city meet capital replacement and new capital needs in an orderly fashion.
2. By forecasting, officials allow enough time for project planning and design. Without a CIP these functions are often rushed, and errors in design are much more likely to result.
3. A CIP can be a helpful fiscal planning tool because forecasting capital demands on local revenues and borrowing power helps a city avoid overextending itself financially during the forecast period and even beyond.
4. A CIP enables a city to schedule the implementation of projects, helping it phase related projects in the most efficient sequence and avoid having to cope with an unmanageable number of major projects at any one time.
5. By identifying major capital requirements before they are needed, a CIP can put city officials in a better position to secure grants, few though they may be, and generally to arrange funding for projects.
6. As already mentioned, a CIP can be an effective springboard for an effort to secure voter approval for general obligation bonds for certain purposes or projects.
7. Having a workable CIP can improve a city's debt rating.

Debt Ratings, Evaluation of Financial Condition, and Forecasting of Resources for Capital Financing

Cities must be able to raise the moneys that they need to undertake capital projects and acquire capital assets. Such moneys may come from annual revenues remaining after current operating needs are met, accumulated capital reserves, bond or other debt proceeds, special assessments or facility fees, federal or state grants, and other sources. Any capital budgeting process should be concerned with the city's bond or debt ratings, its current financial condition, and specifically the ways in which its ability to finance capital needs is likely to change over the planning period covered by the CIP.

Debt Ratings

A debt or bond rating generally evaluates the capacity and the willingness of the issuer to repay debt and to make timely interest payments on debt.[13] North Carolina's cities are rated by several national bond rating agencies—Standard & Poor's Corporation (S & P), Moody's Investors Service (Moody's), and Fitch Investor's Service (Fitch's)—and by the North Carolina Municipal Council, which is an association of banks, securities dealers, bond attorney firms, and regulatory agencies that are involved in the municipal bond market in North Carolina. In rating municipal debt and debt issuers, the rating agencies rely on annual financial reports, annual budgets, CIPs, and other reports and information as well as official offering statements for bond or debt issues themselves.

All three of the national bond rating agencies have headquarters in New York, although each has regional offices in different parts of the country.[14] S & P and Moody's rate nearly all North Carolina local government debt that is sold nationally. Fitch's became active (again) in rating municipal debt in the late 1980s; so far, however, it has rated only a few North Carolina local government debt issues each year. The national agencies evaluate the creditworthiness of a city or any issuer with regard to a specific bond or debt offering. In other words, the rating applies to a specific bond or debt issue rather than to the entity issuing the debt, although the rating on the debt, especially if it is general obligation debt, depends heavily on the strength and the prospects of the issuer. A national debt or bond rating addresses not only the ability and the willingness of the issuer to make debt service payments, but also the legal protection afforded by the bond or the debt contract to investors. Such protection is a function of the contract and of the statutory and constitutional provisions that authorize and regulate this type of debt. A national rating may also take into account credit support, if any is provided, from bond insurance or other sources of guaranty for a debt or bond issue. Bond insurance guarantees to investors the payment of interest and the repayment of principal on an insured bond or debt issue. Insurance from a highly rated national bond insurance company gives the insured debt the rating of the insurance company. The national agencies rate all types of municipal debt: general obligation bonds or notes, revenue bonds, certificates of participation and other debt secured by the asset being financed with the debt, special obligation bonds, and different types of short-term municipal debt.

The national rating agencies use letter rating systems for bonds and other long-term debt. For instance, S & P uses ten general rating categories: AAA, AA, A, BBB, BB, B, CCC, CC, C, and D. The ratings from AA to CCC may be modified by the addition of a plus or minus sign (+ or –) to indicate relative quality within the general categories. The four highest categories, AAA through BBB, are referred to as *investment grade* or *bank eligible* ratings. Banks and certain other financial institutions are not supposed to invest in municipal debt that is otherwise a permissible investment for them unless the debt has a bank eligible rating. Bonds or other long-term debt rated BB or below is regarded as speculative (popularly called *junk bonds*). Debt rated D is in default.

Moody's uses a similar rating system for bonds and long-term debt, although it makes use of nine rather than ten categories: Aaa, Aa, A, Baa, Ba, B, Caa, Ca, and C. Debt in each of the Aa through B groups that has the strongest investment attributes carries an additional rating symbol of 1: Aa1, A1, Baa1, Ba1, and B1. Debt in the first four rating groups is bank eligible. Debt in the lower-rated groups is considered to be speculative.

To secure a rating from a national rating agency for new bonds or debt, a city or any other issuer generally must request it. The Local Government Commission recommends that a North Carolina local government obtain at least one national rating when it sells $1 million to $2 million in debt, and two national ratings when it sells over $2 million. The national rating agencies charge anywhere from several thousand dollars to around $25,000, depending on the size of an issue, for a rating on general obligation bonds. To maintain a national rating, a city must send the agency annual financial reports, budgets, CIPs, and other positive or negative information that bears on its financial condition and prospects and therefore on the rating. If the rating agencies do not receive such information regularly, they will most likely suspend or withdraw their rating for the city's debt. If there is any material change in a city's financial condition, its rating may change. S & P provides *rating outlooks* for all debt that it rates.

These forecast the potential direction of an entity's debt rating. A rating outlook may be *negative*—the rating may be lowered; *stable*—the rating is unlikely to change; *positive*—the rating may be raised; or *developing*—the rating may be raised or lowered.

General obligation bond ratings from the national rating agencies are based on similar criteria, which fall into four areas: economic base, financial performance and flexibility, debt burden and management, and administration and governance. Economic base tends to be the most important element in general obligation ratings from the national agencies. Many of the criteria that enter into debt ratings from the national agencies are discussed under the next heading, Evaluation of Financial Condition.

The North Carolina Municipal Council is located in Raleigh.[15] It rates all cities in the state that have outstanding general obligation bonds, or other publicly traded tax-supported debt[16] such as certificates of participation issued to finance general public improvements. The Council does not rate cities or other local governments that have issued only revenue bonds or debt. Currently the Council maintains ratings on almost 250 North Carolina cities. It also has ratings on about 30 special districts as well as all 100 counties. Council ratings apply to the city or the unit issuing debt rather than to a specific bond or debt issue. Because of this, Council ratings do not reflect bond insurance or other guarantees for specific debt issues. Council ratings focus preponderantly on the ability and the willingness of the issuer to repay debt and make timely payments of interest. The Council uses a numeric rating system that ranges from 0 to 100, with 100 being the highest or best rating. Municipal bonds or debt of a city with a Council rating of 75 or more is considered to be eligible for investment by banks. The Council does not charge a local government for its rating service. Members of the Council pay for ratings through membership fees and assessments. The Council reviews and updates its rating for any unit with outstanding, rated debt at least once every three years or sooner if a unit is marketing new general obligation or publicly offered tax-supported debt. Council staff typically visit a city whenever the Council is reviewing the city's rating.

A Council rating is based on three general factors: general obligation and other tax-secured or -supported debt burden relative to wealth; administrative and financial record, which encompasses budgetary operations, accounting, level of taxes compared with similar units, tax collection, and other areas of financial operations; and payments program and resources, which considers debt structure and ability to make debt payments. Debt burden and structure are very important factors in the Council's rating system.

North Carolina's local governments are generally among the best rated in the country. As of January 1993, only thirty-two cities and counties in the country had AAA general obligation bond ratings from S & P.[17] Eight of these were, and still are as of this writing, North Carolina units. Among these AAA-rated entities are Charlotte, Raleigh, Greensboro, Winston-Salem, and Durham. Because of the importance that economic size and diversity have in determining a general obligation bond rating from one of the national agencies, it is most difficult for cities below 100,000 in population to secure AAA or Aaa ratings. The vast majority of cities in the state have A or BBB general obligation ratings. Only three cities, all small, have had less than bank eligible ratings (BB, Ba, or lower) from either S & P or Moody's in recent years.

The North Carolina Municipal Council's rating system results in few ratings in the 90s; only several of the state's largest cities have such high ratings. Most of the state's cities have ratings in the 80s and the upper 70s. A significant number, though, mostly small cities, have ratings below 75.

Because of their generally excellent debt ratings, the state's cities and other local governments are able to sell their bonds and debt at lower interest rates than local governments in virtually any other state. North Carolina local governments are often able to sell bonds at lower interest rates than comparably rated local governments in other states. The generally excellent credit of the state's cities and other local governments enables them to save millions of dollars in interest costs.

What accounts for the good debt ratings of North Carolina's cities and other local governments? The state's economy has grown and become more diversified. Local government financial management in North Carolina is professional and recognized throughout the country. Good local government leadership, the prevalence of the council-manager form of government, and conservative yet forward-looking budgeting and financial planning also underlie the good bond ratings of the state's local governments. Last but certainly not least, Local Government Commission oversight of debt policies and management, accounting and financial reporting, and budgeting and financial management has contributed greatly to the high local government ratings.[18]

Evaluation of Financial Condition

A city's debt rating and general financial position depend on the size and the strength of the local economy and the financial condition and practices of the city.

Size and Strength of the Local Economy

The local economy is a critical factor in determining the creditworthiness of any local government. The ability to provide services, to raise money, and to pay the cost of capital financing ultimately depends on the health of the local economy. A city's economic base is a function of income and wealth, economic diversity and stability, and the presence of infrastructure that is vital to strong economic performance.

Per capita income is one measure of wealth. Growth in per capita income for a city or the county in which it is located should be compared with that of the state as a whole and with that of other North Carolina jurisdictions of similar size in order to evaluate relative position. Data on per capita income are available from the Bureau of Economic Analysis of the United States Department of Commerce. Retail sales figures, which are another significant measure of wealth and economic activity, are available from the Sales and Use Tax Division of the North Carolina Department of Revenue.

The measure of wealth or economic activity that is most directly related to a city's ability to finance general public improvements is the value of property subject to taxation. Growth in property tax valuation can be compared with that of other cities of similar size. If a city's taxable value is growing relatively slowly, officials should be concerned and determine why: Is the cause underassessment or failure to discover taxable property for the tax rolls? The removal of property from the tax base due to state exemption of certain property or some other reason? A falloff or problems in an industry or an economic sector important to the city's tax base? Some other factor? New construction and industrial growth increase the property tax base of a city. Therefore economic development programs focused on these sectors can be vital in contributing to a city's long-term economic and fiscal well-being.

Economic diversity, which is important for a strong local economy, depends on having several major industries or economic sectors rather than just one. One measure of economic diversity is the level of employment by industry or sector; employment statistics are available from the North Carolina Employment Security Commission. A second measure is the portion of the value of taxable property that comes from a city's largest taxpayer or from a single industrial or economic sector. If more than 10 percent of property tax proceeds are attributed to any single taxpayer or if a significant portion—20 percent or more—of tax revenues comes from one industrial sector (for example, textiles), city officials should monitor the prospects of that industry or sector closely and promote the growth of different types of local economic activity, thereby diversifying the city's tax base.

The economic stability of a city is related to how the local economy holds up in a recession or in the face of general economic problems. One measure of economic stability is the rate of unemployment in the local labor force. This figure can be compared with unemployment rates in other areas, in the state, and in the nation as a whole. The analysis of comparative and historical data on employment can reveal how stable a local economy has been over a long period.

A city's ability to maintain a strong local economy depends on whether it has the infrastructure needed to support economic growth: transportation facilities, utilities, housing, schools, and health care facilities. Important questions with regard to infrastructure include the following: Is the city served by an airport and a railroad? Is it served by an interstate highway? What other roads are available for truck transportation? Are the facilities for water supply and sewage treatment large enough to meet current needs and future growth? What is the age and the composition of the local housing stock? How fast is new housing being built, if at all? Are community college or other technical training facilities adequate, and are their programs responsive to the need of the city and its surrounding region for skilled labor? Will schools and health care facilities be available to serve a growing population, and are the schools giving young people the education they need to function effectively in the workforce and in the community at large?

A city can attempt to strengthen its economic base by fostering economic development and providing the infrastructure needed to support growth. G.S. 158-7.1 gives cities the statutory authority to offer important incentives to industries and other businesses. If successful, economic development programs typically lead to improved financial conditions for the city government itself and also strengthen the city's capacity to finance capital projects. However, the results of economic development efforts are seldom immediate and cannot be guaranteed. (For further discussion of economic development activities, see chapter 20.) A city's financial position and practices are more directly under the control of its officials, and they also affect its ability to acquire and pay the cost of capital financing.

Financial Condition and Practices

A city's financial condition depends on its revenues, expenditures, fund balances or other reserves, outstanding debt, and debt service schedule. Revenues directly or indirectly support all city capital financing. They are necessary to provide current funding for capital outlays financed on a pay-as-you-go basis, to build capital reserves or fund balances to meet capital needs, and to pay debt service on debt obligations incurred to finance capital projects.

One measure of whether revenues are keeping pace with the need for services and capital facilities is growth of important general fund revenues (for example, property and sales and use tax revenues) in relation to growth in the city's population and in general fund expenditures. The property tax is the most general revenue source for most cities. Officials should closely monitor the increase from year to year in property tax revenue and the property tax base. They should know how much revenue growth results from tax-rate increases and how much from growth in the tax base. Separate sources of growth in this base—that is, new construction versus revaluation—should be distinguished.

Expenditures for operating purposes—for example, salaries and wages, fringe benefits, contractual services, and supplies—absorb revenues so they are otherwise not available for capital projects and expenditures. Expenditures for salaries, wages, and fringe benefits account for the largest share of operating expenditures for most city services. Officials can keep track of the number of authorized city positions per 1,000 population, counting part-time positions on a full-time-equivalent basis. This will permit a comparison with similar cities to determine relative staffing levels. Likewise, expenditures per capita for salaries, fringe benefits, and contractual services can be compared with those of similar cities. Officials for a city can compare the city's expenditures per capita for general line-item and functional categories with the averages for all of the state's cities of similar size by referring to the *Fiscal Summary of North Carolina Municipalities*.[19]

The available fund balance for a city at any one point in time consists of its cash plus investments less liabilities, encumbrances, and deferred revenues arising from cash receipts. Chapter 13 discusses fund balance in relation to annual budgeting. All that need be said in this chapter is that a city should maintain some fund balance and reserves for emergency capital replacement purposes. The general fund should have such fund balance or reserves, and enterprise funds should also have them. Moreover, such fund balance or reserves are in addition to the minimum general fund balance that the Local Government Commission recommends local governments carry to support their general fund annual operating budgets, equal to 8 percent of general fund expenditures. Maintaining adequate fund balance is one factor underlying the good debt ratings that North Carolina's local governments enjoy.

Outstanding debt and the annual debt service that a city must pay affect its financial condition and are crucial factors in determining its ability to finance future capital projects. If a city is already heavily in debt and making large annual debt service payments, it is unlikely to be able to borrow major new amounts of money to finance new capital projects. One measure of whether more debt can safely be issued is annual debt service on *net* (non-self-supporting) general obligation and other tax-supported debt, as a percentage of general operating expenditures and debt service. Some authorities say that this should ordinarily not exceed 15 to 20 percent.[20] Most North Carolina local governments hold it to less than 10 percent.

A second measure of safety in borrowing is outstanding general obligation debt as a percentage of the appraised value of taxable property. The statutes in fact set a legal limit on this percentage; according to G.S. 159-55, the net debt for any city may not exceed 8 percent of its taxable property valuation. *Net debt* is total authorized and outstanding general obligation debt plus other forms of general debt (for example, certificates of participation and lease purchase agreements), less debt issued for utility facilities and certain other deductions. (More is written about the calculation of net debt later in this chapter.) Although the legal net debt limit is 8 percent, virtually all cities restrict outstanding net general obligation debt to a percentage far below 8 percent of taxable valuation. For instance, on average, authorized and unissued and outstanding general obligation bonded debt, excluding enterprise debt, as a percentage of appraised property valuation for North Carolina's cities with such debt was only .61 as of June 30, 1994.[21] For cities above 50,000 in population, on average, the percentage was 1.01; and for cities with 1,000–2,499 people, it was .39. Excluding any authorized and unissued debt but including enterprise debt, most of which is paid from utility system revenues, on average, the outstanding general obligation bonded debt as a percentage of tax valuation for North Carolina's cities with such debt was 1.28 as of June 30, 1994.

Of course, one problem with any debt measure stated as a percentage of taxable value is that the latter can change significantly with the revaluation of real property. Before the revaluation a city could have net debt equal to 1.25 percent of taxable valuation. After the revaluation, however, this figure might drop to 1 percent or less. This occurs simply because real property in the unit has been reappraised and has a higher value for tax purposes; it has nothing to do with any change in the existing outstanding or authorized debt.

Per capita debt is another measure widely used to compare the debt burdens of cities and other local governments. As of June 30, 1994, outstanding and authorized and unissued general obligation bonded debt, excluding enterprise debt, for all North Carolina's cities with such debt was $347 per capita. Such debt was $476 per capita for cities above 50,000 in population and $463 for cities with 1,000–2,499 people. Excluding authorized and unissued debt but including enterprise debt, per capita debt for all North Carolina's cities with such debt was $468.[22]

Care must be exercised in interpreting these and other measures of debt burden. For instance, a growing resort town may have issued considerable general obligation debt to provide water, sewer, and other infrastructure. If its permanent resident population is small, its debt per capita will be quite high. On the other hand, the value of the town's taxable property, consisting mainly of expensive vacation homes, may be quite large, causing general obligation debt as a percentage of tax valuation to be modest.

Moreover, these general debt measures are useful for comparing cities only with regard to net general obligation and other debt serviced or paid from taxes and other general revenues. Judgments about a city's ability to carry revenue bonds or other special types of debt must be based on feasibility studies of the projects or enterprise systems financed with the bonds or the debt, and of the specific revenue streams earmarked for debt service on the bonds or the debt.

A city's financial practices also affect its financial position, creditworthiness, and ability to raise financing for capital projects at affordable rates. The most important of these practices are the budget, tax and revenue administration, and accounting and the annual audit. Key questions to ask about the annual budget are as follows: Is the budget enacted by July 1—the start of the budget year—every year? Do actual revenue collections during the year meet or exceed estimates included in the budget? Do expenditures made during the year remain within the appropriations approved in the budget? Does the budget carry any operating reserve in the form of a contingency appropriation, or is there an unappropriated fund balance to meet cash-flow needs and provide for unforeseen expenditures?

A significant measure of effective revenue administration is the percentage of the current property tax levy collected by the end of the fiscal year. The average property tax collection percentage for all North Carolina cities in 1993–94 was 97.4.[23] For cities above 50,000 in population, the average collection percentage was 97.9, and for towns with fewer than 500 people, it was 93.5 for units with electric systems and 97.0 for those without such systems. A collection percentage below 92 indicates significant problems in revenue administration, and the Local Government Commission may not approve a city's bond or debt issue if its collection percentage is less than 90. (Property tax collection is discussed further in chapter 12.)

The General Statutes require all cities to maintain accounting systems in accordance with generally accepted accounting principles and rules and regulations of the Local Government Commission [G.S. 159-25(a)(1)]. Virtually all cities in North Carolina, including the smallest ones, maintain accounting systems that are up to standard. Cities must also undergo an end-of-year independent audit (G.S. 159-34; see chapter 15). Auditors examine accounting systems, financial statements, internal control procedures, and compliance with grant requirements, after which they draft and publish an opinion. An *unqualified* opinion suggests that a city's accounting system and procedures meet the applicable standards. If the auditor renders a *qualified* opinion, the Local Government Commission will normally not approve the issuance of debt by the city.

Forecasting of Resources for Capital Financing

Capital planning must go beyond the evaluation of a city's present fiscal position. It is important to forecast a city's future status and, more specifically, the financial resources that will be available to meet future capital needs. The forecast should cover the same period that the CIP covers. A forecast of financial condition and of capital financing that will be available should first consider how a city's economic base is likely to grow or change in the forecast period, and then trace the effect of the change on annual revenues and operating expenditures. Annual revenues that remain after necessary operating needs are met and an operating reserve is provided, will be available to finance future capital needs. The 1990–91 survey of city budget practices found that of the forty-eight cities above 5,000 in population that were surveyed, nineteen had multiyear revenue and expenditure forecasts. Such forecasting was much more common among the large cities than among the small ones.[24]

Cities can prepare multiyear financial forecasts using a form like that presented in figure 14-2. The form is for a city's general fund and general public improvements. A similar and even simpler form might be used to forecast enterprise revenues, expenditures, and capital financing capacity.

Forecasting of Annual Revenues

Forecasts of annual revenues are usually based on past trends. Because revenues from different sources grow at different rates, a forecast should be made for each major revenue source. In the general fund the key sources for most cities are the property tax, the local sales and use taxes, the utility franchise tax, other state-shared taxes or revenue, sales and services (including charges for collection and disposal of solid waste), licenses and permits, investment earnings, and transfers from utility funds. Most other revenue sources can be combined and forecast together. In an enterprise fund, such as a water and sewer fund, user charges are the major revenue source. They should be projected separately from the handful of other

Figure 14-2
Multiyear Financial Forecast, General Fund

	Two Years Ago Actual	Immediate Past Year Actual	Current Year Estimate	Budget Year Estimate	Planning Years					Totals
					Year 1	Year 2	Year 3	Year 4	Year 5	
Annual Revenues										
Property taxes										
Sales & use taxes										
Utility franchise tax										
Other state-shared revenue										
Sales & services										
Licenses & permits										
Investment earnings										
Transfers										
Other revenues										
Total General Fund Revenue										
Annual Expenditures										
General government										
Public safety										
Streets & transportation										
Culture & recreation										
Community, physical, & economic development										
Environmental protection										
Debt service										
Total General Fund Expenditures										
Net Revenues from General Fund Operations										

significant sources in the fund—for example, assessments and connection fees.

In looking at past revenue trends, growth that resulted from economic expansion must be distinguished from growth that resulted from legal redefinition of the tax base, or revenue (e.g., revaluation), or from changes in the tax rate or rates for user fees. If changes in revenue classifications have been made during the trend period being studied, past classifications must be adjusted to make them consistent with existing ones. In making the revenue forecast, present tax or utility rates will generally be assumed to continue through the forecast period unless a policy is in place that provides for changes in the rates during the forecast period.

Forecasting of Annual Operating Expenditures

Once annual revenues have been projected, the amount that will be used to finance operating expenditures during the forecast period needs to be estimated. This can be done by line-item category for each fund—salaries, fringe benefits, operating expenditures, contractual services, and so on—or by department and program within a fund. If the forecast is done by line-item category for each fund, forecasted amounts are less likely to become a floor or a base for the annual budget requests that department and program managers submit each year. On the other hand, forecasts of expenditures by department and program within a fund are likely to reflect future program and service requirements more accurately than a line-item forecast by fund. Expenditure forecasts should be based on past trends. In some cases the trends can simply be carried forward; in others they will have to be adjusted for changes or new conditions that are likely to prevail in the forecast period.

Forecasting of Annual Debt and Debt Service Requirements

Forecasting outstanding debt and debt service requirements is also essential in determining what capital financing will be available to a city in the future. The goal is to learn how much new debt a city can issue and how much total debt it can carry or have outstanding during the forecast period. Two limits or measures of safety in borrowing have already been discussed. One is annual debt service on net general obligation and other tax-supported debt as a percentage of annual operating expenditures, including debt service, for general government purposes. The Local Government Commission normally arranges debt service schedule on general obligation bonds so that annual debt service declines from year to year until the bonds are fully repaid. A declining debt service schedule, compared with a level or ascending schedule, frees up debt issuance capacity more quickly in the future. Thus debt service on *existing* net outstanding general obligation and other tax-supported debt as a percentage of annual operating expenditures for general purposes should also decline from year to year through the forecast period. This happens not only because annual debt service on such debt is declining, but also because annual expenditures (and revenues) for general purposes typically grow from year to year.

A second measure of safety in borrowing is net general obligation and other tax-supported debt as a percentage of taxable property valuation. Existing outstanding debt is a given figure. It will decline each year during the forecast period as principal payments, which make up part of annual debt service, are made. Taxable property valuation typically will grow during the forecast period. Thus if no new net general obligation or tax-supported debt is issued, such debt as a percentage of taxable valuation will decline during the forecast period.

Capital Financing Methods

Cities, like individuals, have essentially four methods for raising the money necessary to finance capital projects:

1. *Payment from current income.* Revenues earned during the current fiscal year are used to finance projects undertaken during that fiscal year.
2. *Payment from savings.* Revenues earned in earlier fiscal years have been set aside, or reserved, and after a sufficient amount has been accumulated, these savings are used to finance capital projects undertaken during the current fiscal year.
3. *Payment from gifts.* Moneys given to the city (including state and federal grants) are used to finance capital projects.
4. *Payment from borrowed moneys.* Moneys borrowed by the city,

to be repaid in future fiscal years, are used to finance capital projects undertaken during this fiscal year.

The most important of these methods is the last, borrowing. If the capital project is at all large, it will almost always be financed, in whole or in part, by borrowing. Neither current revenues nor reserved moneys are likely to be sufficiently large to finance such a project without borrowed funds; and with the large-scale cutback in the number of federal grant programs, it is unlikely that large amounts of money will be acquired by gift. Therefore this section focuses on borrowing, briefly addressing current revenues and capital reserve funds at the end.

Forms of Security

A city that borrows money has a contract with its lenders, whether they are banks or brokerage houses that lent the money and retained the loan, or holders of bonds or certificates of participation. Under that contract the city agrees to pay the principal and the interest on the loan as they come due and to honor any other promises that it has made as part of the loan transaction. One of the most important provisions of the loan contract is the pledge or the designation of one or more forms of *security*, that to which the lender may look to compel repayment.

North Carolina cities currently may choose among four forms of security when they borrow money. It is appropriate to begin this section with a description of these forms of security because many of the other features of a borrowing flow from the choice that is made with respect to security. The form of security affects what form the loan transaction takes, whether voter approval is required, whether the Local Government Commission or the borrowing unit sells the debt securities, certainly what the credit rating on the loan is and thus what interest rate the borrower will have to pay, and even whether bond counsel is necessary for the loan.

The General Obligation

The strongest form of security that a city can pledge for debt is its full faith and credit, making the debt a *general obligation* of the borrowing government. All the resources of that government stand behind such a pledge, but specifically, a full-faith-and-credit pledge of a North Carolina city is a promise to levy whatever amount of property tax is necessary to repay the debt. (The property tax is singled out because it is the major revenue source over which cities have control; the state's general obligations are in effect secured largely by the state's income and sales taxes.) Because by law there is no statutory limit on the rate of property tax that may be levied for this purpose, such a promise is a pledge of unlimited taxing power.

Three statutes permit cities to incur general obligation debt. G.S. 159-43 through -79, the Local Government Bond Act, authorizes the issuance of general obligation *bonds;* G.S. Chapter 159, Article 9, Part 1 (G.S. 159-160 through -165), general obligation *bond anticipation notes*; and G.S. 159G-18, general obligation *debt instruments.* (Neither general obligation bond anticipation notes nor general obligation debt instruments may be issued without a government's having followed the procedures and met the requirements of the Local Government Bond Act.) These three authorizations are exclusive: G.S. 159-45 provides that "no unit of local government in this State shall have authority to enter into any contract or agreement, whether oral or written, whereby it borrows money and makes an express or implied pledge of its power to levy taxes as security for repayment of the loan," except pursuant to one of the three statutes.

The Revenue-Backed Obligation

A traditional form of security, although much more common nationally than in North Carolina, is a pledge of revenues generated by the debt-financed asset or by the system of which that asset is a part. For example, revenue bonds might be issued for a parking garage and secured by the revenues from charges for parking in the garage; or they might be issued for an expansion of a water system and secured by revenues of the entire system. By law (G.S. 159-91) such a pledge creates a lien on the pledged revenues in favor of the bondholders, and normally the bondholders have the contractual right to demand an increase in the user charges generating the revenues if those revenues prove inadequate to service the debt. The bondholders do not, however, have any right to demand payment from any other source, or to require an increase in taxes, if facility or system revenues continue to be inadequate even after charges are increased.

The nature of the security in a revenue-secured transaction leads to some uses of loan proceeds that are not found in general obligation loans. Two of these are using loan proceeds to pay any interest due to the lenders during the period of construction and to establish a reserve for future debt service payments. One effect of these uses of loan proceeds is that a city borrowing money secured by revenues will normally have to borrow more than it would have had to do had it financed the same project with general obligation debt.

Because the security for the debt is the revenues from the debt-financed asset (or the system of which it is a part), the lenders are naturally concerned about the construction, the operation, and the continued health of that asset or system. This concern is expressed through a series of *covenants*, or promises, that the borrowing government makes to the lenders as part of the loan closing. The most fundamental of these is the *rate covenant*, under which the borrowing government promises to set and maintain the rates, the fees, and the charges of the revenue-producing facility or system so that net revenues will exceed annual debt service requirements by some fixed amount. For example, a common requirement is that the rate structure generate annual net revenues at some specified level—usually between 120 and 150 percent—of either the current year's debt service requirements or the maximum annual debt service requirements during the life of the loan. This margin of safety required by the rate covenant is referred to as *times-coverage* of the loan. Generally, as long as net revenues continue to maintain the required coverage, the borrowing government may modify the rate structure as it pleases. If net revenues fall below the required coverage, however (even if they are still adequate to service the debt), the covenant frequently requires the government to engage an independent consultant to study the operation of the revenue-producing facility or system and recommend changes in the rate structure and in operations necessary to return net revenues to a level above times-coverage. Typically the covenant further requires the government to revise its rate structure in conformity with the consultant's recommendations and permits the trustee (who represents the bondholders) or some percentage of lenders to sue the government to force such a rate revision.

A variety of statutes permit cities to borrow money and secure the loan by a pledge of asset- or system-generated revenues. The principal statute is the State and Local Government Revenue Bond

Table 14-1
Authorized Purposes of Revenue Bonds

Water facilities	Electric facilities
Gas facilities	Public transportation
Solid waste facilities	Airports
Parking	Hospitals
Marine facilities	Stadiums
Auditoriums	Recreation facilities
Convention centers	Stormwater drainage
Economic development	Facilities for the federal government
Sewer facilities	

Act, found at G.S. Chapter 159, Article 5 (G.S. 159-80 through -97), which authorizes the issuance of revenue bonds. G.S. 159-161 permits any government authorized to issue revenue bonds under the aforementioned statute also to issue revenue bond anticipation notes. A second important statute is G.S. 159I-30, which permits cities to issue *special obligation bonds* for solid waste projects. This statute permits the issuance of bonds and bond anticipation notes secured by any revenue source that "does not constitute a pledge of the unit's taxing power," and that language includes revenues generated by the financed asset or system. G.S. 159I-30(b) permits a borrowing government, when the revenue source securing a special obligation bond or note is within its control, "to enter into covenants to take action in order to generate the revenues." Finally, G.S. 159G-18 permits cities to borrow moneys from the Clean Water Revolving Loan Fund for the capital needs of water or sewer systems and to give debt instruments, payable to the state, in evidence of the loan. Among the kinds of security that the borrowing government may give for the loan is a "pledge [of] user fee revenues derived from operation of the benefited facilities or systems." Table 14-1 sets out the purposes for which revenue bonds may be issued.

The Special Obligation

The defining characteristic of the special obligation lies in what it is not: a general obligation. A special obligation is secured by a pledge of any sort of revenue source or asset available to the city, as long as that pledge does not amount to a pledge of the city's taxing

Table 14-2
Revenues Available for a Special Obligation Pledge

Utility Franchise Tax
State Beer/Wine Tax
Local Sales/Use Tax
Inventory Tax Reimbursements

power. Neither the General Assembly nor the courts have definitively established what sorts of pledges, other than a pledge of property taxes, constitute a general obligation, but there is a working understanding in the state's finance community. This understanding focuses on the general obligation as a pledge of the government's taxing power and holds that as long as a city does not pledge *any local tax under its control*, it has not created a general obligation.

Thus in this broad sense a revenue bond is a special obligation because it pledges project revenues and does not pledge taxes of any sort. It is only one kind of special obligation, however; indeed, the term *special obligation*, as used in North Carolina, generally refers to debts secured by something other than project revenues. That something else has usually been the proceeds of one or more kinds of taxes that are levied by some government other than the government making the pledge. Thus, for example, a city might pledge taxes levied by the state and shared with local governments; or it might pledge taxes levied by a county and shared with one or more cities in that county. Table 14-2 sets out the principal sources of such revenue available to cities for a special obligation pledge. In addition, local governments may pledge revenues from nontax sources, such as various user charges.

What are the lender's rights under a special obligation pledge if the borrowing government does not meet its debt service obligations? Because the borrower does not control the levy of any tax that is part of a special obligation pledge, the lender cannot force an increase in the amount or the rate of the tax. Rather, the sole recourse of the lender is to exercise its lien and in essence to attach the pledged moneys on their coming into the possession of the borrower. Thus if the pledge was of a city's share of the state-shared franchise tax, the lender would take possession of those moneys and direct their first, and if necessary exclusive, use to pay debt service. If the moneys were inadequate, the lender would have no other recourse.

Because the debt market perceives the security for special obligation debt as weaker than the security for general obligation debt, the market normally demands of special obligation debt some of the same safeguards demanded of revenue bonds. Therefore if the loan is offered publicly—that is, if it is sold to investors—the borrowing government will almost always be required to establish a debt service reserve fund. As with the fund for revenue bonds, this fund will be initially supplied with money from the loan proceeds. Proceeds of special obligation debt may also have to be used to pay interest during project construction. Whether this is necessary depends on the particular revenues pledged to repayment.

Currently only two statutes specifically authorize a city to borrow money and create a special obligation pledge as security. Both are found in G.S. Chapter 159I. G.S. 159I-13 permits a city that borrows money from the state's Solid Waste Management Loan Fund to secure the loan, among other ways, from "any available source or sources of revenue" as long as the pledge "does not constitute a pledge of the [borrowing] unit's taxing power." G.S. 159I-30 uses similar language to permit a city to issue bonds, for solid waste projects only, with the same sort of security.

The Pledge of the Financed Asset

The final form of security available to North Carolina cities is a pledge of the asset being financed with the proceeds of the loan. Thus a city might secure a loan to construct a parking deck or build an office building by pledging the deck or the office building. Unlike the sources of security discussed earlier, this source is not a stream of revenues. It is not the proceeds from the property tax, the city's share of a state-levied tax, or the revenues from a financed asset. Although the lender will receive the asset if the borrower defaults, that occurs only if there is in fact a default. Both the lender and the borrower will have to look elsewhere for the actual payment of the loan. As a practical matter, both will look to the general revenues of the local government. Therefore loans secured by the financed asset are treated by the market as if they were general obligations, although weaker than the real general obligations of the borrowing government.

No lender wants to rely on the asset as the real security for such a loan. The market does not judge the attractiveness of asset-secured loans on the basis of the suitability of the pledged asset for private use. Rather, the market rates such loans on its perception of the willingness or the unwillingness of the borrower to lose the asset. If the asset is perceived as essential to the continued operation of the city, the loan will be a stronger credit than if the asset is perceived as one the city could lose without much harm to basic operations.

The debt market perceives the security for asset-secured debt as weaker than the security for general obligation debt, so it normally demands of such debt some of the same safeguards demanded of revenue bonds. Therefore if the loan is offered publicly—that is, if it is sold to investors—the borrowing government is almost always required to establish a debt service reserve fund. As with the fund for revenue bonds, this fund will be initially supplied with money from the loan proceeds. Proceeds of asset-secured debt may also have to be used to pay interest during project construction. Whether this is necessary depends on the market's response to that particular financing.

Only two current statutes authorize loans secured by a pledge of the financed asset. The more general is G.S. 160A-20, which expressly permits cities to borrow money for purchases and for construction and to give as the sole security a lien in the financed asset. If the borrowing government defaults on the loan, the lender's sole recourse is to repossess or foreclose on the asset; it may not bring an action to sue the borrowing government for any difference between the amount due and the value of the asset. The second is G.S. 159I-30, which permits a government that issues special obligation bonds for a solid waste project additionally to secure the bonds with a pledge of the financed asset. This statute does not permit a pledge of the asset alone, but only in addition to the special obligation pledge.

Use of a Nonappropriation Clause

Normally if a city borrows money and then during the life of the loan fails to make a scheduled payment of debt service, the city is considered in default on the loan. With asset-secured loans, however, the loan documents will usually give the city the annual choice of appropriating money to meet debt service requirements that year or not appropriating money. If the city chooses not to appropriate money, it will obviously be unable to make its debt service payments that year. Because the loan contract permitted it to make the choice, however, failure to pay debt service in these circumstances is not a default on the loan, but the exercise of a contractual right. The contract provision that gives this right to the borrowing government is known as a *nonappropriation clause.*

Nationally, nonappropriation clauses have become a standard part of asset-secured financings. The market does not exact much of a price for including them in such financings because it does not expect any local government borrower to make use of the clause. If local governments began to exercise this right with any frequency at all, it would quickly become an expensive addition to any financing.

The Structures of the Borrowing Transaction

If a private person wants to borrow money to buy a car or a house, he or she simply goes to the bank and does so, signing a note as evidence of his or her debt. If a city wants to borrow money, however, it can never proceed as simply as that.[25] This section describes the common forms that loan transactions take.

A generation ago, if a North Carolina city borrowed money, it did so through the issuance of bonds. No other structures for borrowing money were available or used. That is no longer true. Although bonds remain the predominant loan form, North Carolina local governments currently borrow money through a variety of transactional structures.

General Obligation Bonds

The traditional mechanism by which cities borrow money is the issuance of *bonds.* A bond itself is simply an evidence of a debt, a fancy IOU, in the same way that the note a person gives his or her bank is the evidence of the bank's mortgage loan to him or her. Historically the bond differed from other evidences of debt in that it bore the seal of the borrower. In current local government finance the essential difference between a bond and a *note* is the length of time for which the underlying debt is outstanding. A note evidences a debt that will fall due in a short time—a few months to a year or, rarely, somewhat longer. A bond evidences a longer debt—from a few years to thirty-five or forty years.

The general obligation bond is the simplest form of borrowing generally available to local governments. The promise of the borrowing government is straightforward—it will levy whatever amount of tax is necessary to pay principal and interest—and can be enforced by the legal action of any bondholder. Furthermore, the promise is relatively unaccompanied by the additional promises characteristic of other forms of security. Therefore the documents generated by a general obligation bond issue are considerably fewer and shorter in length than those generated by other forms of borrowing.

The central document of the proceeding to secure local authorization of a general obligation bond issue is the *bond order*, which is adopted by the city council. The order serves a double purpose. First, it authorizes issuance of the bonds, stating the purpose for which the proceeds will be spent and the maximum amount of bonds that may be issued. If a city is proposing bonds for more than one purpose, it will need a separate bond order for each purpose. Second, the order publicizes the bond issue, not only setting out purpose and amount but also indicating the security for the bonds. As the North Carolina Supreme Court has said, the bond order is "the crucial foundation document which supports and explains" the issue.[26]

The statutory procedure that leads to adoption of a bond order is intended to serve two primary purposes: (1) it concludes with the council's formal authorization of the bond issue; and (2) it provides an opportunity for the public to learn of and comment on the proposed issue and the project or projects it will finance. In fact, however, the procedure is usually a *pro forma* exercise. It does not begin until the city has met informally with the Local Government Commission's staff and received informal approval of the proposed borrowing. The necessary documents are prepared by bond counsel, who also suggest a schedule for the statutory procedure. That schedule is normally established by setting a tentative date for the bond referendum, if one will be necessary, and then counting back from that date. Generally, then, by the time it begins the formal procedure, the city council has already decided to adopt the bond order. Occasionally testimony at the public hearing will cause a council to modify, delay, or drop its plans, but the real opportunity for citizens to comment on the bond issue is the referendum.

Revenue and Special Obligation Bonds

North Carolina law permits bonds to be issued with either of two forms of security besides the general obligation: (1) revenue bonds, which pledge revenues from the bond-financed project; and (2) special obligation bonds, which pledge any revenues available to the issuing government that will not create a general obligation pledge. Because of the nature of their security, neither revenue bonds nor special obligation bonds require voter approval. For that reason the careful statutory procedure that must be followed to issue general obligation bonds (and which is intended to provide public notice of the issue) has no counterpart with these other kinds of bonds. The statutes contain no required procedures at all for council authorization of these bonds, and as a result, the authorization process is legally simple. The documents that underlie such a bond issue, however, are anything but simple, and again the reason is the nature of the security behind the bonds. Furthermore, also because of the nature of the security, revenue and special obligation bond issues require the participation of new entities not necessary to a general obligation issue.

The most important new entity is the *bond trustee*, normally a bank, which represents the interests of the bondholders. When the bonds are issued, the proceeds are paid to the trustee, which controls disbursement of the moneys. Furthermore, the city is frequently required regularly to pay the bond's security—asset revenues or special obligation moneys—over to the trustee, which then makes debt service payments to bondholders. Finally, the borrowing city is often required to secure the trustee's approval of various operational matters, such as changes in consulting engineers or amount of insurance coverage.

As noted earlier in the discussion of security, borrowings secured by revenues or special obligation moneys typically require that the borrowing government agree to a variety of special covenants that protect the lenders. The major part of the issuance process for revenue or special obligation bonds is negotiating these covenants with the *underwriters*, who will sell the bonds, and sometimes with the rating agencies. Once the documents are prepared, the city council simply approves them, and the loan is thereby authorized.

Bond Anticipation Notes

Sometimes a city will authorize a bond issue, but will not wish to borrow the full sum at one time. Alternatively, if the city plans to sell the bonds to the Farmers' Home Administration, the bond sale will not take place until the project is fully constructed. In either case the city might decide to borrow, pursuant to the bond authorization, on a short-term basis. If it does so, it will issue *bond anticipation notes.* These are short-term notes, usually maturing in a year's time, that are primarily secured by the proceeds of the eventual bond issue itself. Because such notes are issued in anticipation of the eventual issuance of bonds, there is no separate authorization process for the notes. The city must, however, receive the approval of the Local Government Commission before the notes are issued, and the commission will sell the notes on the city's behalf.

Installment Purchase Agreements

If the loan is to be secured by the financed asset, it will be structured not as a bond issue but as an *installment purchase agreement* (sometimes called a *lease purchase agreement* or, somewhat less often, a *capital lease*). Even though the government has in fact borrowed money and agreed to pay it back, the documents will describe a transaction in which the government has purchased an asset, agreeing to pay for it over time. The installment payments, however, will be divided into principal and interest components, and they are the equivalent of debt service payments on bond issues. The original reasons for this transactional disguise are no longer necessary, but the form continues from habit.

The statutory procedures incident to entering into an installment purchase agreement are only slightly more elaborate than the total lack of procedure associated with revenue and special obligation bonds. G.S. 160A-20, the relevant statute, requires that if the installment purchase agreement involves real property (either acquisition or construction of it), the city must hold a public hearing on the financing. Otherwise there are no local steps required of the city, and once the documents are prepared, the council may simply approve them and authorize the transaction.

The documentation for an installment purchase agreement varies depending on whether the city borrows from one lender or a few, or from the broad investing public. If the former, which is likely if the loan is to acquire equipment of some sort, the basic document will be the installment purchase agreement itself, often executed on forms developed by the vendor of the equipment or the financing bank.[27] If the loan is larger, however, which is likely if it is to finance a construction project, the transaction becomes considerably more complex.

Certificates of Participation

Once an installment purchase agreement reaches a certain size—currently around $8 or $9 million—it almost certainly has to be publicly sold. That is, rather than the government borrowing the money from a single bank or vendor, the government has to turn to the bond market itself and the millions of individuals, companies, and mutual funds that invest in the market. To reach the market, however, the loan must be divided into much smaller units, afford-able by the various participants in the bond market. With a standard bond issue those smaller units are the bonds themselves, normally issued in denominations of $5,000. As noted earlier, however, a bond is direct evidence of a debt of the unit; because of the transactional form of the installment purchase agreement, bonds cannot be is-sued. Therefore some other investment instrument is necessary, and that instrument is the *certificate of participation.*

The *certificate of participation* (COP) entitles its holder to a share in the periodic payments made by the government under the install-ment purchase agreement; the investor participates in receiving those payments, and the certificate is the evidence of his or her right to do so. Although the legal nature of the COP differs from that of the bond, it has been fully accepted by investors, and the bond mar-ket treats COPs as more or less interchangeable with true bonds.

If a local government borrows through COPs, the documenta-tion for the transaction is probably the most complicated of any of the forms of borrowing. Typically a nonprofit corporation is estab-lished to "sell" the financed asset to the borrowing government. The corporation and the government enter into the installment purchase agreement, which itself is considerably more complicated than an installment purchase agreement made directly with a vendor or a single lender. In addition, there is a thick trust indenture, under which the corporation (not the government) issues COPs and assigns its rights to payments, under the installment purchase agreement, to a trustee; the trustee is then in charge of making payments to the certificate holders.

Debt Instruments and Loan Agreements

Two final forms of borrowing are the *debt instrument* and the *loan agreement*. These are the labels the statutes give to the documents that evidence the debts when a city borrows money from a state agency. Debt instruments are used when cities borrow under the Clean Water program, loan agreements when cities borrow from the Solid Waste Management Loan Fund. Neither program is used very much.

Voter Approval of Borrowing

Article V, Section 4, of the state constitution requires voter approval before a local government may borrow money and secure the loan by a pledge of its faith and credit—that is, before it may borrow money secured by a pledge of its taxing power. The constitution does not require voter approval if any other form of security is used, and therefore voter approval is never necessary for loans secured by revenues, by special obligations, or by the financed asset. In fact, voter approval is not even always necessary for general obligation loans. The following section describes the rules for determining when the voters must, or need not, approve general obligation debt.

Rules for Determining Need for Voter Approval

Refunding Bonds

Refunding bonds are issued to refinance existing debt, usually because interest rates have fallen and the city wishes to reduce its debt service payments. No new debt is being created; rather, one evidence of a single debt is being replaced by another. Therefore the constitution excuses refunding bonds from the requirement of voter approval.

New General Obligation Debt for Certain Purposes

By statute the General Assembly has required that new general obligation debt incurred for a few purposes always be approved by the voters. (That is, debt for these purposes may not be incurred under the two-thirds rule, discussed next.) The purposes in this category are auditoriums, coliseums, stadiums, convention centers, and like facilities; art galleries, museums, and historic properties; urban redevelopment; public transportation; and cable television systems.

Two-Thirds Rule

All other general obligation debt is subject to the *two-thirds rule*, under which cities may incur relatively small amounts of such debt without voter approval. This rule allows a city to issue bonds in an amount up to two-thirds of the amount by which the city's outstanding general obligation indebtedness was reduced in the preceding fiscal year. For example, if a city reduces its net general obligation indebtedness by $900,000 in Year 1, then it may incur general obligation debt up to $600,000—two-thirds of $900,000—in Year 2 without voter approval. The simple thrust of the limitation is to prevent an increase in a government's total indebtedness unless the increase has been approved by the voters.

Several points should be made about the two-thirds rule. First, in determining the amount of debt reduction during a fiscal year, a city counts only principal payments; interest paid is irrelevant. In addition, it is not the amount of principal retired that is counted; rather, it is the net reduction in principal owed. If a city borrows during a fiscal year, it may actually have a net increase in outstanding debt and therefore no two-thirds capacity at all. Second, the city must use its two-thirds capacity in the fiscal year immediately following the year in which the debt was reduced. If it is not used in that immediately following year, the chance to use it is lost; two-thirds capacity cannot be accumulated from year to year. Finally, in using its two-thirds capacity, the city is not restricted in any way by the purposes for which the retired debt was issued. That is, if all a city's outstanding bonds were issued for water or sewer purposes, so that all reductions are in water or sewer debt, a city may still issue two-thirds bonds for any authorized purpose (except those listed earlier as always requiring voter approval). To continue the example, the two-thirds bonds could be issued for streets, park acquisition, a new fire station, and so on.

Public Funds in a Referendum Campaign

A frequent question is, To what extent may a city use city moneys in the campaign for voter approval of a proposed general obligation bond issue? No North Carolina statute or decided case deals with this question, but the law nationally is well settled and is commonly observed in this state. The basic rule is quite simple: public funds may be used to provide information about a bond issue and the proposed project for which the bonds will be issued; public funds may not be used to urge voters to vote yes in the referendum. Obviously differences of opinion may arise about whether a particular expenditure is informational or promotional; cities should be careful to err on the side of caution. There have been a number of cases in other states in which the officials responsible for improper expenditures have been required to repay the money personally. (There do not, however, appear to be any cases in which improper expenditures threatened the validity of a successful vote.)[28]

State Approval of Borrowing

North Carolina is quite unusual among the states in requiring state approval before most local government borrowing transactions. The approval is the responsibility of the Local Government Commission, an agency in the Department of State Treasurer. The commission was created during the Great Depression, when North Carolina had more local governments in default on debt than any other state in the United States. The commission's initial task was to help those defaulting governments out of their fiscal troubles; its task since then has been to ensure, as much as possible, that such a situation does not arise again. Thus the commission's responsibility is to review the borrowing plans of local governments, to judge whether the governments are borrowing only an amount that they will be able to afford to repay, and to approve the borrowing only after it is assured that repayment is indeed within the local government's means.[29]

For most forms of borrowing transactions, commission approval is always necessary: for any kind of bond issue, whether the security is general obligation, special obligation, or project revenues; for bond anticipation notes; and for debt instruments and loan agreements.

The one form of transaction for which commission approval is sometimes not necessary is the installment purchase agreement. Two complementary rules determine when the Local Government Commission must approve installment purchase agreements. First, if the proceeds of the loan will be used to finance improvements to real property, commission approval is always necessary. That is, any *construction* project financed by an installment purchase agreement requires state approval. Agreements that finance *acquisition* of property, whether real or personal, are subject to the second rule. Under this rule, such financings must have state approval if they meet both of two conditions:

1. The agreement must extend for at least five years, or sixty months.
2. The total amount paid by the city under the agreement (which includes both principal and interest) must be larger than a threshold amount: the lesser of $500,000 or 0.1 percent of the total appraised value of property subject to taxation in the city.

Again, both conditions must be met. If an agreement is for only fifty-nine months, it does not require state approval, regardless of the amount of money to be paid by the city. If the amount to be paid is less than the threshold, state approval is unnecessary, regardless of the length of the agreement.

There is one final exception: the statute provides that state approval is never necessary for agreements that finance the acquisition of either motor vehicles or voting machines.

Other Methods of Capital Financing

The introduction notes other forms of capital financing. Any city will finance some capital assets from current revenues. In a small city, such assets may be no more expensive than police cars, whereas in a large city, fire trucks and other expensive personal property may be paid for from current revenues. These kinds of expenditures are treated no differently than any other expenditures included in the annual budget ordinance.

A city might also receive capital financing from a grant or a gift, although this is much less likely now than during the 1970s or earlier. When that occurs, the grantor or the donor normally will specify what uses may be made of the money, and the city will be bound to those specifications. Once received, such moneys are fully public moneys and must be appropriated and accounted for in the same manner as any other public funds.

Finally, a city may save money over time, through establishment of a capital reserve fund. G.S. 159-18 permits cities to establish capital reserve funds for any capital purpose. A city council does this by adopting an ordinance or a resolution that includes at least four points: the purpose or purposes for which moneys will be reserved; the length of time for which moneys will be accumulated; the approximate amounts to be accumulated for each purpose; and the source of the reserved moneys. The council may amend this ordinance or resolution at any time, including changing the purpose for which moneys have been reserved. Moneys may be removed from the fund only for a designated purpose; because only capital purposes can be designated, moneys may not be removed and used for operating expenses. Otherwise, a city has complete flexibility in the use of capital reserve funds.

Authorization of Capital Projects and Expenditures and Appropriation of Funds for Them

Authorization versus Appropriation

Authorization in this context refers to approving a capital project or acquisition; *appropriation,* to making revenues or financing available for expenditure on it. Authorization often occurs by an appropriation, as when annual revenues or fund balances are appropriated to finance an equipment acquisition or a construction project. In such a case the appropriation serves as authorization and provides the funding as well.

In contrast, when bonds are issued to finance a capital project, authorization of the project and appropriation of moneys for it usually take place in separate steps and at different times. For a project financed by general obligation bonds, authorization might be thought to occur when the voters approve the bonds. However, the city council may still choose not to issue the bonds; final authorization occurs only with the decision to issue the bonds, which is typically associated with the letting of major contracts for the project. Once bonds are issued and contracts are let for a project, there is no turning back. Although issuance of bonds constitutes final project approval, it does not of itself appropriate or make the bond proceeds available for expenditure. This must occur in the annual budget ordinance or in a capital project ordinance.

Authorization of capital projects and acquisitions and appropriation of moneys for them also often occur separately when a city has a CIP. In such a case the city council may pass a resolution approving capital projects and expenditures listed in the first year of the CIP as the capital budget for the year. This resolution may be part of a broader resolution approving the entire CIP. Although such a resolution may authorize the projects and the outlays, by itself it does not appropriate moneys for them; this may be done, again, only in the annual budget ordinance or in a capital project ordinance. Of course, if council approval of the projects and the expenditures in the first year of the CIP occurs by incorporation of the projects and the expenditures in the annual budget ordinance, by amendment(s) to the annual budget ordinance, or by enactment of one or more capital project ordinances, then project authorization and appropriation effectively take place in one step and at one time.

Cities occasionally undertake major capital construction projects that take several years to complete. If a multiyear project is financed with revenues that are appropriated in the annual budget ordinance each year during the construction period, project authorization and appropriation of at least part of the funds for the project occur separately. The city council authorizes the full project the first year, but it appropriates from the annual budget ordinance only enough money to meet project expenditures for that year. Then as construction proceeds, the council appropriates enough funds from each year's annual budget to cover project expenditures for that year. This practice is sometimes called *cash-flow budgeting* because appropriations for a project in any year are based on expenditures to be made for the project in that year. Cash-flow budgeting is a less-than-conservative approach to capital budgeting because contracts are let for the full or nearly the full project amount in the year of the project's inception, but appropriations enacted for the project that year cover only expenditures to be made in the year. Nevertheless, such budgeting is legal under the continuing contracts and preaudit statutes [G.S. 160A-17 and G.S. 159-28(a)].

In this last example, if annual revenues are appropriated in a capital project ordinance rather than as part of the annual budget ordinance, authorization and appropriation of the full amount of revenues needed for the project occur at the same time, that is, when the capital project ordinance is passed. Of course, even then, funds can be raised and appropriated initially in the annual budget ordinance and then transferred by council action to the capital project ordinance on a year-to-year basis. Such transfers to the capital project ordinance fund the appropriations already there, not increase them. This approach is favored by staff of the Local Government Commission because it allows the general fund to account for all tax and other recurring revenues.

Use of Capital Project Ordinances

Cities may use their annual budget ordinance or one or more capital project ordinances to appropriate moneys for capital projects or expenditures. Some appropriate all revenues or financing for capital projects and expenditures in the annual budget ordinance or by amendment to it. This method helps to ensure that capital expenditure decisions are coordinated with operating budget decisions. Moreover, because appropriation authority in the annual budget ordinance lasts for only a year, this practice helps to insure periodic review of capital projects under construction.

The disadvantages of appropriating money for capital projects and expenditures in the annual budget ordinance apply mainly to large multiyear projects. One drawback is the incongruity of appropriating funds for a project for only a year at a time, when in fact spending for it will take several years. A more difficult problem is that including major capital projects in the annual budget ordinance can cause the annual budget to fluctuate greatly in amount from year to year so that confusion arises about what amount is budgeted for ongoing operating programs from year to year.

These disadvantages are addressed by using a capital project ordinance. Such an ordinance continues in force until the project is acquired or built. Also, by separating appropriations for capital projects from appropriations for operating expenditures, the distinction is clearer between current expenditures, with their immediate benefits, and capital projects and expenditures, with their long-term benefits.

In general, funds for small recurring capital expenditures should be appropriated in the annual budget ordinance, usually in the general fund or another operating fund, whereas those for major capital projects should usually be appropriated in project ordinances and accounted for in a capital project fund. The dividing line between these types of capital expenditures, however, is not always clear.

G.S. 159-13.2(c) specifies the content of a capital project ordinance. It must "identify and authorize the capital project to be undertaken, identify the revenues that will finance the project, and make the appropriations necessary for the project." The project ordinance should identify each revenue source and specify the amount from each one to be spent for the project. If a project will extend over more than one year and the city includes annual revenues from several years in estimating project revenues, the project ordinance should specify the amount of such revenues that will come from each year's receipts. The Local Government Budget and Fiscal Control Act (G.S. Ch. 159, Art. 3) says nothing about the level of detail for appropriations in a project ordinance. G.S. 159-13(a), however, permits appropriations in the annual budget ordinance to be by project. This would seem to permit a comparable appropriation in a project ordinance—that is, a single one for each project. A city could, of course, appropriate in greater detail.

A separate capital project ordinance may be used for each individual project, or one comprehensive capital project ordinance may be enacted for all new projects authorized by the city council in a particular year. Such a comprehensive capital project ordinance might be passed annually when the council approves new projects in the capital budget for the year. This budget may be taken from the CIP and consist of projects and expenditures in the Budget Year of the five- or six-year forecast made by that program (see figure 14-2 under the heading Capital Improvement Programming, earlier in the chapter).

Implementation: Construction or Acquisition of Capital Assets

The last step in capital budgeting is implementation. Key facets in this phase are managing the funds that are available for a capital project or expenditure; making equipment purchases; designing, contracting for, and constructing buildings or improvements; and accounting for capital construction or acquisition outlays.

The building or the acquisition of capital assets must be timed so that enough cash from the financing sources is on hand to make payments to vendors and contractors as the payments fall due. This can mean delaying major equipment acquisitions and the start-up of construction projects that are financed with annual revenues until the second half of the fiscal year, after most property tax revenue has been collected. If a large construction project is to be built and the financing will come entirely or largely from annual revenues, fund balances or capital reserves may have to be accumulated over several years before construction begins to provide enough money for the project.

If federal or other outside grant money will finance a project but be provided on a reimbursement basis, a city must have its own money to start the project and finance construction until reimbursements start arriving. Such up-front money for grant-financed projects usually comes from city fund balances or capital reserves. Although cities hardly ever use grant anticipation notes, cities are authorized to issue them (G.S. 159-171) to pay for capital projects for which federal or state grant commitments have been obtained. The amount of the notes may not exceed 90 percent of the portion of the grant commitments yet to be received in cash by the city. The Local Government Commission must approve and sell the notes.

Federal Arbitrage Regulations

If tax-exempt bond or debt proceeds are used to finance a capital project, federal arbitrage regulations must be followed to preserve the tax-exempt status of the interest paid on the bonds or the debt. Generally, *arbitrage* refers to profit made by selling securities and investing the resulting proceeds in other, higher-yielding securities. In the case of tax-exempt debt, arbitrage occurs when a governmental or other tax-exempt entity borrows money by selling its tax-exempt debt at a relatively low interest rate, and invests the proceeds in taxable securities that carry higher yields or interest rates.

Federal arbitrage restrictions, which became effective in 1969, and arbitrage rebate requirements, which are based on regulations developed pursuant to the Tax Reform Act of 1986, generally prohibit arbitrage profits on tax-exempt debt—profits made by investing the proceeds of tax-exempt debt in higher-yielding taxable securities.[30] However, under certain conditions the earning of such profits does not violate federal law. Most important, arbitrage profits may be earned from investing the proceeds of governmental tax-exempt debt if (1) the project or the acquisition for which the proceeds will be spent is governmental; (2) the project or the acquisition is under contract within six months after issuance; and (3) 85 percent of the proceeds will be spent within three years. There are certain other conditions or circumstances in which arbitrage profits may be earned on tax-exempt debt.

Even though arbitrage profits may be earned on the proceeds of certain tax-exempt debt, federal arbitrage rebate requirements provide that such profits be rebated to the United States Treasury unless the issuer of the debt qualifies for one of several exceptions. Under these exceptions a rebate of arbitrage profits is not necessary if the issuer of tax-exempt debt—

- Invests the debt proceeds in government tax-exempt obligations or in State and Local Government Demand Deposit Series issued by the United States Treasury; or
- Has general taxing power and sells or issues no more than $5 million of tax-exempt debt in a calendar year and spends the proceeds on governmental activities; or
- Spends the full proceeds, except the lesser of $100,000 or 5 percent of the issue, within six months after issuance; or
- Spends 15 percent of the debt proceeds, less amounts needed for debt service and reserve funds, at the end of six months after issuance, 60 percent of the proceeds at the end of twelve months after issuance, and the full proceeds at the end of eighteen months after issuance; or
- Spends at least 75 percent of the debt proceeds for construction on property to be owned by the issuer, and spends 10 percent of the proceeds within six months of issuance, 45 percent within twelve months of issuance, 75 percent within eighteen months of issuance, and 100 percent, less retainage not to exceed 5 percent of construction proceeds, within two years of issuance. This exception also allows for the *bifurcation* of a debt issue into two components: a non-construction portion to be used for land or other acquisitions, which must be spent within six months to avoid rebate; and the construction portion itself, which must be spent in accord with the two-year schedule just set forth. If the issuer fails to spend the required proportion of debt by any six-month interval, it will have either to rebate to the United States Treasury all arbitrage profits earned on the full debt proceeds or to pay to the Treasury a penalty equal

to 1.5 percent of any portions of the proceeds that should have been spent but were not spent by each six-month interval. The issuer must choose between these options—rebating or paying the 1.5-percent penalty—at the time that it issues or sells the debt.

Clearly, federal arbitrage regulations are very complex. Moreover, they have been modified frequently in recent years. Therefore cities should seek advice from bond counsel, the Local Government Commission, and other competent sources in trying to meet arbitrage restrictions and rebate requirements and in devising an investment plan for tax-exempt bond or debt proceeds. If a city does not comply with the United States Treasury's arbitrage regulations, it might have to pay penalties and interest to the federal government, and if the city fails to rebate arbitrage profits pursuant to regulations, the unit's bonds or debt could lose its tax-exempt status retroactively to the date of issuance.

Because of federal arbitrage regulations and its own longtime practice, the Local Government Commission urges that bonds or almost any form of debt not be sold or issued at least until a city has advertised for and opened the construction bids on the bond- or debt-financed project. The commission needs about ninety days to sell bonds or other debt and deliver the proceeds to a city. A city should contact the commission for the sale at least thirty days before it expects to receive bids on the project. The sale of the bonds will occur about sixty days after this initial contact, and the city will have the bond proceeds about thirty days after that, or not more than sixty days after the bid opening.

Other Considerations

Investment Plan

Adequate management of the financing or revenue proceeds for a major capital construction project typically requires an *investment plan*. The plan should (1) cover the period from the date when cash proceeds for the project begin to be received, to the date when the final disbursement is made; (2) show project receipts, disbursements, and cash balances available by month; (3) lay down a general strategy to guide the investment of balances that are not immediately needed for project payments at any point; and (4) estimate the approximate interest earnings on the investments, calculate arbitrage rebate requirements, if any, and provide for the use of the net earnings.

Bidding for Equipment Acquisitions and Construction Projects

Equipment purchases and construction and repair projects must comply with the applicable North Carolina bidding laws. For example, the purchase, or the lease with option to purchase, of any equipment that costs $20,000 or more and any construction or repair work costing $100,000 or more must be contracted for through formal bid procedures (G.S. 143-129). Further, informal bid procedures—for example, bids secured by telephone—must be used for equipment and projects costing less than the formal bidding minimums, but $5,000 or more (G.S. 143-131). G.S. 143-29 addresses preparation of specifications, solicitation of bids, selection of multiple contractors for different types of work versus a single prime contractor, and use of minority- and women-owned business enterprises on construction projects for buildings. A full discussion of purchasing and contracting laws and procedures appears in chapter 17.

Use of an Architect or an Engineer

Implementing a capital construction project is a complex undertaking. If the project is of any magnitude, a registered architectural or engineering firm is typically employed to prepare plans and specifications, oversee or inspect construction, and advise the city. The architect or the engineer also generally does a feasibility study as an initial step for any utility or enterprise projects. An architect or an engineer must be used when the cost of a project exceeds $45,000 (G.S. 133-1.1). However, if the project is a repair project and involves no structural change, an architect or an engineer is required to prepare plans and specifications only when the cost of the project is more than $100,000.

Architects and engineers are chosen through negotiation or requests for proposals that focus as much on considerations of design and qualifications as on considerations of cost. Indeed, G.S. Chapter 143, Article 3D, makes it the public policy of the state and its local governments to select architects and engineers based primarily on qualifications. Local governments may exempt themselves from this policy when architectural and engineering fees for a project will be less than $30,000 or when local government officials state the reasons for such an exemption.

Architectural and engineering fees are generally charged as a percentage of project costs, ranging from 7 or 8 percent to as much as 12 percent or so, depending on project size and type. Fixed-fee and other arrangements are also sometimes used. The architect or the engineer is responsible for assessing the feasibility of a project, designing it, drawing up blueprints and specifications, preparing and advising on construction contracts, and overseeing construction. For some projects one architectural or engineering firm does the feasibility study, and another plans, designs, and carries out the project. Occasionally a different firm is hired just to oversee and inspect construction. A city should provide guidelines about what and what not to include in the design for a project. Sometimes the architect or the engineer is asked to design *add-ons* or *drops* so that the city can more readily adjust the scope of a project to fit the amount of money available.

Capital Project Fund

A capital project fund should be used to account for the purchase or the construction of a major capital facility. G.S. 159-26(b)(6) requires all local governmental units to use such a fund when bond or other debt proceeds finance part or all of a project. Capital project funds are ordinarily not used to account for the acquisition of equipment and small construction or renovation projects. Such acquisitions or projects are normally budgeted and accounted for in the general fund or another operating fund. A separate capital project fund need not be established for each major project. Multiple projects can be accounted for in one capital project fund. Indeed, a single capital project fund can be used to account for all major general public improvements. However, one or more separate capital project funds should be used for major enterprise system projects.

Additional Resources

Lawrence, David M. *Financing Capital Projects in North Carolina.* Chapel Hill, N.C.: Institute of Government, The University of North Carolina at Chapel Hill, 1994.

Vogt, A. John. *Capital Improvement Programming: A Handbook for Local Government Officials.* Chapel Hill, N.C.: Institute of Government, The University of North Carolina at Chapel Hill, 1977. Although very old and out of print, this guide still provides a useful overview of capital improvement programming. The author is revising and updating the book; a new edition will be available at the end of 1996.

Notes

1. Government Finance Officers Association, *Governmental Accounting, Auditing and Financial Reporting* (Chicago: GFOA, 1994), 318, 330.

2. North Carolina Department of State Treasurer, *Policies Manual* (Raleigh, N.C.: NCDST, October 1990), sec. 20, "Fixed Assets Policy," especially pp. 5–8.

3. NCDST, *Policies Manual,* sec. 20, p. 1, refers to fixed assets as "tangible in nature."

4. GFOA, *Governmental Accounting,* recognizes the appropriateness of including certain intangible property among general fixed assets (p. 104), although its glossary defines a fixed asset as a "long-lived, tangible asset" (p. 330).

5. Accounting for public enterprises follows commercial accounting principles, which provide for the inclusion of intangible as well as tangible property among fixed assets.

6. Bond attorneys have opined that closure and postclosure costs for a landfill are not capital items and therefore may not be financed from bonds issued to finance a landfill.

7. Selected results of this survey are reported in A. John Vogt and Charles K. Coe, "A Close Look at North Carolina City and County Budget Practices," *Popular Government* 59 (Summer 1993), 16–28. The survey, conducted by the Institute of Government in November 1990, focused on preparation of the 1990–91 budget. One hundred and twenty-one cities and counties of different sizes responded to the survey. Seventy-four of these units were cities; of these, only those above 5,000 in population were asked whether they had a CIP. If a city reported having a CIP, follow-up questions were asked about the city's CIP process. Results from some of these follow-up questions are reported further in the chapter.

8. A. John Vogt and Charles K. Coe, unpublished results of 1990–91 survey of North Carolina city and county budget practices, Institute of Government, The University of North Carolina at Chapel Hill, 1991.

9. Vogt and Coe, unpublished results.

10. Vogt and Coe, unpublished results.

11. Vogt and Coe, unpublished results.

12. Vogt and Coe, unpublished results.

13. Standard & Poor's Corporation, *Municipal Finance Criteria* (New York: S & P, 1994), 4.

14. Information presented about the national debt rating agencies draws on S & P, *Municipal Finance Criteria*; Moody's Investors Service, *An Issuer's Guide to the Rating Process* (New York: Moody's, 1993); and conversations with staff of S & P, Moody's, and the Local Government Commission.

15. Information about the North Carolina Municipal Council is based on the council's brochure *North Carolina Municipal Council, Inc.* (Raleigh, N.C.: the Council, undated) and conversations with staff of the council.

16. The term *tax-supported* here means that debt service payments on the debt come from taxes or other general revenue sources rather than from user fees or charges specifically associated with the project being financed with the debt. Tax supported does not necessarily mean tax secured. Debt service payments for a city office building may be paid from taxes or general revenues, but if the debt used to finance the building is certificates of participation, the security for the debt is the building itself rather than any pledge of tax revenue.

17. Standard & Poor's Corporation, *CreditWeek Municipal*, 4 January 1993, 50.

18. The rating agencies have specifically recognized the central contribution of the Local Government Commission (S & P, *CreditWeek Municipal*, 4 January 1993, 50).

19. North Carolina Department of State Treasurer with the assistance of the North Carolina League of Municipalities, *Fiscal Summary of North Carolina Municipalities* (Raleigh, N.C.: the League, 1993).

20. S & P, *Municipal Finance Criteria*, 23.

21. This and the debt percentages that follow it are taken from Local Government Commission, "Analysis of Debt of North Carolina Counties and Municipalities Having Debt at 6/30/94," Memorandum 652 of the North Carolina Department of State Treasurer, November 1994.

22. LGC, "Analysis."

23. Property tax collection percentages for individual North Carolina cities and average collection percentages for North Carolina cities of different sizes are presented in Craig M. Barfield, "Management of Cash and Taxes—Municipalities for the Fiscal Year Ending June 30, 1993," Memorandum 810 of the North Carolina Department of State Treasurer, January 1995.

24. Vogt and Coe, "A Close Look," 26.

25. There are three authorizations in the statutes for special-purpose local governments simply to "borrow money": G.S. 157-9, for housing authorities; G.S. 160A-512(8), for redevelopment commissions; and G.S. 160A-579(13), for public transportation authorities. Of these three authorizations, only that granted to redevelopment commissions has seen any appreciable use, and it has been used only by cities (rather than by redevelopment commissions), which are permitted under G.S. 160A-4565 to exercise any power of a redevelopment commission. Furthermore, although the cities that have used this authority were able simply to approach a bank and borrow the money, the resulting loans were revenue secured rather than general obligations, and the loan documents were anything but simple. In any

event the federal tax provisions that encouraged such loans were repealed in the mid-1980s, and none of these authorizations have seen any use since that time.

26. Rider v. Lenoir County, 236 N.C. 620, 631, 73 S.E.2d 913, 921 (1953).

27. If such forms are used, the borrowing government should review them carefully because they are likely to be particularly protective of the vendor's or lender's interests.

28. The rules on expenditure of public funds in bond referenda are discussed at length in David M. Lawrence, "Use of Public Funds in a Bond Referendum Campaign," *Popular Government* 53 (Spring 1988): 48–49.

29. Cities are subject to one other statutory mechanism that is intended to ensure they do not borrow more than they can repay: the *net debt limitation*. A city determines its net debt by adding together all general obligation debt and installment purchase debt, then subtracting debt incurred for water, electricity, and gas. The resulting sum of outstanding debt may not exceed 8 percent of the appraised value of property in the city subject to taxation. In fact, however, it is quite rare for a city's net debt to exceed 2 percent of its tax base; therefore, as a practical matter, the net debt limitation is unimportant.

30. I.R.C. § 148 (1986). A good summary of federal arbitrage restrictions and rebate requirements appears in Terence P. Burke, *Guide to Arbitrage Requirements for Governmental Bond Issues* and *1994 Supplement to the Guide to Arbitrage Requirements for Governmental Bond Issues* (Chicago: Government Finance Officers Association, 1992, 1994).

15 Fiscal Control and Cash Management

A. John Vogt, David M. Lawrence, and K. Lee Carter, Jr.

Contents

PUBLIC CONFIDENCE in government depends on proper stewardship of public money. The North Carolina Local Government Budget and Fiscal Control Act sets forth requirements for fiscal control that provide a framework for ensuring accountability in a city's budgetary and financial operations. This chapter discusses these requirements. They pertain to the appointment and the role of the city finance officer, the accounting system, control of expenditures, cash management and investments, the annual audit, and audits of federal and state financial assistance to cities.

The Finance Officer

G.S. 159-24 requires that each city have a finance officer, who is legally responsible for establishing the accounting system, controlling expenditures, managing cash and other assets, and preparing financial reports. The Local Government Budget and Fiscal Control Act (LGBFCA) does not specify who is to appoint this official, leaving the decision to each city. In cities without a manager the council normally makes the appointment. City managers are also empowered (by G.S. 160A-148) to appoint the finance officer. By statute the finance officer serves at the pleasure of whoever makes the appointment.

In nearly all cities the official exercising the statutory duties of finance officer carries that title or the title of finance director, but in a few cities this official may have another title, such as accountant or treasurer. The LGBFCA permits the duties of the budget officer and the finance officer to be conferred on one person. In contrast, G.S. 105-349(e) specifies that the duties of tax collector and those of "treasurer or chief accounting officer," by which should be understood finance officer, may not be conferred on the same person, except with the written permission of the secretary of the North Carolina Local Government Commission. This limitation recognizes both the hazards to internal control of one person holding the two offices and the fact that some local government entities are too small to make any other arrangement. If a city wishes to assign both duties to one person, it should contact the commission to discuss the alternative procedures available to strengthen internal controls, and to obtain the secretary's approval. Although the commission has allowed a number of cities to operate under this arrangement, in recent years some approvals have been made with restrictions, such as suggesting that the city contract with the county for property tax billing and collection.

The finance officer's duties are summarized in G.S. 159-25(a): to establish and maintain the accounting records, to disburse moneys, to make financial reports, to manage the receipt and the deposit of moneys, to manage the city's debt service obligations, to supervise investments, and to perform any other assigned duties.

Official Bonds

The finance officer must give "a true-accounting and faithful-performance bond" of at least $10,000 and no more than $250,000, the amount to be fixed by the city council (G.S. 159-29). The usual public official's bond covers faithful performance as well as true accounting. In determining the amount of the bond, the council should seek protection against both a large single loss and cumulative smaller ones. The bond insures the city for losses that it suffers as a result of the actions or the negligence of the finance officer; it offers no insurance or protection to the officer. The city must pay the bond's premium.

G.S. 159-29 also requires that each "officer, employee, or agent . . . who handles or has in his custody more than one hundred dollars . . . at any time, or who handles or has access to the [city's] inventories" be bonded for faithful performance. If separate bonds for individuals are purchased, the $100 minimum should be understood to mean that the bonding requirement applies only to persons who frequently or regularly handle that amount or more. The city council fixes the amount of each such bond, and the city may (and normally does) pay the premium. In lieu of obtaining a separate bond for each employee, cities may purchase a blanket faithful-performance bond. Many cities do so because of the significant savings over the cost of individual bonds. The blanket bond does not substitute for the separate bond required for the finance officer, however.

The Accounting System

A city's accounting system exists to supply information. It provides the manager and other officials with the data needed to ascertain financial performance as well as to plan and budget for future activities with projected resources. The accounting system is also an essential part of internal control procedures. The city council depends on accounting information in making its budgetary and program decisions as well as in determining whether or not they have been carried out.

This kind of information is also valuable to outside organizations and individuals. The investment community and bond rating agencies rely on it as they assess a city's financial condition. State regulatory agencies, such as the Local Government Commission, review financial information to evaluate financial condition and to determine whether cities have complied with the legal requirements regulating accounting and finance. Federal and state grantor agencies use the information to monitor compliance with the requirements of the financial assistance programs that they administer. The media and the public depend on the information to evaluate a city's activities.

City accounting practices are formed in response to (1) the general statutory requirements set forth in G.S. 159-26; (2) generally accepted accounting principles for governments, promulgated nationally by the Governmental Accounting Standards Board (GASB) and other organizations, and in North Carolina by rules and regulations of the Local Government Commission; and (3) cities' own needs and capabilities.

Statutory Requirements

G.S. 159-26 requires that each city maintain an accounting system, which must do the following:

1. Show in detail the city's assets, liabilities, equities, revenues, and expenditures.
2. Record budgeted as well as actual expenditures, and budgeted or estimated revenues as well as their collection.
3. Establish accounting funds as required by G.S. 159-26(b). A *fund* is a separate, self-balancing fiscal and accounting entity having its own assets, liabilities, equity or fund balance, revenues, and expenditures. Governmental activities are grouped into funds to isolate information for legal and management purposes. The types of funds that are set forth in G.S. 159-26(b) for use by c+ities are discussed in chapter 13 of this volume.
4. Use the modified accrual basis of accounting. *Basis of accounting* refers to criteria for determining when revenues and expenditures should be recorded in the accounting system.[1] The *modified accrual basis* generally requires that expenditures be recorded when a liability is incurred (time of receipt) for goods or services provided to the city. This commonly occurs before moneys are disbursed. This type of accounting also requires that revenues be recorded when the revenues are measurable and available. *Measurable* means that they can be reasonably estimated, and *available* means that they will be received within the current fiscal year or soon enough thereafter to be able to pay liabilities of the current fiscal year. In actual practice for various reasons, some revenues are recorded when they are received in cash. For example, property taxes are usually recorded on the cash basis because taxes receivable are not considered to be collectible soon enough after the year's end to meet the availability criterion. Permits and fees are also recorded on the cash basis because they are not considered to be measurable at the year's end. On the other hand, the quarterly sales tax payment received by cities in August is usually recorded as a revenue for the year ending June 30 because the payment can be measured at June 30 and it is received soon

enough after June 30 to be able to pay liabilities at the fiscal year's end.

The modified accrual basis of accounting helps keep financial practices on a prudent footing: expenditures are recorded as soon as the liabilities for them are incurred, and important revenues are not recorded until they have actually been received in cash. In addition, the modified accrual basis enhances the comparability of financial reporting for cities and reduces the opportunity for manipulation of financial information.

5. Record encumbrances that are chargeable against budgeted appropriations. An *encumbrance* is created when a city enters into a contract that will require it to pay money, or when it issues a purchase order. Although the LGBFCA does not explicitly mention any exceptions, in practice, expenditures for salaries and wages, fringe benefits, and utilities are usually not encumbered.

Salaries, wages, and fringe benefits are not encumbered because they are generally budgeted at the full amounts expected for all positions, and this significantly reduces the risk of overexpenditure. Utilities expenditures are normally not encumbered because the amounts are not large and also are not known in advance.

An encumbrance exists as long as the contractor or the supplier has not delivered the goods or the services and the contract or the purchase order is outstanding. While this is the case, the city has not yet incurred a liability to pay for the goods or the services and should not yet record an expenditure. G.S. 159-26(d) requires that a city's accounting system record encumbrances as well as expenditures. This recognizes that the encumbrance is a potential liability, and once the purchase order is filled or the contract fulfilled, a liability for payment is created and an expenditure should be recorded. Although this requirement applies only to cities with more than 10,000 people, the wide use of computerized accounting systems with built-in encumbrance accounting functions has led many smaller cities to record encumbrances.

Generally Accepted Accounting Principles for Governments

Governmental accounting, as a branch of general accounting practice, shares basic concepts and conventions with commercial accounting. However, because of major differences in the governmental environment, a distinct set of national accounting and financial reporting principles has evolved in this field. Currently these are primarily promulgated by the GASB. Established in 1984 with the support of national organizations representing the public accounting profession and government finance officers, the GASB succeeded the National Council on Governmental Accounting (NCGA), which had formerly established generally accepted accounting principles for governmental entities. Although the GASB accepted the NCGA's pronouncements, it has actively set forth additional standards in areas of accounting and finance.

The Local Government Commission plays a key role in setting accounting standards and procedures for local governments in North Carolina. It issues rules and regulations that interpret state statutes as well as national professional standards, and it provides advice about requirements and improvements in accounting and financial reporting practices. The commission's staff focuses much attention on annual financial reports, working closely with local officials and the state's public accounting profession to keep local government accounting systems up-to-date with the increasingly more rigorous reporting and disclosure standards being promulgated by the GASB.

Cities' Own Needs and Capabilities

Cities' own needs and capabilities also shape their accounting and financial reporting systems. For example, a growing number of cities have improved their annual financial reports to the point that they have earned the Certificate of Achievement for Excellence in Financial Reporting, awarded by the Government Finance Officers Association of the United States and Canada to recognize outstanding financial reporting. Although all North Carolina cities issue professionally acceptable annual financial reports, those obtaining the Certificate of Achievement generally provide additional disclosures and also relate current financial conditions and performance to past financial trends.

One component of an accounting system that local governments occasionally neglect is *fixed asset records,* a set of records that accurately reports what fixed or capital assets (items worth more than a specified amount—for example, $500—and having a useful life of longer than a year) the government owns and where they are located. A fixed asset accounting system can provide significant advantages. It helps fix responsibility for the safekeeping of such assets, thereby improving internal control. It also serves as a basis for establishing maintenance and replacement schedules for equipment and for determining the level of fire and hazard insurance that should be carried on buildings and other capital assets. Although almost all cities have developed adequate fixed asset systems, it is important that such systems be maintained once they are established. If not maintained, fixed asset records can become so inaccurate that an independent auditor must qualify the opinion on a city's financial statements. A qualification of the auditor's opinion because of inadequate fixed asset records is a serious problem because it can affect a local government's bond rating and the government's ability to obtain Local Government Commission approval for debt issuance.

Control of Expenditures

Preauditing of Obligations

Through the annual budget ordinance and any project ordinances (see chapters 13 and 14), the city council authorizes the city manager and other officials to undertake programs and projects and to spend moneys. Except for trust or agency funds and internal service funds, which may be excluded from the budget ordinance, G.S. 159-8 directs that no city "may expend any moneys . . . except in accordance with a budget ordinance or project ordinance."

The proper functioning of the budgeting process depends on adherence to the terms of these two types of ordinances. For example, budget and project ordinances are required by law to be balanced. If revenues are raised as estimated and expenditures remain within the appropriations set in these ordinances, deficit spending should not occur. Just as important, these ordinances embody the city's general policies and priorities, which are carried out if the ordinances are followed.

The preauditing of obligations, required by G.S. 159-28(a), is a principal legal mechanism for ensuring compliance with the budget ordinance and each project ordinance. The preaudit rule provides that no obligation may be incurred in an activity accounted for in a fund included in the budget ordinance or for a project authorized by a project ordinance unless two requirements are met. First, the obligation must be authorized; that is, one of the ordinances must contain an appropriation to cover it. Second, the appropriation must not be exhausted; sufficient unspent and unencumbered funds must remain in the appropriation to meet the obligation when it comes due. Only if both requirements are met is the obligation validly incurred.

The Meaning of "Appropriation"

The *appropriations* that may not be overspent without violating the law are the figures that *actually appear* in the annual budget ordinance or a project ordinance. For example, the annual budget ordinance may make appropriations by department. If $260,000 is allotted to the recreation department, that sum is the maximum that the department may spend, and all its expenditures are charged against that figure. Various line items or *objects of expenditure* within the overall departmental appropriation may be overspent without violating the budget ordinance or the Local Government Budget and Fiscal Control Act as long as total departmental expenditures do not exceed $260,000.

In cities where the council makes appropriations by department in the annual budget ordinance, the budget officer, sometimes at the council's direction, imposes a further requirement that each operating department stay within the object-of-expenditure amounts set out in its budget. Typically the budget officer's or the finance officer's permission is needed to exceed these line-item limits. However, such a requirement is administrative rather than legal in nature because the legally binding appropriations in the budget ordinance are made only by department, not by line item.

Encumbrances

To find out whether a particular contract or purchase order will cause an appropriation to be overspent, it is not enough to know the unexpended balance of the appropriation. The preauditor must also ascertain whether contracts or purchase orders are outstanding and chargeable against the appropriation. As already mentioned, an encumbrance is created when a city enters into a contract that will require it to pay money, or when it issues a purchase order. This encumbered portion of an appropriation is as unavailable for a proposed expenditure as if the funds had already been expended: once the contract is completed or the purchase order filled, the encumbrance is replaced by an expenditure. To make the required preaudit, one must know the *unexpended and unencumbered balance* (which is often referred to simply as the *unencumbered balance*) of the proper appropriation.

The Preaudit Certificate

An obligation is invalid if incurred without meeting the preaudit requirements [G.S. 159-28(a)]. For this reason, those who deal with cities—vendors, contractors, consultants, and others—understandably want to be told whether the purchase order that they have received or the contract that they have been offered is a valid obligation. This information is provided by the *preaudit certificate*. G.S. 159-28(a) requires that any contract or agreement requiring the payment of money, and any purchase order for supplies or materials, include on its face "a certificate stating that the [contract, agreement, or purchase order] has been preaudited to assure compliance" with the preaudit requirements, namely, that the budget includes an appropriation for the contract or the agreement and that unspent and unencumbered moneys remain in the appropriation to cover payments in the current year for the contract or the agreement. The certificate, which may be printed or stamped, should read substantially as follows: "This instrument has been preaudited in the manner required by the Local Government Budget and Fiscal Control Act." It must be signed by the finance officer or by a deputy finance officer approved for this purpose by the governing board.

Besides providing some assurance to a vendor, the certificate emphasizes to the person who signs it the importance of the preaudit to the entire budget and fiscal control system. Any finance officer or deputy finance officer giving a false certificate is personally liable for any sums illegally committed or disbursed thereby [G.S. 159-28(e)].

Disbursements

Two Stages of Review

G.S. 159-28(b) outlines a two-stage procedure for approving payment of any "bill, invoice, or claim" (these include any item for which an expenditure may be made). First—and this stage applies to transactions involving moneys in any of the city's funds—the finance officer must determine that the amount claimed is owed to the claimant. Second—and this stage applies only to transactions authorized by the annual budget ordinance or a project ordinance—the finance officer must ascertain that the expenditure is authorized and that either an encumbrance exists for it or a sufficient unencumbered balance remains in the appropriation to pay the claim. Only if the finance officer has made both determinations may the disbursement be made.

The Finance Officer's Certificate

Completion of the two-stage review is evidenced by placing the *finance officer's certificate* on the face of the check or the draft that makes payment. The certificate, which may be printed or stamped on the check, must follow substantially the following form: "This disbursement has been approved as required by the Local Government Budget and Fiscal Control Act." Normally the certificate is signed by the finance officer or by a deputy finance officer approved for this purpose by the council [G.S. 159-28(d)]. Having a deputy finance officer authorized to sign checks is especially important. The absence of the finance officer for sickness or other reasons could delay the issuance of checks if that officer was the only one authorized to sign the certificate.

City Council Approval of Bills, Invoices, or Claims

The LGBFCA authorizes the city council to approve by formal resolution a bill, an invoice, or another claim that has been disapproved by the finance officer. The council may do this only for a valid claim for which an encumbrance exists or an unencumbered appropriation remains in the budget ordinance or a project ordinance, and only by following certain specified procedures. Council members approving invalid payments under this statute may be held personally liable for the payments. These procedures are rarely, if ever, used.

Form of Payment

Payment of obligations by cash is not allowed. G.S. 159-28(d) directs that all bills, invoices, salaries, or other claims be paid by check or draft on an official depository. This statute, by implication, also permits payments by wire transfers from or automated clearing house (ACH) charges to official depositories. Wire transfers are used, for example, to transmit the money periodically required for debt service on bonds or other debt to a paying agent, who in turn makes payments to individual bondholders. ACH transactions are used by a growing number of local governments to make retirement system contributions to the state, to make payroll payments, and to make certain other payments. The state intends to extend the use of the ACH system to most transfers of moneys between the state and local governments that are related to grant programs and state-shared revenues.

G.S. 159-25(b) requires each check or draft to "be signed by the finance officer or a properly designated deputy finance officer and countersigned by another official . . . designated for this purpose by the governing board." The finance officer's signature attests to completion of review and accompanies the certificate described earlier. The second signature may be that of the mayor or some other official. [If the city council does not expressly designate the countersigner, G.S. 159-25(b) directs that it be the mayor.]

The purpose of requiring two signatures is internal control. The law intends that the finance officer review the documentation of the claim and preaudit it before signing the certificate and the check. The second person can independently review the documentation before signing and issuing the check. That two persons must separately be satisfied with the documentation should significantly reduce the opportunities for fraud.

In many cities, however, the second signer does not exercise this independent review, perhaps relying on other procedures for the desired internal control. Recognizing this, G.S. 159-25(b) permits the council to waive the two-signature requirement (thus requiring only the finance officer's signature on the check) "if the board determines that the internal control procedures of the unit or authority will be satisfactory in the absence of dual signatures."

As an alternative to manual signatures, G.S. 159-28.1 permits the use of signature machines, signature stamps, or similar devices for signing checks or drafts. The council must approve the use of such signature devices through a formal resolution or ordinance, which should designate who is to have custody of the devices. For internal control purposes it is essential that this equipment be properly secured. The finance officer or another official given custody of the facsimile signature device(s) by the council is personally liable under the statute for illegal, improper, or unauthorized use of the device(s).

Cash Management and Investments

Daily Deposits

G.S. 159-32 generally requires that "all taxes and other moneys collected or received by an officer or employee of a local government" be deposited daily, either with the finance officer or in an official depository. (Deposits made under the second alternative must immediately be reported to the finance officer.) If an agency is part of a city for purposes of budget adoption and control, it and its officers and employees are also part of the city for purposes of the daily-deposit requirement.

In many cities the daily deposit to an official depository is made before the cutoff time (for example, 1:00 p.m.) set by the depository for crediting interest earnings on deposits made that day. A deposit should be made intact: all moneys collected up to the deposit time should be included. There need be only one deposit per day, although in some cities a second one is made toward the end of the day if substantial moneys are received after the first deposit.

There is a potential exception to the requirement for a daily deposit. If the city council approves, an officer or an employee need make deposits only when moneys on hand amount to $250 or more, although a deposit must always be made on the last business day of each month. Only the council may approve the use of this exception. Managers, finance officers, other officers, or advisory boards or commissions may not authorize it.

Official Depository

All moneys belonging to a city (including those transmitted to a fiscal agent for payment of debt service) must be deposited in an official depository [G.S. 159-31(a)]. The city council designates which banks or financial institutions are to serve as the official depositories. It also decides how many of them there will be. It may so designate any bank, savings institution, or trust company in the state. With the permission of the secretary of the Local Government Commission, the council may also designate a national bank located in another state. For a number of reasons the secretary will approve the use of out-of-state depositories only in rare circumstances. (None are currently approved.)

G.S. 14-234 generally forbids governing board members and other officials involved in contracting to make contracts for the city in which they have an interest. An exception exists, however, for transacting business with "banks or banking institutions." Therefore a city may designate as a depository a bank or a savings institution in which a council member, for example, is an officer, an owner, or a stockholder.

Depository accounts may be non-interest-bearing accounts with unlimited check-writing privileges; interest-bearing accounts with unlimited check-writing privileges (NOW or superNOW accounts); or interest-bearing money-market accounts for which check-writing privileges are restricted. Generally the use of interest-bearing accounts is recommended.

Cities follow a variety of methods in selecting or designating official depositories. Some name each bank and savings institution with an office in the city as a depository and place an account in each. Others maintain just one account, rotating it among the local financial institutions that are qualified to serve as official depositories, changing every year or two according to a predetermined schedule. Although these methods demonstrate a city's support of local financial institutions, they can complicate its cash management procedures, hinder its investment program, and cause it to pay more than it otherwise would for banking services. For these reasons a growing number of cities follow a third method, selecting a bank or a financial institution to serve as the depository through a request-for-proposals process. This method is currently recommended by the Local Government Commission staff. It awards a city's banking business to the institution offering the most in services for the fees charged or for the lowest non- or low-interest-bearing compensating balance that the city must maintain at the financial institution.

Insurance and Collateralization of Deposits

G.S. 159-31(b) requires that funds on deposit in an official depository (except funds deposited with a fiscal agent for the purpose of making debt service payments to bondholders) be fully secured. This is accomplished through a combination of methods. First, city funds on deposit with a bank or a savings institution or invested in a certificate of deposit (CD) issued by such an institution are insured by the Federal Deposit Insurance Corporation (FDIC). If the funds that a city has on deposit or invested in a CD do not exceed the maximum amount of FDIC insurance—currently $100,000 per depositor for interest-bearing accounts and an additional $100,000 per depositor for non-interest-bearing accounts—no further security is required.

Uninsured city funds in a bank or a savings institution may be secured under one of two types of collateral security arrangements. Under the first type the institution places securities with a market value equal to or greater than the city's uninsured moneys on deposit or invested in CDs, into an escrow account with a separate, unrelated third-party institution (usually the trust department of another bank, the Federal Reserve, or the Federal Home Loan Bank). The escrow agreement provides that if the bank or the savings institution defaults on its obligations to the city, then the city is entitled to the escrowed securities in the amount of the default less the amount of FDIC insurance coverage. Under this method the city must execute certain forms and take certain actions to ensure that deposits are adequately collateralized. Responsibility for ensuring that deposits are properly collateralized under this method rests with the finance officer, who should closely supervise the collateral security arrangements.

Alternatively a bank or a savings institution may choose to participate in a pool of bank- and savings-institution-owned securities held by the state treasurer to collateralize state and local government moneys on deposit or invested in CDs with these institutions. In this case it is the institution's responsibility to maintain adequate collateral securities in the pool, although each financial institution's collateral balances are monitored by the state treasurer.

Investments

Cities cannot afford to let significant amounts of cash lie idle in non-interest-bearing depository accounts. Investment income can amount to the equivalent of several cents or more on the property tax rate. G.S. 159-30 makes the finance officer responsible for managing investments, subject to policy directions and restrictions that the governing board may impose. Because of the opportunities and the risks associated with the investments that North Carolina cities may legally make, both national investment authorities and the Local Government Commission recommend that a city council establish general investment policies and restrictions for finance officers to follow.

Such council-adopted policies might, for example, limit the maximum maturities for investments; require the use of informal competitive bidding for the purchase of securities; authorize the finance officer to invest in the cash and/or term portfolios of the North Carolina Capital Management Trust (discussed later); and make clear that safety and liquidity take precedence over yield in the city's investment program. In a growing number of cities, councils are adopting such investment policies.

In conducting their investment programs, finance officers must forecast cash resources and needs, thus determining how much money is available for investment and for how long. They must also investigate what types of investment securities are authorized by law for cities and decide which ones to purchase. If an investment security is to be sold before maturity, the finance officer must make that decision.

Custody of Investment Securities

G.S. 159-30(d) states, "Securities and deposit certificates shall be in the custody of the finance officer who shall be responsible for their safekeeping." Investment securities come in two forms: *certificated* and *noncertificated*. Ownership of certificated investments is represented by an actual physical security. Some commercial paper and most certificates of deposit are issued in certificated form. To obtain proper custody of certificated securities, the finance officer should hold the securities or the certificates in the city's vault or its safe deposit box at a local bank or trust company. Alternatively, certificated securities may be delivered to and held by a city's third-party safekeeping agent, which can be the trust department of a North Carolina bank.

Many investment securities—United States Treasury bills, notes, and bonds as well as almost all federal agency instruments—are not certificated. Ownership of them is evidenced by electronic *book-entry* records that are maintained by the Federal Reserve System for banks and certain other financial institutions, and by the financial institutions themselves. Additionally, for certain other securities the Depository Trust Company in New York maintains the electronic records of ownership. When a city buys noncertificated securities from a bank or a securities dealer, the record of ownership is transferred electronically from the seller or the seller's bank to the city's custodial agent. To obtain proper custody of book-entry securities, a city should have a signed custodial agreement in place with the financial institution that serves as its custodial agent. This financial institution should be a member of the Federal Reserve System and be authorized to conduct trust business in North Carolina. Simply stated, this means that the custodial agent usually will be the trust department of a North Carolina bank that is a member of the Federal Reserve System. Cities may not use securities brokers and dealers and the operating divisions of banks and savings institutions as custodial agents for their investment securities. With the exception of certain repurchase agreements (see note 2), the city's custodial agent may obtain custody of all securities for the city, even those purchased from the operating division of the bank that sells the city the securities. It is essential that a city or its custodial agent obtain custody of all city investments. Major losses from investments suffered by local governments in other states have been due to the failure of those governments to obtain proper custody of their investments.

Authorized Investments

Among the securities or the instruments in which cities invest are CDs or other forms of time deposits approved by the Local Government Commission that are offered by banks, savings institutions, and trust companies located in North Carolina [G.S. 159-30(b), (c)(5)]. CDs issued by banks in the state have traditionally been among the most widely used investment instruments, especially by small and medium-size cities. Some of the other investments authorized by G.S. 159-30(c) include the following:

1. United States Treasury obligations (bills, notes, and bonds), called *Treasuries*, and United States *agency* obligations whose principal and interest are fully guaranteed by the United States Government. Because these are full-faith-and-credit obligations of the United States, they carry the least credit risk—that is, risk of default—of any investment available to cities. As a result, short-term Treasuries are usually lower yielding than alternative investment securities. Long-term Treasuries and Government National Mortgage Association securities (fully guaranteed by the United States Government) can experience significant price variations. This is characteristic of long-term securities; therefore such securities should be carefully evaluated before they are purchased.

2. Direct obligations of certain agencies that were established and/or sponsored by the United States Government but whose obligations are not guaranteed by it. The authorized agencies are listed in G.S. 159-30(c)(2). Examples are the Federal Home Loan Bank Board, the Federal National Mortgage Association, and the Federal Farm Credit System. Direct debt issued by these agencies generally carries very low credit risk, although economic conditions adverse to an agency can create some risk for cities or others who invest in its securities. Some securities of these agencies are not their direct debt and are therefore not eligible investments for North Carolina cities. Moreover, longer-term direct debt of these agencies, although carrying low credit risk, can experience significant price fluctuations before maturity.

3. Obligations of the State of North Carolina or bonds and notes of any of its local governments or public authorities, with investments in such obligations subject to restrictions of the secretary of the Local Government Commission. Because the interest paid to investors on these obligations, bonds, and notes is typically exempt from federal and state income taxes, they generally carry lower yields than alternative investment instruments available to cities. However, should the state and local governments in North Carolina begin to issue significant amounts of securities on which the

interest paid is subject to federal income taxes, those securities would carry higher interest rates than tax-exempt state and local government obligations. This could make these taxable state and local obligations attractive as investment instruments to cities.

4. Top-rated commercial paper issued by United States corporations. Commercial paper is issued by industrial and commercial corporations to finance inventories and other short-term needs. Such paper is an unsecured corporate promissory note that is available in maturities of up to 270 days, although maturities from 30 to 90 days are most common. For any local government to invest in commercial paper, the paper must be rated by at least one national rating organization and earn its top commercial paper rating. If the paper is rated by more than one such organization, it must have the highest commercial paper rating given by each.

   Commercial paper is relatively high yielding, and many cities invest in it. In recent years some commercial paper issuers have been downgraded. This means that their commercial paper is no longer eligible for investment by North Carolina local governments; however, as long as a commercial paper issuer is top rated and the finance officer closely monitors its ratings, the risk is small. City officials should also understand that bank commercial paper is not a deposit and consequently is not covered by insurance and collateralization.

5. Bankers acceptances issued by North Carolina banks or by any top-rated United States bank. *Bankers acceptances* are bills of exchange or time drafts which are drawn on and guaranteed by banks. They are issued to finance international trade or firms' short-term credit needs and are usually secured by the credit of the issuing firm as well as by the general credit of the accepting bank. Most bankers acceptances have terms of 30 to 180 days. Only the largest North Carolina banks issue them, and cities may invest in them. For a city to invest in bankers acceptances of non–North Carolina U.S. banks, the institution must have outstanding publicly held obligations that carry the highest long-term bond rating from at least one national rating organization. If the bank's credit

obligations are rated by more than one such organization, they must have the highest long-term bond rating given by each.

6. Participating shares in one of the portfolios of the North Carolina Capital Management Trust. This trust is a mutual fund established specifically for investments by North Carolina local governments and public authorities. It is certified and regulated by the Local Government Commission, and unlike many state-sponsored investment pools for public entity investments, it is registered with the United States Securities and Exchange Commission, which imposes reporting and other requirements that ensure the safety of money invested in the trust. The trust manages two separate investment portfolios: a money-market portfolio and a term portfolio. The money-market portfolio, which was started in 1982, is intended for the investment of short-term or operating cash balances. The principal value of money invested in a share in this portfolio remains fixed at $1. The term portfolio, which was established in 1987, is intended for moneys that are not subject to immediate need. The principal value of investments in this portfolio fluctuates with changes in market interest rates. Because of this, the term portfolio should primarily be used for the investment of funds that will not be needed immediately or in the short term.

Either portfolio permits the return of funds invested with it within one day of notice; however, the managers of the portfolios do request that local governments provide longer advance notice if large withdrawals will be made. The trust's portfolios may invest only in securities in which local governments may invest under G.S. 159-30(c).

7. Repurchase agreements. A *repurchase agreement* is a purchase by an investor of a security, with the stipulation that the seller will buy it back at the original purchase price plus agreed-on interest at the maturity date. These agreements were once popular for short-term or overnight investments by North Carolina local governments. Unfortunately some local governments in other states suffered substantial losses by engaging in repurchase agreements with unscrupulous securities dealers. As a result, strict laws and requirements

for the safe use of these agreements have been enacted, both in North Carolina and across the country. G.S. 159-30(c) authorizes local governments to invest in repurchase agreements, but only under very limited conditions.[2] These conditions have greatly reduced the cost-effectiveness of local government investments in repurchase agreements, and such agreements are no longer used to any significant degree by cities.

8. Evidences of ownership of, or fractional undivided interests in, future principal and interest payments of *stripped* or *zero-coupon instruments* that are issued directly or guaranteed by the United States Government. These instruments were first authorized as a local government investment in 1987. They are sold at large discounts and pay no interest until maturity. They may be a useful investment vehicle for certain limited moneys, such as those held in a capital reserve fund, that definitely will not be needed until after the instrument matures. However, because they are subject to great price fluctuations before maturity, stripped or zero-coupon securities should not be used for the investment of operating funds. If investments were made in these securities and market interest rates later rose substantially (as they did in 1994), a city that had to cash in the investments before maturity could lose a substantial portion of the principal invested in the securities.

9. Certain mutual funds for moneys held by a city that are subject to the arbitrage and rebate provisions of the Internal Revenue code. The LGBFCA authorizes unspent proceeds from financings subject to the Internal Revenue Code's arbitrage and rebate provisions to be invested in tax-exempt and taxable mutual funds under strict procedures. Operating moneys and proceeds from financings that are not subject to the arbitrage and rebate provisions may not be invested in these mutual funds. Because of the complexity of the federal tax code and the wide variety of available mutual funds, a city should consult with its bond counsel before placing moneys in this type of investment.

10. Derivatives issued directly by one of the federal agencies listed in G.S. 159-30(c)(2) or guaranteed by the United States Government. *Derivatives* refer to a broad range of

investment securities that can vary in market price, yield, and/or cash flow depending on the value of underlying securities or assets, or changes in one or more interest rate indices. Derivatives commonly include mortgage pass-through instruments issued by federal agencies, mortgage obligations "guaranteed" by federal agencies (but not by the United States Government), callable step-up notes, floaters, inverse floaters, and still other securities that go by even more interesting names. It is beyond the scope of this chapter to explain these different types of derivatives. It shall suffice to say that derivatives are generally complex instruments, and many of them are subject to rapid and major changes in value as interest rates change. Local governments in other states have lost vast amounts of money by investing in derivatives. The volume of derivatives available to investors has grown dramatically, and investment brokers and dealers often try to sell various types of derivatives to city and other local government finance officers. Many derivatives are not legal investment instruments for North Carolina's local governments. Those issued directly by one of the federal agencies listed in G.S. 159-30(c)(2) or guaranteed by the United States Government are legal investments. However, many if not most of these are inappropriate as investment vehicles for cities, except in very special circumstances. Even though legal, many of them are subject to extreme price and cash-flow volatility. A finance officer considering investing the city's money in one or more derivatives should do so only pursuant to a city council investment policy that explicitly authorizes such an investment, only if the finance officer understands the nature of the security and the risks associated with it, and only for a short maturity.

Guidelines for Investing Public Funds

Because of great changes and technological innovation in financial markets, weaknesses in certain sectors of these markets, and the availability of many new types of investment instruments, the investment and the general management of public moneys have become very complex. North Carolina cities can avoid many of the problems that have harmed local governments in other states by adhering to the following guidelines in conducting their investment programs:

1. *The investment program should put safety and liquidity before yield.* A city should not put the funds that it is investing at risk of loss for the purpose of obtaining higher investment earnings. The temptation to sacrifice safety for yield is particularly great when interest rates are falling and a city's officials are attempting to maintain investment earnings and revenues. A city should always have funds available to meet payment obligations when they fall due. This requires maintaining adequate liquidity in an investment portfolio and limiting most investments to securities with short-term maturities.

2. *A city should invest only in securities that the finance officer understands.* Many investment vehicles, including most derivatives, are extremely complex. Before purchasing a security, the finance officer should thoroughly understand all its components, especially how its value is likely to change with changes in market interest rates. Whenever the finance officer is considering investing in a type of security that the city has not used before, the finance officer should obtain and study the prospectus or equivalent information for the security and talk to Local Government Commission staff about the nature and the risks of the security.

3. *The finance officer and other officials involved in investing city funds should know the financial institutions, the brokers, and the dealers from which the city buys investment securities.* Investment transactions are made by phone, and investment funds and securities are often electronically transferred in seconds. Funds and securities can be lost or "misplaced" quickly in such an environment. To protect the city, the officials conducting a city's investment program must be sure that they deal only with reputable and reliable institutions, brokers, and dealers. The finance officer should obtain a list of North Carolina local government clients of any firm or person attempting to sell the city investment securities and obtain references from officials in these other governments. The finance officer should also obtain and evaluate current

financial statements from any institution, broker, or dealer that sells or wishes to sell securities to the city. Local governments in other states have lost invested funds because they placed moneys with firms that later went bankrupt and were unable to return the funds. A discussion of how to analyze the financial position of banks and similar financial institutions can be found in the North Carolina Department of State Treasurer's *Policies Manual.*[3] A city should also enter into an investment trading agreement with any firm or person from which it buys investments; model investment trading agreements are used by and are available from several of North Carolina's large cities and counties.

4. *The finance officer should ensure that the city adequately insures or collateralizes all investments in CDs (as well as other deposits in banks), and that it has proper custody of all investment securities.*

5. *The city's investment program should be conducted pursuant to cash management and investment policy approved by the city council.* Such a policy should be based on G.S. 159-30 and related statutes, set forth the council's directions and expectations about which investments will be made and generally how they will be made, and establish general parameters for the receipt, the disbursement, and the management of moneys.

6. *The finance officer should report periodically to the council on the status of the city's investment program.* Such a report should be made annually or more often and show the securities in the city's investment portfolio, the terms or the maturities for investments, and their yields. If possible, average investment maturity and yield should be calculated and also shown in this report.

The Annual Audit

Contents of the Annual Financial Report

G.S. 159-34 requires local governments to have their accounts audited by independent auditors after the close of each fiscal year. The auditor's opinion is contained in the annual financial report, which must include "the [city's] financial statements prepared in conformity with generally accepted accounting principles, all disclosures in the public interest required by law, and the auditor's opinion and comments relating to [the] financial statements."

The annual financial report is a city's responsibility whether it is prepared by the finance officer and his or her staff or by the independent auditor. Nearly all the large cities and some medium-size and small ones now prepare their own financial statements. This requires much work by a city's finance staff, but it can result in significant savings in audit fees.

If a city prepares a comprehensive annual financial report, it will contain three sections: introductory, financial, and statistical. A fourth section consisting of the compliance or single audit reports and schedules may be included. Table 15-1 summarizes the contents of the comprehensive annual financial report. If a city does not prepare a comprehensive report, only the financial section will be found in the annual financial report.

Introductory Section

The introductory section of a comprehensive report includes the transmittal letter, an organization chart, and a list of principal officials. The transmittal letter, which presents an overview of city operations and activities, should be of particular interest to city officials, who may not be aware of all the city does.

Financial Section

The financial section of the annual financial report contains the financial statements, which present information in various formats and levels of detail. Generally the most summarized information is found at the beginning of the annual financial report, and the most detailed data are located in subsequent parts of the report. Combined statements covering all city funds and containing highly summarized information are located at the beginning of the report, before the notes to the financial statements. In the combined statements, information for each type of fund (general, special revenue, enterprise, etc.) is presented in a series of columns, one type to a column. The combining and individual fund statements follow the notes to the financial statements and provide greater detail about city finances. A combining statement shows individual funds of a particular type and a combined total (e.g., each special revenue fund is

Figure 15-1
Contents of a Comprehensive Annual Financial Report

Section	Description
Introductory Section	
Letter of transmittal	Overview of city operations and financial statistics
Organizational chart	Diagram of city's organizational structure
List of principal officials	List of elected and appointed officials
Financial Section	
Auditor's opinion	Independent auditor's opinion on financial statements
Combined financial statements	Summarized information, one column for each type of fund (general, special revenue, etc.)
Notes to the financial statements	Explanations of accounting policies, statutory violations, explanations of financial statement items, etc.
Combining statements	Summarized information, one column for each fund of particular type (e.g., each special revenue fund) and combined-total column
Individual fund statements	Detailed information about individual funds (prior year amounts, budgeted amounts, actual amounts, etc.)
Supplemental schedules	Additional information for such items as fixed assets
Statistical Section	
Statistical tables	Tables, usually on multiyear basis, showing information on property taxes, debt, revenues, expenditures, etc.
Compliance Section (optional)	
Single audit reports	Reports from independent auditor on compliance and internal control
Schedule of findings and questioned costs	Listing of grant findings and questioned costs
Schedule of federal and state financial assistance	Listing of federal and state financial assistance programs

presented in its own column, and a combined total is presented in a final column). Statements for individual funds, such as the general and the water and sewer funds, are also presented. These are usually the most detailed statements and commonly compare actual results with budgeted amounts. Both balance sheets (showing assets, liabilities, and fund balance or fund equity) and operating statements (showing revenues, expenditures, cash flows, and budget-actual comparisons) may be included in the report for each of the three levels of financial statements.

The "disclosures in the public interest" are primarily found in the notes to the financial statements, which are also located in the financial section. The content and the form of the notes are prescribed by the generally accepted accounting principles established by GASB and other organizations. Through written advisory memoranda and illustrative financial statements, the Local Government Commission provides guidance to local officials and their independent auditors on the content of the notes. The notes contain significant information for anyone attempting to interpret the financial statements and understand a city's finances. Disclosures of interest to city officials include such items as the following: statutory violations; budgetary overexpenditures; significant accounting and budgetary policies; and detailed information concerning a city's deposits and investments, fixed assets, and long-term debt.

Statistical Section

The statistical section follows the financial section. It includes multiyear trend information on revenues, expenditures, debt, property taxes, and other items. Economic and demographic data are also reported. This section is useful in analyzing a city's financial trends.

The Auditor's Opinion

The auditor's essential task is to render an independent opinion on the material accuracy and reliability of the financial statements and the notes thereto, as well as on their conformity with generally accepted accounting principles. The auditor opines not that the financial statements and disclosures are perfect, but that they are reliable enough for a knowledgeable reader to use them to make informed judgments about a city's financial position and operations.

The opinion might take one of four forms. First, it may be *unqualified*: the auditor says that the statements present fairly the city's financial position and operations at the close of the fiscal year, in conformity with generally accepted accounting principles.

A *qualified* opinion is a second possibility. If in some way a city's practices vary from generally accepted accounting principles, the opinion will indicate that the statements present fairly the city's financial position except for any such deviation. For example, the city may not have properly accounted for fixed assets. Also, an opinion qualification may be due to a *scope limitation*. This occurs when the independent auditor is unable to perform certain test procedures that are an essential part of the audit. For instance, when a city's accounting system fails to provide adequate documentation for some revenue and expenditure transactions, the auditor's ability to test such transactions is limited. This limitation may result in a qualified opinion.

Third, deviations from generally accepted accounting principles may be so material that the statements as a whole do not present fairly the city's financial position. If that occurs, the auditor renders an *adverse* opinion.

Fourth, and rarely, the auditor may *disclaim* any opinion at all on the statements. In this case the city's accounting system is in such disarray that an opinion cannot be rendered.

Although at one time a significant number of cities received opinions that were other than unqualified, in recent years all but a handful have been receiving unqualified opinions from their independent auditors. Receiving an unqualified opinion is important in part because the Local Government Commission usually requires it before a unit of government may issue debt.

The auditor normally suggests improvements in a city's internal control and financial procedures in a *management letter* that accompanies the audit report. This letter is usually addressed to the governing board. A public document, it typically makes various specific suggestions for improving internal control and financial procedures. These suggestions normally arise from the audit, and the letter is typically delivered at the same time as the annual financial statements. Often the suggestions have been informally made earlier, and some may already have been acted on. Significant weaknesses in internal controls will also be addressed by the independent auditor in the internal control reports that are required as part of the single audit on federal and state financial assistance programs. These are discussed in the next section.

Apart from the management letter, the independent auditor can often be an excellent source of advice on accounting system design, internal control procedures, and finance in general.

Selection of the Independent Auditor

G.S. 159-34 establishes certain requirements and procedures regarding contracting for the annual audit. First, the auditor must be selected by and report to the governing board. The auditor should not report to the manager, the budget officer, or the finance officer.

Second, the council may choose any North Carolina certified public accountant or any accountant certified by the Local Government Commission as qualified to audit local government accounts. In practice, no non-CPA accountants have requested certification or met the requirements for certification to perform local government audits in recent years. City council members should assure themselves that the firm selected to do the audit is familiar with the special features of governmental accounting and auditing. Auditors should be engaged early in the fiscal year so that they can become familiar with the city's procedures and can complete some of the necessary testing before the end of the fiscal year. This also ensures that the auditor can plan the audit engagement and complete it in a timely manner.

In recent years many cities have begun to select the auditor through a *request-for-proposals* (RFP) process. Although this is optional, using an RFP is recommended by the Local Government Commission staff to secure the best audit proposal. Also, selecting an independent auditor through a competitive procurement process is required by federal regulations if a city is allowed by a grant agreement and intends to charge some of the audit costs to the grant. Most cities that use RFPs engage an auditor for a term of three to five years. The RFP should cover both the technical qualifications of a potential audit firm and the firm's cost proposals. Local officials should give more weight to an auditor's technical skills than to its proposed audit fees. References from other local government clients should be requested from an auditor. These references should be contacted so that city officials may obtain information on other local governments' experiences with a potential auditor.

Third, a city's annual contract with an auditor must be approved by the Local Government Commission. Also, invoices for audit services may not be paid until the secretary of the commission has approved them.

Audits of Federal and State Financial Assistance Programs

Federal and state grant and other financial assistance programs may provide moneys to support certain city programs. In the past, individual federal and state agencies providing these moneys would audit a city's expenditure of them to verify that they were spent for the purposes intended and in accordance with prescribed procedures. However, since the mid-1980s the federal government has required local governments to have a *combined financial and compliance audit,* or single audit, on all federal financial assistance programs if a certain amount of revenue from all federal programs was received in a given year. To build on the federal single audit, the 1987 General Assembly, with the support of local officials, passed a law requiring state financial assistance programs to be included with federal programs in a combined single audit. In North Carolina this combined single audit is performed in conjunction with the annual financial audit by the city's independent auditor. Federal and state agencies are allowed to build on the single audit and perform monitoring work on the programs they administer. However, they should not duplicate the work performed by the independent auditor.

The independent auditor issues a number of compliance and internal control reports to disclose findings from the single audit. These reports usually are included in the last section of the annual financial report. The most significant items for local officials in these reports are the internal control weaknesses, findings, and questioned costs identified by the auditor. Internal control weaknesses are usually significant deficiencies and should be corrected unless corrective actions would not be cost-effective. Typically, findings and questioned costs always require corrective action, which may necessitate the repayment of grant funds. City officials' formal responses to findings and questioned costs and material internal control weaknesses are included in the single audit reports.

The Local Government Commission monitors the single audit of grant funds as part of its review of the annual financial report. If the commission staff determines that the single audit reports and schedules are not prepared according to the applicable standards, then the independent auditor may be required to revise them before the annual financial report can be accepted. If the commission staff finds that the single audit is satisfactory, then all state grantor agencies must accept the audit. Subsequent to the acceptance of the annual financial report, if the commission determines that the single audit is not reliable, it may revoke its approval. This opens a city to individual federal and state agency audits.

Additional Resources

Carter, K. Lee, Jr.; Fiscal Management Section, Department of State Treasurer; and S. Grady Fullerton. *Carolina County, North Carolina, Comprehensive Annual Financial Report*, 2d ed. rev. Chapel Hill, N.C.: Institute of Government, The University of North Carolina at Chapel Hill, 1995.

Governmental Accounting Standards Board. *Codification of Governmental Accounting and Financial Reporting Standards as of June 30, 1994.* Norwalk, Conn.: GASB, 1994.

Government Finance Officers Association. *Governmental Accounting, Auditing and Financial Reporting*, 1994 ed. Chicago: GFOA, 1994.

Larson, Corinne, ed. *A Public Investor's Guide to Money Market Instruments.* Chicago: Government Finance Officers Association, 1994.

Lawrence, David M. *Local Government Finance in North Carolina*, 2d ed. Chapel Hill, N.C.: Institute of Government, The University of North Carolina at Chapel Hill, 1990.

Notes

1. Although the LGBFCA requires the use of the modified accrual basis of accounting, it also requires that financial reporting be in conformity with generally accepted accounting principles. Enterprise, internal service, and certain trust funds primarily follow commercial (accrual) accounting standards for financial reporting purposes. A city's annual financial report must both demonstrate compliance with legal requirements and report on operations in conformity with

generally accepted accounting principles; therefore enterprise funds should be reported on both the modified accrual and the accrual basis in a city's financial statements, and internal service and certain trust funds should also be reported on the accrual basis in the annual financial report.

2. The following restrictions apply to local government investments in repurchase agreements: (a) The underlying security acquired with a repurchase agreement must be a direct obligation of the United States or fully guaranteed by the United States. (b) The repurchase agreement must be sold by a broker or a dealer that is recognized as a primary dealer by a Federal Reserve Bank, or be sold by a commercial bank, a trust company, or a national bank whose deposits are insured by the FDIC. (c) The security underlying the agreement must be delivered in physical or in electronic book-entry form to the city or its third-party agent. (d) The value of the underlying security must be determined daily and be maintained, at least, at 100 percent of the repurchase price. (e) The city must have a valid and perfected security interest in the underlying security. This can be achieved through delivery of the security to the city or its third-party safekeeping agent under a written agreement. (f) The underlying security acquired in the repurchase agreement must be free of any lien or third-party claim.

3. North Carolina Department of State Treasurer, *Policies Manual* (Raleigh, N.C.: NCDST, October 1990).

16 City Property: Acquisition, Sale, and Disposition

Ben F. Loeb, Jr., and David M. Lawrence

Contents

AS BUSINESS ENTITIES, cities need to acquire and dispose of property. In acquiring property, cities generally are no different than private persons or corporations, although some acquisition procedures are available only to governments. In disposing of property, cities usually must follow detailed statutory procedures.

Acquisition of Real Property

Cities have broad statutory power to acquire the fee or any lesser interest (such as an easement) in real or personal property for their use or for the use of any of their departments, boards, commissions, or agencies. (Acquisition of personal property, which is generally subject to competitive-bidding requirements, is discussed in chapter 17 of this volume.) Under the General Statutes and the common law, cities may acquire property by the following methods:

1. Gift: a voluntary transfer of property, without any cost to the city
2. Purchase: a voluntary transfer of property, for a price
3. Devise: a voluntary gift of property by a person's last will and testament, without any cost to the city
4. Dedication: a voluntary setting aside of an interest in land,

usually an easement, for public use, which is accepted on behalf of the public by the city

5. Exchange: a voluntary transfer of property for something of equivalent value
6. Lease: a contract giving the city possession of a property for a determinate period
7. Adverse possession or prescription: an involuntary transfer of property, without payment, because of long occupation of the property by the city
8. Eminent domain: an involuntary transfer of property, on payment of just compensation

A city may acquire property as a sole owner or as a joint owner with another government. When it does acquire property, it may not, as a part of the transaction, give a mortgage or another security interest in the property[1] unless a statute specifically permits it to do so.[2] G.S. 160A-20 allows a city to give a security interest in limited circumstances: (1) to the seller of real or personal property to secure the purchase price when the city is paying for the property in installments; (2) to the lender if the city finances such a purchase; and (3) to a construction lender if the loan is structured as an installment purchase contract. (This statute is discussed in detail in chapter 14.) No other statute permits security interests, however; therefore they may not be given in other circumstances.

Eminent Domain

The 1981 General Assembly enacted a new law of eminent domain for private condemnors and local public condemnors, including cities and counties. This act is essentially a General Statutes Commission bill that went through approximately twelve drafts over more than five years. As enacted, it does not affect state agencies. For example, the Department of Transportation continues to use the condemnation procedures set forth in G.S. Chapter 136.

The new law repealed all of G.S. Chapter 40, the eminent domain provisions of G.S. Chapter 160A, and most local condemnation acts (a few have since been added). These repealed provisions were replaced with a new G.S. Chapter 40A. Article 1 of the new act contains general provisions (such as definitions); Article 2 sets forth the condemnation procedures to be used by private condemnors (power companies, railroads, etc.); Article 3 describes the condemnation procedures for public condemnors; and Article 4 concerns "just compensation."

G.S. 40A-1 states in part:

> It is the intent of the General Assembly that the procedures provided by this Chapter shall be the exclusive condemnation procedures to be used in this State by private condemnors and all local public condemnors. All other provisions in laws, charters, or local acts authorizing the use of other procedures by municipal or county governments or agencies or political subdivisions thereof, or by corporations, associations or other persons are hereby repealed. . . .

There are two express exceptions to this broad rule: (1) the new act did not repeal any provision of a local act enlarging or limiting the purpose for which property may be condemned; (2) nor did it repeal any local act creating any substantive or procedural requirement or limitation on the authority of a local public condemnor to exercise the power of eminent domain outside its boundaries. In addition, G.S. 136-66.3 (which authorizes cities to use the Chapter 136 procedure when condemning for a state-highway-system street) was not expressly repealed and apparently survived.

The definitions for Chapter 40A are contained in G.S. 40A-2. The word *property* is given the broadest possible meaning, being defined as any right, title, or interest in land, including leases and options to buy or sell. It also includes rights of access, rights-of-way, easements, water rights, air rights, and any other privilege in or appurtenance to the possession, the use, and the enjoyment of land. *Judge* is defined to include only judges of superior court; therefore district courts have no jurisdiction even when the amount of money in controversy falls within the range normally assigned to district court.

Allowable Purposes of Condemnation

The purposes for which cities may use the power of eminent domain either inside or outside the city are listed in G.S. 40A-3(b):

1. Roads, streets, alleys, and sidewalks (this is in addition to authority under G.S. Ch. 136, Art. 9)
2. Public enterprises listed in G.S. 160A-311[3]

3. Parks, playgrounds, and other recreational facilities
4. Storm sewer and drainage systems
5. Hospital facilities, cemeteries, and libraries
6. City halls, fire stations, office buildings, jails, or other buildings for use by any department, board, commission, or agency
7. Drainage programs and programs to prevent obstruction to the natural flow of streams or to improve drainage facilities
8. Acquisition of designated historical properties
9. Public wharves

A city does not possess the power of eminent domain with respect to property owned by the state of North Carolina unless the state consents to the taking, nor may a city condemn property owned by the federal government. The state's consent is given by the Council of State or by the secretary of administration if the council delegates that authority to him or her. When state property is taken, the only issue is the compensation to be paid (G.S. 40A-5).

Except as otherwise provided by statute, a city may condemn the property of a private condemnor if such property is not in actual public use or is not necessary to the operation of the owner's business. It may also condemn the property of another local or public condemnor if the property proposed to be taken is not being used or held for future use for any governmental or proprietary purpose [G.S. 40A-5(b)].

Prior Offer and Right of Entry

G.S. 40A-4 provides that the power to acquire property by condemnation does not depend on any prior effort to acquire the same property by gift or purchase. Nor is the power to negotiate for the gift or the purchase of property impaired by initiation of a condemnation proceeding.

A condemnor may enter on any lands (but not structures) to make surveys, borings, examinations, or appraisals without filing a complaint, making a deposit, or taking any other action required by G.S. Chapter 40A. However, it must give the owner (at his or her last known address) thirty days' written notice of the intended entry. Also, it must reimburse him or her for any damages resulting from these activities (G.S. 40A-11).

Notice

G.S. 40A-40 requires that a public condemnor notify each owner of its intent to institute an action to condemn property not less than thirty days before it files a complaint. This notice must describe the property to be taken and state the amount estimated by the condemnor to constitute "just compensation."

Complaint and Deposit

A public condemnor institutes action by filing (in the superior court of the county where the land is located) a complaint that contains a declaration of taking. When it files the complaint, the condemnor must deposit a sum of money that it estimates to be just compensation. A summons is then issued. The summons, together with a copy of the complaint and a notice of the deposit, is served on the person or persons named therein in the manner specified by G.S. 1A-1, rule 4. G.S. 40A-41 sets forth the contents for the complaint.

Quick Take

When a city condemns property for certain listed purposes, the title to the property and the right to immediate possession vest when the complaint is filed and the deposit is made (hence the name *quick take* for this procedure). Cities may use the quick-take procedure for such enterprises as electric power generation and distribution systems, water supply and distribution systems, sewage collection and treatment systems, gas production and distribution systems, solid waste collection and disposal systems, cable television, and streets. They may *not* use it for public transportation systems, off-street parking facilities, airports, and certain other purposes [G.S. 40A-42(a)].

Not-So-Quick Take

When quick take is not available to a city, the condemnation proceeds pursuant to G.S. 40A-42(b). Under that subsection, the title to the property specified in the complaint vests in the condemnor (1) when the answer filed by the owner requests only that there be a determination of just compensation, (2) if the owner fails to file an answer within the 120 days specified by G.S. 40A-46, or (3) when the deposit is disbursed in accordance with the provisions of G.S. 40A-44.

The owner may seek an injunction to prevent title from vesting under either subsection (a) or (b) of G.S. 40A-42.

If the owner's answer raises questions other than the amount of just compensation, a judge—on motion and ten days' notice by either party—hears and determines the issues. These issues may include the condemnor's authority to take, questions of necessary and proper parties, the title to land, the interest taken, and the area taken (G.S. 40A-47).

Memorandum of Action and Disbursement

G.S. 40A-43 requires the condemnor, when it files the complaint and deposits the estimated compensation, to record a memorandum of action with the register of deeds in any county where involved land is located. This section also sets out the contents of the memorandum.

When there is no dispute as to title, the persons named in the complaint may apply to the court for disbursement of the deposited money (or any part thereof), "as full compensation or as a credit against just compensation without prejudice to further proceedings to determine just compensation" (G.S. 40A-44).

Answer

The contents of the owner's answer are set forth in G.S. 40A-45. G.S. 40A-46 gives the owner or owners 120 days from the date of service to answer. Failure to answer within this period constitutes an admission that the amount deposited is just compensation and is a waiver of any further proceedings to determine just compensation. In such a case the judge enters final judgment and orders disbursement of the deposited money.

Appointment and Duties of Commissioners

Either the owner or the condemnor may, within sixty days of the answer's being filed, request the clerk of superior court to appoint commissioners to determine just compensation. The clerk then appoints three competent, disinterested persons who reside in the county to serve as commissioners. G.S. 40A-48 requires that they be sworn and then visit the property to appraise its value. The commissioners have the power to inspect the property, hold hearings, swear witnesses, and take evidence as they may deem necessary. When they have completed these tasks, they must file with the court a report substantially as set out in G.S. 40A-48(c).

When the commissioners' report is filed, the clerk mails a copy to each of the parties or their counsel. Either party has thirty days after the report is mailed to file exceptions to it and demand a trial *de novo* by jury on the issue of compensation. If no exception is filed, the judge enters final judgment on a finding that the report awards "just compensation" to the property owners.

Costs and Interest

G.S. 40A-13 requires that the condemnor pay all court costs. In addition, the court in its discretion may award the owner a sum to reimburse him or her for charges paid for appraisers, engineers, and plats if the appraisers or the engineers testify as witnesses and the plats are received in evidence by court order (G.S. 40A-8, -13). The judge also adds interest at the rate of 6 percent from the date of taking to the date of judgment (G.S. 40A-54).

Just Compensation

The determination of just compensation must reflect the value of the property immediately before the complaint is filed (G.S. 40A-63). The measure of compensation for the taking is the property's fair market value unless only part of the tract is taken, in which case the measure of compensation is either (1) the amount by which the fair market value of the entire tract immediately before the taking exceeds the fair market value of the remainder immediately after the taking, or (2) the fair market value of the property taken, whichever is greater (G.S. 40A-64). The value of the property taken does not include an increase or a decrease in value before the date of valuation that is caused by the proposed improvement or project for which the property is taken (G.S. 40A-65).

Sale or Disposition of City Property

City governments generally dispose of property in accordance with the procedures set forth in G.S. Chapter 160A, Article 12 (G.S. 160A-265 through -279). Article 12 authorizes several methods for selling or disposing of property and sets forth the procedures for each one. Before examining these methods, it is useful to discuss one introductory matter: the need for consideration when disposing of city property.

Consideration

Under the North Carolina Constitution it is generally unconstitutional for a local government, including a city, to dispose of property for less than its fair market value.[4] A gift of property or a sale at well below market value constitutes the granting of an "exclusive privilege or emolument" to the person receiving the property, which is prohibited by Article 1, Section 32, of the constitution. Most of the procedures by which a city is permitted to sell or otherwise dispose of property are competitive, and the North Carolina Supreme Court has indicated that the price resulting from an open and competitive procedure will be accepted as the market value.[5] If a sale is privately negotiated, the price will normally be considered appropriate unless strong evidence indicates that it is so significantly below market value as to show an abuse of discretion.[6]

It is not always constitutionally necessary that a city receive *monetary* consideration when it conveys property. If the party receiving the property agrees to put it to some public use, that promise constitutes sufficient consideration for the conveyance.[7] (The receiver in this case is often, but not always, another government.) The General Statutes expressly permit several such conveyances: to governments (G.S. 160A-274), to volunteer fire departments and rescue squads (G.S. 160A-277), to nonprofit preservation or conservation organizations [G.S. 160A-266(b)], and to nonprofit agencies to which the city is authorized to appropriate money (G.S. 160A-279).

Disposition Procedures

G.S. Chapter 160A, Article 12, sets out three competitive methods of sale, each of which is appropriate in any circumstance: sealed bid, negotiated offer and upset bid, and public auction. Article 12 also permits privately negotiated exchanges of property in any circumstance (as long as equal value changes hands) and privately negotiated sales or other dispositions of property in a number of limited circumstances. These various methods of disposition are summarized in the following sections. In undertaking any of them city personnel must remember that the statutory procedure must be exactly followed or the transaction may be invalidated by a court.[8]

Sealed Bids

A city may sell any real or personal property by sealed bid (G.S. 160A-268).

Procedure

The procedure is based on that set forth in G.S. 143-129 for purchasing property, with one modification for real property. An advertisement for sealed bids must be published in a newspaper that has general circulation in the county in which the city is located. Publication must occur one week before the bids are opened if personal property is being sold and thirty days before the bids are opened if real property is being sold. The advertisement should generally describe the property; tell where it can be examined and when and where the bids will be opened; state that a 5-percent bid deposit is required and will be retained if the successful bidder fails to consummate the contract; and reserve the council's right to reject any and all bids. Bids must be opened in public and recorded in the council's minutes. The award is made to the highest bidder.

Comment

This procedure appears to be designed to obtain wide competition by providing public notice and good opportunity for bidders to examine the property. Invitations to bid may be mailed to prospective buyers, just as they are typically sent to prospective sellers in the formal purchasing procedures for personal property. Except for the bid-deposit requirement, this procedure is essentially the one used by the Division of Purchase and Contract in disposing of almost all surplus personal property owned by the state.

Negotiated Offer and Upset Bid

A city may sell any real or personal property by negotiated offer and upset bid (G.S. 160A-209).

Procedure

The procedure begins when the city council receives and proposes to accept an offer to purchase specified city property. (The offer may be either solicited from the offeror or made directly by it on its own initiative.) The council then requires the offeror to deposit a 5-percent bid deposit with the city clerk and causes a notice of the offer to be published. The notice must describe the property; specify the amount and the terms of the offer; and give notice that the bid may be raised by not less than 10 percent of the first $1,000 originally bid, plus 5 percent of any amount above $1,000 of the original bid. Upset bids must also be accompanied by a 5-percent bid deposit. Prospective bidders have ten days from the date on which the notice is published to offer an upset bid. This procedure is repeated until ten days have elapsed without the council's receiving an upset bid. After that time it may sell the property to the final offeror. At any time in the process, it may reject any and all offers and decide not to sell the property.

Public Auction

A city may sell any real or personal property by public auction (G.S. 160A-270).

Procedure

The statute sets out separate procedures for real and personal property sold at public auction. For real property the city council must adopt a resolution that authorizes the sale; describes the property; specifies the date, the time, the place, and the terms of the sale; and states that the council must accept and confirm the successful bid. The council may require a bid deposit. A notice containing the information set out in the resolution must be published at least once and not less than thirty days before the auction. The highest bid is reported to the council, which then has thirty days in which to accept or reject it.

For personal property the same procedure is followed except that (1) the council may in the resolution authorize an appropriate city official to complete the sale at the auction and (2) the notice must be published not less than ten days before the auction.

Comment

Public auction is a traditional method of selling both real and personal property. Open competitive bidding may under some circumstances encourage the offering of higher prices. The possibility of immediately acquiring possession of personal property makes this approach attractive to many buyers.

Exchange of Property

A city may exchange any real or personal property for other real or personal property if it receives full and fair consideration for the property (G.S. 160A-271).

Procedure

After the terms of the exchange agreement are developed by private negotiations, the city council authorizes the exchange at a *regular* meeting. A notice of intent to make the exchange must be published at least ten days before it occurs. The notice must describe the properties involved, give the value of each as well as the value of other consideration changing hands, and cite the date of the regular meeting at which the council proposes to confirm the exchange.

Comment

The exchange procedure is probably most useful in connection with a trade of real property when boundaries must be adjusted or when an individual owns land needed by the city and wants some other tract of city land.

Private Negotiation and Sale: Personal Property

A city may use private negotiation and sale to dispose of personal property valued at less than $10,000 for any one item or any group of similar items (G.S. 160A-266, -267).

Procedure

At a *regular* meeting, the city council by resolution authorizes an appropriate official to dispose of identified property at private sale. The council may set a minimum price, but is not required to do so.

The resolution must be published at least ten days before the sale.

The city council may also establish procedures under which city officials may dispose of personal property valued at less than $500 for any item or any group of similar items without further council action. The procedures may permit one or more officials to declare qualifying property to be surplus, to set its market value, and to sell it by public or private sale. The statute requires the selling official to make a semiannual report to the council on property sold under any such procedures.

Private Negotiation and Conveyance to Other Governments

G.S. 160A-274 authorizes any governmental unit in the state, on terms and conditions determined by the unit, to sell to, purchase from, exchange with, lease to, or lease from any other governmental unit, or enter into agreements with such unit regarding the joint use of, any interest in real or personal property that one or the other unit may own. *Governmental unit* is defined to include cities, counties, the state, school units, and other state and local agencies. The single limitation on this broad authority is that before a county or city board of education may lease real property that it owns, it must determine that the property is unnecessary or undesirable for school purposes; and it may not lease the property for less than $1 per year.[9] Bids or published notices are not required. Thus, when reaching agreements on property with another governmental unit, the city council has full discretion concerning procedure.

Private Negotiation and Sale: Real Property

A city may, in limited circumstances, convey real property to certain nonprofit corporations and associations by private negotiation and without monetary consideration.

Fire or Rescue Services

G.S. 160A-277 permits cities to lease or convey land to volunteer fire departments or rescue squads that is to be used for constructing or expanding their facilities. The city council must approve the transaction by adoption of a resolution at a regular meeting, on ten days' published notice. The notice should describe the property, state its value, set out the proposed monetary consideration or the lack thereof, and declare the council's intention to approve the transaction.

Nonprofit Agencies

G.S. 160A-279 permits a city to convey real or personal property to any nonprofit agency to which it is authorized by law to appropriate funds. (Property acquired through condemnation may not be so conveyed.) The same procedures must be followed as required by G.S. 160A-267 for other private sales.

Architectural and Cultural Property

G.S. 160A-266(b) permits a city to convey, after private negotiation, real or personal property that is significant for its archaeological, architectural, artistic, cultural, or historic associations; for its association with such property; or for its natural, scenic, or open condition. The conveyance must be to a nonprofit corporation or trust whose purposes include the preservation or the conservation of such property, and the deed must include covenants and other restrictions securing and promoting the property's protection. A city making a conveyance under this provision must follow the same procedures as noted earlier for the private sale of personal property.

Lease of Property

A city may lease any property that the city council finds will not be needed during the term of the lease (G.S. 160A-272). The procedure to be followed depends on the length of the lease. The council may, by resolution at any meeting, make leases for one year or less. It may also authorize the city manager or some other administrative officer to take similar action concerning city property for the same period.

The council may lease city property for periods longer than one year and up to ten years by a resolution adopted at a regular meeting, after ten days' published notice of its intention to do so. The notice must also specify the annual lease payment and give the date of the meeting at which the council proposes to approve the action.

A lease for longer than ten years must be treated as a sale of property. It may be executed by following any procedure authorized for selling real property.

Grant of Easements

A city may grant easements over, through, under, or across any of its property (G.S. 160A-273). The authorization should be by resolution of the council at a regular meeting. No special published notice is required.

Sale of Stocks, Bonds, and Other Securities

A city that owns stocks, bonds, or other securities that are traded on the stock exchanges or over the counter by brokers and securities dealers may sell them in the same way and under the same conditions as a private owner would (G.S. 160A-276). It is not limited to the methods outlined earlier.

Warranty Deeds

G.S. 160A-275 authorizes a city council to execute and deliver deeds to any governmentally owned real property with full covenants of warranty when the council determines that it is in the best interest of the city to do so. Council members are relieved of any personal liability arising from the issuance of warranty deeds if their actions are in good faith.

Additional Resources

Lawrence, David M. *Local Government Property Transactions in North Carolina.* Chapel Hill, N.C.: Institute of Government, The University of North Carolina at Chapel Hill, 1987.

Loeb, Ben F., Jr. *Eminent Domain Procedure for North Carolina Local Governments.* Chapel Hill, N.C.: Institute of Government, The University of North Carolina at Chapel Hill, 1984.

Notes

1. Vaughan v. Commissioners of Forsyth County, 188 N.C. 636, 125 S.E. 177 (1896).

2. Brockenbrough v. Board of Water Comm'rs, 134 N.C. 1, 46 S.E. 28 (1903).

3. Public enterprises include electric power generation and distribution, water supply and distribution, sewage collection and treatment, gas generation and

distribution, transportation, solid waste collection and disposal, cable television, parking, airports, and stormwater systems.

4. *Cf.* Redevelopment Comm'n v. Security Nat'l Bank, 252 N.C. 595, 114 S.E.2d 668 (1960).

5. *Id.*

6. Painter v. Wake County Bd. of Educ., 288 N.C. 165, 217 S.E.2d 650 (1975).

7. Brumley v. Baxter, 225 N.C. 691, 36 S.E.2d 281 (1945).

8. Bagwell v. Town of Brevard, 267 N.C. 604, 148 S.E.2d 635 (1966). Some city councils routinely declare as surplus any property that is to be sold. No statute requires such a declaration, however, and it does not appear to be necessary. A city evidences its conclusion that property is surplus by selling it.

9. Although in general, local governments may transfer property among themselves without monetary consideration, the North Carolina Supreme Court has held that a local school board must receive fair consideration whenever it conveys property for some nonschool use, including some other governmental use. Boney v. Board of Trustees, 229 N.C. 136, 48 S.E.2d 56 (1948). The $1 requirement for leases of school property presumably is a legislative determination that this amount is adequate consideration when title to the property remains with the school administrative unit.

17 Purchasing and Contracting

Frayda S. Bluestein and Warren Jake Wicker

Contents

THIS CHAPTER discusses purchasing and contracting in relation to property other than real property. Acquisition of real property is discussed in chapter 16.

Obtaining goods and services for the operation of city government is a major administrative responsibility. In a legal sense this responsibility involves questions of proper authority, adequate authorization for the expenditure of funds, and the making of contracts in accordance with statutory requirements. Administratively the organizational arrangements should be both efficient and legally sufficient.

Authority to Make Purchases and Contracts

A city's power to make purchases and contracts, like other powers, is derived from the legislature and is subject to such limitations and restrictions as the legislature may impose. The basic grant of power with respect to purchasing and contracting is found in G.S. 160A-11, the statute that vests cities with general corporate powers and expressly empowers them to enter into contracts as well as to acquire all kinds of property. Many other statutes authorize cities to perform particular functions and contain other specific contracting powers.

Authorization for Expenditures

A basic requirement with respect to all city contracts is that funds be properly appropriated or authorized to meet contractual obligations. G.S. 159-28(a) provides:

> No obligation may be incurred in a program, function, or activity accounted for in a fund included in the budget ordinance unless the budget ordinance includes an appropriation authorizing the obligation and an unencumbered balance remains in the appropriation sufficient to pay in the current fiscal year the sums obligated by the transaction for the current fiscal year. No obligation may be incurred for a capital project or a grant project authorized by a project ordinance unless that project ordinance includes an appropriation authorizing the obligation and an unencumbered balance remains in the appropriation sufficient to pay the sums obligated by the transaction. If an obligation is evidenced by a contract or agreement requiring the payment of money or by a purchase order for supplies and materials, the contract, agreement, or purchase order shall include on its face a certificate stating that the instrument has been preaudited to assure compliance with this subsection. The certificate, which shall be signed by the finance officer or any deputy finance officer approved for this purpose by the governing board, shall take substantially the following form:
>
> "This instrument has been preaudited in the manner required by the Local Government Budget and Fiscal Control Act.
>
> . . . ."
> (Signature of finance officer)."

An obligation incurred in violation of this subsection is invalid and may not be enforced. The finance officer shall establish procedures to assure compliance with this subsection.

G.S. 159-28 provides further:

> (e) Penalties.—If an officer or employee of a local government or public authority incurs an obligation or pays out or causes to be paid out any funds in violation of this section, he and the sureties on his official bond are liable for any sums so committed or disbursed. If the finance officer or any properly designated deputy finance officer gives a false certificate to any contract, agreement, purchase order, check, draft, or other document, he and the sureties on his official bond are liable for any sums illegally committed or disbursed thereby.

The statute is thus quite clear. Before a contract may be entered into, funds to cover its full amount must be appropriated. The only exception to this requirement is a *continuing contract,* authorized by G.S. 160A-17, which defines it as "some portion or all of which [is] to be performed in ensuing fiscal years." In contracts of this type the statute requires only that funds be appropriated to meet obligations arising in the fiscal year in which the contract is made. The city council must later provide enough money to meet the amount to be paid in ensuing fiscal years for the duration of the contract. Many service and repair contracts, for example, may be of this type. Some may extend for several years; others may simply extend into the fiscal year following the one during which the contract was made.

Goals in City Purchasing

The objective in purchasing by cities is essentially the same as it is with other public agencies and private businesses. The city purchasing organization should be designed to secure—with efficiency—what is needed, when it is needed, and at the lowest possible cost.

This goal does not suggest that every requirement must be anticipated in advance and the necessary goods purchased and stored for use. There are many ways other than operating warehouses to provide goods when they are needed.

Nor does the goal of low cost suggest that only the lowest-priced goods should be purchased. The lowest cost in terms of use may result from the purchase of an item whose initial cost is not the lowest. By the same token it does not always follow that the highest-priced item affords the greatest quality and is the most economical in use. The job of city purchasing is to make rational decisions in buying, after considering price, quality, performance, and other relevant factors.

City purchasing officials are concerned with more than simply making the "right buy." They are also under obligation to buy in the proper manner—the manner prescribed by statute. In North Carolina these statutory requirements foster open competition to save public funds and prevent favoritism in awarding public contracts. These requirements distinguish public buying from private purchasing.

On rare occasions the two major aims of the statutory regulations just noted may conflict. There are times when special prices might be obtained if a procedure that did not prohibit favoritism could be followed, but generally both purposes are served by the statutes. Furthermore, most of the requirements of law are also ones that public officials would impose on themselves even in the absence of law. Awarding public contracts on any basis other than open and free competition could result in charges of favoritism that most public officials would not want to face.

Organization for Purchasing

The city council, under the authority granted by G.S. 160A-146 to organize and reorganize the administration of city government, is responsible for establishing the organization for purchasing. In practice, arrangements vary from a fair degree of centralization and use of a purchasing agent to almost complete decentralization with purchasing done by individual departments. Most large cities have appointed full-time purchasing agents. In many other cities the manager, the finance officer, or another official serves as the purchasing agent, with the degree of decentralization varying from city to city. In some small cities, department heads do practically all the purchasing for their departments.

In operations of any significant size, it is generally considered desirable to appoint a purchasing agent, either someone working exclusively in this position or some other officer designated to serve a dual role. The use of a central purchasing office can result in savings through the following:

1. Lower costs through buying in larger quantities when appropriate
2. Standardization of items in common use, which permits consolidation of needs and buying in larger quantities

3. Improved specifications
4. Increased competition
5. More taking of cash discounts by prompt submission of invoices to finance for approval and payment
6. A closer check on deliveries, with respect to both quantities and condition of goods
7. Improved control over expenditures
8. A closer check on the performance of vendors

Centralizing the purchasing function does not mean the total loss of operational control for department and agency heads. They approve all requisitions for materials and usually consult with the purchasing officer when he or she prepares specifications for goods to be purchased. Thus real control over purchasing decisions is not lost. On the other hand, the availability of personnel who can devote their attention to developing new sources of supply, securing better prices, checking on deliveries, consolidating needs, and watching price trends should save the unit money. The real effectiveness of centralized purchasing, of course, must depend on the competence of the purchasing agent and the cooperation of the various agency and department heads.

The Purchasing Process

Determination of Need

The city council's role is dominant in determining needs—in deciding what goods will be purchased. Through its adoption of the budget, the council has full control over this area. Purchases of major items are probably discussed individually at budget adoption time, especially in small cities. For routine supplies and minor equipment the council usually only approves appropriations for the items and leaves details of specifications to the purchasing agent and the department heads. On major purchases involving contracts let under the formal-bid procedure, the council also exercises control when it awards the contract.

Specifications

Good purchasing practice calls for buying in accordance with carefully developed specifications. However, for purchases of fairly standard items, elaborate specifications are not necessary. Rather, simple standard specifications are needed. For example, an order for "Two dozen pencils" is clearly inadequate; a better description, such as "Two dozen No. 2 wood pencils," is necessary if satisfactory results are to be obtained from the pencils' use and if the best price is to be secured in buying.

Preparing specifications also requires the buyer to determine carefully what is needed. Purchasing items of higher quality than is needed can be just as costly as buying cheap goods that lack the necessary quality. If there is to be real competition—without a misunderstanding about the quality needed, so that all bidders are quoting on the same kind and quality of goods—precise specifications are essential. Finally, when these are provided, the city can safely buy on a low-bid basis from among the bidders who offer products that meet the specifications.

Assistance in preparing specifications is available from a number of sources. Technical personnel in many departments can often write them. Vendors and trade associations of various types are willing to provide specifications of their own products or general ones. A word of caution: model and sample specifications are valuable, but they should not be adopted without examination. It should be determined that they are suitable for the user and do not restrict competition, or they should be appropriately modified.

Buying without Specifications

Although the most desirable method of buying is on specification, there are times when specifications are not available and preparing them is impractical. Two other approaches are then employed: "or equal" and approved-brand list.

"Or Equal"

In using "or equal," a buyer names a particular product as acceptable, and invites bids on this product or any other one equal to it. The named product becomes the standard of quality. Thus the

invitation might be for "Two XYZ's Model D Dips or equal." All bidders, of course, are likely to insist that their product is equal to the
one named. If this happens, the buyer is responsible for deciding
whether this is indeed true, and must be prepared to justify the decision. Some products may be clearly eliminated by bid invitations in
this form, but frequently there will be borderline cases.

Approved-Brand List

The use of an approved-brand list is an improvement over the
"or equal" approach in that the buyer decides in advance which
products are acceptable and satisfy requirements. Price alone can
then be used to choose from among the products listed. Care should
be taken in using this system to see that competition is not unjustifiably restricted and that new products are considered. If the brand
list is too restrictive, the approach will probably not meet the competitive-bidding requirements of the statutes.

Scheduling of Purchases

The materials, the supplies, and the equipment that a city needs
in the course of a year may be bought from day to day, purchased in
advance and stored awaiting use, or obtained under other arrangements. The system adopted will, of course, depend on a number of
factors. Major pieces of equipment as well as batches of supplies and
materials that are used over a relatively long period are usually purchased under *definite quantity contracts* awarded following a separate
advertisement for each trip to the market. For example, most cities
buy a fire engine infrequently and would probably ask for bids on
each one separately. Gasoline for automobiles, on the other hand,
is needed throughout the year, and different arrangements might be
made for its purchase. Office supplies might call for still another
technique. The main approaches used in scheduling purchases of
supplies and materials in regular use are the advance requisition or
requisition schedule, warehouses and stores, and term contracts or
price agreements.

Advance Requisition or Requisition Schedule

Under this system the needs for various supplies or materials are estimated for each department for some period in advance—perhaps six months to a year. Needs of the different departments are consolidated, and a single, large-quantity purchase is made for all needs during the period. Delivery of the goods may be made either to a central storeroom or to small storage cabinets or rooms in the departments. The advantages of this approach are that it usually results in lower prices because of large-quantity buying, supplies are on hand when needed, and paperwork in processing orders is reduced. Where departmental storage facilities are inadequate or permit supplies to be damaged, the advantages of advance requisition may be partially lost.

Warehouses and Stores

Large cities may find that savings will be realized by establishing warehouses or stores. Such operations permit quantity buying and holding of supplies for use as needed. Departmental storage may be eliminated, with orders to the storeroom or the warehouse filled on short notice. Careful establishment of reorder levels for supplies ensures their availability when needed. However, because of the cost of operating warehouses and central stores, small cities may not find central storage advantageous.

Term Contracts or Price Agreements

A *term contract* (or *price agreement*) establishes the price at which a city may buy its needs for a given item from a contractor for a specified period. These are also called *indefinite quantity contracts*. Usually such contracts are let by competitive bidding and are awarded to the lowest bidder. For these contracts the applicable statutory procedure is determined by estimating the cost of items to be ordered under the contract during the contract term. Deliveries are made on purchase orders as city needs arise; thus the supplier becomes the warehousing agent.

In some cases the price is not firm, but tied to an established price. For example, gasoline is frequently purchased under annual term contracts at the pipeline terminal price plus a fixed amount (for transportation, overhead, and profit).

Cities and other public purchasing agencies are making increased use of term contracts. Most state agencies buy under term contracts let by the Division of Purchase and Contract. The combination of quantity buying without warehousing costs makes this type of contracting adaptable to the purchase of many items in frequent use.

Exceptional Purchases

Occasionally a city official needs to make purchases on an emergency basis, usually for special needs that arise when the purchasing office is closed, or because of breakdowns or other emergency situations. Careful attention to purchasing and operating needs will reduce these purchases to a minimum, but regular procedures for them should be established for officials to follow when necessary. Too much emergency purchasing by departmental officials frequently indicates either that the normal purchasing arrangements are not working well or that the city's purchasing procedures are being bypassed. Applicable statutory requirements must be complied with unless the situation meets the definition of emergency in the statute. (See the discussion under the heading Exceptions, later in this chapter.)

Most cities find a need for petty cash funds in some offices to make payments for goods or services (e.g., freight services) that cannot be easily handled through regular channels. Rules should be established for handling these funds and for replenishing them on presentation of proper supporting documents.

Purchase-Order System

Whether purchasing is centralized or decentralized, every city should adopt some form of purchase-order system. Without one it is not easy to meet the requirements of the Local Government Budget and Fiscal Control Act, and internal control over expenditures is exceedingly difficult. Many cities have computerized systems that generate the purchase orders and complete the accounting procedures required by the statutes. Cities without a computerized system use the traditional paper system.

A minimum purchase-order system for decentralized "paper" purchasing provides each department with three-part, prenumbered purchase-order forms. The department head can then keep one carbon for reference and send the original and one carbon to the finance officer. After certifying the availability of funds, the finance officer can send the original to the vendor and retain the other copy for his or her records (either as a memorandum or for encumbrance of funds). With the necessary routing modifications the same purchase-order forms can be used for confirming orders covering emergency purchases or for replenishing petty cash funds. In a centralized system at least one additional copy of the purchase order is needed for the purchasing office.

Assistance in establishing and revising purchasing systems is available from a number of sources, including private consulting firms, the Local Government Commission, and the Institute of Government. Also, the accounting firm employed by the city for the annual audit can usually advise on purchasing procedures and internal control.

Buying under State Contracts

Public schools in North Carolina have long been required to buy under state contracts. Since 1971 it has been the duty of the state Department of Administration also to make its services available to local governments in purchasing supplies, materials, and equipment [G.S. 143-49(6)]. The secretary of the Department of Administration is responsible for adopting rules and regulations covering this procedure. The Division of Purchase and Contract, through which the department acts on purchasing matters, administers this program.

The division maintains over 120 statewide term contracts, each usually covering a twelve-month period, under which some 300,000 individual items of supplies, materials, and equipment may be purchased. The rules provide that any local government wishing to buy under state contracts must place itself in the same position as state agencies that are required to buy under these contracts. The division notifies local governments about the contracts that are made available to them *before the contract is advertised.* Units that wish to participate in the contract must notify the division in writing on the form that the division provides for this purpose. The state solicits bids, awards the contract, and notifies participating local governments of the award(s) at the same time that it notifies state agencies and institutions. Thereafter during the contract period a participating local government simply places orders directly with the vendor as needed. The vendor delivers items and sends invoices to the local government, which pays the vendor directly.

During the contract period a participating local government is obligated to buy all it needs of the items covered from the state contractor under the contract terms and conditions. The contractor, of course, is similarly committed. The local government, however, is not required to purchase a minimum number of the covered items if its requirements change. It may decide to participate for one contract period and then decide to buy elsewhere after the contract expires. It may also choose to participate in one or more contracts, but does not have to participate in all that are available.

The Division of Purchase and Contract does not approve or disapprove orders by a local government. The latter has complete prerogative and responsibility to control the amount of its purchasing.

Vendors will sometimes advise a county or a city that they are the state contract vendor for an item and will offer to sell it at the state contract price, even though the local government has not chosen in advance to come under the state contract. A local government in this situation is *not* automatically free to purchase from the vendor. It must follow the normal competitive-bidding requirements, if any, applicable to the purchase (see the discussion under the heading Statutory Requirements in Purchasing and Contracting, later in this chapter) because it is not a party to the state contract.

Cooperative Purchasing

Cities may join with other cities and with counties in cooperative purchasing under the authority for interlocal cooperation found in G.S. Chapter 160A, Article 20 (see chapter 10 of this volume). Cooperative and joint purchasing actions may range from the joint purchase of a single class of items to the merger of purchasing offices. For example, Guilford County and Greensboro have jointly purchased vehicles. Mecklenburg County and Charlotte have created a joint purchasing department. And in some regions, councils of governments have facilitated cooperative purchasing by groups of cities and counties. Cities have also pooled their needs and cooperatively purchased recycled products in order to realize cost savings from large-quantity buying.

Statutory Requirements in Purchasing and Contracting

Public purchasing must be accomplished in accordance with law. The city council is responsible, either directly or indirectly, for all expenditures of the city and for all contracts that it makes. Cities have broad powers (see G.S. 160A-11) to make such contracts as are necessary to the exercise of their powers and functions. However, these broad powers are limited in that other statutes, and in some instances, court decisions, prescribe the manner in which they may be exercised.

Formal Contracts

Although *formal contracts* is not defined in the statutes, this is the name usually applied to contracts subject to G.S. 143-129—that is, contracts for which a request for bids must be advertised, sealed bids must be received, and awards must be made as prescribed by law.

Coverage

The only contracts that require the use of the formal-bid procedure are those for "construction or repair work" estimated to cost $100,000 or more; and for purchase of "apparatus, supplies, materials, or equipment" estimated to cost $20,000 or more.

Not all contracts are covered by the statute—only the two types just mentioned.[1] Contracts for professional services, such as those of auditors or attorneys, clearly do not fall within the statute, nor do purchases of real property. Contracts for other services, such as insurance or newspaper advertising, also appear to be outside the statute, although good business practice might suggest that a city follow the same procedure in letting these contracts as in letting ordinary construction or repair contracts. Thus the city council is required to follow either the formal or the informal (see the discussion under the heading Informal Contracts, later in this chapter) competitive-bidding procedure in most contracts and may, under its general contracting powers, elect to follow the same procedure on other contracts.

Exceptions

In certain cases the council may set aside the statutory bidding requirements. In an emergency involving the "health and safety" of the people or their property, the council may let contracts without bidding. The courts have interpreted this exception very narrowly, saying that emergencies must be unforeseeable. An example of an emergency that is within the statutory exception is replacement of a city hall roof damaged by a storm. When following the emergency procedure, the council should probably adopt a resolution finding that an emergency exists, documenting its nature, and thus justifying contracting outside the normal procedure. This should be done before the purchase, if possible; otherwise, as soon as possible after the purchase. Council members should remember that although they may decide that an emergency exists and act accordingly, a court reviewing such a decision may declare the city's contract void if it does not agree with them.[2]

The bidding requirements also do not apply to purchases of apparatus, supplies, materials, or equipment from any other governmental unit or agency. Thus city governments may buy goods directly from city, county, state, and federal governments without securing bids. This exception is especially important in acquiring surplus state and federal property.

Purchases of gasoline, diesel fuel, alcohol fuel, motor oil, or fuel oil are exempt from the formal bidding requirements of G.S. 143-129. These may be purchased after receiving informal bids, regardless of the amount of the expenditure.

There is also an exception to the formal-bid requirements for contracts for the design and the construction of certain complex solid waste disposal facilities (G.S. 143-129.2). That statute contains a separate procedure for letting contracts for such facilities.

The final exception is really a limitation on the amount of construction or repair work that a city may undertake with its own forces. Any construction or repair work that will be done by permanent city forces and will have a total project cost (including all labor and materials) of not more than $125,000 may be undertaken without following the competitive-bidding procedure (G.S. 143-135). In addition, a city may undertake a project whose total cost exceeds $125,000 *if* the cost of the *labor* component does not exceed $50,000. (Purchases of apparatus, supplies, materials, or equipment made in connection with the construction or repair work done by the unit's own forces are still subject to the competitive-bidding laws.) Conversely, the city may not undertake with its own forces projects that fall outside the foregoing allowances, nor may it divide projects to bring itself within the statutory limitation and avoid competitive bidding. (A few cities and counties, by special acts, have different limits or requirements.)

Specifications

Purchase of Goods

There are no statutory requirements with respect to specifications for purchases. The council is free to have these written as it deems best except that it cannot do so intentionally or unjustifiably to eliminate competition and thus to defeat the purpose of the competitive-bidding statute. If only one product is suitable and competition is impossible, as may happen, it is generally agreed that a single product or item may be specified, although various suppliers may still compete for the award.

Building Contracts

The council does not have the same freedom concerning specifications for building projects (G.S. 143-128). The statute recognizes three levels of requirements that vary according to the cost of the building project. (Although *building* is not defined in the statute, it clearly does not include horizontal work such as street paving or the installation of water and sewer lines.)

Projects costing $500,000 or more. In the case of building projects that require the expenditure of $500,000 or more, separate bids must be received and separate specifications prepared for each of the following branches of work:

1. Heating, ventilating, air conditioning and accessories, and/ or refrigeration for cold storage (when the cooling load is 15 tons or more of refrigeration)
2. Plumbing and gas fittings and accessories
3. Electrical wiring and accessories
4. General work not included in the three previous branches

When any branch of work is estimated to cost less than $25,000, it may be combined with one of the other branches in receiving bids and letting contracts. This procedure is called the *separate-prime* or *multi-prime* method of soliciting bids and contracting. In addition, and in its discretion, the council may solicit bids on a *single-prime* basis for projects at this level. For contracts costing $500,000 or more, the unit does not have the option of receiving bids only on a single-prime basis.

If both systems are used, the bids under the single-prime system are compared with the sums of the lowest responsible bids received in each branch offered under the separate-prime system when the council makes awards.

Whenever multi-prime contracts are awarded, the city may designate one of the prime contractors as the *project expediter* with special responsibility for developing project schedules and making recommendations to the city on whether payment to contractors should be approved.

Whenever the single-prime method is used, single-prime bidders must identify on their bids the contractors that they have selected for subdivisions or branches of work for (1) heating, ventilating, and air conditioning; (2) plumbing; (3) electrical work; and (4) general work. Single-prime contractors who receive a bid award may not make substitutions of subcontractors named in their bid except with the approval of the awarding authority.

Projects costing $100,000 to $500,000. Projects within this range may be let using either the single-prime or the separate-prime system, but in any case, specifications must be prepared in the separate categories described earlier. Bids may also be solicited and awards made using both systems as described earlier.

Projects costing less than $100,000. None of the requirements in G.S. 143-128 apply to the erection, the construction, the alteration, or the repair of a building when the cost is $100,000 or less. For these contracts the council has complete discretion regarding the form of specifications, the manner of contracting, and the minority-participation goal requirements discussed later.

An additional exception to these requirements authorizes local units to purchase and erect relocatable or prefabricated buildings, regardless of cost, without complying with the requirements of G.S. 143-128 for separate specifications and contracts, and minority

participation. Those requirements do apply, however, to work performed at the construction site of such buildings.

Several 1995 amendments to G.S. 143-128 and G.S. 143-135.26
provide that the State Building Commission may authorize a city
(and other public bodies and agencies) to use an alternative method
of contracting for building construction when the city demonstrates
that a single project cannot "be reasonably completed under the
methods authorized under G.S. 143-128. . ." or for other appropriate reasons as determined by the commission. This authority of the
commission becomes effective on July 1, 1996. The commission may
not waive the competitive-bidding requirements of G.S. 143-129 nor
the minimum number of bids required by G.S. 143-132.

Minority-Participation Goals

G.S. 143-128 also requires local units to adopt verifiable percentage goals for minority business participation in building projects
costing $100,000 or more. The requirement is for a goal, not a quota
or a set-aside. However, local units are also required to adopt guidelines specifying the actions that should be taken to ensure that a
"good faith effort" has been made to attain the goal. In the case of
separate-prime contracts, the guidelines will principally concern the
actions to be taken by the public unit. In the case of single-prime
contracts, the guidelines will principally cover the actions that should
appropriately be taken by the single-prime bidders. A bid may not be
rejected for failure to reach the goal of minority business participation, but one may be rejected if the bidder has not made a good faith
effort to reach it.

Verifiable percentage goal refers to a percentage of the total value
of the building project. The statute sets a 10-percent goal for state
government projects. Local governments set their own goals based
on the availability of minority contractors in their respective regions.

A *minority business* is one in which at least 51 percent of the equity
is owned by minority persons and which is under the active management of one or more minority persons. *Minority persons* are defined
for the purpose of the statute as persons who are black, Hispanic,
Asian American, American Indian, Alaskan Native, or female.

These provisions of G.S. 143-128, it should be noted again,
apply only to building projects. They do not apply to horizontal

construction—for example, paving streets or constructing water lines—nor do they apply to the purchase of apparatus, supplies, materials, or equipment.

Advertising

Bids on contracts subject to the formal procedure must be invited by advertisement in a newspaper that has general circulation in the county in which the city is located. The advertisement must be published once at least a full week before the bids are opened.

G.S. 143-129 stipulates that the advertisement must indicate "the time and place where plans and specifications may be had," specify "the time and place for opening of the proposals," and "reserve to [the governing body] the right to reject any or all proposals." For construction contracts the engineer or the architect may need to advise prospective bidders that they must be properly licensed (G.S. 87-15).

Many bid advertisements contain much more than is required by statute—often needlessly increasing costs. It is not necessary to advertise all contract details and specifications when that information is available elsewhere and when it is impossible, in any event, to bid from the information contained in the advertisement. In short, some purpose other than meeting statutory requirements should be served when long bid advertisements are used.

Bid Deposit

Each formal bid proposal must be accompanied "*at the time of its filing*" (emphasis added) by a bid deposit equal to not less than 5 percent of the bid. The statute lists only four forms of this deposit that are acceptable: cash, a cashier's check, a certified check, or a bid bond from a North Carolina–licensed surety. The city may keep the deposit if the bidder is awarded the contract and fails to execute the contract or to give satisfactory performance and payment bonds (where required by statute or the local government) within ten days after the award. The bid deposit requirement may be waived by the governing board for contracts of less than $100,000 for the purchase of apparatus, supplies, materials, or equipment. The board can waive the requirement for particular contracts, or generally for all purchase contracts under $100,000, but in either case should do so before proposals are received and should notify all bidders.

Opening of Bids

Bids must be opened in public and recorded in the minutes of the governing board. This provision does not necessarily require that they be opened and read before the city council. They may be opened in public by an officer of the city, tabulated, evaluated, and brought before the council for action. A summary of bids is typically recorded in the minutes.

In general, a bid that has been received may be opened at the time set for the opening of bids. However, the basic principles of the sealed-bidding process suggest that it is generally inappropriate to open sealed bids if at the time of the opening, it is known that no award can or will be made—for example, when three bids are required (see the discussion under the heading Number of Bids Required, later in this chapter) and only two are received. In these cases the ethical procedure is to reject and return all bids unopened—something the council may always do. The council may then readvertise the project in a way that places all bidders, including those who did not bid in response to the first advertisement, on an equal footing. To open the bids received after the first advertisement and reveal their contents, could give an advantage to those who waited until the second advertisement to respond.

The only statutory provision that specifically addresses this is G.S. 143-132(b), which prohibits the opening of some bids on building contracts when bids are solicited on both a separate-prime and a single-prime basis. The statute provides, "If there are at least three single-prime bids but there is not at least one full set of separate-prime bids, no separate-prime bids shall be opened." A city council facing a situation in which this provision applies has two choices. First, it may reject all bids and readvertise. A council might take this choice if it wanted to try again to get a full set of separate-prime bids to compare with single-prime bids. (If this choice is taken, ethical practice suggests that the single-prime bids received also be returned unopened.) Second, the council may make the award to a single-prime bidder because the three-bid requirement has been met. A council's choice, of course, will depend on local conditions and its estimates as to which choice better serves the city's interests.

Responsiveness

Before awarding a contract, the city must determine if the bidders are *responsive*. Responsiveness, although not addressed in the bidding statutes, is a threshold determination that must be made before bidders are eligible to receive a contract award. In determining whether bids are responsive, the unit is essentially evaluating whether the bids adequately meet the requirements in the specifications. Some bidders may take exceptions from or offer alternatives to what was specified, and the specifications may reserve to the city the right to waive minor deviations from specifications.

The courts have recognized, however, that there is a limit to the deviation that may be accepted in bids received in a competitive process. As summarized by the North Carolina Court of Appeals, a responsive bid is one which "conforms substantially" with the specifications. A bid cannot be considered to conform substantially with the specifications if it contains a *material variance*, defined by the court as one which gives the bidder "an advantage or benefit not enjoyed by the other bidders."[3] This legal standard makes clear that the limit on waiving variations in bids is based on a principle of fairness and equal treatment among bidders. It makes determining responsiveness an important and sometimes difficult step in the bidding process. Presolicitation and prebid conferences with potential bidders can often reduce the number of questions that arise after bids are received.

Standards in Awarding Contracts

Contracts must be awarded to "the lowest responsible bidder, taking into consideration quality, performance and the time specified in the proposals for the performance of the contract."[4] As used in this sense, the *responsibility* of bidders refers to their capacity to perform the contract, and may include consideration of their experience, the training and the quality of their personnel, their financial strength, other work that they are under contract to finish, and other factors that might reasonably bear on their ability to perform as proposed. For example, a bid to build a water treatment plant received from a small painting contractor who has a general contractor's license but no construction experience, might be subject to question.

The price considered by the city council may vary, depending on the specifications of the request for bids. For example, in some cases the price per unit is submitted and evaluated; in others, *life-cycle costs,* including maintenance, training, and other expenses related to the purchase, are considered.

In addition to considering responsibility and price, a council is authorized to evaluate quality, performance, and completion time. Although the statute is clear that these factors may be considered, this must be done carefully; and if the contract is awarded to other than the lowest bidder on the basis of these factors, a city council is probably well advised to articulate and include in the minutes the grounds for its decision. As a rule, if a board has exercised its best judgment and shown no favoritism, discrimination, or arbitrariness in its decision, the courts will not question its discretion.[5]

Number of Bids Required

G.S. 143-132 requires that for construction and repair contracts estimated to cost $100,000 or more, at least three competitive bids be received after the initial advertisement in order for the city to award a contract. [If several contracts are involved under the separate-specifications statute (G.S. 143-128), the three-bid rule applies separately to each contract.]

In determining if the three-bid requirement has been met when bids are solicited in the alternative between single-prime and separate-prime contracts, the statute provides:

(a) that each *single-prime* bid counts as a bid in each of the four branches of work for which separate-prime bids are solicited, and

(b) that each full set of *separate-prime* bids counts as the equivalent of a single-prime bid.

If the initial advertisement generates fewer than three bids, the city must readvertise. After the second advertisement it may award a contract even if it has received only one bid.

The statute requiring three bids applies only to construction and repair contracts, not to those for the purchase of apparatus, supplies, materials, or equipment. There is no statutory requirement for a minimum number of bids after an initial advertisement for purchase contracts or for construction or repair contracts in the informal range, although some local governments have adopted a rule of this type.

Procedure with Bids Exceeding Funds Available

At times the lowest bid on a proposed contract may exceed the amount of funds available for the project. G.S. 143-129 provides that in such cases the city council may "enter into negotiations with the lowest responsible bidder . . . making reasonable changes in the plans and specifications as may be necessary to bring the contract price within the funds available, and may award a contract to such a bidder [if the bidder will agree] to perform the work at the negotiated price within the funds available therefor." The statute offers no guidance as to what might constitute a reasonable change, leaving this to the discretion of the council acting within the spirit of the competitive-bidding statutes.

If negotiations following reasonable changes fail to bring the contract within limits of available funds, the council is authorized to alter the plans and the specifications and to readvertise the contract.

Performance and Payment Bonds

All formal construction and repair contracts involving more than $100,000 must be executed in writing, and the city must require the contractor to post a performance bond and a payment bond as required by G.S. 44A-25 through -35. Those statutes actually provide that where the total *project* will cost more than $100,000, each contract costing more than $15,000 must be accompanied by a performance and a payment bond in an amount equal to 100 percent of the contract.

The performance bond ensures that the contract will be completed in accordance with its terms, and protects the city. If the contractor defaults, the surety is responsible for seeing that the work is completed.

The payment bond guarantees that payment will be made for all labor and materials furnished or used on the project. This bond is necessary to give workers and suppliers protection equal to what they would have automatically with laborers' and materialmen's liens in private construction—liens to which they are not entitled when public property is involved.

Council members may waive the bond requirement for contracts involving the purchase of apparatus, supplies, materials, or equipment.

In lieu of posting a bond, contractors may deposit money, a certified check, or government securities equal to the contract price. (It is unclear whether two separate deposits are needed if both a performance bond and a payment bond are involved.) If contractors use some form of deposit, the city will then have funds available to complete the work if they default, or to pay for labor and supplies if the contractor fails to do so. The city must act as a surety with respect to any deposits received. The statutes set forth detailed procedures for laborers and materialmen to follow in making claims against bonds and for the surety or the city to follow in making payments from deposits.

Withdrawal of Bid because of Error

Bidders on a construction or repair project who find that they have made an unintentional error in their bids may ask that their bids be withdrawn and their bid securities returned. They must make these requests in writing before the contract is awarded and within seventy-two hours after the bids are opened. The city council must hold a hearing on each request and may allow withdrawal if a clear unintentional error (not involving errors of judgment) is found. Otherwise, the bid security is forfeited. The bidder who makes the request may not receive the contract, even on readvertisement (G.S. 143-129.1).

It is not clear what a city council should do if a bidder claims to have made an error in a bid to provide apparatus, supplies, materials, or equipment. The statutes give no express guidance. However, a court would probably approve the use of a procedure and a standard like those specified by statute for construction contracts, that is, allowing withdrawal when there is clear evidence of an unintentional error. If the evidence is not clear, there are two safe courses for the council. It may reject all bids and readvertise, or it may award the bid to the vendor claiming the error. The vendor then either agrees to perform or forfeits his or her deposit. In the latter case the vendor might sue to recover the deposit on the grounds that the bid was unintended because of the error and that it would be unjust to hold him or her to it. The court would then make the decision about the nature of the error.

Change Orders and Additional Work

Once a construction or repair contract has been let in the proper manner, the contract may be modified in writing by a change order or by a provision for additional work without additional advertisement or bidding as long as the change or the additional work is within the scope of the original construction or repair project (G.S. 143-129).

Informal Contracts

The informal-bidding statute, G.S. 143-131, requires that contracts covered by the statute be let after *informal bids* are received. By common usage, telephone quotations and written quotations are considered informal bids, as would also probably be a catalog price with some evidence to indicate that it is a binding offer. An informal bid is thus one that is not generally secured by a bid deposit, but one that a buyer may nevertheless rely on to compare with other equally reliable price quotations in making a purchasing decision. No newspaper or other published advertisement is required for informal contracts.

Coverage

The informal-contracting procedure required by G.S. 143-131 applies to all contracts for "construction or repair work" and purchases of "apparatus, supplies, materials, or equipment" involving expenditures of $5,000 or more, but less than the threshold for formal contracts as set forth in G.S. 143-129. Under existing statutes this means that construction and repair work costing between $5,000 and $100,000 require informal bids, and contracts for the purchase of apparatus, supplies, materials, or equipment costing between $5,000 and $20,000 must be let in the same manner. As with contracts in the formal-bid range, cities are free to make purchases within the informal range from other governmental units or agencies without receiving informal bids.

For contracts costing less than $5,000, the city may use any procedure it deems appropriate.

Standards in Awarding Contracts

The standards for awarding informal contracts are the same as those for awarding formal ones (see the discussion under the heading Standards in Awarding Contracts, earlier in this chapter). The statute directs that such contracts "shall be awarded to the lowest responsible bidder, taking into consideration quality, performance, and the time specified in the bids for the performance of the contract." Because no advertisement is required for informal bids, they are likely to be received only from vendors who are asked to quote. The purchasing official thus has an opportunity to limit solicitation to bidders deemed to be responsible. In essence, the informal-contracting procedure is designed not to avoid open competitive bidding on public contracts, but to provide an inexpensive and efficient manner of securing competitive bidding for small purchases or small construction and repair contracts.

Record of Bids

The sealed-bidding procedure in letting formal contracts ensures that a record of bids received will be made and that a summary of them will be recorded in the minutes of the city council. The informal-bidding statute does not require that informal bids appear in the council's minutes, but it does direct that a record of all such bids be kept and "be subject to public inspection at any time." The officer who receives the bids should record the date on which each is received, from whom it is received, for what item, and at what price. Special care should also be taken to indicate why an award has been made if it goes to someone other than the lowest bidder.

Performance and Payment Bonds

A performance bond and a laborers' and materialmen's bond for the full amount of the contract must be given for all informal construction or repair contracts over $15,000 when the total project exceeds $100,000 (G.S. 44A-25 through -35). A contractor may deposit money, certified checks, or government securities—just as is the case with formal contracts.

Conflict of Interest

That no man can serve two masters is a principle of human conduct affirmed by St. Matthew[6] and recognized in the English common law for centuries. This principle is widely acknowledged in statutes that make it unlawful for public officials to make, in their official capacity, public contracts in which they have a private interest. North Carolina has several criminal statutes that address this concern, although they are often difficult to interpret and are seldom enforced. City officials should exercise caution and restraint in matters raising conflict-of-interest concerns, for even when the statutory prohibition is not violated, the appearance or the perception of impropriety can erode the public's trust in government and its officials.

The North Carolina legislature first enacted a prohibition of this type in 1825. The central provision of the present statute, G.S. 14-234, is essentially the same as that of the original statute: all persons in a position of public trust who make contracts in which they have a private interest are guilty of a misdemeanor. The rule applies with equal force whether the people involved in making the public contracts are contracting to sell to their public unit (new cars, for instance) or to buy from their unit (for example, used cars at a city surplus-property auction).

Since 1929, however, the legislature has amended the statute several times to restrict its application and to except certain transactions from its coverage. In these instances full disclosure has been substituted for prohibition as a means of protecting the public from conflicts of interest and self-dealing by public officers and employees.

Although the original statute covered any private interest, perhaps regardless of how small, G.S. 14-234 now declares that a person who owns 10 percent or less of the stock of a corporation or other business entity, or who is only an employee of one, is not "interested" in any contract or undertaking with that corporation or other business entity, as that term is used in the statute. G.S. 14-234 does cover a person who is both an employee and an owner of stock, as well as one who is an officer of the private business, with or without stock ownership.

Purchasing personnel in small cities on occasion find that some officials have an interest in a business that is the only local or convenient supplier of some product or service. A 1979 amendment to the statute makes it lawful, in cities with populations of no more than 7,500, for council members to do business with their city. (Elected officials and certain appointed officials in counties in which there was no incorporated place with a population of more than 7,500 in the most recent federal census, may also legally contract with their units. Elected school officials as well as physicians, pharmacists, dentists, optometrists, veterinarians, and nurses appointed to a county social services board, a local health board, or an area mental health board all come within the same exception.) A council member in a city of less than 7,500 may legally contract with his or her city if the contract is approved by the council in a public meeting, the contract is recorded in the council's minutes, and the official involved takes no part in developing the contract and does not vote on its approval. In addition, the sum of all such contracts within any twelve-month period with any single council member may not exceed $10,000 for medically related services and $15,000 for other services or goods; the existence of all such contracts must be reported in the unit's annual audit; and a summary of all such contracts for the past twelve months must be posted quarterly in a conspicuous place in the city hall. Furthermore, contracts covered by the bidding laws (contracts costing more than $5,000 for construction or repair, or for the purchase of apparatus, supplies, materials, or equipment) are not permitted under this exception.

The statute also excepts four transactions from its broad prohibition. To come within any of these four exceptions, the transaction must be approved by a resolution of the governing board, with the concerned member not voting. The first three exceptions permit a city to do business with a bank, a savings and loan association, or a regulated public utility, even if one of the council members has a personal financial interest in any of these organizations. The fourth exception allows an official to receive payment for services, facilities, or supplies provided for needy persons under state or federal assistance programs if (1) the needy persons select the provider, (2) the payment is at the standard rate, (3) the provider takes no part in approving his or her own bill, (4) participation in the program is open to all providers, and (5) the unit's staff or officers exercise no control over which provider is selected by the beneficiary. For example, a physician who is a county commissioner may provide professional services to a person whose medical care is paid for by public funds administered by the county, if all the foregoing conditions are met.

The city council is responsible for all contracts made by the city, whether they are approved directly and separately by the council or made by some officer at its direction. Each council member is thus a party to all city contracts and is prohibited from selling any goods or services to the city while he or she remains a member of the council unless the transaction falls within one of the foregoing exceptions.

If a city employee purchases goods for the city from the private business of a member of the council, and if the council member is absent from the board meeting when the invoice is presented for approval, is the member in violation of the statute? The North Carolina Supreme Court held in such a situation that the board member was guilty of a statutory violation, even though no moral turpitude was demonstrated.[7] The clear rule, then, is that council members may not do business with the cities they serve unless the contract is covered by one of the statutory exemptions. The same rule applies to any other officials, such as purchasing agents or managers who act for the city in their official capacity; they may not contract with themselves to serve private financial interests.

The statute does *not* affect city-appointed officials and employees who are not involved with or in any way responsible for preparing the specifications for or making contracts. Thus, for example, a city recreation department employee who runs a small printing business may provide printing services to the city as long as the employee's official position involves no responsibility for the city's printing contracts.

The statute undoubtedly imposes hardships at times. A council member not covered by any of the exceptions may own the only business in a city that provides certain goods the city needs or may provide them at a considerable discount to the city. Nevertheless, the only course available is to obtain the goods elsewhere, even though to do so may be more expensive.

The prohibition against self-dealing also extends to contracting for personal services. For example, a council member who happens to be an engineer may not contract to supervise the construction of a city building unless the work is done at no charge to the city.

Councils of cities with the mayor-council form of government and populations of less than 5,000 may name one of their members as a department head or to some other position and provide for additional compensation (G.S. 160A-158).

Council members and other officials may occasionally be uncertain whether a particular situation falls within the statute. They are then well advised to seek the counsel of their city attorney or the state attorney general.

Gifts and Favors

North Carolina's gifts-and-favors statute, G.S. 133-32, is quite broad and is designed to discourage the use of gifts and favors to influence the awarding of public contracts. Violation of the statute is a misdemeanor.

It is unlawful for a contractor, a subcontractor, or a supplier who, with respect to any governmental unit, (1) has a current contract, (2) has performed under a contract within the past year, or (3) anticipates bidding on a contract, to make gifts or favors to any officer or employee of a governmental unit who is charged with the following duties: preparing plans, specifications, or estimates; awarding or administering contracts; or inspecting or supervising construction. It is also unlawful for the officer or the employee to accept any such gift or favor.

The statute does not define gift or favor. However, the broad coverage of the statute is apparent from the gifts and the favors that are expressly exempted: honorariums for participating in meetings, advertising items or souvenirs of nominal value, and meals furnished at banquets. Inexpensive pens, calendars, and paperweights bearing the name of the donor firm clearly fall within the exception for advertising items or souvenirs. A gift of a television set or the use of a beach cottage is undoubtedly prohibited. The exemption of meals at banquets from the prohibition suggests that giving free meals under any other arrangement would not be acceptable. The statute does not limit the size of honorariums, but its spirit suggests that an officer or an employee would be prudent not to accept an excessively generous one. The statute is silent on whether an official or an employee may accept reimbursement for expenses incurred in attending a meeting, but because honorariums may be accepted, it seems safe also to accept reimbursement for reasonable expenses required to attend meetings.

The statute also allows city officials to accept "customary gifts or favors" from their friends and relatives. However, officers and employees must report to the head of their governmental unit any gifts or favors from friends or relatives who are contractors, subcontractors, or suppliers and whose gift or favor, except for the friendship or the family relationship, would have been unlawful.

Finally, the statute states that it is not intended to prevent any contractor, subcontractor, or supplier from making donations to professional organizations to defray their meeting expenses, nor to prevent governmental employees who are members of professional organizations from participating in meeting functions supported by such donations that are available to all members.

Building Contracts

A number of statutes, some of which have already been discussed, are concerned with special aspects of contracts for public buildings. The key statutes and their provisions are these:

1. G.S. 87-15 requires that plans and specifications inform prospective bidders that they must be licensed when the cost of the contract will be large enough to limit its undertaking to licensed contractors.
2. G.S. 133-1.1 specifies which public buildings or renovation projects must be designed by registered architects or engineers.
3. G.S. 133-3 directs designers of public buildings to specify in their plans the required performance and design characteristics of materials to be used. When such specifications are impossible or impractical, they must include in their plans at least three items of equal design, if possible, to stimulate competition on all goods and materials used in constructing public buildings.
4. G.S. 143-135 (see the discussion under the heading Exceptions, earlier in this chapter) exempts cities and other political subdivisions of the state from the competitive-bidding requirements on construction and repair projects if the

work is performed by the officers and the employees of the unit concerned and the cost is less than $125,000. This exemption is actually a limit on what a unit may undertake with its own forces. The exemption also extends to a project of any cost if the cost of its labor component is less than $50,000. (Purchases of apparatus, supplies, materials, or equipment needed for the project are still subject to the bidding laws.)

5. G.S. 143-128 (see the discussion under the heading Specifications, earlier in this chapter) requires that separate specifications be drawn and separate bids taken for various types of work on building projects that involve expenditures of $500,000 or more, except for prefabricated buildings.

6. G.S. 153A-164 grants special authorization for the joint construction of public buildings by a county and any city within the county or by two or more counties.

7. G.S. 58-31-40 requires approval of plans for buildings of the state, counties, cities, and public schools by the commissioner of insurance for fire safety.

Procurement of Architectural, Engineering, and Surveying Service

Although professional services are not subject to the competitive-bidding statutes, G.S. Chapter 143, Article 3D, contains some special requirements for the procurement of architectural, engineering, and surveying services. This statute requires (1) that requirements for these professional services be announced; (2) that for each project the public agencies develop a list of qualified firms selected without reference to fee (except for unit price information); and (3) that the agencies then attempt to negotiate a contract with the best-qualified firm on the list. If they are unable to negotiate a contract with the best-qualified firm, then the agencies move to negotiations with the next-best-qualified firm.

City councils may exempt themselves from this requirement on any project for which the professional fee will be less than $30,000, or in their discretion, on any project by stating the reasons therefor. Councils should take these actions by resolution adopted in formal session and should record the action in their minutes.

State Tax Refunds

G.S. 105-164.14(c) authorizes the refund of sales and use taxes that cities pay directly on the purchase of tangible personal property and indirectly on taxable property that contractors may use in erecting public buildings for counties. Refunds are made only when applications are filed as required by the state commissioner of revenue and within six months of the close of each fiscal year.

G.S. 105-446.1 authorizes a refund of the state gasoline tax paid by cities. Applications for these refunds are made to the commissioner of revenue on prescribed forms.

Taxes paid by contractors should be included in the contract amount for purposes of determining the applicable bidding procedure, even if the unit is eligible for a refund.

Minority Contracting

G.S. 143-135.5 declares, "It is the policy of this State to encourage and promote the use of small, minority, physically handicapped and women contractors in state construction projects." The same statute also directs state agencies and political subdivisions to cooperate in carrying out the policy. As noted earlier (see the discussion under the heading Building Contracts), cities are required to establish goals and require good faith efforts to obtain minority participation in building construction projects costing $100,000 or more.

G.S. 160A-17.1(3a) authorizes cities to agree to and comply with requirements established by the federal government and its agencies for participation of minority business enterprises in projects financed by federal grants-in-aid or loans. For these federally funded projects, cities may include in their bid specifications minimum minority-participation requirements and award the contracts only to bidders who meet the requirements. Among bidders doing so, the other award standards set forth in G.S. 143-129 and -131 (see the discussion under the heading Standards in Awarding Contracts, earlier in this chapter) also apply.

Confidentiality of Trade Secrets

Generally, bids received under the procedures described earlier are public records and if received under formal, sealed-bidding procedures, are public after they are opened. However, G.S. 132-1.2 makes it lawful for trade secrets contained in a bid to be kept confidential if the bidder, at the time the bid is submitted, designates the secret and requests that it be kept confidential.

Misuse of Confidential Information

G.S. 14-234.1 makes it a misdemeanor for any state or local government officer or employee to use confidential information acquired in his or her official capacity for personal gain.

Additional Resources

Bell, A. Fleming, II. *Construction Contracts with North Carolina Local Governments.* 2d ed. Chapel Hill, N.C.: Institute of Government, The University of North Carolina at Chapel Hill, 1991 (3d ed. forthcoming).

Council of State Governments. *State and Local Government Purchasing.* 2d ed. Lexington, Ky.: the Council, 1983.

Dobler, Donald W., Lamar Lee, Jr., and David N. Burt. *Purchasing and Materials Management.* 4th ed. New York: McGraw-Hill Book Company, 1984.

Wicker, Warren Jake. *An Outline of Statutory Procedures Controlling Purchasing by North Carolina Local Governments.* Chapel Hill, N.C.: Institute of Government, The University of North Carolina at Chapel Hill, 1990 (with 1995 Supplement).

Notes

1. For a discussion of the coverage of the North Carolina bidding laws, see Frayda S. Bluestein, "Do We Have to Bid This?" *Popular Government* 58 (Winter 1993): 17.

2. Raynor v. Commissioners for the Town of Louisburg, 220 N.C. 348, 17 S.E.2d 495 (1941).

3. Professional Food Serv. Management v. North Carolina Dep't of Admin., 109 N.C. App. 265, 269, 426 S.E.2d 447, 450 (1993).

4. For an extensive discussion of the standards for awards, see Frayda S. Bluestein, "North Carolina's 'Lowest Responsible Bidder' Standard for Awarding Public Contracts," *Popular Government* 57 (Winter 1992): 10.

5. Kinsey Contracting Co. v. City of Fayetteville, 106 N.C. App. 383, 386, 416 S.E.2d 607, 609 (1992).

6. Matt. 6:24.

7. State v. Williams, 153 N.C. 595, 68 S.E. 900 (1910).

IV
Environmental Protection and City Planning

18 Environmental Affairs

Milton S. Heath, Jr.

Contents

IN RECENT YEARS, local governments have increasingly become involved with various aspects of environmental protection and natural resource management. In some instances this takes the form of operating a local regulatory program; in others, of being regulated; in still others, of working cooperatively with other local agencies and with state agencies. This chapter seeks to give city officials a basic acquaintance with their responsibilities and opportunities in this field.

Air Pollution

Under existing federal and state legislation the federal government sets general goals and standards for air quality,[1] whereas the state governments, under close supervision from the federal Environmental Protection Agency (EPA), develop the administrative machinery, or implementation plan, for achieving these goals and standards (G.S. Ch. 143, Art. 21, Pt. 7; Art. 21B, §§ 20-128.1, -183.3). North Carolina's plan was one of the first to be approved by EPA. The state's air and water pollution programs are governed by the Environmental Management Commission (EMC) and staffed by the Division of Environmental Management (DEM) of the Department of Environment, Health, and Natural Resources (DEHNR).

Air quality regulations apply to both private and public sources of pollution. No units of government (federal, state, or local) are exempt from complying with these regulations merely because they are government agencies.

Local Programs

Local governments (cities, counties, and regional groupings of cities and counties) in North Carolina may operate local air pollution control programs, but only if they can demonstrate their ability to do so to EMC's satisfaction. The powers of local programs and the procedure for obtaining state approval are spelled out in G.S. 143-215.112. A city or a county that is interested in conducting or participating in an air pollution control program should review this statute carefully because it sets out the alternatives and the requirements for local programs in some detail.

There were no active *city* air pollution control programs in North Carolina as of January 1, 1995. Forsyth and Mecklenburg counties and the western North Carolina region (Buncombe and Haywood counties) were operating local programs that had full state approval. Cumberland County was operating a local program with partial approval, which covered such functions as open burning, dark smoke control, air quality monitoring, and investigation of complaints.

Land Use and Transportation Control

Several EPA requirements stress the connection between land use and air pollution controls. For example, state air quality implementation plans must include supplementary land use and transportation controls. Also the state must consider the need for air quality maintenance controls in metropolitan areas, and state programs must control *complex sources* of air pollution. (A typical complex source would be a large shopping center with a high level of air contamination from motor vehicles.) On some of these matters, city planning staffs may be able to play an important part in ensuring that a reasonable balance is maintained between the need for air pollution control and the need for development opportunities.

Special mention should be made of one kind of transportation control: vehicle inspection and maintenance (I and M) for the control of pollution from vehicle emissions. When EPA finds that an air quality control region is not attaining national standards for certain pollutants from automobile exhausts, the state that contains the offending *nonattainment area* is required to institute a vehicle I and

M program for the region, or risk losing major federal subsidies. Regular inspections of emission-control systems on all automobiles are the key feature of an I and M program. Federal law allows the state to decide whether these inspections are conducted by state-run, municipally run, or private inspection stations. Whatever method is chosen, motorists in a nonattainment area are required to have their auto emission controls inspected for a fee, and to repair or replace defective controls at their own expense.

In North Carolina as of January 1995, I and M programs were operating in Cabarrus, Durham, Forsyth, Gaston, Guilford, Mecklenburg, Orange, Union, and Wake counties. Inspectors test for emissions of hydrocarbons and carbon monoxide and enforce national standards. Violations of national standards have been detected in other counties, but no I and M programs have been initiated for those counties. The statutes concerning I and M programs are G.S. 20-128.2, 20-183.3 through -183.7, and 143-215.107(a)(6).

Oxygenated and Reformulated Gasoline

A provision of the 1990 United States Clean Air Act Amendments requires the use of oxygenated and reformulated gasoline under some conditions. It is designed to enable the nation and the states to correct persistent nonattainment of ozone and carbon monoxide standards. (Oxygenated gasoline has oxygen-containing additives like ethanol and MTBE, a natural gas derivative. Reformulated gasoline has reduced emissions of volatile organic compounds and toxic chemicals.)

As of January 1, 1995, four North Carolina counties were required to use oxygenated gasoline because of carbon monoxide nonattainment: Durham, Franklin, Orange, and Wake. Local enforcement of oxygenated gasoline requirements was an option under study, but was not in place. No North Carolina counties were required to use reformulated gasoline.

All these arrangements to correct nonattainment conditions are in a state of flux. Continuing studies of air quality conditions showed enough improvement in 1994 to permit EPA to redesignate seven Piedmont Triad counties from a carbon monoxide nonattainment area to an attainment area. EPA has proposed redesignating the Charlotte area from nonattainment to attainment.

Indoor Air Pollution

The original federal and state clean air legislation focused mainly on outdoor air pollution problems. Increasing attention is now being paid to indoor air pollution—for example, problems of asbestos insulation in public buildings and of radon in homes. City and county governments may want to inquire about the current status of programs that address indoor air pollution issues. G.S. 130A-452, passed in 1994, authorizes approved local air pollution control programs to enforce asbestos standards for renovation and demolition, pursuant to EMC rules.

Consistency of Air and Water Pollution Permits with Local Land Use Ordinances

G.S. 143-215.108(f) requires every applicant for an air quality permit covering a new or expanded facility to request each local government having jurisdiction over the facility to determine whether the facility would be consistent with applicable zoning or subdivision control ordinances. If the facility is found inconsistent with a zoning or subdivision control ordinance, EMC must attach to the air quality permit a condition that the applicant comply with this ordinance and other applicable "lawfully adopted" ordinances unless the local government or a court makes a subsequent determination of consistency. A local government must submit its determination to EMC within fifteen days of receipt of a request from EMC, or EMC may consider a permit application without regard to local zoning and subdivision controls. It is not clear what scope of inquiry EMC will or should make to determine whether a local ordinance is lawfully adopted.

This statute is similar to previous legislation that applies to nonmunicipal wastewater discharge permits, contained in G.S. 143-215.1(c)(6). The water quality statute, however, allows EMC to override the local ordinance if it finds that the application has "statewide significance and is in the best interest of the state." As originally introduced, the air quality statute would have allowed EMC the same flexibility, but a Senate committee substitute replaced this quoted language with the requirement to attach a permit condition of compliance with the local ordinance.

Occupational Safety and Health

Some years ago Congress enacted an Occupational Safety and Health Act (OSHA),[2] which imposes standards on employers for the protection of employees' health and safety. Like most federal environmental and health protection laws, OSHA contemplates a coordinated federal-state program, with standards set nationally and administered largely by the states.

Although this chapter does not attempt to cover health legislation generally, it briefly describes OSHA for two reasons. First, OSHA provides, in one sense, the "in-plant" equivalent of the protections established by clean air laws for the outdoor environment. Thus an air quality problem in a factory is likely to be covered by OSHA rather than by clean air laws. Second, there is some overlapping and duplication between OSHA and the environmental protection laws. For example, for the protection of farm workers, OSHA administrators have imposed restrictions on applying pesticides. These restrictions are in addition to (and in some ways may even conflict with) the provisions of pesticide-control legislation (see the discussion under the heading Pesticides, later in this chapter).

North Carolina has adopted the legislation required to put it in a position to administer the OSHA program: the Occupational Safety and Health Law of North Carolina (G.S. Ch. 95, Art. 16). The legislation is administered by the state Department of Labor.

Private employers have been subject to the requirements of OSHA and related state laws since their passage. State and local governmental employers have been required to comply with standards set under these laws since July 1, 1974.

The much-publicized 1991 fire at the Imperial Foods plant in Hamlet led to a strengthening of North Carolina worker safety laws. Among the new laws that directly affect local governments are the following:

1. All employers (public and private) whose *experience rate modifier* (a calculation used in determining workers' compensation premiums) equals or exceeds 1.5 are required to establish workplace safety and health programs. Every such employer must establish an employer-employee safety and health committee with employee-selected representatives. The statute spells out detailed requirements for these pro-

grams (G.S. Ch. 95, Art. 22). A committee is required at each worksite where there are at least eleven employees unless the workers do not report to or work at a fixed location or the labor commissioner permits a variation.

2. The previous exemption of state agencies and political subdivisions from OSHA fines has been repealed. Each local government must report each violation for which it is cited at the next public meeting of its governing board and notify its workers' compensation insurance carrier or risk pool [G.S. 95-137(b)(6)].

Water Pollution (Surface Water)

The basic system of water pollution control is generally similar to the one that operates in the air pollution control field. The federal government provides leadership in setting goals and standards; the state government is largely responsible for providing the machinery to achieve the federal objectives. The North Carolina clean water legislation is codified at G.S. Chapter 143, Parts 1 and 7 and at G.S. 143-215.77 through -215.102. Local government's role in this area has consisted largely of health department programs concerning septic tanks, but local involvement is beginning to expand into emerging fields, such as hazardous waste management and watershed protection.

Federal legislation[3] establishes long-term national water quality goals. The standards required to meet them became increasingly stringent during the last decade as the nation worked toward the objective of achieving recreational water quality for all its water in the mid-1980s. The federal government (EPA) has been working to help the states bring their water pollution control laws and programs into compliance with federal standards. North Carolina's water pollution legislation now complies substantially with federal laws, and the state has enlarged its staff to meet EPA minimum recommendations.

The water pollution laws place important responsibilities on local governments to collect and treat their sewage properly. Local governments, including cities, must obtain permits to discharge their treated sewage to the waters of the United States, just as industries must obtain permits to discharge their treated wastewaters. The permit is obtained from DEM and is known as the *NPDES* (National

Pollution Discharge Elimination System) *permit.* Failure to meet the law's requirements may result in the assessment of heavy penalties on local governments and officials.

During the 1970s and early 1980s, large-scale federal and state subsidies, ranging up to 75 percent or more of the cost, were available to help local governments build sewage treatment plants. Although the days of this extraordinary federal and state largesse are over, some loan funds may still be available. (Financing of water and sewer projects through grants, loans, and other methods is discussed in some detail in chapter 24 of this volume.)

Additional discussion of water pollution control appears under the heading Consistency of Air and Water Pollution Permits with Local Land Use Ordinances, earlier in this chapter.

Sewage Treatment, Including Septic Tanks

Local environmental health specialists (formerly *sanitarians*) employed by county health departments have traditionally been responsible for inspecting and supervising installation of septic tanks and other on-site sewage treatment facilities. In recent years, as septic tanks have been used for larger projects and in more densely built-up areas, these wastes have become an increasing concern for EMC (with its general mandate for water pollution control), for state health authorities in DEHNR, and for local health departments. As a result, jurisdiction over sewage treatment is now divided among state agencies and the local health departments in a fairly complex way. These arrangements have been changed more than once in recent years and may well change again in the near future. The septic tank law is codified at G.S. Chapter 130A, Article 11.

Under 1992 legislation (1) all subsurface on-site wastewater discharge systems are regulated by state and local environmental health agencies—the DEHNR Division of Environmental Health (DEH) and county health departments; and (2) all systems discharging to surface waters or to the surface of the ground (spray irrigation) are regulated by DEM under EMC rules. When EMC has jurisdiction, an EMC permit is required for a sewage system: either an NPDES permit for a sewage discharge system, or a nondischarge permit for a system not covered elsewhere or for system elements such as sewer lines (G.S. 143-215.1). EMC may impose a moratorium on the addition of wastes to a wastewater treatment plant when it determines that the plant is incapable of treating additional wastes.

The Health Services Commission (HSC) is the rule-making body for state environmental health. Under HSC rules, local health departments are delegated routine operating responsibility for the regulatory system. Local departments may also elect to administer their own sewage rules, instead of state rules, if DEH finds that the proposed local rules are at least as stringent as the state's and are necessary to protect public health. (Fewer than five counties now have this approval.) These local rules may incorporate the state's rules together with more stringent local modifications and additions. DEH reviews local rules for consistency with changes in state rules as they are adopted, and examines the enforcement of local rules from time to time [G.S. 130A-335(c), (d)]. EMC may also delegate to local governments authority to approve contracts for sewage and wastewater treatment systems (G.S. 130A-317).

Persons who are subject to DEH or local health department jurisdiction must obtain authorizations and improvement permits for their sewage systems before beginning construction. They must also procure operation permits after the system is in place. Field inspection and tests are required before permits are issued. To reinforce these permit provisions, the on-site wastewater law provides that no permit for electrical or other utility or construction work on a residence or a place of business or public assembly may be issued until the necessary approvals have been obtained (G.S. 130A-337, -338).

In addition to the authority granted to local boards of health to adopt their own sewage rules with DEH approval, these boards have a more general power to adopt "a more stringent rule" in an area regulated by EMC or HSC [G.S. 130A-39(a), (b)]. Health officials have relied on this authority to justify a variety of local rules covering subjects such as wells, package sewage treatment plants, and odor problems from animal feedlots.

Non-Point-Source Pollution

The main thrust of traditional water pollution control programs has been to reduce pollution of streams by *point sources,* such as pipes that discharge the treated sewage of cities. There is growing recognition, however, that runoff from roads, shopping centers, farms, and forests, collectively known as *non-point-source pollution,* is a major contributor to stream pollution. At the national level this recognition is reflected in 1987 amendments to the Clean Water Act[4] that provide for states to present non-point-source water pollution control plans to EPA for early review. These plans are likely to draw heavily on existing state and local programs, such as the North Carolina programs summarized in the following sections.

Sedimentation Pollution

Sedimentation pollution control involves preventing the silting of streams by uncontrolled stormwater runoff from construction projects, logging activities, and so on. In most states (including North Carolina), sedimentation pollution control programs are not administered by the general water pollution control agency.

The Sedimentation Pollution Control Law of 1973 (G.S. Ch. 113A, Art. 4) creates a Sedimentation Control Commission within DEHNR and authorizes it to formulate and supervise a cooperative state-local program to control the pollution of streams by sediment and silt. A principal function of this commission is to review local ordinances and programs for compliance with state standards and criteria. Any city or county that wishes to adopt a sediment-control ordinance should contact the commission, which will provide assistance. About fifteen counties and twenty-four cities have established local ordinances and programs. The administrative arm of the commission is DEHNR's Land Quality Division.

Developers are required to obtain approval of erosion-control plans if they engage in "land disturbing activities that result in a change of natural cover or topography and contribute to sedimentation" of streams [G.S. 113A-52(6), -54(c), -57]. G.S. 113A-57 establishes statewide standards that set buffer zones for lakes and watercourses; limit grades of graded slopes or fills to the angle that can be retained by vegetative cover, devices, or structures; and require erosion-control practices during construction, as well as permanent ground cover for tracts of land larger than one acre that are uncovered in construction.

The Sedimentation Pollution Control Law covers residential, commercial, and industrial construction activities. It exempts agriculture and applies only to forestry activities that do not comply with DEHNR-approved best management practices (BMPs) for water quality. It applies to local and state governmental land-disturbing activities, such as construction projects, as well as to private or commercial work. Generally, governmental activities are regulated directly by the Sedimentation Control Commission; only private and commercial activities can be regulated by a local program.

Agricultural Non-Point-Source Pollution

The exemption of agriculture from the Sedimentation Pollution Control Act left a gap in programs that address stream pollution caused by agricultural runoff. In theory this gap could be filled by the authority of soil and water conservation districts to adopt land use regulations concerning erosion (G.S. 139-9, -10). In practice, however, this authority has never been exercised, probably because of a combination of philosophical reasons and a requirement for referendum approval of any such regulations by vote of two-thirds of the land occupiers of the district.

A more promising approach to controlling agricultural non-point-source pollution has been developed in recent years: the agricultural cost-share program. It provides 75-percent matching grants to encourage farmers to apply BMPs to control soil erosion and runoff from pesticides and fertilizers. The cost-share program is administered by the state Soil and Water Conservation Commission (S&WCC) under guidelines outlined in G.S. 143-215.74, with periodic review by a committee established by G.S. 142-215.74B that reports to the state legislative leadership. At the local level, soil and water conservation districts work closely with farmers in applying BMPs. The districts are responsible for reviewing and approving these practices for individual farms under the conservation compliance, "sodbuster," and "swampbuster" provisions of the 1985 federal farm bill.[5] As a result of these provisions, farmers who want to keep their commodity price supports must either apply the approved BMPs or stop farming highly erodible lands and drained wetlands. The cost-share program began in a few northeastern and Piedmont Triangle counties in the early 1980s. It was gradually extended to its present statewide coverage.

Another element of agricultural non-point-source pollution control is the so-called .0200 rules of EMC.[6] These rules regulate a variety of water-borne wastes that do not discharge into surface waters, under *nondischarge permits*. Amendments in 1993 to the .0200 rules addressed, among other things, potential pollution from intensive livestock operations, such as large hog and poultry feedlots. They set forth a cooperative program involving local soil and water conservation districts, S&WCC, and EMC. In essence, the .0200 rules and related S&WCC rules contemplate these arrangements:

1. The local districts advise farmers about their need to have nondischarge pollution-control systems, to develop animal waste management plans containing approved BMPs, and to get their waste management plans properly certified. Farmers who meet all these requirements are "deemed permitted" under the .0200 rules. New or expanded systems must have certified waste management plans now, and existing systems by December 31, 1997.
2. S&WCC adopts rules concerning approved BMPs and certification of qualified *technical specialists* to review each farmer's animal waste management plan.[7]
3. The technical specialists are responsible for certifying animal waste management plans containing approved BMPs. (Alternatively a farmer may comply with United States Natural Resources Conservation Service guidelines. The Natural Resources Conservation Service was formerly known as the Soil Conservation Service.) The specialist's approval may be set aside by a local district, whose decisions may be reviewed by S&WCC.[8]
4. EMC and its staff administer the nondischarge permit requirements, which they enforce against farmers who do not have certified animal waste management plans.

The 1995 General Assembly enacted additional legislation regulating hog production, including restrictions on the siting of hog houses and lagoons, and a certification law for hog waste applicators.

Stormwater Management

Federal Requirements

A current buzz word in environmental circles is *stormwater management*. For cities this is nothing really new: it is roughly equivalent to municipal storm drainage systems, with some additions and refinements.

The 1987 amendments to the federal Clean Water Act required that large cities (those over 250,000 in population) and medium-size cities (those with 100,000–250,000 in population) obtain NPDES permits covering their stormwater discharges.[9] Deadlines were established for these cities to file applications and obtain permits during 1992 and 1993, and to bring the systems into compliance within the following three years.

Charlotte is the only large North Carolina city on the list; Cumberland County (including Fayetteville), Durham, Greensboro, Raleigh, and Winston-Salem are the only medium-size places. It seems likely, though, that the program will expand to cover smaller communities; they would be well advised to keep in touch with developments on this front.

If small cities and counties are not yet required to obtain permits for their entire storm drainage systems, they (along with large units) are already covered under another part of the federal program, curiously labeled *industrial* activities. Under this label, EPA's stormwater regulations not only cover industrial and commercial activities literally, but also municipal airports, landfills, and motorpool fleet facilities. As of June 1993, all municipal airports were covered, as were uncontrolled landfills.[10] In cities above 100,000 in population, motorpool facilities, controlled landfills, and wastewater treatment plants were covered. All cities should watch for future rule changes concerning industrial facilities.

Two final points should be made about municipal stormwater responsibilities:

1. Any city whose stormwater system contributes to violations of water quality standards is subject to the EPA rules.
2. In addition to being regulated, cities are expected to play regulator in the EPA system: they must adopt, monitor, and enforce citywide stormwater management plans covering all stormwater discharged to their systems.

State Law

Prompted by the 1987 federal amendments, the 1989 North Carolina General Assembly enacted legislation broadening both the municipal and the county enterprise statutes to cover stormwater utility systems. G.S. 160A-311 and 153A-274 now define *public enterprises* to include stormwater and drainage systems. This supplements general ordinance-making and nuisance abatement powers, on which cities had sometimes relied to justify municipal drainage activities. It gives cities and counties the complete range of financing powers that go with the municipal enterprise statutes.[11] The 1994 General Assembly authorized water and sewer authorities to adopt stormwater ordinances [G.S. 162A-6(14c)].

Other Non-Point-Source Pollution-Control Measures

Some counties and cities have begun to include provisions in zoning and other land-use ordinances aimed at reducing non-point-source pollution. Examples include buffer zones around lakes and streams, structural requirements such as silt basins, and limitations on impervious surfaces in developments. Similar provisions have been adopted in Coastal Resources Commission rules covering the twenty coastal counties under the Coastal Area Management Act.

Water Supply (Watershed) Protection

A number of state government programs combine to provide some protection for surface water supply, or *watershed*, areas. Some of these have already been noted: EMC water pollution permits, administered by DEM; the sewage rules administered by health departments; sedimentation pollution control standards; and the agricultural cost-share program for non–point sources of pollution.

The Drinking Water Act (G.S. Ch. 130A, Art. 10), administered by DEHNR, authorizes the setting of maximum contaminant levels for physical, chemical, biological, and radiological contaminants that may affect the public health. It also authorizes watershed protection rules and disinfection rules that are graded according to the nature of the particular water supply source. In addition, there are statutory emergency powers and oil- or chemical-spill response procedures that can be activated by DEM or the secretary of DEHNR in response to spills and other emergencies that jeopardize public water supplies.

In 1989 the General Assembly enacted the Water Supply Watershed Protection Law, which combines minimum state standards for protection of surface water supply watersheds with local land use powers. Since 1989 the statute has been amended, and EMC has adopted the necessary implementing rules and has received and reviewed proposed local ordinances and programs that were required to be presented to it during 1993. The main elements of the resulting watershed protection program are as follows:

1. Streams that may be sources of water supply are placed in one of five classifications, ranging from WS-I for undeveloped watersheds to WS-IV and -V for moderately to highly developed watersheds and their upstream drainage reaches. About 20 percent of the state's land area is located in these watersheds, the majority of it in the Piedmont and mountain areas.

2. Within the WS-II, -III, and -IV classifications there are *general watershed areas* and *critical areas* (where risks associated with pollution are highest) that extend either one-half mile from the normal pool elevation of a reservoir or one-half mile upstream from a water supply intake located directly in a stream. The rules place greater restrictions on activities within critical areas than within general watershed areas.

3. The rules treat WS-I watersheds as pristine areas where no development will be allowed, nor sewer lines, sludge application, landfills, wastewater discharges, or hazardous materials storage, and where BMPs are required for agricultural, forestry, and transportation activities. (Only 0.2 percent of the state's land area lies within WS-I watersheds.) The rules regulate these activities and facilities in varying degrees within WS-II, -III, -IV, and -V watersheds.

    The heart of the rules is their standards for allowable density of development in WS-II, -III, and -IV watersheds. For each of these classifications, local governments may select a low-density option without stormwater controls or a high-density option with stormwater controls. The *most restrictive* low-density option without stormwater controls (for WS-II watershed critical areas) is 2-acre-minimum lots or 6-percent built-upon areas. The *least restrictive* high-density option with stormwater controls (for WS-IV *protected areas*) is development up to 74-percent built-upon area that controls runoff from a 1-inch rainstorm. For the WS-V watersheds (the upper drainage reaches of WS-IV watersheds), there are no restrictions other than in-stream water quality standards that apply to all water supply sources.

4. Cities and counties that contain WS-I water supply water-sheds are essentially bound to maintain these areas in an un-developed state. Cities and counties containing WS-V water-sheds are not bound to restrict development at all in these watersheds.

5. Cities and counties containing WS-II, -III, or -IV watersheds may choose to go with the applicable low-density option or the high-density option with stormwater controls. They may apply the relevant development options either through their zoning, subdivision control, and sediment control ordi-nances or through police power ordinances. EMC has ap-proved a model ordinance as a guide for cities and counties in meeting their requirements for local watershed protec-tion planning under the statute.

    The ultimate sanction available to the state if a city or a county fails to adopt a satisfactory program or to enforce it adequately is a civil penalty of up to $10,000 per month. That is, after notice, EMC may assume responsibility for the program in the affected area and assess the civil penalty to recoup its administrative and enforcement costs.

6. The rules allow expansion of existing single-family resi-dences without any restrictions, and they allowed develop-ment to continue in watershed areas until the applicable deadlines for submission of local watershed plans (from July 1, 1993, to January 1, 1994). The rules also protect vested rights under the 1989 vested rights legislation.

7. The state standards set by this legislation require cities and counties to protect water supply watersheds located within their boundaries whether these watersheds serve their own residents or the residents of other units. That is, County A may be required to protect watershed areas within the county that serve the residents of City X located in neighbor-ing County B.

8. The General Assembly has begun to chip away at the statu-tory scheme by exempting the Ivy River, located in Bun-combe and Madison counties,[12] and by setting a lower clas-sification (WS-IV rather than -III) for the North Toe River, located in Avery and Mitchell counties.[13] It is too soon to tell whether these exceptions will be isolated or will set a pattern for further erosion of the program.

Hazardous Wastes and Low-Level Radioactive Wastes

There is a growing body of federal and state legislation that regulates hazardous waste management, another pollution-control field in which the federal government sets the basic goals, standards, and procedures, and state governments provide much of the machinery to achieve federal objectives. One of the principal federal statutes is the Resources Conservation and Recovery Act (RCRA).[14] It regulates the generation, the transportation, the treatment, and the storage of hazardous wastes under a so-called cradle-to-grave system, which monitors the wastes from the time they are generated through ultimate disposal, relying on a manifest that follows the materials and is filed with regulatory agencies. The 1984 amendments to RCRA contain special regulations concerning underground storage tanks.

Another major federal statute is the Comprehensive Environmental Response Compensation and Liability Act (CERCLA, or *Superfund*).[15] It establishes two funds to help finance removal and disposal of hazardous substances released to the environment, especially substances disposed of to the ground through dumps or otherwise. It also makes those responsible for these releases strictly liable for all costs of removal or remedial action and for damages to natural resources.

North Carolina has statutes that parallel RCRA and CERCLA (G.S. 130A-294 through -309 and 130A-310 through -310.23). Other legislation has made the state a party to the Southeast Interstate Low-Level Radioactive Waste Compact and has established state boards to seek sites for disposal of hazardous wastes and low-level radioactive wastes. These boards also have general responsibility for state hazardous waste management policy. As of early 1994 the only remaining active boards were the Low-Level Radioactive Waste Management Authority and the Pollution Prevention Advisory Council (G.S. Chs. 104F, 104G; G.S. 143B-285.23, note).

Federal legislation goes beyond the regulation of hazardous wastes to the regulation of useful but toxic chemicals that have not reached the waste stream. The lead federal statute on this subject is the Toxic Substances Control Act (TSCA),[16] which establishes a system for regulatory review and clearance of new chemicals that are proposed to be placed on the market, and review of existing chemicals, as well as special regulations concerning PCBs (polychlorinated biphenyls). In addition, the 1986 amendments to CERCLA (which are designated by the acronym SARA) contain complex chemical right-to-know and emergency planning provisions. This subject was already addressed by state legislation in some states, including North Carolina (G.S. Ch. 95, Art. 18).

Some cities (and counties) have adopted ordinances that add local controls on hazardous wastes to the complex set of federal and state laws. These ordinances range from those that merely supplement state inspections and monitoring, to those that regulate small waste-producing sites below the minimum size for state regulation, to those that establish comprehensive procedures for reviewing proposed sites for hazardous waste or low-level radioactive waste treatment and disposal. At least one county has adopted an underground storage tank ordinance.

Any city that is considering a local ordinance on these subjects should examine closely the underlying statutory authority, the possibility of state or federal preemption of the field in question, and the constitutionality of the proposed ordinance. Unless the ordinance takes the form of zoning, the only source of local authority may be the general ordinance-making power (G.S. 160A-174). It may or may not be a legally adequate basis for this kind of local regulation. The general tests for preemption of local ordinances by state or federal laws are set forth in G.S. 160A-174, but several of the state regulatory statutes concerning hazardous waste management contain specific preemption or override provisions of their own that should be considered (see, e.g., G.S. 130A-293).

Solid Waste Regulation

Federal Law

RCRA regulates hazardous wastes from cradle to grave, as already noted. It also regulates management of nonhazardous solid waste in some important ways. RCRA itself prohibits the establishment of new open dumps, requires that existing open dumps be closed, and requires that all solid waste be disposed of in sanitary landfills, be used for resource recovery, or otherwise be disposed of in an environmentally sound manner.

EPA's landfill rules under RCRA go beyond these statutory provisions by requiring monitoring, leachate collection, effective liners, financial responsibility, and closure and postclosure care. They require states to exclude household hazardous wastes from landfills. EPA rules also contain restrictions, such as a ban on receiving sewage sludge in landfills. Collectively these restrictions and requirements are estimated to cost $10 or more per household annually.

State Law

In 1989 the General Assembly began to enact legislation that comprehensively regulates solid waste management by local governments. (The 1989 act is often identified by its original bill number, Senate Bill 111.) County governments are primarily responsible for disposal of solid wastes, but cities are also involved, some more than others. Most cities are responsible for day-to-day collection. Thus a brief summary of state law is warranted:

1. Each county must submit a comprehensive solid waste management plan. Its cities can either cooperate in that plan or submit their own plans. If a city operates the major waste disposal facility in the county, the city may prepare the county plan in cooperation with the county and the other cities in the county.
2. Cities and counties may facilitate cooperation by establishing joint agencies or interlocal agreements under the powers granted in G.S. 160A-460 through -464. They may also create a regional solid waste management authority pursuant to G.S. 153A-421.
3. The General Assembly has adopted a statutory waste-reduction goal that applies to all county solid waste management plans. This goal, on a per capita basis, is a 40-percent reduction by June 30, 2001, of the solid waste stream through source reduction, reuse, recycling, and composting [G.S. 130A-309.04(c)]. The normal baseline year is July 1, 1991, through June 30, 1992, but local governments may use an earlier year in some circumstances.[17]

Groundwater Quality

There is growing concern about protection of groundwater quality, especially in states like North Carolina where many people depend on wells for drinking water. This concern is also reflected nationally. Congress recently enacted legislation concerning underground storage tanks, and in 1986 it amended the federal Safe Drinking Water Act[18] to mandate new federal-state programs for the protection of public water supply well fields and well heads.

In North Carolina there is no comprehensive state law on groundwater quality, only a number of separate laws on the subject that neither collectively nor individually cover most significant groundwater pollution problems. The most nearly comprehensive approach is the North Carolina groundwater classification system administered by DEHNR, which adapts the concepts of an earlier surface water classification system to groundwater conditions and serves as a checkpoint for other decisions (such as landfill siting) that may affect groundwater quality. In addition, wells are to some extent regulated by the Well Construction Standards Act (G.S. 87-83 through -96), by some county well ordinances or health board rules, and by the Capacity Use Areas Law (G.S. 143-215.11 through -215.22). In some individual situations, groundwater quality may also be protected by state solid and hazardous waste regulations (including underground storage tank regulations), septic tank regulations, or radiation protection regulations; or the federal or state oil and hazardous substances spill-control acts.[19] Some of these topics are covered elsewhere in this chapter.[20]

Pesticides

Federal laws and programs set general standards for pesticide control, which must be met by state laws and programs if a state is to retain control over its permit system for the use of pesticides. In 1971, North Carolina enacted a comprehensive law that clearly meets minimum federal standards in most respects (G.S. Ch. 143, Art. 52). Principal elements of the state's program are regulation of the sale and the use of restricted-use pesticides, licensing of dealers who sell restricted-use pesticides, licensing of commercial pesticide applicators and consultants, and registration of pesticides. The North Carolina Pesticide Board is the policy-making agency for the state program, and the commissioner of agriculture has administrative responsibility. EPA is responsible for the federal program.

Local governments are subject to the licensing requirements and regulations of the North Carolina Pesticide Board. Local and state government agencies that use or apply pesticides, as well as commercial operators, must obtain licenses unless they are specifically exempted by law.

Chapter 445 of the 1995 Session Laws preempts local ordinances regulating the sale, the use, or the application of pesticides. (The United States Supreme Court had previously held that the federal pesticide law did not preempt local spraying ordinances.[21] The 1995 state law, however, makes it clear that North Carolina local governments do not have the authority to regulate pesticide sale, use, or application.)

Floodway and Floodplain Management

The *floodway* of a stream is essentially the channel and banks that carry normal stream flow and moderate flooding (defined by statute in North Carolina as the "100-year flood"). The *floodplain* is the broader area receiving and carrying large floods that overflow the banks of a stream and spread out extensively into surrounding areas. It is widely believed that construction and related activities within floodplains, and especially within floodways, should be limited to protect life, property, and the environment.

The state's counties and cities have long had the legal authority under their general zoning powers (for cities, G.S. Ch. 160A, Art. 19, Pts. 1, 3) to adopt floodplain zoning ordinances. Special zones or districts may be established to regulate land use in floodplains, or floodplain management provisions may be added to existing zones. A number of local governments have used the zoning approach to regulate floodplain land uses.

State legislation passed in 1971 (G.S. 143-215.51 through -215.61) specifies in detail the procedure for adopting and administering controls over the use of floodways, as opposed to floodplains. Counties and cities may adopt floodway ordinances under this legislation whether or not they have zoning ordinances, or they may adopt floodway ordinances that supplement floodplain zoning. Once a floodway has been officially delineated, construction is prohibited there without a permit from the appropriate county or city government, except for certain uses that may be made of the land as a matter of right; these include farming, parking areas, recreational areas, streets, utility and railroad facilities, dams, docks, ramps, and temporary accommodations such as those for circuses. Counties and cities must adopt ordinances providing for floodway permits in order to allow any construction within an officially delineated floodway other than construction for the exempted uses.

EMC may trigger local adoption of a floodway permit system by delineating a floodway if a local government does not do so. Except for this authority, however, the state government's role in floodplain and floodway management is generally limited to providing technical assistance to local governments.

The North Carolina Supreme Court in 1983 upheld Asheville's flood hazard district ordinance.[22] The court found that it was a valid exercise of the police power and that there was no regulatory taking of affected commercial properties because the plaintiffs were left with adequate "practical uses" of their land. The Asheville ordinance was a free-standing regulation; it was not part of another ordinance. It established floodway and flood fringe areas, and it set standards for some construction and prohibited other new or improved construction in these areas.

Any floodway or floodplain ordinance that is adopted by a county or a city should take into consideration the Federal Flood Insurance Program, administered by the Federal Insurance Administration (a branch of the Department of Housing and Urban Development—HUD).[23] Under this program, federal mortgage guarantees and other housing assistance programs are not available to communities with flood hazards unless they have adopted approved floodway or floodplain controls. Information on this subject can be obtained from EMC or HUD.

Environmental Impact Statements

The North Carolina Environmental Policy Act of 1971, G.S. Chapter 113A, Article 1, requires that state agencies file environmental impact statements in connection with all "actions involving expenditure of public moneys for projects and programs significantly affecting the quality of the environment." (A similar requirement applies to federal projects and programs under federal law.) A provision in the North Carolina statutes, G.S. 113A-108, authorizes counties and cities by ordinance to require environmental impact statements in connection with "major development projects" (those larger than 2 acres) of private developers and special-purpose governments. The authorization could cover such projects as shopping centers, residential subdivisions, and industrial or commercial developments. A few counties and cities have made use of this authority. A 1986 revision of the state guidelines under the Environmental Policy Act has stimulated further local interest; it provides that "state [permitting] agencies shall consider any information generated by" local governments under the act.[24] A 1991 amendment codified this provision at G.S. 113A-4(2a).

In a case involving Cane Creek Reservoir in Orange County, the North Carolina Court of Appeals held that the state Environmental Policy Act also required preparation of an environmental impact statement for certain local government projects—in particular, for a local water supply reservoir that needed a state permit.[25] The logic of this decision probably extends to, and requires that impact statements be prepared for, other state-licensed local government projects. (After the Cane Creek decision the legislature specifically exempted sanitary landfills operated by local governments from the act, as well as the siting of a superconducting supercollider and the siting of certain prison units.)[26] The Cane Creek case also illustrates the fact that partially overlapping federal, state, and local environmental impact statements may be required for some projects. In that case, separate but similar federal and state impact statements were necessary.

Environmental impact analysis provides an opportunity for a thorough (and sometimes very lengthy) ventilation of the possible environmental consequences of major developments. A city that wants to act to take advantage of this opportunity can either adopt a separate environmental impact ordinance under G.S. 113A-108 or insert similar provisions in its local zoning ordinance or subdivision control ordinance. Which approach is preferable will depend on the city's objectives.

Soil and Water Conservation, Small Watersheds, and Drainage Districts

North Carolina has a soil and water conservation district in each county (except for two multicounty districts covering eight counties in the Albemarle and Pamlico Sound regions). Each district is governed locally by a board of supervisors that is partly elected by the voters of the district and partly appointed by the State Soil and Water

Conservation Commission. A majority of the board is elected. District activities include the following:

1. The basic soil erosion control and land treatment programs that date from the dust bowl era.
2. The agricultural cost-share program for non-point-source water pollution control, and related animal waste control responsibilities, described under the heading Agricultural Non-Point-Source Pollution, earlier in this chapter.
3. Assistance to farmers in preparing farm plans required by the 1985 and 1990 federal farm bills to retain crop price supports.
4. The small watershed (or watershed improvement) program, which assists farmers and other local residents with flooding, farmland drainage, and related water conservation problems. Individual small watershed projects are usually carried out either by counties acting under G.S. 139-41 or by drainage districts acting under G.S. Chapter 156, Subchapter III. Federal and state aid may be available for small watershed projects.[27]

Cities or counties sometimes serve as cosponsors of small watershed or drainage projects, but otherwise cities have no direct responsibilities for soil and water conservation. Cities and counties are *authorized* to assist small watershed programs in any or all of the following ways:

1. By levying property taxes to undertake watershed improvement projects, pursuant to G.S. 160A-209(c)(34) and 153A-149(35)
2. By participating in small watershed projects and contributing funds to projects that provide or protect city or county water supply sources or flood damage protection or drainage benefits to the city or the county, pursuant to G.S. 139-37
3. By issuing bonds to finance water supply storage in small watershed projects, pursuant to G.S. 139-37.1
4. By installing and maintaining recreation facilities or fish and wildlife habitat features in small watershed projects, pursuant to G.S. 139-46.[28]

The Environment and Land Use: Coastal Area Management and Mountain Ridge Protection

The 1974 General Assembly enacted a Coastal Area Management Act (CAMA) (G.S. Ch. 113A, Art. 7). Its basic objective is to establish a comprehensive plan for protection, preservation, orderly development, and management of the coastal area of North Carolina. Twenty counties are covered by the CAMA: Beaufort, Bertie, Brunswick, Camden, Carteret, Chowan, Craven, Currituck, Dare, Gates, Hertford, Hyde, New Hanover, Onslow, Pamlico, Pasquotank, Pender, Perquimans, Tyrrell, and Washington.

The three main features of the act provide as follows:

1. That each of the twenty coastal area counties be covered by a land use plan, preferably prepared by local government and in basic harmony with the plans adopted for the other nineteen coastal area counties. (All the counties have plans.)
2. That all critical areas that need to be considered for protection and possible preservation in each county be designated as *areas of environmental concern.*
3. That any proposed development, change, or other use of land within a designated area of environmental concern be subject to review by means of a development permit procedure. Generally, local governments handle permits for minor developments (in most cases those under 20 acres), and the state Coastal Resources Commission handles permits for major developments.

The thrust of this act is to establish a cooperative state-local program of coastal land management. It is local government's responsibility to establish local land use plans and issue permits for minor development in areas of environmental concern. It is state government's responsibility to adopt guidelines and standards for local land use plans; to establish areas of environmental concern; to issue permits for major developments in areas of environmental concern; and to assume the responsibilities of local governments if and when they do not exercise their powers under the act. Enforcement is a concurrent state-local responsibility. Amendments to the CAMA in the 1980s added two land acquisition elements, the coastal reserve and beach access programs (G.S. Ch. 113A, Art. 7, Pts. 5, 6).

Directly participating in the CAMA program at the state level are the Coastal Resources Commission, the Coastal Resources Advisory Council, and the secretary of DEHNR. The local agencies most involved are the counties, the cities, and the multicounty planning agencies in the twenty coastal area counties.

Coastal cities and counties play an important role in the coastal area management program. Each coastal area city nominates one person to the Coastal Resources Commission, and each county nominates four. Eight representatives of coastal cities and one representative of each coastal county serve on the Coastal Resources Advisory Council. If they wish, coastal area cities and counties may play a role in the planning process, in enforcement, and in beach access programs.

In 1983 the General Assembly enacted a Mountain Ridge Protection Act (G.S. Ch. 113A, Art. 14), which regulates construction of tall buildings along the tops of high mountain ridges. The legislature gave local governments in mountain counties the option of either regulating ridgetop construction through permit systems or allowing the act's prohibitions on this type of construction to go into effect. About two-thirds of the affected counties accepted the state prohibitions. Only one city, Beech Mountain, adopted a city ordinance; one other, Banner Elk, asked its county (Watauga) to enforce the county ordinance inside the city. (The act also allowed mountain counties and cities the opportunity to reject its coverage, but none chose to do so by the statutory deadline.) State government's role under this act is limited to providing technical assistance in identifying and mapping protected mountain ridges.

1995: A Year of Change

The "Contract with America" seeks major changes in the philosophy and the process of environmental regulation at both the federal and the state level. At this writing (August 1995), more has been said than done so far in the Congress and the state legislatures on key elements of the contract, such as imposing risk-based or benefit-cost tests on environmental rules, expediting permit issuance, reducing unfunded mandates, and giving landowners additional protection against regulatory takings.

The 1995 North Carolina General Assembly took several steps toward meeting the objectives of the contract:

1. It required *risk-based analysis* in one program area, the cleanup of discharge from leaking underground storage tanks.[29] [A benefit-cost analysis had previously been required under G.S. 143-215(c) and -215.107(f) for new water and air pollution control rules that were more stringent than federal rules.]
2. It required *expedited review* of air pollution permit applications prepared by engineers.[30]
3. It addressed the *unfunded mandates* issue by imposing a comprehensive set of obligations on the governor's office and state agencies to flag and publicize new federal and state mandates and to minimize their impact on local governments.[31] [This reinforced the existing requirements in G.S. 150B-21.4(b) for fiscal notes on proposed state rules that affect local government.]

To date, Congress has enacted only an unfunded mandate act that relies on the rules of each house to require "full consideration" of unfunded mandate proposals.[32] The act makes it not in order for either house to consider a bill or a committee report proposing an unfunded mandate without an attached Congressional Budget Office statement on the cost of the mandate, or to consider increasing federal mandates to state, local, or tribal government of over $50 million annually without full federal funding. The House has passed and sent to the Senate bills embodying the rest of the contract agenda, together with deep cuts in EPA's budget.

Notes

1. The federal Clean Air Act is codified at 42 U.S.C. §§ 7401–7671q (1983 & Supp. 1995).

2. 29 U.S.C. §§ 651–673 (1985 & Supp. 1995).

3. The primary federal legislation for water pollution control is the Water Pollution Control Act, codified at 33 U.S.C. §§ 1251–1387 (1986 & Pocket Pt. 1995).

4. 33 U.S.C. § 1329 (Pocket Pt. 1995).

5. Food Security Act of 1985, 16 U.S.C. §§ 3811–3836 (1985 & Pocket Pt. 1995).

6. N.C. ADMIN. CODE tit. 15A, subch. 02H, § .0200 (Feb. 1, 1976–Feb. 1, 1994).

7. N.C. ADMIN. CODE tit. 15A, subch. 06F, §§ .0001 through .0005 (eff. March 1, 1994).

8. N.C. ADMIN. CODE tit. 15A, subch. 06F, § .0003 (eff. March 1, 1994).

9. 33 U.S.C. § 1342(p) (1986 & Pocket Pt. 1995).

10. *Uncontrolled landfills* are those that do not meet the runoff requirements of the Resources Conservation and Recovery Act, Subtitle D, 42 U.S.C. § 6941–6949a (1983 & Supp. 1995).

11. For further details on stormwater, see J. Mark Payne, "Stormwater Management: Municipalities' New Requirements under the Clean Water Act," *Popular Government* 58 (Summer 1992): 29. Also, contact the League of Municipalities or the Association of County Commissioners, both of which have counseled local governments extensively about stormwater.

12. 1993 N.C. Sess. Laws ch. 5.

13. 1995 N.C. Sess. Laws ch. 301.

14. 42 U.S.C. §§ 6901–6992k (1983 & Supp. 1995).

15. 42 U.S.C. §§ 9601–9675 (1983 & Supp. 1995).

16. 15 U.S.C. §§ 2601–2629 (1982 & Supp. 1995).

17. A more detailed description of these local and interlocal arrangements can be found in William A. Campbell, "Intergovernmental and Organizational Issues in Solid Waste Management," *Local Government Law Bulletin* no. 54 (January 1994): 1–6. This bulletin also discusses the legal aspects of flow control arrangements and exclusionary devices, some of which have been questioned by the courts on constitutional grounds (pp. 3–4).

18. 42 U.S.C. §§ 300f through 300j-26 (1991 & Pocket Pt. 1995).

19. The federal and state oil and hazardous substances spill-control acts are codified at 33 U.S.C. § 1321 (1986 & Pocket Pt. 1995) and G.S. 143-215.75 through -215.104, respectively.

20. See also Milton S. Heath, Jr., "Ground Water Quality Law in North Carolina," *Popular Government* 52 (Winter 1987): 39–49. This article addresses the subject of groundwater quality law in greater detail. Because of the rapidly changing nature of the groundwater protection field, counties that have concerns about groundwater quality may wish to consult with federal, state, or private experts before addressing those concerns.

21. Wisconsin Public Intervenor v. Mortier, 501 U.S. 597, 111 S. Ct. 2476, 115 L. Ed. 2d 532 (1991).

22. Responsible Citizens in Opposition to the Floodplain Ordinance v. City of Asheville, 308 N.C. 255, 302 S.E.2d 204 (1983).

23. The statutes governing the Federal Flood Insurance Program are codified at 42 U.S.C. §§ 4001–4129 (1994).

24. N.C. ADMIN. CODE tit. 15A, ch. 25, § .0802 (amended eff. May 3, 1993).

25. *In re* Environmental Management Comm'n, 53 N.C. App. 135, 280 S.E.2d 520 (1981).

26. *See* G.S. 113A-1, note; 1987 N.C. Sess. Laws ch. 3, §§ 4, 5.

27. The federal statutes pertaining to small watershed programs are codified at 16 U.S.C. §§ 1001–1009 (1985 & Pocket Pt. 1995).

28. For a general discussion of soil and water conservation, small watersheds, and drainage, see A. Fleming Bell, II, ed., *County Government in North Carolina*, 3d ed. (Chapel Hill, N.C.: Institute of Government, The University of North Carolina at Chapel Hill, 1989), ch. 19.

29. 1995 N.C. Sess. Laws ch. 377.

30. 1995 N.C. Sess. Laws ch. 484.

31. 1995 N.C. Sess. Laws ch. 415.

32. Pub. L. No. 104-4., 109 Stat. 48 (1995).

19 Community Planning, Land Use, and Development

Richard D. Ducker

Contents

THE TERM *community planning* describes a process by which a community (1) determines its goals and objectives; (2) chooses a combination of actions and programs for achieving these goals; (3) carries out its plans and programs in a systematic manner; and (4) evaluates its success and makes necessary adjustments. For most North Carolina cities, community planning means *land use and development planning*. Land use and development planning is an application of the planning process to all public and private activities that affect the use and the development of land and the growth and the character of a community. Some communities prefer to view land use planning as simply an aspect of *community development*, to emphasize that the economic and social development of the community is closely related to its physical development. A few cities view their planning mission as one of *growth management*, to emphasize that the policies, the programs, the incentives, and the regulatory tools for influencing development are at least as important as the plans on which they are based. No matter what it is called, influencing the use and the development of land is an important function of municipal government.

One feature of land use planning that distinguishes it from many other types of public planning is its concern with the performance of the private sector as well as the performance of the public sector. Many local governments view their function as simply to accommodate the growth that the private sector generates and to provide public services wherever and whenever they are demanded. It is also true, however, that the location of a new highway, the extension of utilities, or the standards of a zoning ordinance may strongly influence the location, the type, and the timing of private development. This interplay between public and private activities gives rise to the need for community planning.

A city influences development in four major ways: (1) by providing public programs and services and constructing and maintaining public facilities (streets, utilities, parks, schools, etc.); (2) by regulating the use, the development, and the maintenance of private and public property (zoning and subdivision regulations, a minimum housing code, etc.); (3) by providing direction to induce private parties and other units of government to act consistently with municipal plans and policies; and (4) by extending subsidies, loans, and special incentives to induce private parties to act consistently with municipal objectives. Table 19-1 elaborates on each of these measures.

Table 19-1
Methods Used by Cities for Influencing Land Use and Development

1. Providing public programs and facilities

Estimating needs, selecting sites, and determining sequence and
    timing of capital improvements (e.g., streets and roads)
Influencing pattern of development
  Extending utilities to manage growth
  Protecting future roadway corridors
Establishing capital improvement program (CIP) to link
    budgeting to comprehensive land use planning
Acquiring land and public improvements
  Purchasing sites in advance
  Encouraging donations of land
  Requiring compulsory dedication of land and improvements
    in new developments (e.g., park land, streets, and utilities)
  Requiring compulsory reservation of land
  Imposing impact fees to pay for capital improvements
    required to serve new growth

2. Regulating land use and development

Regulating division of land and construction of community or
    public improvements
  Enforcing land subdivision ordinance
  Adopting utility-extension policies
  Regulating soil erosion and sedimentation control
  Adopting watershed protection ordinance
  Adopting special assessment and cost reimbursement policies
    for public facilities
  Regulating water supply and wastewater disposal systems
  Establishing standards for designing, constructing, and
    accepting subdivision streets
  Enforcing driveway permit regulations
Regulating use and development of land
  Enforcing zoning ordinance
  Adopting watershed protection regulations
  Setting development standards for flood hazard areas

continued on next page

These approaches are often combined. For example, under its
Community Development Block Grant program, a city may install
drainage facilities and make street improvements in a particular
neighborhood. It may also offer subsidized housing rehabilitation
loans to property owners in the affected area. Planners concerned

Table 19-1, *continued*
Methods Used by Cities for Influencing Land Use and Development

2. Regulating land use and development (continued)

Adopting airport zoning
Designating historic landmarks
Adopting special-purpose police-power ordinances
(e.g., governing mobile home parks, outdoor
advertising, and junkyards)
Requiring local environmental impact statements
Adopting roadway corridor official map ordinances
Enforcing State Building Code
Establishing property maintenance and public health and safety
standards
Adopting minimum housing code
Condemning abandoned or unsafe structures
Establishing junked-car program
Controlling weeds and litter
Abating public nuisances

3. Providing direction and leadership

Adopting comprehensive plan and publicizing it
Providing assistance to property owners,
neighborhood groups, environmental groups, and other
nonprofit organizations
Establishing voluntary design guidelines

4. Providing financial incentives

Providing rehabilitation grants and loans for housing
Providing housing rental subsidies
Providing loans and grants for historic preservation
Acting as economic entrepreneur
Engaging in land banking (purchase of land for later resale to
private parties)
Constructing and leasing shell buildings; making site
improvements on privately owned land

about revitalizing a city's central business district may suggest land-scaping plans or building facade designs for downtown merchants who wish to upgrade the area. At the same time the city may use the zoning ordinance to establish sign standards and height limits in the central business district.

Purposes of Community Planning

Community planning is designed to accomplish a variety of important purposes and to offer a number of important benefits. First, the planning process looks to the future. Where no special attention has been given to a city's future needs and capabilities, current problems and political concerns can easily divert the attention of local officials and citizens alike. Elected officials especially may find it easy to become immersed in the day-to-day affairs of government and to give little thought to emerging trends, potential problems, and government capacity to meet the demands for service that lie ahead. For example, some cities have discovered that they have paid insufficient attention to the community's future needs for an expanded water supply and wastewater treatment capacity. Because it anticipates the future, land use and development planning may help municipal officials and citizens avoid such problems and the unnecessarily large costs of correction that this lack of foresight causes.

Community land use planning also suggests a comprehensive approach to community development. Planning is designed to give the community a broad view of itself and help it understand the interrelation of various actions that affect a city's development. Often a community wants to know the likely effect of a projected development. For example, a new highway is to be built on the fringe of a city. The new road may make it easier to travel around the city's perimeter and may stimulate demand for land and utility service along its route. Traffic on streets connecting the new highway with the downtown area may increase, and demand may come for commercial rezoning along the route. If granted, the rezoning may encourage some retail trade to leave the central business district. In addition, the new highway may make one side of town more attractive for residential development because it is now more accessible. The new development may require a new fire station on that side of town. Tracking implications of this sort is a part of planning analysis.

Furthermore, city officials need to understand development relationships so that the actions of various departments and agencies and the general policies of the city may be coordinated. Coordination is fairly easy in small cities: the staff is small and the city council, the mayor, or the city administrator can easily keep track of what is going on. In large cities, however, coordinating all the activities that affect the physical development of the community may be more difficult.

Sound community planning may also help communities avoid inconsistent policies. For example, it may be important to understand that the success of a city's ambitious industrial recruitment drive is connected to the city council's willingness to rezone at least some land for apartments and other forms of rental or temporary housing, or to understand that the opening of a new bypass that offers good locations for a suburban shopping center may damage the effectiveness of a downtown revitalization program.

Community planning can be helpful to the city council and other local bodies in making decisions that affect the city's development. Community planning is really a way of making decisions. It represents a conscious choice by local officials to make development-related decisions that are consistent, predictable, and based on policy. It opens up the possibility that the city council and other boards will view community growth policy as a framework for evaluating individual development-related proposals.

Finally, the planning process provides an opportunity for the public directly to influence the formulation of policy and the decision making that affects a community's development. Successful citizen participation and neighborhood outreach programs emphasize a continuing relationship between government and its citizens. The process may be used to identify citizens' concerns about their community and their views about solutions in a noncrisis environment.

Organization for Municipal Planning

Municipal planning programs involve a number of municipal functions and departments and local boards. The organizational arrangements often differ from one community to another. The most important elements of a local planning program are shown in figure 19-1: the city council, the planning agency, the zoning board of adjustment, and staff assistance.

City Council

The key to the success of any municipal land use and development planning program is the city council. The council exercises a number of powers affecting a land use planning program. It approves the municipal budget and the financing for capital projects

Figure 19-1

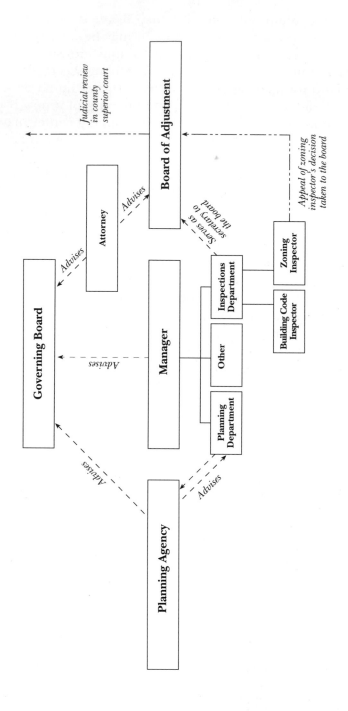

to be undertaken in the current fiscal year. (It may also approve a five- or six-year capital improvement program as an advisory measure; see chapter 14.) The council allocates funds for boards, agencies, and departments that carry out planning-related responsibilities. It approves the location and the design of public buildings and other public facilities. In its legislative capacity the council adopts and amends various land use and development-related ordinances. It may retain for itself authority to issue conditional use permits for certain land uses outlined in the zoning ordinance. The council also affects the city's planning program by the quality of the appointments that it makes to the planning board, the zoning board of adjustment, and other planning-related commissions and agencies. Finally, it has ultimate authority to enforce municipal ordinances, and it approves any legal action taken against violators of the various land use and development-related ordinances.

Planning Board

One of the primary citizen boards that is critical to a local planning program is the *planning board* (also called the *planning commission*). Most North Carolina cities have established a planning board made up of lay members appointed by the city council. Many of the planning board's duties and responsibilities are advisory. The planning board is generally given the responsibility for supervising the development of a city's comprehensive plan. It may arrange for and supervise the preparation of special studies, land use plans and policies, and drafts of ordinances. It may adopt plans and policies, advise the council on them, and recommend ordinances and methods of carrying out plans. In addition, the planning board generally has specific duties in connection with the zoning ordinance. A "planning agency" must prepare and "certify" the draft of a city's original zoning ordinance (G.S. 160A-387). Virtually all city zoning ordinances also grant the planning board a thirty-day opportunity in which to make a recommendation concerning any proposed amendment to the land development ordinance before the council acts on the proposal.

In addition to having advisory responsibilities, a planning board may be delegated the authority to review certain development proposals. As a planning agency, the planning board may be delegated the authority to approve subdivision plats (G.S. 160A-373). The planning board's potential versatility is indicated by the fact that it can take on the duties of certain other agencies if the city council so desires. For example, the council may assign to a planning board any or all of the duties of the zoning board of adjustment (e.g., approval of zoning variances, issuance of conditional use permits, and hearing of appeals from decisions of the zoning official) [G.S. 160A-388(a)]. In addition, if at least two planning board members have demonstrated special interest, experience, or education in history or architecture, the planning board may be designated the municipal historic preservation commission (G.S. 160A-400.7).

North Carolina local governments may also establish a joint planning board representing two or more local units of government. The Winston-Salem/Forsyth County City-County Planning Board and the Charlotte-Mecklenburg Planning Commission are two of the better-known examples of such joint agencies.

Zoning Board of Adjustment

The zoning board of adjustment has three primary responsibilities under North Carolina law [G.S. 160A-388(b),(c),(d)]. First, it interprets the zoning ordinance. Generally this involves hearing appeals from decisions of the zoning enforcement official when an applicant for a permit or another aggrieved party claims that the zoning official has misinterpreted the ordinance. Second, the board of adjustment grants variances to the zoning ordinance. Third, it may be authorized by the city council to grant conditional use permits for certain land uses and types of development outlined in the ordinance. Although it is common for a board of adjustment to be charged with some combination of these duties, it is also possible for any of these responsibilities to be delegated by the city council to the planning agency [G.S. 160A-388(a)]. Virtually all the board of adjustment's major decisions (issuing a variance or conditional use permit or reversing a decision of the zoning enforcement officer) must be made with the concurring vote of four-fifths of its members. Board of adjustment decisions may not be appealed to the council; rather, judicial review of such decisions may be had in county superior court.

Historic Preservation Commission

To initiate special review of development in a historic district or to designate a property as a historic landmark, a city council must appoint a local historic preservation commission (see the section Historic Districts and Landmarks, later in this chapter). The council may assign the functions of a historic preservation commission to a planning agency or to a community appearance commission (see the next section).

Community Appearance Commission

To focus attention on the entire community's aesthetic condition, the city council may appoint a community appearance commission (G.S. 160A-451) and may also participate in forming a joint city-county appearance commission. The commission generally has no permit-granting or mandatory-approval authority; its powers are thus persuasive and advisory in nature (G.S. 160A-452).

Economic Development Commission

To promote local economic development, a city council may establish a municipal economic development commission (G.S. 158-8). The commission, with the help of any staff it hires, may engage in community promotion and business recruitment; provide advice, analysis, and assistance concerning economic and business development matters; and help form nonprofit corporations that develop industrial park sites and shell buildings for relocating businesses.

City Manager

The city manager generally plays an unrecognized role in any land use planning program. In small cities with an administrator, he or she may make recommendations on matters affecting the city's development, enforce planning-related ordinances, and supervise the preparation of plans. In large cities that have a staff planner, the manager may be less directly involved in planning affairs. Still, he or she may coordinate the capital improvement program; administer the housing, community development, transportation, parks and recreation, and inspection programs; make recommendations on annexation and utility-extension plans, downtown revitalization plans, and economic development proposals; and coordinate the interdepartmental staff review of major development projects that come before the council.

Planning Staff

A municipal land use planning program generally needs some professional planning help, which may be provided in any of the following ways:

1. The city may hire staff. Most cities with a population over 10,000 employ at least one staff planner to help execute a land use planning program. Usually planning staff are hired by and ultimately responsible to the city manager, but serve as staff to the planning board and other appointed boards with planning-related responsibilities.
2. The planning board itself may hire staff. The governing body that creates the planning board may authorize it to hire its own full-time staff with funds allocated for this purpose (G.S. 160A-363). Except for joint planning boards that represent more than one jurisdiction, however, this authority has not been used.
3. A city may contract for technical planning services provided by some other local unit of government (G.S. 160A-363).
4. Several local government units may share staff, each jurisdiction retaining its own planning board. Arrangements may be established through an interlocal agreement (G.S. Ch. 160A, Art. 20, Pt. 1).
5. A joint planning board created by two or more local governments may hire staff (G.S. 160A-261, -363). Some of the state's large planning agencies are city-county boards with their own staff. The interlocal agreement establishing the joint planning board determines the financial contributions of each jurisdiction, the manner of appointment of board members, personnel practices affecting staff members, and the way in which work is assigned and supervised.
6. A private consultant may furnish technical assistance. Private planning consultants have been particularly active in prepar-

ing municipal zoning ordinances, economic development plans, and plans for downtown revitalization.
7. A substate regional organization may furnish technical assistance. North Carolina is divided into eighteen regions, each represented by a *lead regional organization* (LRO). LROs in North Carolina take one of three forms: a "regional planning commission" (G.S. 153A-395), a "regional planning and economic development commission" (G.S. 153-398), or a "regional council of governments" (G.S. 160A-475). Most of the LROs provide at least some municipal planning and related technical assistance.
8. The Division of Community Assistance of the North Carolina Department of Commerce may furnish technical assistance. This source provides a broad range of planning and managerial assistance through six field offices. It and its predecessor agencies have prepared a number of land use plans and zoning and subdivision ordinances for communities throughout the state.

Zoning Enforcement Official

In a large city the zoning enforcement official may be charged only with the enforcement of zoning. In small cities the official may also be a building inspector, a city manager or clerk, or a police chief, or may enforce other local ordinances.

Inspection Department

The inspection department is the primary enforcement agency for a variety of development-related ordinances and codes. It typically enforces the State Building Code and sometimes also enforces the minimum housing code. In many cities, both large and small, it also enforces the zoning ordinance.

Community Development Department

In recent years the Community Development Block Grant (CDBG) program has become a key short- and mid-range program for carrying out a city's housing and development objectives in low- and moderate-income neighborhoods. (See chapter 20 for a description of the CDBG program.) Many cities have established a new, separate community development department or office to administer the program. In others the CDBG coordinator may report to the planning director. In some large cities the CDBG program may be administered within a community development division of an umbrella development or planning department.

General Comprehensive Plan (Land Use Plan)

The centerpiece of a local planning program has traditionally been thought to be a *general comprehensive plan*. A general comprehensive plan is designed to give a community an overview of its current physical development and to serve as a guide to its future development policy. Typically the plan includes a sketch of the city's historical development and statistical information about the community, discusses urban development issues and problems, and presents a series of maps displaying both current information and future projections. However, the primary function of the plan document is to outline in writing the policy that the community intends to pursue with respect to growth and development issues and to determine the steps necessary to put this policy into effect. For this reason the process by which the community establishes its development goals and objectives and the extent to which the community develops a consensus about the proper role that local government can play in influencing development is key. The comprehensive plan as a document can be only as effective as the process that has shaped it.

A pivotal component of a general comprehensive plan is the *land use plan*. The land use plan is based on projections of population growth and land development patterns that have implications for public facilities, transportation, and economic development as well as housing, cultural and natural resource protection, and community appearance. In fact, many cities use the terms *general comprehensive plan* and *land use plan* interchangeably.

Land use plans must be prepared for cities in the twenty coastal counties subject to the Coastal Area Management Act. Cities elsewhere in the state are under no similar legal obligation. However, certain rudimentary assumptions about land use must be made if a city is to engage in transportation planning. G.S. 136-66.2 calls for each North Carolina municipality, with the cooperation of the North Carolina Department of Transportation, to prepare a comprehensive street plan (thoroughfare plan). In addition, various state and federal aid programs require local government applicants to prepare a plan (often with land use implications) in order to qualify for assistance.

Uses of the General Comprehensive Plan

If a comprehensive plan is to be used, it must provide some guidance to local governments when they make important development-related decisions. Some jurisdictions automatically refer to the plan when considering rezoning and utility-extension decisions. The zoning statutes say that zoning must be "in accordance with a comprehensive plan" (G.S. 160A-383). This requirement has not been construed to mean that some comparison between the zoning ordinance and an adopted comprehensive land use plan is required. However, there is a growing tendency among the courts to look to documentation outside the land use ordinance itself in determining whether a land use regulatory power is being properly exercised. In addition, some units have bound themselves to follow their own plans.[1]

Strategic Planning

A model that serves as an alternative to comprehensive planning is *strategic planning*. Strategic planning is a process that emphasizes focusing on a few critical issues that are important to the community's future rather than trying to deal with everything at once. It involves looking outward at trends that may affect a community's destiny but be beyond the community's control. Strategic planning is designed to be action oriented so as to show what steps must be taken to achieve goals, who must take them, how much it will cost, and who will pay. It is well adapted to the resolution of economic development and housing issues involving a number of players (government units, businesses, private individuals, and nonprofit organizations) when a distribution of responsibility is necessary and the ability to respond to opportunities is important. Strategic planning is a particularly useful process for making spending decisions. Also, its focus on setting achievable goals and setting timetables for action make it valuable in resolving regulatory issues. Although comprehensive planning is still the primary model used in land use and development planning, it has been substantially influenced by the principles of strategic planning.

Extraterritorial Jurisdiction for Land Use Planning

In North Carolina, as in most other states, a city may exercise jurisdiction in various planning-related matters over areas located outside its boundaries (G.S. 160A-360). Extraterritorial jurisdiction is justified on several grounds: North Carolina annexation laws encourage cities to annex nearby unincorporated urban areas. It is in a city's interest to ensure that areas that will ultimately be brought into the city are (1) developed in a manner consistent with the city's development standards and land use planning objectives, and (2) served by appropriate public facilities. Otherwise, unplanned growth and substandard development may thwart municipal annexation. In addition, even when a city has no annexation ambitions, unplanned growth and substandard development may have detrimental effects on nearby city areas.

In general, a city of any size may establish planning jurisdiction for one mile outside its boundaries. However, North Carolina law does not permit cities to exercise such extraterritorial jurisdiction unilaterally unless there is evidence that the county has not taken the initiative in land use planning. Specifically a city may assume authority outside its limits on its own only if the county is not already enforcing three major types of development regulations in the target area: (1) zoning; (2) subdivision regulations; and (3) the State Building Code [G.S. 160A-360(e)].

Where local governments work cooperatively, other jurisdictional arrangements are also possible. With the board of county commissioners' approval, a city with a population of 10,000 to 25,000 may extend its jurisdiction up to two miles outside city limits, and a city with a population of over 25,000, up to three miles [G.S. 160A-360(a)]. Alternatively, at the city council's request, the county may exercise any of the various land use regulatory powers within the city's extraterritorial jurisdiction or even within the city limits [G.S. 160A-360(d)]. Under a third arrangement a city may not exercise extraterritorial jurisdiction unilaterally, but it and the county may agree on the area in which each will exercise the various powers [G.S. 160A-360(e)].

The land use planning-related powers that may be exercised outside municipal boundaries include (1) zoning, (2) subdivision regulation, (3) enforcement of the State Building Code, (4) minimum housing code regulation, (5) historic district regulation, (6) historic properties designation and regulation, (7) community development projects, (8) jurisdiction of the community appearance commission, (9) acquisition of open space, (10) floodway regulation, and (11) soil erosion and sedimentation control regulation. No city may exercise in its extraterritorial area any power that it does not exercise within its city limits. Also, the boundaries of a city's extraterritorial jurisdiction are the same for all powers.

If a city intends to enforce zoning or subdivision regulations in its extraterritorial area, it must provide some means by which residents of the extraterritorial area may influence the decision making of both the planning agency and the zoning board of adjustment (G.S. 160A-362). A city is directed to ask the county commissioners to appoint some outside members to both the planning agency and the zoning board of adjustment. The number of such appointees and their voting power are determined by the city. If the board of county commissioners does not make these appointments within ninety days after it receives the request, the city council may make them instead.

Zoning

Of all the programs, tools, and techniques associated with land use planning, zoning is perhaps the best known. It may be used to achieve a variety of purposes. First, it can ensure that the community's land uses are properly situated in relation to one another so that one use does not become a nuisance for its neighbors. Second, zoning can ensure that adequate land and space are available for various types of development. Third, it can ensure that the location and the density of development are consistent with government's ability to provide the area with streets, utilities, fire protection, and recreation services. Finally, it can set minimum design standards so that new development reflects aesthetic values, is of appropriate scale, and helps protect privacy.

Zoning involves the exercise of the state's police power to regulate private property in order to promote the public health, the public safety, and the general welfare. It may legitimately be used to protect property values. Zoning can foster economic development and expansion. However, it can also have the effect of restricting competition among commercial activities because the land available for certain uses may be limited. Promotion of the general welfare is a sufficiently elastic purpose to allow the adoption of standards that are justified solely in terms of aesthetics. Because zoning is concerned with the use of property and not its ownership, the identity of owners is generally irrelevant. Permits, approvals, and requirements of zoning "run with the land" and apply to future owners as well as present ones. Similarly, zoning distinctions based on whether property is owner or renter occupied are unenforceable. Zoning may legitimately be used to protect property values, but requirements that new development meet minimum-floor-area standards or cost a certain amount are beyond the scope of zoning and are legally indefensible. A North Carolina city's obligation to accommodate low- and moderate-income housing through its zoning ordinance remains unclear; nonetheless, zoning may not be used as a tool to discriminate on the basis of race or national origin.

Although zoning is primarily a tool for influencing the use of private property, in North Carolina it is also applicable to the construction and the use of buildings by the state and its political subdivisions (G.S. 160A-392). Zoning is prospective in nature: only land uses begun after the ordinance's effective date must comply with all the regulations. However, existing buildings and lots with characteristics that do not comply with the regulations are said to be *nonconforming* (see the discussion under the heading Nonconformities and Amortization, later in this chapter), and a special section of the ordinance deals with nonconformities.

The characteristic of zoning that distinguishes it from most other types of land use regulations is that zoning regulations are different from district to district rather than uniform throughout a city. This feature permits the tailoring of zoning to address development problems, but also means that local governing bodies may be tempted to abuse the power by giving arbitrary and discriminatory treatment to certain property owners.

Basic Elements

A *zoning ordinance* consists of a text and a map or series of maps. The text includes the substantive standards applicable to each district on the map and the procedures that govern proposals for changes in both the text and the map. The zoning ordinance divides the land within a city's jurisdiction into a number of zoning districts. The land in each district is governed by several types of regulations: (1) use regulations; (2) dimensional requirements, including setback and density standards; and (3) other, miscellaneous requirements dealing with off-street parking, landscaping and screening, property access, required public improvements, and signs.

Uses Permitted by Right

If a use is permitted by right, the zoning standards for that use are typically spelled out in specific terms, and the zoning enforcement official grants the applicant routine permission to proceed. In some cases an applicant for a zoning permit must hire a design professional (e.g., an engineer, a landscape architect, or an architect) to prepare a site plan for a use authorized by right. Such a site plan may have to be reviewed by various municipal departments, outside agencies, or a technical review committee made up of representatives of those departments or agencies. In some cities the city council or the planning board approves such a site plan. As a general rule, however, such a site plan must be approved as submitted if it meets municipal standards.

Uses Permitted by Conditional Use Permits

Many jurisdictions contain a variety of uses that merit closer scrutiny because of their scale and effect or their potential for creating a nuisance. These conditional uses may be permissible in a particular district but only at particular locations and then only under particular conditions. *Conditional use permits* (also known as *special use permits* or *special exceptions*) may be issued by the council, the zoning board of adjustment, or the planning agency. Regardless of which body issues the permit, the decision to grant or to deny it must be based on evidence supplied at a quasi-judicial hearing. The zoning ordinance must explicitly list the requirements that the applicant must meet and the findings that the issuing body must make in order for the permit to be issued. If these requirements are met, the board may not refuse to issue the permit. However, it may impose additional conditions and requirements on the permit that are not specifically mentioned in the ordinance. Such conditions may include specifications on the particular use to be made of the property;

sign, parking, or landscaping requirements; requirements that the property owner dedicate land for and construct certain public improvements like streets, utilities, and parks; and specifications dealing with the timing of development. Conditional use permits may be used to deal with small-scale land uses like electric substations and day-care centers or with large-scale developments like shopping centers and group housing developments. Permission to develop or use land in accordance with a conditional use permit runs with the land and applies with equal force to future owners of the property.

Types of Zoning Districts

Most zoning ordinances include three basic types of zoning districts—residential, commercial, and industrial—and a variety of more specialized types of zones—office and institutional, flood hazard, mobile home park, agricultural, and perhaps planned unit development. There may be a number of residential districts, each based on different permissible dwelling types and required lot sizes (or densities).

Zoning districts may also be classified as *general use districts* or *conditional use districts* (also known as *special use districts*). All zoning ordinances include at least some general use districts. Various uses or activities are permitted to locate and operate in a general use district either (1) by right or (2) subject to a *conditional use permit* (sometimes called a *special use permit* or a *special exception*). Generally, any use not specifically listed as permitted is, by implication, prohibited.

The zoning ordinances of some North Carolina cities provide not only for general use districts, but for conditional use districts. Any use of land in a conditional use district is subject to a conditional use permit; there are no uses permitted by right. Thus all development in a conditional use district is subject to discretionary review. In cities that rely on conditional use districts, it is customary for the city council to grant the conditional use permit. This way the council can consider the application for a conditional use permit at the same time that it considers a petition for the rezoning of land to the conditional use district that authorizes such a permit (see also the discussion under the heading Conditional Use Districts, later in this chapter).

Governmental Roles in Zoning

In most cities, zoning involves the city council, a planning board, the zoning board of adjustment, and planning and zoning staff. Collectively these groups carry out the legislative, quasi-judicial, advisory, and administrative functions of a local zoning program. The legislative and quasi-judicial roles of citizen boards in local zoning are a source of some confusion.

Legislative Role

The city council acts in its legislative role when it adopts or amends the zoning ordinance. When it makes the law, such a board has substantial discretion to make decisions as it sees fit. Although a city council must hold a public hearing before it adopts or amends the ordinance, it need not explain its decision or make written findings of fact. The hearing required for legislative action is relatively free of formality. Speakers need not make sworn statements or restrict their statements to topics set forth in the ordinance. City council members may be subject to lobbying efforts before or after the hearing.

Quasi-Judicial Role

Public hearings are also required when three other important types of zoning actions are taken: (1) issuance of variances; (2) issuance of conditional use permits; (3) and appeal of decisions of a zoning official. However, each of these types of cases must be heard in a quasi-judicial proceeding. The decision must be based on the criteria in the ordinance, witnesses must be sworn and offer testimony according to certain rules of evidence, board members may not discuss the case with any of the parties outside the hearing, and the board must make written findings of fact. Thus quasi-judicial hearings (sometimes known as evidentiary hearings) are more formal than legislative hearings and more demanding on those who participate in them. The kinds of cases just identified are generally heard by the zoning board of adjustment. However, if the planning board is assigned the job of hearing any of them or if the city council grants conditional use permits itself, then these boards must also follow quasi-judicial procedures when they hear such cases.

Variances

Because no zoning ordinance can anticipate every land use or development situation that will arise, a zoning ordinance must include a procedure for varying or waiving the requirements of the ordinance when practical difficulties or unnecessary hardships would result from strict enforcement of it. The permission granted by this procedure is known as a *variance.* In most North Carolina cities, granting a variance is the responsibility of the zoning board of adjustment.

Even though zoning regulations may be burdensome on individual property owners, the board of adjustment's authority to grant variances is limited under the law. The board of adjustment lacks the wide legislative discretion that the council has. Often matters that come before it could be handled better by the planning board and the council as proposals to amend the zoning ordinance. To issue a variance, the board must conclude that all of the following are true:

1. If the property owner complies with the provisions of the ordinance, he or she will be unable to enjoy a reasonable return from the property or to make a reasonable use of it.
2. The hardship affecting the property results from the application of the ordinance (not from market conditions or the existence of private restrictive covenants).
3. The hardship is suffered by the applicant's property. (The applicant's personal, social, or economic circumstances are irrelevant.)
4. The hardship does not result from the applicant's own actions.
5. The hardship is peculiar to the applicant's property and does not affect other properties in the same neighborhood. (If a number of properties suffer the same problem, the council should consider amending the zoning ordinance.)
6. The variance is in harmony with the general purpose and intent of the zoning ordinance and preserves its spirit. *Use variances,* which purport to authorize uses of land not otherwise authorized in the district, have been held by North Carolina courts not to be in harmony with the purpose and

the intent of a zoning ordinance and not to preserve its spirit.
7. By granting the variance, the board will ensure the public safety and welfare and do substantial justice.

Nonconformities and Amortization

When land is zoned or rezoned, certain legally existing uses and structures may not conform to the new set of zoning regulations that apply. These nonconformities may take a variety of forms: nonconforming uses, nonconforming buildings (as to height, setback, etc.), and nonconforming lots (as to width, frontage, or area). In addition, a property may be nonconforming with respect to its provisions for off-street parking, its landscaping and buffering features, or the position or the size of advertising signs on it.

It is widely assumed that the policy of zoning is to discourage the perpetuation of nonconformities. However, a close look at many ordinances reveals that most communities take a rather passive approach to elimination of nonconformities. Most ordinance provisions are designed to allow nonconforming uses or structures to continue. There are, of course, restrictions on their expansion or extension. Nonconforming structures may generally not be structurally altered or replaced. Nonconforming uses may generally not be converted to other nonconforming uses, and uses once abandoned may not reopened. Nonetheless, nonconformities have proved to be very resistant to attempts to get rid of them.

A quite different method of treating nonconforming situations involves the concept of *amortization*. Amortization is based on the assumption that the owner of a nonconforming property may be required to come into full compliance with new development standards if the ordinance provides a time period within which the owner may recover the investment made in relying on the former rules. In some cases, amortization may require the removal of a nonconforming use or structure; in other cases it may require the upgrading of a nonconforming use or structure. Amortization provisions are most often applied to nonconforming signs and certain outdoor uses of land (like junkyards) that can be moved to other locations and do not involve entrepreneurial investments of great magnitude. These regulations have been upheld both in principle and in application by the North Carolina courts, overcoming challenges that they violate the landowner's due process rights or that they amount to an unconstitutional taking of private property without just compensation.[2]

Vested Rights

Generally speaking, a project that fails to comply with new ordinance standards may be accorded nonconforming status only if it exists when the new standards become effective. A major issue in zoning law involves how new standards affect construction projects that are begun but not yet completed. If the project is largely a figment of the property owner's imagination, then the project when built will be required to comply with the new standards. If the law allows the owner to complete the project without complying with the new requirements (the project thus becomes nonconforming), the owner has established a *vested right*.[3]

Under North Carolina zoning law there are four ways for a property owner to qualify for protection. The first method is to establish a *common law vested right*. A common law vested right is established if an owner has made substantial good faith expenditures to carry out a project in good faith reliance on a valid project approval. Actual on-site construction is not required. Expenditures of money and binding contracts to purchase land, construction materials, inventory, and equipment qualify. So do expenditures of time, labor, and energy. However, proceeding in good faith requires that the sponsor not work at an extraordinary pace to beat a potential rezoning. In addition, the expenditures must be made in reliance on a valid project approval. A valid zoning or building permit will normally suffice.

The second method was established in 1985 by the General Assembly to provide an alternative form of protection to the property owner that was far easier to apply than the common law vested rights doctrine. G.S. 160A-385(b) simply provides that no zoning ordinance amendment may be applied to property without the owner's consent if a valid building permit for the property has been issued and remains outstanding. This statute does not apply, however, when the adoption of an initial zoning ordinance is involved.

The third method was established in 1990 to allow property owners to establish a vested right still earlier in the development process.

The General Assembly directed local governments to provide for a vested right when a property owner obtained approval of a *site-specific development plan*, a plan for a particular use of land as proposed for a particular site, or a *phased development plan*, a general plan for a large-scale project staged over a long period. G.S. 160A-385.1 provides that approval of a site-specific development plan establishes a vested right for between two and five years, as determined by the city. Approval of such a plan protects against zoning amendments affecting the type and the intensity of use of the property, with certain exceptions. The law also authorizes but does not compel a city to provide for the approval of a phased development plan establishing a vested right for up to five years. However, this statute also does not offer protection from adoption of an initial zoning ordinance.

Finally, a zoning ordinance may, without reference to the specific statutes just described, define the extent to which it applies prospectively. For example, an ordinance provision may provide that projects for which development applications are received or lots recorded before the effective date of newly adopted amendments need not meet their terms.

Special Treatment of Certain Activities

Zoning applies to virtually all uses of property. However, the treatment of certain activities under zoning is especially noteworthy because special state legislation affects the extent to which zoning requirements apply.

Manufactured Housing

Manufactured home is the term used in state and federal law for what used to be called a *mobile home*. These units must be built to special construction standards adopted by the United States Department of Housing and Urban Development. The zoning of manufactured homes is subject to legislation adopted by the General Assembly in 1987 that was designed both to counter the exclusionary tendencies of many local zoning ordinances and to clarify that some special treatment of such units was permitted. G.S. 160-383.1 prohibits a city from adopting zoning regulations that have the effect of excluding manufactured homes from the entire zoning jurisdiction. However, it expressly authorizes cities to adopt special requirements affecting the appearance and the dimensions of manufactured homes that need not also apply to site-built homes. (The law recognizes prior case law holding that a city need not allow manufactured homes in every district in which it allows site-built residences.)

This legislation does not affect *modular homes*. Modular homes are built in a factory, but meet the construction standards of the State Building Code. For zoning purposes they are typically treated in the same manner as site-built residences.

Establishments Selling Alcohol

The sale and the consumption of alcohol are activities beyond the reach of zoning. The sale, the consumption, and the transportation of alcohol are subject to a uniform system of state regulation administered by the North Carolina Alcoholic Beverage Control (ABC) Commission, which controls the issuance of permits for such activities and preempts local zoning. State law provides that the ABC Commission "shall consider" local zoning requirements in determining whether a permit should be issued for an establishment at a particular location. However, it is clear that a city may not use zoning requirements to prohibit the sale or the consumption of alcohol at a particular establishment if the ABC Commission has issued a permit for that activity.

Historic Districts and Landmarks

In its zoning text and on its zoning map, a city may establish a historic district. Before doing so, it must establish a historic preservation commission and undertake an investigation and a report describing the buildings, the sites, and the features that give the proposed district historical, prehistoric, or architectural significance. Once a district is established, no exterior portion of a building or a structure may be erected, altered, relocated, or demolished unless the historic preservation commission issues a certificate of appropriateness for the change, based on the design guidelines and the ordinance criteria adopted for the district. One special power granted to the commission allows it to delay the granting of a certificate of appropriateness for the demolition of a building in a historic district for up to one year after the approval date. During this period the commission and those interested in historic preservation may try to negotiate with the owner to save the building.

The historic preservation commission may also regulate the alteration and the demolition of individual buildings or sites designated as historic landmarks. Landmarks may, but need not necessarily, be located within a historic district. Their demolition or relocation may be delayed for up to one year as well.

Signs and Billboards

The erection and the display of signs and billboards (outdoor advertising displays) have long been subject to municipal zoning. Certain commercial off-premise signs located along particular major federal highways are also subject to requirements imposed by the North Carolina Outdoor Advertising Control Act, which is administered by the North Carolina Department of Transportation. In areas where both sets of regulations apply, it is generally true that municipal sign standards for newly erected signs are much more restrictive and demanding than those adopted by the state, and take precedence.

The Outdoor Advertising Control Act does, however, limit the ability of a city to require the removal of existing nonconforming signs along these highways. It provides that if the Department of Transportation has issued a permit for a sign along the corridors of these federal highways and if local ordinance provisions have made the sign nonconforming, the local government may not require the removal of the sign unless it provides "just compensation" (G.S. 136-131.1). As a result, local sign amortization regulations that require owners of signs to comply with new regulations within a certain number of years but fail to provide monetary compensation for doing so, may not be applied to nonconforming signs located along certain federal highways. Amortization requirements may, however, be applied to signs located elsewhere within a city's zoning jurisdiction.

Watershed Protection

North Carolina's watershed protection legislation, initially adopted in 1989, has important implications for cities whose planning and zoning jurisdiction includes land within the watershed of a public drinking-water supply. This program is designed to protect water supplies from the impurities in the runoff from land within a watershed (non-point sources of pollution). The North Carolina Environmental Management Commission has classified over 200 such watersheds into five water supply categories: WS-I, WS-II, WS-III, WS-IV, and WS-V (see chapter 18 for an explanation of these categories). It has also established statewide minimum watershed protection requirements that apply to the use and the development of land in both the *critical area* of such watersheds and the remainder of the watershed. State law requires affected local governments to incorporate the appropriate land development standards into local zoning, land subdivision, and special-purpose watershed protection ordinances. Perhaps the two primary standards established by state law are the *minimum lot size* for single-family residential lots and the *built-upon-area ratios* for multifamily and nonresidential development. For example, the minimum residential lot size in the critical area of a WS-III watershed is one acre. In such a watershed the portion of the lot that is built upon (i.e., the area with impervious surface) may not exceed 36 percent of the total lot area. The regulations also allow a city to choose a *high-density option*, which permits a property owner to develop a lot more intensively if certain measures are taken to control stormwater.

Amendment of the Zoning Ordinance

Zoning Amendment Process

Unlike many municipal ordinances, a local zoning ordinance may be amended fairly often. Most zoning ordinance amendments are map amendments that change the zoning district classification of particular properties and are known as *rezonings*. However, important alterations may also be made in the ordinance text.

When a city council amends the zoning ordinance, it acts in its legislative capacity. Proposals to amend the zoning ordinance may typically be submitted by anyone—a planning board member, a city council member, a local government agency or commission, or a person in the community whether he or she is a property owner or not. Although state law does not require it, virtually all municipal zoning ordinances stipulate that before the city council may consider a proposed amendment, the planning board must have an opportunity to make recommendations on it. In some communities a zoning amendment petition is received by the planning staff to ensure that the petition is complete before the council decides whether to set a date for a public hearing to consider the proposal. In other communities the council refers the petition to the planning board and holds a public hearing on virtually every such petition submitted to it in good faith. State law requires the council to hold a public hearing before it adopts any zoning ordinance amendment. Notice of this hearing must be published several times in a local newspaper, and in some rezoning cases, notice of the hearing must be sent by first-class mail to the owners of the land to be rezoned and the owners of abutting land.

Substantive Limitations on Zoning Map Amendments

Rezoning is easily one of the most controversial aspects of zoning. Rezoning procedures do not always conform to the expectations that property owners and neighbors have about how zoning should work. Part of the problem is that property owners, neighbors, and local government board members are interested in discussing the nature of the particular use that will be made of land proposed for rezoning. However, most conventional zoning districts provide for a range of permissible uses. North Carolina zoning case law has made it rather difficult for those who participate in rezoning hearings to focus on the specific plans of the petitioner or to have any assurance about the specific way in which the property will be used if the land is rezoned. These difficulties arise from three legal principles established by North Carolina state courts:

1. To be rezoned to a general use district, land must meet the *general suitability* criterion, which requires that the property be suitable for any use permitted in that district. Any rezoning to a general use district that cannot be justified in terms of all the possible uses permitted in the new district is arbitrary and capricious and may be invalidated. Just how demanding this principle can be is illustrated when a petitioner suggests to the governing board that if the land is rezoned, it will be developed in a particular way. A series of North Carolina court rulings demonstrate that a petitioning developer does so at its peril.[4]
2. Ad hoc conditions may not be attached to a zoning amendment. In other words, *conditional zoning* is unenforceable, at least in the context of a rezoning to a general use district. When rezoning a particular property, many city councils

have been tempted to include in the amending ordinance, conditions on the manner of development that apply to the petitioner's land but do not apply to other lands zoned the same way. In doing so, however, councils run afoul of the zoning statute (G.S. 160A-382) that requires regulations to be uniform with respect to all properties within a particular kind of district. Under North Carolina case law, special requirements not spelled out in the ordinance that are added as conditions to a rezoning are invalid and hence unenforceable.[5] The rezoning itself is not necessarily invalid, but the city does not gain the control that it expected over the land of the petitioning property owner.

3.   A local government may not engage in *contract zoning*. Contract zoning involves a transaction in which both the landowner who seeks a rezoning and the governing board itself undertake reciprocal obligations in the form of a bilateral contract.[6] For example, a landowner might agree to subject his property to deed restrictions or make certain road improvements to enhance access to the land if the city council would agree to rezone the land when the landowner took these steps. Contract zoning of this type is illegal because by agreeing to exercise its legislative power in a particular way at a future date, a city abandons its duty to exercise independent judgment in making future legislative zoning decisions.[7]

Special Rezoning Methods and Issues

Conditional Use Districts

The relatively conservative legal doctrines just outlined have encouraged North Carolina cities to find more flexible ways of rezoning land. One such technique combines the discretion offered by the rezoning process with the condition-adding power of the conditional use permit. *Conditional use districts* were first expressly authorized by legislation in 1985 (codified primarily at G.S. 160A-382 and G.S. 153A-342), but several cities and counties were using the technique in the early 1970s.[8] In ordinances that provide for conditional use districts, it is common for each such district to correspond to or "parallel" a conventional general use district. For example, an ordinance that provides for a highway business district (a general use district) may also authorize a conditional use-highway business district. The list of uses that may be approved for a conditional use district typically corresponds to the list of uses allowed in the particular general use district that serves as its parallel. In sharp contrast to a general use district, however, a conditional use district allows no uses by right. Instead, every use allowed in it requires a conditional use permit granted by the governing board. Because of this feature, the statutes prohibit the rezoning of land to a conditional use district unless all the owners of land to be rezoned consent to the proposal. The key feature of the conditional use district as a zoning technique is that the petition for the rezoning to such a district and the application for the conditional use permit required for any development in such a district are generally considered together. The public hearing for the rezoning and the public hearing for the conditional use permit are consolidated.[9] Some cities amend the zoning map and grant the permit with the same vote. Most important, the petitioner or the applicant is encouraged to submit a development plan that indicates the proposed use of the land. If the city council is not pleased with the development proposal, it may choose not to rezone the property. If it is generally pleased with the proposal, it may restrict the use of the land (generally to that proposed by the developer) or mitigate the expected adverse impacts of the development by adding conditions to the conditional use permit, which is granted contemporaneously with the rezoning.

Protest Provisions

North Carolina statutes provide a peculiar but important procedure that allows neighboring property owners to protest rezoning proposals that affect nearby land: a zoning ordinance amendment requires a super-majority vote (three-fourths of all city council members) if enough affected property owners formally protest the proposed rezoning (G.S. 160A-385). The three-fourths vote is required if a protest petition is submitted by the owners of at least 20 percent of the property on one of the sides, on the rear, or across the street from the front of the property. Although the protest procedure is not expressly limited to amendments to the zoning map, it appears to make sense only in this context.

Spot Zoning

Another legal doctrine that limits a city council's discretion in rezoning property involves *spot zoning.* The North Carolina Supreme Court defines spot zoning as

> [a] zoning ordinance or amendment which singles out and reclassifies a relatively small tract owned by a single person and surrounded by a much larger area uniformly zoned, so as to impose upon the small tract greater restrictions than those imposed upon the larger area, or so as to relieve the small tract from restrictions to which the rest of the area is subjected . . . .[10]

Zoning decisions that result in this spot zoning pattern are not necessarily invalid and illegal, however, unless there is no reasonable basis for treating the singled-out property differently from adjacent land. Whether there is good reason for the distinction depends, for example, on (1) the size of the tract; (2) the compatibility of the disputed zoning action with an existing comprehensive zoning plan; (3) the benefits and the detriments of the rezoning for the petitioning property owner, the neighbors, and the surrounding community; and (4) the relationship between the uses envisioned under the new zoning and the uses of adjacent land.[11] Whether a specific instance of spot zoning is illegal depends to a substantial degree on the particular facts and circumstances of the case. In any case the evolving doctrine of spot zoning is consistent with the notion that any rezoning that smacks of favoritism or lacks proper justification risks invalidation.

Confiscatory Zoning

Because zoning is a potent form of land use regulation, zoning requirements may have a drastic impact on a particular property. The constitutional doctrine that comes into play most frequently in this context is the provision of the Fifth Amendment to the United States Constitution that prohibits the *taking* of private property for public use without the payment of just compensation. It has long been true that a law restricting the use of property can have such a confiscatory effect as to constitute a *regulatory taking.* However, it was 1987 before the United States Supreme Court clarified that if a property owner proves such a taking, the remedy is not merely the invalidation of the regulation; the offending government may be held liable in damages for losses suffered by the property owner during the period when the unconstitutional regulation was in effect.[12]

Determining whether an unconstitutional taking has occurred typically depends on a balancing of the interests of the regulating government and the interests of the property owner. Two rules of thumb are clear: (1) If a regulation prevents the use or the development of land to create a common law nuisance (e.g., if a rule prevents new residences from being built in a floodway), such a prohibition is not a taking, regardless of its effect on the value of the property. (2) In contrast, if a regulation does not prevent a nuisance but does prevent an owner from making any practical use of a property or enjoying any reasonable return from it, the restriction amounts to a taking.[13]

Exclusionary Zoning

In general, the term *exclusionary zoning* describes zoning efforts designed to prohibit certain types of land use activities within a jurisdiction. Some communities have tried to exclude completely certain less-popular land uses like junkyards, massage parlors, hazardous waste storage facilities, billboards, mobile homes, other types of low- and moderate-income housing, pawnshops, and nightclubs. Although the courts have not addressed constitutional challenges to exclusionary zoning, at least one North Carolina case suggests that housing types and land use activities that are otherwise legal and do not constitute nuisances per se cannot normally be excluded from a jurisdiction where they would otherwise locate or operate.[14]

Subdivision Regulation

The word *subdivision* usually calls to mind a relatively large residential development of single-family homes. For regulatory purposes, however, subdivision may best be thought of as a process by which a tract of land is split into smaller parcels, lots, or building sites so that the lots or the parcels may eventually be sold or developed or both.

Most subdivision ordinances are based on the premise that the division of land generally signals that the land will soon be developed and used more intensively than it was before subdivision. As a result, those who purchase the subdivided tracts or lots will make more demands for community facilities and services. The platting and the recording of a subdivision map offer a city the opportunity not only to review the design of the resulting lots but also to ensure that the subdivider provides streets, utilities, and other public improvements that will be required to serve the needs of those who purchase the subdivided land.

Subdivision Design

The most fundamental subdivision design considerations concern the arrangement of lots and streets. Ordinance provisions commonly specify minimum lot sizes and lot widths, or require lots to front on a dedicated street for a certain distance. Standards for street design may include width specifications for rights-of-way and pavements, and maximum lengths for blocks and cul-de-sacs; these provisions ensure that emergency vehicles can easily reach any lot and that traffic is not overly concentrated at a particular intersection.

One design consideration that attracts much attention is the balance maintained between adequate access to lots and lot owners' privacy. Although developers and lot purchasers generally value cul-de-sacs for the isolation from traffic that they afford, they may be inappropriate if they make travel especially circuitous, put an excessive burden on existing through streets, or make garbage collection, emergency vehicle response, and street and lot drainage substantially more difficult.

Exactions and the Financing of Subdivision Improvements

The questions of who will finance subdivision improvements and community facilities and how they will be maintained are fundamental to subdivision regulation. Most cities now expect subdividers to provide certain public improvements at their own expense. These *exactions* may take the form of requirements for (1) construction or installation of infrastructural improvements, (2) dedication of land, (3) payment of fees in lieu, or (4) payment of impact fees. Table 19-2 details the city's authority to exact various types of facilities by the different means at its disposal.

Table 19-2
Municipal Authority to Impose Exactions as a Condition of Subdivision
Plat Approval under the General Statutes

Type of Exaction	Type of Community Facility				
	Parks	Utilities	Streets	Schools	Fire Stations
Construction or installation of improvements	Yes	Yes	Yes	Probably not	Probably not
Dedication of land	Yes	Yes, for utility easements	Yes	No	No
Payment of fees in lieu	Yes	No explicit authority	Yes, for street construction	No	No
Payment of impact fees	Possibly	Probably, under public enterprise authority	Possibly	Possibly	Possibly

Forms of Exaction

Construction or Installation of Infrastructural Improvements

Virtually all city subdivision regulations require the subdivider to construct or install certain subdivision improvements. The subdivision enabling statutes (G.S. 160A-372) allow cities to require the "construction of community service facilities in accordance with municipal policies and standards . . . ." *Community service facilities* defies exact definition, but the most commonly required subdivision improvements include streets, curbs and gutters, drainage swales or storm sewers, sidewalks, and water and/or sewer lines.

Subdivision development sometimes provides an excellent opportunity to arrange for streets, utility lines, or stormwater drainage improvements that are designed not only for a particular subdivision but also for future development. If a sewer line must be extended from the end of a sewerage network to a tract being subdivided, the owners of land along the line may wish to connect to it at some future time. A 6-inch water line might adequately serve the particular subdivision, yet it might be wise to lay a 12-inch main in order eventually to serve expected development on the far side of the subdivision. Several approaches are used to allocate costs. If a developer is the first to demand service in a newly developing area, the developer may be required to furnish the line. However, the city may impose acreage fees or other charges on later developers who use the facility, and pay over some of these funds to the original developer in partial reimbursement for all the extra costs that the original developer assumed. Alternatively, if a city requires a subdivider to provide capacity exceeding that necessary to serve the subdivision, the city may pay for the extra capacity from its general funds on the theory that the oversized facilities will benefit the community generally.

Dedication of Land

There are instances in which improvements are required on lands or within easements that the developer does not own or control (e.g., the extension of a water line within an existing public utility easement). More commonly, however, improvements will be made on site. If the improvements are to be available for public use or are to be connected to a public system, the city will require the *dedication* of the land so improved and will accept the dedication only after the improvement has been completed and inspected. For purposes of development approval, then, a dedication is a form of exaction involving a requirement that the developer donate to the public some interest in land for certain public uses. North Carolina law allows cities, as a condition of subdivision plat approval, to require the dedication of sites and easements for streets, utilities, and recreation areas.

Compulsory dedication is based on the assumption that it is often desirable for a public agency to own, control, and maintain the improvements, the facilities, and the open space in a new subdivision. In many instances, however, such government responsibility for control and maintenance is neither possible nor practical. Cities must give careful thought to whether common facilities are made public or are allowed (or required) to remain private.

Payment of Fees in Lieu

An alternative to compulsory dedication and improvement is to require or allow a subdivider to pay a fee that represents the value of the site or the improvement that would otherwise have been dedicated or provided. *Fees in lieu* can be an attractive option when the developer's contribution must be prorated if the exaction is to be fair and legal. G.S. 160A-372 allows a city to provide for fees in lieu of the dedication of recreation areas and for fees in lieu of the construction of road improvements. Because of the administrative burdens in accounting for these funds, relatively few North Carolina cities use this exaction technique.

Payment of Impact Fees

In contrast to the forms of exactions just listed, the use of *impact fees* by North Carolina cities is not expressly authorized by general statute. Several dozen cities are subject to local acts authorizing the use of impact fees, which are also known as *facility fees* or *project fees*. In addition, there is evidence that express enabling legislation authorizing impact fees may not always be needed.[15]

Impact fees are similar to fees in lieu, but generally are established as part of a comprehensive attempt to allocate the costs of a wide range of community facilities to new development. Impact fees can be applied to multifamily residential, commercial, and even office and industrial development; they are rarely restricted in application only to new subdivisions. They are generally collected when building permits are issued, usually just before the development creating the need for new services actually begins, rather than at the time of plat approval.

The validity of a system of impact fees depends on the system's analytical basis. The steps that follow highlight the elements of a plan for the application of impact fees:

1. An estimate is made of the cost of acquiring land for and constructing each new public facility that is within the local government's jurisdiction that must be provided during the planning period (e.g., twenty to twenty-five years), and that will be funded with impact fees. These estimates usually extend far beyond the time horizons used in a typical five- or seven-year capital improvement program.

2. The appropriate distribution of costs is determined on the basis of the costs of each facility that are attributable to, and that should be equitably borne by, both new and existing developments in each zone, service area, or planning district. Such a distribution of costs assumes that the community at large is obliged to provide public facilities such as roads and drainage improvements to serve existing residents at appropriate service standards. These costs are then allocated among the various development sectors—residential, commercial, and industrial.

3. A series of formulas or factors is used to allocate the appropriate portion of costs to each development project. For example, in the case of street improvements, the impact fee may be based on the number of trips generated by the land uses in the proposed development.

4. Once collected, these fees must be placed into trust funds or capital improvement funds, where they are earmarked by both type of facility and zone, service area, or planning district to be served.

5. When the funds reach appropriate levels, they are expended on the facilities for which they were collected so that residents of the new development actually benefit from the facilities. The fees may have to be refunded if they are not spent and facilities are not constructed within a reasonable time.

Exactions and the Constitution

An important dimension of exactions is their constitutional implications. Unless exactions are flexibly applied, they amount to an unconstitutional taking of private property for public use without just compensation. Exactions must be properly and fairly related to the need for the new public facilities generated by a new development.

The United States Supreme Court recently issued a major decision on exactions, one with which North Carolina case law seems to be consistent. In *Dolan v. City of Tigard*,[16] the Court ruled that the United States Constitution requires "rough proportionality" between the impact of the development and the nature and the extent of the exaction. Although precise mathematical calculation is not required, some sort of individualized determination must be made to justify an exaction requirement as it is applied in a particular case. The Court also held that a local government bears the burden of proving that an exaction is constitutional.

Subdivision Review Process

In North Carolina, final approval of subdivision plats may be granted by (1) the city council, (2) the council on recommendation of a planning agency, or (3) a planning agency (G.S. 160A-373). Most cities also review a *preliminary* or *tentative plat.* Because the statutes do not say how a preliminary plat should be reviewed, local units have many choices in organizing the review process.

Preapplication Procedures

Some communities encourage developers first to submit a *sketch plan* or *design plan* to the planning staff or the plat approval agency. The purpose is to bring representatives of local government and the subdivider together so that the local unit can learn what the subdivider has planned and the subdivider can better understand the unit's requirements in approving the subdivision.

Review and Approval of the Preliminary Plat

Normally the next important step in the review process is submission and approval of a preliminary plat. To call a subdivision map submitted at this stage "preliminary" may be misleading because the plat will, in large measure, fix the nature, the design, and the scope of the subdividing activity to follow. Furthermore, it serves as a general blueprint for the installation of whatever improvements or community facilities the developer is to provide. One important aspect of preliminary plat review is the comments and the recommendations obtained from various city and county departments and agencies outside local government before formal action is taken on the preliminary plat.

Review and Approval of the Final Plat

Generally, the final plat is submitted for approval and reviewed by various agencies in much the same manner as the preliminary plat is. In cities where the developer may install improvements after final plat approval, the approval of construction plans may be delayed until the final plat approval stage.

In some circumstances a city may require no preliminary plat at all; only the final plat is reviewed. Many cities classify subdivisions as *major* or *minor* on the basis of the number and the size of the lots involved. Major subdivisions are subject to the two-stage review process described earlier; minor subdivisions (those that do not involve the installation of public improvements and do not have a major impact on the community) are reviewed just once—at the final plat stage.

Once the final plat is approved, the plat must be recorded in the county register of deeds' office before lots may be sold. The register of deeds may not record a plat of a subdivision subject to regulation unless the chair or the head of the plat approval agency has indicated on the face of the plat that it has been approved (G.S. 160A-373).

Guaranteed Developer Performance

In general, a developer may not begin to construct subdivision improvements until the preliminary plat is approved. Once that approval is granted, the developer is obliged to arrange for certain dedications to be made and improvements to be installed or constructed before the final plat may be approved. One way to ensure that streets are properly constructed, and utilities and drainage facilities properly installed, is to withhold final plat approval until these improvements are completed, inspected, and, if appropriate, accepted by the city or another government unit. A much more common practice is to allow final plat approval if the subdivider has provided adequate assurance to the city that improvements will be completed after the final plat is approved. The subdivider may post a letter of credit or some other form of performance guarantee (e.g., a bond or securities held in escrow). Another approach is for a city to withhold the certificates of occupancy for the buildings in a subdivision until the improvements necessary to serve them are ready for use.

Other Regulatory Tools and Techniques

Thoroughfare Planning

In 1987 the General Assembly adopted a series of legislative measures designed to enhance the ability of both cities and the North Carolina Department of Transportation to acquire or protect the right-of-way for proposed new streets and highways. These measures gave cities the power (1) to establish setback requirements for structures based on proposed rather than actual rights-of-way (G.S. 160A-306); (2) to require fees in lieu of road improvements as a condition of subdivision plat approval (G.S. 160A-372); (3) to require the construction of road improvements as a condition of obtaining a municipal driveway permit (G.S. 160A-307); (4) to approve transfers of density to other portions of a development site in order to obtain the dedication of the full right-of-way for a thoroughfare (G.S. 136-66.10, -66.11); and (5) to adopt a roadway corridor official map to reserve a right-of-way for a proposed road (G.S. 136-44.50 through -44.53).

Perhaps the tool that is now being used the most is the municipal driveway permit. Cities may require an applicant for a driveway permit for a city street to provide medians, acceleration/deceleration lanes, and turning lanes if necessary to serve driveway traffic generated by a development.

Another potent but legally risky tool is the roadway corridor official map. A city may adopt an official map ordinance for a road that either is shown on the city's comprehensive street plan and included in the city's capital improvement program, or is a part of the state's Transportation Improvement Program. Once an official map is adopted and recorded, no building permit may be issued for land within the corridor, and no land within the corridor may be subdivided for up to three years after the application for development permission is submitted. A city may adopt an official map for a corridor located either inside its city limits or within its extraterritorial planning jurisdiction. A city is also authorized to acquire the right-of-way for a road shown on an official map even though it is located outside city limits.

Building Code Enforcement

The North Carolina State Building Code, adopted by the North Carolina Building Code Council, applies throughout the state. However, each city and county is responsible for arranging for enforcement of the code within its jurisdiction. The code generally applies to new construction, but it includes a fire code volume that applies to the use of existing buildings and other provisions governing the condemnation of unsafe buildings. The code also provides for the issuance of building permits and certificates of occupancy. These approvals are particularly important in the development and construction processes because they signify not only consistency of plans and work with the requirements of the State Building Code, but also compliance with other state and local regulations applicable to the work.

The North Carolina State Building Code is really a series of eleven volumes adopted at different times and for different purposes. The code applies to all types of new buildings, structures, and their systems and facilities except farm buildings outside city building code enforcement jurisdiction and several other minor classes of property. No city may modify or amend the code as it applies locally unless the Building Code Council approves the modification. However, proposed local amendments to the state Fire Prevention Code that are more stringent than the state code must be approved.

To arrange for local code enforcement services, a city may (1) create its own inspection department; (2) form a joint inspection department with another local unit; (3) hire an inspector from another unit on a part-time basis, with the approval of the other unit's governing board; (4) contract with another unit for the second unit to furnish inspection services to the first; (5) request the county of which it is a part to provide inspection services throughout the city's jurisdiction without any contract between the two; or (6) contract with a certified code enforcement official who is not a local government employee.

Since 1979 no person may enforce the State Building Code without a certificate from the North Carolina Code Officials Qualification Board. Five categories of certified inspectors have been established: building, mechanical, electrical, plumbing, and fire. Each inspector must hold a limited, probationary, or standard certificate for one of three levels of competency (G.S. 143-151.13). All inspectors must complete certain training courses to retain their certification. The

Code Officials Qualification Board may revoke an inspector's certificate for various reasons, including gross negligence.[17]

Minimum Housing Code Enforcement

A city is authorized to adopt its own minimum housing ordinance establishing the standards that any dwelling unit must meet to be fit for human habitation (G.S. 160A-441). The standards may deal with structural dilapidation and defects, disrepair, light and sanitary facilities, fire hazards, ventilation, general cleanliness, and other conditions that may render dwellings unsafe and unsanitary. Most cities try to use this authority to encourage the rehabilitation of substandard housing. If a housing inspector finds after a formal hearing that a dwelling is unfit for human habitation but can be rehabilitated, the inspector may issue an order requiring the building to be repaired, improved, or vacated and closed. If the dwelling cannot be rehabilitated, the inspector may issue an order requiring the dwelling to be removed or demolished. If the property owner fails to comply with such an order after having every reasonable opportunity to do so, the inspector may carry out the order directly. No demolition order may be executed unless the city council enacts an ordinance to that effect for each property to be demolished.

Additional Resources

Brough, Michael B., and Philip P. Green, Jr. *The Zoning Board of Adjustment in North Carolina,* 2d ed. Chapel Hill, N.C.: Institute of Government, The University of North Carolina at Chapel Hill, 1984.

Ducker, Richard D. "Administering Subdivision Ordinances." *Popular Government* 45 (Summer 1979): 20–28.

———. *Dedicating and Reserving Land to Provide Access to North Carolina Beaches.* Chapel Hill, N.C.: Institute of Government, The University of North Carolina at Chapel Hill, 1982.

———. "Federal and State Programs to Control Signs and Outdoor Advertising." *Popular Government* 52 (Spring 1987): 28–42.

———. "Land-Use Planning in Rural Areas." *Popular Government* 46 (Summer 1980): 28–34.

———. "Off-Street Parking in North Carolina Municipalities." *Popular Government* 46 (Summer 1980): 39–42.

———. *Subdivision Regulations in North Carolina: An Introduction.* Chapel Hill, N.C.: Institute of Government, The University of North Carolina at Chapel Hill, 1980.

———. "'Taking' Found for Beach Access Dedication Requirement: *Nollan v. California Coastal Commission.*" *Local Government Law Bulletin* no. 30 (August 1987).

———. "Using Impact Fees for Public Schools: The Orange County Experiment." *School Law Bulletin* 26 (Spring 1994): 1–13.

Ducker, Richard D., and George K. Cobb. "Protecting Rights-of-Way for Future Streets and Highways." *Popular Government* 58 (Fall 1992): 32–40.

Green, Philip P., Jr. *Legal Responsibilities of the Local Zoning Administrator in North Carolina*, 2d ed. Chapel Hill, N.C.: Institute of Government, The University of North Carolina at Chapel Hill, 1987.

———. *Organizing for Local Government Planning in North Carolina.* Chapel Hill, N.C.: Institute of Government, The University of North Carolina at Chapel Hill, 1989.

———. "Questions I'm Most Often Asked: What Is 'Spot Zoning'?" *Popular Government* 51 (Summer 1985): 50–53.

———. "Temporary Damages for a Regulatory 'Taking': *First English Evangelical Lutheran Church v. County of Los Angeles.*" *Local Government Law Bulletin* no. 29 (July 1987).

———. "Two Major Zoning Decisions: *Chrisman v. Guilford County* and *Hall v. City of Durham.*" *Local Government Law Bulletin* no. 34 (November 1988).

Owens, David W. "Amortization: An Old Land-Use Controversy Heats Up." *Popular Government* 57 (Fall 1991): 20–29.

———. "Bias and Conflicts of Interest in Land-Use Management Decisions." *Popular Government* 55 (Winter 1990): 29–36.

———. *Conflicts of Interest in Land-Use Management Decisions.* Chapel Hill, N.C.: Institute of Government, The University of North Carolina at Chapel Hill, 1990.

———. "Land-Use and Development Moratoria." *Popular Government* 56 (Fall 1990): 31–36.

———. *Planning Legislation in North Carolina.* Chapel Hill, N.C.: Institute of Government, The University of North Carolina at Chapel Hill, 1991.

———. *Legislative Zoning Decisions: Legal Aspects.* Chapel Hill, N.C.: Institute of Government, The University of North Carolina at Chapel Hill, 1993.

———. "Zoning Hearings: Knowing Which Rules to Apply." *Popular Government* 58 (Spring 1993): 26–35.

Notes

1. Although not required by state law, a local government may bind itself in its zoning ordinance to grant a special use permit or to rezone property only if the proposal is consistent with the unit's own land development plan. In addition, a subdivision ordinance may require that the dedication of land and the construction of improvements be consistent with the public facilities element of a comprehensive plan.

2. *See, e.g.,* State v. Joyner, 286 N.C. 366, 211 S.E.2d 320, *appeal dismissed,* 422 U.S. 1002 (1975) (validating the amortization of salvage yards and junkyards over three years); Naegele Outdoor Advertising v. City of Durham, 803 F. Supp. 1068 (M.D.N.C. 1992), *aff'd,* 19 F.3d 11 (1994) (validating the amortization of commercial off-premise signs over five-and-one-half years).

3. Technically the term *vested right* applies to a constitutionally protected property right to complete the project. However, for purposes of this discussion the term is used to apply also to the rights of property owners to complete a project based on provisions in state statutes or local ordinances that grandfather projects and that are more liberal than required by the United States Constitution.

4. Allred v. City of Raleigh, 277 N.C. 530, 178 S.E.2d 432 (1971); Blades v. City of Raleigh, 280 N.C. 531, 187 S.E.2d 35 (1972); Hall v. City of Durham, 323 N.C. 293, 372 S.E.2d 564, *reh'g denied,* 323 N.C. 629, 374 S.E.2d 586 (1988).

5. In Decker v. Coleman, 6 N.C. App. 102, 169 S.E.2d 487 (1969), the city council rezoned a property bordering a residential area to permit a shopping center, but made the rezoning subject to a proviso that the developer leave a buffer strip around the development and not cut any access road through this strip into residential neighborhoods. The regulations for the particular commercial zoning district made no mention of such requirements. When the developer ignored these conditions, affected neighbors sought compliance in court. The court held that the conditions were unenforceable because they applied only to this property and not to other land with the same zoning district designation.

6. Chrismon v. Guilford County, 322 N.C. 611, 635, 370 S.E.2d 579, 593 (1988).

7. North Carolina courts have not had the occasion to rule on the validity of such a contract. However, *Chrismon* strongly implies that such contracts are void and unenforceable. *Id.* at 635, 370 S.E.2d at 593.

8. In Chrismon v. Guilford County, 322 N.C. 611, 370 S.E.2d 579 (1988), the North Carolina Supreme Court approved the use of these districts even though the controversy in that case predated the adoption by the North Carolina General Assembly of express enabling legislation for all local governments.

9. It stands to reason that if a legislative hearing and a quasi-judicial hearing are combined, the more demanding requirements of quasi-judicial hearings have to be observed. Most, but not all, cities treat such hearings as quasi-judicial.

10. Blades v. City of Raleigh, 280 N.C. 531, 549, 187 S.E.2d 35, 45 (1972).

11. Chrismon v. Guilford County, 322 N.C. 611, 628, 370 S.E.2d 579, 589 (1988).

12. First English Evangelical Lutheran Church of Glendale v. County of Los Angeles, 482 U.S. 304 (1987).

13. Lucas v. South Carolina Coastal Council, 505 U.S.__, 120 L. Ed. 2d 798, 112 S. Ct. 2886 (1992). *See also* Finch v. City of Durham, 325 N.C. 352, 384 S.E.2d 8 (1989), *reh'g denied,* 325 N.C. 714, 388 S.E.2d 452 (1989).

14. Town of Conover v. Jolly, 277 N.C. 439, 177 S.E.2d 879 (1971) (invalidating special "trailer" ordinance prohibiting mobile homes used as permanent residences anywhere within city limits).

15. The statutes allowing North Carolina cities to finance public enterprises and to fix rates, fees, and charges for services furnished by a public enterprise (G.S. 160A-313, -314) have been held to authorize implicitly the use of impact fees to fund capital improvements to water and sewer systems [South Shell Investment v. Town of Wrightsville Beach, 703 F. Supp. 1192 (E.D.N.C. 1988), *aff'd,* 900 F.2d 255 (4th Cir. 1990)(unpublished)]. In addition, the North Carolina Supreme Court has held that municipal authority must be construed broadly and that the power of

cities to charge *user fees* to recover the costs of reviewing land development proposals may be implied from the zoning, land subdivision control, and other development control enabling statutes [Homebuilders' Ass'n of Charlotte v. City of Charlotte, 336 N.C. 337, 999 S.E.2d 999 (1994)].

16. 512 U.S. ___, 129 L. Ed. 2d 304, 114 S. Ct. 2309 (1994).

17. In a limited number of instances, the owners of new residences have been
successful in convincing the board that an inspector's certificate should be revoked
because of the inspector's failure to inspect adequately the house that they bought
and to detect and have corrected construction mistakes made by contractors.

20 Community Development

Kurt Jenne and David M. Lawrence

Contents

SINCE 1975, cities have undertaken a cornucopia of programs that have combined local, state, and federal resources to improve housing, neighborhood environments, and economic conditions. Among them have been projects that provided new water lines in Tabor City, a new fire station in Sanford, new and rehabilitated housing in Chapel Hill, a new minority-owned neighborhood shopping center in Greensboro, a community health center in Aurora, an employee-owned bakery in New Bern, a transitional shelter for homeless persons in Asheville, and the preservation of historic houses in Tarboro. Although the instruments used in these efforts are variously termed *housing*, *neighborhood improvement*, and *economic development programs*, collectively they make up a coordinated effort called *community development*.

Definition of Community Development

As used in this chapter, *community development* means allocations supported by federal, state, and local governments that seek to improve substandard housing, neighborhood environments, and employment for the benefit of the entire community. This typically includes the federal Community Development Block Grant (CDBG) program, supported by federal, and more recently state, housing subsidy programs for low- and moderate-income families; federal and state assistance for the improvement of local infrastructure; and federal and state support for public-private partnerships to improve employment and economic conditions by promoting economic development. Most of these programs have been successfully integrated with local development functions like capital improvement programs, public works activities, development regulation, building regulation, and many services to residents of the community. The federal CDBG program has formed the core of most of these coordinated efforts since its introduction in 1974, but most cities have come to believe that community development viewed in its broadest terms, with all these resources brought to bear, presents the best prospect for dramatic results.

CDBG: A Foundation for Community Development

The problem of urban slums—deteriorated housing and neigh-borhoods—has motivated city planning and development activities in the United States since the late nineteenth century. Before 1949, most slum eradication movements consisted of efforts to produce good housing under the assumption that as good housing became available, slum houses would become worthless and be torn down. By the late 1940s, however, the federal government saw that it could not produce or subsidize enough new housing to make that process work. Indeed, slums were becoming more valuable because the de-mand for housing was growing faster than the supply of available homes. The federal government also saw that part of the problem lay in *neighborhood effects*; that is, no slum owner wanted to invest in im-proving a rundown house without a guarantee that the neighboring owners would follow suit. Some way was needed to assemble groups of slum properties in order to improve or redevelop them all at once.

The federal government started its official campaign against deteriorated neighborhoods in 1949 with the urban redevelopment programs: land acquisition, slum clearance, and resale of sites to private developers. Over the next twenty years, redevelopment was expanded to include urban renewal—conservation, restoration, and rehabilitation—as an alternative to wholesale clearance (1954); open space, beautification, and historic preservation grants (1961); water, sewer, and neighborhood facilities grants (1965); and integrated physical, economic, and social development under a Model Cities program (1966). In 1968, Congress sought to make it easier for com-munities to apply this smorgasbord of categorical programs through a Neighborhood Development Program (NDP), but communities were frustrated over the complexity, the rigidity, the uncertainty, and the unfairness associated with planning and executing any combina-tion of these and other offerings from the federal government.

Congress responded with Title I of the Housing and Community Development Act of 1974. The act created a Community Develop-ment Block Grant (CDBG) program, which incorporated most of the categorical programs into one instrument with which local govern-ments could fashion programs tailored to their particular needs. To receive funds for any or all of the activities allowed by the program,[1] a community had only to prepare (1) a single plan that included an analysis of housing and neighborhood development needs; (2) a comprehensive strategy to meet those needs, with emphasis on the national objectives of (a) benefiting low- and moderate-income persons,[2] (b) eliminating slums and blight, and (c) meeting urgent community needs; and (3) a documented strategy to meet low- and moderate-income housing needs.[3]

The most significant feature of the block grant program was its dual effect on local control over federally funded community development activities. First, CDBG decentralized decision making nationally. By allowing local discretion in how funds would be spent within the bounds of the eligible activities, the block grant program turned over to the city much of the authority formerly exercised by Congress and the United States Department of Housing and Urban Development (HUD). Cities were no longer bound by separate grant programs in allocating funds among eligible activities, and administrative regulation of how they conducted these activities was greatly reduced.

Second, CDBG centralized decision making locally. By making the general-purpose unit of local government the grantee, the block grant program gave clear and final local authority to the city over how and where to spend funds. This authority formerly had been exercised by agencies that dealt directly with Washington and were immune from control by the local governing body. Many housing authorities and redevelopment authorities had operated quite independently of city councils, and this practice hindered opportunities for political, fiscal, or administrative coordination of their undertakings with related local efforts. Under CDBG these agencies were brought back into the municipal fold through the city council's clear control of the purse strings. As of 1995, ten cities had made one or both of the agencies a department of city government, with their activities directly supervised by the city manager or the mayor. Those that remain as separate authorities often compete with nonprofit corporations for the opportunity to conduct housing and related neighborhood development programs under contract from the cities, which now receive and dispense the grant funds that formerly went directly to housing and redevelopment authorities.

In addition, the requirement to pay specific attention to housing needs as part of a city's block grant proposal provides the means for the city council to improve the coordination of subsidized hous-

Table 20-1
Cities Participating in the CDBG Entitlement Program in North Carolina, 1995

Asheville	Gastonia	Kannapolis
Burlington	Goldsboro	Morganton
Chapel Hill	Greensboro	Raleigh
Charlotte	Greenville	Rocky Mount
Concord	Hickory	Salisbury
Durham	High Point	Wilmington
Fayetteville	Jacksonville	Winston-Salem

ing activities in the community. Taken seriously, the *required comprehensive housing assistance strategy* (CHAS) can guide the council's review of the quantity and the location of subsidized housing throughout the community, from public housing units proposed by housing authorities to subsidized and federally insured units proposed by general-purpose government, nonprofit quasi-public corporations, or private-sector sponsors.

HUD allocates the block grants in two categories: an Entitlement Program and a Small Cities program. The Entitlement Program allocates funds by formula[4] directly from HUD to central cities of metropolitan statistical areas (MSAs), cities with populations over 50,000 outside MSAs, and urban counties with populations over 200,000 net of all entitlement cities within them. The purpose of the entitlement is to ensure that the large urban jurisdictions that historically depended heavily on the federal programs displaced by CDBG would continue to receive a significant level of support for community development activities. Just under 70 percent of HUD's CDBG funds each year are allocated to entitlement jurisdictions, including twenty-one cities (and two counties) in North Carolina in 1995 (see table 20-1).[5]

Most of the remaining 30 percent of funds is allocated among states by formula, to be awarded in competitive Small Cities programs designed by each state around HUD guidelines.[6] In 1995, more than ninety cities and counties undertook projects under the Small Cities program to improve housing, infrastructure, and economic opportunities in local communities around the state.

North Carolina cities' legal authority to conduct community development programs comes not from the federal government, but from the North Carolina General Statutes, even when all the funds come from the federal government. The General Assembly has historically provided legislation necessary for the state's cities to engage in federally funded activities. After the National Industrial Recovery Act was adopted in 1933, the General Assembly passed the Housing Authorities Law (1935) to enable communities to take advantage of federal grants for public housing. This law, as amended, appears as G.S. Chapter 157. In 1951, responding to the broader purposes of the Housing Act of 1949, the General Assembly passed the Urban Redevelopment Law, which, as amended, appears as G.S. Chapter 160A, Article 22. Finally, in response to the Housing and Community Development Act of 1974, the General Assembly passed and later amended G.S. 160A-456 (1975) and G.S. 160A-457 (1977) to permit cities to engage in activities authorized by the federal act, subject to the provisions of other state laws.[7]

Because these statutes were enacted at different times in response to different programs under the rubric of housing and community development, a city's authority to undertake various activities as part of a broadly defined community development effort is not laid out neatly in one place. However, there is considerable authority for cities to undertake a wide variety of community development programs in the major categories of housing, neighborhood development, and economic development.

Housing

The CDBG program's general purpose is the same as that of its predecessors: to eliminate or prevent slums, blight, and deterioration in the community. As with the earlier renewal and redevelopment programs, housing is often regarded as the most direct way to achieve the general objectives of community development. Housing activities now include the provision of low-rent public housing, rehabilitation of owner- and renter-occupied housing, urban homesteading, and new construction. Some of these activities may also be accompanied by the demolition of substandard housing that is beyond repair and the temporary or permanent relocation of residents during the process.

Public Housing

The construction and the operation of subsidized public housing is authorized by G.S. Chapter 157, the housing authorities law. As already noted, this is the earliest form of involvement in housing by cities in North Carolina, dating back to 1935. For a long time it was cities' only involvement in trying to provide standard shelter for low-income families in the community. The housing authorities law remains a significant source of authority for cities to assist both very low income persons through traditional public housing and, more recently, low- and moderate-income families through a variety of subsidy programs for rental and purchase.

G.S. 157-9 authorizes local governments to "prepare, carry out, and operate housing projects." Initially this authorization was for the use of federal funds; however, in 1987 the General Assembly authorized cities to use property tax revenues, without need of voter approval, to support any of the housing programs defined in G.S. 157-3. The definition of *housing project* set out in G.S. 157-3(12) is sufficiently broad to permit a wide variety of activities under a public housing program:

1. Demolition or repair of existing unsanitary or unsafe housing
2. Direct construction, ownership, and operation of housing for low- and moderate-income persons
3. Rent subsidies to low-income persons[8]
4. Financial assistance, including grants, loans, interest supplements, and other means, to low- and moderate-income persons[9] to own or rehabilitate their homes
5. Financial assistance, in the same manner, to public or private developers of housing for low- and moderate-income persons

Until recently the housing authorities law was used primarily to build, operate, and maintain multifamily rental housing for low-income persons who were trying to get a foothold on the first rung of the economic ladder and only secondarily, if at all, to assist the moderate-income "housing poor" or to remedy physical deterioration in cities. Public housing has traditionally been regarded as transitional housing, although its actual performance has increasingly failed to live up to this expectation. Nevertheless, cities that recognize the linkage between individual and family poverty on the one hand and the perpetuation of physically deteriorated housing and neighborhoods on the other, continue to regard public housing as an integral part of potential community development strategies.

In addition, as housing prices have climbed beyond the reach of moderate-income families, some cities have exercised the last two authorities just listed to facilitate the purchase of existing or new homes, both through programs operated by the city itself and through development and mortgage subsidy programs run by private developers, nonprofit organizations, and lending institutions.

Housing Rehabilitation

Authorization for cities to rehabilitate deteriorated housing, found in the housing authorities law as described earlier, is also allowed under redevelopment law (G.S. 160A-512) and under the newer community development law (G.S. 160A-456, -457). The city can directly rehabilitate by doing the work for the owner using outside contractors or its own work crews; by itself acquiring, repairing, and disposing of the property; or by giving a grant, a loan, or a loan subsidy to the property owner. It can also do any of these things through a contract with the housing authority, the redevelopment authority, or a responsible private nonprofit organization. Since 1987, G.S. 160A-457.2 also permits cities to establish urban homesteading programs whereby they may acquire and convey residential property of "little or no value" on condition that the recipient rehabilitate it and live in it for a certain period.

Both owner- and renter-occupied houses can be rehabilitated if the principal beneficiaries are low- and moderate-income persons. A city will sometimes limit its program to owner-occupied houses if the council believes that an apparent subsidy to landlords would be politically unacceptable. In such a case a city can enforce minimum housing code standards under which it can compel the repair of rental houses that do not meet such standards (G.S. 160A-411, G.S. Ch. 160A, Art. 19, Pt. 6). One problem associated with this strategy is that the intended beneficiary, the low-income tenant, can lose. The owner, forced to make improvements, may seek to protect his or her investment and to maintain an adequate return by demanding more rent from the tenant or by seeking another tenant for the upgraded house. In either case the low-income renter might be forced to look for other housing that, unless he or she has rental assistance, will be as substandard as the rehabilitated unit formerly was.

If a city provides rehabilitation grants, loans, or subsidies to landlords, landlords have an incentive to agree to rent-containment and occupancy requirements ensuring that low- and moderate-income tenants benefit from the rehabilitation. Minimum code enforcement provides no such incentive. As a remedy, a city that chooses the enforcement method can use federal rental assistance to subsidize the tenant's rent, either in the newly rehabilitated house or in another higher-quality house elsewhere in the community.

Displacement and Relocation

The city is authorized to deal with other displacement problems that might arise as part of community development activities. When extensive rehabilitation is under way or when a house that is beyond repair is to be demolished, residents may have to be relocated either temporarily or permanently. G.S. 133-5 through -17 (originally enacted in 1971 in accord with the federal Uniform Relocation Assistance and Real Property Acquisition Act) allows the city to help relocated residents with moving expenses, temporary or permanent rental payments, a down payment on the purchase of a house, or a lump sum to buy another house if the permanently displaced family owns the house to be demolished. The law also contains procedural requirements that give reasonable protection to a person or a family displaced by the program.

Support of Housing Programs

Public housing subsidies and block grants have seldom provided enough money to meet a community's total needs for rehabilitating or removing substandard housing and for adequately housing low- and moderate-income citizens. The unit cost of construction and rehabilitation is very high, and a typical block grant allocation, even if it is entirely devoted to housing, usually meets only a fraction of a community's need. Moreover, rent subsidy programs undertaken to promote the rehabilitation of rental properties are expensive and constitute long-term and cumulative commitments that can use up a community's block grant allocation very quickly. Consequently CDBG funds are infrequently used for that purpose. A city typically seeks other federal or state housing funds intended specifically for purchase or rental assistance. A number of cities have set up revolving loan funds with CDBG receipts and other sources so that as assisted families amortize their loans, the city can redirect the income to assist other families. In addition, most communities look for ways to augment federal and state support of housing programs with existing city services in a way that will make them effective and lasting. For example, the effect that housing improvements have on a neighborhood can be increased by channeling the city's housing inspection activities to support block grant and other activities in a target area and by judiciously using the municipal code enforcement powers to supplement financial assistance.

A city can also aggressively use the review and coordination powers given to it by the CHAS. Federal regulations require sponsors of several categories of federally supported housing construction programs to submit proposals for review against the requirements and the priorities outlined in a city's CHAS. This requirement enables the city to coordinate the nature and the location of such proposed projects with its own direct housing activities. Finally, a city can attract or channel investments by private lending institutions into target areas. For example, instead of using the federal CDBG funds for direct loans to individuals for rehabilitation, the city can agree to subsidize loans or mortgages made by lending institutions at market rates. The low-income homeowner can then afford payments of principal and interest while the lender receives a competitive market rate. Also, with voter approval the city can agree to guarantee against defaults on loans made by private lenders in its target areas. Both arrangements are authorized by G.S. 160A-456.

Neighborhood Improvements

When it became clear that replacing substandard housing alone could not overcome the neighborhood effect that forestalled improvement of houses in dilapidated neighborhoods, Congress created the urban redevelopment program as a means of dealing with both housing and its surroundings. Unfortunately the rigidity of the program and other factors resulted in widespread clearance in urban areas without a concomitant replacement of affordable housing—or anything else, in some cases. Many cities saw slum housing replaced only by commercial development. Other cities were left with vast cleared areas in their midst that at best turned into ugly makeshift surface parking lots. The adjustments that came with the new urban renewal program and the supporting categorical programs of the 1960s provided a variety of tools for cities to use in making overall improvements in the environment around the housing that the urban renewal program sought to improve.

The block grant program continues to use the rationale that if a city rehabilitates the houses in a concentrated area, it should also make concurrent improvements in the public facilities that serve those houses; otherwise, the full value of improving the condition of a given house will not be realized and will not be long-lived. Consequently the program encourages cities to undertake neighborhood public improvements to complement housing improvements in their community development target areas. Since 1975, North Carolina cities have tended to emphasize a balanced strategy of housing improvements supported by public facilities, while the majority of states' CDBG programs have primarily funded public facilities projects and a handful have turned to an emphasis on economic development.

Types of Neighborhood Improvements

The kinds of public improvements most commonly undertaken in a target neighborhood in conjunction with housing rehabilitation or construction include the following:

1. Streets: paving, realignment, widening, and extension
2. Curb gutter and driveway cuts: installation, realignment, and rehabilitation
3. Storm drainage: installation, in conjunction with street improvements, or drainage of block centers
4. Sewer: usually installation or rehabilitation of collector lines; also, house connections or outfalls under certain circumstances
5. Water: installation or refurbishment of distribution lines and house connections
6. Open space: common areas, buffers between incompatible uses, and drainage areas
7. Parks: tot lots, play lots, equipped playgrounds, sitting areas, and major neighborhood parks

Authority and Funding for Neighborhood Improvements

Unlike most housing activities, the kinds of improvements just listed are normal and traditional functions of cities in North Carolina, and statutory authority for cities to undertake any of them is clear and well understood. Although the same clear authority exists for other, more general kinds of public improvements like community centers, fire stations, libraries, health centers, and off-street parking, usually it is more difficult to demonstrate that such facilities will benefit primarily low- and moderate-income persons. Consequently block grant funds are less frequently used for the latter activities than for those listed earlier; however, the federally funded projects aimed at revitalizing an area or a neighborhood can be coordinated with the city's capital improvement program (CIP) to ensure that CIP priorities and project scheduling will support the achievement of the community development objectives in the city's target neighborhoods.

Economic Development

Just as cities have realized that housing improvements cannot be very lasting in the absence of neighborhood improvements, so have they realized that providing a safe and sanitary place for a person or a family to live without the economic wherewithal to maintain it is likely to fail in the long run. Therefore economic development, and especially job development, have become more integral to cities' overall strategies to succeed in their community development programs. Moreover, economic development produces widespread benefits for the community, not limited to low- and moderate-income citizens. Economic development provides jobs, improves the city's tax base and other financial resources, and enhances its credit rating, thereby leading to lower borrowing costs and less pressure on the tax rate.

For many years cities (and counties) tended to leave economic development activities to the state and to private agencies, such as chambers of commerce, private power companies, and others. More recently, as natural increases in revenue bases no longer seem capable of keeping up with the cost of providing services, local governments and the state have joined with the private sector to try actively to shape local economies. Cities enjoy fairly broad statutory authority to engage in economic development activities (although there remains some constitutional concern about certain kinds of incentive programs) and can organize their economic development activities in a number of ways. Since 1977 the scope of the CDBG program has embraced economic development as a legitimate activity to be undertaken with grant funds.[10] Before describing city authority and organizational choices, however, it is first useful to set the context by summarizing state and county programs in economic development.

State and County Programs

The state's economic development activities are centered in the Department of Commerce. The department employs a number of persons who work with companies interested in North Carolina to help them locate an industrial or commercial site and to bring their executives together with local officials to discuss local incentives that might be offered to the companies. In addition, the department administers a number of grant and loan programs, including CDBG Small Cities funds for micro-enterprise and large industrial projects, to assist small businesses and to encourage the location and the expansion of large companies in the state. Another agency active in economic development is the Department of Community Colleges, which provides customized training for the employees of new and expanded industries through its Industrial Training Program. A third state agency that plays an important role in economic development is the Department of Transportation, which frequently makes road and highway improvements that encourage both industrial and commercial development.

The state's tax system has also been used to encourage development. Income tax credits are available for companies that create a sufficient number of new jobs, as well as for other companies that invest in new North Carolina businesses. A variety of property tax classifications and exclusions, such as the exclusion for manufacturers' and wholesalers' inventories, are also intended to encourage economic development.

Much of what counties do in economic development parallels the efforts of cities, but counties do have one power not available to cities. They may create special authorities that issue industrial revenue bonds, subject to approval by the Department of Commerce and the Local Government Commission. Such bonds finance the construction of factories and other industrial facilities and are paid for by the companies using the facilities; use of an authority permits issuance of such bonds in tax-exempt form.

Traditional City Authority for Economic Development

There are a number of traditional activities in which cities have engaged to encourage economic development and about which there is no legal dispute. These include employing agents to meet and negotiate with and assist companies interested in locating or expanding in the community, undertaking surveys to identify community strengths and weaknesses, developing strategic plans for economic development, and advertising the community in industrial development publications and elsewhere. Cities have also provided public services and facilities to attract new development and to stimulate economic growth, extending water and sewer lines, expanding water supply and treatment facilities and sewage treatment facilities, and improving streets and roads. Further, a city may acquire property for and build public facilities to complement private development, such as off-street parking adjacent to commercial developments, using the various sources of authority outlined throughout this book.

Direct Incentives

Although cities have been authorized and have undertaken to provide direct incentives to specific industrial and commercial prospects, there have remained some questions about the constitutionality of such incentive programs. The constitutional questions arise from two North Carolina Supreme Court decisions holding that industrial revenue bonds do not serve a public purpose under the state constitution.[11] In those cases the court held that the specific benefit that low-cost industrial revenue bond financing gave to the company whose facilities were being financed outweighed the more general public benefit of increased employment opportunities and enhanced tax base. Although the voters subsequently overruled the decisions by amending the constitution to permit counties to establish county authorities for the issuance of industrial revenue bonds,[12] the amendment is quite narrow. It is not at all certain that the amendment reverses the more general implication of the two decisions: that there is a point along the continuum of governmental assistance to industry at which the special assistance offered to a specific company to entice it to locate in a community becomes so dominant that the private benefit to that company outweighs the public purpose of the assistance.

It has been over twenty years since the more recent of the two supreme court decisions, and the General Assembly has in the interim given cities (and counties) broad statutory authority—possibly extending to the edge of constitutional authority—to assist industry. The basic authorization is found in G.S. 158-7.1. Subsection (b) specifically permits a number of industrial assistance activities, including developing industrial parks, assembling other potential industrial sites, constructing and leasing or selling shell buildings, helping extend public and private utility lines to private facilities, and preparing sites for industrial properties or facilities. Subsection (d2) permits a local government to convey real property to a private company, accepting as consideration for the conveyance the increased property and sales tax revenues that will accrue to the government over the succeeding ten years as a result of improvements by the company to the property. Finally, subsection (a), which has been in the statute since 1925, grants broad authority to "make appropriations for the purposes of aiding and encouraging the location of manufacturing enterprises." Many local governments have relied on this last provision as support for specific incentives not included in subsections (b) or (d2).

G.S. 158-7.1(c) requires any local government that intends to undertake activities specifically listed in subsection (b) first to hold a public hearing on the expenditure in question. If a local government intends to convey property to a private company, whether for monetary consideration or pursuant to subsection (d2), it must first hold a public hearing on the conveyance. Finally, G.S. 158-7.1(f) places a limit on the total investment of a single local government in economic development programs, prohibiting them from exceeding 0.5 percent of the government's tax base.

Economic Development as Part of Community Development

The federal government encourages the use of CDBG funds for economic development consistent with the broad definition of community development established at the beginning of this chapter; however, such activities must meet the test of primarily benefiting low- and moderate-income persons. As a practical matter, the federal government's emphasis has usually been on job development and reversal of physical deterioration in low-income areas. Cities and private businesses are encouraged to enter into cooperative efforts to promote job-producing residential, commercial, or industrial development in their communities.

G.S. 160A-456(a)(2) authorizes all cities to engage in programs concerned with "employment" and "economic development," using either federal and state grants or local funds. As stated earlier, the Department of Commerce also operates two economic development programs under the state's CDBG Small Cities grant program: economic development and a micro-enterprise program. Economic development projects may include a broad range of activities, but the majority of the CDBG funds must be shown to create or retain jobs for low- and moderate-income persons. Funds may be expended for public facilities related to a specific project that can be shown to produce jobs, or they may be loaned to specific businesses through a participating bank, with proceeds from repayment being used to establish and replenish a revolving loan fund used for the same purpose. In addition, the state sets aside funds each year to fund eligible micro-enterprise projects—commercial enterprises with five or fewer employees, one or more of whom own the enterprise. Project funds are used to provide loans, loan guarantees, technical assistance, and business support and training to persons trying to develop such enterprises. These grants may be made either directly to businesses or to one or more local governments that establish a program of assistance for specific projects.

Other Authority to Assist in Economic Development

A city has considerable authority to attract business development by facilitating the location, the preparation, and the transfer of a suitable site in the community. Besides the authority for industrial development activities under G.S. 158-7.1(b), it may acquire land with or without buildings for commercial or industrial development and for public facilities to serve a major private development, under redevelopment law (G.S. 160A-512) if the redevelopment procedures are followed, and under community development law (G.S. 160A-457). If the land to be acquired is "inappropriately developed," the city may dispose of the property to a private developer either directly or after clearing, refurbishing, or adding public improvements to make the site more attractive for development. There are limits, however, on how closely the city may work with a single developer. To dispose of the property that it acquires and improves, the city must follow competitive-bidding procedures whether it operates under redevelopment law or under community development law.[13]

The redevelopment law allows a city to condemn, if necessary, in order to acquire property for any of the purposes identified in the preceding paragraph [G.S. 160A-512(6), -515)], but the community development law does not. When the city acquires land solely for public improvements, its general power of eminent domain may be used for any of the public improvements authorized by the statutes (see G.S. Ch. 160A, Art. 11; improvements are listed in G.S. 160A-241).

Just as with neighborhood improvements, land acquisition and construction for public improvements that are usually authorized for cities when they are undertaken for economic development purposes may be financed by federal funds or by appropriation of local tax revenues without special voter approval. General obligation bonds may be used to finance any improvement authorized by G.S. 159-48, but only with voter approval before issuance. Revenue bonds may be used to finance public service enterprise improvements like sewer, water, or electric utilities or parking facilities built in conjunction with an economic development project. No vote is required for such bonds, but the facility must yield adequate revenue from operations to retire the debt. Just as with housing activities, grants, loans, interest subsidies, loan guarantees, or purchase of property for resale to and development by a private party may be financed by block grant funds without voter approval; but if local property tax revenues are used directly or for debt service related to these activities, a referendum is required as provided in G.S. 160A-209.

No Authority for Tax Breaks

One form of industrial or commercial development and recruitment often used in other states is clearly unavailable in North Carolina: offering special property tax breaks to new industries or businesses. Under Article V, Section 2, of the state constitution, property tax exemptions and classifications may be made only by the General Assembly and then only on a statewide basis. A local government may not constitutionally offer a special classification to a property owner if it is not available statewide. The legislature has not enacted any special classifications for new industrial or commercial development; therefore none can be offered by local economic development officials.

Organization for Community Development

Whether a local community development program consists of only federal block grant activities or a broad range of federal, local, and private activities, it requires effective coordination and management. Meeting federal requirements and private-sector needs and expectations and conducting an effective program requires widespread community involvement on the one hand and concentrated executive control of a complex set of activities on the other. Neither the federal government nor the General Statutes mandate any specific form of organization to carry out a community development strategy in general, although there are specifications and options for the component activities discussed earlier. Each city, then, must use the options available in the General Statutes to accomplish its community development objectives in a way that satisfactorily balances community involvement and executive control, and best suits its local program and circumstances.

City Council

The starting point for organizing for community development activities must be the city council, which has the authority either to undertake directly, or to appoint an appropriate body to undertake on its behalf, all the activities discussed earlier.

Traditionally, even though the governing boards of local housing authorities were appointed by the city's mayor, most operated quite independently of city government. Housing construction and operations were not activities with which general-purpose local governments had much, if any, experience, and with all their funding except for rental income coming from the federal government, their operations relied primarily on federal rules and policies.

In recent years, however, especially as federal support for housing programs has decreased, a number of cities have taken a more assertive role in the operation of their housing authorities. G.S. 157-4.1 and G.S. 157-4.2 offer several alternative organizational arrangements to the traditional independent housing authority. First, under G.S. 157-4.2 a city may retain a separate housing authority, but integrate that authority's budgeting and financial administration activities into those of the city. Under this arrangement the housing authority remains a separate organization with personnel and operating responsibilities under the control of the appointed housing authority board, and the agency is treated like a city department only for purposes of budgeting, accounting, and expenditure control. Two other alternatives eliminate the housing authority altogether: under G.S. 157-4.1 the city council may assign the powers of the housing authority to the redevelopment commission, or the city council itself and the city staff may assume those powers.[14]

The city council has final local authority over all CDBG activities. It must approve the final application for federal funds and formally accept the grant funds and the responsibility for program execution. The state's community development law (G.S. 160A-456, -457) authorizes the city council to exercise directly any of the powers conferred on housing authorities and redevelopment commissions as needed to carry out the block grant program. The city council also holds the ultimate responsibility and statutory authority for most of the locally funded activities that might be part of a community development program, especially neighborhood improvement activities that fall under its general statutory authority for planning, public works, and regulation activities related to public safety, health, and welfare.

The city council may undertake economic development activities itself. When this occurs, it usually grows out of relatively small-scale, discrete programs under CDBG Small Cities economic development grants. For large-scale and long-term economic development efforts, most city councils rely on an appointed commission to do the work on their behalf (see the discussion under the next heading).

Citizen Boards, Commissions, and Committees

Although the city council holds most of the ultimate authority for community development activities, it can make efficient use of citizen interest and expertise by appointing a variety of citizen boards, commissions, and committees for advice or for implementation of program mandates. To help in planning and administering the federal CDBG program, the city council usually finds it very useful to have a citizen advisory body through which to channel public opinion. First, such a body can focus its full attention on the community development program, whereas the council has many other responsibilities. Second, the city council can effectively delegate to the advisory group the time-consuming task of gaining widespread citizen participation in planning. Third, the professional staff can secure from this body a fairly continuous flow of informal comment and information during planning. Finally, the advisory body can supplement professional staff advice with a lay point of view when the program is recommended to the city council.

Although the city council has many options in creating a citizen advisory committee, two arrangements are most common: (1) The council appoints a committee especially for the community development program, apart from any existing boards and commissions. Sometimes such a committee also serves as an umbrella for several subcommittees that represent actual or potential target neighborhoods. (2) The council assigns the community development program to a redevelopment commission already formed under the redevelopment law (G.S. 160A-504). This is done either without changing the status of the commission or by abolishing it (as provided in G.S. 160A-505) and reappointing its members as a nonstatutory advisory committee as described earlier. Either of the latter options is appropriate if a city particularly wishes to draw on the knowledge of an extant commission in formulating a community development program.

Because the city's planning board and its housing authority, if one exists, usually have something to offer to community development, the city council should consider what role (if any) it expects these agencies to play in planning and executing the city's CDBG program. The planning board's work with comprehensive planning and capital improvement planning can be very closely related to the formulation of the community development program. Also, a housing authority's deep knowledge of subsidized housing needs and problems in the community might make it a valuable resource in developing and using a CHAS to coordinate the development of all kinds of assisted housing in and around the city. The city council should also consider whether to ask other boards and commissions (such as the parks and recreation commission, the streets committee, and the public works committee) for advice. Because there is no federal or state prescription for the advisory function, a council can tailor arrangements to its own objectives and circumstances and to the way in which it chooses to balance broad-based citizen participation with the centralized control that is often needed to reach program goals.

Although there are advantages to a city council's taking direct control of housing programs, there are good reasons why some cities have elected to delegate the planning and the operation of these programs to appointed boards. When the new CDBG program gave general-purpose local government the authority over the replacement for the traditional housing and redevelopment programs, officials in many cities felt that they could not do as good a job as the housing and redevelopment authorities had done for years, developing skilled staff, experience, and a trustworthy track record in the process. Probably because construction and operation of public housing is the function that general-purpose local government has the least experience in directly administering, it is not surprising that only ten cities (and a handful of counties) have assumed a direct role in this complex undertaking. Many city councils have continued to use their redevelopment authorities under contract to administer their CDBG programs, while taking a more active role than with previous programs in planning, allocating funds, and monitoring results.

Although the city council may undertake the economic development activities described earlier, using the city staff to centralize management and control, G.S. Chapter 158, Article 2, allows the governing board to appoint an economic development commission. Such a commission is a public agency, but like housing authorities, once it is created and members are appointed, it may act with some independence from the government that created it. Advantages of such a commission include the opportunity to ensure that local business leaders have an active role through their membership on the commission and the possibility of setting such a commission up cooperatively with other jurisdictions to coordinate efforts in one body. One disadvantage is that an economic development commission does not enjoy any authority to own real property and therefore cannot directly undertake some of the incentive programs authorized to cities and counties by G.S. 158-7.1(b).

Some city councils exercise a third option: they delegate their economic development activities to chambers of commerce, committees of 100, or other private nonprofit corporations, limiting the direct role of the public body to one of providing funding in some measure. These private groups share the benefits of an economic development commission in that they permit the involvement of the local business community and facilitate cooperation among several local governments. They also bear two advantages not found with economic development commissions. First, there is no bar to their owning real property; thus they can act directly as developers of industrial parks or shell buildings or can hold industrial sites for conveyance to newly locating companies. Second, because they are private organizations, they can raise private funds within the community and spend those funds without concern for the possible constitutional or statutory limitations that accompany public funds. (Any public moneys appropriated to these organizations, however, retain their public character and remain subject to such limitations.) A possible disadvantage of using these private organizations, depending on how their governing boards are selected, is that they may have considerable independence from local government and therefore might sometimes pursue goals and strategies inconsistent with the wishes of local government officials.

Professional Staff

The variety of ways in which cities have organized to conduct community development programs are characterized by three major approaches: a coordinator, a department, and a task force.

A Coordinator

A community development coordinator is often used in small cities that need few specialized staff. One person is responsible for initiating, negotiating, monitoring, and evaluating the planning and the execution of community development activities by several departments, usually planning, public works, and inspection, and sometimes the rehabilitation staff of a redevelopment authority. Where the coordinator is placed in the administration can be an important consideration. If the person is a member of the planning staff, he or she can certainly integrate the program with other planning activities, but might have little influence on operating departments that carry out the program. If the person is a member of the chief administrator's staff, he or she has more potential clout, but usually only as much as the chief administrator chooses to provide by backing him or her. To date, few cities have combined coordination of federal community development activities and economic development activities in one staff person. It is more common to find a separate coordinator for these two components of community development.

A Department

The city can form a community development department with status equal to that of the more traditional departments that might have a part in the program—public works, inspection, recreation, etc. This arrangement often originates in a city's decision to abolish a separate redevelopment authority that operated urban renewal and Neighborhood Development programs and to bring its housing staff into the city administration to perform housing rehabilitation work. As stated earlier, a number of cities have also brought their housing authority operations under the city organization, either as a separate department or as part of a multifunctional department with broad responsibilities in community development. The multifunctional department might be formed from an existing planning department and from existing building inspection staff, housing inspection staff, engineering staff, housing and redevelopment staffs, economic development staff, or various combinations of all of these. Obviously the more of these functions that the department includes, the more powerful the community development director's influence will be over the performance of tasks that are critical to the program.

A Task Force

A city that takes the broadest possible view of community development—that is, as an endeavor involving almost all city agencies and private-sector organizations from time to time—might adopt a task force approach to planning and managing its programs. Often, primary responsibility for the program goes to a deputy or assistant city manager who, by his or her position, clearly and often acts with the full authority of the manager. This person can organize and supervise department and agency heads who will be responsible for various aspects of program planning and implementation and serve as a critical link to organizations outside city government. The composition of task forces might change over time as the community development program goes through different stages or changes its character. This process tends to be most successful when the city manager delegates effectively and department heads and other staff are comfortable and competent in using team-management techniques.

৯৯ ৯৯ ৯৯

One of the most significant effects of the federal government's block grant programs since 1974 has been a marked improvement in the ability and the inclination of cities to bring a variety of resources to bear on problems of deteriorated housing, declining neighborhoods, and troubled local economies, in a coordinated fashion and with flexibility and sensitivity to special local needs. North Carolina law has complemented federal initiatives by providing cities with the authority they need to take full advantage of available programs. As direct federal financial support has diminished, cities have developed the ability to fashion effective strategies out of local resources, both public and private, to continue these initiatives at the local level.

Additional Resources

Publications

Anderson, Martin. *The Federal Bulldozer: A Critical Analysis of Urban Renewal, 1949–1962.* Cambridge, Mass.: The M.I.T. Press, 1964.

Dommel, Paul R. *From Nation to States: The Small Cities Community Development Block Grant Program.* Albany: State University of New York Press, 1986.

Green, Philip P., Jr. *North Carolina Statutes Related to Lower-Income Housing.* Chapel Hill, N.C.: Institute of Government, The University of North Carolina at Chapel Hill, 1990.

International City/County Management Association. "CDBG Funds: Resource for Innovation." *MIS Report,* vol. 27, no. 2 (February 1995).

Jenkins, Lauretta C. *CDBG: A Creative Link to Small Business Development.* Washington, D.C.: U.S. Department of Housing and Urban Development, 1987.

National Association of Housing and Redevelopment Officials. *Developing Local Housing Strategies under the Housing and Community Development Act of 1974.* Washington, D.C.: NAHRO, 1975.

Organizations

(listed in order of level of relevance)

North Carolina Department of Commerce, Division of Community Assistance, 430 North Salisbury Street, Raleigh, NC 27611

United States Department of Housing and Urban Development, North Carolina State Office, 2306 West Meadowview Road, Greensboro, NC 27407

National Community Development Association, 522 Twenty-First Street, NW, Washington, DC 20006

National Association of Housing and Redevelopment Officials, 1320 Eighteenth Street, NW, Washington, DC 20036

Notes

1. The original thirteen eligible activities defined by the federal law were acquisition of real property; acquisition, construction, reconstruction, or installation of public works facilities and improvements; code enforcement; clearance, demolition, removal, and rehabilitation of buildings and improvements; removal of architectural barriers; payment for loss of rental income associated with relocation activities; disposition of acquired property or its retention for public purposes; provision of public services not otherwise available; payment of the local match for other federal grants; payments to complete an urban renewal project; relocation payments and assistance; community planning and management development; and administrative costs of planning and executing a CDBG program. Economic development was added in 1977, the same year that the Urban Development Action Grant (UDAG) was created, and funding of energy-saving improvements was added in 1980. By 1995 this list had expanded to twenty-five eligible activities, adding to the aforementioned, such activities as assistance to neighborhood-based or community-wide nonprofit organizations, rehabilitation of public housing, support of low- and moderate-income home ownership, and assistance to micro-enterprise.

2. Before July 1990 the law required that at least 60 percent of a grantee's expenditures over a period not to exceed three years had to address this objective. The National Affordable Housing Act of 1990 raised this percentage to 70. Nationwide, most programs exceed this higher requirement.

3. Originally this was called a *housing assistance plan* (HAP). It included a survey of the community's existing housing, an estimate of future housing needs, and realistic goals for meeting those needs. This part of the plan is now called a *comprehensive housing assistance strategy* (CHAS), with some modifications in specific requirements but the same objective as the original HAP.

4. The formula seeks to achieve fair distribution of available funds based on population, degree of poverty, overcrowding of housing, age of housing stock, and population growth lag relative to other metropolitan areas.

5. Besides these twenty-one cities, Cumberland and Wake counties are entitlement jurisdictions.

6. In 1981, all states were given the choice to design and administer their own programs or have HUD administer the programs. North Carolina was one of the first states to assume responsibility for its own program. As of 1995, two states, New York and Hawaii, still chose not to administer their own Small Cities programs, and HUD administers the programs for them.

7. At this writing (1995), legislation pending in the General Assembly would authorize cities and counties to participate in HUD's Section 108 Loan Guarantee Program whereby a grantee could pledge future CDBG allocations as security for private loans in instances when the magnitude of a needed project exceeded the immediate access to grant funds.

8. G.S. 157–9(15a) defines *low-income persons* as those in households with an income no more than 60 percent of the area median family income.

9. G.S. 157–9(15b) defines *moderate-income persons* as those deemed by the entity exercising housing authority powers to require housing assistance because of insufficient personal or family income.

10. The Housing and Community Development Act of 1977 earmarked a portion of CDBG funds at the national level for Urban Development Action Grants (UDAGs) and added economic development to the original list of thirteen eligible activities that could be undertaken with CDBG funds at the local level. When North Carolina took over the Small Cities program in FY 1982, it included a set-aside for economic development activities. Today the allocation of these economic development set-asides is administered by the Commerce Finance Center in the Department of Commerce, while the housing and neighborhood development activities of CDBG are administered by the Division of Community Assistance.

11. Stanley v. Department of Conservation and Dev., 284 N.C. 15, 199 S.E.2d 641 (1973); Mitchell v. North Carolina Indus. Dev. Fin. Auth., 273 N.C. 137, 159 S.E.2d 745 (1968).

12. N.C. CONST. art. V, § 9.

13. G.S. 160A-514(d) governs disposal under the redevelopment statutes, and G.S. Chapter 160A, Article 12, governs disposal under the community development statutes. G.S. Chapter 143, Article 8, governs public building contracts for purposes of making improvements.

14. As of 1995, ten cities had elected to have the council assume these powers directly: Albemarle, Ayden, Chapel Hill, Concord, East Spencer, Edenton, Mount Holly, Murphy, North Wilkesboro, and Shelby. Eight counties had done the same.

V
City Services

21 Law Enforcement

Ronald G. Lynch

Contents

THE PRIMARY PURPOSE of a police department is to protect the lives and the property of both the community's citizens and people who visit and work in the community. This large umbrella covers such functions as answering calls for service, preventing and investigating crimes, enforcing laws, and providing education to reduce the community's fears about its safety.

Kinds of Law Enforcement Agencies

City Departments

Law enforcement powers are conferred on cities by G.S. Chapter 160A, Article 13. North Carolina law is simple and specific in authorizing a city to create a police department. G.S. 160A-281 empowers a city "to appoint a chief of police and to employ other police officers who may reside outside the corporate limits of the city unless the council provides otherwise." The law further allows a city to authorize auxiliary law enforcement personnel, who still must undergo the same training as sworn personnel and must come under the authority and the direction of the chief of police (G.S. 160A-282).

A police officer within the corporate limits of the city has the powers vested in all law enforcement officers by statute and common law. He or she has the power to serve criminal and civil processes and to enforce the ordinances and the regulations of the city and the laws of the state (G.S. 160A-285). This authority applies within the city's corporate limits, within one mile of the city limits, and on any property, wherever located, owned or leased by the city (G.S. 160A-286).

Any city may ask another city for help in emergencies if a prior aid agreement appears in the minutes of both governing bodies. When the assistance is granted, the law enforcement officers who are sent to the requesting municipality have the same authority to make arrests and to execute criminal process in the requesting community as the law enforcement officers of that city (G.S. 160A-288).

The size of a city's police department directly reflects the size of the community. More than 450 of North Carolina's 500 cities have a population of 10,000 or less. Among all cities, 325 have city law enforcement agencies (some of the 220 cities under 1,000 population have none). Of this total, over 60 percent employ ten or fewer police officers. Eighty-five percent of them employ twenty-five officers or fewer; only thirteen cities employ 100 or more.

County Departments

The office of sheriff is established by the North Carolina Constitution. The sheriff, elected directly by the county's voters, operates the sheriff's department independently of the board of county commissioners, except that the commissioners receive and pass on the sheriff's budget and appropriate funds for operating his or her department.

The North Carolina Constitution in no way specifies the sheriff's duties. G.S. Chapter 162 defines the civil duties, but makes no reference to law enforcement functions. Nor does any other statute specify that it is the sheriff's duty to protect life and property. Even so, because the sheriff's office originates in common law, it carries common law responsibilities for providing law enforcement protection.

At one time the sheriff in North Carolina had broader responsibilities than he or she now does. For example, the sheriff was once the county tax collector. Still, the sheriff continues to be both a judicial officer and a law enforcement officer with jurisdiction within city limits. Nonpolice functions performed by the sheriff's deputies include transporting prisoners between jails and courts, serving as bailiffs or court officers, and transporting persons to mental institutions.

Although there were moves during the 1980s to create more county police departments, the moves were not successful. Only two major county police departments in North Carolina (that of Gaston County and the consolidated Charlotte-Mecklenburg department) provide a level of service in their respective counties equal to that provided by a municipal police agency.

State Agencies

State law enforcement agencies operate in specific areas in which it is impractical and expensive for local law enforcement to take complete jurisdiction because of the specialization required. Nevertheless, the local and state agencies must work together closely to accomplish the overall purposes of both.

State Highway Patrol

North Carolina's State Highway Patrol is a division of the Department of Crime Control and Public Safety (G.S. 20-184). It enforces the laws and the regulations respecting travel and use of vehicles on state highways (G.S. 20-188). Patrol officers have the power and the authority of peace officers to serve any warrant or process that issues from the courts, and they may make arrests for violations of any laws that regulate travel and the use of vehicles or highways. Their jurisdiction is statewide, and they are fully authorized to perform any other peace officer's duties that the governor may direct. They may also, at any time on their own motion or at the request of any local police authority, arrest persons accused of highway robbery, bank robbery, murder, or other crimes of violence. Further, they are authorized to make arrests for any crime committed in their presence or on any North Carolina highway.

State Bureau of Investigation

The State Bureau of Investigation is a division of the Department of Justice (G.S. 114-12). It is responsible, under G.S. 114-15, for investigating mob violence; election frauds; violations of Social Security laws and gaming laws; attempted arson; and theft, attempted theft, or misuse of any state-owned personal property, building, or real property. It operates a state crime laboratory (G.S. 114-16), receives criminal statistics (G.S. 114-19), and on request helps municipal law enforcement agencies investigate any crime. It also maintains original jurisdiction in the investigation of drug offenses as defined by G.S. Chapter 90, Article 5.

Governor's Crime Commission

The Governor's Crime Commission is a division of the State Department of Crime Control and Public Safety. Over the past decade the commission's role has changed greatly in response to congressional mandates, the needs of the criminal justice system, and state priorities. G.S. 143B-479 delineates five major goals of the criminal justice system that form the basis of the commission's planning: (1) to reduce crime, (2) to protect individual rights, (3) to achieve justice, (4) to increase efficiency in the criminal justice system, and (5) to increase professional skills. The commission also disburses federal funds.

Criminal Justice Education and Training Standards Commission

The Criminal Justice Education and Training Standards Commission is established under G.S. Chapter 17C. It promulgates rules and regulations and establishes the minimum education and training standards required for all entry-level employment as a criminal justice officer, except for deputy sheriffs, jailers, and other sheriffs' department personnel who are regulated under G.S. Chapter 17E by the Sheriffs' Education and Training Standards Commission. It certifies officer candidates as qualified under the law and establishes minimum standards for certifying criminal justice training schools. It advises in such areas as (1) identifying the types of criminal justice positions that require advanced or specialized training and education and (2) establishing standards for certifying candidates for these positions on the basis of specified education, training, and experience.

Crime Factors and Police Effectiveness

The factors that cause crime are many and varied. Care must be used in comparing the amounts of crime reported in any two cities. The methods used to collect the data often differ, and the reliability of crime statistics varies from city to city. Furthermore, a number of demographic factors that affect the amount of crime in a community are beyond the police agency's direct influence or control: the population's density and size; its composition in terms of age, sex, and race; its economic status; its relative stability; its educational and cultural level; its attitude toward law enforcement; and its religious characteristics and mores.

A police department's effectiveness can best be measured by the absence of incidents that it is charged with preventing. How can it be determined how much crime or how many accidents a police department prevents? The success, the failure, or the efficiency of the police is most often measured by clearance rates, number of arrests, and conviction rates. Domestic security is a precious commodity, and maintaining it is a continuing expense that everyone must share. Police service cannot be reduced to a balance sheet with a final figure representing profit or loss.

Crime Data

Uniform Crime Reporting

A system called Uniform Crime Reporting (UCR) provides a nationwide view of crime in the United States that is based on statistics contributed by local law enforcement agencies. It also serves as a guide for a standard method of crime reporting in most local police agencies. The Federal Bureau of Investigation collects the data on the incidence of crime reported by local law enforcement agencies to a designated office in their state. It then publishes summarized information quarterly and annually for the use of local enforcement agencies and others interested in the crime problem. North Carolina agencies provide monthly data to the Division of Criminal Information (DCI) within the State Bureau of Investigation.

The UCR system has seven categories of criminal offenses known to the police as Index crimes: murder and nonnegligent manslaughter, forcible rape, robbery, aggravated assault, burglary, larceny, and motor vehicle theft. It uses twenty-two additional categories for all other classes of criminal offenses.

Each month the police report the number of Index offenses that became known to them in the past month. *Unfounded* complaints are eliminated from the count before the report is made. Cases *cleared by arrest* and those *exceptionally cleared* are also reported. In the UCR, arrests for all categories of crimes are reported.

Although the UCR reports only Index offenses, local police departments usually report both Index and non-Index crimes. For these reports the following clearance classifications are recommended:

1. *Unfounded.* This classification is applied when the police investigation clearly establishes that no offense actually occurred or was attempted. The recovery of property or the refusal of a victim to prosecute an offender does not mean that the crime did not occur, and in these instances the crime is not "unfounded," but "exceptionally cleared."
2. *Cleared by arrest.* This classification is applied when at least one person is (a) arrested, (b) charged with the commission of the offense, and (c) turned over to the court for prosecution through any of several methods. Several crimes may be cleared by the arrest of one person.
3. *Exceptionally cleared.* This classification is used when the police are not able to follow the three steps outlined under *cleared by arrest*, yet have done everything possible to clear the case. If all of the following questions can be answered yes, then the offense may be listed as an exceptional clearance:
    a. Has the investigation clearly identified the offender?
    b. Is there enough information to support arresting, charging, and turning the offender over to the court for prosecution?
    c. Is the offender's exact location known so that he or she could be taken into custody now?

    d.   Is there some reason beyond police control that stops an officer from arresting, charging, and prosecuting the offender?

For example, an offense can be exceptionally cleared if the offender committed suicide or was killed by police, or if extradition from another state was denied.

Crime Rates in North Carolina

Generally when reports are made concerning crime in North Carolina, they are either individual accounts of a sensational crime or the latest crime statistics that may indicate a substantial change in the number of reported offenses.

Murder, rape, robbery, and aggravated assault are classified as violent (assaultive) crimes. Historically North Carolina has had a relatively high rate of these crimes per 100,000 people. Its murder rate has ranked among the ten- to fifteen-highest state murder rates in the nation. Like homicides elsewhere, homicides in North Carolina tend to involve persons with previous criminal records, and victims are usually friends or families.

Burglary, larceny, and motor vehicle theft are crimes against property. Information collected and analyzed during the past five years shows that North Carolina's property crime rate is increasing faster than the national rate. The state now ranks seventeenth in the United States.

Factors Affecting Crime Rates

Like many other major issues, crime in North Carolina is difficult to forecast accurately. Studies on a national basis, however, show that certain factors have a specific short-term effect on crime rates. For example, a 10-percent increase in the number of youth between the ages of fifteen and twenty-four may bring about an increase of nearly 13 percent in the crime rate. A 10-percent decrease in the employment rate is reflected only slightly in the crime rate—less than a 2-percent increase.

The babies of baby boomers are now beginning to enter their teenage years, and this means that crime rates in North Carolina will probably escalate during the 1990s. Many police agencies are beginning to emphasize the need to deal with youth through such programs as DARE (Drug Abuse Resistance Education), to assist them during this period.

Hiring more law enforcement officers does not seem to reduce crime greatly. Studies indicate that a 10-percent increase in the number of personnel employed by large law enforcement agencies results in only a 1-percent drop in the crime rate.

From 42 to 55 percent of the calls received and answered by a law enforcement agency in the United States are known as miscellaneous service calls. Each community should carefully evaluate these calls to assess whether police departments could use their time more effectively if other city agencies answered the calls and whether the city should even handle such calls. For example, what is the cost to the community in terms of time and money when the police act as bank escorts or funeral escorts? The level of service and the types of calls to which the police department should respond should be set down in a written policy of the city council after careful discussions with the city manager and the chief of police.

Management of a Law Enforcement Agency

Philosophy

It is the responsibility of the chief of police to create an environment in which people can produce at their highest level, continually grow, mature, and feel safe and secure. Further, it is the chief's responsibility to establish high standards of personal behavior. Police chiefs are teachers of their people and are constantly demonstrating by their behavior the values, the beliefs, and the principles of their departments so that all personnel—sworn and nonsworn—may learn to think and act in accordance with the police chief's philosophy. The work environment of the police department should be designed so that the police chief encourages people to use their individual skills. Police chiefs should demonstrate high concern for ethics, justice, and opportunity for others to grow and mature.

Philosophy is the sum of the values and the beliefs of the leader. It is almost impossible to state a philosophy in a short statement. However, philosophy is demonstrated in the behavior of the police chief and his or her commanders.

Values are assumptions about ends which are worth striving for. When combined with beliefs, they develop into a set of principles that can serve as standards for others regarding what is important for police departments.

Beliefs are assumptions about what is true. They are based on a combination of facts and judgments. Beliefs, when combined with values, begin to form a basis for the principles on which a police department must operate.

Principles are statements of right conduct. Principles underlie policies, practices, and procedures. Principles are best stated in a policy manual that gives guidance to all members of the police department, enabling them more effectively to perform and implement day-to-day decisions.

An example of principles that help govern the operation of a police department is the following:

We shall—
1. Do everything within our power and authority to prevent criminal behavior.
2. Promote an open and trusting flow of information within our organization and with the public.
3. Make decisions consistent with legal and ethical standards to guarantee justice to all.
4. Protect the constitutional rights of all persons.
5. Treat all persons with dignity, respect, courtesy, and compassion.

Organization

Organization is the orderly arrangement of functions, personnel, and resources to carry out the institution's purposes, which in law enforcement are to protect the public and provide auxiliary services to it. How a corporate body is organized is very important to its efficiency. The presence or the absence of organizational units and the relationships of these units are critical factors in controlling, coordinating, directing, and supervising an agency.

All police departments have the same basic mission: enforcing the law, that is, protecting citizens from criminal attack and the negligence of others and ensuring the public right to tranquillity and freedom of movement. Naturally, how the department is organized to do this varies from place to place, depending on a community's form of government, the quality of its administrators, the scope and the quality of services expected by the public, and the number and the quality of personnel available to provide the service. Nevertheless, contemporary principles of organization derived from military, government, business, and industrial experiences find use in all police departments, though each department applies them according to its own needs.

Relatively few problems of a police department can be resolved or cured solely by changing the organization. Developing or streamlining a particular structure does not necessarily ensure organizational success. Applying the principles of proper organization cannot, for example, overcome deficiencies in the intelligence and the personal character of personnel, nor alone substitute for the initiative necessary for proper direction and control.

The nature and the form of the basic structure does, however, directly and profoundly influence how efficiently an organization functions. An organizational structure that eases the flow of information in every direction, clearly and understandably depicts the chain of command, and precisely illustrates the organizational and functional relationships in an agency can greatly increase a department's operational and administrative efficiency.

Occasionally an enterprise appears to operate satisfactorily despite a poor organizational structure; however, a close examination of the actual relationships usually reveals that the theoretical organization has no relationship to the structure that actually exists. No enterprise of any size can be effective with a faulty organization.

Common Ways to Group Law Enforcement Activities

There are five common ways to group police activities: by process, by area, by clientele, by time, and by function.

By Process

Grouping police activities by process involves assigning all personnel who use a given type of equipment to one unit. Example: All of those who use the spectrograph are assigned to the crime laboratory.

By Area

Grouping by area—that is, into local commands—is helpful when activities are widespread over any given location. Example: Large cities are geographically and organizationally divided into districts.

By Clientele

Tasks that involve the same group of people lend themselves to specialization. Example: Personnel who deal with narcotic users, juveniles, or burglary suspects are assigned to special units.

By Time

Grouping activities by time is used when a certain function or service must be performed within a specified period. Example: The patrol force works shifts.

By Function

Tasks that share the same methods of work are grouped according to operation and purpose. Example: Depending on how they work and why, personnel are assigned to patrol, investigation, or traffic.

Model Organizational Structures

The following model organizational structures can serve as guides in developing departments of varying sizes. They are presented to indicate the variety of structures developed to serve specific needs. In use they should be adapted to permit expansion and/or consolidation of functions as the need arises.

Very Small Department

Figure 21-1 illustrates a typical organizational structure for a department that employs up to twenty persons. The small staff and the limited resources preclude the establishment of specialized functions. Obviously the easiest way to organize such a department is to assign personnel to shifts.

Small Department

Figure 21-2 shows the recommended structure for departments with 20 to 100 persons. This organization divides the department into three fundamental divisions: Uniformed, Criminal Investigation, and Staff Services. Planning and research, training, and inspection may be performed by the chief or be delegated to someone else.

Medium-Size Department

Figure 21-3 depicts a model organizational structure for departments with 100–300 persons. It retains the division structure, but

Figure 21-1
Model Organizational Structure for a Very Small Police Department
(Up to 20 Persons)

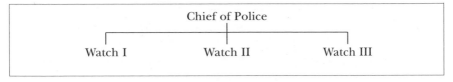

Figure 21-2
Model Organizational Structure for a Small Police Department
(20–100 Persons)

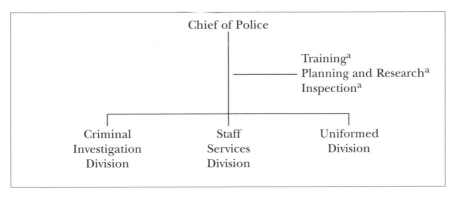

a. Optional functions and relationships

each division contains specialized units. In addition, planning and inspection are also distinct functions.

Large Department

Figure 21-4 shows a proposed organizational structure for a large police agency. As indicated, size alone demands that the structure be different. The inspection and planning functions have each been given separate status, and staff functions have been divided between an Administrative Services Bureau and a Technical Services Bureau. In addition, there is an Operations Bureau that consists of highly specialized activities including the Patrol Division, the Traffic Division, the Criminal Investigation Division, and the Special Operations Division. Specialized activities are especially important in large police agencies. Particular units (bureaus, divisions, etc.) throughout the organizational structure must be specifically identified. Giving entities with equal organizational status different designations confuses their true relationships.

Figure 21-3
Model Organizational Structure for a Medium-Size Police Department (100–300 Persons)

a. Optional functions and relationships

Selection and Employment of Law Enforcement Officers

Qualifications

The minimum qualifications for employment as a law enforcement officer are established under G.S. Chapter 17C and are administered by the Criminal Justice Education and Training Standards Commission. Under present minimum requirements a law enforcement officer must—

- Be a citizen of the United States.
- Be at least twenty years of age.
- Be of good moral character as determined by a thorough background investigation as prescribed.
- Be fingerprinted and be subject to a search of local, state, and national fingerprint files to disclose any criminal record.
- Not have been convicted by any local, state, federal, or military court of a felony, a crime that could have been pun-

Figure 21-4
Model Organizational Structure for a Large Police Department
(Over 300 Persons)

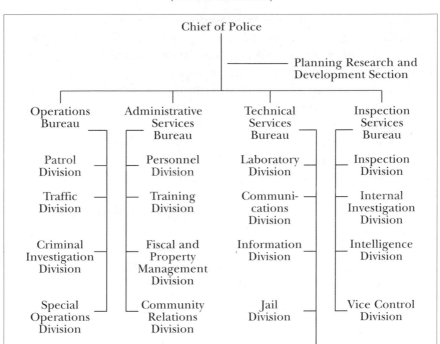

a. Optional functions and relationships

ished by imprisonment for more than two years, or an offense involving moral turpitude.

- Be a high school graduate or have passed the General Educational Development Test indicating high school equivalency.
- Satisfactorily complete the Occupational Aptitude Test administered by the North Carolina Employment Security
Commission for the occupation of law enforcement officer.
- Be examined by a licensed physician or surgeon and meet
physical requirements for properly fulfilling the responsibilities of a law enforcement officer.
- Be interviewed personally, before employment, by the department head or his or her representative(s) to determine

such attributes as appearance, demeanor, attitude, and ability to communicate.

Further, although regulations do not now require this, every candidate for the position of law enforcement officer should be either examined by a licensed psychiatrist or clinical psychologist before employment, or given a battery of psychological evaluation tests to determine his or her mental and emotional suitability to perform the duties of an officer. Also, the commission recommends that every law enforcement recruit, at the time of employment or within twenty-four months thereafter, have been awarded by an accredited institution of higher learning at least six college-semester units of educational credit or nine other units of educational credit.

These are minimum standards for employment. Higher standards are recommended whenever enough qualified applicants are available.

Any agency may choose to set its standards higher. However, the department head or the agency may never employ anyone whose qualifications are below the statutory minimums for the position of law enforcement officer.

The State of North Carolina requires that those who aspire to law enforcement careers complete a probationary period of at least twelve months. A department may extend this period. If during this probationary period, an officer shows traits or behavior that make him or her a liability to the department, he or she should be dismissed without right of appeal. The officer should, of course, be told the reasons for the discharge.

Training

G.S. 17C-8 requires that the Criminal Justice Education and Training Standards Commission establish a Criminal Justice Education and Training System. This system is designed as a cooperative arrangement between the state and local criminal justice agencies and criminal justice education and training schools, both public and private. The system includes the North Carolina Justice Training Academy at Salemburg and all other public or private agencies or institutions in the state that are engaged in criminal justice education and training.

State law now defines entry-level training, requiring that the curriculum contain 240 hours of basic training. Police officers receive basic training at Salemburg, at selected community colleges and technical institutes, and through special programs provided by large police departments like those of Charlotte, Greensboro, and Winston-Salem.

Salaries

There are three ways to determine salaries for police officers. The first relies on what is commonly referred to as the *comparison principle.* Following this principle, one city or town compares the salaries for its officers with those being paid by cities of similar size and in the general region.

The second approach involves the *attract-and-retain principle.* Under this principle, city councils approve a pay scale that will attract potential candidates for the police agency and that provides for raises and benefits sufficient to maintain a low turnover rate.

The third principle is *standard of living.* Under this principle a police officer's salary is determined by the amount needed to maintain the standard of living for middle- to upper-middle-class people living in the individual city. This principle, though followed elsewhere in the United States, is not very popular in North Carolina.

Operations

Patrols and Investigations

The principal function of law enforcement agencies is not to detect offenses, to identify and apprehend violators, to recover property, or to help present the state's case; rather, it is to prevent crimes. The primary means by which this is accomplished is through patrols.

The patrol unit of any local law enforcement department is the agency's greatest user of personnel; only to the extent that the agency cannot achieve its primary objective—eliminating the actual or believed opportunity to commit crimes successfully—are other police services needed. The following are specifically accomplished by patrols:

- Ensuring the safe movement of vehicles and people
- Protecting the lives and the property of the city's residents and visitors

- Maintaining the public order
- Establishing a field reaction force
- Transmitting information to other governmental agencies that operate on less arduous schedules

A uniformed officer patrolling in a marked vehicle can prevent certain types of crimes. Similarly a detective who promptly identifies and apprehends a criminal and takes him or her before a court that swiftly prosecutes and adjudicates the case deters would-be perpetrators.

Some people construe the commission of a crime as a failure by the police department. However, the police simply cannot prevent all crimes. Consequently, following up on incidents is an important continuing activity of a law enforcement agency. How the police conduct these investigations depends on the department's evaluation of their importance, the personnel involved, and the extent of the community's crime problem.

Because a crime must be investigated as soon as it is known, no single unit of the police department can be exclusively responsible for all criminal investigation. Therefore criminal investigation is carried out by both the patrol force and investigators.

Criminal investigations fall into two distinct yet closely interrelated phases: the preliminary investigation, which includes the activities conducted by officers who first arrive at the scene and the functions that immediately follow; and the follow-up or continuing investigation, which involves identifying the perpetrator, recovering stolen property, and preparing the case for court. Whether this follow-up is conducted by a specialized investigative unit or by the patrol officer depends on the offense, the department's total workload, and its size. Most communities cannot afford to have a specialized investigator follow up on every incident or crime. The amount of time that should be spent on a specific case should also be determined by probable success in solving the crime by apprehending the perpetrator and recovering stolen property.

Preliminary Investigations

A preliminary investigation begins when an incident is reported and continues until the point at which a delay is not likely to jeopardize the successful conclusion of the case. It is usually performed by the officer who arrives first at the scene and may include the following steps:

1. Obtain aid for an injured victim.
2. Determine whether a crime has actually been committed, and if so, what crime.
3. Apprehend the suspect if he or she is at the scene, or pursue the suspect if it appears that he or she can be caught by immediate pursuit.
4. Inform the radio dispatcher of the description, the direction of flight, and other information that should be broadcast to other officers engaged in pursuit or search, and to those who might participate.
5. Protect the crime scene and determine whether physical evidence exists, as required by departmental policy or order.
6. Notify appropriate departmental units to assist in collection of evidence, immediate follow-up investigation, etc.
7. Gather information about the crime, the victim, suspects, and witnesses.
8. Search for suspects and witnesses not present at the scene.
9. Determine in detail how the crime was committed, what evidence is available, and to what extent there has been injury or loss.
10. While abiding by legal constraints, obtain written statements at the scene from victims or witnesses and suspects.
11. Record all information clearly and accurately on the appropriate report form(s).

The nature of the patrol force, deployed twenty-four hours a day in radio-equipped patrol cars, makes it the logical unit to be assigned preliminary investigations. The fact that the patrol officer is responsible for the preliminary investigation does not necessarily mean that an investigator should not be directed to a crime scene. Sometimes, particularly for offenses against the person, an investigator is immediately needed at the scene, but usually only when his or her greater skill, knowledge, and freedom of movement are required and when the investigation should be continued without further delay.

Continuing Investigations

The follow-up investigation begins when the preliminary investigation or the patrol officer's activities reach a point that demands the specific skills and freedom of movement of a specialized follow-up investigator. Its basic purpose is to investigate designated serious crimes in order to arrest and convict the offender and to recover stolen property. To carry out the continuing investigation properly, the investigator should do the following:

1. Review, consolidate, and analyze officers' field reports relating to their actions during the preliminary phase.
2. Interview the victim and witnesses again to see whether they have discovered or recalled any other facts since the preliminary interview.
3. Review departmental records to establish modus operandi, known suspects, and other recognized patterns.
4. Interview other sources, including informants, petty criminals, people in the neighborhood, and anyone else who may have information about the suspect or the crime.
5. Check pawnshops, junkyards, retail stores, and other places where stolen property may be sold or advanced.
6. Arrange to obtain results of the scientific investigation when items have been forwarded to the crime laboratory.
7. Arrange for information about the crime, stolen property, and the suspect to be disseminated; prepare lookouts, messages, and wanted posters; distribute handbills to merchants, the news media, and the like.
8. Plan organized police action like raids, neighborhood canvasses, and stakeouts that are aimed at discovering additional physical evidence, witnesses, and information about the suspect.
9. Prepare the case for presentation in court when all information and evidence have been obtained.
10. Confer with prosecuting attorneys to (a) review information and evidence to ensure a complete investigation, and (b) help prepare the case for court.

Assignment of Responsibility

A reasonable policy assigns the entire investigation of noncriminal incidents (except deaths and missing persons) and almost all misdemeanors (except certain vice cases) to the uniformed force. In felony cases the uniformed officer performs the preliminary investigation, and the responsibility for the continuing investigation is transferred to an investigation division or office in agencies that have one.

Allocation of Personnel

Police departments attempt to establish the necessary number of patrol officers in three ways. The first method is comparison: community A compares itself with communities B, C, and D, which are the same size as A. The difficulty with this approach is that the problems faced by communities B, C, and D may be entirely different from those faced by community A. In addition, the level of service demanded by community A may be different from that demanded by communities B, C, and D.

The second method uses a ratio based on the number of sworn personnel per 1,000 people. At present the number is approximately 2.2. This figure is a national average and nothing more. It is not one recommended by any police organization, but results from computing statistics compiled by the Federal Bureau of Investigation under the Uniform Crime Reporting System.

The third and most accurate method is based on the workload. This approach uses the formula demonstrated in table 21-1. It permits a more accurate assessment of the number of officers needed to answer the calls for service that come from a specific community.

Once it is determined how many patrol officers the community needs, the next question is how to distribute these officers during any twenty-four-hour period. Alternatives again are available. The state's small communities usually distribute personnel equally over the three eight-hour time frames. Medium-size and large agencies have begun to use other shift schedules, such as nine- or twelve-hour days with overlapping shifts, depending on the individual community's needs. Some agencies follow a schedule that calls for five days on and two days off. Workload studies have indicated that departments usually handle about 33 percent of their calls during the day, 45 percent during the evening, and some 22 percent on the graveyard shift.

Table 21-1
**Example: Calculating the Number of Patrol Officers Needed for a
Given Community**

Number of calls for service (one year)	25,000	
Average time per call (45 min.)	× .75	
Number of officer hours spent	18,750	
Buffer factor[a]	× 3	
Number of officer hours needed	56,250	
One officer's annual hours[b]	÷ 2,920	
Number of officers needed	19.3	
Assignment availability factor[c]	× 1.7	
Total number of officers needed	32.7	(33.0)

a. Officers spend 33% of their time answering calls, 50% on preventive patrol, and 17% on administrative duties, so the number of hours spent answering calls must be multiplied by 3 to determine the total number of hours of patrol officers' time needed.

b. Eight-hour day × 365 days.

c. Adds allowance for days off, vacations, etc.

When it is known how many officers are needed and which days of the week they will work, the question becomes where they will work. The workload of each watch is analyzed, and beat structures consistent with major thoroughfares and natural boundaries are established. An effort is made to distribute workloads equally among the units. This makes the beat smaller on the evening watch because more cars are available, and larger on the day and midnight watches.

Safeguarding of Information

One major police function is information gathering. Much information is routine in nature, but some is personal and sensitive. Safeguarding information is an important responsibility of the department. Failure to do so can cause irrevocable damage both to a department as a whole and to individuals, and it can ultimately lead to a loss of public confidence in the police organization. In contemplating security the chief must assess the reliability of department personnel as well as unauthorized people.

The records system must be made secure. The information center should be organized to provide physical barriers to unauthorized traffic through it. Only police employees assigned to the records function should have access to the records. Other police personnel should be served at a counter and not permitted inside the center without specific written permission from the chief. Admission to the radio facilities and the teletype room should also be firmly restricted to authorized and properly identified department personnel.

Ordinarily, information should not be given over the phone to an unknown caller. Procedures should be established for handling telephone requests for information.

Special Issues

Community-Oriented Policing

Community-oriented policing is a method of attempting to provide law enforcement services through decentralization with the emphasis on neighborhood contacts between police officers and residents of that part of the community. In the past this approach was referred to as *team policing*.

Implementation of this approach involves assigning a group of officers to a specific geographical area for lengthy periods. It becomes the group's responsibility to develop programs that encourage interactions between police officers and the citizens. Numerous individual projects may be implemented. For example, in Wilmington the city has purchased portable trailers that are moved into specific neighborhoods; when projects such as DARE (Drug Abuse Resistance Education) have been completed, the trailers are moved to other neighborhoods. A general emphasis here is on group meetings between police officers and the citizens. The purpose of such meetings is to help design ways in which police and citizen cooperation can reduce crime and make that portion of the community safer for all people. Another example is the development of the Neighborhood Watch program.

This approach at times delegates to the local residents more control over what is important to them. The police, by providing a professional service, are then able to make the community more enjoyable, safe, and economically sound. The theory behind community-oriented policing is that both the police and the citizens become knowledgeable about what is needed and what can be provided. Each group then interacts in a positive way to provide the essential police services without the conflicts that may arise through centralized bureaucratic red tape.

Problem-oriented policing differs from community-oriented policing in that it is designed for dealing with one specific problem at a time. Community-oriented policing is proactive, whereas problem-oriented policing is reactive. Problem-oriented policing involves careful analysis of where crimes are occurring and what their true causes are. It then directs patrol forces, investigators, and other teams of officers to target areas to work with the community on resolving a specific problem. Although these approaches seem somewhat the same, the emphasis in most cities in North Carolina has been on community-oriented policing, with problem-oriented policing being a part of the overall program.

Civilian and Exempt Positions

A number of tasks in the police service do not require a qualified commissioned police officer and indeed can be better performed by others. The range of positions to be considered is very broad. For example, a qualified secretary can perform the department's clerical tasks better than a police officer can. After study, police administrators will realize that civilian specialists can be employed for several types of agency functions, such as record management, communications, and data processing.

The principle of seeking the best-qualified person to fill a position should always be followed in police operations. Police executives should participate in available management programs so that they can offer the police service progressive administrative techniques.

Well-trained, highly educated, and experienced civilians are ideal for staff positions in planning and research, finance, personnel, training, laboratory, and records. Similarly there may well be sworn police command personnel who can head legal, administrative, public relations, and community relations activities. The advantage in being flexible about filling certain staff positions with either civilians or force personnel is that recruitment for the job can be based primarily on expertise in the field. Also, a properly trained newcomer is likely to bring a fresh approach and be free of limiting, traditional ideas. Furthermore, a well-qualified civilian, in his or her daily communications with the department's sworn personnel, will broaden their perspective. Conversely, the civilian will gain a new understanding of law enforcement problems, and another avenue into the community will be established.

Press Policy

The police department needs a policy for releasing information to the press. Reporters are entitled to receive newsworthy information and be given a summary of current police cases. They can then indicate which of the day's cases they want to review. If releasing information might jeopardize an investigation or prejudice the rights of a defendant in a particular case, the press should be told that the information exists, that an investigation is in process, and that the results will be released at the appropriate time.

An agreement should be reached between the press and the department about what kinds of information warrant a *no publicity* label. Items that fall into this category might include the names of female victims of sex crimes, the names of undercover officers, and so on. If reporters violate the agreement, the matter should be taken up with the newspaper's management. The police should not expect reporters to honor a no-publicity designation merely because a victim does not want publicity.

The departmental policy should clearly indicate who is authorized to discuss police investigations with reporters. Ordinarily these persons include the officers responsible for investigating the case, the supervisor, the section commander, and the chief. Exceptions may sometimes have to be made to this policy, but in each exception the section commander or the chief should decide who should talk to reporters.

Constructive journalism can greatly help law enforcement by emphasizing the agency's positive aspects. However, the department must make it easy for the press to publish information favorable to the department. Press releases covering the goals and the policies of the department, or statements clarifying a major issue or investigation, should be written or approved by the chief. The paper's copy editor will not have to rewrite them—and perhaps inadvertently distort the facts. A copy should be provided for each newspaper and each radio or television station in the community.

Police-Citizen Councils

Although the term *communication* is overworked, the function itself remains the vital link to understanding between the police and the community. The police have a responsibility to the community to lead in a police-community dialogue. When frank and fair conversation is established between the police and the community, misunderstanding and distrust can be eliminated and tensions relieved. The department should take the first steps in this direction by establishing police-citizen councils. Those who serve on the councils can act as a channel of communication between the police and their respective portions of the community. The chief should directly involve his or her line personnel in organizing the councils because their participation is essential to a sound community relations program. Furthermore, the entire department must understand the purpose, the function, and the activities of the councils. Only then will the program succeed.

The chief or the chief's delegate should ask representative community and civic organizations to select a member to participate in the police-citizen council. This method of selection results in a broad, representative sample of the people who live or work in a geographic area.

Community Security

Any crime prevention effort should include strong advice to the public on security precautions for homes, places of business, and motor vehicles. Citizens can take several relatively easy, common-sense measures to reduce the threat of crime to their persons or property. A number of crimes needlessly involve negligence on the part of victims. When they leave home, sensible people will lock their doors and windows securely, leave automatically activated night lights burning during long absences, lock the garage doors, cancel milk and newspaper deliveries, and alert the neighbors or the police to their absence.

Pyramid telephone warning systems are operating in some cities among liquor stores, grocery chains, gas stations, and clothing merchants. For example, when they receive a report of a check fraud, a shoplifting incident, a confidence game, or a robbery, the police warn designated merchants by telephone. Those merchants in turn call others, giving the details of the crime and if possible describing the suspects. Such crimes often are committed in series, and pyramid warnings have often brought about the apprehension of suspects when they tried to strike again. In some places, merchants have rigged a system that sends an alarm to other stores within a four-block radius; once warned, shopkeepers watch for fleeing suspects from their vantage points. This system has sometimes produced information vital to the later identification of suspects.

Educating citizens and business persons on how to avoid becoming victims of crime can be a valuable adjunct to a crime-control program. Such campaigns are sometimes undertaken by the police, other times by interested citizen or business groups. The best ones are often a cooperative effort. The American Association of Federated Women's Clubs and the National Auto Theft Bureau have conducted auto-theft-prevention campaigns in several cities, accompanying the police on their rounds, leaving pamphlets in unlocked cars, and attaching warnings to parking meters on the dangers of leaving keys in the ignition.

Citizens need to remember that crime is possible in their life, and take reasonable steps to limit opportunities for criminal activities. In emergencies they must assume the responsibility for summoning aid for victims or police in distress; they cannot stay free of involvement, yet expect others to protect them. In groups and even as individuals, they can supply desperately needed auxiliary resources to the police, the courts, and correctional officers. Much work remains to be done in developing effective and lasting public education campaigns to persuade citizens to take the few extra precautions that can deter many crimes.

Future Law Enforcement

Municipal police work is a dynamic, changing field of operation, policy formulation, and execution. The municipal governing body must understand and involve itself in this important and visible agency of city government. Understanding must be based on an awareness of the limits to law enforcement in the community and a keen appreciation that although police operations are costly in financial terms, their noneconomic benefits are many.

Future Law Enforcement Officers

Law enforcement officers of the future will be different kinds of persons from those with whom many police managers now deal. Certain attributes that law enforcement officers of the future will need can be identified—attributes that will foster their self-confidence and self-control:

1. They will be able to exercise discretion and judgment, and they will believe that they can overcome the problems they face.
2. They will be service oriented. They will emphasize their interests in helping others in trouble and will be sympathetic and kind toward others.
3. They will know both themselves and others. They will be able to understand what motivates them as a person, to understand the differences between other groups of people and themselves, and to live with these differences.
4. They will be achievement oriented. They will want to do the best job that they can at all times.
5. They will be free of cynicism. They will not feel that the public is their enemy, but will guard against hardness and fight against possible alienation from the community that they serve.
6. They will have endurance, physical ability, and stamina. They will be willing to work hard and long when necessary, and they will have the physical capabilities to succeed under trying conditions.
7. They will have enthusiasm for the law enforcement profession. They will not be eight-hour-a-day persons who dread coming to work each day.
8. They will have a sense of humor. They will be able to laugh at themselves and with others.
9. They will be loyal and honest, even about their own mistakes. Their loyalty will be not to one individual, but to the profession of law enforcement, to a high degree of ethics, and to the department in which they work.
10. They will have speaking and writing skills so that they will be able to communicate effectively with other members of the department as well as with the public.

The Future Chief of Police

To deal with these law enforcement officers, a new type of chief will be needed. This new chief must be skilled in problem solving, flexible, and not bound by tradition. He or she must be able to identify with individual officers and show empathy toward them. The new chief must also be able to deal with situations of conflict, not from fear or necessity, but from a desire to help bring about the growth and the maturity of those in the department. He or she must know how to cooperate, not only with top administrators in the department and with the department's lowest-level personnel, but also with federal, state, and county law enforcement personnel. The chief must also constantly strive to continue individual learning and growth, to be more effective tomorrow than today or yesterday.

The new chief will need human relations skills to run a police department effectively. In the future, chiefs will be adopting techniques like using flatter organizational structures and task forces and promoting decision making at lower levels within the organization.

In the history of the city manager form of government, there has been a general shifting of administrative responsibility from line-operation department heads to specialized administrative agencies or departments like purchasing, finance, and personnel. However, there now seems to be a shift in the opposite direction. More responsibility and accountability are being placed on the police chief. Administrative powers seem to be shifting back into the hands of the police department. One major problem with centralizing functions like personnel administration is that it sometimes forces the chief of police to try to achieve goals that cannot be reached because of the specialized regulations. An example might be a requirement that personnel who are injured in the line of duty take sick leave. A police chief might feel that it is unfair to impose such a requirement on an officer wounded during a gun battle or seriously injured while attempting to save someone's life—that there should be some other type of leave for the officer so that he or she can reserve sick leave for sickness. With such an administrative fiat, recruiting becomes difficult—one single incident can kill morale. Giving police chiefs jurisdiction in such areas as personnel may make them more accountable than they perhaps were.

In the future, more professionals than have done so in the past will probably seek contracts before they accept employment as chief of police. A contract will ensure them of adequate time to accomplish the objectives for which they are being employed.

Future chiefs of police will be held more responsible for productivity, for better use of the taxpayers' dollars, and for a higher level of service with the same number of personnel. Such a change may at first glance seem incongruous, but through better management and operational practices and better personnel allocation systems, these kinds of long-term goals can and will be achieved.

How far the changes will go is hard to predict. One direction, however, seems fairly obvious. Both lower and upper levels of law enforcement personnel will be more qualified to do their respective jobs, and they will be increasingly rewarded for their abilities and production. These rewards will come not only in pay increases and better fringe benefits but also in the way the agency is run. The people within the agency will be able to develop pride, to increase their skills, and to feel worthwhile; they will feel successful through working for a specific police department within the law enforcement profession as a whole.

Additional Resources

Bobb, William J. *Police Personnel Administration*. Boston: Holbrook Press, 1978.

Bobb, William J., and Donald O. Schultz, *Principles of American Law Enforcement and Criminal Justice*. Springfield, Ill.: Charles C. Thomas Publishing Company, 1985.

International City/County Management Association. *Municipal Police Administration*. Washington, D.C.: ICMA, 1989.

Lynch, Ronald G. *The Police Manager*. Cincinnati, Ohio: Anderson Publishing Company, 1993.

National Advisory Commission on Criminal Justice Standards and Goals. *The Police*. Washington, D.C.: the Commission, 1973.

Shanahan, Donald T. *Patrol Administration*. Boston: Holbrook Press, 1977.

Swanson, Charles R., Jr. *Criminal Investigation*. Santa Monica, Calif.: Goodyear Publishing Company, 1992.

22 Fire Protection

Ben F. Loeb, Jr., and Sherman Pickard

Contents

THE BASIC fire service problem confronting city officials today is how to provide an acceptable level of fire service at an affordable cost. In light of firefighters' demands for higher salaries and increased fringe benefits, the cost of mandates under the Occupational

Safety and Health Act, and the rising cost of fire apparatus and fire stations, city officials face the task of finding the revenues to support an acceptable level of fire service.

The Fire Problem in Cities

For city officials the first step in reducing fire losses is to determine the extent and the nature of the local fire problem so that it can be properly attacked. That is, what is there to burn, where is it, and what fire hazards are there?

To understand the fire problem in any city, one must first know what there is to burn. Certain sections of the city may represent a greater fire risk than others. Most cities and towns have three principal types of building construction: fire resistive, masonry and frame, and all frame. The first type has fire-resistive walls, floors, and roofs. The masonry-and-frame type has masonry walls, wood-joisted floors, wooden interior partitions, and wooden roofs. The all-frame type has wood throughout. The type of construction is important because the building's character and arrangement affect not only the fire risk to the building but also the risk to its occupants and contents.

Generally speaking, a city's fire problem will consist of a central business district, usually referred to as the *high-value district*, and single-occupancy facilities that represent a particular problem—for example, lumberyards, bulk oil-storage plants, and public and institutional buildings like schools, hospitals, and nursing homes. Also, outside the central business district lie other mercantile properties, industrial properties, and, of particular interest today, shopping centers.

Single-occupancy dwellings are not considered a serious fire problem to any city in terms of property loss. In a typical city in a normal year, dwellings account for approximately two-thirds of all fires in buildings, but the monetary losses from these fires are relatively small compared with the losses from fires in other buildings. Fires in dwellings, however, are a major concern because the greatest loss of life from fire occurs in residential property.

Of particular significance in identifying the local fire problem is the possibility of group fires and conflagrations. The congestion of buildings in central business districts increases the fire risk, and the arrangement of certain groups of buildings may tend to make a rapidly spreading fire possible. Large buildings of combustible construction so arranged that fire can spread from one floor to another and from one end of the building to the other, form the nucleus of such groups. Even if a building and its neighbors are built of brick or concrete, fire can readily spread from one structure to another through window and door openings.

In summary, a city's fire problem can be described in terms of the buildings within the community that present a fire hazard: how many there are, how they are constructed, where they are, how quickly fire will spread among them, and how likely it is that lives will be lost. The problem can be further characterized by how many impediments there are that might slow up the fire-fighting response, like limited-access highways, railroads, and rivers.

The City Fire Service: An Overview

The fire service is an important function of city government. Its four objectives are (1) to prevent fires, (2) to prevent loss of life and property when a fire starts, (3) to confine a fire to the place where it started, and (4) to extinguish a fire. From the viewpoint of city government, these objectives involve the following: a headquarters staff for budget and payroll, personnel selection and records, clerical support, planning, and public relations; maintenance, including care of apparatus, hoses, and supplies; training, including study of operations; communications, including receipt and transmission of alarms; fire prevention, including inspection services and enforcement of fire laws, codes, standards, and ordinances; and, of course, fire suppression.

These tasks are performed by all fire departments in varying degrees. In large departments they may be further subdivided among various individuals or offices. For example, maintenance services, supplies, and related functions may be handled by separate staffs or by individuals. More than 90 percent of North Carolina city fire departments are staffed entirely or primarily by volunteers, yet all the essentials must be performed, whether by volunteers or regular staff. Cities are not required to have a fire department,[1] but most do.

When a city establishes a fire department, it assumes an implied obligation to provide a reasonable level of fire protection. Courts have ruled that failure to provide adequate facilities or to control a fire does not constitute a liability against a city; nevertheless, people expect the fire department to be reasonably competent in controlling fire, considering the adequacy of equipment, manpower, and water supply along with the nature of the fire and its headway when discovered.

Neither the public nor common and statutory law is entirely clear about where responsibility for fire protection lies—with the individual for his or her own life and property protection or with the public fire department. The limitations that affect the public fire protection service are also not generally understood, even by fire service members. As a result, fire protection agencies often assume tasks that are quite beyond their physical resources and capabilities.

In the public mind and in the credo of the fire service, the prime responsibility of the fire service is to save life and prevent human suffering. In other words, the concept of a fire service capable only of protecting exposures, even though this is a recognized responsibility in fire fighting, would not be acceptable to either the firefighters or the general public. The fire problem is best managed through fire prevention. However, when a fire occurs, the obvious alternative is to extinguish it promptly.

Costs of City Fire Protection

The cost of supporting a municipal fire department can be substantial. (During the 1993–94 fiscal year, total outlays for fire service in Raleigh exceeded $15 million.) Moreover, the total fire cost for a city includes not only the direct outlays for fire protection and the value of the property destroyed, but also the installation and maintenance cost of private fire protection systems, insurance premiums in excess of losses paid, costs of compliance with laws and ordinances enacted in the interest of fire prevention, losses due to disruption of business by fire, and loss of life and personal injury. Not all of these can be measured in dollars and cents. There is no basis for accurately estimating the amount of indirect losses and the various other factors that affect total fire costs, but it is generally assumed that the addition of these other factors makes the cost several times that of the direct fire loss.

The principal costs of direct fire loss are paid by property owners in insurance premiums. These costs indicate the measurable burden that is placed on a city, but give no idea of the indirect and unmeasurable losses, which are frequently larger and often more serious than the direct losses. Fire interrupts a business, causing loss of contracts, dismissal of employees, and a general scattering of customers. Burned property ceases to pay taxes. Every one of the thousands of fire alarms answered each day by fire departments in American cities disrupts already congested traffic, takes people away from their work to watch fire-fighting operations, and imperils the lives of persons in the street.

Legal Aspects of City Fire Protection

G.S. 160A-291 authorizes a city to appoint a fire chief, employ firefighters, organize a fire department, and prescribe the duties of the department. The duties of a fire chief (unless otherwise specified by ordinance or charter provision) are to direct fire-fighting and training activities, preserve the fire apparatus, have fire hazards corrected, and make annual reports to the city council concerning departmental activities (G.S. 160A-292). These statutes allow, but do not require, a city to provide fire protection.

Cities and towns are expressly authorized by G.S. 160A-293 to install and maintain water mains and hydrants, as well as buildings and equipment, inside or outside the city. In addition, personnel and equipment may be sent to protect unincorporated areas pursuant to an agreement between a city and a county or between a city and the owner of property to be protected. (Counties may make payments to cities from tax funds for fire protection furnished to rural areas.) G.S. 160A-293(b) provides that there will be no civil liability on the part of the city or its employees for failure to answer a fire call outside the corporate limits. Also, the city (but not individual firefighters) is exempt from civil liability for acts committed in rendering fire protection outside the city. Employees of city fire departments, while performing services outside the city on the orders of the fire chief or the city council, have the same jurisdiction, authority, rights, privileges, and immunities as they enjoy within the city. One important privilege conferred by this provision is coverage under the North Carolina Workers' Compensation Act [G.S. 160A-293(c)].

Some cities contract to furnish fire protection to rural fire protection districts located in unincorporated areas, whereas others contract with an incorporated volunteer fire department to furnish fire protection to them. The authority to contract for fire protection is contained in G.S. 160A-11 and G.S. 160A-461, which give cities the power to contract or be contracted with; and in the provisions of G.S. 160A-274 and G.S. 160A-277 that authorize cities to lease property, to use real and personal property jointly with another governmental unit, and to lease, sell, or convey land to a volunteer fire department that provides fire protection to the city.

Increasingly North Carolina cities are annexing territory that includes part or all of a rural fire district. The effect of the annexation is often to eliminate or seriously to reduce the tax base supporting the fire department that protects the district. As a result, provisions have been added to G.S. Chapter 160A, Article 4A, requiring cities in some circumstances to enter into a five-year contract with the rural department (to furnish protection in the annexed area) and to assume a part of the department's debt.

Before 1991, cities and counties were authorized (but not required) to adopt a fire prevention code. All the large cities adopted one; many of the small communities did not. Effective July 1, 1991, a statewide fire prevention code was made part of the North Carolina Building Code (G.S. 143-138). This new state code is enforced by city (or county) inspection departments and fire prevention inspectors (G.S. 160A-411 through -438).

Types of Fire Protection and Fire-Fighting Apparatus

Two types of fire protection are available to an urban community. The first is private fire protection, such as automatic sprinklers, automatic fire detection systems, and automatic extinguishing systems like those found in commercial property and other particularly hazardous areas. The second is normally referred to as *public fire defenses*, which consist of a publicly supported fire department, a public water system, a building inspection function, and, to some extent, police protection relating to discovery and reporting of fires.

The two principal types of fire-fighting apparatus are pumpers, or pumping engines, and ladder trucks. The number of pumping engines and ladder trucks in any city will depend on the nature of the local fire problem, the level of fire service desired, and the city's ability to finance the equipment. Pumping engines carry hose and are equipped with a pump, a water tank, and various fire-fighting appliances. Standard pump sizes are 750, 1,000, 1,250, 1,500, and 2,000 gallons per minute. The most popular pumper in North Carolina cities is the 1,000-gallons-per-minute size. The chassis on which the equipment is mounted may be of the commercial type used by industry and business, or it may be custom built by the manufacturer. The major advantage of a well-designed commercial pumping engine is that it will cost less than a comparable custom model.

Ladder trucks, the second type of fire-fighting apparatus, are found in cities that have buildings of three or more stories. Their chief function is to transport the large assortment of tools and appliances needed at fires and the personnel to use them. Usually they carry a ladder that operates automatically to a height of 85 to 100 feet. The ladder is permanently attached to the truck and is raised by power provided from the truck's motor. In recent years some cities have purchased *elevating platforms* in lieu of (or in addition to) the standard automatically raising type of ladder truck. The aerial platform looks like the *bucket trucks* normally used by commercial power companies in constructing overhead lines.

The Fire Department

Types of Fire Departments

North Carolina has three types of city fire departments and many variations of each: (1) career, (2) part career and part volunteer, and (3) all volunteer. A city fire department combines three elements: (1) fire stations, (2) fire equipment, and (3) personnel. The type of fire department and the quantity of the various elements depend on the size of the city, the level of fire protection desired by the citizens, and the city's willingness and ability to finance fire protection.

Organization

To accomplish its objectives, the fire department is usually organized into three broad divisions: administration, fire prevention, and fire suppression.

Administration

The fire chief, the deputy chiefs, and the assistant chiefs are administrative personnel. Their duties include, but are not necessarily restricted to, finance, purchasing, recruiting standards, promotional systems, personnel records, planning, and public relations. The fire chief is the city's fire administrator and is responsible for the department's entire operation. The degree to which the chief delegates authority and assigns responsibility depends on the capability of his or her administrative staff and the organization's size.

Fire Prevention

In small fire departments, fire prevention activities, including the inspection of buildings and the enforcement of codes and standards, may be performed by personnel normally assigned to fire companies. In large cities, prevention activity (and public fire education) is normally carried out by fire company personnel and full-time fire prevention technicians. This group is usually assigned to a "fire prevention bureau," which is an operating division of the department. The number of technicians assigned to this division is determined by the city's size and the level of service desired.

Fire Suppression

More than 90 percent of a city fire department's total personnel are assigned to the fire suppression division. This division consists of fire stations, fire apparatus, and fire suppression personnel. The smallest unit within the fire suppression organization is called a fire company; it usually consists of three to five people on duty at all times assigned to one fire truck. The person in charge of a fire company usually has the rank of company captain or company lieutenant. Cities with twelve or more fire stations may be divided into districts. A district chief has jurisdiction over each district.

Several North Carolina city departments provide, within the fire suppression division, emergency medical first-responder service, hazardous-materials emergency service, and heavy-duty rescue service.

Support Services to the Fire Suppression Division

Three support services are essential to the department's fire suppression mission: training, communications, and maintenance.

Training

Training must be performed in any fire department, regardless of size, whether by full-time training instructors or by company personnel who have dual responsibilities. The city's size usually determines whether a full-time training officer is justified. North Carolina fire departments in cities of 35,000 people or more usually have at least one full-time training officer. The training usually relates to the fire suppression activities only. The local training program is designed around the individual city's fire problems and usually consists of twenty to thirty subjects, ranging from first aid to fire-fighting tactics and strategy. That training program is usually supplemented by fire service training programs offered by the state in both basic and specialized areas.

Communications

An emergency communication system consists of two elements, reporting and dispatching. The most common means of reporting a fire to the fire department is by telephone. More than 95 percent of all fire calls are received in this manner. Another current type of emergency reporting system is emergency telephones strategically located throughout the city. These consist of a pole-mounted box that contains a telephone handset. The caller simply opens the door of the phone box, lifts the handset off the hook, and announces the nature of the emergency. A newer reporting system now being tried in a few states (though not in North Carolina) is the radio reporting system, whereby a radio signal is transmitted from the box location to fire headquarters or to a central communication center.

The communication system's dispatching element consists of a dispatcher's announcing to an individual fire company, over a two-way radio system or an intercom system, the location and the nature of the alarm. In some large cities, only the fire companies that will respond to the call are alerted. In small cities all companies are alerted, regardless of which ones are to respond. Constant communications are maintained between the dispatcher and the fire apparatus by two-way radio. All automobiles used by fire department personnel, including the chief administrator's, are so equipped.

Maintenance

Never before in the history of the fire service has maintenance of apparatus and equipment played a more critical role than it does in today's fire departments. It is said that armies move on stomachs of soldiers; fire service personnel deliver their services with modern apparatus and equipment.

To comply with federal emission control regulations, the manufacturers of diesel engines have had to resort to very sophisticated electronic fuel-injection systems. Extremely sensitive to close setup tolerances, these systems require expensive diagnostic equipment for proper maintenance. This new generation of electronically controlled engines is surely challenging even the best of fire department maintenance personnel.

Another dramatic change has occurred in the design of automatic transmissions for fire-fighting apparatus. Proper shifting relies on a close-tolerance electronic mechanism that is driven by a miniature computer chip. Even a slight drop in battery voltage below the required level results in an engine that will not accelerate and a transmission that will not shift. Again expensive diagnostic treatment is required to keep the apparatus in top working order.

The proper maintenance of the electronic systems of fire-fighting apparatus is therefore of paramount importance. It requires a much higher level of technical service than previously needed.

Finally, reliance on computer-aided dispatch systems and ultra-high-frequency radio communication systems for the delivery of fire department emergency services has added a new dimension to the importance of the maintenance function.

Public Fire Defenses and Fire Insurance Rates

The base fire insurance rates in a given city are determined by the city's fire insurance classification. Engineers of the Insurance Service Office of North Carolina (ISO) inspect the public fire defenses in a city to establish its insurance classification. The ISO is a private organization maintained by the stock fire insurance companies that do business in North Carolina. The standard against which

Table 22-1
Details of the 1980 Fire Suppression Rating Schedule

	Maximum Percent Credit
Fire Alarm System	
Receiving fire alarms	2
Operators	3
Dispatching companies	5
	10
Fire Department	
Number of engine companies	11
Number of ladder and service companies	6
Distribution of companies	4
Pumping capacity	5
Department personnel levels	15
Training	9
	50
Water Supply Capabilities	
Water supply system	35
Size, type, and installation of hydrants	2
Inspection and condition of hydrants	3
	40

a city is inspected is titled Fire Suppression Rating Schedule (FSRS). See table 22-1.

The grading is done strictly on the basis of the department's ability to extinguish fires rapidly, with a minimum loss of life and property. It is not concerned with the economical expenditure of public funds in operating the department. The grading addresses the administrative management of the department only to a very limited extent, and supervision only to the extent that supervisory methods may affect the ability to perform fire-fighting functions.

The better a city's ISO classification, the lower the prices that property owners pay for fire or homeowners insurance. These classifications run from Class 1 through Class 10. In North Carolina, only Greensboro has a Class 1 rating. A 10 essentially means that ISO does not recognize the area as having any fire protection whatsoever. Most North Carolina cities have a fire rating of 3 to 8.

Insurance classifications are based entirely on the FSRS. The current FSRS, which has been in effect since 1980, assigns up to 10 percent to the fire alarm system, up to 50 percent to the quality of the fire department, and up to 40 percent to the water supply capabilities of the area. These are further broken down as shown in table 22-1.

Cities rated 1 through 8 that have questions about their classification should contact the ISO in Raleigh. Cities or other areas whose classification is 9 or 10 should contact the Fire and Rescue Services Division of the North Carolina Department of Insurance in Raleigh.

Additional Resources

Loeb, Ben F., Jr. *Fire Protection Law in North Carolina.* 5th ed. Chapel Hill, N.C.: Institute of Government, The University of North Carolina at Chapel Hill, 1993.

Notes

1. OWASA v. Carrboro, 58 N.C. App. 676, 294 S.E.2d 757 (1982).

23 Streets

Kurt Jenne, Warren Jake Wicker, and David M. Lawrence

Contents

THE DEVELOPMENT of roads and streets has a long history in North Carolina.[1] Many years before the arrival of the first European settlers, Native Americans had developed a system of trails throughout much of the state. The settlers brought with them a well-developed appreciation of the importance of roads in the advancement of any society. Despite this appreciation and increasing attention to road building, some 300 years passed before North Carolina could lay claim to being the Good Roads State.

Historical Development: The "Fifteens" Phenomenon

By coincidence, significant moves have been made in the "fifteens" of the last three centuries. In the early part of the eighteenth century, action was spurred by Church of England missionaries as well as by landowners and commercial interests. In 1715 the colonial legislature adopted a comprehensive plan for laying out roads, constructing bridges, and establishing and maintaining ferries.[2] Responsibility for the development of the plan was placed with local governments—the counties and the cities—where it remained for more than 200 years.

A second push for road improvements came in 1815 under the leadership of State Senator Archibald Murphy of Orange County. In the following years the state chartered private companies to build toll roads, ferries, and bridges along major routes, with state stock ownership in some of them. Most of the roads, however, remained with counties and cities. In the 1840s and the early 1850s the move to toll plank roads emerged.[3] More than 500 miles were constructed at a cost of about $1,500 a mile.

From the early colonial days until the middle of the nineteenth century, roads were often built and maintained by citizens. Typically, all males from age sixteen to sixty were required to contribute their labor, ranging from six to twenty-four days a year. Citizen labor in this fashion, under the direction of overseers, proved less than satisfactory. By the middle of the eighteenth century, some cities had started substituting tax-supported road maintenance for citizen labor. Counties started making the switch later. By the end of the nineteenth century, the requirement for citizen labor on the roads and the streets was ended.

The opening of the twentieth century brought the automobile and increased demand for better roads. (The first cross-country trip by automobile was made in summer 1903—in seventy days. North Carolina first imposed license fees for autos in 1909.) Inspired by the good macadam roads built by George Vanderbilt on his Biltmore estate, the Good Roads Association of Asheville and Buncombe County was organized. Later it expanded into a statewide organization. A key leader of the statewide organization, and its field representative, was Miss Hattie Berry, the secretary of the North Carolina Geological Survey and an Orange County native. The association's efforts were initially directed at improving roads by counties. The increased auto travel and the prospect of federal aid (which started in 1916) resulted in the creation of the State Highway Commission in 1915 with an appropriation of $10,000. It was charged with appointing a state highway engineer who would advise counties on their road-building responsibilities.

Developments since 1915

The next major move came in 1921 when the state assumed responsibility from the counties for the roads connecting the 100 county seats and running through all other cities and towns with a population of 3,000 or more.[4] This first statewide system, which totaled 5,500 miles, was financed by a combination of license fees and a gasoline tax of one cent per gallon.

Between 1921 and 1927 the state issued $115 million in road bonds to build and improve the system. The Great Depression found counties heavily in debt for roads and schools. In 1931, under the leadership of Governor O. Max Gardner, the state took over the remaining county roads—some 45,000 miles.[5]

The 1931 action relieved counties of all road responsibilities except for retirement of their road debt, which was to take another twenty-five years for some counties. The move did nothing for the cities and the towns, however. They remained responsible for all the roads and the streets within their boundaries.

City officials started working for state aid for city streets. The General Assembly responded in 1935 with an appropriation of $500,000 to assist cities in maintaining city streets carrying state highways. Over the years the appropriations increased, reaching $2.5 million in 1949.

The 1949 General Assembly, the first of Governor Kerr Scott's administration, saw two other major actions to improve highways. First, the General Assembly authorized (and the voters approved) the issuance of $200 million in road bonds to improve rural ("farm to market") roads, as promoted by Governor Scott.[6] The proceeds financed the paving of 12,000 miles of rural roads and the stabilizing of another 15,000 miles. Second, the 1949 General Assembly created the State-Municipal Road Commission. Its recommendations led in 1951 to allocation of a part of the state's gasoline tax to municipalities for use on local streets that were to remain municipal responsibilities.[7] The same legislation transferred to the state full responsibility for the construction and the maintenance of some 2,300 miles of roads and streets *within* cities that were part of the state highway system but were being constructed and maintained by cities.

The most recent major highway action came in 1989 during Governor James Martin's administration with the establishment of the North Carolina Highway Trust Fund (G.S. 136, Art. 14). This legislation increased motor fuel and other vehicle taxes and fees to finance a multi-billion-dollar highway improvement program from current receipts of the trust fund. The program projects improvements that would place over 90 percent of the state's population within 10 miles of a four-lane highway, build urban loops, and add funds for rural secondary roads and municipal street aid.

The 1951 arrangement, with modifications for thoroughfare planning in 1959 and several increases in the amount of street aid for cities over the years, remains in place today. Its basic principles are twofold. First, public roads and streets that carry traffic outside, between, into, and through cities are constructed and maintained by the state. Other roads and streets within cities are the responsibility of the cities. Second, streets and highways, both inside and outside cities, are financed primarily from state and municipal shares of vehicle-related revenues. Each motorist, whether driving inside or outside cities in North Carolina, is contributing to the operation of the road or the street on which he or she drives through motor fuel and other taxes.

The Current Street and Highway System

The current public street and highway system in North Carolina totals some 95,000 miles as shown in table 23-1. In round numbers, 82 percent of the mileage is operated by the state, 16 percent by cities, and 2 percent by federal agencies. Of the total mileage some 22 percent is located inside cities.

As notes to table 23-1 indicate, the system is valuable. The estimated current replacement cost is about $100 billion. Given the total value, the outstanding indebtedness for streets and highways is quite small—less than 1 percent of their replacement cost.

Street and highway mileage has shown steady growth over the years—some 26 percent between 1950 and 1990 (see table 23-2). However, the growth in mileage has been far exceeded by increases during the same period in population (63.2 percent), vehicle registration (382.7 percent), and vehicle miles driven (429.5 percent). The short story is one of more roads, much better roads, and greatly increased road use.

Expenditures for streets and highways also have a long record of increases. The mile of plank road constructed in 1850 for $1,500 has

Table 23-1
North Carolina Highway Mileage, January 1, 1992

			Miles	Percentage of Total Miles
State Operated & Maintained by the Department of Transportation			77,155.48	81.0

	Municipal	Nonmunicipal (Rural)	Total
Interstate	234.90	702.34	937.24
Primary	2,188.62	11,208.00	13,396.62
Secondary	3,499.45	59,322.17	62,821.62
Total	5,922.97	71,232.51	77,155.48
Paved	94.2%	80.7%	81.7%
Unpaved	5.8%	19.3%	18.3%

		Miles	Percentage of Total Miles
Operated by Parks and Wildlife		601.14	0.6
Paved	18.8%		
Unpaved	81.2%		
Cities Operated and Maintained by Them		15,380.73	16.2
Paved	94.9%		
Unpaved	5.1%		
Federal Government Parks, Forests, and Military Reservations[a]		2,011.42	2.2
Total		95,148.77	100.0

Source: North Carolina Department of Transportation, Division of Highways, Geographic Information Systems Branch, *Highway and Road Mileage, January 1992* (Raleigh, N.C.: NCDOT, 1992).

Note: The estimated current replacement cost of all state and municipal roads and streets (93,137.35 miles) is $100 billion, or $1.07 million per mile on a statewide basis. This estimate is based on per-mile construction costs that vary from $250,000 for a two-lane, stone-stabilized, unpaved road to $8 million for a four-lane, divided highway in urban areas that is built to Interstate standards. An amount equal to 15 percent of the construction costs is included as the estimated cost of rights-of-way, environmental mitigation, and general administration. On July 1, 1992, state indebtedness for roads was $118.70 million, municipal street debt $476.08 million, for a combined total of $594.78 million. Thus street and highway debt equals less than 1 percent of the estimated replacement cost of the full system. This calculation does not include any outstanding federal government indebtedness for highways, nor private street debt such as that included in mortgages on homes in new subdivisions. Furthermore, the comparison does not take into consideration any physical depreciation of the existing highway facilities. Of course, the value of many roads and streets may well exceed their replacement cost.

a. Mileage on military bases includes only the roads generally open to public travel, not the roads restricted to military personnel.

Table 23-2
Changes in Population, Vehicle Registration, and Highway Mileage, 1950–90

	Year			Percent Change		
	1950	1970	1990	1950–70	1970–90	1950–90
State population (in millions)	4.062	5.084	6.629	25.2	30.4	63.2
Municipal population (in millions)	1.500	2.170	3.195	44.7	47.2	113.0
Vehicle registration (in millions)	1.171	3.208	5.652	174.0	76.2	382.7
Highway mileage (state & mun.)	72,676	85,218	91,914	17.3	7.9	26.5
Lane mileage (state & mun.)	147,000	174,000	196,627	18.4	13.0	33.8
Vehicle miles driven (in billions)	11.852	31.352	62.752	164.5	100.2	429.5
Vehicles per capita	.29	.63	.85	117.2	34.9	193.1
Highway feet per capita	94.5	88.5	73.2	–6.3	–17.3	–22.5
Highway feet per vehicle	327.7	140.3	85.9	–57.2	–38.8	–73.8
Miles driven per capita	2,900	6,200	9,500	113.8	53.2	227.6

Sources: State population for 1950 and 1970 from Bureau of the Census, *Historical Statistics of the United States, Colonial Times to 1970* (Washington, D.C.: U.S. Government Printing Office, 1975), 32; for 1990 from Bureau of the Census, *1990 Census of Population and Housing, North Carolina,* 1990 CPH-1-35 (Washington, D.C.: U.S. Government Printing Office, 1991), table 1, and *1980 Census of Population, Detailed Population Characteristics, North Carolina,* vol. 1, chap. D, pt. 35 (Washington, D.C.: U.S. Government Printing Office, 1983), sec. 1, table 194. Municipal population from North Carolina Department of Transportation, Division of Highways, Planning and Environmental Branch, *Incorporated Municipalities, Municipal Officials, and State Street Aid Allocation, 1950, 1970, 1990* (Raleigh, N.C.: NCDOT, 1950, 1970, 1990). Vehicle registration and miles driven, from North Carolina Department of Transportation, Division of Motor Vehicles, Collision Reports Section, *North Carolina Traffic Accident Facts, 1991* (Raleigh, N.C.: NCDOT, 1992). State highway mileage from North Carolina Department of Transportation, Division of Highways, Geographic Information Systems Branch, *Highway and Road Mileage, January 1992* (Raleigh, N.C.: NCDOT, 1992). Municipal highway mileage for 1950 from John A. McMahon, "Roads and Streets in North Carolina: A Report to the State-Municipal Road Commission," *Popular Government* 17 (September 1950): entire issue; for 1970 and 1990 from NCDOT, *Incorporated Municipalities.* Lane mileage for 1950 and 1970, estimated; for 1990 from NCDOT, *Highway and Road Mileage.*

Note: Municipal streets in 1990 totaled 14,856 miles or 78.44 million feet, for 24.55 feet per capita on the basis of municipal population alone. This compares with the figure of 73.2 highway feet per capita statewide.

been replaced by a rural interstate highway in some places that costs 2,000–3,000 times as much. In 1990 the state and municipal governments expended about $225 per capita in construction and maintenance of the streets and the highways. The 1921 gasoline tax of one cent per gallon has increased seventeenfold, along with comparable increases in registration fees and other vehicle-related charges. Total expenditures for streets and highways in North Carolina for 1990 are reported at $1.5 billion, some 80 percent by the state and 20 percent by cities.[8]

The City Street System

Components

The principal authority for cities to construct, maintain, and operate a city street system is found in G.S. Chapter 160A, Article 15. The system consists of streets, sidewalks, and bikeways.

Streets

Streets are usually the primary means of moving around a city. A city's street system is a circulatory system, like the human circulatory system, by which people and goods reach the vital components of the city—its industrial, commercial, housing, and recreational facilities. Some cities have unusual characteristics that make waterways or rail lines extremely important to their circulation, but for most North Carolina cities, streets are the most important means of movement.

A city's street system contains a variety of street types, each designed to carry a particular volume of traffic in a particular way. Streets usually include more than just the visible pavement. A *right-of-way* extends beyond each side of the pavement. It is controlled by the city and provides room for shoulders, drainage, future widening of the pavement, planting for beautification, or other means of movement, like sidewalks or bicycle paths.

Most streets can be classified into four major categories: freeways, thoroughfares, collectors, and residential streets.

Freeways, or *expressways,* are intended to permit high-speed movement of large volumes of traffic. To help do this, entry and exit are limited to a few carefully chosen places (interchanges). Freeways do not provide direct access to land or buildings. They usually have at least 250 feet of right-of-way, which contains at least 130 feet of pavement, a median strip, and graded shoulders.

Thoroughfares, or *arterials,* are intended to carry a considerable volume of most through traffic and to allow some access to smaller streets, land, and buildings. Often a compromise between these two purposes is struck by putting restrictions on the number and the nature of connections that can be made to the thoroughfare. Four-lane urban thoroughfares require 90–120 feet of right-of-way and are built in a variety of divided or undivided forms.

Collectors are normally busy streets that connect thoroughfares to the smallest streets that serve residential areas. A collector usually requires at least 70 feet of right-of-way and 44 feet of pavement.

Residential streets are intended to provide direct access only to houses or small neighborhood businesses and other facilities that might be found in a residential area. They are intended for low volumes of traffic moving at low speed. Residential streets are usually designed to have 50 feet of right-of-way and 30–32 feet of pavement.

Sidewalks

In the downtown area and in older residential parts of cities, sidewalks usually exist as a normal part of the street system. They are found less frequently in newer residential developments on the fringe of the city and in rural areas. Sidewalks have several functions as a part of the street system. First, they provide safety by separating pedestrians from motor vehicle traffic. This is especially important where there are many pedestrians and vehicles, where vehicle speeds are high, and where lighting or visibility is poor. Second, sidewalks are a convenience to people who choose to walk wherever they want to go. Third, well-maintained sidewalks can improve the appearance of a community when they replace unkempt paths.

Bikeways

As the use of bicycles in a community increases for both recreation and basic transportation, a city often finds that its street system must provide for bikes as well as for motor vehicles and pedestrians. There are three major categories of bikeways: bike paths, bike lanes, and bike routes. A *bike path* is a paved way set aside for bicycles only and prohibited to motor vehicles. Bike paths are often inside the street right-of-way but are almost always clearly separated from the motor vehicle pavement by grade separations, plantings, or other barriers. They should also be separated from sidewalks. *Bike lanes* are usually part of the street pavement, but are separated from motor vehicle lanes by striping, small curbs, or other markings or barriers.

Bike routes usually appear in areas of very light traffic and consist merely of signs to notify motorists that bicycles use the roadway. Bikeways, like sidewalks, are designed to separate bicycle traffic from motor vehicles and pedestrians for safety and convenience. Careful planning is required to make them succeed, for the needs of cyclists are usually not as instinctively clear to decision makers as are the needs of motorists and pedestrians.

Responsibility for the Street System

In North Carolina the responsibility for the municipal street system is shared by the city and the state (G.S. 136-66.1). The state assumes direct responsibility for all streets that are considered to be essential to maintaining travel routes throughout the state—from city to city, and therefore through and around each city. These routes are designated and planned for in the thoroughfare plans that the state prepares with the cooperation of the respective cities. State planners and engineers work with the local elected body or staff to examine the community's growth patterns and projections, to perform traffic surveys, to determine patterns of desired travel, and to suggest locations or improvements for thoroughfares. The city then adopts a plan that may incorporate its own more detailed planning for smaller streets in its system. Once such a plan is adopted by the city and approved by the state, it becomes the city's official thoroughfare plan. At the end of 1992 there were 177 such plans, covering about 230 cities in the state. (Some cities' plans encompass smaller neighbors. The Asheville plan, for example, covers five nearby towns.)

Each thoroughfare plan is reviewed and updated periodically, and along with all the other thoroughfare plans, it serves as the basis for the state's seven-year transportation improvement program. When a thoroughfare is constructed or improved (widened or realigned), the local government usually acquires the necessary right-of-way, and the state performs and pays for all construction associated with the project. Once a thoroughfare is built or designated, the state maintains it. When a city wants to make changes in such features as lane markings, traffic controls, or signs, it must obtain the state's concurrence to do so, but it also usually finds that the state can and will do the work that is required.

Inside the municipal limits, streets other than designated thoroughfares are the city's responsibility. However, the state takes some indirect responsibility for maintaining and improving city streets through its distribution of street aid (Powell Bill) funds to cities. The allocation of these funds is based on the number of miles of streets for which each city is responsible, and its population. The state's responsibility for thoroughfares includes both street improvements and traffic control facilities.

Evaluation of Street System Needs

Whether a city evaluates its street system needs while preparing a state thoroughfare plan or on its own, a number of factors are important in determining these needs.

Growth patterns for the future must be estimated in order to know where residential areas will be located relative to employment and commercial areas. These estimates will suggest both the volume and the location of travel and shipment. In making such a projection, it is almost always necessary to look beyond the city limits.

Travel patterns must be forecast too. This can be done by examining both current travel patterns and anticipated growth patterns.

In projecting future street needs, it is important to consider the *means of travel* that will be available and the ones that people will probably prefer. For example, if many of the people who are included in the calculations of future growth and travel patterns will probably take the bus to work, less street capacity may be called for than if everyone will probably drive an automobile. Trends toward carpooling, vanpooling, and bicycle riding may also reduce the need for street capacity.

The *volume of traffic* that is expected along routes of travel provides a basis for determining the sizes and the types of streets that will be needed. However, *service level* must also be considered—the level of congestion at which a given volume can be handled on a street. For example, a city's traffic volumes at rush hour and during regular hours may be very different. Instead of investing in larger streets oriented to the rush-hour volumes, the city might decide to accept lower service levels—more congestion—at rush hours or to use rush-hour traffic-control measures, which are less expensive than larger streets. Moreover, a city might simply choose to aim for a certain service level to anticipate, or to discourage, development beyond a certain density in the areas served by some streets.

Land use policies should be considered. For example, if the city encourages high-density housing along natural transit corridors, perhaps existing or future bus service could forestall the need to widen some streets. Finally, *plans for public facilities* should be examined to determine whether city recreation facilities, fire station locations, and other service-related plans might affect street system needs.

Priorities for Ranking of Street Improvements

Once a city has determined the needs of its street system and has incorporated them into its own or a state-assisted plan, it must calculate how much it can do over the next year, over the next five years, and so on into the future. Having some idea, either by forecast or by established land use policy, about the timing and the sequence of future development in various areas of the city will help in sorting out future needs.

Few cities will be financially able to provide simultaneously for all future needs as they arise and for maintenance and improvement of the present system. Consequently a number of factors need to be considered in setting priorities among maintenance of existing streets and sidewalks, improvement or rehabilitation of obsolete facilities, and construction of new facilities.

Safety needs usually receive early attention in a street program. Safety considerations might include concerns for patterns of traffic flow as well as for conflicts among users of motor vehicles, pedestrians, and bicyclists.

Convenience may be an important consideration simply in terms of minimizing citizens' dissatisfaction and the adverse economic effects of inconvenience.

Economic development may be affected by the convenience that is afforded to business and industry or by the effects of street improvements on land use patterns. For example, where the city focuses its attention on street improvements might affect whether commercial development occurs downtown or on the periphery.

Fiscal effects might include the relative impact on tax revenues of encouraging or discouraging new development and redevelopment. A consideration of fiscal effects might involve examining the wisdom of accepting grant funds for projects that normally would be done later. It might also entail an analysis of service costs. For example, what economies of maintenance are realized by such measures as preventing clogged storm drains or paving some dirt streets?

Moral obligations are also appropriately included in a city's determination of priorities. These include such considerations as past promises and current needs in recently annexed areas.

Cities will use different criteria for determining priorities and will give them different weights. Nevertheless, taking the criteria into account can help city officials choose among priorities and make intelligent and informed decisions about specific projects to undertake.

Parking

Planning, scheduling, designing, building, and maintaining streets will not by themselves provide adequately for the movement of people and goods throughout a city. The streets provide a pathway for getting from one place to another. However, the drivers' cars must be put somewhere when they arrive at their destinations.

Estimation of Requirements

Estimating parking requirements consists of three major steps: defining the sources of parking needs, defining the magnitude of those needs, and translating the needs into numbers and types of parking facilities. Defining the sources of parking needs includes identifying the facilities or the other uses of land that will attract people. Are there stores, offices, factories, recreation facilities, or schools? What kinds of parking requirements does each kind of land use suggest? Who will use these facilities? Will they travel alone or together, at regular times or random times, and for single or multiple purposes on each trip? Defining the magnitude includes estimating, from the answers to the questions just asked, how many persons will travel to these places each day at what times, and what form of transportation they will prefer or use. Parking needs can then be determined by comparing the demand for parking at various times of day (and sometimes seasons of the year) with the facilities available when the study is made. Normally a careful survey of the use of existing parking will be combined with estimates of total demand, to spot underused capacity in the existing system. Underused capacity might be reserved to accommodate some of the projected demand, or it might suggest some revision of projected demand and the assumptions on which the projection was based.

Determination of the Types of Parking to Provide

Parking can be provided in two ways: spaces on the street or spaces off the street. Once the need for spaces at or around various key locations is determined, the decision can be made about how they will be provided.

On-Street Parking

The use of streets for parking affects their use for traffic movement in three ways. First, curbside parking significantly reduces a street's capacity. At an intersection with a signal, parking on both sides of both streets usually cuts the intersection's—and therefore the street's—capacity roughly in half. Second, curbside parking reduces safety. Vehicles leaving the curb, doors opening into traffic, and pedestrians walking between parked cars are all dangerous concomitants of parking on the street. Third, curbside parking increases service conflict. Curbside space must accommodate not only private cars but also delivery vehicles that need convenient loading zones, buses that need safe and convenient stops, and emergency vehicles that need quick access to buildings and fire hydrants. Furthermore, the alleys that give access to the interior of the block and the crosswalks that permit safe pedestrian crossing of the street all take their slice of curbside space.

Most on-street parking is now parallel; that is, the car is parked parallel to the curb. Angle parking requires a much wider right-of-way for adequate maneuvering room and is generally considered less safe than parallel parking because of the danger of backing into traffic. A community that wishes to establish or keep angle parking probably should do so only if traffic is light and slow. At least 70 feet of pavement should be available if parking on both sides of a street is to be allowed.

Off-Street Parking

If the street system cannot meet parking demand in an area, or if all street capacity is needed to carry traffic, a city might turn to off-street parking instead of or in addition to curbside parking (G.S. 160A-302). Off-street parking can be spaces next to buildings, large surface lots or multistory decks that serve entire areas, or underground garages that serve single buildings or entire areas.

Off-street parking is established in a city in three ways. Any two or more might be used together, depending on the community's needs and circumstances.

Parking Space Required by Land-Use Regulations

Most zoning ordinances include off-street parking requirements for the various categories of land use that they cover. These requirements are usually based on some combination of nationally developed standards or rules of thumb on the number of customer and employee spaces that are likely to be needed for each kind of use and the community's assessment of its own circumstances. The purpose of the requirements is to ensure that buildings, as they are constructed or converted to new uses, do not create more traffic with no place to park, and thus do not add unnecessarily to traffic congestion. Some ordinances require parking on the site of the building; others allow several buildings to pool required spaces in a convenient lot or to earmark the required number of spaces in an existing or planned lot nearby.

Privately Owned Public Parking

This category of parking consists of lots, decks, and garages developed by private firms or individuals to provide off-street parking for a fee to customers or workers in an area. A developer or a private lessee might operate these facilities, or a city might operate them under lease. Parking fees are charged to cover operating costs and profit to the investor.

Publicly Owned Public Parking

These facilities are the same as private off-street facilities, but are either developed, or purchased after development, by a public body—the city or a special authority. Parking fees are charged to cover operating costs and retirement of any public debt used to develop the facilities.

Public Financing of Parking

A variety of means are used to finance public parking that is developed or operated by a public body. On-street parking usually involves little or no acquisition or development expense. It normally uses existing public rights-of-way and existing street pavement. Beyond the small cost of marking spaces, the only costs that a community is likely to incur for curbside parking are for enforcement by city personnel, for parking meters, or for both. Parking meters are the most common means of enforcing time limits for curbside spaces. They also provide a source of revenue to help meet the costs of maintenance and enforcement associated with on-street parking.

Off-street parking is usually a much more costly venture for a city. The city might have to acquire land and construct a lot or a deck. Once the facility is in operation, the city has to control parking and maintain the facility separately from routine street maintenance. Usually the large initial outlays for off-street facilities are covered by bonds, either revenue or general obligation, depending on a variety of factors. Regardless of the type of debt financing used, before the project is undertaken, a city should try to ensure that demand—and therefore use—will provide enough revenue to cover the total cost of developing and operating the facility. Meters may be used on off-street facilities, but attended lots (monitored by persons or machines) are more common as a measure to control turnover and to ensure enough revenue to meet obligations.

Parking on and off the street is intimately linked with the street system and land use in the city. Enough parking must be provided at the right places to facilitate all the daily trips that take place throughout the community. On-street parking competes with that movement. Off-street parking competes for valuable space with the very reason for that movement: productive use of land. Ideally planning for land use, transportation, and parking should be done as an integrated whole, but it seldom is or can be. Nonetheless, a community can benefit by recognizing the relationships among these three elements and consulting its land use and street system plans as it develops its plans for parking.

Table 23-3
Revenue Measures for Financing Street Improvements and
Their Corresponding Financing Principles

Revenue Measure	Financing Principle
Local taxes	Ability to pay
Gasoline taxes	Benefit
Payments from property	
Special assessments	Benefit
Payments in advance	Benefit
Subdivision improvement requirements	Benefit
Impact fees	Benefit

Financing of Street and Sidewalk Improvements

Street and highway financing in North Carolina is shared by the city, state, and federal governments. In 1990 the approximate shares of street and highway funds provided by the three types of governments were federal, 27.5 percent; state, 61.7 percent; and cities, 10.8 percent.[9]

For the past sixty years North Carolina's basic principle for financing highways has called for streets and highways to be financed largely from the gasoline tax and other vehicle-related taxes, licenses, and charges. Because all the federal and state support is derived on this basis, the principle is largely being followed. A part of the city support, however, comes from other than highway-user revenues, and some of this money is derived from assessments for street improvements based on special benefits to property.

Revenue Measures for Financing Improvements

North Carolina's cities have three major revenue measures that may be used to finance street improvements, two of which may also be used to finance sidewalks. The revenue measures and the taxing principle underlying each appear in table 23-3.

General Local Taxes

All cities may levy taxes to finance street and sidewalk improvements (G.S. Ch. 160A, Art. 9). The property tax is the chief local tax, although receipts from a city's auto licenses, privilege license taxes, and dog taxes may be used, as may revenues received from other governments—community development grants and shared taxes, such as sales, franchise, and beer and wine taxes. All the local taxing measures are levied on the ability-to-pay principle. They are extracted according to property ownership or purchases, measures that are assumed to represent financial capacity. Street improvements financed from these measures are not directly related to any special benefits.

Gasoline Tax

Since 1951 the state has shared part of its gasoline tax receipts with cities for use on city streets (but not on sidewalks) (G.S. 160A-41.1). These moneys are the so-called Powell Bill funds. The gasoline tax in principle is a benefit levy. The amount of gasoline purchased, it is assumed, reflects generally the extent of the buyer's use of streets and highways. Thus the more gasoline one buys, the more one uses the highways and the more one realizes benefit.

The original distribution of gasoline tax revenues was based on an allocation to the cities of 0.5 cent of the state's tax per gallon. Half of this allocation was distributed to cities in proportion to their population and half in proportion to their city system street mileage (that is, excluding state-maintained streets within the city). The allocation per gallon was increased to 1 cent in 1971, all the increase being distributed in proportion to population. The 1981 General Assembly increased the cities' share to 1.375 cents of the state's 12-cent tax per gallon, to become effective in 1982, and kept the proportion used in the population-mileage distribution formula at 3 to 1.

An increase in the allocation to 1.75 cents per gallon was made by the 1986 General Assembly, to be effective in 1987. As noted previously, a major highway improvement program was launched in 1989 with the proceeds of its significant tax increases going into the newly established Highway Trust Fund. The act underlying the program also directed that 6.5 percent of the funds (after some minor adjustments) be added to the municipal street aid allocation. The result is a current (1994) allocation that is equal to a fuel tax allocation of approximately 2.2 cents per gallon. In 1951, 386 cities received Powell Bill Funds; by 1994, 492 cities shared in the distribution. Distributions for selected years are indicated in table 23-4.

Many small cities can finance almost all their street expenditures from their state gasoline tax distributions because their streets often

Table 23-4
Distribution of Powell Bill Funds to Cities

Year	Amount per Capita	Amount per Mile
1951	$ 1.51	$ 435.71
1961	1.92	453.12
1971	2.87	612.42
1982	12.69	845.67
1987	16.28	1,141.76
1990	19.09	1,368.88
1994	22.17	1,547.58

Source: North Carolina Department of Transportation, Division of Highways, Program Development Branch, *Incorporated Municipalities, Municipal Officials, and State Street Aid Allocations* (Raleigh, N.C.: NCDOT, 1994), sec. III, p. 3.

do not have curbs and gutters and are built to the less-expensive standards that the state uses outside cities for local roads. Large cities usually install curbs and gutters and build streets wide enough to provide paved parking areas along the curb. These cities usually cannot finance all street expenditures from Powell Bill funds.

Payments from Property

Charges assessed against property are all imposed on the benefit principle. They are designed to recover from the owner of property that is specially benefited by a street or sidewalk improvement at least part of the cost of the improvement. The value added to the property by the improvement often exceeds its cost. The payments from property may be secured in at least three forms by all cities: special assessments, payments in advance, and subdivision improvement requirements. A few cities have a fourth measure available, impact fees.

Special Assessments

Special assessments may be levied against abutting property under a petition procedure set forth in G.S. Chapter 160A, Article 10. Under charter provisions or special legislative acts, some fifty cities have authority to levy special assessments in certain circumstances without a petition. Special assessments may be apportioned against benefited property in proportion to front footage, land area, or value added by the improvement, or on a per-lot basis, or on a combination of these bases. Assessments may be paid as soon as their amount is known or in installments over a period of up to ten years, as the city council provides. Property owned by churches, schools, and other local governments that are exempt from property taxation is subject to special assessment.

Special assessments to meet part of street improvement costs have been widely used, especially by the state's large cities. Small cities use them less frequently. Their use has declined everywhere in recent years as cities and counties have increasingly adopted subdivision improvements requirements that call for street improvements to be made when land is being developed.

Payments in Advance

An alternative approach to the special assessment is payment in advance. Some cities permit owners of abutting property to pay the equivalent of a special assessment before they make the improvement; when no other funds are available, these cities may require such payment in advance if the desired improvement is to be made. When all property owners agree and have adequate funds to make an advance payment, this approach works well. Because these two conditions only rarely occur together, however, most cities normally use the advance-payment approach only in conjunction with other approaches.

Subdivision Improvement Requirements

The third method, subdivision improvement requirements, is the most widely used of the three methods (G.S. Ch. 160A, Art. 19). This approach simply requires the developer of a subdivision to install stipulated street improvements to city standards and then dedicate them to the city. Purchasers of lots, homes, or businesses in the subdivision buy an improved site, and part of the price reflects the cost of the street improvements. The financing in this case is all private. The city treasury reflects neither revenues nor expenditures.

Subdivision improvement requirements have been increasingly used since 1960, both by cities and by county governments for subdivisions outside city jurisdictions for land use regulation. In addition, federal home-financing assistance requirements and state secondary road policies have encouraged at least a minimum level of street improvements in new subdivisions. As a result, most new residential street construction is now financed by developers or property owners directly rather than by public agencies. Large cities are more likely to require improvements than small cities are.

Impact Fees

A few cities have received special authority from the General Assembly to impose impact fees on new development to finance street improvements. Impact fees are usually designed to cover off-site costs that may arise because of new development. The building of a new subdivision, for example, may greatly increase traffic on nearby roads and require that they be widened to handle the increased traffic. Such an improvement, of course, would also benefit current users of the roads. Thus only a portion of the cost of the improvement should be allocated to the new development in the form of impact fees. Calculation of the proper proportion of the cost to impose on new development is not an easy task. Because it will be a fee, not a general tax, it must be imposed carefully and reasonably if it is to survive any legal challenge.

Decisions on Financing Policies

For most cities the chief question in financing street improvements is how much of the cost should be met from local taxes and how much from charges made directly to benefited property. State-shared gasoline tax receipts and other grants that may be available from time to time are, of course, used first. That leaves local taxes and payments from property to cover the balance. Four factors should be considered in deciding which source to use: growth rates, the type of improvement, the relationship of different methods, and past policies.

Growth Rates

Fast-growing cities will probably need to require a larger part of the cost of improvements from developers or property owners through special assessments and payments in advance, than other cities will. Improvement needs in these cities are likely to be relatively high, and if they are met from local taxes (either from current taxes or after borrowing), a tax rate increase may be necessary. Cities that are growing slowly, on the other hand, can often finance street system needs with a stable tax rate.

Type of Improvement

Most cities have policies that take into account the type of street improvement. Residential access streets, for example, are often financed in some way from the benefited property. Collectors and thoroughfares, on the other hand, tend to be financed from general receipts because they serve more than the immediately abutting property. A common practice is to require the owners of property that abuts a nonresidential street to meet the cost of an equivalent residential street and then to meet the remaining cost from general receipts.

Relationship of Different Methods

When both special assessments and subdivision improvement requirements are used to recover street costs from abutting property, an important policy concern is the relationship between assessment policies and subdivision improvement requirements. Generally cities that require developers to finance the full cost of street improvements also tend to recoup most of the cost of constructing new streets that are not in a subdivision under a special assessment program.

Past Policies

Past practices and policies are important concerns in deciding on new ones. A city that has for years financed street improvements from general revenues may find strong objections from affected property owners if the policy is changed to require the benefited property to meet the cost directly. The same objections are also often raised when the proportion of the cost met from benefited property is increased. Giving advance notice of policy changes and providing a period in which citizens may petition for improvement under the old policies is sometimes used as a device for easing the transition.

Some Legal Topics Related to Streets

Definition of *Street*

Highway is the generic term for all ways of passage that are open to the public at large and maintained by public authorities, for both those who are on foot and those who are using vehicles. The word *street* is normally used to refer to highways that are found within urban areas. A city's streets include not only *roadways*—the portions of a street used by vehicles—but also sidewalks, public alleys, bikeways, and downtown malls.[10] The city's basic authority to open and maintain streets, found in G.S. 160A-296, includes all these forms of streets.

Street can occasionally bear a narrower meaning, however, depending on the context. This possibility is best illustrated by the use of the word with respect to state street aid to cities.[11] Part of the state's aid is distributed to cities on the basis of the number of miles of streets maintained by the respective cities. G.S. 136-41.1, however, permits a city to count within its mileage only streets with an average width of at least 16 feet. Thus some city-maintained alleys may not qualify as streets.

Street Property Transactions

Acquisition of Title to Streets

A city may acquire title to a street in one of four ways: purchase (or other voluntary conveyance), condemnation, dedication, or prescription. Purchase and condemnation are no different for a street than for a site for a city hall, an easement for a sewer line, or a watershed for the city's water supply, so there is nothing particular to note with regard to these two methods beyond the discussion of them in chapter 16. The other two methods, however, deserve fuller comment.

Dedication

Dedication consists of an offer by an owner of property to devote (or dedicate) that property to a public use, and the acceptance of that offer by the public. Both elements, the offer and the acceptance, are necessary for a dedication to be complete.

By far the most common procedure for offering a dedication is through subdivision plat approval. Most local subdivision ordinances require the developer to offer to dedicate streets, utility easements, and other public spaces to the public; and the recorded plat for a regulated subdivision typically expressly states the required offer on its face. In areas of the state not subject to local subdivision regulation, the common law reaches a comparable result. Under the common law the preparation of a subdivision plat showing rights-of-way for streets (and other public uses) and the subsequent sale of at least one lot by reference to that plat constitutes an offer of dedication.

Inclusion of an express dedication on the face of a subdivision plat, or, in a common law context, the sale of a lot by reference to the plat, constitutes an offer of dedication, but neither constitutes acceptance of the dedication by the public. For that, the acceptance by proper authorities is necessary.[12] One method of public acceptance is formal action by a public body, such as a city council or the State Board of Transportation, or by its delegate, such as the city manager or public works director. This formal method is preferable to others because it indicates an official decision by the appropriate government to accept the dedication, and it provides a record, such as through the minutes of the public body, of the acceptance.

A city may also, however, indicate acceptance of the dedication simply by beginning to maintain the street.[13] Because the city has no responsibility for maintenance until it accepts the offer of dedication, its undertaking to maintain the street has been held to imply the necessary acceptance.

A third method of acceptance is possible in some states: acceptance through use of the street by the public over a number of years. Recent case law in North Carolina indicates that the method, called *public user*, is not possible in this state.[14]

An owner of property who has made an offer of dedication may withdraw the offer before the public has accepted it and sometimes even after. One way to do this, available when the offer has come through recordation of a subdivision plat, is by subsequently selling lots without reference to the plat.[15] G.S. 136-96 permits a second method. Under this statute, if the public does not open a dedicated street within fifteen years after the offer is made (even if the offer has been accepted), the dedicator may file a notice of withdrawal in the office of the register of deeds. Until that notice is filed, however, the public (city or state) retains the right to accept the offer and open the street, even if more than fifteen years have passed since the offer was made.

A city is the appropriate agency to accept a dedication for a street inside its borders or within its subdivision regulation jurisdiction. [Acceptance of a street outside the city does not obligate the city to maintain it (G.S. 160A-374). In most cases such an acceptance will probably serve for a temporary period—until the street is accepted by the state for maintenance or becomes part of the city by annexation.] The appropriate body to accept a dedication beyond these borders is the State Board of Transportation.

Prescription

Although not often used anymore, one final method of acquisition is by prescription. *Prescription* differs from dedication in that the owner of the property does not intend to offer it for public use. Rather, the public simply uses the property as a street over an extended period—at least twenty years—in a way that is adverse to the interests of the owner, but also known to him or her. The use must be of a specific, definite right-of-way, which must be maintained by the public. If all these elements are met, then acquisition by prescription is possible. In practice this method is rarely used except to confirm title to old streets for which the original title documents are lost.

Closing of Public Streets

Once a city has acquired the right-of-way to a street, it may eventually want to close that street. The street may never have been opened, and closing may be necessary to clear neighboring titles; or the city may wish to relocate the street. Whatever the reason, the city may close a street under the procedure set out in G.S. 160A-299.

The statute requires the city council first to hold a public hearing after it has published notice, mailed notice to owners of abutting property, and posted notice on the street itself. After the hearing, the council must find that the closing is not contrary to the public interest and would not deprive any person of "reasonable means of ingress and egress to his property." The North Carolina courts have held that although owners are entitled to access to the street from their property, they have no right to have traffic pass directly by their property. Thus cutting off access to a street at one end, making that end in effect a cul de sac, does not deny reasonable means of ingress or egress to a property owner along the street.[16] When a street is closed in this fashion, the legal effect is that title to the land involved is divided along the middle of the street, among owners of the abutting land.

Other Uses of a Street Right-of-Way

G.S. 160A-273 permits a city to grant easements "over, through, under, or across . . . the right-of-way of any public street or alley that is not a part of the State highway system" as long as the easement will not "substantially impair or hinder the use of the street or alley as a way of passage." Thus a city is authorized to permit a utility company to lay pipes or to erect poles and string wires in the right-of-way of a street, or to permit the owners of property that abuts a street to join their properties by a bridge across the street. If the city's title to the street is itself but an easement for street purposes (rather than full title in fee simple), however, the city's authority to permit other uses of the right-of-way, such as for laying pipes or erecting wires, is subject to the continuing property rights of the owner of the underlying title. The supreme court has held that utility pipes or poles constitute an additional burden on a street right-of-way, and the owner of the underlying title is entitled to additional compensation, however small that may be. Payment of that compensation, though, is the responsibility of whoever lays the pipes or erects the poles, not the city.[17]

City Liability for Streets

Once a city has assumed control of a street—whether by purchase, condemnation, acceptance of a dedication, or prescription—it becomes responsible for the maintenance and the repair of the right-of-way. This responsibility extends to all portions of the right-of-way, including the roadway, any sidewalk, and any other parts that contain conditions that might be a hazard to the normal use of the roadway or the sidewalk. The city's basic duty is to maintain the street in a "reasonably safe condition" so that it may be used for the purpose for which it is intended.[18] If the city fails to meet this responsibility, by failing to correct or warn against a street condition that renders the street unsafe, it may be held liable to any person injured by the condition. For example, if a street is under excavation, a city generally must set up barriers and lights sufficient to keep a careful traveler from falling into the excavation. Furthermore, the city must keep its streets and sidewalks free from obstructions—whether permanent, such as a private fire hydrant extending from a building, or temporary, such as a pile of bricks being used by a contractor—that present a hazard to vehicles or pedestrians. Although a very large body of case law details the sorts of conditions that might lead to city liability, much of it is old, with recent cases relatively infrequent. This fact suggests that cities are, by and large, meeting their standard of care in maintaining and repairing streets.

Street Names and Numbers

Inherent in the city's "general authority and control" over city streets is the authority to name streets and to establish a system for numbering the houses and the other buildings along streets. Most current naming of streets goes on in new subdivisions, and the typical subdivision ordinance gives attention to street names within the subdivision. This ordinance often requires that any new street that is a clear continuation of an existing street bear the same name as that street, and it prohibits new names that duplicate or sound very much like the names of existing streets. If these conditions are met, the names of the new streets are left to the subdivider. The power to name streets is legislative in nature, however, and therefore the city may change the name of a street at any time.

As noted, cities also have inherent authority to establish a system of house numbers for city streets. Such a system usually begins with *reference streets* that divide the city into quarters—north, south, east, and west. The house numbers then proceed from the reference streets to the city's outer boundaries. Any ordinance that sets up a numbering system must establish frontage intervals so that a new number is given each succeeding interval. Intervals are commonly in the range of 20 to 30 feet, although shorter intervals may be necessary in downtown areas. In addition, the ordinance should also maintain even numbers on one side of the street and odd numbers on the other, in a manner that is consistent throughout the city. (The preferred practice is for the even numbers to be on the right side—low to high—and the odd numbers on the left side, going away from the reference streets.) It is also very desirable to establish the numbers so that the building numbers on parallel streets are comparable.

Franchises

Cities are authorized by G.S. 160A-319 to grant franchises for up to sixty years for the operation of electric, telephone, gas, water, and sewer utilities, and bus lines and other mass transit facilities. The same section permits cities to franchise cable television systems for up to twenty years. In addition, G.S. 160A-304 permits comparable city regulation of taxicab services. (Cities are also authorized to franchise private garbage collectors, parking lot operators, and airports, but in practice these powers are not used.) Because the historical basis and much of the current justification of the power to franchise lie in city control of city streets, the franchising power needs some discussion.

A *franchise* is a special privilege, such as the right to erect poles and string wires in a street right-of-way or to operate a bus line on city streets, that is granted by a city and that may not be exercised in the absence of a franchise.[19] Once granted, the franchise is a contract between its holder and the city and may not be revoked by the city except according to the terms of the franchise.[20] As a contract, it is a property right of great potential value, and for that reason G.S. 160A-76 requires that ordinances granting franchises be adopted twice, at two separate regular meetings of the city council.

Historically the first extensive governmental regulation of public utilities was by cities, through their franchising power. City regulation at this time was comparable to the current state regulation of utilities, including levels and territory of service and rate regulation. In the last half-century, however, state regulation through agencies like the North Carolina Utilities Commission has displaced much of the municipal power to regulate. If there is a conflict between a state-approved tariff and the rates established or approved through a city franchise, the state-approved rates prevail.[21] Indeed, the North Carolina Court of Appeals has held that a city may not require a franchise holder to cease serving customers within the city once the franchise has expired if it is also serving those customers pursuant to a certificate of convenience and necessity from the North Carolina Utilities Commission.[22] The principal continuing justification for city franchising is the regulation of the franchise holder's activities within the rights-of-way of city streets. For example, the franchise may make clear that any excavation or tree cutting is subject to city regulation and inspection; may require the franchise holder to repair fully any street or sidewalk pavement that is removed during an excavation;

and may make clear the city's right to require removal or relocation of utility structures in the right-of-way, at no cost to the city. However, because of the dominant role of the utilities commission in regulating most activities subject to franchise (cable television is not subject to utilities commission regulation), the city's bargaining power is not nearly as strong as it once was.

Additional Resources

Brookings Institution. *Report on a Survey of the Organization and Administration of County Government in North Carolina.* Washington, D.C.: the Institution, 1930.

Ferrell, Joseph S. *Tort Liability of North Carolina Cities and Towns for Street Defects.* Chapel Hill, N.C.: Institute of Government, The University of North Carolina at Chapel Hill, 1965.

Lawrence, David M. *Property Interests in North Carolina City Streets.* Chapel Hill, N.C.: Institute of Government, The University of North Carolina at Chapel Hill, 1985.

McMahon, John Alexander. "Roads and Streets in North Carolina: A Report to the State-Municipal Road Commission." *Popular Government* 17 (September 1950): Entire issue.

North Carolina Department of Transportation, Division of Highways, Planning and Environmental Branch, *Summary of Municipal Local Road and Street Finance Report, June 30, 1990* (Raleigh, N.C.: NCDOT, April 1991).

"Report of the State-Municipal Road Commission." *Popular Government* 17 (December 1950/January 1951): 10–13.

Wager, Paul W. *County Government in North Carolina.* Chapel Hill: The University of North Carolina Press, 1928.

Notes

1. The information in this section is drawn from Hugh Talmage Lefler and Albert Ray Newsome, *North Carolina, The History of a Southern State,* 3d ed. (Chapel Hill, N.C.: The University of North Carolina Press, 1973); Capus Waynick, *North Carolina Roads and Their Builders,* vol. 1 (Raleigh, N.C.: Superior Stone Company, 1952); and Albert Coates's history of North Carolina roads and streets in "Report of the State-Municipal Road Commission," *Popular Government* 17 (December 1950/January 1951): 10–13.

2. 1715 Acts ch. 36.

3. The plank roads were usually 8–10 feet wide. After clearing and grading, *stringers* (heavy sills) were laid lengthwise along the road and sunk into the earth. Across the stringers were placed the planks, usually of pine, 9–16 inches wide and 3–4 inches thick. The planks were then covered with sand. This combination, with

ditches alongside, provided an all-weather road—at least, one much superior to roads that were constructed by simply clearing away the trees.

4. 1921 Pub. Laws ch. 2.

5. 1931 Pub. Laws ch. 145.

6. 1949 N.C. Sess. Laws ch. 1250.

7. 1951 N.C. Sess. Laws ch. 260.

8. Bureau of the Census, *Government Finances: 1989–90* (Preliminary Report), Series GF-90-5P (Washington, D.C.: U.S. Government Printing Office, 1991).

9. These approximations are based on federal and state reports and do not include federal funds for roads on military bases or in national parks and forests. They also do not include private outlays such as subdivision streets that are constructed by developers and dedicated to the state or some city. County governments may provide front-end money pending the collection of special assessments for improving subdivision streets in unincorporated areas.

10. Parsons v. Wright, 223 N.C. 520, 27 S.E.2d 524 (1943).

11. The uses to which state street aid may be put are listed in the discussion of sources of revenue in chapter 11.

12. Owens v. Elliott, 258 N.C. 314, 128 S.E.2d 583 (1962).

13. Foster v. Atwater, 226 N.C. 472, 42 S.E.2d 592 (1946).

14. *Owens,* 258 N.C. 314, 128 S.E.2d 583; Bumgarner v. Reneak, 105 N.C. App. 362, 413 S.E.2d 565 (1992).

15. Rowe v. Durham, 235 N.C. 158, 69 S.E.2d 171 (1952).

16. Wofford v. North Carolina State Highway Comm'n, 263 N.C. 677, 140 S.E.2d 376 (1965).

17. Van Leuven v. Akers Motor Lines, 261 N.C. 539, 135 S.E.2d 640 (1964).

18. Fitzgerald v. Concord, 140 N.C. 110, 52 S.E. 309 (1905).

19. Shaw v. City of Asheville, 269 N.C. 90, 152 S.E.2d 139 (1967).

20. Boyce v. City of Gastonia, 227 N.C. 139, 41 S.E.2d 355 (1947).

21. Corporation Comm'n v. Henderson Water Co., 190 N.C. 70, 128 S.E. 465 (1925).

22. Duke Power Co. v. City of High Point, 22 N.C. App. 91, 205 S.E.2d 774 (1974).

24 Water and Wastewater Services

Warren Jake Wicker

Contents

WATER AND WASTEWATER services are both the most important and the most widely provided enterprise services of North Carolina cities. Both are traditional city government services in North Carolina and throughout the world. The aqueducts and large sewers of ancient Rome rank among civilization's early major public works.[1]

Colonial cities provided water by means of public wells. The earliest piped public water supply in North Carolina was developed in 1778 in Winston (which later joined with Salem).[2] Oak pipes brought the water into the community from its source a mile away. Raleigh also used oak pipes for its first system, which was completed in 1818.[3] Expansion of the services was slow, however. In 1888 twelve communities reported having public water supplies: Asheville, Charlotte, Concord, Durham, Fayetteville, Goldsboro, Greensboro, Raleigh, Salem, Salisbury, Wilmington, and Winston. Most of these were privately owned, but a trend for city governments to take over the systems was already established.

By the end of the nineteenth century, about two dozen cities had water systems, and fewer still had wastewater (sewer) systems.[4] The *Municipal Year Book* for 1902 reported on water and sewer services in the state's twenty-three cities with populations over 3,000 in 1900. Three—Edenton, Kinston, and Washington—had no public water systems. Of the remaining cities, twelve owned their water systems, and eight, including Raleigh and Wilmington, were served by private companies.

Thirteen of the twenty-three cities reported having sewer systems. Only one, Wilmington, was owned by a private company. None had sewage treatment. In all cases the cities reported that their "crude sewage" was being discharged into creeks and rivers. A few cities—Goldsboro and Wilmington, for example—reported that "sewage purification" was under consideration. Charlotte was facing two suits for water pollution from sewage.

The twentieth century has seen a steady expansion of water and sewer services and increased state and federal efforts to make water safer for human consumption and to improve the quality of water in streams and lakes. Services were significantly expanded during the booming 1920s. Oddly the 1930s, following the Great Depression, also saw expansion of municipal water and sewer works, much of it because of the financial assistance available under the federal Emergency Relief and Construction Act and through the Public Works

Administration. Urban growth following World War II, together with increased state and federal regulatory activity, saw more expansion of services.

Although cities have been the chief local governmental providers of water and wastewater services, special needs and circumstances led in the middle of the century to the involvement and the use of other public agencies. Sanitary districts were first authorized in the 1920s, with the provision of water and sewer services a major focus (G.S. Ch. 130A, Art. 2). Counties (G.S. Ch. 153A, Art. 15) were authorized to provide these services in 1955, the same year in which water and sewer authorities (G.S. Ch. 162A, Art. 1) were first authorized. The creation of metropolitan sewage districts (G.S. Ch. 162A, Art. 5) was authorized in 1961, and the creation of metropolitan water districts (G.S. Ch. 162A, Art. 4) in 1971. County service districts (G.S. Ch. 153A, Art. 16), through which water and sewer services may be provided, were first authorized in 1973. Authority to create county water and sewer districts (G.S. Ch. 162A, Art. 6) dates from 1977.

The environmental movement of the 1970s added further stimulus to the expansion of services, greatly aided by federal and state funds. The grants under Public Law 92-500 (the "201" program) for water pollution control were important in building and improving wastewater treatment facilities. State Clean Water Bonds ($300 million in 1972, $230 million in 1977, and $145 million in 1993) also added financial support for expanded services. Following the 1987 amendments to the federal Clean Water Act, North Carolina's General Assembly created the Clean Water Revolving Loan and Grant Fund in the Department of Environment, Health and Natural Resources (G.S. Ch. 159G). Federal and state grants and loans are channeled through this fund.

The Current System of Water and Wastewater Services

The 1990 census found that some 65 percent of all North Carolina housing units were served by public or private water systems; most of the remainder used private wells. The same census found that about 50 percent of the housing units were connected to a public or private sewer system.[5] Of those not connected, most used septic tanks or other on-site systems.

The Division of Environmental Health reports that in 1993 there were some 10,500 public water systems in North Carolina.[6] This figure includes all systems that are required to report on quality tests of their water. A great majority of them are private and serve a single business, industry, campground, or other such facility.

Among local governments, cities are the chief providers of public water service.[7] Over 400 of the state's 520 cities provide water service. Other local governments providing water service include 42 counties, at least 16 sanitary districts, smaller numbers of water and sewer authorities and county water and sewer districts, and 1 metropolitan water district. Federal and state governments are also important providers with respect to their own facilities: military bases, parks, hospitals, and others.

The state's utilities commission regulates private water systems serving ten or more customers. In 1991 there were 1,182 of these serving an estimated population of 263,000.[8]

The dominance of local governments in providing wastewater services is even greater than their role in providing water.[9] Among the 520 cities, 310 report that they provide sewer services. Other local units providing services include approximately 20 counties and 5 other types of local governments. As with water, the state and federal governments often provide service to their own facilities, and a large number of small treatment plants are owned by private parties to serve hotels, campgrounds, private schools, motels, shopping centers, country clubs, and subdivisions.

In 1991 there were 268 private sewer systems subject to regulation by the state's utilities commission.[10] They served an estimated 82,000 people.

Most of the people in North Carolina live in housing with complete plumbing: hot and cold piped water, a flush toilet, and either a bathtub or a shower. The 1990 census found that 98.5 percent of the housing units in the state had complete plumbing.[11] This figure represents a major improvement in the past fifty years. In 1940 only 24 percent of the state's housing units had complete plumbing.

When the number of housing units with complete plumbing is viewed in connection with the number of units served by public water and sewer systems, it is clear that from 35 to 49 percent of the housing units with complete plumbing are served by private wells, septic tanks, or some other form of on-site water or sewer facility.

City and county governments have been extending public systems rapidly, but because of the state's dispersed population, on-site facilities continue to be very important. Some 37,000 new on-site wastewater units, overwhelmingly septic tanks, were installed in 1991–92, only a slight decline from the number installed in previous years.[12]

The Regulatory Framework

All cities are authorized to provide water and wastewater services (G.S. Ch. 160A, Art. 16). As noted earlier, the great majority of cities do so. When they do, they become subject to extensive federal and state regulations.[13]

Water Supply and Treatment

The North Carolina Department of Environment, Health, and Natural Resources (DEHNR) is chiefly responsible for administering both state and federal regulations. Its Division of Environmental Management classifies the state's surface waters and designates those that are appropriate to be used as drinking-water supply sources. The Public Water Supply Section of DEHNR's Division of Environmental Health is responsible for approving public water supply plans. The same division is responsible for monitoring the safety of all public water supplies under the federal Safe Drinking Water Act. Finally, the state requires that all water supply systems have certified water plant operators (G.S. Ch. 90A, Art. 2). Local governments are also responsible under state legislation (G.S. 143-214.5) for watershed protection—important for protecting both public surface-water supplies and general water quality.

Wastewater Treatment and Discharge

The general structure for wastewater regulation is quite similar to that for regulation of water supply and treatment. Federal legislation has established the long-term goals for national water quality. In short, the surface waters are to be swimmable and drinkable. The Environmental Protection Agency is the federal actor, but most of its requirements are administered by the state. Key in this is the Division of Environmental Management's administration of the NPDES (National Pollution Discharge Elimination System) permits. Thus all discharges of municipal sewage to the surface waters must meet the standards necessary for the stream classification set by the state. The division also regulates discharges to the ground surface (spray irrigation). Regulation of subsurface discharges of sewage and other wastewaters is the responsibility of the Division of Environmental Health at the state level and the county health departments at the local level. Operators in charge of wastewater treatment plants must be certified by the state (G.S. Ch. 90A, Art. 3).

Financing of Water and Wastewater Services

Revenue Sources

City governments in North Carolina have six principal types of revenues that may be used to finance water and wastewater services. These are set out in table 24-1, together with the general principle of revenue raising that the use of each represents. All water and wastewater services provided by city governments in North Carolina are financed using one or more of these revenue measures.

Local Taxes and Nontax Funds

The property tax and the local sales tax are the two chief local tax measures (G.S. 160A-209; G.S. Ch. 105, Arts. 39, 40, 42). The sales tax is listed here because city officials usually view it as a local tax. It is, in fact, levied by counties, and a share of the receipts is distributed to cities by the state. (It is thus, properly speaking, a shared revenue from county governments. Because a portion of the proceeds of the counties' levies goes into a statewide kitty for distribution, the local sales tax also has some appearance of a state-shared tax.) Both are classified in economic terms as ability-to-pay taxes, because the amount that each taxpayer contributes is based on the value of the taxpayer's property and on how much the taxpayer spends on taxable goods. The value of the property and the amount of spending are assumed to reflect the taxpayer's ability to pay. For neither tax is the taxpayer's obligation related to his or her use of the water and wastewater systems or his or her direct benefit from them.

Table 24-1
Sources of Funds for Financing Water and Sewer Services and
Their Revenue-Raising Principles

Source of Funds	Principle
Local taxes (and nontax funds)	Ability to pay
Service rates and charges	Benefit
Availability charges	Benefit
Payments from property	Benefit
Special assessments	
Subdivision improvement requirements	
Payments in advance	
Acreage charges	
Impact fees	
Special connection charges	
Special service charges (tap fees,	
hydrant rentals, etc.)	Benefit
Funds from other governments	Ability to pay

The two 0.5-percent local sales taxes authorized in 1983 and 1986 have partial earmarking. Cities receiving these proceeds must use part of them for water and sewer capital improvements or debt service: 40 percent of the proceeds for the first five years after their levy and 30 percent for the next five years (G.S. 105-487, -504). Cities that have no need to use the proceeds for water and sewer purposes may establish their absence of need with the Local Government Commission and receive authorization to use the proceeds for other city purposes.

Cities may also use nontax funds—interest earned, receipts from the sale of property, and the like—for water and wastewater purposes unless they are earmarked by law for other purposes. To the extent that a city uses nontax funds for water and wastewater purposes, they are not available for other uses in regard to which they would take the place of tax funds. Thus they are classified here as the equivalent of tax funds.

User Rates and Charges

These charges, authorized by G.S. 160A-314, are the monthly or quarterly charges made to utility customers on the basis of their consumption of water or use of the sewer system. In most systems the amount of the charge reflects the amount of use and thus is related to the benefit the customer receives directly.

Two changes are taking place in the type of rate structure used. The first trend is away from the traditional declining-block rate structure to one of uniform unit pricing. The declining-block system, supporters contend, reflects economies of scale. Those who use large amounts of water add more to the scale of production and should receive the benefit of their contribution to lower average costs. The traditional system, for example, often provides for a minimum monthly charge that carries with it a fixed quantity of water—say, $7.00 for 3,000 gallons. The next 10,000 gallons might be priced at a lower figure, say, $1.25 per 1,000 gallons. At the top of the range, perhaps 50,000 or 100,000 gallons per month, the unit price might drop to only a fraction of the basic unit price. Critics of this system claim that it does not encourage the conservation of water and that a system of uniform unit pricing is more equitable. Any savings from economies of scale should be shared proportionally among all users, not just among large users. Many cities have moved in this direction, with a basic charge that covers either some small number of units or standard customer costs (billing, collecting, meter reading, etc.), followed in both cases by uniform unit prices through the remaining range of consumption.

The second change is a trend to uniform pricing throughout the service area. Most North Carolina cities have for many years charged higher rates to customers outside their boundaries than to those inside. The practice started because at one time substantial local tax support was given to these utilities, especially for sewers. These funds came, of course, from taxes levied only on the property inside the city. Because property of outside customers was not taxed, a higher utility charge was imposed so that their contribution to the systems would match the total of inside customers. In the past thirty years most cities have moved to a utility approach in financing water and wastewater systems. Under this approach, utilities are financed by some combination of rates and charges applying to customers and benefited property. Some cities use no local tax funds; others use such funds only to a limited degree. Thus the desire to secure equal contributions from customers inside and outside municipal boundaries can be achieved without a rate differential.

Some cities also instituted the higher outside rates to create an inducement for annexation during the period when annexation was subject to a referendum among those proposed for annexation. Those being annexed would face a property tax increase that would be offset, at least in part, by a drop in their utility rates. Although voting on annexation is no longer used, the rate differential is still considered significant by many officials.

Finally, substantial contributions to municipal water and wastewater services have been made in recent years from county, state, and federal governments. Outside customers, of course, are taxpayers in all these governments and thus have shared in the financing of these grants and assistance to cities.

All these changes have increased the pressure on cities to establish rate structures that are uniform throughout their service areas.[14]

Availability Charges

Under G.S. 160A-317, cities may require owners of improved property located within the city and within a reasonable distance of the city's water or sewer lines to connect their premises to the lines, and the city may fix the charges for the connection. In lieu of requiring the connection, the city may require owners to make periodic payments of an availability charge. Such an availability charge may not exceed the minimum periodic charge under the city's standard rate structure. Owners who have adequate wells or septic tanks, for example, may prefer this charge to the cost of connection and the use of the city's system. At the same time the charge assures the city of some revenue to support the system. (A few systems impose a charge that is termed an availability charge, but is, in fact, an impact charge. See the discussion under the heading Impact Fees, later in this chapter.)

Payments from Property

The presence of water and sewer lines provides special benefits to the property that the lines serve. Increasingly cities and counties in North Carolina are adopting financing polices that require the owners of abutting property to bear all or part of the cost of installing the water and sewer lines to serve their property. The six devices listed under the heading Payments from Property, in table 24-1, are those used most often for securing payments from abutting property owners. Terminology is not standard. Some of the devices may have other names in some places.

Special Assessments

The use of special assessments is authorized by G.S. Chapter 160A, Article 10. A special assessment is a charge against property for part or all of the cost of making an improvement. It is in the nature of a tax. Once a special assessment is made against a lot or a tract, that property is available to satisfy the payment of the special assessment in the same manner found with property tax levies. The major advantages of the special assessment are that the property stands behind the charge and a city may allow installment payments of the assessment for a period of up to ten years. The chief disadvantage is that a city must provide the front-end money to make the improvement. Such funds may come from bond proceeds, a revolving fund, capital reserves, or current appropriations.

No petition of the property owners is required. Interest on unpaid assessments may be set by the city council, not to exceed 8 percent. Assessments may be apportioned according to frontage on the lines, acreage, or the increased value of the improvement to the property, or on a per-lot basis. The theory supporting special assessments is that the presence of the water or sewer line adds value to the property; thus the charge is made against vacant properties as well as against improved properties.

Subdivision Improvement Requirements

Subdivision improvement requirements are normally a part of a city's subdivision ordinance (G.S. Ch. 160A, Art. 19). When a city uses subdivision improvement requirements, the developer must install utilities to the city's specifications and dedicate them to the city when they are complete. The financing is thus normally a private matter, and the funds to install the facilities do not flow through the city's treasury. The cost of these subdivision improvements, it is assumed, is passed on to those who buy property in the subdivision. As with special assessments, that cost becomes part of the cost of the developed lot or tract. This approach to the financing of water and sewer lines is widely used by cities. From a city's financing perspective, it is the simplest method of all.

Payment in Advance

When a city plans to make an extension but does not want to use special assessments, under the authority of G.S. 160A-314, it may permit property owners to pay in advance for the extension so that the city will have funds available to make the improvement. The charge is usually on the basis of front footage and at a level that would correspond with what would be imposed if special assessments were used. This method is useful when the city does not have the necessary front-end funds available, the extensions are short, and the property owners are able to pay in advance.

Acreage Charges

Acreage charges have been used by some North Carolina cities for more than forty years under the general authority of G.S. 160A-314. They are often a form of impact fee in that they are designed to cover part of the cost of off-site facilities. Typically the acreage charge covers part of the cost of the large water distribution and sewage collection lines that lie between the treatment plants and the property being directly served. Subdivision improvement requirements or special assessments, for example, are used to meet the cost of the lines immediately serving a lot or a tract. The acreage charge recovers from the property owner a share of the cost of the major lines that are also necessary to provide full service to his or her property. Charges are usually based on net acreage—excluding rights-of-way and property donated for public purposes, such as park lands and school sites. Charges typically vary from $500 to $1,000 an acre.

Impact Fees

Impact fees are charges imposed on new development to meet a share of the capital cost of off-site facilities required to provide water and sewer services to a given property. They may be imposed under the general authority of G.S. 160A-314. As noted earlier, these might be termed acreage charges when the off-site facilities are major water transmission or sewage collection lines. Impact fees may also be imposed to recover a share of the cost of water and wastewater treatment plants.

The impact fee is sometimes viewed as a buy-in charge, by which a new customer pays a share of the cost of facilities that were constructed by previous customers. If the proceeds of current rates are being used for capital expansion or debt service, the impact fee should be based only on the debt-free portion of the facilities. Both new and old customers will contribute to debt service and capital expansions alike to the extent that these are financed from current service charges.

The impact fee at other times is viewed as an appropriate way to develop capital reserve funds. In this case, it is argued that the new customer will use a portion of the capacity of the existing water treatment plant, for example, thus hastening the day when the plant will require expansion. The impact fee may thus be directed to a capital reserve for that purpose.

Those who support the use of impact fees suggest that their use more fairly distributes the total cost of the utility systems than is the case when the off-site costs are principally financed through user charges alone.

Those who view impact fees negatively often point first to the cost of developing a fair system and the small amount of funds derived from each individual lot. Because these are fees rather than taxes, it is legally necessary that they not be arbitrary, discriminatory, or unreasonable. This means that the basis for the charges must be carefully and reasonably calculated. Skeptics also note that the average cost for all users is reduced when a new customer uses part of any excess capacity, as long as his or her contribution to the system's revenues exceeds the cost of his or her service. Without any new customers the existing debt service on facilities, for example, will be met by old customers. New customers sometimes share these costs and lower the average cost for all customers. Thus, imposing impact fees may conflict with a desire for growth in the number of customers. Some cities (and systems) want growth; others do not. In each case a city's long-term objectives are important in determining policies. (Country clubs typically impose impact fees of the buy-in variety; churches tend not to do so.)

Special Connection Charges

Special connection charges, imposed under the authority of G.S. 160A-314 and known by a variety of names, are used to recover utility extension costs from the property being served. In most cases they are a substitute for one of the devices described earlier, or a combination of two or more of them. For example, a city that does not impose special assessments might use a special charge at the time of connection to collect the same amount and on the same basis, or the city might use a single connection charge that would equal the sum of a special assessment and an acreage charge.

Special Service Charges

The operation of a utility system involves a number of services that are provided directly for the benefit of particular customers: making a tap and setting a meter, turning services on and off, installing a private fire hydrant or a sprinkler connection, providing temporary service, and the like. These changes are authorized under G.S. 160A-314. Special charges, set at a level to cover costs, are often made for these services.

Funds from Other Governments

In past years significant amounts of money for water and wastewater facilities have been made available through federal and state grants and loans and county appropriations. More recently the amounts of federal and state grants and loans have declined. Under the state and federal tax systems, these funds are raised largely from state and national taxpayers through the individual and corporate income taxes and the general sales tax, all of which are levied on the ability-to-pay principle. County contributions have usually been made to encourage industrial development or to finance jointly the extension of services, and are largely derived from countywide property and sales tax receipts.

To the extent that contributions from other governments are used to finance water and sewer services, these services are being supported on a countywide, statewide, or nationwide basis by some taxpayers who are not being served directly by any utility system that receives the funds. This approach to financing water and sewer utilities is similar in principle to that used in financing education, social services, parks and recreation, and many other general governmental functions.

Financing Approaches

Self-Supporting Systems

As the foregoing discussion suggests, cities may use many different combinations of revenue measures to finance water and sewer services. Differing views about need and equity as well as different community conditions and traditions lead to various

Table 24-2
Typical Mix of Revenue Measures Used in a Self-Supporting
Water and Sewer System

Element of Cost	Revenue Measures
Supply and treatment works	User charges and impact fees, plus grants when available
Major lines	Acreage charges and impact fees, plus grants when available
Minor lines	Special assessments, subdivision improvement requirements, payments in advance, and special connection charges
Operation and maintenance	User and availability charges
Special services	Special service charges

financing arrangements. A community actively seeking new industrial growth may be less inclined to impose high extension costs on
users than one with a no-growth bent. A city that has a tradition of
financing all extensions from taxes and user charges may find it difficult to change to the use of special assessments.

Nevertheless, there has been a trend since the 1950s toward making city water and sewer services self-supporting insofar as the local
share of the financing is concerned. (Most cities have been willing to
accept state and federal funds when these are available.) This trend
has undoubtedly been encouraged by citizens' resistance to property
tax increases and the demand for expansion of other services—fire
protection, law enforcement, sanitation, etc.—that are traditionally
supported from general taxation. Cities with self-supporting utility
systems have tended to adopt policies that relate elements of system
cost to particular revenue measures, as shown in table 24-2.

Not all cities that have self-supporting systems use all the revenue
measures in the manner shown in table 24-2. Most cities, for example, do not use impact fees or acreage charges, and thus the importance of user charges in these cities is relatively greater. Also,
some cities use general tax receipts to some degree. In these cities,
tax revenues are most likely to be used for capital cost and debt service, particularly on treatment works.

A hypothetical example illustrates the meaning of the financing
approach outlined in table 24-2 for the individual water customer.

(The levels of charges, while not untypical, are given for purpose of illustration; they will vary from system to system.)

Initial Charges	Amount
Special assessment for line in front of property ($15 per foot for 100 feet)	$1,500
Service connection and meter (cost)	400
Acreage charge (for share of major lines serving area: $1,000 per acre for 0.5 acre)	500
Total	$2,400
Monthly Charges	
User charges based on water consumption (for costs of water supply and treatment, operation and maintenance, and administration	$ 15

A similar set of charges for sewer service would be found in cities using this financing approach.

Reimbursement Agreements

Many cities require private developers not only to install the water and sewer facilities within their developments, but to extend the major lines necessary to reach their developments from existing city facilities. Typically these are constructed to city standards and are designed to serve the intervening property as well as the new development. In these cases some cities enter into reimbursement agreements with the initial developer. The agreements call for the city to make its standard acreage and other charges for those who connect to the intervening lines and to reimburse the initial developer for the portion of the cost of the major line that exceeds what would have been necessary to serve his or her own development. Reimbursements usually cover only the original cost (without interest) and are made only for five to ten years. Thereafter the same charges are imposed on those who connect, but the city retains the proceeds. It is thought that financing realities demand that a developer fully discount any reimbursement that might (or might not) be received after these periods. Thus a cutoff date has little influence, if any, on a developer's decision about undertaking a development.

Financing of Capital Improvements

North Carolina statutes authorize cities to use various long-term financing methods in providing water and sewer facilities. These include issuance of general obligation and revenue bonds, entry into lease-purchase agreements, making of installment purchases, creation of capital reserve funds, and appropriations from current receipts. (See chapter 14 for a full discussion of the procedures to be followed in using each of these approaches.)

As implied in the earlier discussion, the basic question in utility financing is, Who should pay? That is, should the cost of a particular capital facility be borne by the taxpayers of the city? By county, state, or federal taxpayers? By the utility's customers through user charges? By the customers who receive special services? By the owners of benefited property? By some combination of the foregoing, and, if so, in what proportion for each?

Once the decision is made about who should pay, a city arranges for long-term financing to secure the funds to construct the facility. Long-term financing allows the customers and the taxpayers who will pay for the facility to do so over some period.

A city's first choice is between pay-before-you-go and pay-as-you-go financing, that is, between paying before the use of a facility and paying during the use of one. (This designation describes what happens, but is different from the traditional—and inaccurate—use of the pay-as-you-go term.)

The two pay-before-you-go approaches are appropriations from current receipts and use of capital reserves. In both of these approaches the customers or the taxpayers lay out the funds before the facility is constructed. With the first the time between payment and outlay is brief. As a result, current appropriations are likely to be used principally for comparatively small capital outlays. If capital reserves are used, payments into these by customers or taxpayers may have extended over several years.

The true pay-as-you-go approaches permit the customers or the taxpayers to pay for a capital improvement (or acquisition) for a period after it is constructed (or purchased) and during its use in providing services. Two of these, the lease-purchase agreement and the installment purchase, are usually used for capital financing over a relatively short period, usually five years or less. General obligation bonds and revenue bonds are the appropriate vehicles for long-term financing when the customers or the taxpayers need a long period—say, ten to thirty years—to amortize the cost of a capital improvement. (Bond anticipation notes may be used during construction of major capital facilities. They are liquidated from the proceeds of general obligation or revenue bonds that are typically sold near the completion of construction. See chapter 14.) North Carolina cities may use revenue bonds in long-term financing, but do so infrequently. General obligation bonds are preferred because they usually have slightly lower interest rates and lower issuance costs. Furthermore, the restrictive general obligation debt limits often found in other states are not present in North Carolina. Thus the practice here is to use general obligation bonds even if, as is usually the case, debt service on the bonds is to be met totally from utility revenues. Revenue bonds have been used by a few cities to avoid a referendum by the voters, which is usually necessary for a general obligation bond issue of significant size.

City-County Relationships

As noted earlier, county governments have become increasingly involved in providing water and sewer services in the latter half of this century. The demand for county action in providing utilities has arisen principally because of the growth of suburban areas. For orderly and healthful development in these areas, water and sewer services must be present before extensive development takes place. Although many cities have extended services to areas outside their boundaries without county participation, needs have frequently developed in areas where the nearby cities have not been in a financial position to make the extensions, and funds from private developers and industries have also been inadequate. The result has been increasing joint action by city and county governments.

This common approach, stressing municipal ownership and operation of facilities and county participation in financing, is in accord with the principles underlying North Carolina's annexation procedures and the division of governmental powers and functions among the state, counties and cities. These principles call for the extension of municipal boundaries and the full range of municipal types of services (such as water and sewer services and higher levels of law enforcement, fire protection, street construction and maintenance, and solid waste collection) to areas that are becoming urban in character.

Although specific arrangements for joint city-county action in providing utility services have varied greatly, they may be classified into five general approaches.

The first type of joint action involves county appropriations to meet part of the cost of extending services outside municipal boundaries. County assistance in providing service to new industries has been prominent in these joint actions. The cities own and operate the lines from the beginning. Early arrangements between Raleigh and Wake County, for example, followed this pattern.

Counties have also built facilities and leased them to cities for operation. This sharing of revenues through the lease arrangement permits the county to recover its capital costs while the city involved meets its operating expenses. This pattern has been used between Hickory and Catawba County for line extensions and between Durham and Durham County for sewer lines and wastewater treatment facilities to serve the Research Triangle Park. A few of these arrangements in the past have called for the city to purchase the portion of lines or other facilities in areas annexed by the city. Care should be exercised in drafting such annexation provisions to make sure that their implementation will not create financial stress for either the city or the county government. This aspect of an agreement should not impair a city's ability to annex, nor result in county opposition to annexation because of negative financial results for the county. Among the many units that have used this general approach are Reidsville and Rockingham County and Goldsboro and Wayne County.

In the third approach, currently the most common one, the county is reimbursed for its contribution to the capital costs of extending services. In some cases the reimbursement may come from acreage charges or other connection charges; in other cases, at least in part, from the rates charged customers.

A few counties have constructed water supply works or wastewater treatment plants and provided "wholesale" service to cities within their boundaries and "retail" service to customers along the lines outside cities. Examples of this approach may be found in Anson, Dare, and Jones counties.

The final pattern of city-county cooperation involves the creation of joint departments. Leading examples are those of Asheville and Buncombe County, Charlotte and Mecklenburg County, and Winston-Salem and Forsyth County. All three of these joint departments were established under the Interlocal Cooperation Act (G.S. Ch. 160A, Art. 20), and each would be considered a joint agency under G.S. 160A-462 except that it is administratively a part of the city government. In all three cases the joint operations have advisory boards that to a considerable extent determine policy. (The Asheville-Buncombe agency is known as a water authority, but as noted, it is organized under the Interlocal Cooperation Act, not the Water and Sewer Authorities Act.) Given the hundreds of examples of city-county cooperation in providing utilities, the future will likely bring more mergers of activities into joint departments.

City-County Financing Agreements

Because situations differ, the arrangements made between cities and counties in jointly financing water and sewer services will necessarily vary from place to place. Although no standard agreement can be recommended, some factors are listed that should be kept in mind and, when necessary, included in such agreements. Special conditions may sometimes call for consideration of factors not listed.

1. Responsibility for financing the cost of construction should be set forth. This cost may be borne by one unit or shared by all units; or certain portions of an improvement may be financed by one unit and other portions by the remaining unit or units.
2. Ownership of all facilities and rights in all easements should be established.
3. If initial ownership is with the county and the county will not operate the facilities, the possible future transfer of the ownership should be anticipated.
4. The agreement should specify any change in ownership that would take place if the city annexed areas in which the facilities are located; or it should anticipate any problems that might arise if ownership did not rest with the city after annexation.
5. The procedure and the circumstances under which further extension of any facility may take place should be covered.

Any unit might be authorized to extend on its own, or joint approval might be required.

6. The unit that is to prescribe the specifications for all facilities should be established. Specifications should cover the size and the quality of all materials used and the location of all facilities.

7. The level of rates, fees, and other charges to customers should be agreed on. This agreement would include the level of water rates, tap fees, acreage charges, fire protection charges and other miscellaneous charges. Either stipulated rates or rates scaled to those charged inside the city might be used. The authority and the procedures for changing rates and charges should be covered.

8. Any changes that might be made in the levels of rates or other fees and charges if the city annexed the area where the facilities are located, should be anticipated with regard to both the initial financing and the financing of future extensions.

9. The source and the amount of all reimbursements to the county or the city, if any, should be set forth, including the term during which reimbursements are to be made.

10. Responsibility for operation, maintenance, and control of the facilities, including control of taps and collection of all rates and charges, should be established.

Notes

1. In Greek mythology, Hercules, as one of his labors, was required to clean the stables of King Augeas of Elis in a single day. This was not a small task. The stables were occupied by some 3,000 oxen and had not been cleaned in thirty years. Hercules, however, was equal to the job. He diverted two streams through the stables and "flushed" them clean in a day—an achievement probably never matched by any other wastewater engineer! Furthermore, he established himself as an administrator of extraordinary capability. He cleared all the permitting and environmental impact hurdles in a matter of minutes by maneuvering to have the approving authorities direct him to undertake the task.

2. David H. Howells, *Historical Account of Public Water Supplies in North Carolina* (Raleigh, N.C.: Water Resources Research Institute of the University of North Carolina, 1989), 2.

3. Howells, *Historical Account*, 2.

4. M. N. Baker, ed., *The Municipal Year Book 1902* (New York: The Engineering News Publishing Company, 1902), 128–32.

5. Bureau of the Census, *1990 Census of Population and Housing. Summary Social, Economic, and Housing Characteristics,* 1990 CPH-5-35 (Washington, D.C.: U.S. Government Printing Office, 1992), table 12.

6. North Carolina Department of Environment, Health, and Natural Resources, Division of Environmental Health, unpublished computer printout, August 1993.

7. The figures cited here are based on unpublished reports of the North Carolina League of Municipalities and the divisions of Environmental Management and Environmental Health, North Carolina Department of Environment, Health, and Natural Resources. The data from the different sources are not always complete and are sometimes in conflict. It is believed that the figures given are conservative and would be close to the exact figures, were they known.

8. From not-yet-published 1991 Report of the Commission.

9. The comments in note 7 with respect to the information on water services also apply to the information on sewer services.

10. From not-yet-published 1991 Report of the Commission.

11. Bureau of the Census, *1990 Census of Population and Housing,* table 12.

12. Steve Steinbeck, On-Site Wastewater Branch, Division of Environmental Health, Department of Environment, Health, and Natural Resources, interview with author, 24 August 1993.

13. See chapter 18, "Environmental Affairs," for a more detailed discussion of state and federal regulatory provisions.

14. A model approach to both inside-outside pricing and municipal annexation was created in the early 1980s by Charlotte, Mecklenburg County, and the other cities within the county. At that time Charlotte's and the county's utility systems were merged, the cities in the county adopted annexation agreements, and Charlotte and the county agreed that the water and sewer rates would be equalized over ten years. Since then the Charlotte-Mecklenburg Utility Department has taken over the water and wastewater systems of most of the smaller cities in the county. These actions have removed rate structures, extension policies, and annexation as subjects of possible conflict between cities and between the cities and the county government.

25 Other Enterprises: Solid Waste, Electricity, Gas, Airports, Public Transportation, and Stormwater

Warren Jake Wicker

Contents

CITY GOVERNMENTS in North Carolina are authorized to operate ten enterprises (G.S. Ch. 160A, Art. 16):

1. Solid waste collection and disposal systems
2. Electric power generation and distribution systems
3. Gas generation and distribution systems
4. Airports
5. Public transportation systems
6. Stormwater and drainage systems
7. Water supply and distribution systems
8. Sewage collection and treatment systems
9. Off-street parking facilities
10. Cable television systems

The first six of these ten enterprises are covered in this chapter. Water supply and distribution systems and sewage collection and treatment systems are discussed in chapter 24. Off-street parking facilities are discussed in chapter 23. No special discussion of cable television systems is provided in this book. Although North Carolina cities are authorized to own and operate cable television systems as enterprises with all the general powers outlined for other enterprises, only one city, Morganton, has done so. Cities have instead franchised private firms to provide cable service, as authorized in G.S. 160A-319.

Cities may own and operate all these enterprises both inside and outside their boundaries and may grant franchises for operation of the enterprises within their city limits. They may also condemn land needed for enterprise operations and issue both general obligation and revenue bonds (except for cable television) to finance enterprise facilities. Property taxes (only after voter approval in the case of cable television and public transportation systems) may be levied to finance them, and most other general city revenues may also be used for these purposes. Rates, fees, and charges may be established for all the enterprises, and special assessments may be levied to finance three of them: water, sewage, and stormwater systems. Finally, cities may join with other cities or with counties and other public bodies to own and operate the enterprises. In short, cities have very broad powers with respect to the enterprises and great flexibility in organizing to provide them and in financing them. Moreover, some cities, by special act or charter provisions, have additional powers and flexibility with respect to some of the enterprises.

Once a city owns these enterprises, it may sell, lease, or discontinue operation of seven of them only with voter approval unless the sale or the lease is to another governmental unit. This restriction does not apply to three of the enterprises: airports, off-street parking facilities and solid waste collection and disposal systems.

Solid Waste Collection and Disposal

Solid waste collection and disposal (once called *garbage collection and disposal*) is a traditional service offered by North Carolina cities. Over much of the state's history, the service would be more accurately described as "collection and removal"; disposal in the manner now considered essential was not practiced. Removal was frequently to open dumps, sometimes with burning to reduce the accumulation of waste.

The *Municipal Year Book* for 1902[1] provided exceedingly brief descriptions of garbage services for the state's twenty-four largest cities. A sample of the entries indicates the range of practices at that time:

Concord: "Collected by contract; used as fertilizer."

Durham: "Collected by day-labor; dumped."

Goldsboro: "Collected by day-labor; hauled out of city."

Greensboro: "Collected by day-labor; cremated."

Raleigh: "Collected by day-labor; hauled to city farm and burned."

Winston and Salem: "Collected by contract and day-labor; burned."

Increasing attention to disposal developed after World War II. It initially manifested itself in moves to replace open dumps with sanitary landfills. The environmental movement, which may roughly be dated as starting with the publication of Rachel Carson's *Silent Spring* in 1962, increased attention to solid waste. A decade later the energy crisis arrived with the Middle East oil embargo. It too brought increased emphasis on the conservation of all types of natural resources and underscored the value of waste reduction and recycling.

Significant state technical assistance to local governments was first offered in the 1930s by the State Board of Health's Sanitary Engineering Division.[2] Efforts to improve the management of wastes continued, but progress was slow. A survey in 1968 found 479 disposal sites being operated. Of these, only 23 were determined to operate in a manner that provided reasonable protection of the public health. State and local efforts were then directed at improving landfill operations. By the mid-1970s most of the open dumps had been eliminated and consolidated into 160 landfills that were operating in an approved manner.

The Resource Conservation and Recovery Act (RCRA), passed by Congress in 1976 in a flood of environmental legislation, brought more attention to and increased restriction on waste disposal.[3] The major step affecting municipal landfills, however, came with the 1984 amendments to RCRA.[4] This legislation required states to implement permit programs to ensure that municipal solid waste landfills complied with federal criteria for such landfills.[5] The Environmental Protection Agency (EPA) has responsibility for determining if state programs are adequate. North Carolina developed a permitting plan that EPA determined to be adequate on October 7, 1993.[6]

The North Carolina requirements for landfills are a major part of the state's solid waste program. The basis for the program is found in G.S. Chapter 130A, Article 9, originally enacted in 1989, but the subject of numerous amendments since that time. (The general citation is often to the 1989 legislation in its original bill form, Senate Bill 111.)

The chief provisions of the state's solid waste management program and legislation are these:

1. The solid waste management hierarchy (from most to least desirable) is as follows:
    a. Waste reduction at the source
    b. Recycling and reuse
    c. Composting
    d. Incineration with energy production
    e. Incineration for volume reduction
    f. Disposal in landfills
2. Goals for the reduction of waste going into landfills are 25 percent by June 30, 1993, and 40 percent by June 30, 2001.
3. The state must prepare a solid waste management plan (completed in February 1992) and update it every three years. Counties must prepare a plan consistent with the state plan. Cities must cooperate in the preparation of county plans, or prepare one of their own.
4. Counties and cities must report to the state on their solid waste management activities by December 1 of each year. A status report on solid waste management in North Carolina is prepared each year by the Department of Environment, Health, and Natural Resources, Division of Solid Waste Management, as required by G.S. 130A-309.06.
5. A Solid Waste Management Trust Fund was established with a fee on the sale of tires, a tax on virgin newsprint, plus other revenues. Counties receive 68 percent (increasing to 90 percent on June 30, 1997) of the funds to pay for scrap tire disposal. The remainder goes to support state solid waste activities.
6. Local governments must determine the full cost of their

solid waste management activities and inform their citizens of that cost.

7. Banned from disposal in landfills are used motor oil, lead acid batteries, tires, antifreeze, white goods, appliances, aluminum cans, steel cans, and yard wastes.

Rules covering the collection and the disposal of solid wastes, prepared by the Division of Solid Waste Management, may be found in the North Carolina Administrative Code, Title 15A, Subchapter 13B.

Considerable progress has been made in the past few years in meeting the more stringent state and federal disposal requirements. The second annual report[7] on the status of solid waste management in North Carolina gives a current picture:

- Some 6.8 million tons of municipal solid waste were generated in North Carolina in 1992. This was approximately one ton per capita per year.
- Sixty local governments—twenty-two counties and thirty-eight cities—had source reduction programs under way in fiscal year 1992.
- Four hundred eighty-three local governments had recycling programs in fiscal year 1992. They reported recycling 436,544 tons of materials that year.
- Holding permits at the end of fiscal year 1992 were 110 municipal solid waste landfills, 150 land-clearing and inert debris landfills, 9 incinerators, 14 yard waste–composting facilities, 11 mixed waste–processing facilities, 17 transfer facilities, and 94 scrap tire collection sites.

By October 1993, twenty lined, high-tech landfills (meeting the rules relating to siting, design, operation, financial assurance, closure, and postclosure care) had been permitted, and the applications of an additional nine landfills meeting the same standards were under review.[8] Of the twenty-nine agencies involved, one was a city, seven were private corporations, and twenty-one were county governments.[9] Unlined landfills that do not meet the new standards are closing rapidly. More than fifty had been closed by the end of fiscal year 1993.[10] No disposal of solid wastes in unlined landfills will be allowed after January 1, 1998.

Since 1965 a major change in local responsibility for solid waste disposal has occurred. Before that time, most medium- and large-size cities owned and maintained their own landfills or other disposal sites. State and federal programs to improve solid waste disposal have encouraged a shift to fewer landfills that meet high environmental standards. Although the proportion of landfills that are owned and operated by private firms is increasing, most are still owned by counties. Typically each landfill serves several cities as well as unincorporated areas of a county. Many serve more than one county, and a few very large private landfills serve several counties and the cities therein. Some of the county-owned landfills are operated by the county; a few by a city; and some by private firms under contracts with a county or with two or more cities and counties jointly. Usually each city makes some payment to meet its share of the cost. The payments may be based on population, the quantity of waste, or a negotiated share. In a few counties the landfill is county operated and financed, and no charge is made to either cities or private haulers that use it.

Although cities have broad authority to provide solid waste services both inside and outside their boundaries, only a few have provided service outside. Those few have usually done so only within a limited area near their boundaries.

North Carolina cities also generally provide the collection service with city forces, although a 1993 survey by the North Carolina League of Municipalities (NCLM) found that an increasing number were contracting with private firms to provide collection services.[11] Some small cities provide no collection service; citizens and businesses are served under individual agreements with private collectors.

Collection frequency for residential areas varies from one to three times per week. The traditional pattern has been twice-weekly collection. That pattern is changing, however. The 1993 NCLM survey found over 60 percent of the cities collecting household wastes once a week. With improved collection equipment and rising costs, more cities will probably move to once-a-week collection in residential areas.

Although the historical practice was to collect solid waste from the rear of the house in residential areas, the NCLM survey found that over two-thirds of the cities were collecting from the curb. The advent of large-capacity roll-out containers made the switch feasible (but not always without political fallout). Curb collection costs the city less than collection from the backyard because the resident helps to move the waste. Most cities with curb collection make special provisions for people who are physically unable to move their waste to the curb.

Similar differences also prevail with respect to collection from commercial and industrial establishments and collection of leaves, household furnishings, and other special items. Large cities usually require commercial establishments, apartment units, and other places with lots of waste to use central containers (dumpsters) that can be handled with special transport equipment, and most cities do not collect wastes from industrial processes or from construction sites or clearings, leaving this service to private firms or collectors. Most cities do remove dead animals.

A city's policies, practices, and regulations relating to collection, storage, and control of solid wastes are usually set forth in an ordinance. The ordinance typically establishes the various classes of service; defines the minimum standards for containers and prescribes their placement; prescribes placement of leaves, refuse, and other materials; specifies charges and penalties; and defines the wastes to be collected.

Explosive, radioactive, and other hazardous wastes have become a major concern in the past few years. The principal state programs for collecting and disposing of them are carried out under the Solid Waste Management Act (G.S. Ch. 130A, Art. 9) and the Hazardous Waste Management Commission (G.S. Ch. 130B). Such authority as the city has for regulating how these materials are handled appears in G.S. 160A-183, -185, and -303.1.

Although the statutes list solid waste service as an enterprise, most cities do not operate it as one. Rather, most cities have traditionally financed it from general taxation and budgeted for the service in their general fund. The sanitation division—the name most often applied to the work unit that provides the service—is typically part of the public works department.

The costs of solid waste services are principally in collection. The average distribution of costs among the cities reporting in the 1993 NCLM survey was as follows:

Collection	63.6%
Disposal	35.5
Other	0.9
Total	100.0%

To finance this service, cities may use property and sales tax receipts and other revenues not earmarked for a particular purpose, as well as fees and charges. Over much of the state's history, cities financed garbage collection and disposal from general revenues. That practice has been changing, however. Many cities have long made special charges for special or extra services, but before 1980 only a few imposed a general charge designed to meet most or all of the cost of solid waste collection and disposal. By 1993, however, almost half of the cities had general charges for residences and businesses, according to the NCLM survey. The typical residential charge at that time was about $5 a month.

Although the use of fees is increasing, their place in the total financing picture is still limited. In the cities responding to the NCLM survey, fees and charges were reported to meet only about 20 percent of the total costs of solid waste collection and disposal. The major advantage of the general charge is that it relieves the property tax. Because the charge can also be scaled to the level of service received—the amount of waste collected and the frequency of collections—some citizens see financing by charges as more equitable than financing by general taxation. The disadvantages are the additional costs for collecting the charge, the regressive character (more regressive than the property tax) of the charge, and the fact that a cutoff of service to enforce payment is not a satisfactory remedy.

As noted earlier, resource recovery programs are now widespread among North Carolina cities. The programs are still expensive as compared with disposal in the standard landfill, however. Respondents to the NCLM survey reported that the sale of recyclables, on the average, met less than 10 percent of the total cost of their recycling programs. Even when allowances are calculated for costs not incurred in landfill disposal, the programs are comparatively expensive. The programs are encouraged by legislators and others because they think that alternative disposal costs will increase and, equally important, that markets for recyclables will improve. If their assumptions prove correct, sometime in the future the programs' revenues will equal their costs. Furthermore, the earth has a finite quantity of some resources, and conservation and recovery of these are justified by the probable needs of future generations.

Electric Service

North Carolina cities have been authorized to provide electric service since the early days of electric power development. Seventy cities (as of 1993) own and operate electric distribution systems. In addition, one city, Lake Lure, owns and operates a hydroelectric generation plant, but sells its output to Duke Power Company, which is the distributor of electric power for the city and the surrounding area. These cities, in operating their electric systems, have all the general enterprise powers noted earlier, including establishing rates and charges (which are not subject to state regulation), using tax funds, borrowing, and condemning land.

Legislation enacted in 1965 (G.S. 160A-331 through -340) allocates service areas for electric providers in urban areas. Under this legislation, cities not now providing electric service are unlikely to be able to add the service in the future. Furthermore, expansion of existing service to surrounding areas by cities currently operating electric distribution systems is often restricted by the legislation, which gives preference in serving new areas to the providers who are nearest.

Under the authority of the Joint Municipal Electric Power and Energy Act (G.S. Ch. 159B), cities may jointly own and develop facilities for generating and transmitting electricity. Fifty-one of the state's cities operating electric distribution systems purchase their power through one of the two joint power agencies that they have created under this authority. As members of the joint power agencies, they own a share of plants constructed and operated by Duke Power Company and Carolina Power and Light Company. The other nineteen cities that distribute electricity purchase power wholesale from a private power company or through a neighboring city that is a member of one of the joint agencies. Only one city, Fayetteville, has significant generating capacity, enough to meet about half of its demand. A few others have supplementary generating facilities that are employed to shave peak demand and thus to lower the cost of purchased power.

Sixty-four of the cities operating electric distribution systems belong to ElectriCities of North Carolina, an association that provides consulting, technical assistance, and management services to its members. Nonmember cities are Enfield, Fayetteville, Highlands, Lake Lure, Oak City, Waynesville, and Windsor.[12]

The eight cities with the largest operating revenues in 1992 (more than $30,000,000) were Fayetteville, Gastonia, Greenville, High Point, Kinston, New Bern, Rocky Mount, and Wilson. Some small cities also provide electricity. Among them are Bostic, Fountain, Hamilton, Hobgood, Hookerton, Macclesfield, Oak City, and Waltonsburg, all of which had operating revenues in 1992 of less than $500,000.[13]

At one time many electric systems were operated by commissions appointed by the city council, but separate from the general city government. Only Fayetteville and Greenville now use such commissions. Other cities provide electric service through their central city administrations.

Cities providing electric service do so on a self-supporting basis. In fact, earnings from each city's electric fund are typically transferred to its general fund and help to keep the municipal property tax rate lower than it might be otherwise. In 1992, sixty-four of the cities made such transfers. For the median city, they were equal to some 17 percent of its general fund revenues.[14]

Although electricity revenues are important to the general fund, their regular use can pose a financing problem for a city operating an electric distribution system that wishes to annex an area served by another electric supplier. In this case the city would realize no increase in electricity revenues to support its increased general fund obligations. A similar problem is posed if such a city annexes an area in which it already provides electric service. Again, its general fund obligations increase, but without a comparable increase in electricity earnings.

Natural Gas Service

Natural gas in North Carolina is distributed by four private companies regulated by the North Carolina Utilities Commission, and by systems owned and operated by eight cities.[15] The four regulated companies are North Carolina Gas Service (a division of Pennsylvania and Southern Gas Company), North Carolina Natural Gas Company, Piedmont Natural Gas Company, and Public Service Company of North Carolina. The eight cities are Bessemer City, Greenville, Kings Mountain, Lexington, Monroe, Rocky Mount, Shelby, and Wilson.

In 1991 the four companies and the eight municipal systems provided service in 80 of the state's 100 counties and made service available to about 80 percent of the state's population. In the same year the eight cities served 7.0 percent of the 629,672 natural gas customers in the state, collected 10.1 percent of the $615 million in gas sales revenues, and distributed 11.0 percent of the 143 million dekatherms of gas sold.

The gas services in the eight cities all contribute to the cities' general fund from earnings that exceed operating costs. Except in Greenville, they are all operated as regular city departments. Greenville provides gas service through a separate commission that also operates the electric and water and sewer services.

Airports

In 1929, just over twenty-five years after the Wright Brothers made their first flights in Kitty Hawk, North Carolina's cities and counties were authorized to own and operate airports (G.S. Ch. 63).[16] Their initial powers were broad and have since been enlarged. Cities may levy taxes for airports, issue bonds to finance facilities, condemn land for airport facilities, and join with other cities or counties in supporting and operating airports. They may also create subordinate boards or commissions to manage airport operations, or lease the airports to be operated privately. A few other arrangements have been authorized. For example, the Raleigh-Durham airport is operated by an authority created by special act. Members of the authority board are appointed by the four participating governments: Wake and Durham counties and Raleigh and Durham cities. The Charlotte airport, the state's largest, is operated as a regular city department, but with strong policy guidance from an advisory commission.

Although the exact number of airports in North Carolina is not known, the North Carolina Department of Transportation (NCDOT) estimates that there are over 400 airports and airstrips, the majority of which are privately owned personal-use airstrips in rural areas.

There are some 115 publicly owned airports in the state. Of these, 75 are open to general public use; the remaining 40 landing areas are not. In the latter group are such facilities as military airports, local hospital heliports, and state airports used for forest fire fighting.

Of the 75 airports owned by public bodies and open to general public use, 31 are administered by an airport authority or commission. Seven of these are operated by a single-government commission. The other 24 are creations of multiple units of governments, usually a city and a county, such as the Burlington-Alamance Airport Authority. Six of the 24, however, reflect the joint action of more than two units. For example, the Rocky Mount–Wilson Airport Authority is a joint operation of the cities of Rocky Mount and Wilson and three counties, Edgecombe, Nash, and Wilson.

Of the remaining 44 publicly owned airports open to general public use, 1 is operated directly by the federal government, 3 are operated directly by state agencies, 18 are operated directly by a city, and 22 are operated directly by a county. Of the 40 airports operated directly by a city or a county, 36 have some sort of advisory board or committee.

NCDOT estimates that about one-third of the city airports generate enough revenues to meet operating expenses. Only the airports served by major airlines are fully self-supporting for both operations and most capital improvements.

Local appropriations and state and federal aid are used to meet the remaining capital outlays and, for most of the airports, to supplement operating expenses. These small airports have modest needs. Their annual operating costs are usually restricted to utilities, grass cutting, and limited pavement and building maintenance.

Technical assistance and information on airport matters are available through NCDOT's Division of Aviation.

Public Transportation Systems

Public transit systems in North Carolina cities began over a century ago with privately owned horse-drawn coaches.[17] These gave way to electric trolleys, which in turn were replaced by motor buses. The electric trolleys were often operated by power companies. In several cities the power companies, as a part of their franchises, continued to provide transit services after the switch to buses. The end of this arrangement came in 1991 when Durham and Greensboro took over the bus systems in their cities from Duke Power Company. City government activity in public transit is fairly recent, dating from 1967, when Asheville and Wilson first began to subsidize the bus systems in their cities.

Public transit systems operate in sixteen cities. Their 1991 populations varied from Salisbury's 23,770 to Charlotte's 422,410. In addition, the cities and the counties in the Research Triangle area have created the Research Triangle Regional Transit Authority, which operates buses between the Research Triangle Park, Chapel Hill, Durham, and Raleigh. All seventeen systems use motor buses.

Three organizational approaches are found among the city-owned systems: direct city operation, city contract with a private firm for operation, and general management by an authority created by the city. For example, the Chapel Hill and Greenville systems operate as a regular city department. In Charlotte and Durham the city council retains general control, but contracts with a private firm for operation. Greensboro, Raleigh, and Winston-Salem (under special-act authorizations) have created independent authorities to supervise and set policies for the transit systems. In all three cases these authorities have also contracted with a private firm to operate the systems.

Cities may issue revenue bonds for public transportation purposes. With approval of the voters they may also levy property taxes and issue general obligation bonds.

The public bus systems in North Carolina are not self-supporting.[18] Operating revenues in 1993 for the state's seventeen systems were $.44 per passenger, compared with operating costs of $1.34 per passenger. That is, a net cost of $.90 per passenger had to be met from other sources, principally local appropriations and state and federal aid. Federal aid has been available for several years for planning, capital, and operating expenditures. State aid for planning and capital outlays has also been available for several years, and in 1993–94 it became available for operating assistance as well.

The seventeen units' fixed-route systems boarded almost 31 million passengers on 389 buses (peak hour) that covered 13.75 million miles in 1993. Farebox revenue (about 96 percent of total operating revenue) accounted for some 26 percent of total operating expenses. The net operating deficit per passenger was $1.34.[19]

The sharing of costs between riders and local, state, and federal taxpayers varies from system to system and from year to year. Variations are influenced heavily by the size of capital grants. North Carolina has systems in five urban areas with populations of more than

200,000: Chapel Hill, Charlotte, Durham, Fayetteville, and Raleigh. In 1992, federal grants met from 75 to 80 percent of the capital expenditures for these systems. Federal support for operating expenses varied from 8 to 38 percent. Farebox receipts in the five systems met from 21 to 32 percent of operating expenses.[20]

Chapel Hill's 1992 experience represents a year in which state and federal capital grants were modest.[21] In that year some 47 percent of the system's total cost was met from local revenues: 25 percent from the farebox and 22 percent from local taxes and other revenues. Federal grants accounted for 34 percent of the required revenues, state grants for the remaining 19 percent.

Although bus ridership has been increasing slowly, it is still too low to support the systems from operating revenues. In 1993 the statewide ridership was 1.94 passengers per mile of fixed-route bus operations.[22] If the average passenger rides 3 miles, city buses are carrying an average of 5.82 passengers at all times.

In 1993, fourteen cities operated dial-a-ride, or demand-response, services as a part of their transit systems.[23] A chief purpose of these systems is to serve persons with special needs that cannot adequately be met by the fixed-route systems because of location or physical impairments. The fourteen systems in that year boarded about 650,000 passengers, tallied some 2.5 million bus miles, and recovered some 8 percent of their costs from the farebox. The operating deficit per passenger was $5.68.

Given the levels of ridership and the levels of fares that riders are judged to be willing to pay, most observers conclude that continued subsidy of both capital and operating expenses of city transit systems will be needed.

Stormwater and Drainage Systems

The need to protect people and property from stormwater damage has faced most cities as long as there have been cities. Dense urban development increases runoff from storms. Streets become storm sewers unless open ditches, gutters, drains, culverts, bridges, and other devices are used to handle the flow from rains. Improvements in drainage ways are often needed to protect private homes and businesses as well as public properties. Clearing of stream banks and building of canals, dikes, and levees are appropriate in many places.

For much of history, protection from the physical onslaught of stormwater has been the primary concern. In more recent times, stormwater concerns have been broadened to include the improvement of water quality in streams, lakes, and other bodies of water.

In 1972 the federal Clean Water Act established the National Pollution Discharge Elimination System (NPDES).[24] The NPDES program (administered in North Carolina by DEHNR's Division of Environmental Management) requires a permit for all point-source discharges of wastewaters into surface waters.

Amendments to the act in 1987 extended the permitting requirements to cover discharges from nonpoint sources, or stormwater runoff, into surface waters by certain industrial activities and large cities with separate storm sewer systems.[25] Initially, only cities serving a population of 100,000 or more are covered. In 1993 this encompassed only six North Carolina cities: Charlotte, Durham, Greensboro, Fayetteville, Raleigh, and Winston-Salem. Extension of the regulations to smaller cities is expected in the future.[26]

The chief requirements for covered cities are as follows:

1. Prepare and implement a comprehensive stormwater management plan to control the level of pollutants in stormwater to the maximum extent possible.

2. Adopt ordinances to prohibit illicit discharges to separate stormwater systems, to control pollutant discharges to their stormwater systems, and to provide a right of entry on private property for inspections.

3. Inspect and monitor discharges.

There is no model for the kinds of measures that may be used. Each city develops arrangements that fit its particular needs and circumstances. Several agencies have developed guides and suggestions.[27]

Among the measures that may be appropriate are drainage systems, settling ponds, holding basins, ground surface treatments designed to reduce runoff, use of porous pavements, requirements for the removal of chemical pollutants, spill control, and remediation programs.

Obviously these activities can be expensive. In 1989, G.S. Chapter 160A, Article 15, was amended to add stormwater systems to the list of municipal enterprises. This action brought with it the full range of financing alternatives and other powers available for enterprises. G.S. 160A-314 authorizes charges against property for stormwater control programs as for other enterprises. However, the amendment also includes some special requirements in the case of "schedules of rates, fees, charges and penalties" for providing stormwater services. Such charges may vary according to the use of the property: residential, commercial, or industrial. Other characteristics that may be considered in developing classes of charges are the size of the property, the quality and the quantity of runoff from the property, the characteristics of the watershed into which stormwater from the property drains, and any other factor that affects the stormwater system.

Charges may not exceed the cost of providing the service. Where the jurisdictions of two governments (say, a city and a county) overlap, both may not levy charges on the same property. By forming joint arrangements, however, one of the units may make appropriate charges. Furthermore, schedules of charges for stormwater service may be adopted only after a public hearing on the proposed schedule. This requirement does not apply to other enterprises.

Cities have revenue measures other than fees and charges that may be used to finance stormwater services. G.S. 160A-209 authorizes the levying of property taxes for this purpose. G.S. Chapter 160A, Article 23, lists stormwater services as one of the purposes for which a municipal service district may be established. G.S. Chapter 160A, Article 10, allows the use of special assessments. Finally, state street aid (Powell Bill) funds may be used for stormwater improvements within street rights-of-way.

Charlotte's stormwater program, initiated in 1993 and coordinated with Mecklenburg County's program,[28] was the first in the state under the new regulations. Its experiences and program arrangements are probably similar to those that other cities may anticipate. Charlotte found that it has in place a 2,400-mile drainage system (much underground) located on both public and private property. Many of the drainage pipes are over eighty years old. The cost of the needed repairs to the systems is estimated to be greater than $100 million. The city plans to spend $13–$15 million a year for the first five years to repair and maintain the system. Priority in repairing is based principally on the severity of the condition's impact on water quality. Repairs to private property require that adequate easements be granted to the city.

Charlotte's program is largely financed from charges, but supplemented by some $2.5 million a year in property tax receipts. Charges are based on the amount of impervious surface (buildings, driveways, patios, walkways, and other structures) on each property. Annual charges are the total of $5.76 per property, plus approximately $.01 per square foot of impervious surface. Billing is monthly as a part of the water bill. The charge for a typical single-family home is $2.60; a business with 1 acre of hard surface faces a monthly charge of $35.82.

Notes

1. M. N. Baker, ed., *The Municipal Year Book, 1902* (New York: The Engineering News Publishing Company, 1902), 128–32.

2. North Carolina Department of Environment, Health, and Natural Resources, *North Carolina Recycling and Solid Waste Management Plan: Volume II, State Strategy* (Raleigh, N.C.: NCDEHNR, February 1992), 1-1.

3. 42 U.S.C. § 6901–6992 (1995).

4. *Id.*

5. 40 C.F.R. § 258 (1995).

6. 58 Fed. Reg. 52,305 (7 October 1993).

7. North Carolina Department of Environment, Health, and Natural Resources, *North Carolina Solid Waste Management: Annual Report, July 1, 1991–June 30, 1992* (Raleigh, N.C.: NCDEHNR, 12 December 1993).

8. Report of Dexter R. Matthews, Chief, Solid Waste Section, Division of Solid Waste Management, to the Environmental Management Commission, 28 October 1993.

9. Report of Dexter R. Matthews.

10. Report of Dexter R. Matthews.

11. Lee M. Mandell and David S. Kaplan, *What Are We Doing with Garbage—1993?* (Raleigh, N.C.: North Carolina League of Municipalities, 1994). The information in these paragraphs on collection practices is from this report of an NCLM survey in July 1993. The survey covered some 75 percent of cities with populations above 2,500, and about 30 percent of cities below that population level.

12. Dell Johnson, ElectriCities of North Carolina, telephone conversation with author, 3 May 1994.

13. North Carolina Department of State Treasurer, State and Local Government Finance Division, "Memorandum No. 779, Statistical Information on Electric System Operations," 19 March 1993.

14. NCDST, "Memorandum No. 779."

15. The information in this section is from North Carolina Utilities Commission, *North Carolina Utilities Commission: 1993 Report*, vol. 24 (Raleigh, N.C.: the Commission, 30 June 1993).

16. The information in this section, current as of the end of 1992, was

provided by the North Carolina Department of Transportation, Division of Aviation, from unpublished records and reports.

17. The information in this section was drawn from North Carolina Department of Transportation, Public Transportation Division, *Urban Fixed-Route Transit Systems, Rural General Public Transportation Systems,* and *Human Service Transportation Systems,* 1992–93 (Raleigh, N.C.: the Division, 1994). The division also develops information on intercity buses, taxis, carpooling, vanpooling, park-and-ride, passenger trains, ferries, bicycling, and state and federal aid programs.

18. Operating information of transit and transportation systems for 1992–93 was tabulated by NCDOT, Public Transportation Division, 1993.

19. NCDOT, 1993.

20. United States Department of Transportation, Federal Transit Administration, *Transit Profiles: Agencies in Urbanized Areas Exceeding 200,000 Population, for 1992* (Washington, D.C.: USDOT, 1993), 29, 75, 76, 78, 203.

21. USDOT, *Transit Profiles,* 1993.

22. NCDOT, 1993.

23. NCDOT, 1993.

24. 33 U.S.C. §§ 1251–1376 (1995).

25. 33 U.S.C. § 1342 (1995).

26. 40 C.F.R. § 122.26 (1994).

27. See, for example, *Stormwater Management Guidance Document,* a manual prepared for the North Carolina Division of Environmental Management by the Water Quality Group at North Carolina State University, 1993. Authors were J. A. Arnold, D. E. Line, S. W. Coffey, and J. Spencer. Another is *Stormwater Management in North Carolina: A Guide for Local Officials,* prepared by William M. Eaker of the Land-of-Sky Regional Council, Asheville, N.C., 1994.

28. The information in these paragraphs about the Charlotte program is from an educational brochure, *The Rain in Our Drains,* issued by Charlotte-Mecklenburg Stormwater Services in 1993.

26 Parks and Recreation

Candace Goode

Contents

THE GENERAL ASSEMBLY ... declares that the public good and the general welfare of the citizens of this State require adequate recreation programs, that the creation, establishment, and operation of parks and recreation programs is a proper governmental function, and that it is the policy of North Carolina to forever encourage, foster, and provide these facilities for all its citizens.[1]

The development of public parks and recreation activities as a local government function in the United States stems from the public park and playground movement that began in such large cities as

Boston and Chicago in the 1890s. Since the early days of settlement houses, the provision of parks and recreation services has generally been regarded as a proper municipal responsibility. Not until the late 1960s did parks and recreation become an accepted county function. In 1992 in North Carolina, 131 cities and 57 counties provided full-time recreation services for their citizens.

Generally, cities that have parks and recreation programs tend to spend more on them per capita than do counties that have such programs. In 1992 the average per capita expenditure by cities with parks and recreation programs was $59.94, based on a total statewide outlay of $108.44 million; the average per capita expenditure by counties was $9.99, based on a total statewide outlay of $1.29 million.[2] For cities, these levels of expenditures are near the national average; for counties, slightly below the national average. In the nation and in North Carolina, local governments spend more for parks and recreation than state governments do. In the nation in 1990, local governments accounted for 82.7 percent of state and local government expenditures for parks and recreation. In North Carolina the local government share was even higher–87.7 percent.[3]

The size and the scope of local recreation programs vary greatly across North Carolina. Large cities such as Raleigh and Greensboro operate a wide range of programs from youth athletics to activities for older adults, with full-time staffs of 276 and 184 and total budgets of $18.26 million and $11.56 million, respectively. On the other hand, small cities often provide parks and recreation services with one to three full-time employees and seasonal staff. Some municipal programs are responsible for managing both parks and recreation programs, whereas others operate strictly recreation programs. In some cases municipal departments are being asked to expand their programs to provide some level of recreation services to noncity residents. At least ten of the state's municipal parks and recreation departments provide services to noncity residents through joint agreements with county governments.

City parks and recreation services are not uniform, in either type of activity or level of service. Some are primarily oriented toward team league sports, whereas others offer a variety of arts, crafts, music, dance, aquatics, drama, boating, environmental education, and wellness programs for all ages. Many cities have a system of ball fields, tennis courts, golf courses, community centers, greenways, and aquatic facilities. Others may provide only one or more park sites with limited facilities. Some communities not only have built their own recreation facilities, but using the Community Schools Act of 1977, have opened up schools for a variety of recreational uses. Local parks and recreation departments are also expanding their offerings to include nontraditional services such as after-school child care programs, literacy programs, and child care for parents participating in recreation programs. Although each recreation department is unique, all recreation departments are working toward the goal of improving the quality of life for their residents by providing quality parks and recreation services.

Authority to Provide Parks and Recreation Services

Cities provide parks and recreation services to the citizens of North Carolina under the authority granted by the Recreation Enabling Act, G.S. Chapter 160A, Article 18. The statute defines *recreation* broadly for purposes of the enabling act:

> "Recreation" means activities that are diversionary in character and aid in promoting entertainment, pleasure, relaxation, instruction, and other physical, mental, and cultural development and leisure time experiences. (G.S. 160A-352)

This legislation authorizes local governments to do the following:

1. Establish and conduct a system of supervised recreation;
2. Set apart lands and buildings for parks, playgrounds, recreational centers, and other recreational programs and facilities;
3. Acquire real property, either within or without the corporate limits of the city or the boundaries of the county, including water and air rights, for parks and recreation programs and facilities by gifts, grant, purchase, lease, exercise of the power of eminent domain or any other lawful method;
4. Provide, acquire, construct, equip, operate, and maintain parks, playgrounds, recreation centers, and recreation facilities, including all buildings, structures, and equipment necessary or useful in connection therewith;
5. Appropriate funds to carry out the provisions of the Article;
6. Accept any gift, grant, lease, loan, bequest, or devise of real or personal property for parks and recreation programs. Devises, bequests, and gifts may be accepted and held subject to such terms and conditions as may be imposed by the grantor or trustor, except that no county or city may accept or administer any terms that require it to discriminate among its citizens on the basis of race, sex, or religion.

The law also provides for cities to operate a parks and recreation system as a line department or to create a policy-making parks and recreation commission.

Land needed for local recreation programs or for parks is ordinarily acquired with local property tax revenues, although under some circumstances federal and state grants are available. Bonds may be used to acquire parks and recreation facilities and to pay for them over time. General obligation bonds are usually more appropriate for this purpose than revenue bonds. Property may also be acquired by gift or donation. Although the statute allows cities to acquire parks and recreation sites by condemnation, this power is rarely used.

Cities may require subdivision developers to dedicate or reserve recreation areas to serve residents of the proposed subdivision (G.S. 160A-372). The requirement may be imposed only as part of a subdivision ordinance adopted by the city to guide and regulate subdivision development. The rationale for it is that each developed subdivision both increases the demand for recreation and open space and removes open space through land development. The subdivider is thus required to furnish such space for the city in relation to the need the subdivider creates. The subdivider ordinarily passes the economic cost on to purchasers of subdivision lots. Once the land is dedicated, the cost of maintaining it falls on the city.

A subdivision ordinance that requires dedication or reservation of land should indicate the amount of land per subdivision that must be dedicated (such as 5 percent of the total area), its location, and perhaps some standard relating to its degree of improvement. The ordinance should include some provisions to ensure that the land is well suited and properly located for recreation purposes. North Carolina cities may also require developers to provide funds in lieu of land so that additional recreation lands may be acquired to serve the new developments.

The General Statutes contain another authority for cities to acquire open space: G.S. Chapter 160A, Article 19, Part 4. The law authorizes cities to preserve for public access or enjoyment open areas of significant scenic or aesthetic value that might otherwise be lost because of rapid urban growth and development, and it expressly declares the acquisition and the preservation of open space to be a public purpose of municipalities. It authorizes cities to spend public funds to acquire open spaces, but not to acquire open-space land by condemnation. Local governments may acquire outright ownership of open space or any lesser interest, such as a conservation easement.

A local unit may acquire a conservation easement for open space like farmland, preserving the scenic characteristics of the property for public enjoyment without opening it to public access or granting public access.

Open space is an area (1) that is characterized by great natural scenic beauty or (2) whose openness, natural condition, and present state of use, if retained, would enhance the present or potential value of abutting or surrounding urban development or would enhance or maintain the conservation of natural or scenic resources. Open space includes undeveloped land in an urban area that has value for (1) parks and recreation purposes, (2) conservation of land or other natural resources, or (3) historic or scenic purposes (G.S. 160A-407).

In 1994 the North Carolina General Assembly established the Park and Recreation Trust Fund (PARTF) (G.S. 113-44.15). Under this fund was established a matching-grant program for local government units for local parks and recreation purposes. Annually, 20 percent of the funds appropriated to the Department of Environment, Health, and Natural Resources from PARTF will be allocated to local governments. The grants will be awarded for the sole purpose of providing local recreation opportunities to the public. The types of projects that may be funded include fee-simple acquisition of real property for preservation of natural areas and future recreation development; projects for construction, expansion, and renovation or repair of both outdoor and indoor recreation facilities; and projects for construction of support facilities and improvements that support primary recreation facilities.

Organization

A city council may provide parks and recreation services through one of three alternatives: (1) a line department within city government, (2) a policy-making parks and recreation commission, or (3) a joint agreement with another city or with a county.

A Line Department

The most common organizational method used in North Carolina is to organize parks and recreation as a line department of the city. When this approach is used, the parks and recreation department is usually administered by an executive who reports to the city manager or the city council. The city council may establish and appoint a parks and recreation advisory board. This board has no policy-making authority, but can provide a link between the citizens and department staff, the city manager, and the city council. An advisory board is most useful when it represents all the city's major interests, communities, and population groups.

A Policy-Making Parks and Recreation Commission

Second, the city council may establish a parks and recreation department and appoint a policy-making parks and recreation commission to oversee departmental operations. This commission then has the responsibility for the department's organization, personnel, fiscal matters, areas and facilities, programs, and other functions. The commission members report directly to the city council. The commission may be established by an ordinance, which ordinarily spells out the commission's general powers and duties, including its relationships to the city council and its finances.

A Joint Agreement

The city may also elect to enter into a joint agreement with another city or with a county to provide recreation services for its residents. This type of arrangement is authorized by G.S. 160A-335. The future is likely to bring more joint agreements between cities and counties to provide parks and recreation services because of their common purposes and their desire to provide the services as efficiently as possible.

The authority of a municipal government to enter into joint agreements with other governmental entities or agencies to provide parks and recreation services is an important right. A city that does not wish to hire and maintain its own staff may contract with another city or with the county for the use of certain parks and recreation facilities by its residents or for professional staff support from the other unit, or it may agree to set up a joint parks and recreation agency with the other unit. These arrangements are authorized by G.S. 160A-355 and G.S. Chapter 160A, Article 20, Interlocal Cooperation. Contracting for support personnel or services is a satisfactory arrangement when one or two units of government are in effect "buying" the use of park facilities for their residents or seeking professional staff support from another unit's program, and when a second full-time staff person is not feasible or a second policy-making body not needed. Certain contents of the contract are specified in G.S. Chapter 160A, Article 20. The contract must state its purpose and duration and the arrangement for handling the ownership of real property. It should also provide for its own amendment and termination.

A joint agency with its own staff may also be established under G.S. Chapter 160A, Article 20. This approach can provide services that would be impossible or too expensive for any one local unit to provide with its own resources. It can take advantage of the wider population and tax base of several units. Administrative cost can generally be reduced, making more money available for programs and services. The professional staff can be appointed either by one unit or jointly by all participating units. The agency is funded by appropriations from participating units. Title to real property can be held jointly or can continue to be held by the individual participating units. As when services are provided by contract, the contract establishing the joint agency should specify the agency's purpose, duration, organization, appointment of personnel, financing, amendment, and termination.

The Community Schools Act of 1977 (G.S. Ch. 115C, Subch. IV, Art. 13) allows a city to arrange with a local school board for use of school property to meet community needs. A city can agree with a school board to use school gymnasiums, playgrounds, and fields for its recreation programs and thus partially avoid having to construct or acquire expensive capital facilities.

Finally, G.S. 160A-274 allows a city to contract with any other "governmental unit" of the state of North Carolina to sell, buy, lease, or convey real or personal property, with or without consideration, or to agree to joint use of that property. This statute facilitates the maximum and most-efficient use of all governmental property. Action under it can be taken by resolution of a unit's governing board, and local units may dispense with the procedural restrictions imposed on them when they dispose of property under other statutes. Under this statute a city might lease a playground from a school board under a long-term lease that qualifies the city for federal grant assistance in developing the property as a parks and recreation facility.

Financing

Before the 1973 revision of Article V of the North Carolina Constitution, recreation was not considered a "necessary expense" and could not be financed by property tax revenues without a vote of the people. Under the revised constitution and enabling legislation enacted pursuant to it in 1973, public parks and recreation are among the purposes for which counties and cities may levy property taxes without a vote, subject to an overall limitation of $1.50 on the property tax rate. Cities may also allocate to parks and recreation any other revenues whose use is not restricted by law.

Although local parks and recreation departments are primarily funded through property tax revenues, they do receive operating and capital improvement moneys from other sources. In 1992 the municipal departments participating in the 1992 *Municipal and County Parks and Recreation Services Study* reported receiving their funding from the sources indicated in table 26-1.

Because of limited federal, state, and even local funding for parks and recreation, city departments are exploring innovative alternative sources of funding for facilities and programs. In the future there will be increased reliance on user fees, use of occupancy-tax revenues for recreation facilities as part of tourism development programs, publication of gift catalogs to allow donors to give particular needed items to parks and recreation programs, partnerships between local government and private business to build recreation facilities, and establishment of local foundations and trust funds.

Parks and Recreation Planning

Parks and recreation facilities and services, like any other government function, must be planned if they are to operate efficiently and economically as well as provide an appropriate level of service. The need for parks and recreation land should be anticipated so that appropriate sites can be located near user populations and open land can be acquired where necessary while land prices are still low enough that the site is affordable for parks and recreation purposes. Local parks and recreation departments are being encouraged to develop comprehensive planning documents that will help guide the development of recreation facilities and purchase of lands to meet

Table 26-1
Funding Sources of Municipal Parks and Recreation Services, 1992

Source	Amount (in thousands)	Percent
General Fund (taxes, some fees)	$87,627	82.2
Gifts	528	.5
Fees and charges	12,689	11.9
Grants	922	.9
Concessions	975	.9
Mandatory Land Dedication Fund	309	.3
Other	3,599	3.4
Total	$106,649	100.1

Source: Scott Payne, *Municipal and County Parks and Recreation Services Study* (Raleigh, N.C.: North Carolina State University, Recreation Resources Service, 1992), 2.

the needs of local residents. Professional planners and consultants recommend different sizes of facilities that can be put to a variety of uses. Thus a neighborhood may have a small open park, a segment of the city may have a larger facility, and the city as a whole may have one or more large, multipurpose facilities. Possible expansion should be considered when sites and buildings are first acquired and constructed. Effective planning can anticipate where future sites should be reserved against possible incursion from population growth and annexation patterns.

Trends in Public Recreation

Changes in the state's population patterns, economic growth, changes in the political arena, and new social issues have had and will continue to have a major influence on the management and the provision of public parks and recreation. Because of community concern for at-risk youth, quality day care, the homeless, and other social issues, municipal recreation departments are beginning to organize nontraditional recreation programs such as after-school child care, day care for older adults, literacy programs, and a variety of self-help classes for children and adults. As the demand for day-care services increases, local recreation departments will be asked to play a role in providing quality day-care opportunities for working parents and their children. Departments will have to respond with programs beyond their traditional summer day camps, playground programs, or just open community centers. Some local departments will be operating licensed child care facilities. Others will provide facilities for private groups to operate needed child care programs.

As the population ages, the demand for recreation programs and services for older adults will increase. North Carolina is affected not only by the aging of the baby boomers but by the influx of older adults retiring to North Carolina. This older population will demand recreation programs and services to meet its needs. Older adults will influence the types of recreation facilities built and the program mix. The aging population will present several challenges. On one end of the continuum, the baby boomers who are retiring early and remaining healthy will expect a full range of recreation opportunities beyond the traditional senior programs. At the other end of the continuum, as people live longer and the need for day care for older adults increases, the public will turn to parks and recreation agencies for assistance.

Public parks and recreation professionals are also facing an environment of increased government regulations. Constraints on hazardous-waste disposal, rules governing pesticide application, Occupational Safety and Health Administration standards for blood-borne pathogens, guidelines for playground safety, and the Americans with Disabilities Act are just a few regulations, guidelines, and laws that parks and recreation professionals must address. New regulations are affecting not only program delivery and staffing but facility design. The challenge facing parks and recreation professionals is how to implement or comply with many of the new regulations without additional financial resources.

Another trend in recreation is the emphasis on risk management. In an era of increasing concern about litigation, parks and recreation systems are being forced to address the issues of liability and safety.[4] Departments must be concerned with the safety of employees, particularly those who work with toxic chemicals, and the safety of participants. In the future, more professional staff and volunteers will be trained and certified as part of an overall effort to improve the quality of services. Risk-management plans are becoming a necessity.

The next twenty years will bring an increase in the number of merged municipal and county parks and recreation systems. The organizational structure of local parks and recreation systems is beginning to change. In counties with both municipal and county parks and recreation departments, the opportunity to merge exists. Although a dozen or more parks and recreation departments provide services to both city and county residents, the Charlotte Parks and Recreation Department and the Mecklenburg County Parks and Recreation Department have been among the few to merge in recent years.

Funding continues to be a concern for parks and recreation professionals. Perhaps the most critical area of concern is the funding of capital improvements. Moneys from the Land and Water Conservation Fund continue to be available at a reduced level, forcing local communities to depend almost entirely on bond issues to generate revenue for capital development. To date, most recreation bond issues have passed,[5] but will that trend continue? In the future, cities will need to investigate alternative financing for capital development projects such as joint agreements with other private and governmental agencies. As the demand for recreation services and facilities increases, local departments will have to find a way to meet those needs in an environment of static tax rolls, modest growth rates, and limited federal and state funding.

As America moves toward the twenty-first century, the scope of recreation services will continue to broaden. Collaborative efforts with other agencies will increase as local departments respond to community needs. The types of persons employed by parks and recreation departments will expand to include not only the traditional parks and recreation majors, but people with majors in early childhood development, nutrition, computer science, and gerontology. Local parks and recreation services will change as life-styles, resources, and demographics change.

Additional Assistance

The primary source of assistance for local governments that either provide local parks and recreation services or are contemplating the establishment of a parks and recreation department is the Recreation Resources Service. The Recreation Resources Service is a division of the Parks, Recreation and Tourism Management Department, North Carolina State University, and is funded through an agreement with the Division of Parks and Recreation, North Carolina Department of Environment, Health, and Natural Resources. It provides a wide range of technical assistance to local parks and recreation agencies. Services include educational workshops on topics such as playground safety, the Americans with Disabilities Act, and athletic field maintenance; training of parks and recreation advisory board members; publication of technical assistance manuals, directories, and a monthly job bulletin; applied research; evaluative studies of parks and recreation agencies; production of park conceptual maps; and provision of individual technical assistance. The North Carolina League of Municipalities and the Institute of Government can also help with legal, budgetary, and financial aspects of parks and recreation services.

Notes

1. Recreation Enabling Act of 1945, codified as G.S. Chapter 160A-351.

2. Scott Payne, *Municipal and County Parks and Recreation Services Study* (Raleigh, N.C.: North Carolina State University, Recreation Resources Service, 1992).

3. Bureau of the Census, *Government Finances: 1989–90, Preliminary Report* (Washington, D.C.: Government Printing Office, September 1991).

4. See chapter 9 for a discussion of a city's expenditure for personal injuries sustained in a city parks and recreation program.

5. H. D. Sessoms, ed., *Introduction to Leisure Services in North Carolina* (Dubuque, Iowa: Kendall/Hunt Publishing Company, 1990), 100.

27 Other Services and Functions

Warren Jake Wicker

Contents

THIS CHAPTER briefly examines several functions and activities that are performed by only a limited number of cities. Small numbers of cities are still involved in financing hospitals and establishing armories. Larger numbers (but a minority of all cities) have been involved in the alcoholic beverage control systems and in providing ambulance and rescue services. In between are modest numbers of cities that support cemeteries, art galleries and museums, and auditoriums, coliseums, and convention centers.

The Alcoholic Beverage Control System

G.S. Chapter 18B, Regulation of Alcoholic Beverages, covers manufacturing, sale, transportation, use, and possession of alcoholic beverages in the state. The system that G.S. Chapter 18B establishes has developed largely since adoption of the Twenty-First Amendment to the United States Constitution in 1933, which repealed the Eighteenth Amendment prohibiting manufacture or sale of alcoholic beverages in the United States.[1] The casual observer might well conclude that labeling the complex arrangements a "system" is excessively generous.

Five classes of beverages are subject to regulation under G.S. Chapter 18B:

1. *Malt beverage:* beer, ale, and similar beverages containing between 0.5 percent and 6 percent alcohol by volume
2. *Unfortified wine:* wine with an alcohol content of not more than 17 percent by volume
3. *Fortified wine:* fermented wine whose natural alcoholic content has been augmented by brandy, but which contains not more than 24 percent alcohol by volume
4. *Spirituous liquor:* whiskey, gin, rum, brandy, and other distilled spirits
5. *Mixed beverage:* mixed beverages, ranging from bourbon on the rocks to Bloody Marys to fancy cocktails

General administration of the law is the responsibility of the North Carolina Alcoholic Beverage Control (ABC) Commission, a state agency. The ABC Commission has three members appointed by the governor. The ABC Commission's chief functions are to warehouse all beverages sold in the local ABC stores, set the prices of beverages sold in the stores, enforce the ABC laws, review the operations of local ABC systems, and issue ABC permits to private establishments that sell regulated beverages (G.S. 18A-203).

North Carolina's approach is usually characterized as a *local option system* because the sale of alcoholic beverages is initially approved by citizens in an election held in a city or a county. The elections may be held countywide or in individual cities.

The system's design anticipates that the county will be the primary unit for making decisions about the availability of alcoholic beverages, but in some circumstances the city becomes the jurisdiction in which elections are held (G.S. 18A-600).

Counties may hold four kinds of elections: (1) on the sale of malt beverages, (2) on the sale of unfortified wine, (3) on the establishment of ABC stores, or (4) on the sale of mixed beverages (liquor by the drink). A county may hold an election on the sale of mixed beverages only if it already has ABC stores (or if ABC stores are approved in the same election held on the sale of mixed beverages).

City elections and operation of ABC stores take place when there have been no county elections or when the county voters have rejected one or more alcoholic beverage alternatives. City elections may be initiated by the city council or by a petition from at least 35 percent of the city's registered voters. City elections on ABC issues are conducted by the local board of elections (city or county) that conducts other types of city elections.

A city election on the establishment of ABC stores may be held only if the city (a) has at least 500 registered voters and (b) is located in a county that does not operate ABC stores.

A city may hold an election on the sale of malt beverages or unfortified wine only if there has already been a countywide election in which a proposal to allow the sale of these beverages has been rejected and either (a) the city has a population of at least 500 or (b) the city operates ABC stores.

A city may hold an election on the sale of mixed beverages only if it has at least 500 registered voters and either (a) the city operates ABC stores (or their operation is approved at the time of the election on the sale of mixed beverages) or (b) the city is located in a county that operates ABC stores and in which a mixed beverage election has been held and has failed to secure approval of the voters.

A vote in either county or city elections to approve the establishment of ABC stores carries with it approval of the sale of fortified wines. There is no separate election on the sale of fortified wines.

Spirituous liquors are sold only in county or city ABC stores. Some ABC stores also sell fortified wines. Malt beverages, unfortified wines, and fortified wines may be sold in grocery stores, restaurants, and other places properly licensed within jurisdictions where their sale has been approved in the necessary elections.

By the middle of 1995, actions taken under the arrangements just described had resulted in widespread sale of alcoholic beverages in the state.[2] Some type of alcoholic beverage could legally be sold in all or parts of 95 of the state's 100 counties. The 5 totally "dry" counties were Clay, Graham, Mitchell, Yadkin, and Yancey. In these counties none of the five classes of alcoholic beverages could legally be sold.

Eleven counties in 1995 were completely "wet." That is, each of the counties (except Guilford) operated ABC stores, and within them all the classes of beverages had been approved for sale. These counties were Brunswick, Craven, Cumberland, Durham, Guilford, Mecklenburg, New Hanover, Onslow, Orange, Pender, and Wake.

In the other 84 counties, varying arrangements were found. Many of them involved cities. A total of 113 cities operated ABC stores in counties that did not have ABC stores countywide.

In 104 cities, malt beverages had been approved for sale. These cities were in counties where the sale of malt beverages had not been approved countywide.

In 76 cities the voters had approved the sale of mixed beverages. These cities were in counties where there were either county or city ABC stores but mixed beverages (liquor by the drink) had not been approved on a countywide basis.

The city council in a city that operates ABC stores appoints members of the local ABC board. Under the general law, G.S. 18B-700, each local board has three members who serve three-year staggered terms. In some cities, however, local acts provide for larger boards. The local board is completely independent of the city; it is not a part of the city government. The local board is responsible for management of the local system. Its principal duties are hiring and firing employees, enforcing ABC laws and regulations, buying and selling alcoholic beverages, arranging for store sites, and issuing purchase-transportation permits (G.S. 18B-701).

The state's ABC system realizes revenues from state-imposed taxes and special charges, and from profits from sales in the local stores. In general, the state receives the tax revenues and a portion of the charges, and the local systems keep the profits from the stores. G.S. 18B-805 sets forth detailed directions to local boards on the distribution of their gross receipts. The directions cover operating expenses and working capital as well as the sharing of special fees and charges. Portions of the profits from the local stores must be expended for purposes specified in the statutes. Other portions, those that remain after all the statutory distributions have been made, are available for use by city and county governing bodies.

Under the general law, local boards must spend 5 percent of their profits on enforcement of liquor laws. They are also required to distribute some 7 percent of their profits to support alcoholism or substance abuse programs. Many local acts, however, have modified this requirement. Most cities are required, under local acts, to share their ABC profits with the county government, the schools, or other designated public agencies.

Ambulances and Rescue Squads

Under the Emergency Medical Services Act of 1973 (G.S. Ch. 143, Art. 56), the Department of Human Resources is responsible for establishing and maintaining "a program for the improvement and upgrading of emergency medical services throughout the State." The North Carolina Medical Care Commission adopts rules, regulations, and standards for the various types of emergency medical service vehicles and for the certification of emergency medical technicians and ambulance attendants (G.S. Ch. 131E, Art. 7). All emergency medical service vehicles must be permitted, and all emergency medical service personnel must be certified. An *ambulance* (an emergency medical service vehicle) is a vehicle that is designed to transport persons who are "sick, injured, wounded, or otherwise incapacitated or helpless" and may need medical care while being transported (G.S. 131E-55). The program is administered by the Office of Emergency Medical Services of the Department of Human Resources.

The basic scheme for local arrangements, set forth in G.S. 153A-250, makes county government the key player in the delivery of emergency medical services. This statute authorizes counties, by ordinance, to franchise ambulance services throughout their jurisdictions. The county boards of commissioners may also establish schedules of fees and charges for the services. More than one operator may be franchised in a county.

In lieu of franchising operators (in all or parts of a county), a county may own and operate an ambulance service as a line department of the county government. Alternatively a county may create an ambulance commission and vest in the commission the authority to operate an ambulance service.

Pursuant to G.S. 153A-250(c), a city has the same power as a county *if* (a) the county in which the city is located has adopted a resolution authorizing the city to provide and franchise ambulance services or (b) the county, after being requested by the city to provide for ambulance services within the city, has not done so. A city's authority to provide services covers only the territory within its boundaries. Like a county, a city that has been authorized to operate ambulance services may do so as a line department of the city government or through an ambulance commission that it may create. Cities may levy property taxes to support ambulance services [G.S. 160A-209(c)] and issue general obligation bonds to finance the purchasing of equipment [G.S. 159-48(c)(22)].

A county, if it wishes to do so, may preempt a city's authority to operate or franchise ambulances after notice to the city. Thus a city's operation of services must initially be approved by a county, and the county may end the operation in its discretion. This relationship, of course, reflects a basic approach that is designed to make services available to all citizens of the state and that assumes that primary county responsibility for the services at the local level is most likely to achieve that goal.

The Office of Emergency Medical Services reports that in early 1995 there were 1,648 emergency service vehicles permitted in the state.[3] One-third of them (544) were owned and operated by a governmental unit. Among the governments in the picture, counties were the chief players, operating 449 of the governmental vehicles, or 82.5 percent. Federal agencies operated 19 vehicles, or 3.5 percent, and state agencies operated 13, or 2.4 percent. The remaining 63 vehicles, or 11.6 percent, were permitted to cities. Some fifteen cities directly provided ambulance services.

Two-thirds of the emergency medical service vehicles in the state in early 1995 were operated by other agencies: nonprofit volunteer organizations, fire departments, hospitals, industrial corporations, and private for-profit companies. Most of these were franchised by counties.

The Office of Emergency Medical Services is also responsible for testing and certifying the personnel who operate emergency medical service vehicles. In May 1995 a total of 27,511 individuals held some form of certification. Of these, 2,235 were certified as ambulance attendants, 17,592 as emergency medical technicians (EMTs), and 7,684 in four other specialized EMT classifications. The initial training required and the continuing education necessary to maintain certification are usually provided by community colleges and technical institutes or special training staffs in the operating units.

Rescue squads in North Carolina are usually formed as nonprofit volunteer organizations. Rescue squads' vehicles are designed and equipped to rescue persons at sites of accidents, fires, drownings, and disasters. Rescue vehicles are not designed to transport the sick and the wounded and thus are not subject to permitting by the Department of Human Resources.

It is common for a single department to provide more than one of the three chief emergency functions: ambulance (emergency medical services, EMS), rescue, and fire. A 1994 survey by the North Carolina Association of Rescue and Emergency Medical Services covered 462 departments, or about three-fourths of those in the state. Functions provided by these departments were as follows:

Function	Percentage
EMS and rescue	54.2
EMS, rescue, and fire	22.9
EMS only	15.1
Rescue and fire	5.2
Rescue only	1.3
EMS and fire	1.3
Total	100.0

The same survey found that in 1994 the average department (squad) had thirty-five members, responded to 1,770 calls, and had a budget of almost $300,000. Sources of funds were as follows:

Source	Percentage
County appropriations	56.4
City appropriations	11.7
Fund raisers	11.3
Donations	9.7
Other	10.9
Total	100.0

Some rescue squads are exclusively volunteer organizations; others have some paid personnel; and still others are operated fully by paid personnel. Relatively few cities operate rescue squads directly.

Rather, cities support them financially. G.S. 160A-487 authorizes cities to support rescue squads that operate both within and outside their boundaries. Cities may levy property taxes to support rescue squads [G.S. 160A-209(c)]. Cities may also lease, sell, or convey land to volunteer rescue squads, on which the squads may build or expand facilities (G.S. 160A-277), and under G.S. 160A-279, cities may appropriate property to rescue squads providing services within the cities.

Armories

Cities (and counties) in North Carolina are authorized to acquire property suitable for use as an armory or on which an armory might be constructed (G.S. 127A-165). They are also authorized to make appropriations for the purpose of building armories, either alone or to supplement funds available for that purpose from the state and federal governments (G.S. 127A-167). All such property may be leased or conveyed to the state of North Carolina for use by the North Carolina National Guard and other properly organized militia organizations.

Cities may levy property taxes to support the acquisition of property for armories or to build armories, but only after receiving approval from their voters in a referendum [G.S. 160A-209(e)]. Cities may also issue general obligation bonds to finance the provision of armories [G.S. 159-48(b)(21)].

The Division of the National Guard, a part of the state's Department of Crime Control and Public Safety, is responsible for the general management and the administration of armories and related facilities in the state. Title to all of them is now in the state, with two exceptions: one is leased from Kinston and one (in Wilmington) is leased from the federal government.[4]

Current (1995) funding for new armories is shared among federal, state, and local governments. The land for a new armory must be provided by one or more local governments. The cost of site preparation is shared evenly between the state and one or more local governments. The federal government, subject to specific appropriations by Congress, provides 75 percent of the construction cost. The remaining 25 percent of the construction cost is shared between the state and local governments.

Armories are also available for general community uses under rules and regulations established by the local unit commander. The national guard encourages use of the facilities by local governments and private groups.

Arts Programs and Museums

North Carolina cities have broad authority in providing arts programs and museums. G.S. 160A-488 authorizes cities (and counties) to establish and support museums, art galleries, and arts centers as long as the facilities are open to the public. As used in this statute, *arts* refers "to the performing arts, visual arts, and literary arts and includes dance, drama, music, painting, drawing, sculpture, printmaking, crafts, photography, film, video, architecture, design and literature, when part of a performing, visual or literary arts program."

The support may include purchasing works of art as well as providing buildings and meeting operating and maintenance expenses. Moreover, cities may operate such programs directly or contract with any public or nonprofit private organization to establish and operate them. Cities may levy property taxes to support the programs and issue general obligation bonds to finance the acquisition or the construction of museums and other arts facilities.

Over 100 cities in the state make significant contributions to the support of arts programs and museums. A few, such as Farmville, Gastonia, and Winston-Salem, operate some facilities directly. Most cities, however, have agreements with private nonprofit associations through which they direct their support.

Auditoriums, Coliseums, and Convention Centers

G.S. 160A-489 authorizes cities to establish and support public auditoriums, coliseums, and convention centers. Support includes the acquisition and the construction of these facilities and their operation, maintenance, and improvement. Cities may use any funds they have available whose use is not otherwise limited by law. Under G.S. 160A-209(c) they may levy property taxes to support auditoriums, coliseums, and convention centers. They may also issue general obligation bonds [G.S. 159-48(b)(3)] and revenue bonds (G.S. Ch. 159, Art. 5) if needed to build these facilities.

Local officials agree that outlays for auditoriums, coliseums, and convention centers are investments in economic development, cultural opportunities, and tourism. Rarely are such facilities fully self-supporting from revenues of the activities and the events presented in them. A facility is usually considered financially successful if it produces enough revenues to cover all operating and maintenance costs. Whereas small and medium-size cities may have facilities adequate for small conferences and sports events, only the large cities in the state have facilities adequate to handle major conventions and conferences and large sports events.

In some cities the operation of the facilities is part of the general administrative arrangements, and the directors report to the city manager. In other cities a separate board has been created and given general responsibility for supervising the operation of the facilities, including appointment of management personnel.

Cemeteries

Concern for the proper burial of the deceased has been almost universal throughout history. Well-maintained cemeteries evidence respect for the dead, are often significant in connection with religious burial rituals, and are important in safeguarding the public health.

State officials in North Carolina estimate that there are more than 35,000 active, inactive, and abandoned cemeteries in North Carolina. This tabulation includes family, church, private, and public cemeteries.[5] The number of cities that maintain cemeteries is not known, but is probably 200 or so.

State law generally regulates the operation of cemeteries and the removal and the reinterment of remains (G.S. Ch. 65). Privately owned and operated perpetual care cemeteries are subject to the rules and the regulations of the North Carolina Cemetery Commission (G.S. Ch. 65, Art. 9). Municipal cemeteries, along with those operated and maintained by religious organizations, are not subject to regulation by the state.

Cities are authorized to own, operate, and maintain cemeteries both within and outside their boundaries and may take over abandoned cemeteries within their boundaries (G.S. Ch. 160A, Art. 17). A city may directly operate a city cemetery, or the council may appoint a board of trustees, transfer the cemetery to the board, and vest in the board full authority for operating and maintaining the cemetery. A city may adopt rules and regulations with respect to the operation of its cemetery, establish a schedule of fees and charges, and levy property taxes for the cemetery's support. A board of trustees, if established, has the same powers except that its support from tax funds is secured through annual appropriations from the city.

Municipal cemeteries are increasingly viewed as a cultural and recreational amenity. When attractively landscaped with flowers, shrubs, and trees, they provide open space, a quiet place for walking, a serene setting for those interested in gaining insights into the social indicators reflected in headstones and monuments, and a resource for genealogical investigations. In some cities, cemeteries are operated as a part of the parks and recreation department.

Hospitals

North Carolina cities have broad authority to provide hospital services (G.S. 131-5 through -14.1). They may build, operate, and support all types of hospitals. Support includes leasing hospitals to other governmental agencies or private corporations, both for-profit and nonprofit. Cities may issue general obligation bonds (G.S. 159-48) and revenue bonds (G.S. Ch. 159, Art. 9) to finance the construction of hospitals and other medical facilities. Property taxes may be levied for hospital purposes (G.S. 160A-209).

North Carolina cities initiated hospital activities after the Civil War, but very few cities were involved during the nineteenth century.[6] Activities increased in the twentieth century, reaching their peak after World War II. Most hospital support in this century has been from county governments, and in the past twenty years most county hospitals have been leased or conveyed to private nonprofit organizations. Counties continue to be responsible for much of the construction of facilities, but not for operation. In 1993 there were 124 general acute care hospitals in the state. They had 22,094 beds and an average occupancy rate of 55.5 percent.[7] Fewer than a dozen of these 124 hospitals were significantly supported by city governments.

Notes

1. For a brief history of the development of North Carolina's approach to the control of alcoholic beverages, see Ben F. Loeb, Jr., "ABC Law: The Rise and Fall of Local Option," *Popular Government* 58, no.4 (Spring 1993): 36–42.

2. The information in this paragraph and the paragraphs that follow it is from ABC Commission, unpublished computer printout, 18 May 1995.

3. The information in this paragraph and the paragraphs that follow it was provided by Hadley Whittemore, Office of Emergency Medical Services, Department of Human Resources, and Gordon Joyner, secretary-treasurer, North Carolina Association of Rescue and Emergency Medical Services, May 1995, from unpublished records.

4. Major Danny Hassell, assistant construction and management officer, North Carolina National Guard, telephone interview with author, 3 May 1995.

5. Donna Kelly, North Carolina Cemetery Survey, Department of Cultural Resources, telephone interview with author, 1 May 1995.

6. For a brief history of the development of hospitals in North Carolina, see Anne Dellinger, "Hospitals," in *State-Local Relations in North Carolina*, ed. Charles D. Liner (Chapel Hill, N.C.: Institute of Government, The University of North Carolina at Chapel Hill, 1985), ch. 5.

7. North Carolina Department of Human Resources, Division of Facility Services, *Draft 1995 State Medical Facilities Plan* (Raleigh, N.C.: NCDHR, 1994).

Appendix: County Government in North Carolina

David M. Lawrence

Contents

ALTHOUGH this is a book about city government in North Carolina, the reader cannot fully understand the role, the powers, and the responsibilities of cities without knowing something about county government. North Carolina's 100 counties are, like the state's cities, general-purpose units of local government. Chapter 1 of this book details how much alike the two types of units have become in recent years, both in services that they are authorized to—and do—provide and in systems of management. Important functional and organizational differences remain between cities and counties, however.

The functional differences arise mainly from the basic fact that the state's counties, unlike its cities, cover all the state's territory and include all its citizens. Thus from North Carolina's earliest years, county governments have been used as a means of carrying out some of *state government's* responsibilities. For many years, county officials collected the state's taxes, constructed and maintained the state's roads, and operated the state's court system. Of course, the state long ago assumed primary responsibility for these functions, but it has continued to look to county governments to help finance and administer some of them. Therefore, although it has long been possible to say of cities that there are few functions or services that they must by law provide, that can never be said of counties: counties are required by law to provide many functions and services. Viewed from within the state's governmental structure, these are state-mandated county functions. Viewed from outside that structure, these functions are part of a larger scheme under which citizens have assigned certain functions to counties to perform, others to the state to provide directly, and still others (the largest number) to the state and counties to provide jointly.

Beyond acting as agents of state government, counties—because they cover the entire state—have assumed primary responsibility for a number of functions that are traditionally considered local government's and that are needed by all, whether they live in an urban, suburban, or rural area. Thus some functions that were formerly city responsibilities are now county responsibilities. Public health, hospitals, libraries, and solid waste disposal are examples of functions that originally were primarily provided by cities and are now primarily provided by county governments.

The organizational differences between counties and cities lie in the role of the board of county commissioners, each county's governing board. Whereas a city council normally may initiate and direct policy throughout city government, a board of county commissioners may not. In a number of functional areas—schools, social services, health, and law enforcement are among the most prominent—policy control lies largely with more-or-less independent boards or officers or with the state. The only commissioners' responsibility that includes all of county government is financial: setting financial policy and determining the level of local financial support (subject to mandated minimum levels in some cases) to be given each county service.

The remainder of this appendix describes each function of government for which primary local government responsibility rests with counties rather than with cities.

Education

Public Schools

The responsibility for public elementary and secondary education in North Carolina is shared by the state government, the local boards of education, and the boards of county commissioners. The primary responsibility, both for policy making and for financing, rests at the state level with the General Assembly and the State Board of Education. Local responsibility is divided between the school board and the board of county commissioners. Broadly speaking, the school board makes educational policy, and the board of county commissioners, in making county financial policy, determines the amount of county financial support for public education. In application, of course, the division of responsibility is not that simple. In determining the amount of county funds to be available for education, the county commissioners do influence educational policy. The school boards that are dissatisfied with the share of county resources allocated to them may take their case beyond the commissioners to the courts. There is, in fact, a very complex division of responsibility that varies in detail from county to county.

Each county has at least one school administrative unit. By general law, each county is a county school administrative unit, under the control of the county board of education. In addition, there are currently (in 1995) nineteen other school administrative units, each created by the General Assembly in the territory in and around one or more cities in one or more contiguous counties. (This territory is therefore deleted from the county administrative unit.) These additional units are called *city administrative units*, though cities have nothing to do with supporting them or (with rare exceptions) operating them.

Each county or city unit is governed by its own board of education. All the county school boards are elected, as are the boards of most of the city school units. These local boards appoint the local superintendent, the teachers, the principals, and other employees of the unit; prepare the school budget; adopt local school policies; and oversee the implementation of local policies, the state's educational programs, and the state's rules and regulations governing enrollment of students. Unlike school boards in most other states, North Carolina school boards do not have the power of taxation. In this state the board of county commissioners is the local tax-levying authority for the schools. In 1995, these 119 local school boards had responsibility over approximately 2,000 separate schools in which some 1,111,000 students were enrolled.

Since 1933, primary financial responsibility for the state's public school system has rested with state government. In 1992–93 some 68 percent of total public school support (including both current operating expense and capital costs) was paid by state appropriations; local governments met about 23.5 percent, and the federal government about 8.5 percent.[1] The proportions of state, local, and federal support, of course, differ from unit to unit. The state's money goes primarily to meet current operating expenses. The Basic Education Program, authorized in 1985, with full implementation scheduled for 1995, includes special funding that is designed to provide a comparable basic educational opportunity to students in every unit. The state provides some additional operating funds to small and low-wealth school units. Local moneys are used to meet most of the system's capital requirements and to supplement the state's support for operations. About once a decade for the past forty years, local capital outlays have been supplemented by statewide bond issues. In addition, some state capital funds are available through the Public School Building Capital Fund and the Critical School Facility Needs Fund. Although local support accounts for only about 25 percent of total public school expenditures, the counties allocate from 50 to 75 percent of their funds for school purposes. Federal support of the schools goes mainly to support specific current programs and to assist units that are heavily impacted by federal installations such as military bases.

Total public school expenditures (including current expenses, capital outlay, and debt service) in 1992–93 were approximately $5.6 billion. Of this sum, 61.1 percent was raised by the state, 7.7 percent by the federal government, and 31.2 percent by counties and the local schools. The average total expenditure per student for 1992–93 was about $5,075.

Community Colleges and Technical Institutes

The sort of general picture that holds for the state's system of public schools holds for its system of community colleges and technical institutes. Primary policy-making and financial responsibility rests with the General Assembly, the State Board of Community Colleges, and the president of the North Carolina System of Community Colleges, who also serves as head of the State Department of Community Colleges. Local responsibility is shared by each institution's board of trustees and the board of county commissioners, in much the same manner as local responsibility for public schools is shared by school boards and county commissioners.

The community college system, established in 1963, originally comprised two types of institutions: community colleges offering two-year college transfer work; and technical institutes emphasizing technical training. In the past thirty years many institutions that started as technical institutes have enlarged their offerings to include college transfer work. All fifty-eight institutions in the system are now known as community colleges. At the state level they are under the control of the State Board of Community Colleges, which makes policy for the system, appoints the president of the State Community College System, and approves the appointment of presidents of the fifty-eight individual institutions. Local administrative authority is vested in a board of trustees with powers and responsibilities comparable to those of a local school board. Like the school board, it depends on the local tax-levying authority (or authorities) of the board(s) of county commissioners for local financial support.

The City's Role

Cities have neither powers nor responsibilities with respect to the operation of the community college system. As a general matter, the same statement is true of the public school system. As already explained, despite their names, city school boards for the most part have no relationship with city government. (In a few cities these boards are appointed by the city council; and a few city councils levy school supplemental taxes for city administrative units.) The basic financial responsibility for operating both county school systems and city school systems rests with the board of county commissioners.

Social Services

Although social services are often thought of strictly in terms of public assistance, they are in fact much more than that. Besides the basic programs of public assistance, like Aid to Families with Dependent Children and Food Stamps, social services include an array of other programs such as Medicaid, various protective services for children and disabled adults, placement services (such as adoption and foster care) for children, and day care.

The basic shape of social services in all states is determined by the federal government, primarily through the Social Security Act of 1935 as amended. State legislation is structured to implement the federal requirements that are a condition for receiving the very large amounts of federal funds that support the programs. The federal legislation requires that federally supported public assistance programs be provided statewide and be uniformly administered throughout the state. The federal government lets the states decide (1) what the relative shares of state and local matching contributions will be and (2) whether the program will be administered by the state or the county. Because North Carolina has chosen county administration, subject to state control, each county must establish and finance a social service program at a minimum level set by the state. Statewide in 1992–93, an estimated 1 million persons (or a little less than one in every six) in the state received some form of assistance through the various social service programs.

Each North Carolina county has a board of social services of three or five members, as determined by the board of county commissioners. All members are appointed: one (or two, depending on the board's size) by the State Social Services Commission, one (or two) by the board of county commissioners, and the third (or fifth) by the other members. Although this board is largely advisory, it does appoint the county director of social services, who in turn appoints the other employees of the county department. The county social service department is subject to closer control by the State Division of Social Services (part of the Department of Human Resources) than by the county commissioners or the county manager.

The board of county commissioners' principal role in social services is financial, and even in this realm its actions are constrained. The federal government provides varying percentages of support for the various programs of social services and leaves the amount and the relative shares of state-local support to be determined by the states. In North Carolina the General Assembly makes those decisions through the biennial appropriation process. Once the decisions have been made, however, the federal requirement of statewide uniformity in support of the federally supported programs obliges the counties to meet a specific percentage of nonfederal social service costs. That is, there is a state-mandated minimum level of support that all counties must meet with their social service appropriations, and the General Statutes give the State Department of Human Resources the power to ensure that the mandated minimum is met.

For 1995–96 the Division of Social Services estimated statewide social service costs of $4.61 billion. Of this amount the division estimated that 67.4 percent of the funds would be supplied by the federal government, 25.9 percent by the state government, and 6.7 percent by counties.

Public Health, Mental Health, and Hospital Services

Public Health Services

Each North Carolina county is required to provide public health services by one of three methods: through a county department, through a district health department that includes two or more counties, or by contract with the state. The services provided by a local health department, which vary somewhat from department to department, include collecting vital statistics; enforcing state sanitation regulations for restaurants, hotels, summer camps, and other public establishments; enforcing septic tank and other on-site sewage disposal regulations; offering clinical services to adults, pregnant women, and children; conducting health education programs; and providing immunization and communicable disease control.

The state, through the Department of Environment, Health, and Natural Resources (DEHNR), affects local health programs in several ways. DEHNR advises local health department employees, and the Commission for Health Services requires local departments to enforce its regulations. Also, DEHNR administers the allocation of federal funds to the local departments and, as a condition of state funding of health departments, enters into a contract with each county that includes certain minimum standards for departmental operations.

Although cities were once authorized to operate health departments, that authority has been repealed, and public health is now entirely a county function at the local level. The principal local public health agencies are the board of health and the health department. A county may have its own board of health, or it may be served by a district health board, along with one or more other counties. In 1995, seventy-nine counties had a single-county board; the other twenty-one counties were served by eight district boards.

The commissioners in a county served by a single-county health board appoint one of themselves and ten other persons to the eleven-member health board. The commissioners of each county served by a district health board appoint one of themselves to that board, and these members then appoint enough other persons to make up a health board of fifteen persons. In either event the board of health is the policy-making body for the health department. It adopts regulations, comparable to city ordinances, relating to public health; it recommends the levels of fees for health services to the county board of commissioners; it (in most counties) reviews the health department budget for transmittal to the county commissioners; and it appoints the local health director.

As with education and social services, the county commissioners' primary role with respect to health services is to provide the local financial support for the program. The commissioners have considerable flexibility in deciding on the level of local support, the only constraint being the minimum standards set out in administrative rules of DEHNR's Division of Health Services. However, whereas it is not the primary source of support for schools and social services, the county is the chief provider for public health operations, accounting for as much as 75 percent of the support in some cases. The state ranks second and the federal government third in providing the remaining funds.

Mental Health Services

Community mental health services are provided through area mental health, developmental disabilities, and substance abuse authorities. An authority's activities include outpatient therapy, inpatient services, follow-up care for persons discharged from state mental hospitals, counseling services for children in schools, group homes for emotionally disturbed adolescents and mentally retarded adults, and alcoholism and drug prevention and treatment programs.

The organization and the nature of mental health services have been strongly influenced by federal requirements, imposed as a condition of federal financial assistance. The State Commission for Mental Health, Developmental Disabilities, and Substance Abuse Services (in the Department of Human Resources—DHR) sets the minimum standards that local programs must meet. These standards are then administered by DHR, and compliance at the local level is a condition of receiving state and federal funding.

Local administration is under the control of the area authority, which is governed by the area mental health, developmental disabilities, and substance abuse board. There are twenty-five authorities that serve two or more counties. The board of commissioners in each county served by a multicounty authority appoints one of its members to the area board; these members then appoint the remaining members. In a single-county area (sixteen in 1995) the entire board is appointed by the county commissioners. In either case the statutes require that various consumer interests and professional specialties be represented on the area authority board. The board prepares and submits to the state an annual plan for operations. This becomes the basis for a Memorandum of Agreement between the board and the state, under which state assistance is received. The board also appoints, with state approval, the director of the area authority; the director then appoints the authority's other employees, subject to standards set by the State Personnel Act and the board.

The statutes characterize an area authority as a separate political subdivision, and county government's role is largely limited to providing local financial support. The commissioners are relatively free to determine the level of support that they will provide, but need to remember that the amount of state and federal aid is based on each county's financial capacity and its level of local support. Local mental health expenditures are financed (in the order of their share of support) by the state (some 54 percent in 1995), county and local service receipts, and the federal government. As a practical matter, cities are not involved in mental health programs.

Hospitals

According to a tabulation by the North Carolina Hospital Association, North Carolina had 172 licensed hospitals in 1995. Of these, 135 provided general acute care, 27 offered psychiatric care, and the other 10 provided specialty services. Some 88 are privately owned and operated; 37 are owned by counties; another 16 are owned by other local governments (sometimes jointly with a county); 14 are owned by the state; and the remainder are owned by federal agencies, churches, and other parties. On an average day, some 23,000 persons (about 3 of each 1,000 in the state) are receiving inpatient care at one of these hospitals, which have a total of some 35,000 beds.

Although both counties and cities are authorized to own and operate hospitals, hospital services have become largely a county function, reflecting the fact that hospital services are needed by all citizens, whether or not they reside inside a city. In recent years the typical arrangement has been for a county to finance, through the issuance of bonds, the construction of a hospital and then to lease it to a separate agency (most often a nonprofit corporation whose directors are appointed by the board of county commissioners) for operation. This separate agency then operates the hospital in a manner largely independent of county control. The operation of a hospital can be financed almost entirely from receipts, including third-party payments from insurance carriers and Medicaid and Medicare, and the county's involvement is usually limited to contributing an annual sum to pay for treatment of medically indigent patients and providing funds for retiring hospital debt. When hospital revenues are sufficient to retire the debt (as they often are), the only county responsibility is indigent care.

Law Enforcement, the Courts, and the Medical Examiner

The Sheriff

The North Carolina Constitution requires that each county elect a sheriff. In most counties, sheriffs and their deputies provide law enforcement; serve process, enforce judgments, and otherwise act as officers of the court; and administer the county jail. (In Gaston County the sheriff's normal duties have been split. The Gaston sheriff has all the normal duties except for law enforcement, which has been placed with a county police force under the control of the board of commissioners. Mecklenburg County also had a county police force until 1993, when it was merged with the Charlotte police department to form a countywide department that operates under the city.)

The sheriff has jurisdiction to enforce the criminal law throughout the county, including within the boundaries of cities and towns located in the county. As a practical matter, most sheriffs restrict their law enforcement activities to areas within their county but outside the boundaries of cities with organized police departments. Sheriffs, in their law enforcement and court-related duties, generally operate independently of the board of county commissioners. As with a number of other county functions, the commissioners' involvement in these activities is largely financial. Through the annual budget ordinance they determine the level of financial support that the sheriff's office is to receive. Within the limits of that support, the sheriff has by statute the "exclusive right to hire, discharge, and supervise the employees in his office." (A sheriff's deputies, however, must meet state-established standards for law enforcement officers that are comparable to those that city police officers must meet.)

The sheriff and the board of county commissioners more nearly share responsibility for operation of the county jail. The commissioners build, maintain, and finance it; the sheriff administers it. Both are responsible for seeing that the jail and its operation adhere to state-established standards for physical condition and sanitation and for the feeding, the medical care, and other treatment of the inmates. The state inspects each local jail twice a year and, if the state standards are not met, may order the facility to be closed. (If that is done, the county must keep its prisoners in the jail of a neighboring county and pay the cost of doing so.)

The Courts

Courts in North Carolina are a state-operated system comprising three divisions: the Appellate Division, the Superior Court Division, and the District Court Division.

The Appellate Division has two courts. The supreme court, as its name suggests, is the highest court in the state. It hears appeals from lower courts regarding questions of law and is the final authority on constitutional law. It has seven justices elected in partisan, statewide elections for overlapping eight-year terms. The court of appeals, the second court in the Appellate Division, is also not a trial court and hears only appeals about matters of law. It has twelve judges elected in the same manner as the justices of the supreme court. It exists to take part of the appellate workload from the supreme court. Unlike the justices of the supreme court, the judges of the court of appeals do not sit together, but in rotating panels of three judges each.

The Superior Court Division has original jurisdiction for all felonies, misdemeanors appealed from the district courts, civil actions involving more than $10,000, and certain other cases. As of June 1995, there were ninety-one regular superior court judges, who are at present also elected on a partisan, statewide basis for eight-year terms. (Statewide election of superior court judges is being challenged in federal court.)

The District Court Division has 189 judges (as of June 1995), who are elected from their districts in partisan elections for four-year terms. District courts have original jurisdiction for civil cases involving less than $10,000, juvenile and domestic relations matters, probable cause hearings in felony cases, involuntary commitments for persons with mental illness, and nonjury misdemeanor cases.

Also in the District Court Division are some 650 magistrates, who handle minor civil and criminal cases. Magistrates in each county are appointed by the resident superior court judge for two-year terms.

The state's court system is now largely a responsibility of state government. The Administrative Office of the Courts administers it. Its director is appointed by the chief justice of the supreme court.

The state pays the full operating costs of the system, including the salaries of judges, district attorneys, public defenders, magistrates, and clerks. The county's sole remaining responsibility, albeit an important one, is to provide the physical facilities for the district and superior courts. (A few cities that are not county seats are also seats of district courts; in these cities the municipal government is responsible for providing court facilities.) A portion of the fees charged in each civil and criminal case is earmarked to be used for providing court facilities, but these fees do not meet the entire cost. Thus counties (and certain cities) must look to their general revenues to meet their court system responsibilities.

The Medical Examiner

The statutes require each county to have one or more medical examiners, who are physicians appointed to that post by the secretary of human resources. At present there are about 600 medical examiners in the state, most serving part-time. The medical examiner's responsibility is to investigate each death "apparently by criminal act or default, or apparently by suicide, or while an inmate of any penal or correctional institution, or under any suspicious, unusual or unnatural circumstances." The medical examiner may order an autopsy (as may the state's chief medical examiner) whenever "it is advisable and in the public interest."

A county medical examiner is part of a statewide system administered by the chief medical examiner, who is appointed by the secretary of human resources. The state finances the central services of the system, but counties are responsible for paying the local medical examiner's fee for each investigation of a deceased person who was a county resident, and any autopsy fee in such a case. (The state pays the fee in all other investigations.) The costs of the medical examiner system are met in roughly equal shares by the state and the counties.

A few counties (thirteen in 1995) still elect coroners, whose duty is to investigate unattended or questionable deaths to determine whether they probably resulted from a criminal act or default. In those counties the coroner must work along with the medical examiner, but most counties have found that the latter official is sufficient and have obtained from the General Assembly special ("local acts") legislation that has eliminated their coroner's position.

The Register of Deeds

A register of deeds is elected in each county. This officer is responsible for registering or filing documents relating to land transactions, such as deeds, mortgages, subdivision plats, and the like; for issuing marriage licenses; for filing security agreements arising from commercial transactions; and for maintaining a variety of other records. The responsibilities of the office are largely established by statute.

As noted, the register of deeds is an elected official and by statute has the "exclusive right to hire, discharge, and supervise the employees in his office." The county commissioners' role with respect to the operations of the register of deeds is essentially financial. The fees that the register charges are set by statute and are uniform statewide; if those fees are insufficient to meet the expenses of the office, the county finances the balance.

Agricultural Extension

Agricultural extension is a cooperative program of the federal government (through the United States Department of Agriculture), state government (through North Carolina State University), and county government. The primary mission of agricultural extension remains dissemination of the research findings of North Carolina State University and other universities throughout the country in the areas of agriculture and home economics. As the state has urbanized, however, the audience has increasingly become urban and suburban homeowners rather than full-time farmers and their families.

Under the standard agreement entered into between the Agricultural Extension Service at North Carolina State University and each county, the decisions on extension personnel are reached jointly by state and county officials. The service develops standards for each professional position, advertises for and interviews candidates, and makes a recommendation to the county commissioners; the commissioners then make the appointment. Funding for the statewide program is shared by all three levels of government. In 1993–94 the statewide cost of the extension programs was some $68 million, or just under $10 per capita. The state provided 45.9 percent of the program's financial support, the federal government 22.0 percent, and county governments 24.7 percent; the remaining 7.4 percent came from private sources.[2] The state and federal moneys pay a portion of the salaries of professional personnel in the county offices; they also fund specialized staff services at the state level and the many booklets that the extension agencies publish and distribute.

Libraries

Although the earliest public libraries were supported by cities, and cities retain statutory authority to operate public libraries, provision of library services has become largely a county function in North Carolina. Therefore, even though counties are not required to provide library services and cities are not prohibited from doing so, it is appropriate to discuss libraries in this appendix on county government.

Public libraries are operated pursuant to G.S. Chapter 153A, Article 14, which authorizes operation of multiple-county library systems as well as operation of single-county systems. In 1995, fifty-one counties had single-county systems, and forty-nine counties in various combinations operated fifteen regional libraries. (There were also nine independent municipal libraries.) Although a county or a city may operate a library as a line department directly under the unit's manager, most units with libraries have established library boards of trustees and delegated to them much of the responsibility for library operations. G.S. 153A-266 permits a unit to delegate to such a board the authority to appoint the chief librarian and other employees (the chief librarian must be certified by the State Library Certification Board), to establish a schedule of fines, to extend library privileges to nonresidents, and generally to supervise operation of the library system. The unit's governing board remains responsible for appropriating the funds for the library's operation and, of course, for appointing the library's trustees.

Most library funding comes from local government. In some cases the county assumes full financial responsibility for library services. In others, one or more of the cities in the county may contribute to the operation of the county system—often, in small cities, by providing a building for a branch library. A certain amount of state aid (and a smaller amount of federal aid) is available for local library systems, distributed through a series of formula grants by the

Division of State Library of the State Department of Cultural Resources. In 1993–94, local library expenditures statewide were about $96 million, or some $13.50 per capita. Local sources provided 87 percent of these funds, state government 13 percent, and federal assistance 2 percent.

Notes

1. North Carolina Department of Public Instruction, *1994 North Carolina Public School Statistical Profile* (Raleigh, N.C.: NCDPI, 1994), 49.

2. Richard Phillips, Associate Director, Cooperative Extension, North Carolina State University, telephone conversation with author, 14 August 1995.